P9-DFO-838

CYCLING NEW ZEALAND

Nicola Wells
Neil Irvine
Ian Duckworth

LONELY PLANET PUBLICATIONS
Melbourne • Oakland • London • Paris

NEW ZEALAND

NORTHLAND
Magnificent kauri forests, beautiful harbours, significant historical and cultural sites

COROMANDEL PENINSULA
Spectacular coastline, rugged mountain ranges and superb beaches

EAST CAPE RIDE
One of the world's great coastal rides – spectacular scenery, traffic-free roads and quaint villages

ROTORUA
Maori culture, gushing geysers, bubbling mud pools and NZ's first dedicated mountain bike park

MT TARANAKI
Cycle around it, climb it or just stare at it, Mt Taranaki is a sight to behold

PACIFIC OCEAN

TASMAN SEA

200 km
100 mi

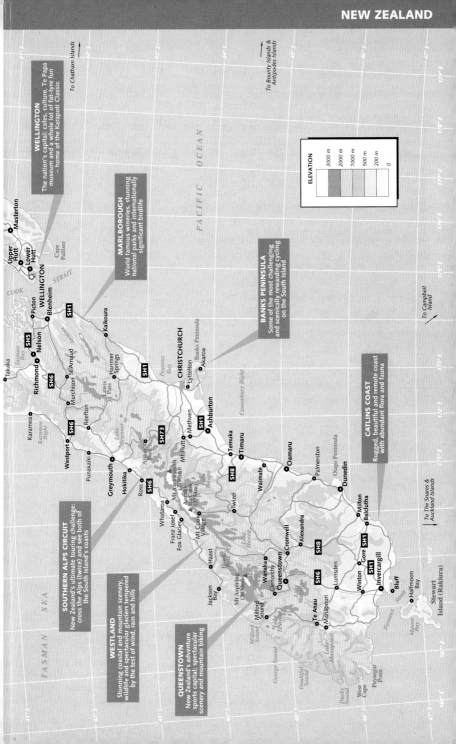

NEW ZEALAND

WELLINGTON
The nation's capital: cafes, culture, Te Papa museum and a whole lot of fat-tyre fun – home of the Karapoti Classic

MARLBOROUGH
World famous wineries, stunning national parks and internationally significant birdlife

BANKS PENINSULA
Some of the most challenging and scenically rewarding cycling on the South Island

CATLINS COAST
Rugged, beautiful and remote coast with abundant flora and fauna

SOUTHERN ALPS CIRCUIT
New Zealand's ultimate touring challenge: cross the Alps (twice) and see both of the South Island's coasts

WESTLAND
Stunning coastal and mountain scenery, wildlife and spectacular glaciers tempered by the test of wind, rain and hills

QUEENSTOWN
New Zealand's adventure sports capital; spectacular scenery and mountain biking

ELEVATION
3000 m
2000 m
1000 m
500 m
200 m
0

To Chatham Islands

To Bounty Islands & Antipodes Islands

To Campbell Island

To The Snares & Auckland Islands

PACIFIC OCEAN

TASMAN SEA

COOK STRAIT

Masterton
Upper Hutt
Lower Hutt
WELLINGTON
Picton
Blenheim
Cape Palliser
Takaka
Nelson
SH5
Richmond
SH6
Murchison
St Arnaud
Hanmer Springs
Kaikoura
SH1
Karamea
Reefton
SH6
Westport
Punakaiki
Greymouth
Hokitika
Ross
SH6
Whataroa
Franz Josef
Fox Glacier
Mt Cook Village
Haast
Jackson Bay
Mt Aspiring (3030m)
Glenorchy
Wanaka
Queenstown
SH6
Te Anau
Manapouri
Milford Sound
Lewis Pass
Arthur's Pass
Mt Hutt
SH73
Mt Somers (1688m)
Aoraki/Mt Cook (3754m)
Methven
SH1
Ashburton
CHRISTCHURCH
Lyttelton
Akaroa
Banks Peninsula
Pegasus Bay
Canterbury Bight
Temuka
SH1
Timaru
SH8
Twizel
Waimate
Oamaru
Palmerston
Otago Peninsula
Dunedin
Cromwell
Alexandra
SH8
Milton
Balclutha
SH1
Lumsden
SH6
Winton
Gore
SH1
Invercargill
Bluff
Halfmoon Bay
Stewart Island (Rakiura)
Mason Bay
West Cape
Puysegur Point
Dusky Sound
George Sound
Doubtful Sound
Milford Track
Lake Manapouri
Foveaux Strait

Cycling New Zealand
1st edition – July 2000

Published by
Lonely Planet Publications Pty Ltd A.C.N. 005 607 983
192 Burwood Rd, Hawthorn, Victoria 3122, Australia

Lonely Planet Offices
Australia PO Box 617, Hawthorn, Victoria 3122
USA 150 Linden St, Oakland, CA 94607
UK 10a Spring Place, London NW5 3BH
France 1 rue du Dahomey, 75011 Paris

Photographs
Many of the images in this guide are available for licensing from
Lonely Planet Images.
✉ lpi@lonelyplanet.com.au

Main front cover photograph
The long and not so winding road, Canterbury (Chris Mellor)

Small front cover photograph
Moke Creek, near Queenstown (David Wall)

Back cover photographs (from left to right)
Moke Creek, near Queenstown (David Wall)
Old Dunstan Trail, Otago (David Wall)
Otago Central Rail Trail, Otago (David Wall)

ISBN 1 86450 031 X

text & maps © Lonely Planet 2000
photos © photographers as indicated 2000
Wind information on page 20 was supplied by (NIWA) The National
Institute of Water and Atmospheric Research Ltd, New Zealand.

Printed by Craft Print Pte Ltd, Singapore

Contents

2 Contents

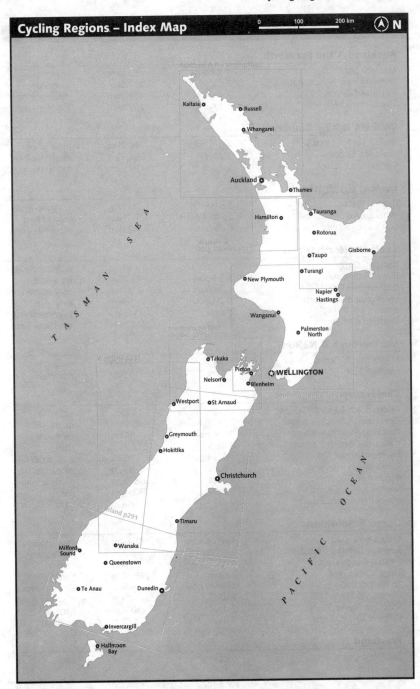

Cycling Regions – Index Map

The Rides	Duration	Distance	Standard
Auckland & the Far North			
Muriwai Beach	3-4 hours	62.8km	easy-moderate
Seabird Coast & Hunua Ranges	2 days	133.5km	moderate
Northland Circuit	7 days	462.1km	moderate-hard
The Coromandel	5 days	259.8km	moderate-hard
Waikato & King Country			
Raglan via Four Brothers	2½-4 hours	46.9km	moderate
Waitomo Circuit	3 days	254.3km	moderate-hard
Cambridge Circuit	5-8 hours	99.8km	moderate-hard
Eastern North Island			
Central Plateau	2 days	133km	easy-moderate
Whakarewarewa Forest	up to 2 hours	3.5-16km	easy to hard
East Cape Circuit	6 days	473km	moderate-hard
Southern North Island			
Karapoti Gorge	1-2 hours	14km	easy-moderate
Rimutaka Incline	2-3 hours	41.2km	moderate
Baring Head Coast	2-3 hours	37km	easy-moderate
Wellington Scenic Circuit	2-2½ hours	38km	easy
Around Mt Taranaki	3 days	145km	easy-moderate
Stratford Circuit	7 days	447.9km	moderate-hard
Marlborough & Nelson			
Marlborough Circuit	5 days	331km	moderate
Farewell Spit	3 days	153km	moderate
Canterbury			
Christchurch Parks & Gardens	1½-2½ hours	15.8km	easy
Christchurch Beaches & Hills	2½-3½ hours	45.9km	moderate
Port Hills Mountain Biking	2-2½ hours	16km	moderate
Kaikoura Coast & Hanmer Springs	6 days	512.8km	hard
Hanmer Springs Off-Road	1½-2 hours	20km	easy-moderate
Canterbury Hinterland	4 days	285km	moderate
Mackenzie Country	4 days	315.9km	moderate-hard
Southern Alps Circuit	8 days	692.4km	hard
Banks Peninsula Circuit	4 days	170km	hard
Otago & Southland			
Otago Peninsula	3-4½ hours	68.6km	easy-moderate
Swampy Summit Circuit	3-4 hours	30km	moderate-hard
Central Otago Circuit	4 days	233km	hard
The Catlins Coast	3 days	269.1km	hard
To Bluff & Back	3½-5½ hours	60km	easy-moderate
Invercargill Hinterland	2 days	147km	easy-moderate
Southern Scenic Route	3 days	308km	hard
Western Otago Circuit	3 days	206km	moderate-hard
Westland			
The West Coast	6 days	563.7km	hard

The Authors

Nicola Wells

Nicola lives in Melbourne and grew up in regional Victoria. With an honours degree in ecology, she has had various writing and research-based jobs, worked for a successful bicycle advocacy group and done a stint in a bike shop.

She rode a bike while living in Sweden, aged 12, and redis-covered cycling at university, where she became passionate about the environmental, social and health benefits. It is still her main transport, preserver of sanity and preferred mode for travel. She has toured in Australia, New Zealand and the UK.

Her other passions include classical music, especially singing (which, she regrets, is not terribly compatible with cycle touring), and food (which is). She has a particular weakness for good coffee.

Neil Irvine

Neil's account of his first serious cycle tour from Sydney to Brisbane via the Pacific Cycle Trail was published in 1981. Soon afterwards he found himself editing the magazine in which the article appeared. He founded *Australian Cyclist* magazine in 1989 and was editor until 1998, a career punctuated by cycle tours abroad with his features editor/wife, Alethea.

Neil has toured extensively – by road bike, mountain bike and tandem – in Australia, North America, Europe and NZ. His interests include involvement in lobbying for better cycling conditions at local, state and national level, and a love of the challenges of distance and mountains. He has completed the 1200km Paris-Brest-Paris ride three times, and also the Raid Pyrénéen, a 790km, 28-pass traverse of the French Pyrenees. Lately his riding has been more gentle, with a child-seat on the back, as he introduces his young son, Alexander, to the pleasures of cycling.

Ian Duckworth

Ian is a native of Perth, Western Australia. During a year off from uni he discovered the joys of cycle touring when he traded in his train ticket for a bicycle, spending several months pedalling around the back roads of Europe. On his return to Australia he set about exploring his own back yard by bike, a journey that culminated in the publication of his first book. Having traded in a career in law to be a full-time travel writer, Ian plans to see a lot more of the world from his bicycle seat. This is his first title for Lonely Planet.

FROM THE AUTHORS

Nicola Wells I'd particularly like to thank Jonathan Kennett for his generosity and assistance with the History of Cycling and Mountain Biking sections. Thanks too, to Robert from the Cycling Advocates' Network, Patrick Morgan, Stephen Knight, Richard Oddy, Iain Dephoff, Bruce O'Halloran and contributors to 🖳 www .mountainbike.co.nz and 🖳 www.kennett.co.nz. I'm indebted to Bert McConnell for his historical material, to Clare Simpson, Ron Shepherd and especially to John and Briar Gregory for their valuable and varied assistance.

I'm grateful to all the Kiwis who offered information, advice and stories, including Phil from the Treehouse, Steve from Ground Effect, Craig from Mountain Biking Adventures, Phil from 1WD, Geoff Mellsop, Stuart Burgess from NIWA, Bob McDavitt from METSERVICE, Vaughan from Whangarei and lots of bike shops – especially Pack 'n' Pedal and Bike Barn in Newtown, Auckland.

Big thank yous to Joanne and Mike in Auckland and Richard from Hamilton for taking in a stranger and to Gael for setting it up.

I'm blessed with supportive friends and am particularly grateful to my family, Milly and Gael who've been angels, Peter for his support and advice, and Richard and Lesley.

Finally, I'd like to thank Darren Elder at Lonely Planet, whose encouragement, support and collaboration throughout has been a pleasure.

Neil Irvine It would not have been possible for me to undertake this project without the tremendous support of my wife Alethea, of my parents Bob and Dulcie, and of Alethea's parents Bill and Mary, who all kept the household under control while I was absent and during the long writing process.

There are too many people in NZ to thank, so I will thank the entire population of the South Island for their friendliness, helpfulness and enthusiasm. There is so much positive energy on one not-so-small island.

Thanks are also due for early inspiration and spiritual guidance to a great cycle tourist and cycling writer, Britain's Nick Crane.

Finally, I would like to dedicate my section of the book to the memory of two keen fellow cyclists – Aussie Bob Chorley, who would have loved cycling NZ, and Kiwi Ken Everett, who *did* love cycling NZ, as well as lots of other places.

This Book

Nicola Wells was the coordinating author of *Cycling New Zealand* and wrote the introductory chapters and the Auckland & the North, and Waikato & King Country chapters. Neil Irvine wrote the Canterbury, Otago & Southland, and Westland chapters. Ian Duckworth wrote the Eastern North Island, Southern North Island, and Marlborough & Nelson chapters.

The Your Bicycle chapter was written by Darren Elder with contributions by Nicola Wells, Neil Irvine and Sally Dillon. The Health & Safety chapter was written by Nicola Wells, Dr Isabelle Young, and Kevin Tabotta from the Tasmanian Institute of Sport.

Material from the 9th edition of Lonely Planet's *New Zealand* guide, by Peter Turner, Jeff Williams, Nancy Keller and Tony Wheeler, was used for parts of this book.

From the Publisher

Cycling New Zealand, the first in Lonely Planet's new series of cycling guides, has been a long time in the planning, writing and researching. The series was developed by a team from Lonely Planet's Outdoor Activities Unit in Melbourne including Emily Coles, Sally Dillon, Teresa Donnellan, Sue Galley, Chris Klep, Andrew Smith, Nick Tapp and project manager Darren Elder, assisted by Paul Clifton and Nicola Wells. The cover design for the series was developed by Jamieson Gross, Vicki Beale, Simon Bracken, David Kemp and Tamsin Wilson.

Andrew and Darren coordinated the mapping and editing of this book, while Teresa helped oversee operations. Emily Coles, Janet Austin, Adam Ford, Brigitte Ellemor and Sally also assisted with editing; Verity Campbell, Tony Fankhauser and Glenn van der Kniff assisted with mapping.

Matt King coordinated the illustrations, drawn by Martin Harris and Don Hatcher. Mathew Burfoot designed the book and laid it out; Tim Uden and Andrew Tudor provided QuarkXPress assistance; Dan Levin and Geoff Rasmussen wrote computer programs to automate our processes. The staff of LPI, in particular Fiona Croyden, Brett Pascoe, Valerie Tellini and Louise Poultney, also lent valuable assistance.

Jeff Crowe from Sport: The Library provided the studio, technical knowledge and patience when shooting the photographs used in the Your Bicycle chapter. A crew from Cannondale USA and Cannondale Australia provided the bicycles for the Your Bicycle chapter; thanks to Nick Goljanin, Bill Conradt, Tom Armstrong and Matt Moon. Christie Cycles, Hawthorn, and Swim Bike Run, St Kilda, built the bicycles up and provided technical assistance; thanks to Ian and Richard, in particular.

Maps & Profiles

Most rides described in this book have an accompanying map that shows the route, services provided in towns en route as well as any attractions and possible side trips. These maps are oriented left to right in the direction of travel; a north point is located in the top right corner of each map. The maps are intended to stand alone but could be used together with one of the commercial maps recommended in the Planning section for each ride.

We provide a profile, or elevation chart, when there is a significant level of climbing and/or descending on a day's ride; most of the time these charts are included on the corresponding map but where space does not permit they accompany the text for that day. These charts are approximate and should be used as a guide only.

MAP LEGEND

Note: not all symbols displayed below appear in this book

CUE SHEET SYMBOLS

Continue Straight	Left Turn	Point of Interest	Traffic Lights
Right Turn	Veer Left	Mountain, Hill	Roundabout
Veer Right	Return Trip	Caution or Hazard	Side Trip

MAP SYMBOLS
[ON RIDE MAPS]

Bike Shop	Hostel	Point of Interest
Cafe, Takeaway Food	Hotel, Motel, B&B	Restaurant
Camping	Information	Store, Supermarket
Airport	[ON CITY MAPS]	Post Office
Church	Hospital	Zoo
	Museum	

POPULATION

CAPITAL — National Capital	LARGE Medium — City	Town, Village
CAPITAL — State Capital	Town Village — Town	Urban Area

ROUTES & TRANSPORT

Freeway, Tunnel	Train Line, Train Station
SH6 — Highway, Route Number	Underground Train
Secondary Road	Metro
Street, Minor Road	Tramway, Bus Terminal
Unsealed Road	Cable Car, Chairlift
Lane	Ferry

CYCLING ROUTES

Main Route
Alternative Route
Side Trip
Previous, Next Day
Bikepath, Track

HYDROGRAPHIC FEATURES

Coastline, River, Creek	Dry Lake, Salt Lake
Canal	Spring, Rapids
Lake	Waterfalls

TOPOGRAPHIC FEATURES

Cave
Cliff
Mountain
Pass, Saddle

AREA FEATURES

Building	Beach
Cemetery	Glacier
National Park, Forest	Swamp

BOUNDARIES

International
State
Disputed

Cue Sheets

Route directions in this book are given in a series of brief 'cues', which tell you at what kilometre mark to change direction and point out features en route. The cues are placed on the route map, most of the time with a profile, or elevation chart. Together these provide all the primary directions for each route in one convenient reference. The only other thing you need is a cycle computer.

To make the cue sheets as brief as we can, yet still relatively simple to understand, we've developed a series of symbols (see the Map Legend on p9) and the following rule:

Once your route is following a particular road, continue on that road until the cue sheet tells you otherwise.

Follow the road first mentioned in the cue sheet even though it may cross a highway, shrink to a lane, change name (we generally only include the first name, and sometimes the last), wind, duck and climb its way across the country. Rely on us to tell you when to turn it.

Because the cue sheets rely on an accurate odometer reading we suggest you disconnect your cycle computer (pop it out of the housing or turn the magnet away from the fork-mounted sensor) whenever you deviate from the route.

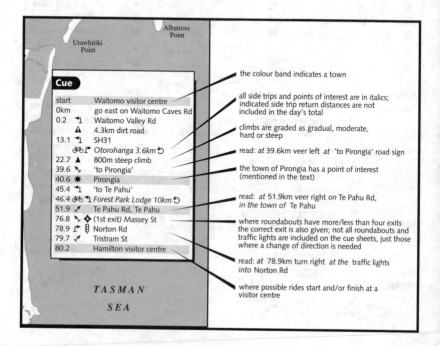

Foreword

HOW TO USE A LONELY PLANET GUIDEBOOK

The best way to use a Lonely Planet guidebook is any way you choose. At Lonely Planet we believe the most memorable travel experiences are often those that are unexpected, and the finest discoveries are those you make yourself. Guidebooks are not intended to be used as if they provide a detailed set of infallible instructions!

Contents All Lonely Planet guidebooks follow roughly the same format, including the cycling guides. The Facts about the Destination chapters give background information ranging from history to weather. Facts for the Cyclist gives practical information on the destination. Health & Safety covers medical advice and road rules. Basic bicycle maintenance is addressed in Your Bicycle. Getting There & Away gives a brief starting point for researching travel to/from the destination. Getting Around gives an overview of the transport options when you arrive.

The peculiar demands of each destination determine how subsequent chapters are broken up, but some things remain constant. We always start each ride with background and getting to/from the ride information. Each day's ride is summarised and the highlights en route detailed in the text, and locations noted on the map and cue sheets. A selection of the best sights and places to stay and eat in each start and end town are also detailed.

Heading Hierarchy Lonely Planet headings are used in a strict hierarchical structure that can be visualised as a set of Russian dolls. Each heading (and its following text) is encompassed by any preceding heading that is higher on the hierarchical ladder.

Entry Points We do not assume guidebooks will be read from beginning to end, but that people will dip into them. The traditional entry points are the list of contents and the index. In addition, the cycling guides also have a table of rides and a map index illustrating the regional chapter break-up.

There is also a colour map that shows highlights. These highlights are dealt with in greater detail in the Facts for the Cyclist chapter, along with planning questions and suggested itineraries. Each chapter covering a geographical region also begins with a map showing all the rides for that region. Once you find something of interest turn to the index or table of rides.

ABOUT LONELY PLANET GUIDEBOOKS

The process of creating new editions begins with the letters, postcards and emails received from travellers. This correspondence often includes suggestions, criticisms and comments about the current editions. Interesting excerpts are immediately passed on via newsletters and the Web site, and everything goes to our authors to be verified when they're researching on the road. We're keen to get more feedback from organisations or individuals who represent communities visited by travellers.

Lonely Planet gathers information for everyone who's curious about the planet – and especially for those who explore it first-hand. Through guidebooks, phrasebooks, activity guides, maps, literature, newsletters, image library, TV series and Web site we act as an information exchange for a worldwide community of travellers.

Research Authors aim to gather sufficient practical information to enable travellers to make informed choices and to make the mechanics of a journey run smoothly. They also research historical and cultural background to help enrich the travel experience and allow travellers to understand and respond appropriately to cultural and environmental issues.

Authors don't stay in every hotel because that would mean spending a couple of weeks in each medium-sized city and, no, they don't eat at every restaurant because that would mean stretching belts beyond capacity. They do visit hotels and restaurants to check standards and prices, but feedback based on readers' direct experiences can be very helpful.

Many of our authors work undercover, others aren't so secretive. None of them accept freebies in exchange for positive write-ups. And none of our guidebooks contain any advertising.

Production Authors submit their raw manuscripts and maps to offices in Australia, USA, UK or France. Editors and cartographers – all experienced travellers themselves – then begin the process of assembling the pieces. When the book finally hits the shops, some things are already out of date, we start getting feedback from readers and the process begins again ...

WARNING & REQUEST

Things change – prices go up, schedules change, good places go bad and bad places go bankrupt – nothing stays the same. So, if you find things better or worse, recently opened or long since closed, please tell us and help make the next edition even more accurate and useful. We genuinely value all the feedback we receive. Julie Young coordinates a well-travelled team that reads and acknowledges every letter, postcard and email and ensures that every morsel of information finds its way to the appropriate authors, editors and cartographers for verification.

Everyone who writes to us will find their name in the next edition of the appropriate guidebook. They will also receive the latest issue of *Planet Talk*, our quarterly printed newsletter, or *Comet*, our monthly email newsletter. Subscriptions to both newsletters are free. The very best contributions will be rewarded with a free guidebook.

Excerpts from your correspondence may appear in new editions of Lonely Planet guidebooks, the Lonely Planet Web site, *Planet Talk* or *Comet*, so please let us know if you *don't* want your letter published or your name acknowledged.

Send all correspondence to the Lonely Planet office closest to you:

Australia: PO Box 617, Hawthorn, Victoria 3122
USA: 150 Linden St, Oakland, CA 94607
UK: 10A Spring Place, London NW5 3BH
France: 1 rue du Dahomey, 75011 Paris

Or email us at: ✆ talk2us@lonelyplanet.com.au

For news, views and updates see our Web site: ⌨ www.lonelyplanet.com

Introduction

Much of New Zealand looks as though it came straight out of a postcard. The country has a well deserved 'clean and green' reputation, and although the natural environment has changed significantly in the 200 years since European colonisation, the proportion of land protected in national parks and wilderness areas is one of the highest in the world.

Indeed, the stunning scenery makes cycling a joy – and while the country is not overly large, it's certainly varied. The two main islands are quite different, both in scenery and character, and each is worthy of exploration. The North Island is more populated and is a stronghold of Maori culture, while NZ's English and Scottish heritage pervades much of the South Island.

On the North Island, you can cycle through lush, semitropical bush, past some of the world's oldest trees, round exquisite harbours, over rugged mountain ranges, along stunning coastlines, and then soak in hot springs, check out the geysers around thermally active Rotorua, get down and dirty on some of the many excellent mountain bike trails and explore the moonscape of Mt Ruapehu.

The cooler South Island is dominated by the Southern Alps. The scenery is stunning here – you'll find cool temperate rainforests, snow-capped mountains, glaciers, lots of icy-blue rivers, picturesque lakes and (more) beautiful coastal scenery, including the exquisite Milford and Marlborough Sounds. Kaikoura is a famous spot for whale-watching.

If you want some fun off the bike, adventure activities – such as bungy jumping, white-water rafting, skydiving, jet-boating and much more – are on offer just about anywhere.

NZ is an easy country in which to travel, geared for tourism (particularly adventure and nature-based) without being spoiled and trashy. The people are friendly, there's a good range of affordable accommodation, food is plentiful and fresh, and the wine is

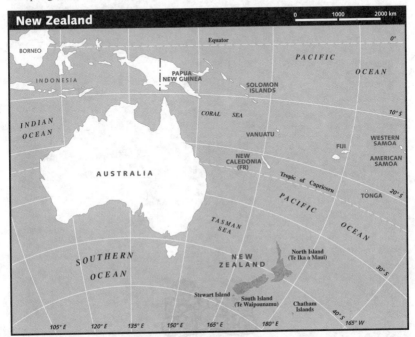

excellent. There are plenty of quiet roads and uncrowded beauty spots. It's a place where you can rough it – head out to the back country on a self-sufficient adventure – or ride in style: enjoying beautiful scenery by day, complemented with fine food and wine and a comfortable bed to retire to at night.

Facts about New Zealand

HISTORY

c 950 AD – The legendary Polynesian navigator Kupe discovers NZ and names it Aotearoa (Land of the Long White Cloud), before returning home to the Polynesian ancestral homeland of Hawaiki, near Tahiti.

c 1300-1400 – A succession of great canoes leave crowded Hawaiki for Aotearoa. Each canoe group establishes its own territory.

1642 – The Dutch explorer Abel Tasman sails up the west coast and names the land Niuew Zeeland after the Netherlands' province of Zeeland. Several of his crew are killed.

1769 – James Cook circumnavigates both islands in the *Endeavour* and claims the land for the British Crown. French explorer Jean François Marie de Surville sails round NZ at the same time.

1790s – European sealers and whalers introduce firearms, diseases and prostitution to the battle-loving Maori. By 1830 the Maori population has fallen dramatically.

1814 – Samuel Marsden introduces Christianity and is followed by other missionaries. The Maori language is recorded in writing for the first time, in a translation of the Bible.

early 19th century – As the rate of settlement from Europe and Australia increases, relations between Maori and Pakeha (Maori term for Europeans) and lawfulness in general deteriorate.

1820 – The overseas kauri timber trade begins when British naval ship HMS *Coromandel* takes a load from the Coromandel Peninsula. The use of kauri timber for boat and other building purposes will lead to a 90% reduction of NZ's forests.

1830 – The UK despatches James Busby from Australia to Kororareka as the British Resident. His job is to protect British settlers and keep law and order. This role is made difficult, however, without the support of forces, arms or authority.

1840 – Captain William Hobson is sent from the UK to replace Busby and persuade the Maori chiefs to relinquish their sovereignty to the British Crown. A treaty is drawn up and more than 400 Maori gather at Waitangi in the Bay of Islands to hear it read. After debate and amendments, the Treaty of Waitangi is signed by Hobson and 45 Maori chiefs on 6 February. More than 500 chiefs sign it in the next seven months. Hobson proclaims British sovereignty and establishes his capital at Kororareka (now Russell).

Under the terms of the treaty, still hotly debated today, the chiefs cede their sovereignty to the Queen of England in exchange for granting their people the citizenship rights and duties enjoyed by British citizens. The treaty guarantees the Maori possession of their land and stipulates that they can only sell it to the Crown.

1841 – The nation's capital is moved to Auckland.

1845 – Conflict occurs both between Maori and Pakeha, as more settlers demand their own land, and within Maori communities, as chiefs sell land belonging to whole tribes. Open warfare breaks out in Northland.

1852 – The Constitution Act divides the country into six provinces, each to administer local government and take responsibility for land sales. The Maori, meanwhile, become increasingly reluctant to sell land.

1856 – NZ becomes a self-governing British colony.

1859 – In the Waikato region around Hamilton on the North Island, the tribal chiefs unite to elect a Maori King and resist European settlement until the 20th century.

1860-69 – The British regard the Waikato King movement as open rebellion. They take a year to defeat the Waikato Maori, who retreat to an area south of Waikato, now called King Country. Pressure between Maori and Pakeha escalates into fully fledged wars in many regions, known collectively as the Land Wars. After defeating the Maori, the government confiscates huge parcels of Maori land. This, coupled with new legislation allowing private land sales, gradually results in the loss of prime Maori land over the rest of the 19th century.

1860s – While conflicts stunt development in the North Island, farming and the discovery of gold help the South Island become the main area of settlement.

1865 – Wellington becomes the national capital.

1867 – The Maori people are given the vote.

1876 – Provincial governments are abolished and power is centralised in Wellington.

1877 – The Treaty of Waitangi is ruled a 'simple nullity' by Chief Justice Prendergast, denying it any legal status.

late 19th century – European settlement continues and NZ becomes a productive agricultural country. Refrigerated ships enable meat to be sold in Europe, and NZ becomes England's 'efficient off-shore farm'.

1890s – Far-sighted social reforms are initiated, including old-age pensions, minimum wage structures and introduction of arbitration courts and child health services. Meanwhile, the decline in the Maori population and their loss of traditional culture continues.

1893 – Women are given the vote, 25 years before the UK or USA.

1907 – NZ becomes a dominion (a self-governing part of the British Empire).

early 20th century – NZ fights for the UK in the Boer War, WWI and WWII.

postwar years – Demand for agricultural products contributes to NZ's high per-capita income.

1947 – NZ becomes independent from the UK.

1950-3 – NZ sends troops to the Korean War. Australia, NZ and the USA sign the ANZUS defence pact, pledging mutual aid in the event of attack. NZ also joins the anti-communist South-East Asia Treaty Organisation.

1971 – NZ joins the South Pacific Forum to discuss common problems with other Pacific governments. Around this time, NZ is directing increasing amounts of aid to Pacific countries.

1970s-80s – Along with much of the rest of the world, NZ's economy slumps. However, during this period Maori culture experiences a resurgence (see Society & Conduct later in this chapter).

1975 – The Treaty of Waitangi is reconsidered, the Waitangi Act is passed and a tribunal established to investigate Maori land claims. Financial reparations are eventually made to many Maori tribes whose lands were found to have been unjustly confiscated.

1983 – NZ and Australia sign an agreement permitting unrestricted trade between the two countries. NZ increasingly sees itself as a Pacific nation, rather than the UK's offshore farm. Asia, the Pacific and the USA are important trading partners.

1984 – A Labour government is elected and undertakes radical economic restructuring (see Economy later in this chapter); NZ takes a strong anti-nuclear stand by refusing entry to nuclear-equipped US warships and leading Pacific opposition to French nuclear testing at Mururoa Atoll.

1985 – French secret service agents sink the Greenpeace ship *Rainbow Warrior* in Auckland Harbour.

1990 – The National Party is elected, following rising unemployment and instability within the Labour Party. Economic reform continues,

with greater privatisation of government utilities, substantial cuts to welfare and deregulation of the labour market.

1993 – The election sees the National Party scrape through, holding government by one seat. Through a referendum, the population elects to adopt a Mixed Member Proportional (MMP) voting system, based on the German model.

1995 – NZ is again at the forefront of international protests as the French resume Pacific nuclear testing; NZ boat *Black Magic* wins the America's Cup yacht race.

1996 – Following the election, the National Party forms a coalition government with the minority NZ First Party.

1997 – National Party leader Jim Bolger is replaced by Jenny Shipley, NZ's first woman prime minister, in a bloodless coup.

1998 – A power blackout in Auckland lasts several weeks; Jenny Shipley continues to lead the National Party in a minority government after the coalition dissolves.

1999 – The Labor Party wins government in coalition with the (left leaning) Alliance Party with the support of the Greens. Helen Clark becomes NZ's first elected woman prime minister.

History of Cycling

Bicycles arrived in NZ not too far behind the early European settlers. The first bike to be introduced was a velocipede, in 1869. The first racing clubs began in the 1870s and by the 1880s pioneers were using penny farthings to travel stock routes.

Pneumatic tyres were introduced in the early 1890s, by which time cycling had been

NATIONAL LIBRARY OF NEW ZEALAND

Dressed in uniform and equipped with the best bikes of the era (circa 1914), Christchurch's South Durham St district nurses are ready to roll.

embraced by the women's movement. Bicycles were liberating for women since they provided an independent means of transport and demanded less restrictive clothing. Kate Sheppard, a prominent feminist (look out for her on the $10 note), was also a keen cyclist. The Atalanta Cycling Club for women was established in 1892 – also the year in which the first NZ cycling magazine was launched.

In 1916 NZ sent a cyclist company to fight for the UK in WWI, along with 201 bicycles to be used for training and as transport into battle.

Amateur cycling clubs began to form in the 1920s. Manakau Amateur Cycling Club, based in Auckland, became the country's largest. Originally planned as a touring club when it was formed in 1924, it quickly became competitive. In 1938 a group from the club toured the Coromandel Ranges in preparation for the Empire Games in Sydney, Australia – in which kiwi John Brown finished a close second in the road race.

Bear in mind that conditions in the early days of racing were much harder than they are today. Roads were mostly rough and unsealed, and until the 1930s bikes had no gears. Riders tackled courses with 28 inch wooden rims and 'balloon' 1½ inch tyres – the width of modern mountain bike tyres – and fixed wheels made coasting a luxury of the future.

In spite of this, those tough early riders managed to cover long distances surprisingly quickly – in the early 1930s riders were finishing 100 mile races (about 160km) in little more than five hours (that's around 19 miles, or 31km, an hour)!

During the 1930s freewheels and limited gearing came into use, hand brakes became compulsory, superior Reynolds 531 tubing (made in England) was developed and 27 inch tubular tyres became common. At this stage, few could afford imported cycles and most bikes were made in NZ by the various frame builders springing up around the country. Some popular makes included Gamage and Jones, based in Christchurch, and, from Auckland, early Fleetwings, Comet and Leader. Malvern Star, imported from Australia towards the end of the decade, became popular as the bicycle used by (already) legendary Australian cyclist Hubert Opperman.

Early on, amateur cycling was controlled by the NZ Amateur Athletics Association, but after a campaign led by the Manakau Amateur Cycling Club, a separate national cycling body, Cycling New Zealand, was formed in 1933. Races such as from Timaru to Christchurch offered generous prize money and were a good way to make ends meet during hard times. Cyclists travelled as far as Australia to ride in major events

Cycling continued to grow in popularity into the 1930s. However, with the outbreak of WWII many of the fit young cyclists were snapped up by the forces and cycling activity waned.

The Auckland Cycle Touring Association formed in 1948. However, with increasing motorcar ownership in the postwar boom, cycling did not develop a great deal for a couple of decades.

It was not until the 1970s, as people began to worry about pollution and the depletion of fossil fuels, that bike use in NZ, as well as the USA and UK, again started to rise. NZ was heavily dependent on imported petroleum and the proportion of its imports used for powering vehicles was among the highest in the world. At about this time, 10-speed bikes became widely available.

Morrison Industries Ltd and AG Healing Ltd were the two major bike manufacturers and, by the 1970s, NZ companies were also manufacturing cycle clothing and equipment such as panniers and helmets.

Various groups formed in NZ to campaign for better cycling facilities, often from an environmental standpoint and generally focussing on bikes as transport. While progress in such a car-centric country remained slow, cyclists were beginning to be recognised by planning authorities as legitimate road users.

Once celebrated as the 'Copenhagen of the Pacific', Christchurch again became known as NZ's bike capital. The Bicycle Planning Committee in Christchurch began in 1975 and initiated Bike Week, still held annually in February. It includes activities such as races that pit car against bike during peak hour traffic.

Cycling advocacy has continued into the 1990s. Late in the decade a number of the cycle advocacy groups affiliated to form the Cycling Advocates Network (CAN) and environmental issues remain a strong focus.

The mountain biking community is also vocal about conservation issues.

With its rugged terrain and relative abundance of bush, mountain bikes took off early in NZ. In 1984, as mountain bikes were developing in the USA, Healing Cycles imported 15 mountain bikes and soon began manufacturing its own Mountain Cat brand. Two years later, Paul Kennett ran the first national mountain bike race – now the annual Karapoti Classic, the biggest mountain bike race in the southern hemisphere. By the late 1980s there was a strong and growing local mountain biking scene, and Kiwi mountain bikers were competing successfully overseas.

Mountain biking has continued to boom throughout the 1990s. Mountain bikes now dominate the bike shop floor; the Kennett brothers' 'bible', *Classic New Zealand Mountain Bike Rides*, first printed in 1991, is (at the time of research) into its third edition; and in 1997 the six summer races of the New Zealand National Mountain Bike Association (NZMBA) Nationals series became official UCI (international) events.

GEOGRAPHY

NZ stretches 1600km from north to south. It consists of two large islands around which are scattered some smaller islands, plus a few far-flung islands hundreds of kilometres away. NZ's territorial jurisdiction extends to the mostly uninhabited islands of Chatham, Kermadec, Auckland, Antipodes, Snares, Solander, Bounty and Tokelau in the Pacific and to the Ross Dependency in Antarctica.

The North Island (115,000 sq km) and the South Island (151,000 sq km) are the two major landmasses. Stewart Island, with an area of 1700 sq km, lies directly south of the South Island. The country is 10,400km south-west of the USA, 1700km south of Fiji and 2250km east of Australia, its nearest large neighbour. Its western coastline faces the Tasman Sea, the section of the Pacific Ocean which separates NZ and Australia.

NZ's land area (268,000 sq km) is greater than that of the UK (244,800 sq km), but smaller than that of Japan (377,800 sq km). With only 3,540,000 people, almost 70% of whom live in the five major cities, NZ has a lot of wide open spaces. Its coastline, with many bays, harbours and fiords, is long in comparison to its landmass.

A notable feature of NZ's geography is the great number of rivers. There's a lot of rainfall in NZ and all that rain has to go somewhere. The Waikato River in the North Island is NZ's longest river (425km).

Also in the North Island, the Whanganui River is the country's longest navigable river, which has always made it an important waterway. NZ also has many beautiful lakes; Lake Taupo is the largest and Lakes Waikaremoana and Wanaka are two of the most beautiful.

GEOLOGY

Both the North Island and South Island have some high mountains, formed by two distinct geological processes associated with the westward movement of the Pacific tectonic plate.

When one tectonic plate slides underneath another one, it forms a subduction zone. The North Island is on the southern reaches of the subduction zone where the oceanic Pacific plate slides beneath the continental plate. The resulting volcanic activity has created a number of large volcanoes and thermal areas, and some equally impressive volcanic depressions.

A rough 'line' of volcanoes, some of which are still active, extends south from the steaming Whakaari (White) Island in the Bay of Plenty past Mt Putauaki (Edgecumbe) and the highly active thermal areas in and around Rotorua and Lake Taupo. The latter was formed by a gigantic volcanic explosion in 186 AD and still has thermal areas bubbling away nearby. South of Lake Taupo are the North Island's spectacularly large volcanoes Tongariro, Ruapehu, Ngauruhoe and the smaller Pihanga. Farther south-west is the lone volcanic cone of Mt Taranaki (Egmont). Port Nicholson, Wellington's harbour, was formed by a giant crater, now filled by the sea. Other parts of the North Island also contain evidence of volcanic activity; in Auckland, for example, there are more than 50 volcanic cones, including most of its famous 'hills' (One Tree Hill, Mt Eden etc) that rise up from the plains.

The North Island has some ranges of hills and mountains produced by folding and uplift, notably the Tararua and Ruahine ranges in the southern part of the North Island. In general, though, most of the high places of the North Island were formed by volcanic activity. In the island's centre there's a high plateau.

In the South Island the geological process is different. Here the two tectonic plates are smashing into each other, resulting in a process called 'crustal shortening'. This has caused the Southern Alps to rise as a spine, virtually extending along the entire length of the South Island. Thrust faulting, folding and vertical slips all combine to create a rapid uplift of the Southern Alps. Though the Southern Alps receive a lot of rainfall, the rate of uplift is enough to keep pace with the erosion and the mountains continue to rise by as much as 10mm a year. Most of the east side of the South Island is a large plain known as the Canterbury Plains. Banks Peninsula, on the east coast, was formed by volcanic activity and joined to the mainland by alluvial deposits washed down from the Southern Alps.

CLIMATE

Lying between 34°S and 47°S, NZ is in the Roaring Forties latitude. The prevailing wind is from the Tasman Sea, blowing west to east year-round, ranging from gentle, freshening breezes to occasional raging gales in winter. It's a relatively warm and moisture-laden breeze. However, when the wind comes up from the south, it's from Antarctica and is icy; a southerly wind always means cold weather.

Mountains shape the prevailing westerlies into generally west or south-west winds on the west coast, and generally north-west winds along the east coast of the country. You are more likely to encounter strong wind if you are in the mountains, in gaps between the mountains (such as Cook Strait) or on protruding bits of coast, like Taranaki or any of NZ's peninsulas.

The South Island's geography also creates a wind pattern in which the prevailing wind, after losing its moisture, blows eastwards as a dry wind, gathering heat and speed as it blows downhill and across the Canterbury Plains towards the Pacific coast. In summer this katabatic, or föhn, wind can be hot, dry and fierce. In the Grey River valley on the South Island's west coast there's another kind of downhill wind, locally called 'the Barber'.

The windiest season is spring (September to November), while autumn (March to May) is calmest. The other factor that influences NZ's wind pattern is the El Niño/La Niña effect: whereas El Niño winds are west and south-westerly, a La Niña year tends to be less windy (except in Northland) and the wind is from the east.

Because of their different geological features, the North and South islands have two distinct rainfall patterns. In the South Island, the Southern Alps act as a barrier for the moisture-laden winds coming across the Tasman Sea, creating a wet climate on the west side of the mountains and a dry climate on the east side: the annual rainfall on the west side is more than 7500mm but is only about 330mm on the east.

In the North Island, the western sides of the high volcanoes get a lot more rain than the eastern sides but the rain shadow is not as pronounced, as there is not such a complete barrier as the Alps. Rainfall is more evenly distributed over the North Island, which averages around 1300mm per year.

It is a few degrees cooler in the South Island than the North Island. Winter is from June to August and summer from December to February. But there are regional variations: it's quite warm and pleasant up in the Northland region at any time of year, although in summer it can be humid. Higher altitudes are always considerably cooler, and it's usually windy in Wellington, which catches the winds whistling through Cook Strait.

Snow is mostly seen in the mountains, where it can fall above the bushline any time of year. However, in the South Island there can be snowfalls even at sea level, particularly in the extreme south. Some of the plains and higher plateaus also receive snow in winter, notably the Canterbury Plains in the South Island and the high plateau around Tongariro National Park in the North Island, especially on the 'desert' (east) side. Snow is seldom seen near sea level on the west coasts and not at all in the far north.

One of the most important things travellers need to know about the NZ climate is that it's a maritime climate, and weather travels quickly over the narrow landmass. This means the weather can change with amazing rapidity. If you're out at high altitudes, for example, the extreme changeability of the weather can be a life-or-death matter.

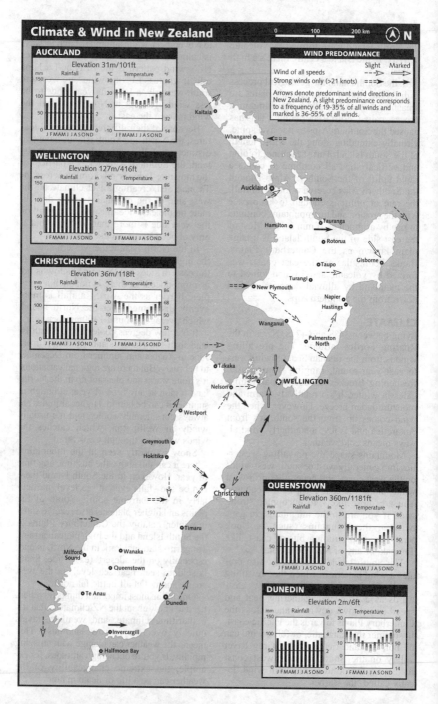

For more detailed regional information, see the Climate section in individual rides chapters. For on-the-spot weather information, see Weather Information in the Facts for the Cyclist chapter.

ECOLOGY & ENVIRONMENT

NZ, isolated from other lands for 70 million years, developed its own unique flora and fauna. Geological records indicate that 150 million years ago NZ was part of the supercontinent of Gondwanaland, along with Australia, Antarctica, Africa and South America.

Since separating from the other continents, NZ's plant and animal life evolved in the absence of mammalian predators (the only native land mammals are bats) and many of its bird species have evolved without flight.

The arrival of Polynesians around 1000 years ago and, in particular, Europeans 200 years ago brought about massive change to the natural environment.

The Maori hunted to extinction the moa and used fire extensively to clear land for agriculture (mainly sweet potato, or *kumara*). They also fished and hunted other birds (some of which are also now extinct).

The first Europeans were sealers and whalers who hunted the seal and whale populations to almost nothing. They were followed by timber cutters greedy for kauri timber – particularly prized for ship building – and settlers who simply cleared the forests to make way for pasture.

Both Polynesians and Europeans introduced weeds and, perhaps more seriously, mammals, which led to the destruction of habitat and decimation of bird populations. James Cook intentionally introduced pigs and goats and, in the latter part of the 19th century, the mostly English middle-class settlers (with some government encouragement) brought in animals and fish for sport. Others were later introduced in an attempt to control those which had become pests.

With no natural predators, these adaptable mammals (Australian brush-tail possums, cats, rats, goats, pigs, rabbits, weasels and stoats) are difficult to control and, by hunting birds, stealing eggs or simply browsing in large numbers, remain a serious threat.

Despite the overwhelming numbers, there are attempts to control these introduced pests by methods such as hunting and poison baiting.

Conservation

Perhaps because human habitation has been so recent (and remains relatively sparse), NZ has a deserved reputation as one of the last remaining clean, green, wilderness areas of the world.

After the plundering of early settlers, New Zealanders had begun to recognise the need for conservation by the 1880s, when nature reserves were declared and laws were passed concerning wildlife protection. In 1910 botanist Leonard Cockayne wrote, 'However little the average New Zealander may know about the plants of his country, there are few who cannot raise some enthusiasm regarding the 'bush', as the forest is everywhere called ...'. In 1923 the Native Bird Protection Society was founded by Captain Val Sanderson. Now called The Royal Forest and Bird Protection Society (🖳 www.forest-bird.org.nz), it is NZ's largest conservation group with 40,000 members. Other groups include Greenpeace New Zealand, the New Zealand Native Forests Restoration Trust, Friends of the Earth and Native Forest Action.

Nonetheless, forestry, farming and fishing, traditional cornerstones of the country's economy, remain important (see Economy later in this chapter) and the economic pressure to exploit natural resources continues to threaten the natural environment. The long-term lease of forests by multinational companies is a visible example.

However, the strong conservation ethic means that new logging contracts and proposed developments, such as laying roads through sensitive areas, are highly controversial, and in 1991 the Resource Management Act was passed, which has made approval for such projects significantly more difficult to obtain.

The government body responsible for conservation is the Department of Conservation (DOC) or, as it is known by its Maori name, Te Papa Atawhai. Along with its responsibility for administration of national and forest parks, hundreds of reserves, wildlife refuges and sanctuaries, DOC also has an extensive species preservation program (see also Endangered Species in the Flora & Fauna section later in this chapter).

National Parks & Reserves

NZ was the fourth nation to introduce a system of national parks, following Maori chief Te Heuheu Tukino IV's offer of land to the NZ government, as a gift for all people, in 1887.

The country now has 13 national parks: Urewera, Tongariro, Egmont and Whanganui in the North Island; and Abel Tasman, Kahurangi, Nelson Lakes, Arthur's Pass, Paparoa, Westland, Mt Cook, Mt Aspiring and Fiordland in the South Island. Te Wahipounamu World Heritage Region in the south-west of the South Island encompasses Mt Aspiring, Westland, Mt Cook and Fiordland national parks.

Other natural areas have been designated forest parks in a system designed to preserve wilderness areas, yet enable them to be used for other purposes, including timber harvesting and recreation (in contrast to national parks, where preservation is paramount). There are also three maritime parks, along with numerous forests and scenic reserves.

FLORA & FAUNA

Because it evolved in isolation over 70 million years, NZ's native flora and fauna are, for the most part, not found anywhere else in the world. It claims the world's largest flightless parrot (kakapo), the only truly alpine parrot (kea), the oldest reptile (tuatara), some of the biggest earthworms, the smallest bats, some of the oldest trees, and many of the rarest birds, insects and plants in the world. While two small bats are the only native land mammals, NZ is notable for its birds – many of them flightless.

NZ's flora and fauna has been shaped, over millions of years, by periods of glaciation and warming, along with volcanic activity. However, probably the greatest impact (certainly the most rapid) has been human settlement and the accompanying introduction of new plants and animals. Wild pigs, goats, possums, wallabies, rabbits, dogs, cats and deer have all made their mark on the native wildlife, and gorse, broom, blackberries and agricultural weeds have infested huge areas of land.

Endangered Species

More than 50 animal species have become extinct since humans arrived in NZ and 150 native plants are threatened. Animals that are now endangered or threatened include flightless birds such as the kakapo – the world's largest parrot whose courtship ritual is amazing – the takahe, the black stilt and even the kiwi, as well as frogs and the Hooker's sea lion.

DOC has an extensive program to save threatened species from extinction. An effective strategy is the relocation of endangered species to pest-free islands or mainland areas isolated by terrain fences or subject to intensive management, known as 'mainland islands'.

The NZ nature conservation space Web site (💻 www.naturespace.co.nz/species) has more about the conservation of endangered species and about native species in general.

GOVERNMENT & POLITICS

The governmental structure of NZ is modelled on the British parliamentary system. However, unlike the UK, NZ only has a lower house. The government runs on a party system, with the major parties being National (conservative) and Labour.

Secret ballot elections are held at least triennially, using (since 1996) a system of limited proportional representation. The party winning the most seats is asked to form government and its leader becomes the prime minister. All citizens of 18 or more years of age are eligible to vote and, although it's not compulsory, generally about 80% do.

NZ is a constitutional monarchy, with a resident governor-general representing the reigning British monarch as head of state. An independent judiciary makes up another tier of government.

ECONOMY

NZ is a modern country which enjoys a standard of living equivalent to that of other 'developed' countries. The NZ economy has undergone a radical restructuring since 1984, moving from a government-involved, welfare-state economy towards a private open-market economy.

By the 1980s NZ had lost its traditional agricultural market in the UK, incurred huge foreign debts, and the economy was stagnant and restricted by government controls.

Restructuring involved deregulating the financial market, reducing tarrifs, encouraging

New Zealand's Flora & Fauna

When the Polynesians first arrived, much of New Zealand would have been covered in evergreen forest. About 70% remained when Europeans arrived in the early 19th century.

Though the diversity of NZ's vegetation is enormous, the main forest types are hardwood, kauri and beech.

The podocarps (trees such as rimu, totara, kahikatea, miro and maitai) are part of the ancient *Podocarpaceae* family, which evolved before flowering plants. The podocarp-hardwood forests are probably surviving examples of a vegetation type common in both hemispheres before the great Ice ages. These temperate rainforests are found on both islands, although there is considerable variation in terms of species.

The podocarps tower above hardwoods such as tawa (dominant in the north), kamahi (in the south), pukatea, hinau and maire, while tree ferns, small trees, shrubs and mosses form the middle and lower storeys.

Kauri forests, too, are highly diverse, with many herbs, mosses and lichens growing on the kauri trees themselves. Podocarp and hardwood species are often also present. The gigantic, long-lived kauri trees are only found in Northland and on the Coromandel Peninsula. Because their excellent timber was sought in the early days of settlement, much of the land that was once covered in kauri forest is now bare. However, some areas of forest remain and a handful of awe-inspiring trees believed to be 1000 or 2000 years old still survive in the Waipoua Forest in Northland's west (see the Northland Circuit ride in the Auckland & the North chapter).

The pohutukawa or NZ native Christmas tree

Beech forest is the most plentiful forest type, since it was not highly sought after for its timber and much of it is now protected in national parks. The *Nothofagus* (beech) species found in NZ are very similar to those found in South America, adding weight to the Gondwanaland theory. Beech forests are found on both islands. Some exist as pure stands, while elsewhere several beech species grow together, or with podocarps, hardwoods and/or softwoods. Ferns and mosses flourish in beech forests.

Ferns are a prominent feature of the NZ bush. The largest of the 80 species is the mamaku, or black tree fern, which grows to 20m. The ponga (silver tree fern), growing to 10m, is the national symbol, adorning the jumpers of NZ sports representatives.

Other vegetation communities include northern coastal forest – look out for the beautiful pohutukawa (also called the New Zealand Christmas tree) and NZ's mangrove species – and subalpine and alpine regions, which support a wide range of species, including herbs, alpine shrubs, snow tussocks and flowers.

Birds The endemic avifauna of NZ is not immense, but it evolved in relative peace with very little threat and no large competitors. As a result, ground-dwelling birds such as parrots, kiwis and moas not only survived, but thrived.

The balance was altered by the arrival of humans and the predatory species that both Maori and Europeans introduced. Many species vanished in a 'blink of the eye' relative to NZ's evolutionary history.

The NZ bird you *won't* see today is the famous moa, a huge, ostrich-like creature growing up to 4m high. Hunted out by the Maori, they were extinct for several centuries before Europeans arrived – you can see moa skeletons and reconstructions in many NZ museums.

Birds that you are likely to spot on the road include the deep blue pukeko (a swamp hen with a bright red beak), tui and, circling above, the NZ falcon. Kiwis, the national symbol, are

New Zealand's Flora & Fauna

shy, nocturnal creatures, and although you may hear them, you are unlikely to see one except in captivity – among the best places to see them are at the Moana Zoo, near Greymouth, or the Otorohanga Kiwi House, near Hamilton.

With so much coastline, NZ is also home to a variety of sea birds, some, such as the gannet, performing amazing migratory journeys just weeks after hatching. You can see gannet colonies at close quarters during breeding season, at Muriwai Beach (see the Muriwai Beach ride in the Auckland & the North chapter), Cape Kidnappers (North Island) and Farewell Spit (see the Farewell Spit ride in the Marlborough & Nelson chapter). The Seabird Coast, south-east of Auckland, is another excellent spot for bird-watching (see the Seabird Coast & Hunua Ranges ride in the Auckland & the North chapter).

MARTIN HARRIS

Listen for the extraordinary song of the tui.

Marine Mammals Perhaps one of the greatest delights of a trip to NZ, especially the South Island, is a chance to observe the wealth of marine mammals. Of the 76 species of whales and dolphins in the world, tiny NZ is blessed with 35, including the largest and smallest of the toothed whales and dolphins – the sperm whale and the Hector's dolphin. There are also baleen whales, seals and sea lions.

No longer does the blood of these species stain NZ waters. They attract not the bludgeon and harpoon, but the entranced eyes of tourists. The dollars pouring into Kaikoura and elsewhere are worth many times the money made by the previous slaughter.

Other Fauna Growing to 60cm, the tuatara is a lizard-like relic from the dinosaur age, found on protected offshore islands or in captivity at the Wellington Zoo, Otorohanga Kiwi House and Southland Museum, Invercargill.

NZ has no snakes and only one spider that is dangerous to humans, the rare katipo. There are three frog species, none of which can croak! The sandfly *(te namu)*, the most ubiquitous of nuisances, is abundant in South Westland and Fiordland. The fearsome-looking wetas, although quite large invertebrates, fall prey to the European rat and most species are confined to protected islands.

Bats were the only mammals to reach NZ before the arrival of humans. There are two species: the long-tailed and the short-tailed bat.

Though NZ's native freshwater fish are generally fairly small, the country is known as an angler's paradise, largely due to the proliferation of introduced species such as trout. Offshore, there is a great variety of tropical and cold-water fish species, along with crustaceans such as crayfish.

ANN JEFFREE

The tuatara is a 'living fossil' – its ancestors possibly existed up to 260 million years ago.

foreign investment and borrowing, abolishing agricultural subsidies and reforming the taxation system by introducing a goods and services tax (GST), while lowering company and personal income taxes.

The initial changes resulted in a drop in the NZ dollar, an influx of foreign capital, even larger capital speculation, and an increase in private foreign debt. Foreign competition drove out inefficient, government-protected industries.

The bubble burst in 1987 with the worldwide stock market collapse. Inflation and unemployment topped 10%, growth was nonexistent and the country questioned the restructuring.

Labour was replaced by a conservative government which continued with free-market reform. Welfare programs were cut, privatisation was increased and, most significantly, the labour market was deregulated.

The economy showed dramatic improvement in the second half of the 1990s: the government ran a budget surplus and reduced public debt, growth had risen to around 4% (although this had levelled off by the end of the decade), inflation was low and unemployment around 7.5%.

The reforms have had a major effect on NZ's economy and society. Though still overwhelmingly reliant on agriculture for export income (principal exports are meat, dairy products, fish, forest products, fruit and vegetables and wool; main imports are machinery and mechanical appliances, electrical machinery and equipment, textiles, motorcars and other goods), NZ has managed to diversify its economy. Business efficiency and profit has increased in the manufacturing, finance and service industries. Tourism is another major source of foreign revenue; manufacturing and small-scale industry are also important.

NZ now has a broader world outlook, both in its trade and in general. Since 1960, when the UK bought more than half of NZ's exports, NZ has shifted its focus elsewhere, especially to Asia. Australia is now NZ's single-largest trading partner.

The reforms have also had their pitfalls. As the corporate philosophy engulfs NZ, the once-sacrosanct ideals of equality in society have lapsed. Income disparity has grown substantially. In the new user-pays NZ, social services have been sold off to private enterprise, usually resulting in higher charges and the axing of some nonprofitable services.

POPULATION & PEOPLE

New Zealand's population of around 3.8 million is comprised of 72% NZ European (Pakeha), 15% NZ Maori, about 6% Pacific Island Polynesian and 5% Asian (mostly Chinese and Indian). The proportion of Maori, Polynesians and Asians, however, is increasing in relation to NZ's European population.

More than a quarter of all New Zealanders dwell in Auckland, which is more than the entire population of the South Island.

ARTS

NZ has a multifaceted arts scene, with both Maori and Pakeha engaged in all kinds of traditional and modern arts. Although there are distinct 'Maori arts' and 'European arts', Pakeha may carve bone or paint in Maori styles; Maori songs, poi dances and some Maori language are taught in all schools; and Maori people have excelled in such traditionally European arts as theatre and music. Dame Kiri Te Kanawa, a Maori, is one of the world's best-known operatic divas (see the 'Dame Kiri Te Kanawa' boxed text in the Eastern North Island chapter).

Music, from classical to rock, jazz, blues and Irish, is performed in larger cities, and you can even find interesting music played in smaller towns.

There's a lively literary scene (see Literature later in this chapter), poetry readings and live theatre. Wellington is particularly known for its theatre scene, with traditional, improvisational and avant-garde theatre companies. Visual arts and crafts – both contemporary and traditional – can be seen in museums, galleries and commercial outlets throughout the country.

Maori Arts

Maori arts are dramatic in many ways and include practices perhaps unfamiliar to those of European background.

Traditionally, Maori history was preserved in long, specific and stylised songs and chants. As is common in the practice of oral history, oratory, song and chant developed to become a magnificent art in Maori culture. The many rituals associated

NATIONAL LIBRARY OF AUSTRALIA

Maori art includes finely-detailed carving of wood and bone, usually to fashion weapons.

with Maori protocol are also quite stylised – such as the traditional *haka* (war chant) and *wero* (challenge) you'll be greeted with if you visit a *marae*, the traditional meeting place for a tribe. The Maori arts of song and dance include some special features such as the poi dance and action songs. Martial arts, using a variety of traditional weapons and movements, are highly developed and very skillful.

Other Maori arts include crafts such as wood, bone and jade carving, basketry, weaving and a distinctive form of wall panelling known as *tukutuku*, which can be seen on marae buildings and in Maori churches. You'll see woodcarvings, tuku-

tuku and distinctive styles of painting in most Maori meeting houses.

Literature

NZ has an active literary scene. Internationally known Katherine Mansfield (1888-1923) was born and raised in NZ, but did most of her writing in England.

Frank Sargeson (1903-82) is probably as well known as Mansfield in NZ, but less so overseas. Maurice Shadbolt has written several fine historical novels about NZ; best known is probably the prize-winning *The Season of the Jew*, about the Northland Land Wars.

Janet Frame's autobiography became famous after being made into the film *An Angel at My Table* by acclaimed Kiwi director Jane Campion.

Other favourite authors include Shonagh Koea, Maurice Gee, Fiona Kidman, Owen Marshall, Philip Temple and mystery writer Dame Ngaio Marsh.

Children's literature is a particularly fertile area of writing, with many NZ writers achieving international success.

Good references include the *Oxford History of New Zealand Literature in English*, edited by Terry Sturm, or the *Penguin History of New Zealand Literature*, by Patrick Evans.

For short stories see the *Oxford Book of New Zealand Short Stories*, edited by Vincent O'Sullivan, and *Some Other Country: New*

New Zealand Rock Music

New Zealand rock music doesn't begin and end in Dunedin, although over the past 10 to 15 years you could be forgiven for thinking so. In terms of innovative and alternative music, Dunedin (equated by some North Americans with Athens, Georgia, home of the B-52s and mega band REM) is NZ's music capital.

Bands whose success began in Dunedin and continued overseas include the Verlaines, Straightjacket Fits, the Clean and the Chills. Other well known acts were the Able Tasmans, the Bats and the Headless Chickens.

In the 1970s and 80s, Split Enz was NZ's best known and most successful band. Originally an unusual and eccentric group, their style became more mainstream in the 80s.

Like many other NZ bands who achieved success, Split Enz eventually relocated to Australia and soon found they were referred to as 'a great Australian band'. After their break-up in the mid-1980s, band member Neil Finn formed another successful 'Australian' band, Crowded House (at least Crowded House had one Australian member).

Te Awamutu, south of Hamilton in the North Island, was the boyhood home of the Finn brothers, Neil and Tim, and is alluded to in the Crowded House song *Mean to Me*. Fans can analyse the brothers' roots on a walk through the town (keyed maps are available from the information centre).

Zealand's Best Short Stories, chosen by Marion McLeod & Bill Manhire. Trudie McNaughton compiled *In Deadly Earnest*, a collection of fiction by NZ women.

Maori & Pacific Literature Despite the orally based Maori culture, NZ is experiencing a movement of dynamic Maori literature. *Te Ao Marama*, two volumes on contemporary Maori writing, includes an anthology of Maori literature (written and oral) and a series of prominent Maori authors examining crucial issues affecting Maori people. The editor, Witi Ihimaera, is a prolific Maori author.

Keri Hulme's *The Bone People* won the British Booker McConnell Prize in 1985; she has also published several other novels and poetry.

Controversial author Alan Duff writes about Maori people in modern NZ society. His first novel, *Once Were Warriors*, was made into an award winning, internationally acclaimed film.

Other significant Maori authors include novelists Apirana Taylor and Patricia Grace and poet Hone Tuwhare. NZ also has some important Pacific islander authors. Samoan Albert Wendt is one of the finest. He has published novels, poetry and short stories. Niuean John Puhiatau Pule has written about the Pacific islanders' experience in NZ.

Poetry James K Baxter is possibly the best known NZ poet. Others include RAK Mason, Allen Curnow, Denis Glover, Hone Tuwhare and the animated Sam Hunt. *Contemporary New Zealand Poetry Nga Kupu Titohu o Aotearoa*, edited by Miriama Evans, Harvey McQueen & Ian Wedde, is an excellent collection of NZ poetry written both in English and Maori. Wedde and McQueen also edited the comprehensive *Penguin Book of New Zealand Verse*.

Cinema

The history of NZ film doesn't really begin until the late 1970s. From some early stumbling attempts, notable feature films such as *Sleeping Dogs* (1977), *Bad Blood* (1981), *Smash Palace* (1981) and the comedy *Came a Hot Friday* (1984) have launched the careers of NZ directors and actors.

Other films of note include *Utu* (Revenge; 1983), an amateurish but break-through Maori film, *Meet the Feebles* (1989), *The Quiet Earth* (1985), *Goodbye Pork Pie* (1980), the animated *Footrot Flats* (1986) and art-house *Vigil* (1984).

However, it wasn't until the Cannes and Academy Award success of Jane Campion's *The Piano* (1993) that the world noticed NZ's by then accomplished movie industry. Since then, *Once Were Warriors* (1994), a brutal tale of modern urban Maori life, stunned movie-goers around the world; and Peter Jackson's *Heavenly Creatures* (1994), based on a famous 1950s case of matricide, also achieved critical acclaim.

Campion is NZ's best-known director. *An Angel at My Table* (1990), based on Janet Frame's autobiography, shows the fine character development typical of all of her films.

SOCIETY & CONDUCT

NZ culture is essentially European, shaped by the early settlers who held strongly to their British traditions. However, Maori culture, always integral, is a strong and continuing influence.

A growing diversity of migrants and a wider global outlook has profoundly influenced contemporary NZ society. Resurgent Maori culture, along with the new corporate philosophy, have also prompted NZ to revise its world view. More than ever, the country is exploring its identity and its place in the world.

New Zealanders are intensely proud of their country. Aware of their country's small size and relative insignificance on the world stage, national achievements, particularly world-beating sporting achievements, are greeted with great fanfare. NZ also values its independence and is not afraid to take on the world, as it has done in its anti-nuclear stance, a policy that eventually became so widely supported that not even conservative governments have been game to reverse it, despite intense international pressure.

To the visiting cyclist, New Zealanders are a friendly and easy-going lot.

Perhaps due to the social liberalism of the late 19th century, there appears to be little in the way of class division and social instability, at least *within* the Pakeha population, although the impact of economic rationalism may eventually change that as social services are cut back.

Traditional Culture

The Maori are the original Polynesian settlers of NZ, migrating from the islands of the South Pacific. As such, Maori language and culture is closely related to that of other Polynesian peoples.

The term Maori has only applied to NZ Polynesians since the arrival of Europeans. Maori society was tribal and the Maori referred to themselves in terms of their *iwi* (tribe), such as Ngati Kahu, or 'Descendents of Kahu'. The tribes were headed by a supreme chief, but often of more relevance was the *hapu* (sub-tribe or clan), and the village structure based around family groups.

Whakapapa (genealogy) determines everyone's place in the tribe, so ancestral and family ties are critical. The marae is where the tribe gathers – it's the focus of Maori culture. It is here that ancestors are as present as the current generations.

Traditional Maori society was irrevocably damaged by British colonisation and the accompanying land appropriation and cultural dominance. During the 1860s, race relations dived with the Land Wars. However, since the turn of the century, the Maori people have actively sought to strengthen their political voice and improve their lot. Despite disparities in education, wealth and power between Maori and Pakeha, Maori people have enjoyed greater acceptance and equality under the law than the indigenous peoples of many other European colonised countries.

With the postwar economic boom, the promise of jobs brought many Maori to the cities where they mixed with Europeans as never before. But assimilation, encouraged by the government, also meant the dominance of European culture and although Maori culture survived, they lost contact more than ever with their language and traditions.

In the late 1960s a new Maori voice arose and called for a revival in Maoritanga (Maori culture). Young activists combined with traditional leaders to provide a new direction, calling for the government to address Maori grievances. The contentious Treaty of Waitangi, always on the Maori agenda, came to the fore as never before.

The focus on Maori issues spurred the government to give the Maori language

Maori Religion & Society

Maori oral histories tell of the discovery of New Zealand around 950 AD by the Polynesian navigator Kupe, who sailed from Hawaiki, the 'ancestral homeland', to the land later named 'Aotearoa' – Land of The Long White Cloud.

Maori societies revolved around the *iwi* (tribe) or *hapu* (sub-tribe). Ancestor worship was important and long genealogies *(whakapapa)*, often stretching back to one of the canoe groups of the Great Migration, were committed to memory.

Maori religion was complex, with a variety of gods representing the sea, sky, mountains, war, agriculture etc. The priests *(tohunga)* could communicate with the gods and knew the rituals associated with offerings, but were also responsible for maintaining the history, genealogy, stories and songs of the tribe.

Essential to Maori religion and society were the notions of *mauri* (life force) and *wairua* (spirit) that reside in all things, and *mana* (spiritual power or prestige). *Tapu* (taboos) applied to forbidden objects, such as sacred ground or a chief's possessions, and also to actions or even people proscribed by the tribe.

One of the best ways to promote the mana of a tribe was through battle, so the Maori had a highly developed warrior society. War had its own worship, sacrifices, rituals, dances and art forms. Tribes engaged in numerous battles over territory, for *utu* (revenge) or for other reasons, with the losers often becoming slaves or food. Eating an enemy not only delivered the ultimate insult but also passed on the enemy's life force or power. The Maori built defensive villages, or *pa*, to which they retreated when attacked. These fortresses were built on terraced hill tops with concentric defensive walls. If the outer wall was breached, the defenders could retreat to the next fortified inner terrace.

The higher classes were decorated with intricate tattoos – women only had *moko* (facial tattoos) on their chins, while high-ranking men not only had tattoos over their entire face but also over other parts of their body (especially their buttocks).

Marae Etiquette

Increasingly these days, visitors to New Zealand are being given the opportunity to experience traditional Maori culture by being granted permission to visit a *marae*.

Strictly speaking, the marae is the open area in front of the *whare hui* (meeting house) but the term is often loosely used to describe the buildings as well. Either way, it is a place that is sacred to the Maori and should be treated with great respect.

Some of the customs and conventions of the marae are:

• that it is a place to stand *(turangawaewae)*
• that it is a place of kinship *(whanau-ngatanga)*, friendship *(manaakitanga)*, love *(aroha)*, spirituality (wairua) and the life force (mauri)
• respect for elders *(whakarongo ki nga kaumatua)*
• that it is a place where life and death merge, where the living *(te hunga ora)* give great honour to the dead *(te hunga mate)*
• the preservation and use of the Maori language *(Maori reo)*.

A welcoming ritual *(Te Powhiri Ki Te Manuhiri)* is followed every time visitors *(manuhiri)* come onto the marae. Manuhiri bring with them the memories of their dead. The hosts *(tangata whenua)* pay their respects to the deceased of the manuhiri, likewise the manuhiri to the tangata whenua. The ceremony removes the *tapu* (taboo) and permits the manuhiri and tangata whenua to interact. The practice varies from marae to marae. Note that shoes must be removed before entering a whare hui.

Te Powhiri Ki Te Manuhiri may proceed as follows: a welcoming call *(karanga)* by women of the tangata whenua to the manuhiri. It could also include a ceremonial challenge *(taki or wero)*.The manuhiri reply to the karanga and proceed on to the marae. They pay their respects and sit where indicated, generally to the left (if facing outwards) of the whare hui.

Welcoming speeches *(mihi)* are given by the tangata whenua from the threshold *(taumata tapu)* in front of the meeting house. Each speech is generally supported by a song *(waiata)*, generally led by the women. When the mihi is finished the manuhiri reply. The tapu is deemed to have been lifted from the manuhiri when the replies are finished. The manuhiri then greet the tangata whenua with handshakes and the pressing of noses *(hongi)*. In some places the hongi is a single press, in others it is press, release, press.

Before the manuhiri leave the marae they make farewell speeches *(poroporoaki)* that take the form of thanks and prayer.

Once invited into the marae you will be extended every hospitality. You are now part of an extended family. Remember though, if you do receive hospitality such as food and lodging, it is customary to offer a *koha*, or donation, to help towards the upkeep of the marae.

greater prominence in schools and the media, to institute the Race Relations Act banning discrimination and, in 1975, to introduce the Waitangi Tribunal to investigate Maori land claims. However, in 1994, to try and extricate itself from the terms of the tribunal, the government proposed a massive once and for all 'fiscal envelope' of $1 billion to pay out all Maori land claims over the following 10 years.

Though the Maori population is now overwhelmingly urban and largely integrated into European society, the growing interest in Maoritanga has brought about a renaissance of Maori language, literature, arts and culture. More Maori are returning to the marae, the main focus for Maoritanga, learning the language and taking an interest in their whakapapa.

Many Pakeha also have a growing awareness of Maori culture. Certainly, government and intellectuals have embraced the new Maori revival, and see an understanding of Maori culture and at least a basic knowledge of Maori as an advantage. However, there is an undercurrent of unease in the wider community, especially with radical Maori aspirations that call for Maori sovereignty – the establishment of a separate Maori government and judicial system.

Though NZ is not the utopia of racial harmony it is sometimes portrayed as, there is no denying the genuine attempts by the European community to accommodate Maori aspirations. The overall good relations between both communities continue, and NZ's record on race relations remains justifiably strong.

Dos & Don'ts

The protocol surrounding a visit to a Maori marae is important. It is extremely offensive to enter a particular marae (including the land surrounding the buildings) unless you

have been invited and welcomed onto it. (Be careful that you don't accidentally waltz onto a marae in search of somewhere to fill your water bottles!)

Once you've been welcomed onto a marae in a Te Powhiri Ki Te Manuhiri (welcoming ceremony), you are considered part of it and are free to visit at any time. However, you must always enter by the front door.

As more Maori land claims are settled, many spiritual places are being returned to Maori ownership or closed to the public. They are generally well signed. If you come across such areas, it is important to respect the wishes of the traditional owners and not enter, without permission.

Place Names

Many place names have a clear Maori influence. These include:

anatoki – axe or adze in a cave; cave or valley in the shape of an axe
awa – river or valley
ika – fish
iti – small
kahurangi – treasured possession or special greenstone
kai – food
kainga – village
kare – rippling
koura – crayfish
manga – branch, stream or tributary
mangarakau – plenty of sticks; a great many trees
manu – bird
maunga – mountain
moana – sea or lake
moko – tattoo
motu – island
nui – big
o – of
one – beach, sand or mud
onekaka – red-hot or burning sand
pa – fortified village
papa – flat, broad slab
parapara – the soft mud used for dyeing flax
patarua – killed by the thousands; site of early tribal massacres

pohatu – stone
puke – hill
rangi – sky or heavens
rangiheata – absence of clouds; a range seen in the early morning
repo – swamp
roa – long
roto – lake
rua – hole, two
takaka – killing stick for parrot, or bracken
tane – man
tata – close to, dash against or twin islands
te – the
totaranui – place of big totara trees
uruwhenua – enchanted objects
wahine – woman
wai – water
waikaremumu – bubbling waters
waingaro – lost; waters that disappear in certain seasons
wainui – big bay or many rivers, the ocean
waka – canoe
wero – challenge
whanau – extended family
whanga – bay or inlet
whare – house
whenua – land or country

Try a few – Whanga-roa is 'long bay', Roto-rua is 'two lakes', Roto-roa is 'long lake' and Wai-kare-iti is 'little rippling water'. All these names with 'wai' in them – Waitomo, Waitara, Waioru, Wairoa, Waitoa and so on – are associated with water.

However, words don't always mean the sum of their components. If you're interested, *A Dictionary of Maori Place Names*, by AW Reed, is a superb reference.

LANGUAGE

NZ has two official languages: English and Maori. English is the language you will usually hear spoken, but Maori, long on the decline, is making a comeback. There are advantages in knowing a little Maori, not only because of the Maori terms in everyday use, but because so many places in NZ have Maori names.

Try these common Maori greetings:

Haere mai!
   Welcome!
Kia ora.
   Hello, good luck, good health, thank you

Pronunciation

If you find yourself cycling through a place called Ngaruawahia or Tauteiihiihi, you may feel a little lost – but know the basics of pronunciation and at least you'll be able to tell someone where you are. Their length is one reason why some place names initially seem so unpronounceable, but break them into syllables and they become relatively simple.

Pronunciation of most consonants in Maori is similar to English. The Maori **r** is a flapped sound with the tongue near the front of the mouth, but not rolled.

Two special consonant sounds are **ng**, pronounced as in the English suffix '-ing' (sing, running etc); and **wh**, which should be pronounced like a soft English 'f'. This pronunciation is used in many (but not in all) place names, such as Whakatane and Whakapapa.

Correct pronunciation of vowels is all-important:

a   as in 'but' (short 'a')
e   a sort of combination sound, between 'get' and 'bait' (long 'e')
e   as in 'get' (short 'e')
i   as in 'it' (short 'i')
o   a shorter sound than 'o'
u   as in 'foot' (short 'u')

Vowels are often used in combination, in which case each vowel is pronounced. For example, Maori is pronounced mah-or-ree; but kauri is pronounced kah-oo-ree.

Syllables always end in a vowel and there is never more than one vowel in a syllable. So Tauteiihiihi breaks into ta-u-te-i-ih-i-ih-i.

There are many Maori language references available (including some Maori-English dictionaries) and one of the best is *Say it in Maori*, a pocket-sized book compiled by Alan Armstrong.

Facts for the Cyclist

HIGHLIGHTS

There are so many beautiful places to cycle in New Zealand. To make the most of them, keep away from the main highways – the most bland way to get from A to B – and, unless you like crowds, rows of motels and spending lots of money, don't spend all your time around the main tourist centres like Rotorua, the Bay of Islands and Queenstown. These towns often make a good base with plenty of tourist attractions, but there are far nicer parts of the country to cycle.

Best Coastal Scenery

The dramatic seascapes and quiet, sealed Pacific Coast Highway (SH35) between Opotiki and Waihau Bay make the East Cape Circuit on Eastern North Island a genuine contender for the title of best coastal tour in the world.

Less rugged but incredibly pretty are the sparkling turquoise waters of Marlborough Sounds seen from the cliff-hugging road on the Marlborough Explorer.

Another beauty is the Coromandel Peninsula, where you are never far from delightful little beaches, including Hot Water Beach near Whitianga.

Best Mountain Scenery

The Around Mt Taranaki tour provides a 360° view of the majestic Fuji-like cone of Mt Taranaki – even after three days of circumnavigation, it's hard to tear your gaze away.

The Tongariro Crossing walk (on the Central Plateau tour) affords breathtaking close-up views of the big volcanic peaks of Mt Ruapehu, Mt Ngauruhoe and Mt Tongariro, and the surrounding awe-inspiring Martian landscape.

The ride into Milford Sound on the Southern Scenic Route takes you along glacier-carved valleys between massive mountains and over the Divide into colossal Cleddau Canyon, before emerging at sea level with the mighty Mitre Peak towering before you.

Best Alpine Cycling

The Southern Alps Circuit from Porters Pass to Arthur's Pass keeps you above 500m for about 70km, while (with good wet weather gear) riding in the rain over Haast Pass on the West Coast ride can be an almost spiritual experience.

Best Descent

The freewheeling descent from Takaka Hill (791m) on the Farewell Spit ride is memorable both for its fine views and duration – 15km on the Motueka side! By the time it's over, your hands are ready to drop off from squeezing the brakes and you're taking the hairpin bends like a Grand Prix motorbike champion.

Best Ascent

The 12.5km from the Waipoua River (80m) to Wairau Summit (387m) on the Northland Circuit involves 7km of continuous climbing, but the gentle gradient and splendour of the surrounding kauri forest make it a joy.

For a challenge, try the Crown Range Rd climb on the Western Otago Circuit. NZ's highest highway features a solid 3.7km ascent reminiscent of the classic hairpin climb in the French Alps, the Alpe d'Huez, followed by another 9km stretch (partly on gravel) to the crest (1100m) with views over Queenstown and the Kawarau valley.

Best Fitness Challenge

The Banks Peninsula Circuit from Christchurch will test your stamina and determination with a series of cruel climbs, plunging descents and some extraordinarily rough, narrow and winding gravel sections. The volcanic geology and views, however, are among the most memorable on the South Island.

Most Remote

With a scenic 20km section of very rough gravel, the 50km Raglan-Kawhia road is slow-going and there are only a few dwellings along the way. Though sealed, the section from Kawhia to Te Anga is also sparsely populated.

To the south of North Island, the Stratford-Wanganui Circuit includes long, isolated stretches of countryside punctuated by virtual ghost towns like Whangamomona. The

East Cape Circuit is another good choice for quiet roads.

Best Mountain Biking

There are heaps of great mountain biking areas in NZ, but the Whakarewarewa Forest near Rotorua is a mecca for enthusiasts, as are the hills around Wellington.

On the South Island, the Nelson and Hanmer Springs areas are a fat-tyre heaven, while Christchurch is blessed with fantastically varied mountain bike terrain.

Best Wildlife Spotting

For marine mammals, you can't beat the Kaikoura Coast & Hanmer Springs Circuit on the South Island. The Seabird Coast on the Seabird & Hunua Ranges ride is great for spotting – you guessed it – sea birds; and in summer you can visit the amazing gannet colonies on the Muriwai Beach ride or at Farewell Spit, home to thousands of migratory waders from the Arctic Tundra.

Thousands of glow-worms can be seen at the Waitomo Caves on the Waitomo Circuit.

SUGGESTED ITINERARIES
One Week

If you are feeling fit, ride the East Cape Circuit on the North Island or the West Coast ride on the South Island; if you're less so, the Northland Circuit in the North and the Marlborough Explorer on the South Island are slightly easier alternatives.

Two Weeks

From Auckland, take a bus to Thames (or do the Seabird Coast & Hanua Ranges ride) and take on the challenge of the Coromandel Peninsula ride, branching off to Rotorua and then linking up with the East Cape Circuit.

On the South Island, a hard but rewarding 14 days of riding could include the six-day West Coast ride from Wanaka to Greymouth, coupled with the Southern Alps Circuit.

Alternatively, follow up the West Coast ride with the Farewell Spit and/or Marlborough Explorer rides.

One Month

On the South Island, warm up with the Marlborough Explorer, then do either the Catlins Coast ride (Dunedin to Invercargill) or the Southern Scenic Route. Make sure you ride the West Coast ride, followed by the Southern Alps Circuit, including the Kaikoura Coast/Hanmer Springs ride (ending at Christchurch instead of Greymouth).

On the North Island, do the Northland Circuit and head over to the Coromandel Peninsula via the Seabird Coast, continuing east to the East Coast Circuit. Follow that with biking and other activities in the Central Plateau area, perhaps combining the Central Plateau ride with the Tongariro Crossing walk. If you've time, head back west to ride the Waitomo Circuit and visit the glow-worm caves.

Two Months

Plan according to the time of year in which you're travelling. Between February and March start with the cooler South Island and go north as the weather cools down. In November and December, tour the North Island first.

On the South Island, ease into the saddle with the relatively flat Canterbury Hinterland ride, followed by the Mackenzie Country and Catlins Coast rides and the Southern Scenic Route. Take time out around Te Anau and Queenstown for walking or sightseeing. Continue your tour with the West Coast ride and Southern Alps Circuit, finishing with the Marlborough Explorer. Squeeze in the Kaikoura Coast & Hanmer Springs ride along the way!

If you're heading in a south-north direction on North Island, check out the mountain bike routes around Mt Wellington, then push on through the East Cape ride. Head over to Rotorua for more mountain biking, sightseeing and other activities, before doing the Central Plateau ride, linking to the Stratford-Wanganui Circuit and Around Mt Taranaki rides. Walk the Tongariro Crossing and climb Mt Taranaki, then clean up the Waitomo Circuit before heading to the Coromandel Peninsula. Ride to Auckland via the Seabird Coast & Hunua Ranges ride, and finish up with the Northland Circuit.

PLANNING
When to Cycle

NZ's busiest tourist season is during the warmer months from around November to April. Peak season is the summer school holidays from 20 December to late January.

Avoid cycling through tourist areas and beach towns during this period: not only is accommodation heavily booked and expensive, but that delightful deserted country road becomes the highway from hell. Easter, Labour Day weekend in late October and the mid-year school holidays are other busy times to avoid.

The ideal time for cycling is from late February to April, when the roads and tourist centres are less crowded. Later in spring (October to early December) is another possibility, though autumn tends to be calmer and drier (see Climate in the Facts about New Zealand chapter).

Areas that are not particularly touristy (such as the Waikato, Wanganui and Taranaki areas of the North Island) are good for cycling in summer – though cyclists from cooler climates may find the North Island too hot or humid for cycling in February.

It is possible to cycle in the north right through winter – especially around Northland and the Coromandel Peninsula. The days are short, though, and it gets cooler at night, so take warm clothes – particularly if you are intending to camp.

Unless you're a die-hard, most of the South Island is too cold for cycling during the winter months. Snow can fall at higher altitudes any time between March and November, and in snow and icy conditions the pass roads may close. Some accommodation, transport services and activities close in winter due to lack of patronage.

Maps

The best cycling maps are a series of District Maps (1:350,000) put out by the New Zealand Automobile Association (AA). Frustratingly, while these are available free to AA members and members of affiliate organisations, they are not given (or even sold) to anyone without a membership card. District Maps are only available from AA offices and agents.

The AA also sells maps and small road atlases at an adequate scale for cyclists through bookshops, newsagents and travel centres: the *Glovebox Edition* (1:810,000) costs $14.20 and *Classic Edition* (1:600,000) sells for $23.70.

Land Information New Zealand produces a series of Terrain Maps (1:250,000) which contain limited topographical information, but do not show road names and tend to be less accurate than AA maps, particularly concerning road surfaces.

What to Bring

Weight and weather protection are essential factors to consider when choosing equipment. You'll notice every extra gram on the uphill stretches, so don't take anything you don't really need – and go for lightweight equipment wherever possible. Exposure to the elements can be a serious hazard in NZ; waterproof clothing and gear will minimise danger and discomfort.

The Your Bicycle chapter has some handy tips on how best to organise your gear in panniers.

Clothing Wear padded bike shorts, known to cyclists as 'knicks'. These are designed to be worn without underwear to prevent chafing. If you don't fancy yourself in Lycra, you can get 'shy shorts' – ordinary looking shorts with sewn-in lightweight, padded knicks.

In colder weather, you'll need Lycra tights over your knicks, or padded thermal 'longs'. Another option is to get a pair of legwarmers, which are usually also made of Lycra and are easily removed if things warm up. You can also get arm-warmers.

Sunburn is a serious hazard in NZ (see Medical Problems & Treatment in the Health & Safety chapter) and long sleeves provide the best protection. To avoid overheating, though, you need something light and breathable. Some cycling tops are made from synthetic fabrics like CoolMax and Intercool, which are specially designed to keep you cool. Silk is another alternative. While cotton is cool, it dries slowly and as a result is useless when the weather suddenly gets cold and wet.

Sunglasses are essential cycling wear, not only to minimise exposure to UV radiation, but to shield your eyes from insects and prevent them from drying out in the wind. A peaked helmet cover also provides a little sun protection and a bandanna is useful to soak up sweat.

Go for bright or light-coloured clothing; not only is it cooler, but it maximises your visibility – NZ drivers are not known for their safety-consciousness. A fluorescent top or visibility vest will make sure that you're seen early.

Because the weather can change so quickly in NZ, it's important to always carry warm and waterproof clothing. Don't underestimate the danger of exposure. Layering (wearing several thin layers of clothing) is the most practical way to dress in cooler weather. Start with a lightweight cycling or polypropylene top, followed by a warmer insulating layer, such as a thin synthetic fleece jacket (these are lightweight and dry quickly), and a rainproof jacket.

There are some excellent waterproof, yet 'breathable' cycling jackets on the market. Gore-Tex is probably the best known fabric used in making jackets. Other fabrics such as Silmond or Activent are compact, lightweight and excellent for light rain, but won't stand up to a steady downpour.

Wear fingerless cycling gloves: the padded palms reduce the impact of jarring on your hands, which can lead to nerve damage; they also prevent sunburn and protect your hands in case of a fall.

In cold weather you may also need full-finger gloves (either thin polypropylene gloves, which can be worn with cycling gloves, or more wind and/or rain resistant ones). You can also buy thermal socks and neoprene booties to go over your shoes, so you can feel your toes on those cold mornings. A close-fitting beanie under your helmet will help to keep you warm.

Helmets are compulsory in NZ. Make sure that yours fits properly (the helmet should sit far enough forward that only 3 to 4cm of your forehead is exposed; it should be firm but not tight once the strap has been fastened). If it has been in a crash, replace it.

Cycling shoes are the way to go (or next best, stiff-soled ordinary shoes). Stiff soles transfer the power from your pedal stroke directly to the pedal. Spongy soled running shoes are inefficient at doing this and are likely to leave your feet very sore.

Off the Bike The clothing you carry for off the bike depends a bit on the type of accommodation you plan to use.

If you're camping, it's essential to have adequate protection against the cold, particularly on the South Island outside the summer months. Pack thermal underwear (tops and bottoms), socks and underwear, a warm top such as a synthetic fleece, a hat and gloves.

Cold weather gear is also important, but less critical if you're staying indoors. New Zealanders are a pretty relaxed bunch, so casual clothes are fine, though you may want to pack something better if you plan on eating in smart restaurants.

Take a separate pair of shoes for when you're off the bike. In summer, you can probably get away with sandals unless you're at higher altitudes.

Camping Equipment If you're planning to camp, you'll need a lightweight, waterproof tent, sleeping mat and warm sleeping bag. Especially if you're camping in the mountains, use a down or good-quality synthetic bag, rated from at least 0° to 5°C. Carry a torch (or bike light), cooking and eating utensils and water containers; and you may want to bring a portable stove and fuel container.

Fuel may not be carried on aircraft, but is readily available in NZ. White gas (known as shellite or white spirits), methylated spirits and kerosene are available from petrol stations, hardware shops and some supermarkets. Gas cartridges can be purchased at outdoor supply shops in larger centres.

Another useful thing to pack into a pannier is a daypack for use on excursions.

Buying Locally Kiwis make some good cycle clothing as well as general outdoor gear. Ground Effect (☎ 03-379 2623, toll-free in NZ ☎ 0800 655 733 or in Australia ☎ 1800 14 33 00; ✉ ernie@groundeffect.co.nz) is a Christchurch mail-order cycle clothing company that makes reasonably priced, quality garments minus all the advertising that appears on most cycle jerseys. Contact the company for a copy of its catalogue.

Bike Shops In NZ, bike shops tend to be very good, particularly those in the larger towns and cities. Many of these (such as Pack 'n' Pedal, Hedgehog, Pins and Bikebarn) are chains, with good service and well laid-out shops. The staff are generally active cyclists who are happy to provide advice.

In smaller centres, bike shops are often combined with a lawn mower or general sports shop; the range of parts is generally limited and the interest in cycling variable.

Shimano produces a useful free pamphlet, *Cycling in New Zealand*, available from

Equipment Check List

This list is a general guide to the things you might take on a bike tour. Your list will vary depending on the kind of cycling you want to do, whether you're roughing it in a tent or planning on luxury accommodation, and on the time of year. Don't forget to take on board enough water and food to see you safely between towns.

Bike Clothing
- [ ] cycling gloves
- [ ] cycling shoes and socks
- [ ] cycling tights or leg-warmers
- [ ] helmet and visor
- [ ] long-sleeved shirt or cycling jersey
- [ ] padded cycling shorts (knicks)
- [ ] sunglasses
- [ ] thermal undershirt and arm-warmers
- [ ] T-shirt or short-sleeved cycling jersey
- [ ] visibility vest
- [ ] waterproof jacket & pants
- [ ] windproof jacket or vest

Off-Bike Clothing
- [ ] change of clothing
- [ ] spare shoes or sandals
- [ ] swimming costume
- [ ] sunhat
- [ ] fleece jacket
- [ ] thermal underwear
- [ ] underwear and spare socks
- [ ] warm hat and gloves

Equipment
- [ ] bike lights (rear and front) with spare batteries (see torch)
- [ ] elastic cord
- [ ] camera and spare film

- [ ] cycle computer
- [ ] day-pack
- [ ] medical kit* and toiletries
- [ ] sewing/mending kit (for everything)
- [ ] panniers and waterproof liners
- [ ] pocket knife (with corkscrew)
- [ ] sleeping sheet
- [ ] small handlebar bag and/or map case
- [ ] small towel
- [ ] tool kit, pump and spares*
- [ ] torch (flashlight) with spare batteries and globe – some double as (front) bike lights
- [ ] water containers
- [ ] water purification tablets, iodine or filter

Camping
- [ ] cooking, eating and drinking utensils
- [ ] clothesline
- [ ] dishwashing items
- [ ] portable stove and fuel
- [ ] insulating mat
- [ ] matches or lighter and candle
- [ ] sleeping bag
- [ ] tent
- [ ] toilet paper and toilet trowel

* see the 'First Aid Kit' boxed text in the Health & Safety chapter; 'Spares & Tool Kit' boxed text in the Your Bicycle chapter

---

bike shops, which lists bike shops around the country (it's not an exhaustive list, but it's a pretty good guide).

Mountain bikes dominate the shop floor in NZ. Hybrid bikes are also widely available, but outside Trek and Cannondale's models traditional touring bikes are only available custom-made.

Many shops offer a 'buy back' scheme, whereby you can sell a bike back to the shop you bought it from for up to 50% of the purchase price. This is an excellent deal; it can be cheaper than hiring and is generally a better option than the second-hand market, which is a bit hit-and-miss. The buy back schemes apply to bikes only, not to panniers and other equipment.

You may be able to pick up second-hand equipment through hostels, from other cyclists off-loading gear at the end of their trips. There are also a couple of second-hand shops around, like the Secondhand Sport Shop (☎ 09-366 4555), 14 Upper Queen St, Auckland, that sell touring equipment.

For a decent hybrid bike or rigid mountain bike you'll need to pay from $800 to $1200, though you can get a cheap one for around $500. Panniers cost $130 to $350 a pair (you can pick up good local brands such as Tika or Cactus for around $200 to $250); and a good pannier rack is about $75. Other equipment (new), including gloves, lock, pump, combination tool, chain lube, helmet, knicks and cycling top, will set you back another $400 to $550.

Some shops have reasonable second-hand bikes, but the better option is probably to try the Buy Sell Trade & Stolen! section of the New Zealand Mountain Bike Web site (🖳 www.mountainbike.co.nz).

Outdoor Shops Being a country of outdoor enthusiasts, NZ has lots of outdoor shops and manufactures quality equipment. Bivouac and Kathmandu are major chains with shops throughout the country and Pack 'n' Pedal (☎ 09-522 2161), 436 Broadway, Newmarket, sells camping equipment as well as bikes. NZ-made tents include the Great Outdoors Cycle two-person tent from $225 and the excellent Macpac 1 to 2 person 'Microlight' from $500. You can buy a reasonable butane gas stove for around $50 or a multi-fuel stove for $200.

Hiring Locally A surprising number of bike shops do not hire bikes, though in the major centres and popular touring areas you can generally find someone who will. The usual price is from around $30 per day and $100 per week for a fairly standard rigid-fork mountain bike (some have front suspension and, in good mountain biking areas, you may find full-suspension mountain bikes).

Panniers are less frequently for hire, especially outside popular cycle touring areas. A few entrepreneurial types, however, have set up companies that hire both bikes and panniers for touring. They often advertise in the city hostels and may, like the Mountain Bike Hire Company in Auckland (see Information under Auckland in the Auckland & the North chapter), bring the bike to your hostel door; others operate through shops.

TOURIST OFFICES
Local Tourist Offices
Almost every city or town has a tourist information centre. Many are united by the Visitor Information Network (VIN), affiliated with the New Zealand Tourism Board (NZTB). These bigger information centres have trained staff, abundant information on local activities and attractions, and free brochures and maps. Staff also act as travel agents, booking almost all activities, transport and accommodation. Use the centres: they are an excellent resource.

Their only problem is that they can be understaffed and some are too busy. They may devote most resources to their booking facilities because self-funding is the name of the game in NZ and these centres rely on the 10% they take from bookings. Most operators prefer you to book directly with them. Also, a few (very few) operators don't pay to be listed with the centres, so information on their services may not be available.

Smaller tourist offices funded by local councils or business communities don't have the resources of the VIN network and are usually staffed by volunteers. Though the staff may not take bookings, they can answer most queries and are helpful.

Tourist Offices Abroad
The New Zealand Tourism Board (NZTB), whose role is to promote tourism to NZ, has representatives in various countries around the world. Its head office is at PO Box 95, Wellington (☎ 04-472 8860), and its overseas offices include:

Australia
  (☎ 02-9247 5222) Level 8, 35 Pitt St, Sydney, NSW 2000
Germany
  (☎ 69-971 2110) Friedrichstrasse 10-12, D-60323 Frankfurt am Main
Hong Kong
  (☎ 2526 0141) Unit 1601 Vicwood Plaza, 199 Des Voeux Road C
Japan
  Osaka: (☎ 6-268 8335) Meiji Seimei Sakaisuji Honmachi Building, 2nd floor, 1-7-15 Minami Honmachi, Chuo-ku, Osaka 541
  Tokyo: (☎ 3-5381 6331) Shinjuku Monolith, 21st floor, 2-3-1 Nishi Shinjuku, Shunjuku-ku, Tokyo 163-09
Singapore
  (☎ 738 5844) 391 Orchard Rd, Ngee Ann City, 15th floor, Tower A, Singapore
UK
  (☎ 020-7930 1662) New Zealand House, The Haymarket, London SW1Y 4TQ
USA
  (toll-free ☎ 800-388 5494)
  California: 501 Santa Monica Blvd, No 300, Santa Monica, CA 90401
  New York: 780 Third Ave, Suite 1904, New York, NY 10017-2024

VISAS & DOCUMENTS
Passports & Visas

Everyone needs a passport to enter NZ. If you enter on an Australian or NZ passport, or a passport containing an Australian or NZ residence visa, your passport must be valid on arrival. All other passports must be valid for at least three months beyond the time you intend to stay in NZ, or one month beyond the intended stay if the issuing government has an embassy or consulate in NZ able to issue and renew passports.

Australian citizens or holders of current Australian resident return visas do not need a visa or permit to enter NZ and can stay indefinitely if they do not have any criminal convictions. Australians do not require a work permit.

Citizens of the UK, and other British passport holders who are able to show they have permanent UK residency, do not need a visa; they are issued on arrival with a visitor permit to stay for up to six months.

Citizens of the following countries do not need a visa and are given a three month, extendable visitor permit upon arrival:

Austria, Belgium, Brunei, Canada, Czech Republic, Denmark, Finland, France, Germany, Greece, Iceland, Indonesia, Ireland, Italy, Japan, Kiribati, South Korea, Liechtenstein, Luxembourg, Malaysia, Malta, Monaco, Nauru, the Netherlands, Norway, Portugal, Singapore, South Africa, Spain, Sweden, Switzerland, Thailand, Tuvalu, USA.

Citizens of all other countries require a visa to enter NZ, available from any NZ embassy or consular agency. Visas are normally valid for three months.

To qualify for a visitor permit on arrival or for a visa, you must be able to show:

- Your passport, valid for three months beyond the time of your intended stay in NZ.
- Evidence of sufficient funds to support yourself for the time of your intended stay, without working. This is calculated at a rate of NZ$1000 per month (NZ$400 per month if your accommodation has been prepaid) and can be in the form of cash, travellers cheques, bank drafts or American Express, Bankcard, Diners Club, MasterCard or Visa credit cards.
- Onward tickets to a country where you have right of entry, with firm bookings if travelling on special rate air fares.

Evidence of sufficient funds can be waived if a friend or relative in NZ sponsors you (ie will guarantee your accommodation and maintenance). Requirements can change, so always check the situation before departure.

Visa Extensions Visitor permits can be extended for stays of up to nine months, if you apply for further permits and meet normal requirements. 'Genuine tourists' and a few other categories of travellers can be granted stays of up to 12 months.

Apply for extensions at any New Zealand Immigration Service office in Auckland, Manukau, Hamilton, Palmerston North, Wellington, Christchurch and Dunedin.

Be careful not to overstay, as it can mean deportation. Extensions are easy to get, provided you meet the requirements.

Onward Tickets

In order to be granted a visitor permit to NZ, visitors (other than Australian citizen) travelling on special rate air fares will need an onward ticket and bookings to a country where they have right of entry.

Travel Insurance

A travel insurance policy to cover theft, loss and medical problems is a good idea. Some policies offer lower and higher medical-expense options; the higher ones are chiefly for countries, such as the USA, that have extremely high medical costs. There is a wide variety of policies available, so read the small print. Most cover loss of baggage, sickness, accidental injury or death, and cancellation costs in the event that your trip is cancelled due to accident, illness or death, concerning either yourself or a family member.

Some policies specifically exclude 'dangerous activities' that can include scuba diving, motorcycling, even walking, so check carefully what it says about cycling and any other activities you might undertake in NZ.

You may prefer a policy that pays doctors or hospitals directly rather than you having to pay on the spot and claim later. If you have to claim later, make sure you obtain and keep all documentation – bills and medical certificates, or police reports. Some policies ask you to call back (reverse charges) to a centre in your home country where an immediate assessment of your problem is made. Check the policy covers ambulance costs or an emergency flight home.

Other Documents

No special documents other than your passport are required in NZ. Since no vaccinations are required to enter NZ, an international health certificate is not necessary.

Bring your driver's licence. As long as you're over 21, a full, valid driver's licence from your home country is all you need to rent and drive a car in NZ. Members of automobile associations should bring their membership cards – you'll need it to receive the excellent AA free maps (see Maps in the Planning section earlier in this chapter).

An ISIC card (International Student Identity Card) entitles you to certain discounts, particularly on transport. Even better is an International Youth Hostel (YHA) card, which is well worth having even if you don't intend staying in hostels. This card provides a 50% discount on standby tickets for domestic air travel and a discount of up to 30% on major buslines, plus dozens of discounts on activities. A VIP Backpackers Card offers the same benefits and can be bought in NZ or Australia from VIP hostels.

All important documents (passport data page and visa page, travel insurance policy, travellers cheques, air/bus/train tickets etc) should be photocopied before you leave home. Leave one copy with someone at home and keep another with you, separate from the originals.

It's also a good idea to store the details of your vital travel documents in Lonely Planet's free online Travel Vault in case you lose the photocopies or can't be bothered with them. Your password-protected Travel Vault is accessible online anywhere in the world. You can create it at the Lonely Planet Web site (🖳 www.ekno.lonelyplanet.com).

EMBASSIES & CONSULATES
NZ Embassies & Consulates

NZ embassies and consulates in other countries include:

Australia
(☎ 02-6270 4211, fax 6273 3194) Commonwealth Ave, Canberra, ACT 2600. A consulate is also located in Sydney.

Canada
(☎ 613-238 5991, fax 238 5707, ✆ nzhcott@istar.com) Suite 727, Metropolitan House, 99 Bank St, Ottawa, Ont K1P 6G3. A consulate is also located in Vancouver.

France
(☎ 01 45 00 24 11, fax 01 45 01 26 39, ✆ nzembru@bru@compuserve.com) 7ter, rue Léonard de Vinci, 75116 Paris

Germany
(☎ 30-206 210, fax 206 2114) Friedrichstrasse 60, 10117 Berlin. A consulate is also located in Hamburg.

Ireland
(☎ 1-676 2464, fax 676 2489) 46 Upper Mount St, Dublin 2

Japan
(☎ 3-3467 2271/5, ✆ nzemb@gol.com) 20-40 Kamiyama-cho, Shibuya-ku, Tokyo 150. A consulate is also located in Osaka.

Netherlands
(☎ 70-346 9324, fax 363 2983) Carnegielaan 10, 2517 KH The Hague

South Africa
(☎ 12-342 8656, fax 342 8640) 2nd floor, Block C, Hatfield Gardens, 1110 Arcadia St, Hatfield, Pretoria

UK
(☎ 09060-100 100, fax 020-7839 4580) New Zealand House, The Haymarket, London SW1Y 4TQ

USA
(☎ 202-328 4848, fax 667 5227, ✆ nzemb@dc.infi.net) 37 Observatory Circle NW, Washington, DC 20008. Consulates are also located in Los Angeles and Seattle.

Embassies & Consulates in NZ

Foreign embassies and consulates in NZ include the following:

Australia
(☎ 04-473 6411) 72-78 Hobson St, Wellington

Canada
(☎ 04-473 9577) 61 Molesworth St, Wellington

France
(☎ 04-472 0200) Willis Corroon House, 1-3 Willeston St, Wellington

Germany
(☎ 04-473 6063) 90-92 Hobson St, Wellington

Ireland
(☎ 09-302 2867) 2nd floor, Dingwall Building, 87 Queen St, Auckland

Japan
(☎ 04-473 1540) 3-11 Hunter St, Wellington

Netherlands
(☎ 04-473 8652) 10th floor, Investment Centre, cnr Featherstone & Ballance Sts, Wellington

South Africa
(☎ 04-474 4953) 80 The Terrace, Wellington
UK
(☎ 04-472 6049) 44 Hill St, Wellington
USA
(☎ 04-472 2068) 29 Fitzherbert Terrace, Wellington

CUSTOMS

Customs allowances are 200 cigarettes (or 50 cigars or 250g of tobacco), 4.5L of wine or beer and one 1125mL bottle of spirits or liqueur.

Goods up to a total combined value of $700 are free of duty and GST. Personal effects are not normally counted. If you do not exceed your $700 passenger concession, and do not have any alcohol or tobacco in your possession, you can import two extra bottles of duty-free liquor.

As in most places the customs people are fussy about drugs. In a bid to prevent any nasties from damaging wilderness areas or threatening its important primary industries, NZ customs is also strict when it comes to dirt, plants and animals. Clean your bike carefully before you bring it, as well as tents, sleeping bags and shoes; if they don't pass the quarantine inspection, you'll be delayed while they are cleaned. Remember that you cannot carry fuel or gas for camping stoves on the plane.

MONEY
Currency

NZ's currency is dollars and cents. There are $5, $10, $20, $50 and $100 notes and 5c, 10c, 20c and 50c, $1 and $2 coins. Unless otherwise noted, all prices quoted in this book are in NZ dollars.

There are no limitations on the import or export of foreign currency. Unused NZ currency can be changed to foreign currency before you leave the country.

Exchange Rates

The currencies of Australia, the UK, USA, Germany and Japan are all easily changed, and at consistently good rates, in NZ. Most banks will exchange these and up to 30 other currencies, but exchange rates may be lower for less frequently changed currencies.

Naturally, exchange rates are subject to change and may vary between currency sellers. As at February 2000, they were:

country	unit		dollar
Australia	A$1	=	NZ$1.19
Canada	C$1	=	NZ$1.22
euro	€1	=	NZ$0.51
France	1FF	=	NZ$0.29
Germany	DM1	=	NZ$0.97
Japan	¥100	=	NZ$1.48
South Africa	R1	=	NZ$1.79
UK	UK£1	=	NZ$2.89
USA	US$1	=	NZ$1.79

Exchanging Money

Cash Banks are open from 9.30 am to 4.30 pm from Monday to Friday. Exchange rates may vary a few cents between banks.

For long stays, it may be worth opening a bank account. Westpac and the Bank of New Zealand (BNZ) have many branches around the country and having a card for 24-hour ATM access is often more convenient (if there's one in town – not always the case in smaller towns). Get an ATM card before you go – it will be much more difficult to arrange without a fixed address in NZ and some banks are more cooperative than others.

Travellers Cheques Travellers cheques are always the safest way to carry money and their exchange rate is slightly better than that for cash in NZ. American Express, Visa, MasterCard and Thomas Cook travellers cheques are widely recognised. At most banks there's no service charge for changing travellers cheques. Country businesses may not be willing to take travellers cheques, especially if they are not in NZ dollars.

ATMs Some banks allow ATM access to overseas savings accounts, via networks such as Cirrus and Plus, but check with your bank before departure to see if this facility will be available to you in NZ. ATMs are available in most (but not all) NZ towns.

Credit Cards Credit cards are a convenient way to carry money if you avoid interest charges by always keeping your account in the black and your bank doesn't charge exorbitant fees. Get a card with a PIN number attached for ATM withdrawals (but check whether there are fees for this).

Visa, MasterCard and Australian Bankcard credit cards are the most widely recognised and are honoured by thousands of retail outlets. You can get cash advances over the counter at banks or through ATMs that display Visa or MasterCard symbols.

American Express is less widely recognised – for cash you must go to one of their offices in the main cities.

International Transfers It's a good idea to authorise somebody at home to access your account so that they can arrange a bank draft if you need emergency cash; or you may be able to instruct your bank to send a draft to a particular branch of bank in NZ. A telegraphic transfer is quicker, but more expensive than a transfer by mail.

An easier way to get emergency cash is for someone at home to deposit money into your credit card account, which you can then withdraw as a cash advance. If your credit card is linked to a savings account, you may also be able to use phone banking facilities to transfer money yourself.

Moneychangers Moneychangers work in the major tourist areas and at airports. They have slightly longer weekday hours and are usually open on Saturday and sometimes Sunday. Rates may be competitive but are usually less than the banks. Thomas Cook offices have competitive rates and change a wider variety of currencies than most banks.

Security
While NZ is relatively crime-free, it still pays to be careful with your money. Don't leave it sitting in a pannier pocket or handlebar bag and take particular care in tourist areas.

Costs
While it is possible to travel quite economically in NZ, it's just as easy to spend up big. If you stay in hostels, it will cost around $14 to $20 per person, per night. Tent sites are around $9 to $12 per person at motor camps, and less at basic Department of Conservation (DOC) camp sites. Guesthouses and B&Bs charge around $70 a night for two, but it *can* be that much per person. Cheaper hotels charge about $35/50 for singles/doubles, while motels start at $60 to $70 for two.

Hostels, motor camps and motels have kitchens for guests' use, allowing you to cook – a big money saver. While you'll get a light takeaway meal from around $5, it's difficult to find a substantial evening meal for less than $15 – at most mid-priced restaurants, mains are around $20.

An average three to five-hour bus ride might cost around $30 (less with an approved Backpacker/YHA card) plus $10 for your bike.

While activities such as tramping, swimming and bird-watching cost nothing, others, like bungy jumping, rafting or whale watching, can really eat into a travel budget.

Tipping
Tipping is becoming more widespread, although many Kiwis still regard it as a rather odd, foreign custom and something to be discouraged. Nevertheless, it is on the increase, mostly in the major tourist centres. You should tip in a restaurant (not in a simple cafe) if you feel you have received exceptional service. The tip should be about 5% to 10% of the bill.

Taxes & Refunds
GST (Goods and Services Tax) adds 12.5% to the price of just about everything in NZ. Prices quoted almost invariably include GST, but look out for any small print announcing that the price is GST exclusive – which means you'll be paying more than the stated price.

POST & COMMUNICATIONS
Post
NZ post shops are open from 9 am to 5 pm on weekdays. You can have mail addressed to you care of 'Poste Restante, CPO' in whatever town you require (CPO stands for Chief Post Office). Mail is usually held for 30 days.

Within NZ, standard post costs 50c; delivery time is two days between major centres, and a bit longer for rural areas. Or there's Fast Post, promising next-day delivery between Auckland, Wellington and Christchurch, and two-day delivery for rural areas.

For international mail, use Fast Post. Just affix a Fast Post sticker or use a Fast Post envelope. This way it costs $1 to send a postcard anywhere in the world.

Telephone
Most pay phones in NZ are card-operated; they accept $5, $10, $20 or $50 phonecards (standard or prepaid), available from any

shop displaying the lime-green 'phonecards available here' sign, as well as many hostels. Prepaid phonecards offer discounted rates for long-distance calls. There are some pay phones in the larger cities that accept credit cards.

Lonely Planet's eKno Communication Card (see the insert at the back of this book) is aimed at independent travellers and provides budget international calls, a range of messaging services, free email and travel information – for local calls, you're usually better off with a local card. You can join online (🖳 www.ekno.lonelyplanet.com) or by phone from NZ by dialling ☎ 0800-114478.

Check the eKno Web site for joining and access numbers from other countries and updates on super budget local access numbers and new features.

Larger cities have calling centres that advertise discounted overseas rates – and they're more private than a street phonebox. You pay at the counter after making your timed call.

Emergency calls are not charged. Toll-free numbers in NZ are preceded by the ☎ 0800 code, but card phones may require you to insert a card, even though the call is not charged. Mobile phone numbers are preceded by the ☎ 025 code and are charged at a higher rate.

Directory assistance in NZ	☎ 018
Emergency (police, ambulance and fire brigade)	☎ 111
International direct dial access code	☎ 00
International directory service	☎ 0172
Local and national operator	☎ 010
NZ country code	☎ 64
Reverse-charge international calls	☎ 0170

Area Codes The area or STD code for the whole of the South Island and Stewart Island is ☎ 03. The North Island has various regional STD codes: ☎ 09 in Auckland and Northland; ☎ 07 in the Coromandel Peninsula, Bay of Plenty, Waikato and Central Plateau; ☎ 06 in the East Coast, Wanganui, Manawatu and Taranaki regions; and ☎ 04 in and around Wellington. If dialling within a region, you still have to use the area code between towns, often for a town just a few kilometres down the road.

Fax

Many hotels, motels and even hostels have fax machines. Most centres of any size offer fax services, as do post shops. The charge for sending a fax is about $5, plus the telephone toll charges. Receiving a fax costs around $1 per page.

Email & Internet Access

Email and Internet use is becoming increasingly common throughout the country. Cybercafes are popping up in cities as well as in some smaller towns. You can also send and receive email (as well as accessing the Internet) at some hostels, motels, libraries and universities.

To access your own email account from any Net-connected machine in NZ, you'll need to have on hand three pieces of information: your incoming (POP or IMAP) mail server name, your account name and your password. Your ISP or network supervisor will be able to give you these.

Alternatively, open a free Web-based email account such as Hotmail (🖳 www.hotmail .com) or Yahoo! Mail (🖳 mail.yahoo.com), which can be accessed by any computer with a standard browser.

INTERNET RESOURCES

The World Wide Web is a rich resource for travellers. You can research your trip, hunt down bargain air fares, book hotels, check on weather conditions or chat with locals and other travellers about the best places to visit (or avoid!).

There's no better place to start your Web explorations than the Lonely Planet Web site (🖳 www.lonelyplanet.com). Here you'll find succinct summaries on travelling to most places on earth, postcards from other travellers and the Thorn Tree bulletin board, where you can ask questions before you go or dispense advice when you get back. You can also find travel news and updates to many of our most popular guidebooks, and the subWWWay section links you to the most useful travel resources elsewhere on the Web.

BOOKS

The Arts section in the Facts about New Zealand chapter discusses NZ literature in general. There has also been much written about natural history and the outdoors in NZ. Whitcoulls and London Bookshops are two large chains with a wide variety of books, including sections specialising in

New Zealand on the Net

There is a wealth of information on the Internet about New Zealand. Once you've browsed the Lonely Planet Web site (💻 www.lonelyplanet.com), try some of these other useful addresses:

Web site	address	content
NZ Government Online	www.govt.nz	general country information, government statistics and regulations
Government Statistics	www.stats.gov.nz	1999 Year Book with general information on the economy, tourism, environment etc
AraNui	www.lincoln.ac.nz/libr/nz	a great links site to just about everything
Destination NZ	url.co.nz/nzl.html	best place to start for information on accommodation, transport, activities etc
NZ Tourism Board site	www.purenz.com	themed sections on different ways to experience NZ
Akiko	nz.com	news, general information and links
NZ White Pages	www.whitepages.co.nz	telephone directory
Cycling sites		
NZ Mountain Bike Web	www.mountainbike.co.nz	forums and links for touring as well as mountain biking
The Kennett Brothers	www.kennett.co.nz	the personal site of these NZ cycling gurus has loads of information and links
Cycling New Zealand	www.cyclingnz.org.nz	the national road and track racing site with news, events, results etc
Cycling Advocates Network	www.kennett.co.nz/can	cycling issues, bicycle advocacy, touring and media stories on cycling etc

NZ books. The larger cities have a good selection of other general and specialist bookshops. Many towns also have second-hand bookshops.

Different publishers in different countries publish books in different editions, but most of the books listed in this section will be available in NZ bookshops.

Lonely Planet

New Zealand is a 700 page general travel guide to the country by Jeff Williams & Christine Niven. *Tramping in New Zealand* (400 pages), by Jim DuFresne, details nearly 50 walks (tramps) throughout the country. Andrew Stevenson's *Kiwi Tracks: A New Zealand Journey* offers insight and gentle humour about NZ, its people and his fellow backpackers on one man's escape from everyday life into the wilderness.

Cycling

Classic New Zealand Mountain Bike Rides, by Paul, Simon & Jonathan Kennett, is a well produced 350 page guide to the coun-try's best mountain biking. Known as 'the Bible', it's widely available from bike shops and bookshops.

The Kennett brothers are also writing a book on the history of cycling in NZ.

General

For a bit of historical background on NZ, try *A History of New Zealand,* by Keith Sinclair, or *New Zealand Historical Atlas: Visualising New Zealand – Ko Papatuanuku e Takoto Nei* – edited by Malcolm McKinnon and the most exciting NZ publication for years.

Two Worlds: First Meetings between Maori and Europeans 1642-1772, by Anne Salmond, is an account of the first points of contact between the Maori and the European explorers.

The 19th century Maori Land Wars are looked at in a new and interesting way in *The New Zealand Wars,* by James Belich. Christopher Pugsley's *Anzac* is a pictorial account of the NZ troops' involvement in the ill-fated Gallipoli campaign in 1915 during WWI, an important part of the national psyche.

Maori: A Photographic and Social History, by Michael King, and *The Old-Time Maori* (1938), by Makereti, explore the history of the Maori people.

The controversial Treaty of Waitangi is the subject of many books, including *The Treaty of Waitangi* and *An Illustrated History of the Treaty of Waitangi,* both superbly written by Claudia Orange. Several books have been written about the Greenpeace ship *Rainbow Warrior,* sunk by the French government in Auckland Harbour in 1985. *Making Waves: The Greenpeace New Zealand Story* by Michael Szabo is one.

Some of the most fascinating history has been told through biography. *The Dictionary of New Zealand Biography* is a multi-volume collection of hundreds of short NZ biographies. Or there's *A People's History: Illustrated Biographies from The Dictionary of New Zealand Biography, Volume One, 1769-1869,* edited by WH Oliver.

Three biographies about Maori elders are particularly interesting. *Eruera: The Teachings of a Maori Elder* is by Eruera Stirling, as told to Anne Salmond; *Te Puea* and *Whina,* both by Michael King, explore the lives of two influential Maori women.

The Book of New Zealand Women – Ko Kui Ma Te Kaupapa, edited by Charlotte Macdonald, Merimeri Penfold & Bridget Williams, is an anthology of over 300 biographical essays.

Barry Crump, a favourite NZ character, is the author of many popular books published in the 1960s, including the autobiographical *The Life and Times of a Good Keen Man. Being Pakeha,* by Michael King, is the autobiography of one of NZ's foremost Maori historians, himself a Pakeha. Other autobiographies include *An Autobiography,* by the poet Lauris Edmonds; and Maori elder, Mihi Edwards' *Mihipeka: Early Years* and *Mihipeka: Time of Turmoil.*

Maori Culture In recent years NZ has experienced a renaissance of interest in Maori culture, a subject covered by many excellent books. Language books are mentioned in the Language section of the Facts about New Zealand chapter.

Some useful references for learning about Maori culture include: *Te Marae: A Guide to Customs & Protocol,* by Hiwi & Pat Tauroa – good if you're visiting a marae; the more scholarly *Hui: A Study of Maori Ceremonial Gatherings,* by Anne Salmond; *Te Ao Huri-huri: Aspects of Maoritanga,* edited by Michael King; *Tikanga Whakaaro: Key Concepts in Maori Culture,* by Cleve Barlow; and *Maori Customs and Crafts,* compiled by Alan Armstrong.

A number of good books have been written about the rich legends, stories and myths of the Maori people. The illustrated *Maori Myths and Tribal Legends,* retold by Antony Alpers, is particularly good, and others include the illustrated *Maori Myth and Legend,* by AW Reed, and *Traditional Maori Stories,* introduced and translated by Margaret Orbell.

A Land Apart: The Chatham Islands of New Zealand, by Michael King and Robin Morrison, is a good book of photographs, history and stories of the Chatham Islands. *Moriori: A People Rediscovered,* also by King tells about the Moriori people of the these remote islands and debunks some of the common notions about them.

Photography There are numerous coffee-table books of NZ photographs, with titles like *New Zealand – the Glorious Islands, Beautiful New Zealand* and so on. Two of NZ's best photographers, Craig Potton and Robin Morrison, have published a number of books.

Art & Architecture There are plenty of high-quality art books on NZ's well known artists and Maori arts and crafts. Try the magnificent *Taonga Maori: A Spiritual Journey Expressed through Maori Art,* by the Australian Museum (Sydney).

Architecture is not what people usually think of when contemplating NZ, but *The New Zealand House,* by Robert van de Voort (photographer) & Michael Fowler (architect), presents a fascinating variety of NZ home architecture.

Cartoons No overview of NZ publishing could be complete without mention of the country's favourite comic strip, *Footrot Flats,* by Murray Ball. Dozens of books have been published over the years featuring the adventures of The Dog, his master, Wal, and NZ farm life.

NEWSPAPERS & MAGAZINES

There is no national paper, although the *New Zealand Herald* (Auckland), *Dominion* (Wellington) and *Press* (Christchurch) have wide circulations. Backing up the city newspapers are numerous local dailies – some OK, some not. The closest to a national weekly newsmagazine is the *Listener*, an excellent publication which provides a weekly TV and radio guide, plus articles on the arts, social issues and politics. International publications such as *Time* and *Newsweek* are available almost anywhere.

NZ Bike magazine covers on and off-road cycling, with articles on racing, touring, events, technical information and health plus interviews and information from clubs and associations.

RADIO & TV

There are four commercial TV stations (only a couple may be received in some areas), plus Sky, a subscriber television service with news, sports, documentary and movie channels. Cable (subscriber) television has recently been introduced.

Many regional or local commercial stations broadcast on the AM and FM bands; there's also a national noncommercial news station (The National Radio) and a noncommercial classical music station, Concert FM.

WEATHER INFORMATION

Detailed wind information is available from the National Institute of Water and Atmospheric Research (💻 www.niwa.cri.nz) and from the Web site of the Meteorology Department at Victoria University of Wellington (💻 www.geo.vuw.ac.nz/meteorology).

For weather updates, call the Metphone service: ☎ 0900 999 07 for Waikato, Taupo and the Bay of Plenty; ☎ 0900 999 09 for the far north; ☎ 0900 999 04 for Wellington; ☎ 0900 999 06 for the rest of the North Island; and ☎ 0900 999 03 for the South Island.

PHOTOGRAPHY & VIDEO

Photographic and video supplies, equipment and maintenance are all readily available in NZ, but prices are generally higher than in other countries. Video recorders in NZ operate on the PAL system.

Fuji and Kodak are the most popular films, with Agfa also available. Film and processing prices can vary, so it pays to shop around. For prints, one-hour photo developing shops are all over NZ. Slide film is very expensive and processing usually takes about a week.

The native bush in NZ is dense and light levels can be very low – 400 ASA film will help.

TIME

Being close to the international date line, NZ is one of the first places in the world to start the new day. NZ is 12 hours ahead of GMT (Greenwich Mean Time) and UTC (Universal Time Coordinated) and two hours ahead of Australian Eastern Standard Time.

In summer NZ observes daylight-saving time, where clocks are put forward by one hour on the last Sunday in October; clocks are wound back on the first Sunday of the following March. Ignoring daylight-saving time, when it is noon in NZ it is 10 am in Sydney, 9 am in Tokyo, 8 am in Singapore, midnight in London, 8 pm the previous day in New York and 5 pm the previous day in San Francisco.

ELECTRICITY

Electricity is 230V, 50Hz, as in Europe and Australia; Australian-type flat three-prong plugs are used. Appliances designed for DC power supply or different voltages will need a transformer.

WEIGHTS & MEASURES

NZ uses the metric system: distance is measured in kilometres or metres, height is also in metres, weight in kilograms, and temperature in degrees Celsius. Occasionally, you'll encounter vestiges of the British imperial system, in use until 1967. A metric conversion table is printed on the inside back cover of this guide.

LAUNDRY

Laundrettes are relatively uncommon in NZ, but virtually every accommodation place provides a coin-operated washing machine and dryer; you can wash a full load of clothes for about $2 and dry it for $2, using coins or tokens.

WOMEN CYCLISTS

NZ is quite an easy country for women travellers and plenty of women cycle alone with very few hassles. Women should, however, exercise the same degree of caution as they would anywhere – don't walk or camp alone in isolated areas at night, for example.

NZ male cyclists are generally very supportive of women and encourage them to get involved. Women are very active in the racing and mountain bike scene.

In 1998 two women won Cycling New Zealand's Cyclist of the Year awards: Suzy Pride (road) and Sarah Ulmer (joint track winner with Glen Thomson).

Kathy Lynch is pretty much a household name in NZ thanks to her long and brilliant cycling career.

There are women's bike clubs (one is WOMBACS – the Women on Mountain Bikes and Coffee Society) and women only activities – check out the Women's Forum on the NZMTBA Web site (⌨ www.mountainbike.co.nz/forums/women).

GAY & LESBIAN CYCLISTS

Homosexuality was finally decriminalised in 1985 and it is now unlawful to discriminate against a person on the grounds of their sexual orientation in regards to access to and provision of goods, services, employment and so on.

Auckland has the biggest concentration of the country's gay and lesbian organisations and is home to the annual HERO festival held in February. Wellington holds the Devotion Festival in November.

The New Zealand Gay & Lesbian Tourism Association (NZGLTA; ☎ 04-384 1877 or ☎ 0800 367 429, fax 384 5187, ✉ secreta riat@nzglta.org.nz), PO Box 11582, Wellington 6001, promotes gay and lesbian tourism in NZ. Travel Gay New Zealand (fax 04-382 8246, ⌨ www.webnz.com/tpac/gaynz) is a reservation service for gay destinations and accommodation.

Touring with Children

Children can travel by bicycle from the time they can support their head and a helmet, at around eight months. There are some small, lightweight, cute-looking helmets around, such as the L'il Bell Shell. To carry an infant to toddler requires a child seat or trailer. Child seats are more common for everyday riding and have advantages of being cheaper, easier to move as a unit with the bike and letting you touch and talk to your child while moving.

Disadvantages, especially over long distances, can include exposure to weather, the tendency of a sleeping child to loll, and losing luggage capacity at the rear. The best makes, such as the Rhode Gear Limo, include extra moulding to protect the child in case of a fall, have footrests and restraints, recline to let the child sleep and fit very securely and conveniently onto a rack on the bike.

With a capacity of up to 50kg (versus around 18kg for a child seat), trailers can accommodate two bigger children and luggage. They give better, though not always total, protection from sun and rain and let children sleep comfortably. Look for a trailer that is lightweight, foldable,

conspicuous (brightly coloured, with flag) and that tracks and handles well. It's also handy to be able to swap the trailer between bikes so adults can alternate towing and riding beside the trailer. Child trailers tend to be preferred for serious touring, but may be illegal in some places, for example, Western Australia. Trailers or seats are treated as additional luggage items when flying.

Be sure that the bike to which you attach a child seat or trailer is sturdy and low-geared to withstand – and help *you* withstand – the extra weight and stresses.

PETER HINES

With 'kiddy cranks', tandems are a good long-term solution for including children in your touring holidays.

DISABLED CYCLISTS

NZ generally caters well for disabled travellers. Most hostels, hotels and B&Bs etc have wheelchair access and disabled bathrooms, as required by law for new establishments. Many government facilities and tourist attractions are similarly equipped. Disabled travellers usually receive discounts on transport.

A good place to start is the Disability Information Service (☎ 03-366 6189, fax 379 5939), 314 Worcester St, Christchurch. Its has a separate postal address: PO Box 32-074, Christchurch.

SENIOR CYCLISTS

Senior travellers over 60 receive a discount on most transport; proof of age may be required. Discounts on attractions, activities and other services may also be available but sometimes only for NZ citizens. Many B&Bs are run by older couples, delighted to meet older travellers from overseas.

CYCLING WITH CHILDREN

NZ is an ideal country to travel with children. Health problems are not a major issue and many attractions and activities cater for children.

Hostels don't really cater for children, but also don't discourage them. YHA hostels are better set up for families and often have specific family rooms set aside, but families can also get a four-bed share room to themselves in most backpackers. B&Bs are mostly for couples and some even ban children. Motels, and particularly camping grounds, are well set up for children and often have playgrounds and games rooms. Children cost extra on top of double rates, but the charge is usually half the per extra adult rate at motels and camping grounds.

Touring with Children

From the age of about four, children can move on to a 'trailer-bike' (effectively a child's bike, minus a front wheel which hitches to an adult's bike) or to a tandem (initially as 'stoker', as the rider at the back is called, with 'kiddy cranks', or crank extensions) – this lets them assist with the pedalling effort. The tandem can be a long-term solution, keeping you and your child together and letting you compensate if the child tires.

Be careful of children rushing into touring on a solo bike before they can sustain the effort and concentration required. Once they are ready and keen to ride solo, at about age 10 to 12, they will need a good quality touring bike, properly fitted (A$300, US$200, UK£130 up).

The British publication *Encycleopedia*, by Alan Davidson et al, is a good guide to quality trailers, trailer-bikes and tandems available from manufacturers around the world.

Bike touring with children requires a new attitude as well as new equipment. Be sensitive to their needs – especially when they're too young to communicate them fully. In a seat or trailer, they're not expending energy and need to be dressed accordingly. Take care to keep them dry, at the right temperature and protected from the sun.

Keep their energy and interest up. When you stop, a child travelling in a seat or trailer will be ready for action, so always reserve some energy for parenting. This means more stops, including at places like playgrounds. Older children will have their own interests and should be involved in planning a tour.

Before setting off on a major journey, try some day trips to check your set-up and introduce your child to cycling.

Children need to be taken into account in deciding each day's route – traffic and distances need to be moderate and facilities and points of interest adequate. Given the extra weight of children and their daily needs, you may find it easier to leave behind the camping gear and opt for indoor accommodation or day trips from a base or series of bases. The very fit and adventurous may not need to compromise to ride with children, but those who do will still find it worthwhile.

As with other activities, children bring a new perspective and pleasure to cycle touring. They tend to love it.

Alethea Morison

Mountain Biking in New Zealand

New Zealanders got onto the mountain bike idea not too many years after it was born in the US. In 1984, the NZ company Healing Cycles imported 15 Shogun mountain bikes and soon began building its own. By 1986 the first national mountain bike race was held in the Akatarawa Range, north of Wellington; this was the forerunner of the Karapoti Classic, now the biggest mountain bike race in the southern hemisphere (see 'The Karapoti Classic' boxed text in the Southern North Island chapter).

Many kiwis are passionately involved in the sport of mountain biking and, not surprisingly, considering the country's population, everyone seems to know each other in the NZ scene. The Kennett brothers, Paul, Simon and Jonathan, who have been in it since the beginning, appear to have achieved guru status. Famous for their book, *Classic New Zealand Mountain Bike Rides*, they also organise events, including the Karapoti Classic, and are active mountain bike and environmental advocates and consultants. Web design is another spoke to their wheel and you'll find their tyre prints right through the virtual NZ bike environment.

The New Zealand Mountain Bike Association (NZMBA) was formed in 1988 to promote mountain biking nationally, for recreation and competition. It aims to represent the interests of all mountain bikers in NZ, promote the off road code, promote protection and preservation of the natural environment and organise and sanction events. The association also lobbies regionally for continued access to public recreation lands.

Mountain biking continues to increase in popularity and, while the participation in the sport is not yet comparable to that of rugby and cricket, there is certainly a healthy national scene. By the mid-1990s, Karapoti Classic entries had to be restricted to 1000; and in 1997, some events on the national series were added to the international (UCI) calendar.

While it's still a male-dominated sport, it's no boys club: women seem to be encouraged to get out there. One who has is Kathy Lynch, something of a local hero, whose claims to fame include winning the Karapoti Classic eight times, setting the course record and (at 39!) finishing 8th in the inaugural cross-country mountain bike event at the 1996 Atlanta Olympics.

Access

The growing popularity of mountain biking has led DOC to commit resources to developing a workable system of land access and conservation of natural areas. A strong conservation ethic is common among kiwi mountain bikers and local bike clubs often work together with land owners/managers to build custom bike tracks – there are some excellent custom built mountain bike parks in NZ.

Also check out Lonely Planet's *Travel with Children* by Maureen Wheeler.

CYCLING ORGANISATIONS

The national road and track racing body, the Cycling New Zealand Federation (☎ 04-801 8753, fax 801 8754), PO Box 1057, Wellington, also incorporates BMX New Zealand and the New Zealand MTB Association, PO Box 13734, Christchurch.

The Cycling Advocates Network (CAN; ☎ 04-385 2557, ✉ can@actrix.gen.nz), PO Box 11-964, Wellington, is made up of affiliated organisations and works to promote cycling in various forms.

For details of Web sites, see the 'New Zealand on the Net' boxed text earlier in this chapter.

The Auckland Cycle Touring Association's Web site (🖳 mysite.xtra.co.nz/~cammac/) lists upcoming rides and information about the club.

BUSINESS HOURS

Office hours are generally Monday to Friday from 9 am to 5 pm. Most government offices are open from Monday to Friday from 8.30 am to 4.30 pm. Shops are usually open from Monday to Friday from 9 am to 5 pm plus Saturday morning (9 am to 12.30 pm), with

Mountain Biking in New Zealand

Currently, the issue of land access works through self-regulation. Mountain bikers are expected to respect any restrictions to access, which may be in place for a variety of conservation, cultural, social or commercial reasons. The system, though not without it's hiccups, seems generally to work pretty well. If you go mountain biking, make sure you respect any restrictions, even if you don't understand or agree with them; flouting the system may lead to a more restrictive situation in the future.

Like the NZ landscape in general, the terrain for mountain biking is enormously varied; you can come across anything, including soft sand, packed clay, single tracks, 4WD tracks, gravel roads, steep ups and downs, relatively flat areas, unrideable bits, native forests, pine plantations and some fabulous custom-built tracks. One place that you cannot ride, however, is away from formed roads in national parks.

This Book

Several mountain bike rides have been described in this book, all in areas where you can hire a decent mountain bike. Most of them don't require high-level skills and experience, but they will give you a taste of what's out there.

If you want to do more, the latest edition of *Classic New Zealand Mountain Bike Rides*, by Paul, Simon and Jonathan Kennett, is the definitive guide.

Off-Road Code

If you're mountain biking in NZ, you should also abide by the off-road code. In addition to the code remember to never ride alone, always tell someone where you're going and when you'll be back, and always carry adequate food and water, a first-aid kit and a repair kit. Also see the Safety on the Bike section in the Health & Safety chapter.

- **Yield** – the right of way to other non-motorised recreationalists
- **Use** – caution when overtaking another, and make your presence known well in advance
- **Maintain** – control of your speed at all times
- **Stay** – on designated trails only
- **Ensure** – stock or wildlife stay calm
- **Leave** – no trace; respect public and private property
- **Always** – wear an approved helmet when riding
- **Support** – land access organisations

Nicola Wells

late-night shopping to 9 pm one night of the week, usually Thursday or Friday. Many small convenience stores (or dairies) stay open for much longer hours and many of the larger supermarkets are open seven days a week until 8 pm or later.

PUBLIC HOLIDAYS & SPECIAL EVENTS

Though it seems odd to northern hemisphere folk, it is summer at Christmas time in NZ. And this is the main school holiday period – which means lots of crowds and higher prices. Shorter school breaks during the year are less hectic but also busy.

Public holidays include:

January
New Year's Day and the next day (1st & 2nd)
February
Waitangi Day or New Zealand Day (6th)
March/April
Good Friday and Easter Monday (variable dates)
April
Anzac Day (25th)
June
Queen's Birthday (1st Monday)
October
Labour Day (4th Monday)
December
Christmas Day and Boxing Day (25th & 26th)

In addition, each province has its own Anniversary Day holiday. Province holidays (dates can vary) include: Wellington, 22 January; Auckland, 29 January; Northland, 29 January; Nelson, 1 February; Otago, 23 March; Southland, 23 March; Taranaki, 31 March; Hawkes Bay, 1 November; Marlborough, 1 November; Westland, 1 December; and Canterbury, 16 December.

When these holidays fall between Friday and Sunday, they are usually observed on the following Monday; if they fall between Tuesday and Thursday, they are held on the preceding Monday.

Some of the more noteworthy cultural events and festivals include:

January
Auckland Anniversary Day Regatta
Held on Waitemata Harbour.
Summer City Program
Two months (January and February) of festivals and entertainment around Wellington.

February
Marlborough Food & Wine Festival
Held in Blenheim, one of NZ's best wine areas, on the 2nd weekend.
Art Deco Festival
Held in Napier, the Art Deco 'capitol' of NZ, on the 3rd weekend it is a festival of balls, dinners, fancy dress and Art Deco tours.
International Festival of the Arts
Held in Wellington on even-numbered years – a month of national and international culture.

Aotearoa Traditional Maori Performing Arts Festival
Held every two years (odd numbered years) in Wellington.

March
Wildfoods Festival
Held in Hokitika. The festival features tasty and healthy wild food from the land and sea.
Pasifika Polynesian Festival
Auckland – traditional arts, entertainment, sports and food celebrating Auckland's Pacific communities.

November
Canterbury Show Week
Held in Christchurch.

December
Festival of Lights
Held in New Plymouth over Christmas. Features the annual light-up of the town and a lighting display at Pukekura Park.

There are a plethora of smaller annual special events held all over NZ; each little town seems to have its annual show (fair), often involving sports like racing horses on the beach, wheelbarrow and sugar bag races, and wood-chopping and sheep-shearing contests.

CYCLING ROUTES
Route Descriptions
This guide aims to cover the best areas for cycling touring on roads that NZ has to

---

Cycling Events

New Zealanders are very keen participants when it comes to the outdoors and usually make the country's few annual cycling events incredibly successful. The major NZ cycling events are:

- **Rainbow Rage** (March) – The Rainbow Rage is a non-competitive 106km mountain bike ride to Hanmer Springs via the Rainbow Valley Road.
- **Karapoti Classic** (March), Wellington – Probably the most famous annual mountain bike race in the Southern Hemisphere (see 'The Karapoti Classic' boxed text in the Southern North Island chapter).
- **Great Lake Cycle Challenge** (November), Lake Taupo – This non-competitive ride is the country's largest cycling event and typically attracts around 5000 entrants, each riding anything from 40 to 320km.
- **Hamilton to Whangamata** (November) – A direct road route via Karangahake Gorge, which began as a fun event but now includes a competitive option.

In addition, there is a thriving road, track and mountain bike racing scene and a calendar of each of the national series events for these sports can be found on the Cycling New Zealand Web site (🖳 www.cyclingnz.org.nz).

offer. Rather than offering a comprehensive route from one end of the country to the other, it describes a series of discrete rides, each short enough to be feasible for a visitor with limited time. Routes link easily to one another, ensuring continuity for extended trips. Various transport options (including by bike) for getting to and from each ride are discussed.

The rides have been designed to make carrying camping gear and food optional. Each ride is broken into a set number of days, with accommodation and food options available at each day's destination. Alternative destinations are also indicated for many of the rides.

Standards

Each ride is graded according to its difficulty in terms of distance, terrain, road surface and navigation. The grade appears in the Table of Rides at the beginning of the book and in the facts box in the introduction to each ride.

Grading is unavoidably subjective and is intended as a guide only; the degree of difficulty of a particular ride may vary according to the weather, the weight in your panniers or how hungry and tired you are.

Easy These rides involve no more than a few hours riding each day, over *mostly* flat terrain with good, sealed road surfaces, and are navigationally very straightforward.

Moderate These rides present a moderate challenge to someone of average fitness; they are likely to include some hills, two to six hours riding each day and may involve some unsealed roads and/or navigation.

Hard These are for fit riders who want a challenge; they involve long daily distances and/or challenging climbs, may require negotiation of rough and remote roads and present navigational challenges.

Times & Distances

Each ride is divided into stages and we've suggested a day be spent on each stage. In some cases the distance for a particular stage is relatively short, but other attractions in the region warrant spending extra time – distance junkies may decide to condense two stages into one day.

The directions for each day's ride are given in terms of distance from the starting point (specified in the cue sheets).

A suggested riding time has been given for each day's riding. Because individual riding speed varies widely, these should be used as a guide only. They only take into account the actual riding time – not time taken for rest stops, taking photographs or eating – and are generally based on an average riding speed of between 12 and 20km/h (sometimes lower, depending on the terrain or road surface).

Cue Sheets

See the Foreword for more information on cue sheets.

Elevation Charts

See the Foreword for more information on elevation charts.

ACTIVITIES

New Zealanders love the outdoors and one of the special attractions of visiting NZ is that there are heaps of activities to do. Some of them are expensive; others cost nothing.

Classic New Zealand Adventures, by Jonathan Kennett et al, has information on lots of adventure activities; and if you're planning on doing a few expensive activities, check out an organisation called New Zealand Outside (☎ 03-326 7516, fax 326 5518, 🖳 www.webnz.com/outside), PO Box 17673, Christchurch. They've got a directory of over 300 outdoor activities, and you'll receive substantial discounts on many of them if you buy their discount card for $29.95.

Tramping

Tramping (that's Kiwi for walking) is a great way to get right into NZ's wild areas and is very well supported. The country has thousands of kilometres of tracks – many well marked, some only a line on the map. Tramping is made easy by NZ's excellent network of huts, enabling trampers to avoid lugging tents and cooking gear. Many tracks are graded, though others are only for experienced, fit walkers.

There are literally hundreds of tracks to be enjoyed all over NZ. The most walked are the Abel Tasman Coast Track, the Routeburn, the Milford, the Tongariro Northern

Circuit, the Kepler, and Lake Waikaremoana. These tracks do draw in the crowds, especially in summer, while equally fine but unknown tracks are all but deserted.

If you want to avoid the crowds, DOC offices and park headquarters can advise and help you plan some enjoyable walks on lesser known tracks. DOC offices are in every city and in dozens of towns, and give free information about tramping in their areas. Every national, forest and maritime park has its own DOC headquarters.

There are also council parks, farm parks, regional parks and more, all of which have walks (in NZ a walk is defined as a fairly easy day walk or less, often suitable for families, while a tramp is a longer trek that requires you to be suitably equipped and where some experience may be necessary).

Be aware that tramping can be quite a dangerous activity if you are not well prepared. Almost every year inexperienced or inadequately equipped tourists die. Some trails are only for the experienced, and weather conditions are changeable, making high-altitude walks subject to snow and ice even in summer. Always check weather conditions, and always carry adequate warm and waterproof clothing, water and food. Consult and register your intentions with a DOC office before heading off on the longer walks. Above all, heed their advice.

Jim DuFresne's *Tramping in New Zealand* is another Lonely Planet guide, with descriptions of nearly 50 walks, of various lengths and degrees of difficulty, in all parts of the country.

DOC also produces leaflets that outline thousands of walking tracks throughout the country.

Fishing

NZ is renowned as one of the great sportfishing countries of the world, thanks largely to the introduction of exotic species. The lakes and rivers of central North Island are famous for trout fishing, especially Lake Taupo and the rivers that feed it (see the Eastern North Island chapter). The rivers and lakes of the South Island are also good for trout, notably the Mataura River, Southland. The rivers of Otago and Southland also have some of the best salmon fishing in the world.

Saltwater fishing is also a big attraction for Kiwi anglers, especially in the warmer waters around the North Island. Ninety Mile Beach and the beaches of the Hauraki Gulf are good for surfcasting. The Bay of Islands and Whangaroa in Northland, Tutukaka, near Whangarei, Whitianga on the Coromandel Peninsula and Mayor Island in the Bay of Plenty are noted big game-fishing areas.

The colder waters of the South Island, especially around Marlborough Sounds, are good and the Kaikoura Peninsula is great for surfcasting.

Fishing gear can be hired in areas like Taupo and Rotorua, and a few sports outlets in other towns also hire equipment, but serious enthusiasts may wish to bring their own. Rods and tackle may have to be treated by NZ quarantine officials.

A fishing permit is required to fish on inland waters and are sold at sport shops. Local visitors centres and DOC offices have more information about fishing licences and regulations.

Many books have been written about fishing in NZ. John Kent has written the *North Island Trout Fishing Guide* and the *South Island Trout Fishing Guide*. Tony Orman, a renowned NZ author and fisherman, has written *21 Great New Zealand Trout Waters*; and for surfcasting, check out *Surfcasting: A New Zealand Guide*, by Gil Henderson.

Marine-Mammal Watching

Kaikoura, on the north-eastern coast of the South Island, is the country's best marine-mammal watching location. The main attraction is whale-watching tours, and there is swimming with dolphins and seals.

Nature being what it is, there's no guarantee of seeing any specific animal on any one tour. In general, sperm whales are most likely to be seen from October to August, and orcas from December to March. Most of the other animals are able to be seen year-round.

Dolphin swimming is common across NZ, with dolphins around the North Island at Whakatane, Paihia and Whitianga, and in the Marlborough Sounds and off Fiordland on the South Island.

Jet-Boating

NZ is the home of the amazing jet-boats, invented by CWF Hamilton in 1957. The boats are ideal for use in shallow water and white water; the instant response of the jet enables the boats to execute 360° spins almost within the length of the boat – making for hair-raising rides on NZ rivers.

Just about every riverside and lakeside town throughout NZ has a jet-boat company that runs trips. The Shotover and Kawarau rivers near Queenstown and the Buller near Westport are renowned jet-boating rivers on the South Island; the Dart River is less travelled but also good. In the North Island, the Whanganui, Manganui-a-te-Ao, Motu, Rangitikei, Kaituna and Waikato rivers are excellent for jet-boating. At Waitomo you can drive your own tiny jet-boat and at Broadlands, Waikato, you can ride as a passenger in an exhilarating sprint-jet.

Rafting

There are almost as many white-water rafting possibilities as there are rivers in NZ. And there is no shortage of companies to take you on a heart-pounding, drenching, exhilarating and spine-tingling ride down some wild, magnificent rivers.

Rivers are graded from I to VI, with VI meaning 'unraftable'. The grading of the Shotover canyon varies from III to V+ depending on the time of year, the Kawarau River is rated IV and the Wairoa River is graded III to V. The rafting companies supply wet suits and life jackets.

Rafting trips take anything from one hour to three days and cost between about $75 and $130 per person per day. Be aware that people have been killed in rafting accidents – check at local tourist offices for the best and safest times for rafting. There are risks in all such adventure activities, but safe rafting will always to some extent depend on your fellow crew; ie the other amateurs in the boat with you.

Sea Kayaking

Sea kayaking is very popular. Renowned sea kayaking areas are the Hauraki Gulf, Bay of Islands and Coromandel in the North Island and, in the South Island, the Marlborough Sounds and along the coast of the Abel Tasman National Park, where sea kayaking has become a viable and popular alternative to walking the Abel Tasman Coastal Track.

Fiordland has become a popular destination for those wishing to hone their sea kayaking skills. Tour operators in Te Anau, Milford and Manapouri arrange spectacular trips on the lakes and through the fiords.

Scuba Diving

The Bay of Islands Maritime and Historic Park and the Hauraki Gulf Maritime Park in the North Island, and the Marlborough Sounds Maritime Park in the South Island, are obvious attractions, but both islands have many more diving possibilities.

NZ has two marine parks for interesting diving. The Poor Knights Islands, off the coast near Whangarei, is reputed to have the best diving in NZ. The Sugar Loaf Islands, another interesting reserve, is off Back Beach in New Plymouth, not far from the city centre.

Coastal Fishes of New Zealand: A Diver's Identification Guide, by Malcolm Francis, is a field guide to all the fish a diver in NZ is likely to encounter. For more information, contact the NZ Underwater Association (NZUA; ☎ 09-849 5896), PO Box 875, Auckland.

Surfing

With its thousands of kilometres of coastline, NZ has excellent surfing possibilities. Swells come in from every angle and, while any specific beach will have better surfing at some times of the year than at others, there's good surfing to be found *somewhere* in NZ at any time of the year.

Raglan's 2km-long left-hander is NZ's most famous wave, but areas closer to Auckland also have great surfing. Dunedin is one of the best spots in the South Island, especially in summer and autumn, but there are hundreds of possibilities. Among the guidebooks on surfing in NZ, look out for *The New Zealand Surfing Guide,* by Mike Bhana, and *A Guide to Surf Riding in New Zealand,* by Wayne Warwick.

Bungy Jumping

Bungy jumping was made famous by Kiwi AJ Hackett's bungy dive from the Eiffel Tower in 1986. His company alone has sent many thousands of people hurtling earthward from bridges over scenic NZ rivers with nothing between them and kingdom come but a gigantic rubber bungy cord tied to their ankles. No doubt about it, it's a daredevil sport, and the adrenalin rush can last for days. But it's all very well organised, with every possible precaution and attention to safety.

The historic Kawarau Suspension Bridge near Queenstown attracts the most jumpers; it's 43m above the Kawarau River. A more spectacular dive spot is Skippers Canyon Bridge, 71m above a narrow gorge on the Shotover River, also near Queenstown. Highest of the lot near Queenstown is the 102m Pipeline where the first bounce brings you up to the height of the Skippers Bridge! That jump will cost you $135 (others start below $100). Among the cheapest is at the Waiau River Bridge near Hanmer Springs, close to Christchurch. Jumping is also done in the North Island at Taupo, 45m above the scenic Waikato River, and on the Rangitikei River near Mangaweka.

Bird-Watching

NZ is a bird-watcher's paradise in a relatively small area, with many unique endemic species, interesting residents and wave upon wave of visitors.

Some of the best places for bird-watching are Ulva Island (Stewart Island), the Catlins Forest Park and south-east coast, Fiordland and the forests of Westland, Otago Peninsula, Cape Farewell, Marlborough Sounds, Te Urewera National Park, the Firth of Thames and the Coromandel, Tiritiri Matangi and Little Barrier islands, and the forests and coasts of Northland. A number of islands are wildlife refuges where threatened birds are protected; special permission is needed to visit.

Two good guides are *A Field Guide to New Zealand Birds,* by Geoff Moon, and *Birds of New Zealand: Locality Guide,* by Stuart Chambers.

ACCOMMODATION

NZ has a wide range of accommodation, but there is one catch: the Kiwis are great travellers. It's wise to book ahead, particularly in the main tourist areas at peak times: the summer holidays from Christmas to the end of January, and Easter. At these times prices rise in the beach resorts and other popular destinations, and finding a room can be difficult. International tourism also puts a strain on accommodation from October to April, particularly during February and March.

Accommodation guides include the *AA Accommodation Guide,* which lists mostly motels and is available from bookshops or from AA offices, where it's free to members (or members of affiliate associations overseas); and Jason's accommodation directories (budget or motel), available for free from motels and motor camps, or for sale at bookshops. Other useful publications are listed in this section.

One of the best resources for accommodation information is the local information centre, found in almost every town of any size. Most also act as booking agents for accommodation; you can fax them from overseas for information and accommodation bookings.

Camping & Cabins

Kiwi camping grounds and motor camps are some of the best in the world; they are found almost everywhere, often in prime locations, such as right on the beach.

They have excellent facilities with tent sites plus on-site vans and cabins of different degrees of luxury, and tend to be well equipped: most have communal kitchens and dining areas – good places to meet other cyclists. Stoves, kettles and toasters are generally provided, though you may have to supply your own cooking and eating utensils (ask at the office – there's often a spare set you can borrow). They also have laundry facilities and, often, TV rooms. Though it's best to bring your own sleeping bag, most places also hire linen if you're staying in cabins.

Tent sites are usually charged at a per-person rate, typically around $9 to $12 per adult. But rates may be for a minimum of two people with an additional charge for each extra person, or are sometimes just a straight site charge.

At most sites the kitchen and showers are free but a few have coin-operated hotplates and hot showers. Laundry facilities (if available) are generally coin-operated. In many camping grounds, the only place for your bike is locked to a tree, but some places will allow you to take bikes inside cabins.

Camping becomes less practical in NZ in winter, especially in the south.

A good guide is the *New Zealand Camping Guide,* by Kerr & Hansen. Separate

North and South Island volumes cover almost every motor camp, and DOC and regional camping ground in the country.

DOC Camping Grounds DOC operates over 120 camping grounds around NZ, often in beautiful locations. Its camping grounds are in reserves and national parks, maritime parks, forest parks and farm parks – DOC offices have lists.

Standard DOC camping grounds are basic, with minimal facilities including cold running water, toilets, fireplaces and not much else, but they also have minimal charges (around $2 to $6 per adult). Serviced camping grounds are more luxurious and cost around $6 to $9. Informal camping grounds are free, but have almost no facilities, apart from a cold-water tap and places to pitch tents. Some DOC camping grounds are fully serviced like motor camps and have on-site managers.

Local DOC offices have details of facilities, and can advise you on what you need to take and whether to book in advance. Most operate on a first come, first served basis, and fees are paid by a self-registration system. Since the low fees are used for the maintenance of the camping grounds, it's important to pay them (usually into an honesty box) even when there's no warden.

DOC also operates numerous back country huts, most of which can only be reached on foot. DOC offices have details.

Cabins & Tourist Flats Many camping grounds and motor camps have cabins. Standard cabins are simply free-standing rooms with bare mattresses. You provide your own sleeping gear and towels, or linen can usually be hired. Rooms cost around $30 to $40 for two. The minimum rate is generally for two, plus a minimal charge for each additional person; however, some charge per person, making them reasonable for singles. Some places will allow (clean) bikes inside.

Many motor camps now offer hostel-style bunkrooms, often a cabin filled with dorm beds that are generally around $15 per person and often empty. Alternatively, backpacker beds are offered in two, three or four-bed cabins.

Better equipped cabins are called 'tourist flats'. Closer to motel standard, they have kitchens and/or bathrooms and may be serviced, with linen provided. On-site caravans (trailer homes in US parlance) are another camping-ground possibility. Many camping grounds also have regular motel rooms or an associated motel complex.

Hostels

Hundreds of hostels offer cheap accommodation all over NZ. At a hostel you rent a bed, usually for around $15 to $18 a night. Bunkrooms, some segregated, generally sleep four or more people – some sleep more than 10; and almost all have some twin or double rooms. Sometimes single rooms are offered, though they are rare and, unless the hostel is empty, you'll have to pay for a double. Many hostels also offer tent sites (generally around $10 per person). All hostels have a communal kitchen, laundry, dining area and lounge area.

Most will find somewhere secure to put your bike – though in some it may be in a laundry that is not locked until 11 pm.

Hostels are divided into two camps – YHA hostels and private hostels or backpackers. Intense competition has compelled the NZ YHA to update its image and ditch the chores, curfews and some of the outdated ways traditionally associated with YHAs. Though the offices are often closed during the day, communal facilities are available and you can still leave your gear if you arrive outside office hours.

Hostels vary enormously. Some are purpose-built, with excellent facilities; at the other end are small, cramped places, not really adequate for large numbers. Good managers make a hostel – some are right on the ball, promote a congenial atmosphere and offer travel services. Many of the hostels, YHA and private, are just brilliant.

In the peak season, it is essential to book at least a day in advance, especially for twin or double rooms, which are limited compared with dormitories. Even dormitories fill up, despite the tendency of some hostels to cash in and pack the dorms to overflowing with beds.

Many hotels, motor camps and even some motels are cashing in on the backpacker boom and also offer backpacker accommodation, often at cheaper rates than the hostels. They can be good value but are often anonymous and lack the atmosphere of a hostel. Many motor camps, though, especially in the main tourist areas, have good communal areas where travellers meet.

Take a sleeping bag. At independent backpackers, bedding usually costs extra. YHA hostels provide bedding for free; you just have to ask for it.

YHA Hostels The YHA in NZ produces the free annual *YHA Accommodation Guide* with details of all its NZ hostels; it is available at all NZ YHA hostels and travel centres. Otherwise try your national YHA or the NZ YHA national office (☎ 03-379 9970, fax 365 4476, 🖳 www.yha.org.nz), PO Box 436, Christchurch. The YHA also goes under the banner of Hostelling International (HI), but the term YHA is still more common in NZ.

YHA hostels are open to members, and while nonmembers can also stay, they pay extra. Join the YHA in your home country or in NZ at any YHA hostel for $24. If you have a YHA card, make sure you bring it, even if you don't want to stay in hostels. Flashing your YHA card will bring discounts on buses (up to 30%), airlines and many activities.

Associate YHA Hostels are privately owned premises affiliated to the YHA, which are also open to nonmembers at the same rates.

Hostels can be booked ahead directly by phone, through the New Zealand YHA offices, through another hostel (for a $1 fee) or through the Internet. You may need to pay in advance – and if you cancel at short notice, you may not receive a full refund.

Backpackers The many backpackers (private or independent hostels) generally have the same facilities and prices as YHA hostels.

A couple of well prepared and up-to-date booklets (in which hostels pay to be included) list many of the private hostels. The BBH guide *Budget Backpackers Hostels New Zealand* is an excellent resource, with details and prices of the biggest selection of backpackers throughout NZ; it's available through member hostels, Auckland and Christchurch international and domestic airports, visitor centres, the Rainbow Lodge (☎/fax 07-377 1568), 99 Titiraupenga St, Taupo, or Foley Towers (☎/fax 03-379 3014), 208 Kilmore St,

Christchurch. The guides are also on the Internet (🖳 www.backpack.co.nz).

The *VIP Backpackers Accommodation Guide* also lists a wide range of hostels. All those listed are members of the VIP network; a VIP Card ($25) gives you $1 off at VIP hostels, plus discounts similar to those offered on a YHA card. The VIP accommodation guide is available at VIP hostels and visitors centres, or you can contact the VIP network directly: ☎ 09-827 6061, fax 09-827 6013, 🖃 nztravel@iprolink.co.nz, PO Box 80021, Greenbay, Auckland.

YMCA & YWCA Hostels YMCA and YWCA hostels in larger cities offer rooms, from the no-frills to quite luxurious, and are generally reasonably priced. Some are single-sex only, but most take both men and women. Although the emphasis is on long-term accommodation for young people coming to study or work in the 'big city', they do provide accommodation in the crowded summer season when their long-term residents go home or on holiday. Accommodation is often in single or twin rooms.

B&Bs & Guesthouses

B&B accommodation in private homes is by far the biggest category of accommodation. B&Bs are sprouting up everywhere – everyone with a spare room in their house seems to be getting in on the act.

The best publication for B&B listings is the *New Zealand Bed & Breakfast Book* by J & J Thomas, available in NZ bookshops and updated annually. Though the blurbs are the often overstated estimations of the owners, it has by far the biggest listing of B&Bs, with prices and details on facilities. Local visitors centres also have lists of B&Bs.

Although breakfast is definitely on the agenda at the real B&B places, it may or may not feature at guesthouses. Breakfast may be 'continental' (ie not much) or a substantial meal of fruit, eggs, bacon, toast, tea and coffee. Many guesthouses pride themselves on the size, quality and 'traditional value' of their breakfasts. If you like to start the day heartily, it's worth considering this when comparing prices. A big breakfast is worth at least $10 per person at a decent cafe.

Guesthouses may be spartan, cheap, ultra-basic 'private' (unlicensed) hotels.

Most are comfortable, relaxed but low-key places, patronised by people who don't enjoy the impersonal atmosphere of many motels. Others are very fancy indeed.

Guesthouses are often slightly cheaper than B&Bs. B&Bs usually start at around $40 a single, if available, or $60 a double – which will get you a standard room with share bathroom. Doubles with attached bathroom start at around $80. While some B&Bs are simply a room in the family home (sometimes called homestays), others are very luxurious and cost well over $100. Most can find somewhere to store your bike safely.

Many B&Bs also offer an evening meal for an extra charge. A few B&Bs have a kitchen where guests can do their own cooking.

WWOOF

If you have plenty of time but little money and want to see the countryside, try WWOOFing. Willing Workers on Organic Farms (WWOOF) is an organisation of more than 300 organic farms. By joining, you receive a list of farms that will offer you free food and accommodation in exchange for your work. You must contact farms several days in advance by telephone or letter (you can't just turn up) and you're generally obliged to stay at least three days (but it makes a good break from the saddle).

To join WWOOF and receive the booklet, contact Janet and Andrew Strange (☎ 03-544 9890, ✆ wwoff@wwoof.co.nz), PO Box 1172, Nelson.

Hotels

Many traditional, older-style pubs have rooms, but they are often just a sideline enterprise and the main emphasis is on the bar. You may also have to carry your bike upstairs or leave it outside. At the cheapest pubs, singles/doubles might cost as little as $20/30, though $30/50 is more common, while at the more luxurious city hotels, a room is more likely to be around $80 or more.

The pubs can be good value and often have plenty of character. Some now also have 'backpackers rooms' that usually cost about half the normal hotel rate. These are regular hotel rooms without the frills. They may also be rooms awaiting renovation (ie very shabby indeed).

Many economical older hotels are listed in the free *Pub Beds* brochure, which brings a good discount when presented at participating hotels. It's published by Pub Beds (PO Box 101 291, North Shore Mail Centre) and is available at many NZ hotels and visitor centres.

Motels

NZ motels have all the facilities of motels everywhere, and more. Many motel units have fully equipped kitchens, though some studio units only have a fridge, and tea and coffee-making equipment. Most motels provide you with a small carton of fresh milk and often have a laundry or swimming pool for guests.

Many visitors find NZ motels a definite notch below international standards, as they often date from the 1960s and look like it. Though comfortable enough, they are drab, prefabricated affairs. Newer motels are often cheap constructions but usually brighter with better decor, and some are definitely luxurious.

Motel rooms typically cost around $60 to $70 a double, plus $10 to $15 for every extra person. The more luxurious new motels charge around $80 and up. The difference in price between a double or single room, if there is one, is usually minimal. In tourist towns, motels can really hike up their prices during the main tourist season. On the other hand, when it is quiet they may give discounts. Some motels are quite used to cyclists and are happy to find somewhere safe for your bike; others look doubtful and suggest you'd be better off at the motor camp.

A motor inn is part motel, part hotel, offering motel-style accommodation, usually with a bar and restaurant.

FOOD

NZ is blessed with a large variety of fresh, quality food. Once regarded as 'an efficient offshore farm' for England, it is still a big producer of meat, dairy products, fruit and vegetables; fish and seafood are also abundant. The English influence on cuisine is obvious – meat or fish and a vegetable accompaniment still form the basis of the typical kiwi diet. However, the country's culinary horizons have broadened immeasurably in recent years. The major cities and tourist towns have a range of other cuisines and fashionable cafes on offer.

For more specific advice on your day-to-day nutritional requirements while cycle touring, see Nutrition in the Health & Safety chapter.

Local Food

There's not much of a national cuisine, though they're big meat eaters – and a NZ steak is every bit as good as an Aussie or American one. *Kumara* (Polynesian sweet potato) is something of a national vegetable – it was widely cultivated by the Maori and remains a major crop, particularly in Northland. Then, of course, there is kiwi fruit; once the obscure Chinese gooseberry, it was a marketing success story of the 1980s. NZ is also renowned for its dairy products: milk, cheese, cream – and the ice cream that's available at every corner dairy.

With all that coastline it's not surprising that NZ's seafood is excellent; it's widely available in restaurants and cafes. Green-lipped mussels are easily the best in the world – and cheap – and there are oysters, scallops or crayfish. Saltwater fish favourites include hoki, hapuka, groper, snapper and kingfish. Try catching your own freshwater fish (see Fishing in the Activities section earlier in this chapter).

Where to Eat You can get a steak or fish and chips just about anywhere. The choice is more limited if you want vegetarian food, and even a wholesome carbohydrate-based meal can be surprisingly hard to find in some places – you might need to ask for extra potatoes with your steak instead.

Steak and seafood mains in a moderately priced restaurant typically cost around $22 (less in a pub bistro), but international cuisines and vegetarian meals are generally a cheaper bet. In the cities and larger towns, there are plenty of restaurants serving Italian, Middle Eastern, Indian, Thai, Japanese and Mexican food. You'll often find mains for around $12 to $20. In the hinterlands, Chinese restaurants still predominate over any other sort of international cuisine but, while good-value and hearty meals are offered, the Kiwi version of Chinese can be a bland travesty of the real thing.

Fast Food NZ has plenty of fast-food joints, including those symbols of US culinary imperialism: McDonald's, Pizza Hut and KFC. Or try traditional Kiwi favourites: fish and chips, and hot meat pies.

Fish and chips is an English institution that NZ excels at. Not only can you get some superb fresh fish, deep fried in batter, but fish and chip shops also offer mussels, scallops, oysters, *paua* (abalone) fritters and other seafood delights, served with hot, crisp chips. (For Americans, 'chips' in NZ are thickly cut french fries.) Try kumara chips for a variation.

Other fast food popular in NZ include nachos, potato skins and hamburgers like the great 'Kiwi burger' with a fried egg, beetroot and salad.

Cafes & Tearooms NZ's traditional cafes or coffee shops, called tearooms, are nothing to get excited about. Tea, scones and white bread sandwiches, or Devonshire teas, which include a pot of tea, one or two scones, jam and whipped cream, are standard fare.

Food in the more fashionable cafes is likely to be focaccia or panini filled with salad, pastrami or marinated vegetables; croissants, quiche, gourmet pizza, muffins and sinfully rich desserts.

Self-Catering

With so much quality food produced locally, it's easy to eat well in NZ and you'll save yourself a lot of money by cooking your own. If you're using hostels, you'll often find herbs and spices provided; they ask for coin donations to keep up the service.

NZ has several large supermarket chains – Pack 'N Save, New World and Woolworths, for example – and they're usually open seven days a week until around 8 pm. Large supermarkets are found in the cities and in towns that serve a large rural community. Many of them have an excellent bulk food section, where you can fill your bags with exactly the amount of pasta, rice, nuts etc that you need.

In smaller towns, try the corner dairy or Four Square minisupermarket. They generally sell a bit of everything, including snacks like muesli bars and giant cookies. You won't find food in bulk here and it's more expensive. Many towns also have a greengrocer, which is generally a better place to look for such things as fresh food than the Four Square.

Cookie Time

Mmmmm … cookies!

After discovering how good New Zealand's giant chocolate chip cookies were, I was never without one in my pannier pocket. Then I tried the muesli bars and I reckon they've got to be the perfect on-road snack: they taste great (raspberry is the best); the chocolate chips are nice and generous; and they're compact – well, too much at once isn't good just before a big hill, anyway.

At the Cookie Time factory in Christchurch I found out about the feel-good Cookie Time tale – little guy turned success story. Apparently, it all started as a one-man band in 1983, but the founder's brother came on board to keep everything on the financial rails and it's been a roaring success ever since. The company even has a marketing mascot, the Cookie Muncher (who looks suspiciously like *Sesame Street*'s Cookie Monster to me).

Not content with just baking giant chocolate chip cookies and muesli bars (did I say giant? You ain't eaten nothin' yet …) these guys decided they'd make a culinary bungy jump into the *Guinness Book of Records* by baking the world's biggest cookie. With 2 tonnes of butter, 4½ tonnes of flour and 24,000 eggs, this extremely giant cookie was 25m in diameter!

Nicola Wells

Bulk health food shops and organic grocers are quite common in rural 'alternative lifestyle' areas. While these are generally more expensive than supermarkets, they often sell in bulk.

Don't get caught out if you're travelling through country areas after hours and on weekends. Often, there's something open seven days, but it's not uncommon for the only store for miles to close at midday on Saturday and not reopen until 9 am Monday morning.

For really fresh food at discount prices, take advantage of the roadside produce stalls in farming areas. As well as selling delicious fruit and vegetables, the friendly farmer may even fill your honey container or provide you with individual eggs.

DRINKS
Nonalcoholic Drinks

NZ tap water is, in all but a few instances, clean, delicious and safe (why anyone would buy bottled water is a mystery). Not so for water taken from streams – it's recommended you sterilise it before drinking.

While New Zealanders are great tea drinkers, they have only recently become interested in good espresso coffee. Fashionable cafes have espresso machines and most can make passable coffee – but it's becoming more common to find cafes which care about making a good brew and some which even roast their own beans. If you like lots of milk, cafe latte in NZ comes in a huge bowl-like cup; also popular is the mocchacino – hot chocolate with a shot of espresso. The best coffee is mostly – but not exclusively – in the cities. If you're desperate, you'll find some sort of coffee in all but the tiniest towns.

In addition to the usual carbonated drinks and fruit juices, caffeinated 'energy' drinks seem to be the latest thing filling the drinks fridge shelves. Beware of drinking caffeinated drinks or tea and coffee in place of water to prevent dehydration. Caffeine is a diuretic which causes the body to lose water through urination, so even more water is required to counteract the effect of caffeinated drinks.

Spirulina is a health drink popular in trendy or healthy cafes and available in the drinks section or in powder form from the supermarket. It's a seaweed powder, generally mixed into fruit juice (turning it a dark green colour), that is reputedly high in vitamins.

Sports Drinks Sports drinks such as PowerAde are widely available in dairies and supermarkets. For a discussion of the benefits of sports drinks, see Hydration in the Health & Safety chapter.

Alcoholic Drinks

Beer Almost all the beer is now brewed by only two companies, NZ Breweries and DB

The New Zealand Wine Industry

Although early European settlers first planted grapes in New Zealand more than 150 years ago, it wasn't really until the early 1980s that the wine industry took off in a big way. Much of the country is blessed with ideal growing conditions: plenty of warm sunshine, light rains and long autumn ripening periods. The proximity of most growing areas to the ocean means that grapes are warmed by the clear sunlight during the day and cooled by sea breezes at night, an ideal climatic pattern resulting in wines characterised by high levels of fruit, intensity and flavour.

The variety that first gained NZ the respect and attention of international wine lovers was Sauvignon Blanc, a style perfected in the Marlborough region. Quite unlike other Sauvignons, it has been described in wine parlance as having 'a uniquely juicy, sappy flavour; a powerful combination of pungent gooseberries, cats and asparagus.' After a glass or two to wash down some fresh local seafood, it's not hard to see what all the fuss is about.

Grapes are generally harvested by machine in March and April, with Gisborne usually picking ahead of Hawkes Bay, Marlborough and Canterbury. It's common for winemakers to blend grapes from different vineyards to achieve the desired character and complexity.

Look out for some superb wineries in the major wine producing regions of Gisborne (excellent Chardonnay, Sauvignon Blanc and Gewurztraminer), Hawkes Bay (stylish Rieslings, Chardonnay, Sauvignon Blanc, Cabernet Sauvignon and Merlot), Martinborough (high quality Pinot Noir, Sauvignon, Cabernet Sauvignon and Merlot), Nelson (luscious Sauvignon Blanc and Chardonnay), Canterbury (Riesling, Chardonnay and Pinot Noir) and Marlborough (superior Sauvignon Blanc). In the Auckland region, Waikato and Otago also produce some top drops.

Breweries. Steinlager, the various types of DB (Bitter, Export etc) and Lion Red are the most popular.

Small boutique breweries are popular and found in the main cities and towns. The best of the boutique beers are from Marlborough and Nelson – Pink Elephant and Mac's.

In a pub the cheapest beer is on tap. You can ask for a 'seven', originally seven fluid ounces but now a 200mL glass; a 'handle', a half-litre or litre mug with a handle and often called a pint or half-pint (old ways die hard); or a jug, which is just that.

Drinks at public bars are the cheapest, while lounge or fancier bars tend to mark their drinks up more, but prices vary widely. In public bars you can pretty much wear anything, but lounge bars have a lot of 'neat dress required' signs.

Wine NZ has a thriving wine industry and many wineries have established international reputations, particularly the white wines.

The best known regions are Marlborough, noted for its Sauvignon Blanc (for a trip through wine-growing country, see the Marlborough Explorer ride in the Marlborough & Nelson chapter), and Hawkes Bay, noted for its Chardonnay. Winery visits and tours are popular in these places and, of course, there's free wine-tasting.

An unusual NZ speciality is kiwi fruit wine. There are lots of varieties – still and bubbly, sweet and dry – and even a liqueur.

Health & Safety

Keeping healthy on your travels depends on your predeparture preparations, your daily health care while on the road and how you handle any medical problem that develops. While the potential problems can seem quite frightening, in reality few cyclists experience anything more than a bit of soreness, fatigue and chafing. The sections that follow aren't intended to alarm, but they are worth a skim before you go.

Before You Go

HEALTH INSURANCE
Make sure that you have adequate health insurance. For details, see Travel Insurance in the Visas & Documents section in the Facts for the Cyclist chapter.

IMMUNISATIONS
You don't need any vaccinations to visit New Zealand. However, it's always wise to keep up to date with routine vaccinations such as diphtheria, polio and tetanus – boosters are necessary every 10 years and protection is highly recommended.

FIRST AID
It's a good idea at any time to know the appropriate responses to make in the event of a major accident or illness, and it's especially important if you are intending to ride off-road in a remote area. Consider learning basic first aid through a recognised course before you go, and including a first aid manual with your medical kit.

Although detailed first aid instruction is outside the scope of this guidebook, some basic points are listed in the section on Traumatic Injuries later in this chapter. Undoubtedly the best advice is to avoid an accident in the first place. The Safety on the Bike section at the end of this chapter contains tips for safe on-road and off-road riding, as well as information on how to summon help should a major accident or illness occur.

PHYSICAL FITNESS
Most of the rides in this book are designed for someone with a moderate degree of cycling

First Aid Kit

It's wise to carry a small medical kit or at least share one between your group. A possible kit could include:

First Aid Supplies
- [ ] **sticking plasters (Band Aids)**
- [ ] **bandages & safety pins**
- [ ] **elastic support bandage** for knees, ankles etc
- [ ] **gauze swabs**
- [ ] **nonadhesive dressings**
- [ ] **small pair of scissors**
- [ ] **sterile alcohol wipes**
- [ ] **butterfly closure strips**
- [ ] **latex gloves**
- [ ] **syringes & needles** – for removing gravel from road-rash wounds
- [ ] **thermometer** (note that mercury thermometers are prohibited by airlines)
- [ ] **tweezers**

Medications
- [ ] **anti-diarrhoea** and **anti-nausea drugs**
- [ ] **antifungal cream** or **powder** – for fungal skin infections and thrush
- [ ] **antihistamines** – for allergies, eg hay fever; to ease the itch from insect bites or stings; and to prevent motion sickness
- [ ] **antiseptic powder** or **solution** (such as povidone-iodine) and **antiseptic wipes** – for cuts and grazes
- [ ] **nappy rash cream**
- [ ] **calamine lotion, sting relief spray** or **aloe vera** – to ease irritation from sunburn and insect bites or stings
- [ ] **cold** and **flu tablets, throat lozenges** and **nasal decongestant**
- [ ] **painkillers** eg aspirin or paracetamol (acetaminophen in the USA) – for pain and fever

Miscellaneous
- [ ] **insect repellent, sunscreen, lip balm** and **eye drops**
- [ ] **water purification tablets** or **iodine**

Getting Fit for Touring

Ideally, a training program is individualised to a person's objectives, specific needs, fitness levels and health. However, if you have no idea how to prepare for your cycling holiday these guidelines will help you better prepare so you can enjoy it more.

When preparing your training schedule consider the following:

Foundation You will need general kilometres in your legs before you start to expose them to any intensive cycling. Always start out with easy rides and give yourself plenty of time to build toward your objective.

Tailoring Once you have the general condition to start your specific preparation, remember to tailor some of your training rides to the type of ride or tour you will be embarking on. Someone preparing to do a three week ride will require a different approach to someone building fitness for a one day or weekend ride. Some aspects to think about are the ride length (distance and days), terrain, climate and weight to be carried in panniers.

Recovery Adaptation to a training program actually occurs during recovery time so it's important to ensure that you do the right things in between rides. Recovery can take many forms, but the simple ones are best. These include getting quality sleep, eating an adequate diet to refuel the system, doing recovery rides in between hard days (using small gears without pushing yourself), stretching and a relaxing bath. Other forms include recovery massage, spas and yoga.

If you have no cycling background the following program will help you get fit for your cycling holiday. If you are doing an easy ride (each ride in this book is rated; see Cycling Routes in the Facts for the Cyclist chapter), aim to at least complete Week 4; for moderate rides complete Week 6; and complete the program if you are doing a hard ride. Weekend cyclists may start at Week 3, while those who ride up to four days a week may choose to start at Week 5.

	Monday	Tuesday	Wednesday	Thursday	Friday	Saturday	Sunday
Week 1	10km*	–	10km*	–	10km*	–	10km*
Week 2	–	15km*	–	15km*	–	20km*	–
Week 3	20km*	–	20km*	25km*	–	25km*	20km†
Week 4	–	30km*	–	35km*	30km†	30km*	–
Week 5	30km*	–	40km†	–	35km*	–	40km†
Week 6	30km*	–	40km†	–	–	60km*	40km†
Week 7	30km*	–	40km†	–	30km†	70km*	30km*
Week 8	–	60km*	30km†	–	40km†	–	90km*

* steady pace (allows you to carry out a conversation without losing your breath) on flat or undulating terrain
† solid pace (allows you to talk in short sentences only) on undulating roads with some longer hills

The training program shown here is only a guide. Ultimately it is important to listen to your body and slow down if it's getting too hard. Take extra recovery days and cut back distances when you feel this way. Don't panic if you don't complete every ride, every week; the most important thing is to ride regularly and gradually increase the length of your rides as you get fitter.

For those with no exercise background, be sure to see your doctor and get a clearance to begin exercising at these rates. This is especially important for those over 35 years of age with no exercise history and those with a cardiac or respiratory condition of any nature.

Remember to be specific with your training program. If your trip involves carrying 20kg in panniers then incorporate this weight into some training rides, especially some of the longer ones.

Kevin Tabotta

fitness. As a general rule, however, the fitter you are, the more you'll enjoy riding. It pays to spend time preparing yourself physically before you set out, rather than let a sore backside and aching muscles draw your attention from some of the world's finest scenery.

Depending on your existing level of fitness, you should start training a couple of months before your trip. Try and ride at least three times a week, starting with easy rides (even 10km to begin with, if you're not already cycling regularly) and gradually building up to longer distances. Once you have a good base of regular riding behind you, include hills in your training (you'll appreciate hill fitness in NZ) and familiarise yourself with the gearing on your bike. In the last week or two, do at least one 60 to 70km ride with loaded panniers.

As you train, you'll discover the bike adjustments you need to make to increase your comfort – as well as any mechanical problems.

Staying Healthy

The best way to have a lousy holiday (especially if riding a bike) is to become ill. Heed the following simple advice and the only thing you're likely to suffer from is contented satisfaction from a challenging effort.

Reduce the chances of contracting an illness by washing your hands frequently, particularly after working on your bike and before handling or eating food.

HYDRATION

You may not notice how much water you're losing as you ride, because it evaporates in the breeze. However, don't underestimate the amount of fluid you need to replace – particularly in warmer weather. The magic figure is supposedly 1L per hour, though many cyclists have trouble consuming this much – remembering to drink enough can be harder than it sounds. Sipping little and often is the key; try to drink a mouthful every 10 minutes or so and don't wait until you get thirsty. Water 'backpacks' can be great for fluid regulation since virtually no physical or mental effort is required to drink. Keep drinking before and after the day's ride to replenish fluid.

Use the colour of your urine as a rough guide to whether you are drinking enough. Small amounts of dark urine suggest you need to increase your fluid intake. Passing reasonable quantities of light yellow urine indicates that you've got the balance about right. Other signs of dehydration include headache and fatigue. For more information on the effects of dehydration, see Dehydration & Heat Exhaustion later in this chapter.

Water

While tap water is almost always safe to drink in NZ, the intestinal parasite *Giardia lamblia* has been found in water from lakes, rivers and streams. Giardia is not common but, to be certain, water from these sources should be purified before drinking. For more information on giardiasis, see Infectious Diseases later in this chapter.

The simplest way of purifying water is to boil it thoroughly. Vigorously boiling for five minutes should be satisfactory.

Simple filtering will not remove all dangerous organisms, so if you can't boil water treat it chemically. Chlorine tablets will kill many pathogens, but not giardia. Iodine is very effective in purifying water and is available in tablet and liquid form, but follow the directions carefully and remember that too much iodine can be harmful. Flavoured powder will disguise the taste of treated water and is a good idea to carry if you are spending time away from town water supplies.

Sports Drinks

Commercial sports drinks such as Gatorade and PowerAde are an excellent way to satisfy your hydration needs, electrolyte replacement and energy demands in one. Often it's difficult to keep eating solid fuels day in day out on long rides but sports drinks, because of their (simple) carbohydrate source, can supplement these energy demands and allow you to vary your solid fuel intake a little for variety. The bonus of course is that your water needs are being met at the same time and those all important body salts lost through perspiration get restocked as well.

If you don't like the taste of a particular sports drink, try another. Most have similar recipes and the only difference is the flavouring; what you eat and drink while riding should work for you and suit your tastes. A good idea is to trial any sports drinks on your training rides before you fly to NZ and when you find one you like, take adequate supplies with you.

Most sports drink brands also come in two forms: premixed (sold in corner diaries and minisupermarkets) and in powder form (usually only sold in larger supermarkets). Drinking the premixed drinks all the time will be expensive, so mix your own using the powder. Don't mix the drinks too strong (follow the instructions) because, in addition to being too sweet, too many carbohydrates can actually impair your body's ability to absorb the water and carbohydrates properly.

A cool drink is easier for your body to absorb than a warm one.

If you have two water bottles on your bike (and you should), it's also a good idea to fill one with sports drink and the other with plain water. This will give you a way to clear your mouth of the sticky sweet taste you often get from sports drinks.

NUTRITION

One of the great things about bike touring is that it requires lots of energy, which means you can eat more. Depending on your activity levels it's not hard to put away huge servings of food and be hungry soon after.

Because you're putting such demands on your body, it's important to eat well – not just lots. As usual, you should eat a balanced diet from a wide variety of foods. This is easy in NZ, with so much fresh food

Avoiding the Bonk

The bonk, in a cycling context, is not a pleasant experience; it's that light-headed, can't-put-power-to-the-pedals weak feeling that engulfs you (usually quite quickly) when your body runs out of fuel.

If you experience it the best move is to stop and refuel immediately. It can be quite serious and risky to your health if it's not addressed as soon as symptoms occur. It won't take long before you are ready to get going again (although most likely at a slower pace), but you'll also be more tired the next day so try to avoid it.

The best way to do this is to keep your fuel intake up while riding. Cycling for hours on end burns considerable body energy and replacing it is something that needs to be tailored to each individual's tastes. The touring cyclist needs to target foods that have a high carbohydrate source. Foods that contain some fat are not a problem occasionally, as cycling at low intensity (when you're able to ride and talk without losing your breath) will usually trigger the body to draw on fat stores before stored carbohydrates.

Good on-bike cycling foods include:

- bananas (in particular) and other fruits
- bread with jam or honey
- breakfast and muesli bars
- rice-based snacks
- pre-packaged high carbohydrate sports bars (eg PowerBar, Cliff Bar etc)
- sports drinks

During lunch stops (or for breakfast) you can try such things as spaghetti, cereal, rice cream, pancakes, baked beans, sandwiches and rolls.

It's important not to get uptight about the food you eat. As a rule of thumb, base all your meals around carbohydrates of some sort, but don't be afraid to also indulge in local culinary delights.

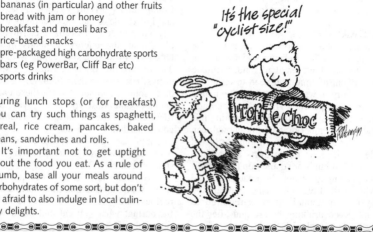

It's the special "cyclist size!"

widely available (see Food in the Facts for the Cyclist chapter).

The main part of your diet should be carbohydrates rather than proteins or fats. While some protein (for tissue maintenance and repair) and fat (for vitamins, long-term energy and warmth) is essential, carbohydrates provide the most efficient fuel. They are easily digested into simple sugars, which are then used in energy production. Less-refined foods like pasta, rice, bread, fruits and vegetables are all high in carbohydrates.

Eating simple carbohydrates (sugars, such as lollies or sweets) gives you almost immediate energy – great for when you need a top-up (see the 'Avoiding the Bonk' boxed text); however, because they are quickly metabolised, you may get a sugar 'high' then a 'low'. For cycling it is far better to base your diet around complex carbohydrates, which take longer to process and provide 'slow-release' energy over a longer period. (But don't miss the opportunity to indulge guiltlessly in cakes and that delicious NZ ice cream every now and then …)

Cycle Food: a Guide to Satisfying Your Inner Tube, by Lauren Hefferon, is a handy reference for nutrition and health advice, and practical recipes.

Day-to-Day Needs

Eat a substantial breakfast – wholegrain cereal or bread is best – and fruit or juice for vitamins. If you like a cooked breakfast, include carbohydrates (such as porridge, toast or potatoes) and try to avoid foods high in fat, which take longer to digest.

Bread is easy for lunch, topped with ingredients like cheese, peanut butter, salami and fresh salad vegetables. If you're in a town, filled rolls or focaccia make for a satisfying meal (chips or pizza with their high fat content, on the other hand, will feel like a lump in your stomach if you continue straight on).

Keep topping up your energy during the ride. PowerBars are a long-lasting, uncrushable and conveniently packaged source of (variably edible) carbohydrates for the road. They don't contain any 'magic' dietary properties, however, and are more expensive than standard snack foods. Bananas, dried fruit and muesli bars, or NZ's excellent muffins, will give you the same wholesome energy boost.

Try and eat a high carbohydrate meal in the evening. If you're eating out, Italian, Mexican, vegetarian or Asian restaurants tend to offer more carbohydrate-based meals.

Rice, pasta and potatoes are good staples if you're self-catering. Team them up with fresh vegetables and ingredients such as instant soup, canned beans, fish or bacon. Remember that even though you're limited in terms of what you can carry on a bike, it's possible with some imagination and preparation to eat delicious as well as nutritious camp meals.

CYCLING AILMENTS
Saddle Sores & Blisters

While you're more likely to get a sore bum if you're out of condition, riding long distances does take its toll on your behind. To minimise the impact, always wear clean, preferably padded bike shorts (known as 'knicks'); shower as soon as you stop and put on clean clothes. Brief, unfitted shorts can chafe, as can underwear (see Clothing in the Facts for the Cyclist chapter). Moisturising or emollient creams or baby nappy rash cream also help guard against chafing – apply liberally around the crotch area before riding. For information on the correct adjustment of your bike seat, see the Your Bicycle chapter.

If you do suffer from chafing, wash and dry the area and carefully apply a barrier (moisturising) cream.

You probably won't get blisters unless you do a very long ride with no physical preparation. Wearing gloves and correctly fitted shoes will reduce the likelihood of blisters on your hands and feet. If you know you're susceptible to blisters in a particular spot, cover the area with medical adhesive tape before riding.

Knee Pain

Knee pain is common among cyclists who pedal in too high a gear. While it may *seem* faster to turn the pedals slowly in a high gear, it's actually more efficient (and better for your knees) to 'spin' the pedals – that is, use a low enough gear so you can pedal quickly with little resistance. For touring, the ideal cadence (number of pedal strokes per minute) ranges from 70 to 90. Try to maintain this cadence even when you're climbing.

It's a good idea to stretch before and after riding, and to go easy when you first start riding each day. This reduces your chances of injury and helps your muscles to work more efficiently.

You can also get sore knees if your saddle is too low or if your shoe cleats (for use with clipless pedals) are incorrectly positioned. Both are discussed in greater detail in the Your Bicycle chapter.

Numbness & Backache

Pain in the hands, neck and shoulders is a common complaint, particularly on longer riding days. It's generally caused by leaning too much on your hands. Apart from discomfort, you can temporarily damage the nerves and experience numbness or mild paralysis of the hands. Prevent it by wearing padded gloves, cycling with less weight on your hands and changing your hand position frequently (if you have flat handlebars, fit bar ends to provide more hand positions).

When seated your weight should be fairly evenly distributed through your hands and seat. If you're carrying too much weight on your hands there are two ways of adjusting your bike to rectify this: either by raising the height of your handlebars or, if you are stretched out too much, fitting a smaller stem (talk to your local bike shop). For more guidance on adjusting your bicycle for greater comfort, see the Your Bicycle chapter.

Fungal Infections

Warm, sweaty bodies are ideal environments for fungal growth, and physical activity, combined with inadequate washing of your body and/or clothes, can lead to fungal infections. The most common are athlete's foot (tinea) between the toes or fingers, and infections on the scalp, in the groin or on the body (ringworm). You can get ringworm (which is a fungal infection, not a worm) from infected animals or other people.

To prevent fungal infections, wash frequently, use talcum powder and dry yourself carefully. Change out of sweaty bike clothes as soon as possible.

If you do get an infection, wash the infected area at least daily with a disinfectant or medicated soap and water, and rinse and dry well. Apply an antifungal cream or powder like tolnaftate. Expose the infected area to air or sunlight as much as possible, avoid artificial fibres and wash all towels

and underwear in hot water, change them often and let them dry in the sun.

Staying Warm

Except on extremely hot days, put on another layer of clothing when you stop cycling – even if it's just for a quick break. Staying warm when cycling is as important as keeping up your water and food intake. Particularly with wet or sweaty clothing, your body cools down quickly after you stop working. Muscle strains occur more easily when your body is chilled and hypothermia can result from prolonged exposure (for prevention and treatment, see Hypothermia later in this chapter). Staying rugged up will help prevent picking up chest infections, colds and the flu.

It's not advisable to cycle at high altitude during the winter months; however, with NZ's changeable weather, you *can* get caught suddenly in bad weather at any time of year, especially in the mountains. No matter when you go, always be prepared with warm clothing and a waterproof layer. Protect yourself from the wind on long downhill stretches – stuffing a few sheets of newspaper under your shirt cuts the chill considerably.

Medical Problems & Treatment

ENVIRONMENTAL HAZARDS
Sun

Because the ozone layer is relatively thin over NZ, the sun is fiercer than in other parts of the world. You can get sunburnt quite quickly, even on cool or cloudy days. You are most at risk during spring and summer and at higher altitudes.

Take sun protection seriously – unless you want to be fried and increase your chances of heatstroke and skin cancer. Here are some tips:

• Cover yourself wherever possible: wear a long-sleeved top with a collar, and a peaked helmet cover – you may want to go the extra step and add a 'legionnaire's flap' to your helmet to protect the back of your neck and ears. Make sure your shirt is sunproof: very thin or loosely woven fabrics still let sun through. Some fabrics are designed to offer high sun protection.

- Use high protection sunscreen (30+ or higher). Choose a water resistant 'sports' sunscreen and reapply every few hours as you sweat it off. Don't forget to protect your neck, ears, hands and feet if wearing sandals. Zinc cream is good for sensitive noses, lips and ears.
- Wear good sunglasses; they will also protect you from wind, dust and insects and are essential protection against sticks and flying objects if you're mountain biking.
- Sit in the shade during rest breaks.
- Wear a wide-brimmed hat when off the bike.

Mild sunburn can be treated with calamine lotion, aloe vera or sting-relief spray.

Heat

Treat heat with respect. NZ is temperate but can get very hot in the north, so don't set yourself a demanding touring schedule as soon as your arrive; take things lightly until you acclimatise.

Dehydration & Heat Exhaustion Dehydration is a potentially dangerous and generally preventable condition caused by excessive fluid loss. Sweating and inadequate fluid intake are common causes of dehydration in cyclists, but others include diarrhoea, vomiting and high fever – see Diarrhoea later in this chapter for details on appropriate treatment in these circumstances.

The first symptoms are weakness, thirst and passing small amounts of very concentrated urine. This may progress to drowsiness, dizziness or fainting when standing up, and finally, coma.

It's easy to forget how much fluid you are losing via perspiration while you are cycling, particularly if a strong breeze is drying your skin quickly. Make sure you drink sufficient liquids (see Hydration earlier in this chapter). Refrain from drinking too many caffeinated drinks like tea, coffee and some soft drinks (which act as a diuretic, causing your body to lose water through urination) throughout the day; don't use them as a water replacement.

Dehydration and salt deficiency can cause heat exhaustion. Salt deficiency is characterised by fatigue, lethargy, headaches, giddiness and muscle cramps; salt tablets may help, but adding extra salt to your food is probably sufficient.

If one of your party suffers from heat exhaustion, lie the casualty down in a shady spot and encourage them to drink slowly but frequently. If possible, seek medical advice.

Heatstroke This serious and occasionally fatal condition can occur if the body's heat-regulating mechanism breaks down and the body temperature rises to dangerous levels. Continuous periods of exposure to high temperatures and insufficient fluids can leave you vulnerable to heatstroke.

The symptoms are feeling unwell, not sweating very much (or at all) and a high body temperature (39° to 41°C or 102° to 106°F). Where sweating has ceased, the skin becomes flushed and red. Severe, throbbing headaches and lack of coordination will also occur, and the sufferer may be confused or aggressive. Eventually the victim will become delirious or convulse.

Hospitalisation is essential, but in the interim get the casualty out of the sun, remove their clothing, cover them with a wet sheet or towel and then fan continuously. Give them plenty of fluids (cool water), if conscious.

Hypothermia

Hypothermia is a real danger in NZ because of the extremely changeable weather and the low winter temperatures.

Hypothermia occurs when the body loses heat faster than it can produce it and the core temperature of the body falls. It is surprisingly easy to progress from very cold to dangerously cold due to a combination of wind, wet clothing, fatigue and hunger, even if the air temperature is above freezing.

Symptoms of hypothermia are exhaustion, numb skin (particularly toes and fingers), shivering, slurred speech, irrational or violent behaviour, lethargy, stumbling, dizzy spells, muscle cramps and violent bursts of energy. Irrationality may take the form of sufferers claiming they are warm and trying to take off their clothes.

To prevent hypothermia, dress in layers (see Clothing in the Facts for the Cyclist chapter). A strong, waterproof outer layer is essential. Protect yourself against wind, particularly for long descents. Eat plenty of high-energy food when it's cold; it's important to keep drinking too – even though you may not feel like it.

To treat mild hypothermia, first get the person out of the wind and/or rain, remove wet clothing and replace it with dry, warm clothing. Give them hot liquids – not alcohol – and some high-kilojoule, easily digestible food. Do not rub victims: instead, allow them to slowly warm themselves. This should be enough to treat the early stages of hypothermia; seek urgent medical treatment. Early recognition and treatment of mild hypothermia is the only way to prevent severe hypothermia, which is a critical condition.

INFECTIOUS DISEASES
Diarrhoea
Simple things like a change of water, food or climate can all cause a mild bout of diarrhoea, but a few rushed toilet trips with no other symptoms are not indicative of a major problem. More serious diarrhoea is caused by infectious agents transmitted by faecal contamination of food or water, by using contaminated utensils or transmission directly from one person's hand to another. Paying particular attention to personal hygiene, drinking purified water and taking care of what you eat are important measures to take to avoid getting diarrhoea while touring.

Dehydration is the main danger with any diarrhoea, particularly in children or the elderly, as dehydration can occur quite quickly. Under all circumstances fluid replacement (at least equal to the volume being lost) is the most important thing to remember. Weak black tea with a little sugar, soda water, or soft drinks allowed to go flat and diluted 50% with clean water are all good. With severe diarrhoea a rehydrating solution is preferable to replace minerals and salts lost. Commercially available oral rehydration salts (ORS) are very useful; add them to boiled or bottled water. In an emergency you can make up a solution of six teaspoons of sugar and a half teaspoon of salt to a litre of boiled or bottled water. You need to drink at least the same volume of fluid that you are losing in bowel movements and vomiting. Urine is the best guide to the adequacy of replacement – if you have small amounts of dark-coloured urine, you need to drink more. Keep drinking small amounts often. Stick to a bland diet as you recover.

Gut-paralysing drugs such as diphenoxylate or loperamide can be used to bring relief from the symptoms, although they do not actually cure the problem. Only use these drugs if you do not have access to toilets, eg if you *must* travel. These drugs are not recommended for children under 12 years, or if you have a high fever or are severely dehydrated.

Seek medical advice if you pass blood or mucus, are feverish or suffer persistent or severe diarrhoea.

Another cause of persistent diarrhoea in travellers is giardiasis.

Giardiasis
This intestinal disorder is contracted by drinking water contaminated with the Giardia parasite. The symptoms are stomach cramps, nausea, a bloated stomach, watery and foul-smelling diarrhoea, and frequent gas. Giardiasis can appear several weeks after you have been exposed to the parasite. The symptoms may disappear for a few days and then return; this can go on for several weeks. You should seek medical advice if you think you have giardiasis, but where this is not possible, tinidazole or metronidazole are the recommended drugs. Treatment is a 2g single dose of tinidazole or 250mg of metronidazole three times daily for five to 10 days.

Amoebic Meningitis
This very serious disease can be a danger if you bathe in natural hot thermal pools. Fortunately, it's no danger if you know how to protect yourself from it.

The amoeba that causes the disease can enter your body through the orifices of your head, usually the nose but occasionally the ears as well. Once it gets inside the nose it bores through the tissues and lodges in the brain. It's easy not to catch the disease – just keep your head out of water!

Symptoms of amoebic meningitis may have a slow onset – it could be several days or even several weeks before the first symptoms are noticed. Symptoms may be similar to the flu at first, later progressing to severe headaches, stiffness of the neck, hypersensitivity to light and even coma. It can be treated but it has a high mortality rate; seek urgent medical treatment.

BITES & STINGS
Bees & Wasps
Wasps are a problem in some places in NZ. They are attracted to food, especially at picnic sites; late summer is the worst time of

year for them. There are many wasps in beech forests.

Bee and wasp stings are usually painful rather than dangerous. However, in people who are allergic to them severe breathing difficulties may occur and urgent medical care is required. Calamine lotion or a commercial sting relief spray will ease discomfort and ice packs will reduce the pain and swelling.

Mosquitoes & Sandflies

Mosquitoes appear after dusk. Avoid bites by covering bare skin and using an insect repellent. Mosquitoes may be attracted by perfume, aftershave or certain colours. They can bite you through thin fabrics or on any small part of your skin not covered by repellent.

Another NZ insect that can drive you wild is the sandfly, a tiny black creature found in inland areas as well as around the coast, where it lives in bushes, trees or grasses. Sandfly bites occur mainly on the feet and ankles. Wearing shoes, thick socks and plenty of insect repellent is not only advisable but practically a necessity where sandflies are present.

The most effective insect repellent is called DEET, an ingredient in many commercially available repellents. Look for a repellent with at least a 28% concentration of DEET. Note that DEET breaks down plastic, rubber, contact lenses and synthetic fabrics, so be careful what you touch after using it. It poses no danger to natural fibres.

Spiders

The only poisonous spider, the retiring little katipo spider, can be fatal, but rarely is. Antivenin is available from most hospitals and is effective even if administered as long as three days after being bitten. The venomous female has a shiny black body, about 6mm long, with a bright red patch on the rear of the abdomen. It is found in all NZ coastal areas except for the far south, weaving a small, dense web close to the ground, just back from the high-tide zone.

WOMEN'S HEALTH

Cycle touring is not hazardous to your health, but women's health issues are relevant wherever you go, and can be a bit more tricky to cope with when you are on the road.

If you experience low energy and/or abdominal or back pain during menstruation, it may be best to undertake less strenuous rides or schedule a rest day or two at this time.

Gynaecological Problems

If you've got a vaginal discharge that is not normal for you with or without any other symptoms, you've probably got an infection.

- If you've had thrush before and you think you have it again, it's worth self-treating for this (see the following).
- If not, get medical advice, as you will need a laboratory test and an appropriate course of treatment.
- It's best not to self-medicate with antibiotics because there are many causes of vaginal discharge, which can only be differentiated with a laboratory test.

Thrush (Vaginal Candidiasis) Symptoms of this common yeast infection are itching and discomfort in the genital area, often in association with thick white vaginal discharge (said to resemble cottage cheese). Many factors, including diet, pregnancy, medications and hot climatic conditions can trigger this infection.

You can help prevent thrush by wearing cotton underwear and loose-fitting bicycle shorts; maintaining good personal hygiene is particularly important when wearing cycling knicks. It's a good idea to wash regularly, but use a pH-neutral soap (soaps with a high acidity or alkalinity can increase the chance of it occurring). If you have thrush a single dose of an antifungal pessary (vaginal tablet), such as 500mg of clotrimazole is an effective treatment. Alternatively, you can use an antifungal cream inserted high in the vagina (on a tampon). Antifungal cream can be used in addition to a pessary to relieve vulval itching. A vaginal acidifying gel may help prevent recurrences.

If you're stuck in a remote area without medication, you could use natural yoghurt (applied directly to the vulva or on a tampon and inserted in the vagina) to soothe and help restore the normal balance of organisms in the vagina.

Urinary Tract Infection

Cystitis, or inflammation of the bladder, is a common condition in women. Symptoms include burning when urinating and having to urinate urgently and frequently. Blood can sometimes be passed in urine.

If you think you've got cystitis:

- Drink plenty of fluids to help flush the infection out; citrus fruit juice or cranberry juice can help relieve symptoms.
- Take a non-prescription cystitis remedy to help relieve the discomfort. Alternatively, add a teaspoon of bicarbonate of soda to a glass of water.
- If there's no improvement after 24 hours despite these measures, seek medical advice because a course of antibiotics may be needed.

TRAUMATIC INJURIES

Although we give guidance on basic first aid procedures here remember that, unless you're an experienced first aider and confident in what you're doing, it's possible to do more harm than good. Always seek medical help if it is available, but if you are far from any help, follow these guidelines.

Cuts & Other Wounds

Here's what to do if you suffer a fall while riding and end up with road-rash and a few minor cuts. If you're riding in a hot, humid climate or intend continuing on your way there's likely to be a high risk of infection, so the wound needs to be cleaned and dressed. Carry a few antiseptic wipes in your first aid kit to use as an immediate measure, especially if no clean water is available. A small wound can be cleaned with an antiseptic wipe (only wipe across the wound once). Deep or dirty wounds need to be cleaned thoroughly, as follows:

- Make sure your hands are clean before you start
- Wear gloves if you are cleaning somebody else's wound
- Use bottled or boiled water (allowed to cool) or an antiseptic solution like povidone-iodine
- Use plenty of water – pour it on the wound from a container
- Embedded dirt and other particles are able to be removed with tweezers or flushed out using a syringe to squirt water (you can get more pressure if you use a needle as well); this is especially effective for removing gravel
- Dry wounds heal best, so avoid using antiseptic creams that keep the wound moist; instead you could apply antiseptic powder or spray
- Dry the wound with clean gauze before applying a dressing – alternatively, any clean material will do as long as it's not fluffy (avoid cotton wool), because it will stick

Any break in the skin makes you vulnerable to tetanus infection – if you didn't have a tetanus injection before you left, you'll need one now.

A dressing will protect the wound from dirt, dust and flies. Alternatively, if the wound is small and you are confident you can keep it clean, leave it uncovered. Change the dressing regularly (once a day to start with), especially if the wound is oozing, and watch for signs of infection.

If you have any swelling around the wound, raising the affected limb can help the swelling settle and the wound to heal.

It's best to seek medical advice for any wound that fails to heal after a week or so.

Major Accident

Crashing or being hit by a motor vehicle is always possible when cycling. When a major accident does occur what you do is determined to some extent by the circumstances

Bleeding Wounds

Most cuts will stop bleeding on their own, but if a blood vessel of any size has been cut it may continue bleeding for some time. Wounds to the head, hands and at joint creases tend to be particularly bloody.

To stop bleeding from a wound:

- Wear gloves if you are dealing with a wound on another person
- Lie the casualty down if possible
- Use your fingers or the palm of your hand to apply direct pressure to the wound, preferably over a sterile dressing or clean pad
- Apply steady pressure for at least five minutes before looking to see if the bleeding has stopped
- Raise the injured limb above the level of your heart
- Put a sterile dressing over the original pad (don't move this) and bandage it in place
- Check the bandage regularly in case bleeding restarts

Never use a tourniquet to stop bleeding as this may cause gangrene – the only situation in which this may be appropriate is if the limb has been amputated.

you are in and how readily available medical care is. However, remember that emergency services may be different from what you are used to. If you are outside of a major town they may be very much slower at responding to a call, so you need to be prepared to do at least an initial assessment and to ensure that the casualty comes to no further harm. First of all, check for danger to yourself. If the casualty is on the road ensure oncoming traffic is stopped or diverted around you. A basic plan of action is:

- Keep calm and think through what you need to do and when
- Get medical help urgently, phone ☎ 111
- Carefully look over the casualty in the position you found them (unless this is hazardous for some reason, eg on a cliff edge)
- Check for pulse (at the wrist or on the side of the neck), breathing and major blood loss
- If necessary (ie not breathing or no pulse), and you know how, start resuscitation
- Check the casualty for injuries, moving them as little as possible; ask them where they have pain if they are conscious
- Take immediate steps to control any obvious bleeding by applying direct pressure to the wound
- Make the casualty as comfortable as possible and reassure them
- Keep the casualty warm if necessary by insulating them from cold or wet ground (use whatever you have to hand, such as a sleeping bag)
- Don't move the casualty if a spinal injury is possible

Safety on the Bike

ROAD RULES
The NZ government publication *The Bike Code* is available for $9.95 from bookshops or its Web site (🖳 www.itsa.govt.nz/cyclists/index.html) and explains the rules and regulations for cyclists. Some important things to note are that helmets are compulsory, as are reflectors and lights when cycling in low light. You may be fined for riding without these items.

Ride on the left side of the road in NZ and use hand signals for right turns. Be careful of the quirky 'give way to the right' rule whereby traffic turning left at an intersection must give way to those turning right. There are no 'free' left turns unless they are marked.

Use bike lanes, which are marked in some areas, and the sealed shoulder (where it occurs) on major roads. Always ride in single file if the road is busy, narrow or winding. Only ride two abreast where it is safe and don't ride on footpaths (sidewalks) unless they are approved cycle lanes.

RIDING OFF-ROAD
While the mountain bike rides in this book are not far from civilisation, you should always remember one of the first rules about mountain bike riding: never do it alone. It's not uncommon for people to go missing in the NZ bush, either through injury or after losing their way. It's best, if possible, to go in a small group – four is usually considered the minimum number. This way, if someone in the group has an accident or is taken ill, one person can stay with the casualty and the others can go for help.

Always tell someone where you are going and when you intend to be back – and make sure they know that you're back. Take warm clothing, matches and enough food and water in case of emergency. Carry enough tools with you so that you can undertake any emergency bicycle repairs (see the Your Bicycle chapter for advice on a basic toolkit).

Carry a map and take note of your surroundings as you ride (terrain, landmarks etc), so that if you do get lost, you're more likely to find yourself again. If you get really lost, stay calm and stop. Try and work out where you are or how to retrace your route. If you can't, or it's getting dark, find a nearby open area, put on warm clothes and find or make a shelter. Light a fire for warmth and assist searchers by making as many obvious signs as you can (such as smoke, brightly coloured items or symbols made with wood or rocks).

EMERGENCY PROCEDURES
If you or one of your group has an accident (even a minor one) or falls ill during your travels, you'll need to decide on your best course of action – this is not always easy. Obviously, you will need to take into consideration your individual circumstances, including where you are and whether you have some means of direct communication with emergency services, such as a mobile phone.

Tips for Better Cycling

These tips on riding technique are designed to help you ride more safely, comfortably and efficiently:

- Ride in bike lanes if they exist.
- Ride about 1m out from the edge of the kerb or from parked cars; riding too close to the road edge makes you less visible and more vulnerable to rough surfaces or car doors opening without warning.
- Stay alert; especially on busy, narrow, winding and hilly roads it's essential to constantly scan ahead and anticipate the movements of other vehicles, cyclists, pedestrians or animals – and keep an eye out for potholes and other hazards as well.
- Keep your upper body relaxed, even when you are climbing.
- Ride a straight line and don't weave across the road when you reach for your water bottle or when climbing.
- To negotiate rough surfaces and bumps, take your weight off the saddle and let your legs absorb the shock, with the pedals level (in the three and nine o'clock positions).

At Night
- Only ride at night if your bike is equipped with a front and rear light; consider also using a reflective vest and/or reflective ankle bands.

Braking
- Apply front and rear brakes evenly.
- When your bike is fully loaded you'll find that you can apply the front brake quite hard and the extra weight will prevent you doing an 'endo' (flipping over the handlebars).

Climbing
- When climbing out of the saddle, keep the bike steady; rock the handlebars from side to side as little as possible.
- Change down to your low gears to keep your legs 'spinning'.

Cornering
- Loaded bikes are prone to sliding out on corners: approach corners slowly and don't lean into the corner as hard as you normally would.
- If traffic permits, take a straight path across corners; hit the corner wide, cut across the apex and ride out of it wide – but never cross the dividing line on the road.
- Apply the brakes before the corner, not while cornering (especially if it's wet).

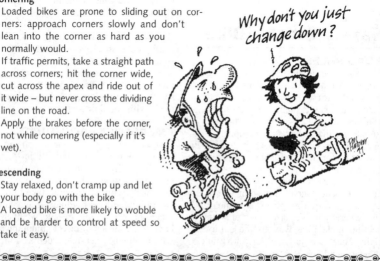

Why don't you just change down?

Descending
- Stay relaxed, don't cramp up and let your body go with the bike
- A loaded bike is more likely to wobble and be harder to control at speed so take it easy.

Tips for Better Cycling

- Pump the brakes to shed speed rather than applying constant pressure, to avoid overheating the rims, which can cause your tyre to blow.

Gravel Roads

- Avoid patches of deep gravel (often on the road's edge); if you can't, ride hard, as you do if driving a car through mud.
- Look ahead to plan your course; avoid sudden turning and take it slowly on descents.
- Brake in a straight line using your rear brake and place your weight over the front wheel if you need to use that brake.
- On loose gravel, loosen your toe-clip straps or clipless pedals so you can put your foot down quickly.

Group Riding

- If you're riding in a group, keep your actions predictable and let others know, with a hand signal or shout, before you brake, turn, dodge potholes etc.
- Ride beside, in front or behind fellow cyclists; don't overlap wheels. If either of you moves sideways suddenly it's likely both of you will fall.
- Ride in single file on busy, narrow or winding roads.

In Traffic

- Obey the rules of the road and signal if you are turning.
- Look at the wheels to see if a car at a T-junction or joining the road is actually moving or not.
- Scan for trouble: look inside the back windows of parked cars for movement – that person inside may open the door on you.
- Look drivers in the eye; make sure they've seen you.
- Learn to bunny hop your bike (yes, it can be done with a fully-loaded touring bike; just not as well) – it'll save you hitting potholes and other hazards.

In the Wet

- Be aware that you'll take longer to slow down with wet rims; exercise appropriate caution.
- When descending apply the brakes lightly to keep the rims free of grit/water etc and allow for quicker stopping.
- Don't climb out of the saddle (unless you want a change); shift down a gear or two and climb seated.

On Bikepaths

- Use a bell or call out to warn others of your approach on bikepaths.

Some basic emergency guidelines are:

- Use your first aid knowledge and experience, as well as the information in this guide if necessary, to make a medical assessment of the situation.
- For groups of several people, the accepted procedure is to leave one person with the casualty, together with as much equipment, food and water as you can sensibly spare, and for the rest of the group to go for help.
- If there are only two of you, the situation is trickier and you will have to make an individual judgement as to the best course of action in this situation.
- If you leave someone, mark their position carefully on the map (take it with you); you should also make sure they can be easily found by marking the position with something conspicuous, such as bright clothing or a large stone cross on the ground.
- You can try attracting attention by using a whistle or torch, lighting a smoky fire (use damp wood or green leaves) or waving bright clothing; shouting is tiring and not very effective.

The uncertainties associated with emergency rescue in remote wilderness areas should make it clear to you how important careful planning and safety precautions are, especially if you are going in a small group.

Emergency Numbers

In New Zealand there is only one number for all emergency services:

☎ 111 – emergency number (ambulance, police or fire brigade)
☎ 0800-735 466 – ambulance advice line

YOUR
BICYCLE

Fundamental to any cycle tour you plan is the bicycle. In this chapter we look at choosing a bicycle and accessories, setting it up for your needs, learning basic maintenance, and loading and carrying your gear. In short, everything you need to gear up and get going.

CHOOSING & SETTING UP A BICYCLE

The ideal bike for cycle touring is (strangely enough) a touring bike. These bikes look similar to road bikes but generally have relaxed frame geometry for comfort and predictable steering; fittings (eyelets and brazed-on bosses) to mount panniers and mudguards; wider rims and tyres; strong wheels (at least 36 spokes) to carry the extra load; and gearing capable of riding up a wall (triple chainrings and a wide-range freewheel to match). If you want to buy a touring bike, most tend to be custom-built these days, but Cannondale (🖳 www.cannondale.com) and Trek (🖳 www.trekbikes.com) both offer a range of models.

Of course you can tour on any bike you choose, but few will match the advantages of the workhorse touring bike.

Mountain bikes are a slight compromise by comparison, but are very popular for touring. A mountain bike already has the gearing needed for touring and offers a more upright, comfortable position on the bike. And with a change of tyres (to those with semi-slick tread) you'll be able to reduce the rolling resistance and travel at higher speeds with less effort.

Hybrid, or cross, bikes are similar to mountain bikes (and therefore offer similar advantages and disadvantages), although they typically already come equipped with semi-slick tyres.

Racing bikes are less appropriate: their tighter frame geometry is less comfortable on rough roads and long rides. It is also difficult to fit wider tyres, mudguards, racks and panniers to a road bike. Perhaps more significantly, most racing bikes have a distinct lack of low gears.

Tyres Unless you know you'll be on good, sealed roads the whole time, it's probably safest to choose a tyre with some tread. If you have 700c or 27-inch wheels, opt for a tyre that's 28–35mm wide. If touring on a mountain bike, the first thing to do is get rid of the knobby tyres – too much rolling resistance. Instead, fit 1–1½ inch semi-slick tyres or, if riding unpaved roads or off-road occasionally, a combination pattern tyre (slick centre and knobs on the outside).

To protect your tubes, consider buying tyres reinforced with Kevlar, a tightly woven synthetic fibre very resistant to sharp objects. Although more expensive, Kevlar-belted tyres are worth it.

Pedals Cycling efficiency is vastly improved by using toe clips, and even more so with clipless pedals and cleated shoes. Mountain bike or touring shoes are best – the cleats are recessed and the soles are flexible enough to comfortably walk in.

🔧 Fold & Go Bikes

Another option is a folding bike. Manufacturers include: Brompton (🖳 www.phoenixcycles .com), Bike Friday (🖳 www.bikefriday.com), Slingshot (🖳 www.slingshotbikes.com) and Moulton (🖳 www.alexmoulton.co.uk). All make high-quality touring bikes that fold up to allow hassle-free train, plane or bus transfers. The Moulton, Brompton and Slingshot come with suspension and the Bike Friday's case doubles as a trailer for your luggage when touring.

Touring Bike

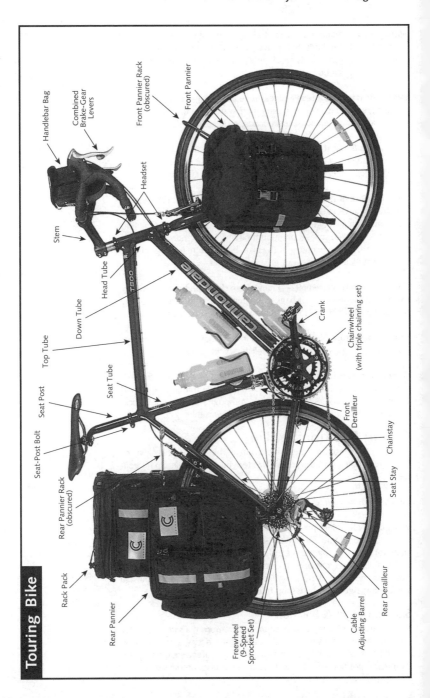

Handlebar Bag

Combined Brake-Gear Levers

Front Pannier Rack (obscured)

Front Pannier

Headset

Stem

Head Tube

Down Tube

Top Tube

Crank

Chainwheel (with triple chainring set)

Seat Tube

Front Derailleur

Seat Post

Chainstay

Seat-Post Bolt

Rear Pannier Rack (obscured)

Seat Stay

Rack Pack

Rear Derailleur

Rear Pannier

Cable Adjusting Barrel

Freewheel (9-Speed Sprocket Set)

Mudguards Adding mudguards to your bike will reduce the amount of muddy water and grit that sprays you when it rains or the roads are wet. Plastic clip-on models are slightly less effective but not as expensive, and they can be less hassle.

Water Bottles & Cages Fit at least two bottle cages to your bike – in isolated areas you may need to carry more water than this. Water 'backpacks', such as a Camelbak, make it easy to keep your fluids up.

Reflectors & Lights If riding at night, add reflectors and lights so you can see, and others can see you. A small headlight can also double as a torch (flashlight). Flashing tail-lights are cheap and effective.

Pannier Racks It's worth buying good pannier racks. The best are aluminium racks made by Blackburn. They're also the most expensive, but come with a lifetime guarantee. Front racks come in low-mounting and mountain bike styles. Low-mounting racks carry the weight lower, which improves the handling of the bike, but if you're touring off-road it is a better idea to carry your gear a bit higher.

Panniers Panniers (see pp92–4) range from cheap-and-nasty to expensive top-quality waterproof bags. Get panniers that fit securely to your rack and watch that the pockets don't swing into your spokes.

Cycle Computer Directions for rides in this book rely upon accurate distance readings, so you'll need a reliable cycle computer.

Other Accessories A good pump is essential. Make sure it fits your valve type (see p82). Some clip on to your bicycle frame, while others fit 'inside' the frame. Also carry a lock. Although heavy, U- or D-locks are the most secure; cable locks can be more versatile.

Riding Position Set Up

Cycling is meant to be a pleasurable pursuit, but that isn't likely if the bike you're riding isn't the correct size for you and isn't set up for your needs.

In this section we assume your bike shop did a good job of providing you with the correct size bike (if you're borrowing a bike get a bike shop to check it is the correct size for you) and concentrate on setting you up in your ideal position and showing you how to tweak the comfort factor. If you are concerned that your bike frame is too big or small for your needs get a second opinion from another bike shop.

The following techniques for determining correct fit are based on averages and may not work for your body type. If you are an unusual size or shape get your bike shop to create your riding position.

Saddle Height & Position

Saddles are essential to riding position and comfort. If a saddle is poorly adjusted it can be a royal pain in the derriere – and legs, arms and back. In addition to saddle height, it is also possible to alter a saddle's tilt and its fore/aft position – each affects your riding position differently.

Saddle Tilt Saddles are designed to be level to the ground, taking most of the weight off your arms and back. However, since triathletes started dropping the nose of their saddles in the mid-1980s many other cyclists have followed suit without knowing why. For some body types, a slight tilt of the nose might be necessary. Be aware, however, that forward tilt will place extra strain on your arms and back. If it is tilted too far forward, chances are your saddle is too high.

Fore/Aft Position The default setting for fore/aft saddle position will allow you to run a plumb bob from the centre of your forward pedal axle to the protrusion of your knee (that bit of bone just under your knee cap).

Fore/Aft Position: To check it, sit on your bike with the pedals in the three and nine o'clock positions. Check the alignment with a plumb bob (a weight on the end of a piece of string).

Saddle Height The simplest method of roughly determining the correct saddle height is the straight leg method. Sit on your bike wearing your cycling shoes. Line one crank up with the seat-tube and place your heel on the pedal. Adjust the saddle height until your leg is almost straight, but not straining. When you've fixed the height of your saddle pedal the cranks backwards (do it next to a wall so you can balance yourself). If you are rocking from side to side, lower the saddle slightly. Otherwise keep raising the saddle (slightly) until on the verge of rocking.

The most accurate way of determining saddle height is the Hodges Method. Developed by US cycling coach Mark Hodges after studying the position of dozens of racing cyclists, the method is also applicable to touring cyclists.

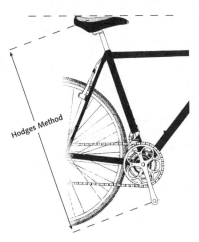

Hodges Method

Standing barefoot with your back against a wall and your feet 15cm apart, get a friend to measure from the greater trochanter (the bump of your hip) to the floor passing over your knee and ankle joints. Measure each leg (in mm) three times and average the figure. Multiply the average figure by 0.96.

Now add the thickness of your shoe sole and your cleats (if they aren't recessed). This total is the distance you need from the centre of your pedal axle to the top of your saddle. It is the optimum position for your body to pedal efficiently and should not be exceeded; however, people with small feet for their size should lower the saddle height slightly. The inverse applies for people with disproportionately large feet.

If you need to raise your saddle significantly do it over a few weeks so your muscles can adapt gradually. (Never raise your saddle above the maximum extension line marked on your seat post.)

Handlebars & Brake Levers

Racing cyclists lower their handlebars to cheat the wind and get a better aerodynamic position. While this might be tempting on windy days it doesn't make for comfortable touring. Ideally, the bars should be no higher than the saddle (even on mountain bikes) and certainly no lower than 75mm below it.

Pedals

For comfort and the best transference of power, the ball of your foot should be aligned over the centre of the pedal axle (see right).

If using clipless pedals consider the amount of lateral movement available. Our feet have a natural angle that they prefer when we walk, run or cycle. If they are unable to achieve this position the knee joint's alignment will be affected and serious injury may result. Most clipless pedal systems now have some rotational freedom (called 'float') built in to allow for this, but it is still important to adjust the cleats to each foot's natural angle.

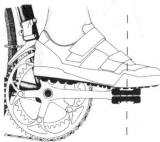

Comfort Considerations

Pedal Alignment: The ball of your foot should be over the centre of the pedal axle for comfort and the best transfer of power.

Now that you have your optimum position on the bike, there are several components that you can adjust to increase the comfort factor.

Handlebars come in a variety of types and sizes. People with small hands may find shallow drop bars more comfortable. Handlebars also come in a variety of widths, so if they're too wide or narrow change them.

With mountain bike handlebars you really only have one hand position, so add a pair of bar-ends. On drop bars the ends should be parallel to the ground. If they're pointed up it probably means you need a longer stem; pointed down probably means you need a shorter stem.

On mountain bikes the **brake levers** should be adjusted to ensure your wrist is straight – it's the position your hand naturally sits in. For drop bars the bottom of the lever should end on the same line as the end section.

Getting the right **saddle** for you is one of the key considerations for enjoyable cycling. Everybody's sit bones are shaped and spaced differently, meaning a saddle that suits your best friend might be agony for you. A good bike shop will allow you to keep changing a new (undamaged) saddle until you get one that's perfect. Women's saddles tend to have a shorter nose and a wider seat, and men's are long and narrow.

Brake Levers: Adjust your drop bars so the end section is parallel to the ground and the brake lever ends on this same line.

If you feel too stretched out or cramped when riding, chances are you need a different length **stem** – the problem isn't solved by moving your saddle forward/aft. Get a bike shop to assess this for you.

🔧 Record Your Position

When you've created your ideal position, mark each part's position (scratch a line with a sharp tool like a scribe or use tape) and record it, so you can recreate it if hiring a bike or when reassembling your bike after travel. The inside back cover of this book has a place to record all this vital data.

MAINTAINING YOUR BICYCLE

If you're new to cycling or haven't previously maintained your bike, this section is for you. It won't teach you how to be a top-notch mechanic, but it will help you maintain your bike in good working order and show you how to fix the most common touring problems.

If you want to know more about maintaining your bike there are dozens of books available (*Richard's Bicycle Book*, by Richard Ballantine, is a classic) or inquire at your bike shop about courses in your area.

Predeparture & Daily Inspections

Before heading off on tour get your bike serviced by a bike shop or do it yourself. On tour, check over your bike every day or so; inspect the following in particular:

- **Bolts & Screws** – tighten all bolts and screws regularly (especially pannier racks and water-bottle cages)
- **Brakes** (see pp86–7) – check pads for wear and alignment with rim; squeeze brakes to ensure they are adjusted to stop you
- **Chain** – clean and relube it regularly (see pp84–5)
- **Tyres** – check tyre pressure; visually inspect for cuts (including sidewall) and/or foreign objects such as embedded glass or nails
- **Wheels** – check they're true and no spokes are broken (see pp90–1)

Spares & Tool Kit

Touring cyclists need to be self-sufficient and should carry some spares and a basic tool kit.

Multi-tools (see right) are very handy and a great way to save space and weight, and there are dozens of different ones on the market. Before you buy a multi-tool though, check each of the tools is usable – a chain breaker, for example, needs to have a good handle for leverage otherwise it is useless.

Adjustable spanners are often handy, but the trade-off is that they can easily burr bolts if not used correctly.

The bare minimum:
- ☐ pump – ensure it has the correct valve fitting for your tyres
- ☐ water bottles (2)
- ☐ spare tubes (2)
- ☐ tyre levers (2)
- ☐ chain lube and a rag
- ☐ puncture repair kit (check the glue is OK)
- ☐ Allen keys to fit your bike
- ☐ small Phillips screwdriver
- ☐ small flat screwdriver
- ☐ spare brake pads
- ☐ spare screws and bolts (for pannier racks, seat post etc) and chain links (2)

For those who know what they're doing:
- ☐ spoke key
- ☐ spare spokes and nipples (8)
- ☐ tools to remove freewheel
- ☐ chain breaker
- ☐ pliers
- ☐ spare chain links (HyperGlide chain rivet if you have a Shimano chain)
- ☐ spare rear brake and rear gear cables

Always handy to take along:
- ☐ roll of electrical/gaffer tape
- ☐ nylon ties (10) – various lengths/sizes
- ☐ hand cleaner (store it in a film canister)

Fixing a Flat

Flats happen. And if you're a believer in Murphy's Law then the likely scenario is that you'll suffer a flat just as you're rushing to the next town to catch a train or beat the setting sun.

Don't worry – this isn't a big drama. If you're prepared and know what you're doing you can be up and on your way in five minutes flat.

Being prepared means carrying a spare tube, a pump and at least two tyre levers. If you're not carrying a spare tube, of course, you can stop and fix the puncture then and there, but it's unlikely you'll catch that train and you could end up doing all this in the dark. There will be days when you have the time to fix a puncture on the side of the road, but not always. Carry at least two spare tubes.

1 Take the wheel off the bike. Remove the valve cap and unscrew the locknut (hex nut at base; see Valve Types) on Presta valves. Deflate the tyre completely, if it isn't already.

2 Make sure the tyre and tube are loose on the rim – moisture and the pressure of the inflated tube often makes the tyre and tube fuse with the rim.

3 If the tyre is really loose you should be able to remove it with your hands. Otherwise you'll need to lift one side of the tyre over the rim with the tyre levers. Pushing the tyre away from the lever as you insert it should ensure you don't pinch the tube and puncture it again.

4 When you have one side of the tyre off, you'll be able to remove the tube. Before inserting the replacement tube, carefully inspect the tyre (inside and out); you're looking for what caused the puncture. If you find anything embedded in the tyre, remove it. Also check that the rim tape is still in

Valve Types

The two most common valve types are Presta (sometimes called French) and Schraeder (American). To inflate a Presta valve, first unscrew the round nut at the top (and do it up again after you're done); depress it to deflate. To deflate Schraeder valves depress the pin (inside the top). Ensure your pump is set up for the valve type on your bike.

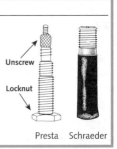

Unscrew

Locknut

Presta   Schraeder

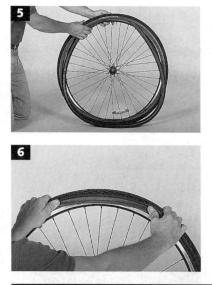

place and no spoke nipples (see pp90–1) protrude through it.

5 Time to put the new tube in. Start by partially pumping up the tube (this helps prevent it twisting or being pinched) and insert the valve in the hole in the rim. Tuck the rest of the tube in under the tyre, making sure you don't twist it. Make sure the valve is straight – most Presta valves come with a locknut to help achieve this.

6 Work the tyre back onto the rim with your fingers. If this isn't possible, and again, according to Murphy's Law, it frequently isn't, you might need to use your tyre levers for the last 20–30cm. If you need to use the levers, make sure you don't pinch the new tube, otherwise it's back to Step 1. All you need to do now is pump up the tyre and put the wheel back on the bike. Don't forget to fix the pucture that night.

Fixing the Puncture

To fix the puncture you'll need a repair kit, which usually comes with glue, patches, sandpaper and, sometimes, chalk. (Always check the glue in your puncture repair kit hasn't dried up before heading off on tour.) The only other thing you'll need is clean hands.

1. The first step is to find the puncture. Inflate the tube and hold it up to your ear. If you can hear the puncture, mark it with the chalk; otherwise immerse it in water and watch for air bubbles. Once you find the puncture, mark it, cover it with your finger and continue looking – just in case there are more.

2. Dry the tube and lightly roughen the area around the hole with the sandpaper. Sand an area larger than the patch.

3. Follow the instructions for the glue you have. Generally you spread an even layer of glue over the area of the tube to be patched and allow it to dry until it is tacky.

4. Patches also come with their own instructions – some will be just a piece of rubber and others will come lined with foil (remove the foil on the underside but don't touch the exposed area). Press the patch firmly onto the area over the hole and hold it for 2–3 minutes. If you want, remove the excess glue from around the patch or dust it with chalk or simply let it dry.

5. Leave the glue to set for 10–20 minutes. Inflate the tube and check the patch has worked.

Chains

Chains are dirty, greasy and all too often the most neglected piece of equipment on a bike. There are about 120 or so links in a chain and each has a simple but precise arrangement of bushes, bearings and plates. Over time all chains stretch, but if dirt gets between the bushes and bearings this 'ageing' will happen prematurely and will likely damage the teeth of your chainrings, sprockets and derailleur guide pulleys.

To prevent this, chains should be cleaned frequently (see the 'Squeaky Clean' boxed text).

No matter how well you look after a chain it should be replaced regularly – about every 5000–8000km. Seek the advice of a bike shop to ensure you are buying the correct type for your drivetrain (the moving parts that combine to drive the bicycle: chain, freewheel, derailleurs, chainwheel and bottom bracket).

If you do enough cycling you'll need to replace a chain (or fix a broken chain), so here's how to use that funky-looking tool, the chain breaker.

1 Remove the chain from the chainrings – it'll make the whole process easier. Place the chain in the chain breaker (on the outer slots; it braces the link plates as the rivet is driven out) and line the pin of the chain breaker up with the rivet.

2 Wind the handle until the rivet is clear of the inner link but still held by the outer link plate.

3 Flex the chain to 'break' it. If it won't, you'll need to push the rivet out some more, but not completely – if you push it all the way out, you'll have to remove two links and replace them with two spare links. If you're removing links, you'll need to remove a male and female link (ie, two links).

4 Rejoining the chain is the reverse. If you turn the chain around when putting it on you will still have the rivet facing you. Otherwise it will be facing away from you and you'll need to change to the other side of the bike and work through the spokes.

Join the chain up by hand and place it in the breaker. Now drive the rivet in firmly, making sure it is properly lined up with the hole of the outer link plate. Stop when the rivet is almost in place.

5 Move the chain to the spreaders (inner slots) of the chain breaker. Finish by winding the rivet into position carefully (check that the head of the rivet is raised the same distance above the link

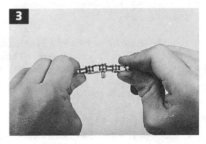

plate as the rivets beside it). If you've managed to get it in perfectly and the link isn't 'stiff', well done!

Otherwise, move the chain to the spreaders on the chain breaker and gently work the chain laterally until the link is no longer stiff.

If this doesn't work (and with some chain breakers it won't), take the chain out of the tool and place a screwdriver or Allen key between the outer plates of the stiff link and carefully lever the plates both ways. If you're too forceful you'll really break the chain, but if you're subtle it will free the link up and you'll be on your way.

Chain Options

Check your chain; if you have a Shimano HyperGlide chain you'll need a special Hyper-Glide chain rivet to rejoin the chain. This will be supplied with your new chain, but carry a spare.

Another option is to fit a universal link to your chain. This link uses a special clip to join the chain – like the chains of old. You'll still need a chain breaker to fix a broken chain or take out spare links.

Squeaky Clean

There are loads of chain lubes on the market these days. Most require you to degrease your chain and then place a drop or two of the lube on each link, while others come in spray packs.

One of the most convenient ways to keep the chain clean and squeak-free when touring involves using WD40 to degrease and lube the chain. There are some combination degreaser-lubes on the market but few work as well or are as convenient (to buy and carry) and inexpensive as WD40. However, if you're aghast at this suggestion, substitute your favourite spray lube for WD40 (after degreasing it).

Spray the WD40 on the whole chain liberally while holding a rag behind to catch the excess spray. Make sure you direct the spray into the links. Firmly hold the wet area of the rag over the chain and pedal the drivetrain backwards several times. WD40 works well as a degreaser and what you're doing here is cleaning off the grit and grime.

Now apply a coating of lube back on the chain, so give a clean area of the rag a long spray of WD40 and hold it over the chain as you pedal the drivetrain backwards again.

WD40 is a very light lubricant so you'll need to repeat the process every couple of days.

Irrespective of what lubricant you use, if you've been riding in the rain for an extended period clean the chain and relube it – most lubricants claim to be great if it rains, but few really are.

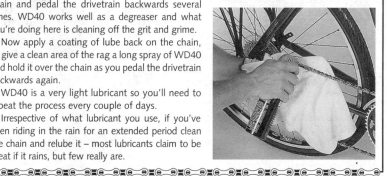

Brakes

Adjusting the brakes of your bike is not complicated and even though your bike shop will use several tools to do the job, all you really need is a pair of pliers, a spanner or Allen key, and (sometimes) a friend.

Check three things before you start: the wheels are true (not buckled), the braking surface of the rims is smooth (no dirt, dents or rough patches) and the cables are not frayed.

Begin by checking that the pads strike the rim correctly: flush on the braking surface of the rim (see right and p87) and parallel to the ground.

Calliper Brakes

It's likely that you'll be able to make any minor adjustments to calliper brakes by winding the cable adjusting barrel out. If it doesn't allow enough movement you'll need to adjust the cable anchor bolt:

1 Undo the cable anchor bolt – not completely, just so the cable is free to move – and turn the cable adjusting barrel all the way in.

2 Get your friend to hold the callipers in the desired position, about 2–3mm away from the rim. Using a pair of pliers, pull the cable through until it is taut.

3 Before you tighten the cable anchor bolt again, check to see if the brake lever is in its normal position (not slack as if somebody was applying it) – sometimes they jam open. Also, ensure the brake quick-release (use it when you're removing your wheel or in an emergency to open the callipers if your wheel is badly buckled) is closed.

4 Tighten the cable anchor bolt again. Make any fine-tuning to the brakes by winding the cable adjusting barrel out.

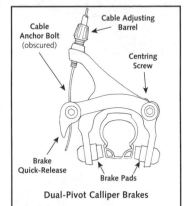

Dual-Pivot Calliper Brakes

(Labels: Cable Anchor Bolt (obscured); Cable Adjusting Barrel; Centring Screw; Brake Quick-Release; Brake Pads)

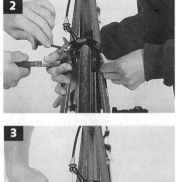

 Brake Cables

If your brakes are particularly hard to apply, you may need to replace the cables. Moisture can cause the cable and housing (outer casing) to bond or stick. If this happens it's often possible to prolong the life of a cable by removing it from the housing and applying a coating of grease (or chain lube) to it.

If you do need to replace the cable, take your bike to a bike shop and get the staff to fit and/or supply the new cable. Cables come in two sizes – rear (long) and front (short) – various thicknesses and with different types of nipples.

Cantilever Brakes

These days most touring bikes have cantilever rather than calliper brakes. The newest generation of cantilever brakes (V-brakes) are more powerful and better suited to stopping bikes with heavy loads.

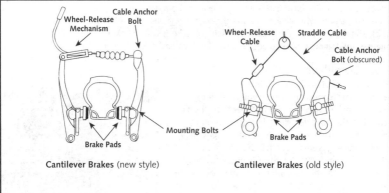

Cantilever Brakes (new style)   **Cantilever Brakes** (old style)

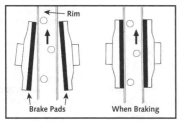

Cantilever Brake Toe-In: This is how the brake pads should strike the rim (from above) with correct toe-in.

On cantilever brakes ensure the leading edge of the brake pad hits the rim first (see left). This is called toe-in; it makes the brakes more efficient and prevents squealing. To adjust the toe-in on cantilever brakes, loosen the brake pad's mounting bolt (using a 10mm spanner and 5mm Allen key). Wiggle the brake pad into position and tighten the bolt again.

If you only need to make a minor adjustment to the distance of the pads from the rim, chances are you will be able to do it by winding the cable adjusting barrel out (located near the brake lever on mountain bikes and hybrids). If this won't do you'll need to adjust the cable anchor bolt:

1 Undo the cable anchor bolt (not completely, just so the cable is free to move) and turn the cable adjusting barrel all the way in. Depending on the style of your brakes, you may need a 10mm spanner (older bikes) or a 5mm Allen key.

2 Hold the cantilevers in the desired position (get assistance from a friend if you need to), positioning the brake pads 2–3mm away from the rim. Using a pair of pliers, pull the cable through until it is taut.

3 Before you tighten the cable anchor bolt again, check to see if the brake lever is in its normal position (not slack as if somebody was applying it) – sometimes they jam open.

4 Tighten the cable anchor bolt again. Make any fine-tuning to the brakes by winding the cable adjusting barrel out.

Gears

If the gears on your bike start playing up – the chain falls off the chain-rings, it shifts slowly or not at all – it's bound to cause frustration and could damage your bike. All it takes to prevent this is a couple of simple adjustments: the first, setting the limits of travel for both derailleurs, will keep the chain on your drivetrain, and the second will ensure smooth, quick shifts from your rear derailleur. Each will take just a couple of minutes and the only tool you need is a small Phillips or flat screwdriver.

Front Derailleur

If you can't get the chain to shift onto one chainring or the chain comes off when you're shifting, you need to make some minor adjustments to the limit screws on the front derailleur. Two screws control the limits of the front derailleur's left and right movement, which governs how far the chain can shift. When you shift gears the chain is physically pushed sideways by the plates (outer and inner) of the derailleur cage. The screws are usually side by side (see photo No 1) on the top of the front derailleur. The left-hand screw (as you sit on the bike) adjusts the inside limit and the one on the right adjusts the outside limit.

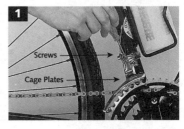

Front Derailleur: Before making any adjustments, remove any build up of grit from the screws (especially underneath) by wiping them with a rag and applying a quick spray (or drop) of chain lube.

After you make each of the following adjustments, pedal the drivetrain with your hand and change gears to ensure you've set the limit correctly. If you're satisfied, test it under strain by going for a short ride.

Outer Limits Change the gears to position the chain on the largest chainring and the smallest rear sprocket. Set the outer cage plate as close to the chain as you can without it touching. Adjust the right-hand limit screw to achieve this.

Inner Limits Position the chain on the smallest chainring and the largest rear sprocket. For chainwheels with three chainrings, position the inner cage plate between 1–2mm from the chain. If you have a chainwheel with two chainrings, position the inner cage plate as close to the chain as you can without it touching.

Rear Derailleur

If the limit screws aren't set correctly on the rear derailleur the consequences can be dire. If the chain slips off the largest sprocket it can jam between the sprocket and the spokes and could then snap the chain, break or damage spokes or even break the frame.

The limit screws are located at the back of the derailleur (see photo No 2). The top screw (marked 'H' on the derailleur) sets the derailleur's limit of travel on the smallest sprocket's (the highest gear) side of the freewheel. The bottom screw ('L') adjusts the derailleur's travel towards the largest sprocket (lowest gear).

Outer Limits Position the chain on the smallest sprocket and largest chainring (see photo No 3). The derailleur's top guide pulley (the one

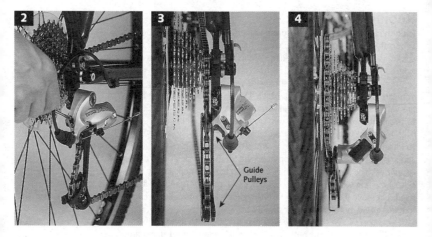

Guide
Pulleys

closest to the sprockets) should be in line with the smallest sprocket; adjust the top screw ('H') to ensure it is.

Inner Limits Position the chain on the largest rear sprocket and the smallest chainring (see photo No 4). This time the guide pulley needs to be lined up with the largest sprocket; do this by adjusting the bottom screw ('L'). Make sure the chain can't move any further towards the wheel than the largest sprocket.

Cable Adjusting Barrel

If your gears are bouncing up and down your freewheel in a constant click and chatter, you need to adjust the tension of the cable to the rear derailleur. This can be achieved in a variety of ways, depending on your gear system.

The main cable adjusting barrel is on your rear derailleur (see photo No 5). Secondary cable adjusting barrels can also be found near the gear levers (newer Shimano combined brake-gear STI levers) or on the downtube of your frame (older Shimano STI levers and Campagnolo Ergopower gear systems) of some bikes. Intended for racing cyclists, they allow for fine tuning of the gears' operation while on the move.

Raise the rear wheel off the ground – have a friend hold it up by the saddle, hang it from a tree or turn the bike upside down – so you can pedal the drivetrain with your hand.

To reset your derailleur, shift gears to position the chain on the second smallest sprocket and middle chainring (see photo No 6). As you turn the crank with your hand, tighten the cable by winding the rear derailleur's cable adjusting barrel anti-clockwise. Just before the chain starts to make a noise as if to shift onto the third sprocket, stop winding.

Now pedal the drivetrain and change the gears up and down the freewheel. If things still aren't right you may find that you need to tweak the cable tension slightly: turn the cable adjusting barrel anti-clockwise if shifts to larger sprockets are slow, and clockwise if shifts to smaller sprockets hesitate.

Replacing a Spoke

Even the best purpose-made touring wheels occasionally break spokes. When this happens the wheel, which relies on the even pull of each spoke, is likely to become buckled. When it is not buckled, it is considered true.

If you've forgotten to pack spokes or you grabbed the wrong size, you can still get yourself out of a pickle if you have a spoke key. Wheels are very flexible and you can get it roughly true – enough to take you to the next bike shop – even if two or three spokes are broken.

If you break a spoke on the front wheel it is a relatively simple thing to replace the spoke and retrue the wheel. The same applies if a broken spoke is on the non-drive side (opposite side to the rear derailleur) of the rear wheel. The complication comes when you break a spoke on the drive side of the rear wheel (the most common case). In order to replace it you need to remove the freewheel, a relatively simple job in itself but one that requires a few more tools and the know-how.

If you don't have that know-how fear not, because it is possible to retrue the wheel without replacing that spoke *and* without damaging the wheel – see Truing a Wheel (below).

1 Remove the wheel from the bike. It's probably a good idea to remove the tyre and tube as well (though not essential), just to make sure the nipple is seated properly in the rim and not likely to cause a puncture.

2 Remove the broken spoke but leave the nipple in the rim (if you it's not damaged; otherwise replace it). Now you need to thread the new spoke. Start by threading it through the vacant hole on the hub flange. Next lace the new spoke through the other spokes. Spokes are offset on the rim; every second one is on the same side and, generally, every fourth is laced through the other spokes the same way.

3 With the spoke key, tighten the nipple until the spoke is about as taut as the other spokes on this side of the rim. Spoke nipples have four flat sides – to adjust them you'll need the correct size spoke key. Spoke keys come in two types: those made to fit one spoke gauge or several. If you have the latter, trial each size on a nipple until you find the perfect fit.

Truing a Wheel

Truing a wheel is an art form and, like all art forms, it is not something mastered overnight. If you can, practise with an old wheel before leaving home. If that's not possible – and you're on the side of the road as you read this – following these guidelines will get you back in the saddle until you can get to the next bike shop.

1 Start by turning the bike upside-down, so the wheels can turn freely. Check the tension of all the spokes on the wheel: do this by

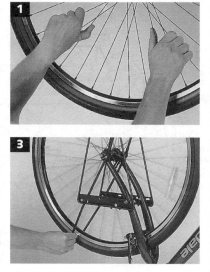

squeezing each pair of spokes on each side. Tighten those spokes that seem loose and loosen those that seem too tight. Note, though, the spokes on the drive side of the rear wheel (on the same side as the freewheel) are deliberately tighter than the non-drive side.

2 Rotate the wheel a couple of times to get an idea of the job at hand. If the wheel won't rotate, let the brakes off (see pp86–7).

3 Using the chalk from your puncture repair kit, mark all the 'bumps'. Keep the chalk in the same position (brace the chalk against the pannier rack or bike's frame) and let the bumps in the wheel 'hit' the chalk.

4 In order to get the bumps out you'll need a constant point of reference – to gauge if the bumps are being removed. Often, if it is not a severe buckle, you can use a brake pad. Position the brake pad about 2–3mm from the rim (on the side with the biggest buckle).

5 With your spoke key, loosen those spokes on the same side as the bump within the longest chalked area, and tighten those on the opposite side of the rim. The spokes at the start and the finish of the chalked area should only be tightened/loosened by a quarter-turn; apply a half-turn to those in between.

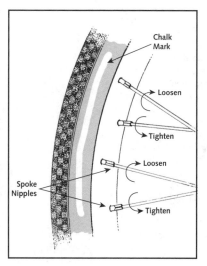

Chalk Mark

Loosen

Tighten

Loosen

Spoke Nipples

Tighten

6 Rotate the wheel again; if you're doing it correctly the buckle should not be as great. Continue this process of tightening and loosening spokes until the bump is as near to gone as you can get it – as the bump is removed turn the nipples less (one-eighth of a turn on the ends and a quarter-turn in between). Experienced exponents can remove buckles entirely, but if you can get it almost out (1mm here or there) you've done well.

7 If the wheel has more than one bump, move onto the second-longest chalk mark next. As each bump is removed you might find it affects the previous bump slightly. In this case, remove the previous chalk mark and repeat Steps 4–6. Continue to do this until all the buckles are removed.

Don't forget to readjust the brakes.

If you've trued the wheel without replacing the broken spokes, have them replaced at the next bike shop.

Loading Your Bicycle

If you've ever been to Asia and seen a bike loaded with boxes piled 2m high or carrying four, five or six people, plus a chicken or two, you'll realise that there are more ways to carry your gear than would otherwise seem. More realistic options for you come from a combination of front and rear panniers, a handlebar bag or trailer.

'Credit-card tourists', who are intent on travelling lighter, further and faster and who are happy to stay in hotels or hostels, can get by with a handlebar bag and/or rear panniers (see top right). The downside to this configuration is poor bike-handling; the steering feels particularly 'airy'. It's possible to adopt the 'lighter, further, faster' principle and still camp, but it means frugal packing.

If you want to be more self-sufficient or you're carrying 20kg or more, you'll probably find it easier (and your bike will handle better) with front and rear panniers. The tried-and-tested configuration that works best for a touring bike is to use four panniers: two low-mounting front panniers with two high-mounting rear panniers (see bottom right). The only other thing you might want to add is a small handlebar bag for this book, snacks, sunblock, money, camera etc.

This combination, with a few light but bulky items on the rear rack (eg, tent, sleeping mat etc), allows you to carry a large load and still have predictable and manageable bike-handling.

If you're riding a mountain bike and riding off-road you'll probably want high-mounting front panniers to give you more clearance.

Pannier Configurations: the four pannier system is the best way of carrying your gear and having a bike that handles well; packing light saves weight but the compromise is poor bike handling.

Packing Your Gear

It's frequently said that, in packing for a cycle tour, you should lay out everything you need to take and then leave half of it behind. The skill is in knowing which half to leave behind. Almost as much skill is needed in organising the gear in your panniers. Here are some tried and tested tips.

Compartmentalise Pack similar items into nylon drawstring bags (stuff sacks), to make them easier to find again (eg, underwear in one, cycling clothes in another, and even dinner food separated from breakfast food). Using different coloured stuff sacks makes choosing the right one easier.

Waterproof Even if your panniers are completely waterproof, and especially if they're not, it pays to put everything inside heavy-duty plastic bags. Check bags for holes during the trip; replace them or patch the holes with tape.

Reduce Flood Damage If your panniers are not waterproof and they pool water, you can reduce problems by putting things that are unaffected by water, say a pair of thongs, at the bottom of the bag. This keeps the other stuff above 'flood level'. Try using seam sealant on the bags' seams beforehand, too.

Load Consistently Put things in the same place each time you pack to avoid having to unpack every bag just to find one item.

Balance the Load Distribute weight evenly – generally around 60% in the rear and 40% in the front panniers – and keep it as low as possible by using low-mounting front panniers and packing heavy items first. Side-to-side balancing is just as critical.

Group Gear Pack things used at the same time in the same pannier. Night/camp things like your mat, sleeping bag and pyjamas, which you don't need during the day, could all be in the bag most difficult to access – likely to be on the same side as the side of the road you are riding on, since you will probably lean that side of the bike against a tree, pole or roadside barrier.

Put all clothing in one pannier, if possible, sorted into separate bags of cycling clothes, 'civilian' clothes, underwear, wet weather gear and dirty clothes. Keep a windproof jacket handy on top for descents.

In the Front Food and eating utensils are convenient to have in a front pannier along with a camping stove. Toiletry items, towel, first-aid kit, reading material, torch and sundry items can go in the other front bag.

In the Pockets or Bar Bag Easily accessible pockets on panniers or on your cycling shirt are useful for items likely to be needed frequently or urgently during the day, such as snacks, tool kit, sun hat or sunscreen. A handlebar bag is good for these items if your panniers don't have pockets, but remember that weight on the handlebars upsets a bike's handling.

Keep Space Spare Remember to leave some spare space for food and, if using a Camping Gaz stove or the like, for the fuel canister. Be mindful when packing foods that are squashable or sensitive to heat and protect or insulate them – unless you're working on a gourmet pasta sauce recipe that includes socks.

Another Option – Trailers

Luggage trailers are gaining in popularity and some innovative designs are now on the market. By spreading the load onto more wheels they relieve the bike and can improve rolling resistance. Their extra capacity is a boon for travelling on a tandem or with a young family. They can be combined with racks and panniers, but the hitch (point it connects with the bike) of some trailers may interfere with your panniers, so check first.

Two-wheeled trailers are free standing and can take very heavy loads including babies and toddlers. Often brightly coloured, they give a strong signal to car drivers who tend to give you a wide berth. However, their relatively wide track can catch a lot of wind and makes them ungainly on rough, narrow roads or trails.

Single-wheeled trailers such as the BOB Yak share the load with the bike's rear wheel. They track well and can be used on very rough tracks and may be the only option for full suspension bikes. The load capacity of these units is somewhere between that of a bike with a rear rack only and a fully loaded (four panniers plus rack-top luggage) touring bike.

Prevent 'Internal Bleeding' Act on the premise that anything that can spill will, and transfer it to a reliable container, preferably within a watertight bag. Take care, too, in packing hard or sharp objects (tools, utensils or anything with hooks) that could rub or puncture other items, including the panniers. Knives or tools with folding working parts are desirable.

Fragile Goods Valuables and delicate equipment like cameras are best carried in a handlebar bag, which can be easily removed when you stop. Alternatively, carry these items in a 'bum bag', which will accompany you automatically.

Rack Top Strap your tent lengthways on top of the rear rack with elastic cord looped diagonally across from front to rear and back again, and maybe a third short one across to anchor the rear end. Be sure the cords are well-tensioned and secure – deny their kamikaze impulses to plunge into the back wheel, jamming the freewheel mechanism, or worse.

What to Look for in Panniers

Panniers remain the popular choice for touring luggage. They offer flexibility, in that one, two or four can be used depending on the load to be carried and they allow luggage to be arranged for easy access.

Many people buy a rear rack and panniers initially, and it is wise to buy the best quality you can afford at this stage. These bags will accompany you on all of your tours as well as day-to-day shopping and commuting trips for years to come.

The attachment system should be secure, but simple to operate. That big bump you hit at 50km/h can launch a poorly designed pannier and your precious luggage.

The stiffness of the pannier backing is another concern – if it can flex far enough to reach the spokes of the wheel the result can be catastrophic. Good rack design can also help avoid this.

The fabric of the panniers should be strong and abrasion- and water-resistant. You can now buy roll-top panniers, made from laminated fabrics, that are completely waterproof. Bear in mind that these bags are only waterproof until they develop even the smallest hole, so be prepared to check them and apply patches occasionally. Canvas bags shed water well, but should be used in conjunction with a liner bag to keep things dry. Cordura is a heavy nylon fabric with excellent abrasion resistance. The fabric itself is initially waterproof, but water tends to find the seams, so using a liner bag is a good idea once again.

Pockets and compartments can help to organise your load, but the multitude of seams increase the challenge of keeping the contents dry in the wet. A couple of exterior pockets are great for sunscreen, snacks and loose change that you need throughout the day. Carrying front panniers as well as rear ones allows more opportunities to divide and organise gear.

When fitting rear panniers check for heel strike. Long feet, long cranks and short chainstays will all make it harder to get the bags and your body to fit.

Getting There & Away

AIR

The overwhelming majority of visitors to New Zealand arrive by air. Although six airports handle international flights, most international flights go through Auckland. Wellington and Christchurch also receive flights from Australia.

Round the World Tickets

Round-the-World (RTW) tickets are popular – and are great if you want to cycle in several countries. They are often real bargains, and can work out to be no more expensive or even cheaper than an ordinary return ticket.

Circle Pacific tickets use a combination of airlines to circle the Pacific – combining Australia, NZ, North America and Asia. As with RTW tickets, there are advance purchase restrictions and limits to the number of stopovers. Air New Zealand sometimes offers good deals on tickets departing from Los Angeles that don't include Asia but do include NZ, Australia and many small Pacific islands.

The USA & Canada

Most flights between the USA and NZ are to/from the USA's west coast. Most travel through Los Angeles but some are via San Francisco. If you're coming from elsewhere in the USA, your travel agent can arrange a discounted 'add-on' fare to get you to your departure city and check the conditions for domestic carriage of your bike.

Excursion (round-trip) fares are available from various airlines but are more expensive than those from travel agents. Cheaper 'short life' fares are frequently offered for limited periods. The easiest way to get a cheap air fare from the USA is through a travel agency selling discounted fares; these fares can be about US$950/1500 return in the low/high season from Los Angeles or about US$1325/1914 return from New York. It costs a comparable US$1245 to fly from Los Angeles to Sydney with a stopover in NZ in the low season.

Two of the most reputable discount travel agencies in the USA are STA and CIEE. Both are international travel agencies with many offices throughout the USA and in other countries. The magazine *Travel Un-*

limited (PO Box 1058, Allston, MA 02134) publishes details of the cheapest air fares and courier possibilities departing from the USA for destinations all over the world.

If you want to visit other Pacific destinations on your way to or from NZ, carefully compare the stopover possibilities offered by each airline. For example, Air New Zealand LA-Auckland flights offer an excellent variety of stopover options – you can visit Honolulu, Tahiti, Rarotonga, Western Samoa, Tonga and Fiji quite cheaply.

In Canada, the *Vancouver Sun* and the Toronto *Globe & Mail* carry travel agents' ads. Much of the same advice about travel between the USA and NZ applies to Canada, especially stopover options.

Australia

The NZ cities with flights to and from Australia are Auckland, Christchurch and Wellington. Freedom Air flies to and from Dunedin, Palmerston North and Hamilton. Australian cities with flights to NZ are Brisbane, Cairns, Coolangatta (Gold Coast), Canberra, Adelaide, Hobart, Melbourne, Perth and Sydney. Air New Zealand, Qantas Airways and United Airlines (Sydney and Melbourne only) are the main carriers. Smaller carriers include Garuda Indonesia and EVA Airways (Taiwan) from Brisbane and Aerolineas Argentinas, Thai Airways International, Royal Tongan Airlines and Polynesian Airlines from Sydney.

Typical high/low-season economy return fares include: Sydney-Auckland A$399/599, Sydney-Christchurch A$449/645, Perth-Auckland A$799/989, Perth-Christchurch A$799/1145, Melbourne-Auckland A$459/645 and Melbourne-Christchurch A$459/699.

In Australia, STA and Flight Centre are major dealers in cheap air fares and have branches in all major cities. Otherwise, check the travel agents' ads in the *Yellow Pages*.

The UK

London-Auckland return tickets can be found in London bucket shops for around UK£605 in the low season and UK£1150 in the high season. Some stopovers are permitted on this sort of ticket. Depending on

Packing for Air Travel

We've all heard the horror stories about smashed/lost luggage when flying, but a more real threat to cycle tourists is arriving in a country for a two week tour and finding their bike with broken wheels or in little bits spread out around the baggage carousel. Fixing a damaged bike could take days, and the delay and frustration could ruin your holiday.

How do you avoid this? Err on the side of caution and box your bike. Trust airline baggage handlers if you want (we're told some people actually do) and give your bike to them 'as is' – turn the handlebars 90°, remove the pedals, cover the chain with a rag or bag (to protect other people's baggage) and deflate your tyres (partially, not all the way) – but is it worth the risk? If you want to take that sort of a risk do it on your homeward flight, when you can get your favourite bike shop to fix any damage any time.

Some airlines sell bike boxes at the airport, but most bike shops give them away. Fitting your bike into a box requires a few simple steps and only takes about 15 minutes:

1 Loosen the stem bolt and turn the handlebars 90°; loosen the clamp bolt(s) and twist the handlebars as pictured.

2 Remove the pedals (use a 15mm spanner, turning each the opposite way to how you pedal), wheels and seat post and saddle (don't forget to mark its height before removing it).

3 Undo the rear derailleur bolt and tape it to the inside of the chainstay. There's no need to undo the derailleur cable. You can remove the chain (it will make reassembly easier) but it isn't necessary.

4 Cut up some spare cardboard and tape it beneath the chainwheel to prevent the teeth from penetrating the floor of the box and being damaged.

5 Remove the quick-release skewers from the wheels and wrap a rag (or two) around the cluster so it won't get damaged or damage anything else.

If you run your tyres at very high pressure (above 100psi), you should partially deflate them – on most bikes this won't be necessary.

6 Place the frame in the box, so it rests on the chainwheel and forks – you might want to place another couple of layers of cardboard underneath the forks.

Most boxes will be too short to allow the front pannier racks to remain on the bike; if so, remove them. The rear rack should fit while still on the bike but may require the seatstay bolts to be undone it pushed forward.

Packing for Air Travel

Side View

ALL PHOTOS JEFF CROWE SPORT THE LIBRARY

7 Place the wheels beside the frame, on the side opposite the chainwheel. Keep the wheels and frame separate by inserting a piece of cardboard between them and tying the wheels to the frame (to stop them moving around and scratching the frame).

8 Slot the saddle and seatpost, your helmet, tools and any other bits and pieces (eg tent, sleeping bag) into the vacant areas. Wrap the skewers, chain and other loose bike bits in newspaper and place them in the box. Add cardboard or newspaper packing to any areas where metal is resting on metal.

9 Seal the box with tape and write your name, address and flight details on several sides.

Now all you need to do is strap your panniers together and either take them with you as carry-on luggage or check them in.

Top View

Bike Bags

If you're planning on travelling between regions via train, plane or bus then consider taking a bike bag. The simplest form of zippered bike bag has no padding built into it, is made of Cordura or nylon, and can be rolled up and put on your rear pannier rack and unfurled when you need to travel again.

Some of the smaller ones require you to remove both wheels, the front pannier racks, pedals and seatpost to fit inside the bag. However, these make for (relatively) easy and inconspicuous train, plane or bus transfers so the extra effort is worthwhile.

which airline you travel with, you may fly across Asia or across the USA. If you travel via Asia you can often make stopovers in places like India, Bangkok, Singapore and Australia; in the other direction, stopover possibilities include places like New York, Los Angeles, Honolulu or a variety of Pacific islands. Stopover options vary depending on the airline you use.

Since NZ is about as far from Europe as you can get, it's not much more expensive to continue round the world rather than backtracking. Agents can organise you an RTW route through the South Pacific from around UK£750.

Check the travel page ads in the *Times*, *Business Traveller*, the weekly 'what's on' magazine *Time Out* or give-away papers like *TNT*. Good, reliable low-fare specialists are Trailfinders and STA. Quest Worldwide and Bridge the World are also worth trying.

Continental Europe

Frankfurt is the major arrival and departure point for NZ flights, with connections to other European centres.

There are many bucket shops on mainland Europe where you can buy discounted air tickets. The international student and discount travel agencies STA and Council Travel also have a number of offices in various European countries. Any of their offices can give you the details on which office might be nearest you. In Amsterdam, make sure your travel agent has an 'SGR' certificate or you may never see your money again.

Asia

There are far more flights between NZ and Asia than in the past. Cities with direct flights to Auckland include Tokyo, Hong Kong, Singapore, Denpasar (Bali) and Taipei, and there are connecting flights to most other places. Many of the connecting flights have stopovers in Australia. There are also a few direct flights to Christchurch including flights to/from Tokyo and Singapore.

Ticket discounting is widespread in Asia, particularly in Hong Kong, Singapore and Bangkok; Hong Kong is probably the discount air ticket capital of the region. There are a lot of fly-by-nighters in the Asian ticketing scene so care is required when choosing a travel agent. STA, which is reliable, has branches in Hong Kong, Tokyo, Singapore, Kuala Lumpur and Bangkok.

SEA

Apart from cruise ships, no regular passenger services to NZ are available.

Cycle-Friendly Airlines

Not too many airlines will carry a bike free of charge these days – at least according to their official policy. Most airlines regard the bike as part of your checked luggage. Carriers working the routes to NZ through Europe, Asia and Australia usually allow 20kg of checked luggage (excluding carry-on), so the weight of your bike and bags shouldn't exceed this. If you're over the limit, technically you're liable for excess-baggage charges.

Carriers flying routes to NZ through North America use a different system. Passengers are generally allowed two pieces of luggage, each of which must not exceed 32kg. Excess baggage fees are charged for additional pieces, rather than for excess weight. On some airlines a bike may be counted as one of your two pieces; others charge a set fee for carrying a bike, which may then be carried in addition to your two other pieces. Check whether these fees are paid for the whole journey, each way or per leg.

When we looked into the policies of different carriers, we found that not only does the story sometimes change depending on who you talk to – and how familiar they are with the company's policy – but the official line is not necessarily adhered to at the check-in counter. If a company representative or agent reassures you that your bike travels for free, ask them to annotate your passenger file to that effect. If your flight is not too crowded, the check-in staff are often lenient with the excess charges, particularly with items such as bikes.

The times when you are most likely to incur excess baggage charges are on full flights and, of course, if you inconvenience the check-in staff. If you suspect you may be over the limit, increase your chances of avoiding charges by checking in early, being well organised and being friendly and polite – a smile and a 'thank you' can go a long way!

ORGANISED TOURS

Many companies around the world run organised cycling tours of NZ. The Internet is a good place to get an idea of what's around. There are also several NZ-based companies (see the Getting Around chapter).

Based in the USA, Backroads (☎ 800-462 2848, ⌨ www.backroads.com), 801 Cedar St, Berkeley, CA 94710-1800, is an impressively professional outfit, which runs a well supported tour of the South Island. The 15 day trip from Nelson to Queenstown, with lodgings, almost all meals, van shuttles and transport fares included, starts at US$3398. Custom-built Cannondales can be hired for US$190.

Gerhard Meng of Gerhard's Bicycle Odysseys (☎ 503-223 2402, fax 503-223 590, ⌨ www.since1974.com/zealand.html), 921 SW Morrison/426, Portland, OR 97205, USA, personally accompanies cyclists on a two week tour from Christchurch to Queenstown (US$3295). All accommodation and most meals are provided.

Women Tours (☎ 800-247 1444, ☻ info@womantours.com), which is also US-based, offers several tours of the South Island each year and caters specifically for the needs of women.

In the UK, Pacific All-Way Tours (☎ 01494-432 747, fax 432 767, ☻ john@allways.co.

uk), 7 Whielden St, Old Amersham, Buckinghamshire, HP7 0HT, is an agent for the US company Pedaltours and can organise several itineraries on both islands to suit all levels of fitness.

Also in the UK, the Cyclists' Touring Club (CTC; ☎ 1483-417 217, ☻ cycling@ctc.org.uk), Cotterell House, 69 Meadow, Godalming, Surrey, GU7 3HS, coordinates a large number of independently organised, well priced tours to around-the-world destinations (including NZ), led by experienced volunteer members.

Warning

The information in this chapter is particularly vulnerable to change: prices for international travel are volatile, routes are introduced and cancelled, schedules change, special deals come and go, and rules and visa requirements are amended. You should check directly with the airline or a travel agent to make sure you understand the conditions of your ticket. The details given in this chapter should be regarded as pointers and are not a substitute for your own careful, up-to-date research.

Getting Around

AIR

New Zealand's major domestic airlines are Air New Zealand (☎ 0800 737 000 or ☎ 09-357 3000) and Ansett New Zealand (☎ 0800 267 388 or ☎ 04-471 1051). Air New Zealand also extends its service through part ownership or cooperation with smaller airlines, such as Mt Cook Airline, Eagle Air and Air Nelson, which form the Air New Zealand Link.

Apart from the major operators, there are many local and feeder airlines. These include flights from Auckland to Great Barrier Island with Great Barrier Airlines, Southern Air's hop between Invercargill and Stewart Island and Air Chatham's flights to the Chatham Islands from Christchurch or Wellington.

Cost

If you're short of time, it's worth considering travelling by air. The smaller airlines, in particular, are a reasonable alternative to ferries to the various islands; Soundsair's $50/95 one-way/return fare (plus $15 per bike) across Cook Strait works out even cheaper than the faster *Lynx* ferry.

Air New Zealand and Ansett New Zealand offer various discounts on domestic flights –

up to 60% on special advance purchase return flights. International Student Identity Cards (ISIC) and International Youth Hostel (YHA) cards get you a 50% discount on standby tickets. Generally, it's cheaper to buy domestic flight tickets once you get to NZ rather than from your home country.

Both airlines charge $20 to carry your bike.

Carrying Your Bicycle

Most airlines advise that bikes will only be carried subject to space. However, getting your bike on board is rarely a problem except on some of the smaller aircraft's more popular flights (Auckland to Great Barrier Island on Friday evening or back on Sunday, for example). It's worth checking when you book whether it's likely to be a crowded flight – and let the airline know you'll be bringing a bike.

On smaller aircraft you're often required only to remove your front wheel, strapping it to the rear wheel, lower the seat and turn the handlebars. The larger operators stipulate removing pedals, partially deflating the tyres and covering the chain. Some people use boxes or bike bags for added protection (see

---

'Will You Take a Bike?'

Carrying bicycles when travelling is really a bit of a pain. You can tell by the look on bus drivers' faces, as you bring your beloved steed to be loaded – or from a glance at most transport companies' bicycle policies: bikes must often be semi-dismantled, they cost extra and may not be taken at all. After all, aren't bikes big, awkward, heavy and dirty things with sharp bits that scratch other passengers' baggage?

But we enlightened types – who realise that a bike is the key to freedom and adventure – don't want to be thwarted by bike-unfriendly terms and conditions. So we've got to be clever about using the system.

In many cases, particularly with airlines, the official policy is just that, it's there to cover the company, but is not necessarily strictly adhered to, especially outside the peak periods.

As a rule, the way to get your bike transported as quickly, easily and cheaply as possible is to make things as quick, easy and hassle-free as possible for the transport company. Book early, be there in plenty of time, have your gear neatly packed, your bike clean (boxed, if necessary) and with tools handy to dismantle it if required.

While you can be unlucky and strike someone who is a stickler for official policy (or is just having a bad day), the personal touch can often go a long way. Smiling, saying 'thank you' – the stuff your parents taught you – generally encourages lenient behaviour. Of course, being uncooperative or bumbling around makes it easy for the person at the desk to sock you for the full amount or simply say 'sorry, we can't fit you on'.

the 'Packing for Air Travel' boxed text in the Getting There & Away chapter). In any case, make sure you're at the check-in desk in plenty of time.

BUS

Buses are the most popular form of public transport in NZ – simply because they go everywhere. There are generally conditions about carrying bikes, but in most cases it's relatively easy to get your bike from A to B.

Bus Companies

There are dozens of bus companies throughout the country, but InterCity (☎ 09-913 6100, 🖳 www.intercitycoach.co.nz) is the main national operator. InterCity buses go to almost all bigger towns and the main tourist areas. Other larger operators include Newmans (☎ 09-309 9738); White Star (☎ 06-758 3338); Northliner Express (☎ 09-307 5873), on the North Island only; and on the South Island only, Mt Cook Landline (☎ 0800 800 286).

Local operators offer more limited services. Both the North and South islands have small shuttle services. Buses on main routes usually run at least daily, although on some routes, weekend services may be limited or nonexistent.

The Getting to/from the Ride sections and Gateway City sections in the regional chapters have specific bus information.

Shuttle Buses A number of small shuttle-bus companies offer useful services. These services are typically cheaper and friendlier than those offered by the larger companies.

North Island In the North Island, there are shuttles around the East Cape, Coromandel Peninsula, and up into Northland:

Magic Bus (☎ 09-358 5600) bills itself as 'the transport network for the independent traveller', offering a variety of services on the North and South Island, picking up at many backpacker lodges.
Alpine Scenic Tours (☎ 07-378 7412) operates between Turangi and the Tongariro National Park, with stops at various spots in the park that are useful for trampers, and extension services to Taupo and Rotorua.
Northliner Express (☎ 09-307 5873) offers backpacker rates for services to Northland and the Bay of Islands

White Star (☎ 06-758 3338) has runs between New Plymouth and Wellington on the North Island; in the South Island between Christchurch and Nelson via Lewis Pass

South Island In the South Island, there are shuttle services between Christchurch and Akaroa, Nelson and the Nelson Lakes, Queenstown and Te Anau/Milford Sound, and Westport and Karamea:

Knightline (☎ 03-547 4733), between Motueka, Nelson and Picton
Compass Coachlines (☎ 03-578 7102), between Picton and Christchurch
Atomic Shuttles (☎ 03-322 8883), between Picton, Christchurch, Queenstown, Dunedin and Invercargill, Greymouth and Wanaka
South Island Connection (☎ 03-366-6633), Christchurch to Picton and Dunedin
Nelson Lakes Transport (☎ 03-547 5912), between Nelson and St Arnaud (for the Nelson Lakes National Park area)
Wadsworths Motors (☎ 03-522 4248), between Nelson and Tapawera and St Arnaud
Kahurangi National Park Bus Service (☎ 03-525 9434), between Golden Bay, Abel Tasman and Kahurangi national parks, Motueka and Nelson
Coast to Coast Bus Service (☎ 0800 800 847), between Christchurch and Greymouth, passing through Arthur's Pass National Park
Kiwi Discovery (☎ 03-442 7340), between Christchurch and Queenstown
Topline Tours (☎ 03-249 8059), between Te Anau and Queenstown
Spitfire Shuttle (☎ 03-218 7381), between Te Anau and Invercargill, including Manapouri, Tuatapere and Riverton

Reservations

It's a good idea to book by phone at least a day or two in advance (earlier during peak times), although you can often leave it until the day to pay for and/or pick up your ticket (you can also pay in advance by credit card or mail).

Tell the bus company when you book that you have a bike. It's worth asking whether they can reserve a place for it, but don't expect a definite answer as most operators carry bikes subject to space being available (see Carrying Your Bicycle later in this section).

Costs

There is a slight fare variation between companies, but they are generally fairly similar.

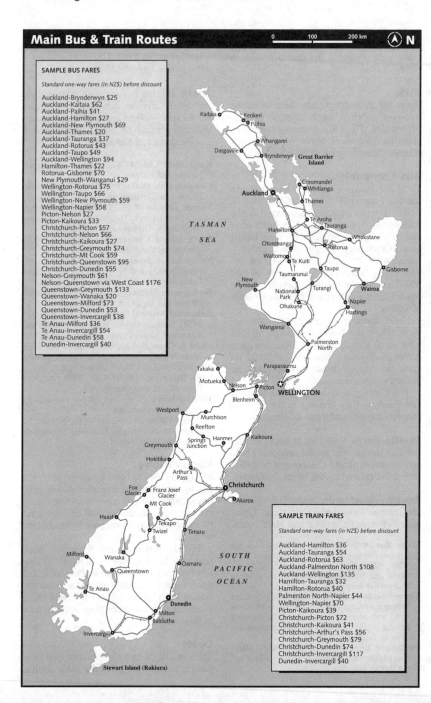

Main Bus & Train Routes

0   100   200 km   N

SAMPLE BUS FARES

Standard one-way fares (in NZ$) before discount

Auckland-Brynderwyn $25
Auckland-Kaitaia $62
Auckland-Paihia $41
Auckland-Hamilton $27
Auckland-New Plymouth $69
Auckland-Thames $20
Auckland-Tauranga $37
Auckland-Rotorua $43
Auckland-Taupo $49
Auckland-Wellington $94
Hamilton-Thames $22
Rotorua-Gisborne $70
New Plymouth-Wanganui $29
Wellington-Rotorua $75
Wellington-Taupo $66
Wellington-New Plymouth $59
Wellington-Napier $58
Picton-Nelson $27
Picton-Kaikoura $33
Christchurch-Picton $57
Christchurch-Nelson $66
Christchurch-Kaikoura $27
Christchurch-Greymouth $74
Christchurch-Mt Cook $59
Christchurch-Queenstown $95
Christchurch-Dunedin $55
Nelson-Greymouth $61
Nelson-Queenstown via West Coast $176
Queenstown-Greymouth $133
Queenstown-Wanaka $20
Queenstown-Milford $73
Queenstown-Dunedin $53
Queenstown-Invercargill $38
Te Anau-Milford $36
Te Anau-Invercargill $54
Te Anau-Dunedin $58
Dunedin-Invercargill $40

SAMPLE TRAIN FARES

Standard one-way fares (in NZ$) before discount

Auckland-Hamilton $36
Auckland-Tauranga $54
Auckland-Rotorua $63
Auckland-Palmerston North $108
Auckland-Wellington $135
Hamilton-Tauranga $32
Hamilton-Rotorua $40
Palmerston North-Napier $44
Wellington-Napier $70
Picton-Kaikoura $39
Christchurch-Picton $72
Christchurch-Kaikoura $41
Christchurch-Arthur's Pass $56
Christchurch-Greymouth $79
Christchurch-Dunedin $74
Christchurch-Invercargill $117
Dunedin-Invercargill $40

TASMAN SEA

Kaitaia
Kerikeri
Paihia
Whangarei
Dargaville
Brynderwyn
Great Barrier Island
Auckland
Coromandel
Whitianga
Thames
Te Aroha
Hamilton
Tauranga
Whakatane
Otorohanga
Rotorua
Waitomo
Te Kuiti
Taupo
Gisborne
Taumarunui
New Plymouth
National Park
Turangi
Wairoa
Ohakune
Napier
Hastings
Wanganui
Palmerston North
Paraparaumu
Takaka
Motueka
Nelson
Picton
WELLINGTON
Blenheim
Westport
Murchison
Reefton
Hanmer
Kaikoura
Greymouth
Springs Junction
Hokitika
Arthur's Pass
Fox Glacier
Franz Josef Glacier
Christchurch
Mt Cook
Akaroa
Haast
Tekapo
Twizel
Timaru
Milford
Wanaka
Oamaru
SOUTH PACIFIC OCEAN
Queenstown
Te Anau
Dunedin
Milton
Balclutha
Invercargill
Stewart Island (Rakiura)

Smaller shuttle companies tend to offer cheaper fares than the major coachlines. However, the major companies do offer substantial discounts: YHA/VIP cardholders often receive up to 30% off and InterCity offers limited Saver and Super Saver fares with the standard fare discounted by 30% and 50%, respectively (special conditions apply). Advance bookings and return tickets may also be discounted.

Most companies charge from $5 to $10 one way for bikes.

Carrying Your Bicycle

The overwhelming majority of bus companies cover themselves by stating that bicycles will be carried subject to space available. In general, you're more likely to have trouble during school holiday periods and on commuter services. Arriving at the depot in plenty of time (at least 15 minutes prior to departure), being neatly packed and ready to board, will increase your chances of getting on.

Most companies' official policies also state that bicycles must have pedals removed, handlebars turned and chains covered to avoid damaging other passengers' luggage. While many drivers will take your bike fully assembled, make sure you have the requisite tools to dismantle it quickly if required. On larger coaches, bikes are stowed underneath in the luggage area, but many of the smaller shuttles have a bike rack on the back.

TRAIN

Trains are a good alternative to buses, but it depends where you want to go. NZ's nationwide rail network, operated by Tranz Scenic, only covers a few main routes: Auckland to Wellington, Tauranga or Rotorua; Wellington to Napier; and Christchurch to Picton, Invercargill or Greymouth.

Tranz Metro operates suburban services in Auckland (☎ 09-366 6400) and Wellington (☎ 04-801 7000), which are the best way to get to the start of rides on the city fringe.

As with buses, both Tranz Scenic and Tranz Metro advise that bicycles will only be carried subject to space – and not at all on some peak hour suburban services.

There are more details on train services in the relevant regional chapters – or pick up the free Tranz Scenic booklet with fares and timetables at train stations and visitor centres.

Reservations

To be sure of a seat, Tranz Scenic advises booking tickets at least 24 hours in advance. However, for cheaper fares you may need to book three or four weeks ahead and some services, such as the TranzAlpine from Christchurch to Greymouth, book out weeks in advance during summer. Phone reservations (☎ 0800 802 802 or ☎ 64 4-498 3303 from overseas) can be made daily between 7 am and 9 pm. Bookings can also be made at most train stations, travel agents and information centres.

If you do take a punt and just turn up, be there at least 20 minutes before the scheduled departure, since trains can depart early from some stations if all pre-booked passengers have been checked in.

No reservations are necessary on suburban services; tickets are purchased on the train from the conductor.

Costs

Standard fares on trains are generally a bit more expensive than buses. Like buses, however, there are substantial discounts available for train travel. YHA/VIP (and various NZ backpacker organisations) card holders and seniors are eligible for 30% discounts, children 40% and students 20%. Tickets on 'no frills' carriages can save you up to 50% of the standard fare. There are also limited Saver and Super Saver fares (discounted by 30% and 50%, respectively), but you must book in advance and they're only available during off-peak periods.

Bikes cost $10 (one way) per train service with Tranz Scenic; they are carried free on Tranz Metro suburban services.

Carrying Your Bicycle

Unlike most other transport, Tranzrail will guarantee to transport bicycles that have been pre-booked. But (yes, there's a but), most services will only book a maximum of two bikes in advance – and the spots tend to fill up early. Any others have to chance it on the day that there's luggage space.

Again, be prepared in case you're asked to remove pedals, turn handlebars, and cover your chain.

CAR

Driving is pleasant in NZ: distances between towns are relatively short, and the roads are well signposted and in good condition (unless you head into the back country where some can be unsealed and rough). Petrol (gasoline) is reasonably expensive at about 80 cents a litre (US$1.70 a gallon).

New Zealanders drive on the left side of the road. Buy yourself a copy of *The Road Code* from AA offices and bookshops.

Beware of theft from cars, particularly in isolated parking areas for scenic spots and walks. Don't leave valuables in the car.

Car Rental

You'll need to be at least 21 years old and have a valid, unrestricted driving licence from your home country. The major car-hire companies – Avis, Budget, Hertz – have extensive fleets of cars with offices in most towns. Smaller companies often have much cheaper deals, but mostly have older cars and less flexible hire conditions.

BOAT

Being a country of many islands and harbours, NZ has plenty of ferries. There are quick, cheap trips across harbours that would take hours to ride around; longer rides out to small islands; and, of course, the scenic trip across Cook Strait (see Getting There & Away in the Gateway Cities sections of the Marlborough & Nelson and Southern North Island chapters for details of this service).

ORGANISED RIDES

Several companies run guided cycling tours around NZ. They are generally small-group, set-itinerary affairs, although some offer customised tours. Most include motel accommodation, vehicle support, optional bike hire and some or all meals. Tours generally range from one to three weeks in length; some are on-road, others off-road; and some combine cycling with other activities.

For an all-inclusive tour, expect to pay $1500 to $2000 per week, with double/twin share accommodation – for singles, add another $300 or so. Less luxurious tours, aimed at the backpacker market, are around $300 per week. The NZ Tourist Board Web site (🖳 www.purenz.com) lists a number of tour operators. Look up cycling in the 'Thrill Zone' themed section.

Companies with a wide range of tours include New Zealand Pedaltours (☎ 09-302 0969, fax 302 0967, 🖳 www.pedaltours .co.nz), PO Box 37-575 Parnell, Auckland; Adventure South New Zealand Cycle Tours (☎ 03-332 1222, fax 332 4030, 🖳 www.ad vsouth.co.nz), PO Box 33153 Christchurch; Flying Kiwi Wilderness Expeditions (☎ 03-573 8126 or ☎ 0800 692 396, fax 573 8128, 🖳 webnz.com/flying_kiwi/), Koromiko, RD3, Blenheim, has a backpacker-style touring arrangement with a combination of bussing, biking and hiking; and Pacific Bicycle Tours (☎ 03-389 0583, 🖳 www.bike-nz .com), whose Web site is also in German.

City Cycle Hire (☎ 0800 343 848, 🖳 www .cyclehire-tours.co.nz), 137 Sparks Rd, Hoon Hay, Christchurch, offers a range of tours with budget options and organises rides with a self-guided itinerary.

Others offer a smaller range of bicycle tours among a variety of other activities. They include Natural High Adrenalin Dealers (☎ 03-546 6936; 🖳 www.natural-high.co.nz); Rest New Zealand Tours (☎ 09-486 0636, 🖳 www.restnztours.co.nz), PO Box 33-457 Takapuna, Auckland; and Naturally New Zealand Holidays (☎ 0800 101 301 or ☎ 09-480 0580), 21 Birkenhead Ave, Birkenhead, Auckland.

Auckland & the North

This chapter features a number of rides around the two narrow peninsulas separated by the Hauraki Gulf at the northern end of the North Island. Surrounded by harbours, Auckland sits near the base of the finger-shaped Northland. The smaller Coromandel Peninsula is to Auckland's east.

Superb coastal scenery is a highlight of the rides in this chapter. Mangroves and almost tropical vegetation give an island paradise flavour, and the awe-inspiring kauri forests are unique to Northland and the Coromandel Peninsula. Bird enthusiasts will particularly enjoy the Muriwai Beach ride and the Seabird Coast, while the far north (from Kaitaia to the Bay of Islands in Northland) should be visited by anyone interested in Maori culture or colonial history.

HISTORY

The beautiful and bountiful north was the first region to be settled by Maori and Europeans. The fertile land around present-day Auckland was prized by the Maori, and a tribe had settled there by 1350. Not content to let one tribe have all the pickings, however, others moved in and the area was ravaged by warfare and epidemics. The area was almost deserted by the time Europeans (who had also noted the area's good soil and fine harbour) chose it for their national capital in 1840. The population of Northland, however, still has the greatest proportion of Maori anywhere in New Zealand.

The north is also where European colonisation began. It was here that early sealers and whalers based themselves and where first permanent contact with the Maori was made. Samuel Marsden, the first missionary, arrived at Matauri Bay near Whangaroa in 1814, soon after the kauri timber trade began. Over the next century, wholesale logging was to decimate the kauri forests covering much of Northland and the Coromandel Peninsula. Gum-digging, gold mining (on the Coromandel Peninsula) and, of course, farming were other major industries.

Russell, in the Bay of Islands, was the nation's first administrative centre; and nearby Waitangi was the site of the historic treaty signing in 1840. Auckland, declared capital in that same year, remained so for a mere 25 years before Wellington took over the title.

NATURAL HISTORY

Narrow peninsulas, convoluted harbours and countless bays and beaches characterise the northern regions of NZ. While Northland is geologically one of the oldest and most stable areas in NZ, the Waitakere Ranges to Auckland's west, the Hunuas to

---

In Summary

Area Codes
- ☎ 09 – Auckland & Northland
- ☎ 07 – Coromandel Peninsula

Highlights
- Sea birds at the **Firth of Thames** and **Muriwai Beach**
- **Northland** giant kauri trees
- **Hot Water Beach** thermal springs
- Historic **Bay of Islands**

Special Events
- **Auckland Anniversary Day Regatta** (January), Waitemata Harbour
- **Waitangi Day Ceremony** (6 February), Bay of Islands
- **Pasifika Polynesian Festival** (March), Auckland

Terrain
Predominantly undulating, the only flats are near the Firth of Thames.

Dangerous Surf

⚠ There are many beautiful beaches around the Coromandel Peninsula and the Northland, but take care when you're swimming and ask the locals about the safest areas. Tourists drown every year by underestimating the power of the surf, most notably at the Coromandel Peninsula's famous Hot Water Beach.

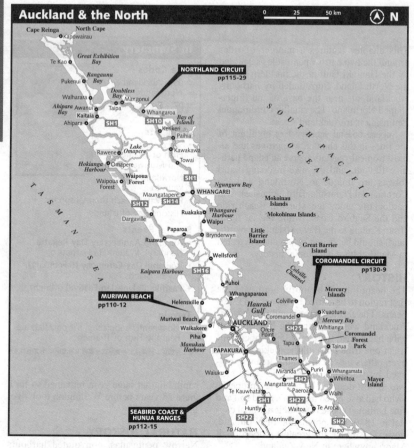

Auckland & the North

0   25   50 km

N

NORTHLAND CIRCUIT
pp115-29

COROMANDEL CIRCUIT
pp130-9

MURIWAI BEACH
pp110-12

SEABIRD COAST &
HUNUA RANGES
pp112-15

Cape Reinga • Kāpowairau
North Cape
Te Kao
Great Exhibition Bay
Pukenui
Rangaunu Bay
Walharara
Doubtless Bay
Mangonui
Ahipara Bay   Awanui   Taipa
Kaitaia
Ahipara
Whangaroa
SH1   SH10   Bay of Islands
Kerikeri
Paihia
Lake Omapere
Rawene   Kawakawa
Hokianga Harbour   Omapere   Towai
Waipoua Forest
Waipoua Forest   SH1
Ngunguru Bay
Maungatapere   WHANGAREI
SH12   SH14
Mokoinau Islands
Ruakaka   Whangarei Harbour
Dargaville   Waipu
Mokohinau Islands
Paparoa   Brynderwyn
Little Barrier Island
Ruawai
Wellsford
Great Barrier Island
Kaipara Harbour   SH16
Colville Channel
Puhoi
Whangaparaoa
Mercury Islands
Helensville
Hauraki Gulf
Colville
Muriwai Beach
Coromandel
Kuaotunu
Waikakere
Orere Point
Mercury Bay
Whitianga
Piha
AUCKLAND
SH25   Coromandel Forest Park
Manukau Harbour
Tapu   Tairua
PAPAKURA
Thames
Waiuku
Miranda   Puriri   Whangamata
Mangatarata   SH2   Whiritoa
Mayor Island
Te Kauwhata   Paeroa   Waihi
SH1   SH27
Huntly   Waitoa   Te Aroha
SH22   Morrinville   SH2
To Hamilton   To Taupo

TASMAN SEA

SOUTH PACIFIC OCEAN

the south-east and the Coromandel Range were formed more recently. Sixty volcanoes have erupted around Auckland in the last 100,000 years, and hot springs at Miranda on the Firth of Thames and Hot Water Beach on the Coromandel's east coast suggest that there is still activity beneath the surface.

With the end of the last ice age, the rising sea flooded valleys, creating beautiful harbours, notably the Bay of Islands. Kaipara Harbour on Northland's south-west coast is NZ's largest, enclosed on the southern end by the 50km-long Muriwai Beach. Between the Hunua Ranges and the Coromandel Peninsula are the shallow mudflats of the Firth of Thames.

The beautiful coastal scenery is one of the main attractions of the far north and

Coromandel Peninsula. The Bay of Islands is especially famous, although there are many other scenic, sheltered bays and superb beaches that are less touristy along the entire coast.

Much of Northland and the Coromandel Peninsula was covered in forests (predominantly kauri, with patches of podocarp and hardwood) at the beginning of European settlement. The Maori had, however, already cleared patches of land for agriculture using fire, creating areas of grassland and scrub, notably around Auckland.

With kauri in high demand, the timber industry flourished during the 19th century. This, along with further land clearing by English settlers, resulted in the loss of most of the original forest. The best remaining stands can

Fresh-Air Travelling

There's a certain pleasure in following your nose down a country road. Bus and car travellers really miss out on that patchwork of roadside smells that so enriches the cyclist's journey.

The tangy, almost blackberry-like scent of the white umbelliferous flowers that are everywhere in Northland is periodically overpowered by the spiciness of a *kumara* (Polynesian sweet potato) paddock, the heady sweetness of wild ginger (an introduced pest), a paddock of pungent cattle or a fresh pine forest. Such delights are sure to satisfy the soul of any olfactory hedonist!

But a fresh-air traveller's journey is not without its hazards. A major risk on NZ roads is copping the crap from a passing sheep truck! Perhaps worse is an incident that occurred as I cycled through a sparsely populated farming district one day. The only traffic was a guy above me in a plane, spraying crops. Spewing heaven-knows-what from its innards, the plane flew up and down the paddock and, though the pilot kindly halted the deluge to cross the road, the gentle breeze carried it right to me ...

Nicola Wells

be seen along Northland's west coast and covering much of the Coromandel Range.

There are some excellent birdwatching opportunities in this area. Muriwai Beach, west of Auckland, is the breeding site of a gannet colony; while the Firth of Thames is a birdwatchers' paradise, with dozens of sea bird species. Riding along inland roads you're likely to see falcons circling above and pukekos (a swamp hen with dark blue feathers and a red beak) hurrying for cover.

CLIMATE

As the region closest to the equator, the far north is also the warmest region in the country. Even in winter the average minimum temperature in Auckland doesn't drop much below 10°C (50°F). The mild winters make it an excellent choice for cycling during the cooler months. Summer, when the average maximum temperature is 22°C (72°F), is the driest period, although

the air can sometimes be moist enough to feel almost tropical. Indeed, tropical cyclones *can* occur between January and March, bringing strong wind and rain.

Although the prevailing wind, particularly on the west coast, is west to southwesterly, there is plenty of variation – in a La Nina year, for instance, the wind is generally from the east.

INFORMATION
Information Sources

Visitor centres and DOC offices, listed in the Gateway Cities section and for individual rides, are excellent information sources.

Place Names

In keeping with its high Maori population, the far north has many Maori place names to get your tongue around. However, the pronunciation rules (see Language in the Facts about New Zealand chapter) are not always consistent. While Whangarei is generally pronounced '**fong**-a-**ray**', some locals say '**wong**-a-**ray**', and Whangamata seems generally to be '**wong**-a-ma-**tah**'.

GATEWAY CITIES
Auckland

Auckland is the arrival point for many visitors to NZ. Surrounded by water, the city sits on the narrow stretch of land between the Manukau and Waitemata Harbours and the Hauraki Gulf. It's a real harbour city – often dubbed the 'City of Sails'. The America's Cup yacht race was contested here in 2000.

The city itself is built on and around a series of old volcanoes. While there is good cycling around the region, Auckland itself is not one of NZ's better cycling cities. Apart from the hills, traffic can often be heavy, street signs are not always obvious and there are few bicycle facilities.

Nevertheless, plenty of locals get around by bike and lobby the authorities for better facilities – and it is worth riding around the harbour.

Information The Auckland visitor centre (☎ 09-366 6888, fax 366 6893), 24 Wellesly St West, is near Aotea Square. It's open from 8.30 am to 5.30 pm weekdays (until 6 pm in summer) and from 9 am to 5 pm on weekends. Alternatively, there's an information kiosk (open daily from 9 am to 5 pm) in the

Queen Elizabeth II Square at the harbour end of Queen St, and a visitor centre (☎ 09-275 6467) in the airport's international terminal.

DOC has an information centre (☎ 09-379 6476, fax 379 3609) at the Ferry Building; the main DOC office (☎ 09-307 1465) is in the Sheraton Complex, on the corner of Liverpool St and Karangahape Rd.

There are free maps of the city in several tourist information booklets, such as Jason's *Auckland: What's On* and the AA's *What to See & Do*. Specialty Maps (☎ 09-307 2217), 58 Albert St, is a good source for touring and topographical maps. The AA (☎ 09-377 4660) at 99 Albert St, near the corner of Victoria St, also has a range of maps.

Post restante is held at the chief post office, in the Bledisloe Bldg on Wellesley St West near the Queen St corner.

You can access the Internet at Net Central Cyber Cafe (☎ 09-373 5186), 5 Lorne St; the Live Wire Internet Cafe (☎ 09-356 0999), 1st floor, Mid City Complex, 239 Queen St; Discount Dialling (☎ 09-355 7300), 7 Fort St, which has private phone booths; the YHA travel centre, USIT (☎ 09-379 4224, 🖳 www.usitbeyond.co.nz), 18 Shortland St; and at Auckland Central Travel (☎ 09-358 4874) in Auckland Central Backpackers, 9 Fort St.

Auckland has some excellent bike shops, many of which have buy-back schemes (see Buying & Hiring Locally in the Facts for the Cyclist chapter). In Newmarket, the helpful Pack 'n' Pedal (☎ 09-522 2161, fax 522 2163), 436 Broadway, also sells camping equipment. Pins Cycles Royal Oak (☎ 09-6256549), 725 Mt Albert Rd, is another good option.

The only shop claiming to specialise in touring is Adventure Cycles (☎ 09-309 5566, fax 309 4211, 🖂 adventurecycles@xtra.co.nz), 1 Fort Lane, but the staff couldn't offer much advice when we visited. It has second-hand bikes, however, and hires bikes and panniers.

For a good range of second-hand equipment, try the Secondhand Sport Shop (☎ 09-366 4555), 14 Upper Queen St.

If you want to hire a bike, the Mountain Bike Hire Company (☎ 09-358 4885), 10 Norwood Rd, Bayswater, will deliver bikes and gear to you. Bike hire costs $70 per week or $210 per month, plus around $10 per week for panniers. Book at least a few days ahead.

Mountain Biking Adventures (☎ 025-284 4644) hires good front-suspension mountain bikes for $30/50/85 a day/weekend/week and takes groups. Haere Mai Bikes (☎ 09-486 1517 or ☎ 631 5973, fax 631 5934) has day/weekend hire for $30/58 (extra for gear and delivery) and group tours.

Things to See & Do The **Auckland Museum** (☎ 09-306 7067), set in the middle of Auckland Domain, the park opposite the city centre, has interesting displays on Maori culture and the war memorial museum has recently been extensively refurbished. The **New Zealand Maritime Museum** (☎ 09-358 3010), on the downtown waterfront, explores 1000 years of NZ's seafaring history. **Kelly Tarlton's Underwater World & Antarctic Encounter** (☎ 09-528 1994), 6km from the centre at 23 Tamaki Drive, is a unique aquarium experience. The **Auckland Art Gallery** (☎ 09-307 7700), corner of Kitchener and Wellesley Sts East, has an extensive collection of local art. The 328m-high **Skytower** (☎ 09-912 6000), corner of Federal and Victoria Sts, offers spectacular views from the top. Alternatively, spend a little more effort (but no money) climbing **Mt Eden** (196m), the region's highest volcanic cone, for superb views of the entire Auckland area.

A good way to explore Auckland is to ride the **50km Route**, a pleasant circuit around the harbour, inner parks and suburbs (stop off at Kelly Tarlton's and Mt Eden on the way). Pick up a free *50km Route* map at the visitor centre.

Inquire at the visitor centre about adventure activities in and around Auckland, including **urban rap jumping** (face-down abseiling from the Novotel Hotel), **scuba diving**, **abseiling** and others.

There are good **swimming** beaches on the east coast along Tamaki Drive – try Mission Bay and St Heliers (both are on the 50km Route). Both the Auckland and DOC visitor centres have information about **walks** in and around Auckland.

Harbour cruises are a great way to appreciate the area – you can take a short ferry ride to picturesque Devonport on the north shore, or out to one of the many islands in Hauraki Gulf. Fullers (☎ 09-367 9111, 🖳 www.fullers.co.nz), in the Ferry Building, is the biggest operator, running a range of cruises. The free *Guide to the Gulf* booklet has information about its services and other activities. **Waiheke Island** is one of the larger islands, for which Fullers produces the useful *Bike Waiheke* pamphlet (includes a map of the island).

Places to Stay All Auckland's camping grounds are away from the central area. The closest to the city is *Remuera Motor Lodge & Inner City Camping Ground (☎ 09-524 5126, 16 Minto Rd)*, off Remuera Rd, 8km south-east of the city centre. Tent sites are $12 per person and self-contained motel units are $79.

Hostel accommodation is plentiful in the city and inner suburbs, but it pays to book ahead, especially in summer. Hill-climbing is unavoidable to reach the hostels out of the central city, but these are often quieter and more pleasant.

The *Georgia Parkside Backpackers (☎ 09-309 8999; 189 Park Rd, Grafton)* has some tent sites. Dorm beds start at $17 and doubles from $21 per person; there's also a lockable bike shelter.

Parnell Lodge YHA Hostel (☎ 09-379 3731, cnr Earl & Churton Sts) is an excellent larger hostel with a purpose-built bike shed. Dorms cost from $17; doubles are $22.

In Ponsonby, try the friendly *Brown Kiwi (☎ 09-378 0191, 7 Prosford St)*, with dorm beds from $17 and doubles from $20. Bikes are stored in a garage on the adjoining block.

In the city, the large and busy *Auckland Central Backpackers (ACB; ☎ 09-358 4877, 9 Fort St)*, has excellent facilities including a bike storeroom, a travel agency and Internet access; there's a budget travellers cafe adjoining. Per person, dorms cost from $16, doubles from $18 and singles from $33.

Pick up the *Bed & Breakfast: Auckland Region* from the visitor centre for a listing of B&Bs around Auckland.

Aspen Lodge (☎ 09-379 6698, 62 Emily Place) is a pleasant, unassuming and centrally located B&B, opposite a park. Singles/doubles are $52/75 with a continental breakfast. Bikes can be stored in rooms (ask for a lower-floor room) or in the linen store. More elegant is the Art Nouveau-style *Birdwood House (☎ 09-306 5900, 41 Birdwood Crescent)*, 60m off Parnell Rd. Phone ahead to book rooms from $110/130.

The *City Central Hotel (☎ 09-307 3388, cnr Wellesley & Albert Sts)* has rooms/studios for $79/99, with tea and coffee facilities.

The bright and clean *Parnell Inn (☎ 09-358 0642, 320 Parnell Rd)* has rooms with ensuite bathroom from $75/80, or request a self-contained unit ($120).

Close to the airport, the *Airport Pensione (☎ 09-275 0533, 1 Westney Rd)* offers B&B plus transport to/from the airport from $50/60.

Places to Eat In the city, Lorne St (which becomes High St north of Victoria St) is a good place to start. On the corner of High and Victoria St East, the *Southern Cross Bakery* has delicious heavy Danish rye loaves ($5). Across the road, the *Paneton* serves good coffee and baked goods.

The *Sierra Cafe (☎ 09-366 4720, cnr Lorne & Victoria St East)* also has excellent coffee. The cafeteria-style *Simple Cottage Restaurant (☎ 09-303 4599, 50 High St)* has generous helpings of reasonably priced wholesome vegetarian food. *Pizza Pizza (☎ 09-309 3333, 57 Lorne St)* has regular pizzas from $8.50. Upstairs is smoke-free.

The inner city suburbs of Ponsonby and Parnell are great eating spots, with a range of cuisines on both Ponsonby and Parnell Rds. *The Other Side Cafe and Bar (☎ 09-366 4426, 320 Parnell Rd)*, adjoining the Parnell Inn, has reasonably priced breakfast, lunch and dinner menus with a German influence (mains from $12.50 to $16.50). Parnell Rd also has a number of good *Italian restaurants* with pasta mains for around $18.

The *Atomic Cafe (☎ 09-376 4954, 121 Ponsonby Rd)* has the best coffee in town plus good cycling food like brown rice porridge, delicious pizza by the slice and good, heavy sandwiches (both $5). The Swiss *BakeHaus* at 242 Ponsonby Rd *has* a range of serious breads. There's another *BakeHaus* on Broadway in Newmarket.

Getting There & Away As the largest city in NZ, Auckland also has plenty of transport options.

Air Air New Zealand (☎ 09-357 3000), Ansett New Zealand (☎ 09-302 2146) and Mt Cook Airline (☎ 09-309 5395) connect Auckland with the other major centres in NZ. Local operators, such as Great Barrier Airlines (☎ 09-275 9120) and Waiheke Air Services (☎ 09-372 5001) also have flights into and out of Auckland.

Auckland airport is about 21km west of the city centre. There's a free shuttle bus between the international and domestic terminals.

Keep your bike in its box as the ride to the city from the airport is not particularly attractive and involves busy roads. Door-to-door shuttle buses are a better bet. Super Shuttle (☎ 0800 727 747 or ☎ 09-307 5210) and Johnston's Shuttle Link (☎ 09-275 1234) each charge $15 per person one way ($9 from a hostel) plus $5 per bike.

Airbus (☎ 09-275 7685) runs every 20 minutes from the airport to the Downtown Airline Terminal (☎ 09-275 9396), 86 Quay St, with scheduled stops along the way. The 50 minute trip costs $12 one way plus $6 for bikes.

A taxi from the airport to the city will cost around $40. Warn the company that you have a bike when you phone.

Train Tranz Scenic (☎ 0800 802 802) runs services from Auckland to Hamilton ($36 one way), Wellington ($135), Rotorua ($63) and Tauranga ($54) by train, with connecting services to Napier. Substantially reduced fares are available with advance booking, YHA/VIP membership and for off-peak services. Bikes cost $10.

Tranz Metro (☎ 09-366 6400) runs suburban passenger services to Waitakere in the north-western outskirts and Papakura in the south from Monday to Saturday.

The Auckland train station (☎ 0800 802 802), on Beach Rd, east of the city centre, is a neglected-looking couple of platforms tucked away behind a grand old station building, now used for student housing.

Bus InterCity (☎ 09-913 6100) runs services from the Sky City coach terminal at 102 Hobson St to just about everywhere in NZ. It's Web site (🖳 www.intercitycoach.co.nz) has detailed timetable and fares information. Newmans (☎ 09-309 9738) also operates from Sky City and has a good North Island network and a more limited South Island service that runs along the east coast.

Northliner Express (☎ 09-307 5873) runs services to Northland and is based in the Downtown Airline Terminal at 86 Quay St. Also operating from the terminal, the Little Kiwi Bus Co (☎ 0800 759 999) has buses to Hamilton, Rotorua, Tauranga, Mt Maunganui, Wellington and Auckland airport.

Auckland Region

Good riding is not far from Auckland, a city surrounded by harbours, fertile farmland and scenic ranges. Two rides – to Muriwai Beach, north-west of Auckland, and around the Hunua Ranges and Seabird Coast, south-east of the city – are both good opportunities to see migratory sea birds.

Muriwai Beach

Duration	3-4 hours
Distance	62.8km
Difficulty	easy-moderate
Start/End	Waitakere

This day ride to Muriwai Beach, on Auckland's rugged west coast to the north of the Waitakere Ranges, is a good warm-up ride through fruit and wine growing country. Like other beaches on the west coast, Muriwai's astonishing black sand, rich in iron, is a legacy of coastal volcanoes.

A colony of Australasian gannets is one of the main attractions at Muriwai. Crowded together, the birds 'nest' on exposed rocky ledges. By the end of January, when the chicks are only one to two months old, they will set out on their journey across the Tasman to Australia. During spring, you may also see New Zealand fur seals lazing on the rocks below the gannets.

PLANNING
When to Ride
The best time to see the gannets is in spring and summer, but the ride can be done year-round. Traffic and beach crowds are lighter on weekdays.

GETTING TO/FROM THE RIDE
Waitakere
Train Tranz Metro (☎ 09-366 6400) runs a suburban passenger service to Waitakere Monday to Saturday, which takes about 48 minutes. Waitakere line trains depart Auckland train station every 30 minutes between 6.15 am and 6.15 pm during the week and hourly from 7.15 am on Saturday. The last train back departs Waitakere station at 7.05 pm.

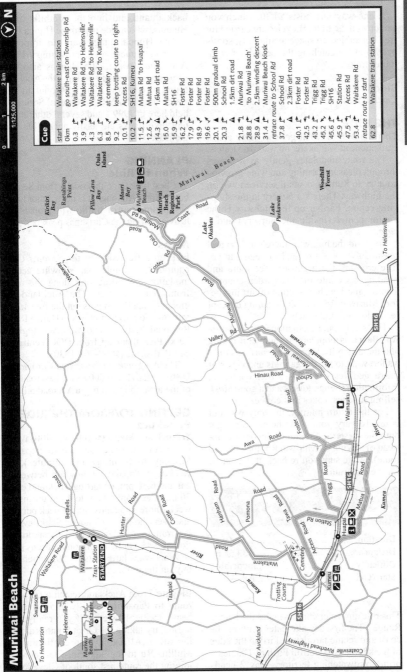

Muriwai Beach

Cue

	start	Waitakere train station
⌐	0km	go south-east on Township Rd
⌐	0.3	Waitakere Rd
⌐	3.9	Waitakere Rd 'to Helensville'
↗	4.3	Waitakere Rd 'to Helensville'
↘	6.3	Waitakere Rd 'to Kumeu'
↘	8.5	at cemetery
↘	9.2	keep trotting course to right
↘	10.1	Access Rd
←	10.2	SH16, Kumeu
↗	11.5	Matua Rd 'to Huapai'
⌐	12.6	Matua Rd
↘	14.3	1.6km dirt road
↗	15.0	Matua Rd
⌐	15.9	SH16
⌐	16.2	Foster Rd
⌐	17.9	Foster Rd
⌐	18.9	Foster Rd
⌐	19.6	Foster Rd
	20.1	500m gradual climb
←	20.3	School Rd
		1.5km dirt road
↗	21.8	Muriwai Rd
⌐	28.8	'to Muriwai Beach'
	28.9	2.5km winding descent
⌐	31.4	Muriwai Beach kiosk
		retrace route to School Rd
⌐	37.8	School Rd
		2.3km dirt road
↘	40.1	Foster Rd
⌐	42.5	Foster Rd
⌐	43.2	Trigg Rd
↗	45.2	Trigg Rd
←	45.6	SH16
↘	45.9	Station Rd
↗	47.5	Access Rd
⌐	53.4	Waitakere Rd
		retrace route to start
	62.8	Waitakere train station

A one-way fare costs $4.30, which you can buy on the train. Bicycles are carried for free but subject to space availability, so it's best to avoid catching the peak-hour commuter trains.

Bicycle From central Auckland? Forget it. Catch a train.

THE RIDE

There is only a small *general store* and a card phone at Waitakere: no water, no toilets.

The route undulates gently as it passes through pleasant farming and wine-growing country to **Kumeu**, a small service town on the highway. There's a *bakery* in the shopping centre. Farther up the highway is the visitor centre (inside the nursery) and a *cafe*.

To avoid the highway, there's a short and reasonably good dirt road to negotiate before crossing the highway once more and heading back into market garden country. There's another short section of dirt just before Muriwai Rd. A 2.5km winding descent leads down to the beach.

The sandy pine plantation behind **Muriwai Beach** is popular for mountain biking and the beach itself has great surf. It's only a short walk to see the **gannets** and views of the rugged west coast. The settlement has an information shelter, toilets and a good *kiosk* selling lunches, cakes and coffee.

For the return journey, the only way out is up. To vary your route home, turn right onto the western, dirt end of School Rd, instead of staying on Muriwai Rd (the outward route). Make sure you're back at Waitakere for the last train.

Seabird Coast & Hunua Ranges

Duration	2 days
Distance	133.5km
Difficulty	moderate
Start/End	Papakura

This ride almost circumnavigates the Hunua Ranges. The first day alternates between the coast and scenic farmland, skirting the edge of the strangely beautiful Firth of Thames – prime birdwatching territory. Day 2 heads back inland and into the foothills of the Hunuas, with a side trip to the Hunua Falls.

The Hunua Ranges are an important water catchment area, providing 61% of Auckland's water. The Hunuas also have some good mountain biking – the Auckland round of the New Zealand Mountain Bike Association (NZMBA) National Series was held here in 1999 – and several other mountain bike tracks are easily accessible from the ride.

PLANNING
When to Ride

The best time to do this ride is from September to April. Although it is not a major tourist destination, tourist traffic will probably be heavier during the Christmas peak period.

Maps

Pick up a free copy of the *Seabird Coast* pamphlet, a simple map showing accommodation and attractions along the route, from visitor centres. The Auckland Regional Council also puts out the free *Mountain Bike Routes* pamphlets to Hunua Range Regional Parkland and Waharau Regional Park. Pick them up from DOC centres or call ParksLine (☎ 09-303 1530).

The AA *South Auckland and Coromandel* District Map (1:350,000) is the best road map of the area, followed by an AA road atlas.

GETTING TO/FROM THE RIDE
Papakura

Train Tranz Metro (☎ 09-366 6400) runs a suburban passenger service to Papakura Monday to Saturday (47 minutes). On weekdays, Papakura trains run between 6 am and 6.30 pm, departing Auckland every 30 minutes from 10 am to 4 pm during the week (more frequently during peak periods) and every hour from 7 am on Saturday. The last train to Auckland departs Papakura station at 5.45 pm (6.15 pm on Saturday).

A one-way fare costs $4.30, which you buy on the train.

Bicycle From Auckland, catch a train; the route to Papakura is hilly and often has heavy traffic. However, if you really want to ride, try taking the Great South Rd, turning off to Alfriston, then continuing via Mullins Rd to the Takanini-Clevedon Rd, joining the route just south of Clevedon.

Seabird Coast & Hunua Ranges

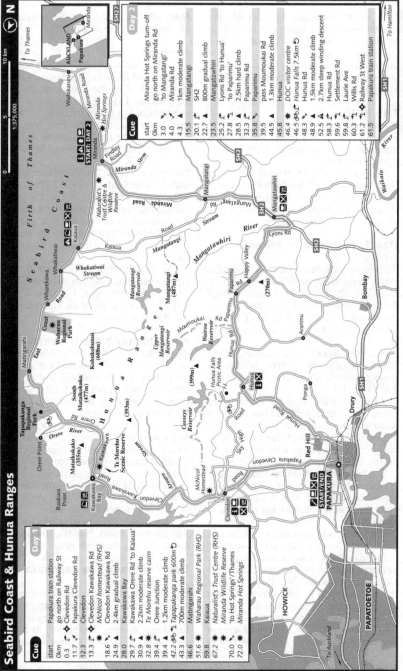

	Cue		Day 1
	start		Papakura train station
▲	0km	⌐↑	go north on Railway St
◆	0.3	⌐↑◆	Clevedon Rd
	11.7	⌐↑	Papakura Clevedon Rd
☀	12.3		Clevedon
	13.3	⌐↑◆	Clevedon Kawakawa Rd
☀	18.6	▶	McNicol homestead (RHS)
	24.9	◀	Clevedon Kawakawa Rd
▲			2.4km gradual climb
	28.0		Kawakawa Bay
	29.7	⌐↑	Kawakawa Orere Rd 'to Kaiaua'
▲	30.9		2.2km moderate climb
☀	32.8	⌐↑	Te Morehu reserve cairn
▲	39.4		Orere Junction
▲	39.4	◀	1.2km moderate climb
⤿	42.2	☍⤿	Tapapakanga park 600m ↻
▲	43.3		700m moderate climb
	46.6		Matingarahi
	51.6		Waharau Regional Park (RHS)
	59.8		Kaiaua
☀	67.2		Naturalist's Trust Centre (RHS)
▶	70.0	▶	Miranda Wildlife Reserve
			'to Hot Springs'/Thames
☀	72.0	☀	Miranda Hot Springs

	Cue		Day 2
	start		Miranda Hot Springs turn-off
▲	0km		go north on Miranda Rd
⌐↑	3.0	↘	'to Mangatangi'
	4.0	◀	Miranda Rd
▲	4.3		1km moderate climb
	15.5		Mangatangi
	20.1	⌐↑	SH2
▲	22.7		800m gradual climb
	23.5		Mangatawhiri
⌐↑	25.2	⌐↑	Lyons Rd 'to Hunua'
◀	27.8	◀	'to Paparimu'
▲	28.5		2.5km hard climb
⌐↑	32.3	⌐↑	Paparimu Rd
	35.8	↘	Paparimu
▲	39.5		pass Moumouka Rd
◀	44.5	◀	1.3km moderate climb
	45.8		Hunua
☀	46.4		DOC visitor centre
⤿	46.5	☍⤿	Hunua Falls 7.5km ↻
◀	48.3	↘	Hunua Rd
▲	48.9		1.5km moderate climb
◀	52.5	◀	2.7km steep winding descent
⌐↑	58.3	⌐↑	Hunua Rd
⌐↑	59.6	⌐↑	Settlement Rd
◀	59.8	◀	Laurie Ave
⌐↑	60.3	⌐↑	Willis Rd
◆	61.2	◆	Railway St West
	61.5		Papakura train station

To join the Coromandel Circuit ride, described later in this chapter, leave the ride at Miranda (the end of Day 1) and continue south around the Firth of Thames, before joining SH25 and heading north to Thames from Kopu. Thames is about 30km from Miranda.

THE RIDE
Papakura

Papakura, at the end of the metropolitan train line, is a retail centre 30km south of central Auckland.

Papakura Cycles (☎ 09-298 7772), 29 Broadway, is about 200m from the train station. Head west along Wood St and turn right into Broadway. There are also a couple of *cafes* and a *bakery* close by.

Day 1: Papakura to Miranda
4-6 hours, 72km

After leaving Papakura, farmland undulates gently to the sleepy seaside town of Kawakawa Bay (28km) before a climb through the Te Morehu Scenic Reserve and down to the pancake-flat Seabird Coast. Traffic is relatively light, especially after Kawakawa Bay.

The **homestead** (now a museum) of the McNicol family who, in 1865, became the area's first white settlers, is over the Clevedon River (14km).

After Kawakawa Bay, the ride is more scenic. Once through the **Te Morehu Scenic Reserve**, red-painted farm buildings lend an almost Scandinavian air to the rolling farmland, though the ponga ferns covering the nearby hills are distinctively NZ.

The **Tapapakanga Regional Park** (42.2km) is rich in Maori and European history, with archaeological sites, carved posts and an early homestead. Permits are required to *camp* (☎ 09-366 2166).

The Coromandel Peninsula is visible across the Firth of Thames at Matingarahi (46.6km).

In the foothills of the Hunua Ranges, the **Waharau Regional Park** has walks and some challenging mountain bike rides. Some of the land is owned by Maori tribes; respect them by staying on designated routes.

Kaiaua is the only place for meals on the East Coast Rd. *Kaiaua Fisheries Licensed Seafood Restaurant & Takeaways* (☎ 09-232 2776) won the national fish and chip competition in 1995 and the *Bay View*

Hotel (☎ 09-232 2717) has a restaurant, take-aways and bar snacks.

Miranda

Miranda is hardly a town – the Hot Springs complex and adjoining holiday park make up the bulk of it. The shallow mudflats of the Firth of Thames, rich in worms and crustaceans, is a haven for birds. Up to 60 species are recorded each year, including the wrybill, New Zealand dotterel and Arctic species that have flown south for winter.

Things to See & Do The **Miranda Naturalist's Trust Centre** (☎ 09-232 2781), 5km north of the Hot Springs on East Coast Rd, has displays and information about many of the birds seen in the area and where to spot them. **Bird-watching** is best on the incoming tide, which pushes the birds closer to the shore.

The **Hot Springs** complex (☎ 07-867 3055), open daily, has open and covered hot pools, and private spas. The $6 charge is waived when you stay at the Miranda Holiday Park next door.

Places to Stay & Eat At *Miranda Holiday Park* (☎/fax 07-867 3205), next to the Hot Springs complex, dorm beds are $20 per person, tent sites are $12 and the self-contained motel units are $100 a double. Bikes are locked out the back. Book ahead for indoor accommodation.

The pleasant, modern *Miranda Naturalist's Trust Centre* (☎ 09-232 2781) has beds for $15 per person (with a shared kitchen); a self-contained apartment costs $45, but there is limited bedding available.

B&Bs in the area include *Miranda Bed & Breakfast* (☎ 09-232 77350), about 2km west of Miranda on Findlay Rd.

You can only get limited rations (including bread and milk) from the Hot Springs *kiosk*, so bring food with you.

Day 2: Miranda to Papakura
3½-5 hours, 61.5km

From the Hot Springs complex, retrace the route from Day 1 for 2km before heading inland through the orchard country south of the Hunua Ranges. The country is rolling and the roads are narrow lanes. Make sure you stop off at one of the excellent orchards for some fresh fruit or honey.

At 20.1km you join SH2 for 5km. It is busy, but there's a wide shoulder. Mangatawhiri seems an unlikely spot for a medieval castle, but *Chateau Creme Delight* does its best – and it's the last spot to buy food (sandwiches, hot food, ice cream, coffee and basic supplies) until Papakura.

Back off the highway, there's little traffic as the route heads through farm country in the foothills and valleys skirting the Hunua Ranges. It's pleasant country – as you'd expect with names like Happy Valley. Moumoukai Rd (39.5km) is the turn-off to several great **mountain bike tracks**.

The **DOC centre** in Hunua on the corner of Lockwood Rd and Hunua Rd is worth a visit. As well as information on the area's natural history, there's an excellent display of Maori and Pakeha history. The pretty **Hunua Falls** (see Side Trip) makes for an great lunch spot.

In the last 10km to Papakura, there's a climb through Hunua Gorge and a lovely winding downhill through Ponga ferns. Make sure you're back in time to catch the last train!

Side Trip: Hunua Falls
25-35 minutes, 7.5km return
Not far off the main route, Hunua Falls is a great spot for a picnic, swim or walk. To get there, turn right into Whites Rd (46.5km), then right into Falls Rd. The ride is relatively easy, ending with a swooping downhill – you'll have to climb up the same hill on the way out.

Northland

Northland is famous for the Bay of Islands – and beautiful it is. The area was noted by both Maori and Europeans for its spectacular harbour and natural abundance; according to James Cook it had 'every kinds of refreshments'. It's also largely geared towards tourists. If that's not your thing, don't despair – there are plenty of quieter treasures, like the beautiful Hokianga Harbour and the awesome kauri forests on the west coast.

Cape Reinga, at the northern end of a narrow sandy peninsula, has particular spiritual significance for the Maori. According to legend, the souls of the dead travel north towards the Polynesian ancestral homeland;

at Cape Reinga, they look back on Aotearoa (the Maori name for New Zealand), their corporeal home, before farewelling it forever. (However, contrary to popular belief, Cape Reinga is not the northernmost point of the mainland – that's Surville Cliffs, 30km to the east.)

Northland Circuit

Duration	.7 days
Distance	.462.1km
Difficulty	.moderate-hard
Start	.Brynderwyn
End	.Whangarei

A feast of natural beauty, history and culture, this ride takes in kauri forests, superb coastal scenery and the settings of some of the nation's earliest and most significant Maori and European events.

If history and culture is your thing, plan to spend a rest day around the neighbouring towns of Paihia, Russell and Waitangi, and perhaps another in Kaitaia. If you prefer the natural environment, walking, or staying away from tourists, rest at Waipoua, the Hokianga Valley or Kahoe Farm.

Traffic is not heavy on SH12 – except during the summer school holiday period. The west coast is more remote than the east, and the west coast section of this ride has been divided into a couple of shortish days. This is because both the kauri forest and the Hokianga area are too lovely to rush through. And also because the terrain is most challenging in this section. However, if you are pressed for time (and fit), Day 2 could be extended to Omapere and Day 3 from Omapere to Kaitaia, thus shortening the tour by a day.

PLANNING
When to Ride
Northland is temperate enough to ride year-round, although it is probably best from February to May and October to December. From Christmas to the end of January is the holiday season, when roads and accommodation are more crowded.

Maps
The AA *Auckland and Whangarei* District Map (1:350,000) is excellent, while the AA

Bay of Islands Leisure Map (1:139,200) is also very useful. The Land Information *Whangarei* and *North Cape* Terrainmaps (1:250,000) indicate topography but don't include road names, and road surfaces may be inaccurate.

GETTING TO/FROM THE RIDE
Brynderwyn

Bus InterCity (☎ 09-913 6100), Northliner Express (☎ 09-307 5873) and Newmans (☎ 09-309 9738) all run services from Auckland. Auckland to Brynderwyn costs $25 plus $10 per bike for the two hour trip.

Bicycle It's best not to ride from Auckland to Brynderwyn: the route is hilly and SH1 is very busy with no shoulder to shield you from the trucks. The alternative route, via Helensville in the west, is much quieter, but no less hilly and not as pretty as the country farther north. If you insist on riding all the way, however, this is the route to take.

Catch the suburban train to Waitakere, follow the Muriwai Beach ride to Kumeu, continue on SH16 to Waimauku, then turn north towards Helensville via SH16 or the quieter back roads. From Helensville it is a strenuous 59km to Wellsford, followed by 28km on SH1 to Brynderwyn.

Whangarei

Bus InterCity (☎ 09-913 6100), Northliner Express (☎ 09-307 5873) and Newmans (☎ 09-309 9738) all run several services between Whangarei and Auckland. The 2¾ hour trip costs around $30 plus $10 per bike.

Bicycle If you want to ride, SH1 is the only option from Whangarei for about 38km. From here, turn off the highway onto Cove Rd and take the pretty coast road through Waipu and Waipu Cove to Mangawhai. Continue south through Te Arai, turning west and back onto SH1 about 7km north of Wellsford – from here veer right, following the signs to Helensville. Follow SH16 from Helensville back to Kumeu and retrace the Muriwai Beach ride back to Waitakere.

THE RIDE
Brynderwyn

Brynderwyn is 100km north of Auckland, at the intersection of SH1 and SH12. It's little more than a petrol and tea stop for people motoring up SH1 and has a petrol station, *tea-rooms*, cardphone and *motel* – and that's it.

Day 1: Brynderwyn to Dargaville
3½-5½ hours, 72.5km

The first half of the route is through rolling green dairy country with a couple of moderate hills. After the plains of the Wairoa River, about 10km before Ruawai, it's dead flat all the way to Dargaville.

After 17km, look to the south for views of the Pahi River, following a 1.7km steady climb. The Paparoa Oakleigh Rd turn-off, which leads to the old Paparoa post office (now a *guest house*), is on the descent. Over the bridge is the pretty township of Paparoa.

Northland has a large Maori population and you'll see a number of road signs to *maraes* (traditional ancestral Maori villages). There are strict rules about marae etiquette, particularly regarding visitors (see the 'Marae Etiquette' boxed text in the Facts about New Zealand chapter).

The superb **Matakohe kauri museum** (☎ 09-431 7417) is a 2km side trip off the route. It's full of information about the kauri industry during its heyday. It's a great introduction to the kauri country the route is about to pass through. There's a *tearoom* nearby.

Soon after Matakohe, are the pancake-flat plains and farmland around Ruawai. Cows, corn and *kumara* (Polynesian sweet potato) are Ruawai's most obvious industries (kumara stalls are everywhere), along with fishing. Judging by the tacky welcome sign, folks here don't take themselves too seriously.

The brooding Tokatoka Hill is the main landmark as the route follows the Wairoa River to Dargaville.

Dargaville

Dargaville lies on the Wairoa River, which runs into Kaipara Harbour. Once an important river port for the export of kauri timber, Dargaville today is a quiet agricultural service town – and while it doesn't appear to be as kumara-centric as Ruawai, Dargaville claims the Kumara Capital title.

Information Dargaville's visitor centre (☎ 09-439 8360), 65 Normanby St, is open weekdays in summer from 8.30 am to 5 pm and on weekends from 9.30 am to 4.30 pm. Winter hours are weekdays between 10 am and 4 pm.

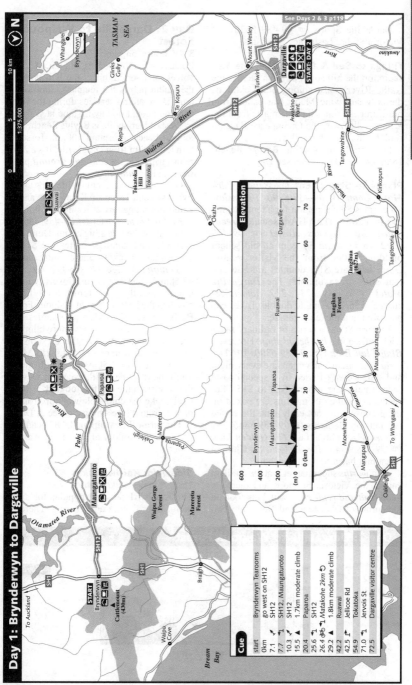

Day 1: Brynderwyn to Dargaville

Cue

start	Brynderwyn Tearooms
0km	go west on SH12
7.1	↗ SH12
7.7	↗ SH12, Maungaturoto
10.3	↗ SH12
15.5	▲ 1.7km moderate climb
20.4	Paparoa
25.6	← SH12
26.4	← Matakohe 2km ↺
29.2	▲ 1.8km moderate climb
42.2	Ruawai
42.5	↱ Jellicoe Rd
54.9	Tokatoka
71.0	← Jervois St
72.5	Dargaville visitor centre

Elevation

Dargaville Sports (☎ 09-439 8520), 92 Victoria St, has basic bicycle spares.

Things to See & Do The **Maritime Museum**, on the hill south of town (across the Kaihu River), has, among other exhibits, the only surviving Maori war canoe from pre-European times and the masts from the *Rainbow Warrior*, the Greenpeace flagship sunk by the French in 1985.

For details on visiting **Baylys Beach**, 18km east of Dargaville, see Day 2.

Places to Stay & Eat The *Selwyn Park Motor Camp* (☎ 09-439 8296, 10 Onslow St) charges $9 per person for a tent site and $15 in a dorm. The YHA-associate *Greenhouse Backpackers Hostel* (☎ 09-439 6342, 13 Portland St) is in an old school building 100m from the visitor centre. Dorm beds are $15, doubles are $36 and tent sites are available. The *Dargaville Motel* (☎ 09-439 7734, 217 Victoria St) charges $55/75 a single/double. Bikes can be stored in a lockable garage.

Victoria St has a series of ordinary sandwich cafes and a *hot bread shop*. However, *Blah Blah Blah* (☎ 09-439 6300, 101 Victoria St) is great – it's open late every night and staff weren't fussed by a special pasta order (mains are around $12 to $15). Focaccia and delicious muffins are baked on the premises (but not early) and the coffee is good. Try *Belushis* (☎ 09-439 8866, 102 Victoria St) for breakfast. *The Golden Lion* (☎ 09-439 8940, 108 Victoria St) Chinese restaurant has a $10 smorgasbord.

Woolworths supermarket is at the northern end of the Victoria St shops and there's a good *fruit and vegie shop* with bulk food on the corner of Gladstone and Normanby Sts.

Day 2: Dargaville to Waipoua Forest
3-4½ hours, 54.5km
Relatively flat for the first 28.5km, Day 2 involves some serious hills – the 3km slog after the Kaihu pub is the toughest climb of the tour. There are no services during the ride – and don't count on buying food at Waipoua.

West of Dargaville is **Baylys Beach**, NZ's longest beach at around 100km. To see it, turn left 4.9km from Dargaville. It's a 26km return trip. It has a *camping ground* plus a *store* and *restaurants*.

Other diversions include side trips to Kai-Iwi Lakes and Trounson Kauri Park, and the **woodturning gallery** at Kaihu (28.4km).

Kaihu Farm hostel (☎ 09-439 4004) is at the top of the ride's big climb. Dorm beds cost $15 and doubles/singles are $18/25. There's also breakfast and evening meals.

Waipoua Lodge (☎ 09-439 0422) at 47.5km is just before the lovely winding descent into the kauri forest. More luxurious than the DOC cabins at Waipoua Forest, B&B here is $95 to $125 for doubles.

If you can bear to do any more climbing, take the Lookout Road on the left soon after you enter the Waipoua Forest park. After a climb (160m in 1.5km) on rough gravel, you'll be rewarded with excellent views of the park from the **old fire lookout**. Alternatively, take the enjoyable walk up from the picnic ground (see Things to See & Do).

The turn-off to Waipoua DOC headquarters is at the bottom of the hill at Waipoua River.

Side Trip: Kai-Iwi Lakes
1½-2½ hours, 28km return
The Kai-Iwi Lakes are popular for swimming, trout fishing and boating. There are

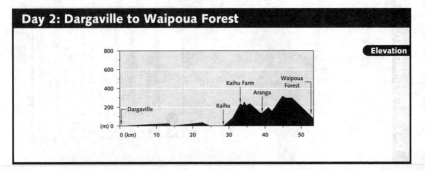

Day 2: Dargaville to Waipoua Forest

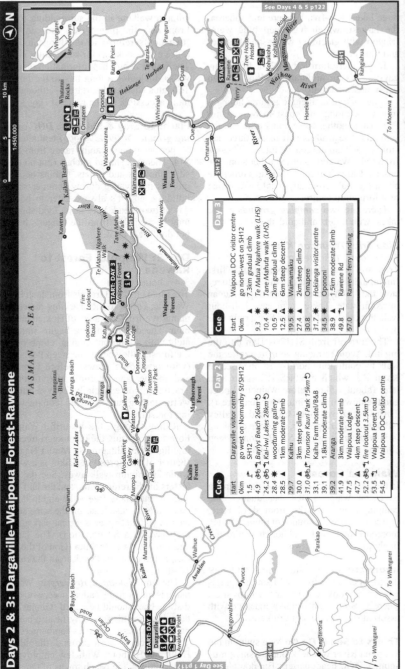

Days 2 & 3: Dargaville–Waipoua Forest–Rawene

Day 2

Cue		
start		Dargaville visitor centre
0km	↰	go west on Normanby St/SH12
1.5		SH12
4.9	🚲 🍴	Baylys Beach 26km ↻
24.2	🚲 🍴	Kai-Iwi Lakes 28km ↻
28.4	✱	woodturning gallery
28.5	▲	1km moderate climb
29.7		Kaihu
30.0	▲	3km steep climb
31.0	🚲 🛏	Trounson Kauri Park 15km ↻
33.1		Kaihu Farm hostel/B&B
39.1	▲	1.8km moderate climb
39.2		Aranga
41.9	▲	3km moderate climb
47.5		Waipoua Lodge
47.7	△	4km steep descent
52.2	🚲 ⚲	fire lookout 3.5km ↻
53.5	↱	Waipoua Forest road
54.5		Waipoua DOC visitor centre

Day 3

Cue		
start		Waipoua DOC visitor centre
0km		go north-west on SH12
9.3	▲	7.3km gradual climb
10.4	✱	Te Matua Ngahere walk (LHS)
10.5	✱	Tane Mahuta walk (LHS)
12.5	△	2km gradual climb
19.5	△	6km steep descent
27.4	▲	2km steep climb
30.8		Waimamaku
31.7	✱	Omapere
34.5	✱	Hokianga visitor centre
38.9	▲	Opononi
49.8	↱	1.5km moderate climb
57.0		Rawene Rd
		Rawene ferry landing

three lakes: Kai-Iwi, Waikere and Taharoa, the largest, which has deep blue water fringed with gleaming white-sand beaches and pine groves.

To get there turn left 24.2km from Dargaville. It's an undulating 14km ride on partly unsealed road.

Other activities include a three hour return walk along the coast to Maunganui Bluff (it's another three hours return to the summit). The walk is part of the three-day Hokianga-Waipoua coastal track – it begins from Lake Waikere, a little farther along the unsealed stretch of road. Pick up a brochure about the walk from any local DOC office or information centre.

There are two *camping grounds* at the lakes, with toilets and cold showers.

Side Trip: Trounson Kauri Park
1-1½ hours, 15km return

Trounson Kauri Park is Northland's first 'mainland island' project, which aims to restore the 450-hectare reserve to a pre-human invasion state. There is an easy half-hour walk through beautiful kauri forest right near the road (lock your bike).

The turn-off from SH12 is 1km into the big hill. Avoid retracing your steps after the walk by continuing north-west on unsealed Katui Rd, which meets SH12 again 8km later (about 1.5km before Waipoua Lodge and the downhill run into Waipoua Forest). This alternative route travels the valley rather than the ridge and, although climbing is inevitable, it avoids SH12's long, steep climb (but also the ridge-top views).

Waipoua Forest

In the heart of the forest, beside the Waipoua River, the Waipoua DOC headquarters and camping ground are 1km from SH12. Here, you can sleep to the sounds of running water, morepork owls and – although you're unlikely to see them – kiwis.

Information The visitor centre (☎ 09-439 0605), open daily from 8.30 am to 6 pm, is where to book cabins and camp sites. There's also a food vending machine with assorted snacks and soft drinks.

Things to See & Do Go for a **swim** in the Waipoua River or check out the small **museum** at DOC headquarters. But don't leave

without **walking** in the surrounding forest. From near the picnic area you can walk (two hours return) to the forest lookout (once a fire lookout) for spectacular views. The visitor centre has information on other walks, including a long trek to the famous Te Matua Ngahere kauri tree – although it's more accessible on the route of Day 3.

Places to Stay & Eat At the *DOC camping ground* (☎ 09-439 0605) tent sites are $7 per person and cabins range from $8 to $14. There's a shared kitchen (but no utensils), showers and toilets. Cabins book up months in advance during summer school holidays, and it's always safer to book a day or two ahead. Very basic food supplies may be available from the ranger's house, but don't rely on it.

Day 3: Waipoua Forest to Rawene
3-4½ hours, 57km

The route on Day 3 travels from deep in the Waipoua Forest to the sparkling dunes and mangrove-fringed waters of Hokianga Harbour. The day's climbing begins immediately with a long but gradual climb out of the forest, followed by the steep Pakia Hill (with rewarding views) before Omapere and another gentler climb after Opononi. Traffic is not especially heavy, but it's worth starting early to avoid it on the winding forest road.

Riding through the beautiful Waipoua Forest and visiting the giant kauri trees is a highlight. Breathtaking **Te Matua Ngahere** (Father of the Forest) at 9.3km is a worthwhile 20 minute walk away. See the **Four Sisters** on the return walk, and the half-hour walk to the **Yakas Tree** – the eighth largest kauri in NZ – also leads off the same access path. A volunteer guards the car park against theft (worth a $2 donation). The largest kauri in NZ, **Tane Mahuta** (God of the Forest), is three minutes walk from the road at 10.4km.

The tiny *Hokianga Brewery* in Waimamaku is run by a guy called Innes, who quips that his beer should be called 'Ginnes'. Although beer is his speciality, he also brews a passable espresso and fries hamburgers.

The pace is slow around the idyllic Hokianga Harbour. With few employment opportunities, the beach towns of Omapere and Opononi are relatively depressed. Alternative lifestylers and artists seem to flourish, however – the local galleries have some fine work on display. There's a range of accommodation, but make sure you boil water at Omapere and Opononi – this is one of the few regions in NZ where tap water is not guaranteed against giardia.

Tiny Opononi became nationally famous in 1955 through Opo, a friendly dolphin who performed tricks and played with children. She died tragically, but can be seen on video at the **Hokianga visitor centre** in Omapere (31.7km) or enshrined in stone outside the Opononi pub.

Rawene

Rawene is a little village on a point jutting into Hokianga Harbour. The main village, a series of attractive heritage buildings clustered around the ferry wharf, is 2.5km beyond the hospital on the hill that rather imposingly heralds the entrance to town.

Some of Rawene's buildings date from the days of early European settlement, including Clendon House, built in the late 1860s, and the hotel, which was built the following decade.

The Hokianga Ferry (☎ 09-401 21010) crosses the harbour from Rawene to the Narrows (on the Kohukohu side) hourly from 7.30 am to 7.30 pm (earlier in winter); and from the Narrows to Rawene on the hour between 7.45 am and 8 pm (every half hour between 7.30 and 9.30 am). The 15 minute trip costs $1.50 with a bike.

Information There is no visitor centre at Rawene, but the Hokianga visitor centre in Omapere (open daily from 8.30 am to 5 pm) has information about the region.

Rawene's post office is in the small supermarket by the ferry wharf.

Things to See & Do Surrounded by a majestic harbour, Rawene is a pretty spot to kick back and relax (and everybody else here appears to do just that). The **Boatshed Gallery & Cafe** (☎ 09-405 7728), near the wharf, has some excellent local arts and crafts. Just up the road is historic **Clendon House** (☎ 09-405 7874), one of the earliest buildings in Rawene and built by local magistrate James Clendon. A little farther on is a **mangrove boardwalk**.

Places to Stay & Eat The *Rawene Motor Camp* (*☎ 09-405 7720, 1 Marmon St*) is before the hill down to the wharf. It has tent sites for $8, on-site vans for $12 and cabins for $18 per person. The historic *Masonic Hotel* (*☎ 09-405 7822*), 500m from the wharf, has singles/doubles for $30/40.

The down-to-earth and friendly *Boatshed Gallery & Cafe* (see Things to See & Do) has delicious trendy lunches for around $8 and excellent coffee and muffins (but closes at 5pm). The *Masonic Hotel* (*☎ 09-405 7822*) has counter meals for $13.50; mains in the restaurant cost from $16 to $23. Fish and chips from the *take away* around the corner are good (but it closes early). *Hokianga Wholefoods*, next to the *supermarket*, has organically grown vegies and health food.

Kohukohu On the other side of the harbour, the *Tree House* (*☎ 09-405 5855*), 2km north-west of the ferry terminus, is a real travellers rest – perfect for a relaxing day off. Tent sites are $10 per person, dorm beds cost $16 and cabins from $25.

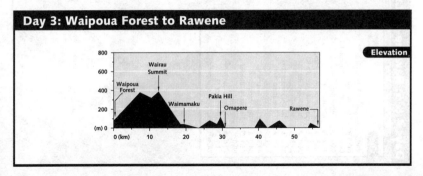

Day 3: Waipoua Forest to Rawene

Days 4 & 5: Rawene-Kaitaia-Whangaroa

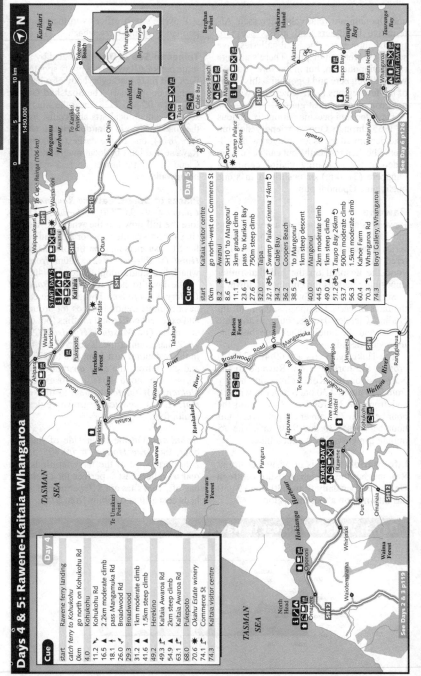

Cue — Day 4

start	Rawene ferry landing
	catch ferry to Kohukohu
0km	go north on Kohukohu Rd
4.0	Kohukohu
11.2	Kohukohu Rd
16.5	2.2km moderate climb
18.1	pass Mangamuka Rd
26.0	Broadwood Rd
29.3	Broadwood
31.2	1km moderate climb
41.6	1.5km steep climb
49.2	Herekino
49.3	Kaitaia Awaroa Rd
54.9	2km steep climb
63.1	Kaitaia Awaroa Rd
68.0	Pukepoto
70.6	Okahu Estate winery
74.1	Commerce St
74.3	Kaitaia visitor centre

Cue — Day 5

start	Kaitaia visitor centre
	go north-west on Commerce St
0km	
8.2	SH10 'to Mangonui'
8.6	Awanui
11.1	3km gradual climb
23.6	pass to Karikari Bay'
27.6	750m steep climb
32.0	Taipa
32.1	Swamp Palace cinema 14km ↰
34.2	Cable Bay
36.2	Coopers Beach
38.5	'to Mangonui'
	1km steep descent
40.0	Mangonui
44.5	2km moderate climb
49.0	1km steep climb
51.2	Taupo Bay 26km ↰
53.7	500m moderate climb
56.3	1.5km moderate climb
60.4	Kahoe Farm
70.3	Whangaroa Rd
74.3	Boyd Gallery, Whangaroa

See Day 6 p126

See Days 2 & 3 p119

Day 4: Rawene to Kaitaia
4-6 hours, 74.3km

Day 4 is via the lightly trafficked scenic route to Kaitaia. Unless you've already crossed the harbour, the day starts with a picturesque 15 minute ferry ride. From the northern ferry terminus, the road continues round the picturesque mangrove-fringed harbour, gently undulating. The charming village of Kohukohu nestles in among the hills. Keep an eye out for birds such as pukekos and herons.

Although it's not quite halfway, the small town of **Broadwood** is a good spot for lunch; it has the last *shop* en route before Kaitaia (other than the Herekino pub). There are a couple more hills as you pass through rolling farmland to Herekino. Enjoy the views of the mountains of **Herekino Forest** while you're riding beside them on the (relative) flat – pretty soon you're climbing again, through the Herekino Gorge.

The road undulates a little after Wainui Junction, but the last 5km into Kaitaia are more or less flat. Check out **Okahu Estate** (70.6km), NZ's most northern winery.

Kaitaia

Kaitaia (population 4800) is the far north's commercial centre. It's also the jumping-off point for tours to Cape Reinga. However, the town itself has little character or charm. If you're planning a rest day, don't spend it here, unless you want to do a trip to the cape.

The town has significant populations of both Maori (there's an excellent cultural centre) and Dalmatians (immigrants from West Croatia who came to dig kauri gum). Ahipara, south-west of Kaitaia, is known for its massive 'gumfields', which flourished last century.

Information The visitor centre is in Jaycee Park, Commerce St, 200m from the turn-off from Redan Rd. It's open daily from 8.30 am to 5 pm; only to 12.30 pm on winter weekends.

The DOC office (☎ 09-408 2100) is at 127 North Rd. Check your email at Hackers Internet Cafe (☎ 09-408 4999, 🖳 www.hackers.co.nz), 84 Commerce St. Several banks with ATMs are on Commerce St.

Cycle Sport 'N' Heat Shop (☎ 09-408 2460), 167 Commerce St, is reputedly the best in Northland for repairs – and the only bike shop until Kerikeri on Day 6.

Things to See & Do Check out the Maori cultural centre **Te Wero Nui** (☎ 09-408 4884), behind KFC on Commerce St. It's a tourist-focused centre teaching aspects of Maori culture.

Kaitaia is the best place from which to take a **Cape Reinga tour**. Although the Cape is not actually the northernmost point of the mainland, it is the point at which the Tasman Sea meets the Pacific Ocean and it does have an end-of-the-world feel to it. Sand Safaris (☎ 0800 869 090) and Harrison's Cape Runner (☎ 0800 227 373) organise day trips that also include **sand tobogganing**.

Alternatively, go **mountain biking** at the Ahipara gumfields – ask the DOC (☎ 09-408 2100) for more information and maps. Stick to the 4WD tracks to avoid damaging the fragile sandscapes.

Places to Stay & Eat The *Kaitaia Motor Camp (☎ 09-408 1212, 67 South Rd)* has cheap tent sites at $5 per person. At *Main Street Backpackers (☎ 09-408 1275, 235 Commerce St)* the owner is on-hand to teach

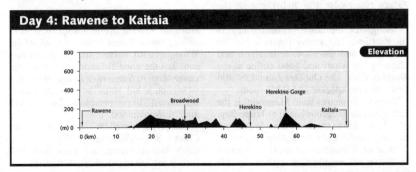

Day 4: Rawene to Kaitaia

visitors about Maori culture. Dorms here start at $13 per person and single/doubles are $30/34. The *Hike & Bike YHA* (☎ 09-408 1840, 160 Commerce St) has dorms from $14 for members and doubles are $40. Bikes can be locked in the storeroom if you ask.

The friendly *Wayfarer Motel* (☎ 0800 118 100, 231 Commerce St) charges from $55 for a self-contained unit. There's a spa, and a lock-up garage.

The *Golden Crumb Bakery* is towards the southern end of the Commerce St shops. Farther south is *Maisey's* cafe (☎ 09-408 4934), where you can get late meals and coffee. Try *Steve's Snapper Bar* (123 Commerce St) for good-value fish and chips or pizza, or the *Sea Dragon* (☎ 09-408 0555) Chinese restaurant. There are also a few *pubs* serving meals. If you're desperate, Kaitaia also has *McDonald's* and *KFC*.

Pak 'N Save is in the middle of town and *Wholefoods Organics* is towards the northern end of the shops (or you can pick up cheap organic vegetables from the Saturday morning *market*).

Day 5: Kaitaia to Whangaroa
4-6 hours, 74.3km

After the flat 8km to Awanui, the road rocks and rolls through pleasant farmland with no major climbs, but lots of ups and downs. The coast is never far away, however, and there's a series of beach towns to visit before descending to Whangaroa Harbour.

Check out the **mural** at Awanui before turning onto SH10. Legend has it a local woman who'd made millions in an Australian brothel initiated it.

The Oruru public hall, 7km up the river from Taipa, has been taken over by a local movie buff and turned into the quaint **Swamp Palace cinema** (☎ 408 7040), should the need for a movie strike.

Mangonui, the last town on the bay, is the prettiest. The visitor centre is on the waterfront and there's excellent fish and chips by the wharf and good coffee at the *Dolphin Cafe*. The *Old Oak Inn* (☎ 09-406 0665) has backpacker and B&B rooms.

Eleven kilometres from Mangonui is the turn-off to the gorgeous beach of **Taupo Bay**. The 13km ride to the small town is over undulating terrain and a final steep descent.

West of Whangaroa, at 60.4km, is an alternative accommodation option for the night. *Kahoe Farm* (☎ 09-405 1804) is a beautiful old kauri farmhouse with dorm beds for $16 and doubles for $37. The hospitality and Italian cooking is a treat (order the home-made bread the night before you leave). Activities include the **Tara Tara challenge** – a 5km ride followed by a 2km run up Tara Tara Rock (the record is under 23 minutes) – and kayaks are also available.

From here, it's relatively flat and pleasant ride to Whangaroa around the harbour.

Whangaroa
Whangaroa is another picturesque inlet, surrounded by high rugged cliffs and curious-looking hills. Not only was this a site of early European settlement – early missionaries set up shop here, as did kauri loggers – but one of the first Maori canoes is also said to have landed in the area.

Information Called the Boyd Gallery, the general store (☎ 09-405 0230) is also an informal tourist information office. The closest bank is the ANZ at Kaeo, 2.7km south of the Whangaroa turn-off (on the route of Day 6).

Things to See & Do There are lots of great **walks** in the area: climb St Pauls Rock from Whangaroa or take the longer walk to Lane Cove and up the Dukes Nose for great **views** of the harbour.

Whangaroa is a popular **game fishing** town – and the water really is a great place from which to explore this area: the Sunseeker Lodge has free kayaks and Northland Sea Kayaking (☎ 09-405 0381) runs day tours out to Tauranga Bay. Spend a day sailing on the **yacht** *Snow Cloud* (☎ 09-405 0523) or go **diving** in Whangaroa Harbour and see the wreck of the *Rainbow Warrior*.

Places to Stay & Eat The *Whangaroa Harbour Retreat Motor Camp* (☎ 09-405 0306), about 2.5km before the wharf on Whangaroa Rd, has tent sites for $9 per person. Try the good fish and chips from the *camp shop*. At *Sunseeker Lodge* (☎ 09-405 0496), on a hill 500m beyond the wharf, dorms cost $15 per person, doubles are $36 and self-contained units are $90. The *Whangaroa Motel* (☎ 09-405 0022), on Church St overlooking the Big Gamefish Club, has self-contained units from $90 (prices are lower outside peak season).

The **Marlin Hotel** (☎ 09-405 0347) does breakfast, lunch and dinner, or you can gain temporary membership to eat at the **Big Gamefish Club** (☎ 09-405 0399). For a Texan chilli meal outside town, try **Janits Texas Diner** (see Day 6). The **general store** also has a good range of stock.

Day 6: Whangaroa to Paihia
3-4½ hours, 55.9km

From Whangaroa the route follows the Kaeo River and, after climbing out of the valley, drops down again to the fruit-growing region surrounding historic Kerikeri and Paihia, the main tourist town on the Bay of Islands.

Just outside Whangaroa is **Janits Texas Diner**. Not what you'd expect amid such unTexan mangroves, mist and mountains, but Janit (whose Daddy was a Texan) makes terrific chilli con carne, along with sodas and breakfasts (from 7.30 am).

There's a **bakery** and **supermarket** in the little town of Kaeo. The visitor centre is in the **Old Saddlery Tearooms**. Almost 2km

The Rainbow Warrior

A relatively insignificant nation, in international terms, New Zealand made world headlines in 1985 when the Greenpeace flagship *Rainbow Warrior* was blown up in Auckland Harbour by French saboteurs.

Backed by their government, the mission of the French secret service agents was to prevent the *Rainbow Warrior* from sailing to Tahiti to protest against French nuclear testing. After collecting explosives from a yacht in the far north (which had picked them up from a submarine), the agents posed as tourists, driving to Auckland in a Kombi van, and attached the explosives to the ship.

Green campaigner Fernando Pereira was killed in the blast. There was uproar in France – not because the French government had conducted an act of terrorism on the soil of a friendly nation, but because the secret service had bungled the operation – two of the agents were caught.

The skeletal remains of the *Rainbow Warrior* were taken to rest in the waters of the beautiful Cavalli Islands, east of Whangaroa, while the masts stand at the maritime museum in Dargaville.

on, the road climbs for 6km – sometimes steeply – out of the valley, passing a turn-off to Puketi Forest on the way. The **Puketi Forest** is one of Northland's largest areas of native forest, home to populations of kaka, kiwi, kokako and bats. For information about walking and mountain biking in the area, see the DOC pamphlet *Puketi & Omahuta Forests*.

The turn-off to Kerikeri is just past the shops at Waipapa (see Side Trip). The **Cottle Hill Winery** (☎ 09-407 5203), 7.2km from Waipapa, serves a good ploughman's lunch.

The road undulates to Puketona junction, turn-off point to the Bay of Islands. The bay won't be visible until you're almost there – it's obscured by a couple of hills.

Side Trip: Kerikeri
30-50 minutes, 10.7km return

Kerikeri is primarily a service town for the surrounding agricultural district, but it's also the site of NZ's oldest surviving building, the wooden **Kemp House**, built in 1821 as part of the country's second mission station. The influence of the well-heeled English settlers is still evident. There's also an authentic reproduction of a **pre-European Maori village**.

After the shops at Waipapa, turn left onto Waipapa Rd. Turn right at the end of Waipapa Rd and head downhill to the visitor centre and historic buildings. The Kerikeri Rd shopping area is on the way back to SH10. There are plenty of cafes, making it a good lunch spot. Try the **Cathay Cinema Cafe** for good coffee, cakes and meals. Keri Mowers Saws & Cycles (☎ 09-407 7040) is on Cobham Rd. Look out for the **Makana Confections chocolate factory** (☎ 09-407 6800) on the way out of town.

Bay of Islands

There are three settlements in the area that are of interest. Paihia, originally settled as a mission station, is the tourist hub of the Bay of Islands. It's only a small town, but is geared towards the summer rush with lots of accommodation, restaurants and tours.

Russell, the nation's first administrative centre, has retained a bit more charm and character and is only a short ferry trip away. Ferries to Russell depart from the wharf every 20 minutes between 7 am and 10 pm (to 7 pm in winter). All three ferry services

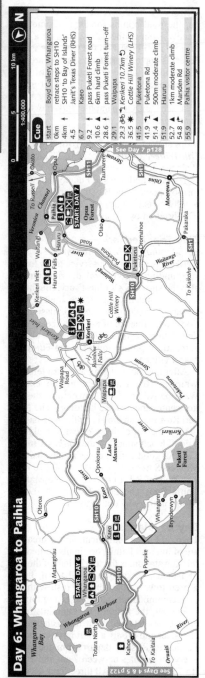

Cue		
start		Boyd Gallery, Whangaroa
		retrace steps to SH10
0km		SH10 'to Bay of Islands'
4km	↑	Janit's Texas Diner (RHS)
4.5	←	Kaeo
6.7	↑	pass Puketi Forest road
9.2	↑	6km hard climb
10.6	←	pass Puketi Forest turn-off
28.6	↑	
29.1		Waipapa
29.3	⚷	Kerikeri 10.7km ↺
36.5	✳	Cottle Hill Winery (LHS)
41.5		Puketona
41.9	↰	Puketona Rd
51.4	▲	500m moderate climb
51.9		Haruru
52.7	▲	1km moderate climb
54.8	↲	Marsden Rd
55.9		Paihia visitor centre

charge $3 one way, and only the *Bay Belle* charges for bikes ($1.50).

The town of Waitangi, just north of Paihia, lends its name to the Treaty of Waitangi, which provided the basis for British annexation of NZ. It was signed here by Maori chiefs and a representative of the British government on 6 February 1840.

Information The Bay of Islands information centre (☎ 09-402 7345, fax 402 7314, ✉ paivin@nzhost.co.nz) is in the Maritime Building by the wharf on Marsden Rd in Paihia. It's open daily from 8 am to 8 pm from December to February, with earlier closing hours at other times. The Bay of Islands Maritime & Historic Park DOC visitor centre (☎ 09-403 7685) is in Russell on the corner of Pitt St and The Strand.

There are ASB and ANZ banks at Paihia, and Russell has Westpac and a Bank of New Zealand. Check email at the visitor centre or the Boots Off Traveller's Centre (☎ 09-402 6632), on Selwyn Rd in Paihia.

Things to See & Do At the Waitangi National Reserve, about 2km north of the visitor centre along Marsden Rd, the **Treaty House** has been preserved as a memorial and museum. Close by is the beautifully carved **whare runanga** (Maori meeting house), built to mark the centenary of the treaty, and the Maori war canoe *Ngatokimatawhaorua*, the world's largest canoe. There's an audiovisual presentation about the treaty at the visitor centre on the reserve. **Kelly Tarlton's Shipwreck Museum** is near the bridge to the reserve.

Take a ferry ride to Russell. There are some interesting **historic buildings**, a **museum** and **walks**. Pick up a copy of *Russell: Kororareka* or the free *Russell Heritage Trails* pamphlet from the visitor centre in Paihia.

You can walk from the Waitangi National Reserve to **Haruru Falls** and there are a number of other good **walks** around the Bay of Islands. The DOC visitor centre has more pamphlets and information about longer walks in the area.

Paihia has a multitude of tours and activities on offer. Not surprisingly, the bay itself is a major focus. Ask at the visitor centre about the various **cruises** that pick up at Paihia and Russell, **jet boat** Hole in the Rock rides and half-day or longer **sailing** trips. **Dolphin swimming** is also popular and operates all year. The bay is a great spot for **scuba diving, sea kayaking** and **fishing**. You can also take a **seaplane flight**.

Places to Stay & Eat Both Paihia and Russell have plenty of accommodation and eating options.

Paihia South of town on the corner of Mc-Murray and Seaview Rds is the *Park Lodge Caravan Park (☎ 09-402 7826)*. Tent sites cost $10 per person, which includes use of the swish Park Lodge hotel's saltwater pool.

Paihia has plenty of hostels. Away from the Kings Rd 'backpacker strip', the friendly *Mayfair Lodge (☎ 09-402 7471, 7 Puketona Rd)* has dorms/doubles for $16/17.50 per person, limited tent sites ($10 per person), a spa and a shed for bikes. The *Centabay Lodge (☎ 09-402 7466, 27 Selwyn Rd)* has $16 dorm beds, as well as tourist lodge accommodation.

The *Sands Motel (☎ 09-402 7707, fax 402 6217, 136 Marsden Rd)* has single/double studios for $65/145.

Pizza Pasta Ruffino (☎ 09-402 7964, 39 Williams Rd) has pasta and pizzas for around $11. In the mall, *Jazz Cafe & Diner (☎ 09-402 7653)* has Mexican burritos (vegetarian available) with salad for $7 and good-value burgers and steaks. On Marsden Rd, *Caffe Over the Bay (☎ 09-402 8147)* is a good bet for breakfast, reasonably priced mains and a vegetarian selection. The *Blue Marlin Diner (☎ 09-402 7590)*, in the main shopping strip, has cheap breakfasts, grills and take-away.

The *Bread Shed* bakery and *supermarket* are neighbours on Williams Rd, and there's a *fruit shop* in the mall.

Russell If you're camping, the *Russell Holiday Park (☎ 09-403 7826)*, north-east of the ferry terminal on Long Beach Rd, has tent sites for $12 and shared cabins at $16 per person.

The *Russell Lodge (☎ 09-403 7640, cnr Chapel & Beresford Sts)* has four-bed ensuite units for $18 per person or singles/doubles for $30/44. There's also a self-contained unit for $100. *Motel Russell (☎ 0800 240 011 or ☎ 09-403 7854, fax 403 8001, 16 Matauwhi Bay Rd)* has doubles starting at $75. Bikes are locked in an enclosed area. The *Abba Villa* B&B *(☎ 09-402 8066, 21 School Rd)* charges $48/80 a room and will lock bikes in the shed.

The unlicensed *Verandah Cafe (☎ 09-403 7167)* in the traders mall has mains from $15 to $20. Also in the traders mall is a *bakery*, a *bulk grocery* and *fruit shop* and a good *take away* with burgers, Asian food and pizza.

For style, try the restaurant in the *Duke of Marlborough Hotel (☎ 09-403 7829)* on the waterfront.

Waitangi At the Treaty Grounds in Waitangi, the *Waikokopu Cafe* has mains for around $14.50.

Day 7: Paihia to Whangarei
4-5 hours, 73.6km

After the first 10km of Day 7, the route tracks inland and the sea won't come into view again until Whangarei. Tourist glitz is left behind as you head through laid-back, no-airs-and-graces farm country. There are also some interesting limestone formations along the way.

The road starts to climb soon after leaving Paihia. There are a couple of hills – and some nice vistas – before a long, steep downhill leads to open rolling farmland (take care here – you're sharing the road with tour buses).

Kawakawa is an unpretentious country town. The main incentive to detour into the centre is the excellent espresso and cakes at the *Trainspotting Cafe* (watch out for the tourist steam train from Opua), or for an emergency visit to Turton Sports & Cycles (☎ 09-404 0632).

After Kawakawa, the route is on SH1 all the way to Whangarei, but the traffic is light. There's a steepish climb as the road ascends a ridge with views of steep, bushy valleys.

The **Waiomio Glow-Worm Caves** turn-off is 3.3km south of Kawakawa. Known in Maori as Te Ana-O-Roku, the caves are owned and run by the Kawiti family, descendants of the Ngapuhi tribe. Tours (☎ 09-404 1256) cost $10 and there's a 10 minute walk to the caves. The office is only 300m off SH1 on Waiomio Rd, and you can leave your bike here while you see the caves.

Just before Hikurangi (54.3km) are the bizarre rocks of **Waro Limestone Reserve**. The 20 minute walk is worth the effort.

The route ends with a nice long descent through the suburbs of Whangarei; look out for the quick turn onto Tarewa Rd.

Day 7: Paihia to Whangarei

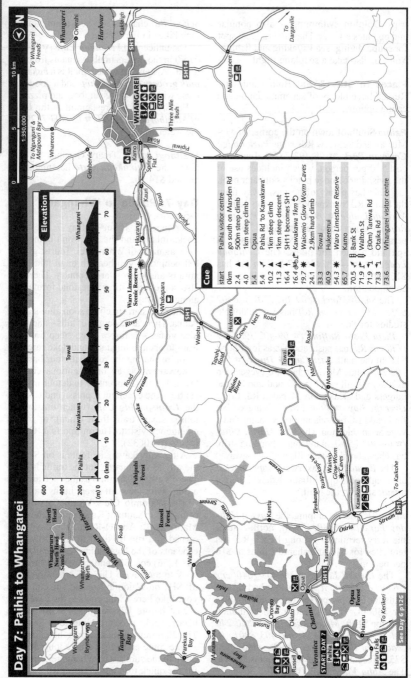

Elevation

Cue	
start	Paihia visitor centre
0km	go south on Marsden Rd
2.4	500m steep climb
4.0	1km steep climb
5.4	Opua
5.4	Pahia Rd to Kawakawa'
10.2	1km steep climb
11.3	1km steep descent
16.4	SH11 becomes SH1
16.4	Kawakawa 1km
19.7	Waiomio Glow Worm Caves
24.1	2.9km hard climb
33.3	Towai
40.9	Hukerenui
54.3	Waro Limestone Reserve
65.7	Kamo
70.5	Bank St
71.9	Walton St
71.9	(30m) Tarewa Rd
73.3	Otaika Rd
73.6	Whangarei visitor centre

Maori culture is an integral part of New Zealand and a strong and growing influence over the country and its people. Central to Maori culture are the arts: dances such as the poi, action songs, martial arts, carving, as well as the very distinctive painting often best illustrated in *marae*.

Waitemata Harbour and Auckland

Art Gallery, Auckland

Westhaven Marina, Auckland

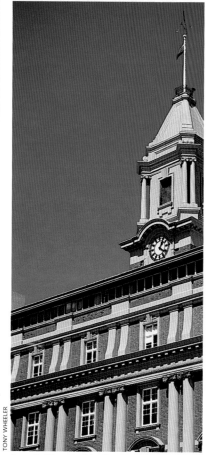

Ferry Building, Auckland

Whangarei

Whangarei is Northland's major city, with a population of 45,000. Built around a deep harbour, the city is surrounded by forested hills – there are several nearby reserves – and the area's rich soil supports many farms and orchards.

Information The visitor centre (☎ 09-438 1079), together with the DOC office (☎ 09-430 2007, ✉ whangareivc@doc.govt.nz), is 1.7km south of the city centre on Otaika Rd (SH1).

Hedgehog Bikes (☎ 09-438 2521), 29 Vine St, is good for repairs and advice. Motocat Cyclery (☎ 09-438 1168) is at 70 James St. Ask here for details of the Parahaki Mountain Bike Club and Marsden Wheelers road racing club.

Cable Action Cybercafe (☎ 09-430 7470), on the corner of James and Quay Sts, is open daily till 9 pm.

Things to See & Do The **Whangarei Town Basin** is an attractive area along Quay St next to the harbour where boats from all over the world are moored. The renovated waterfront area houses several **museums** and **galleries**.

There are plenty of **walks** through the **scenic reserves** around town. Pick up the free *Whangarei Walks* pamphlet from the visitor centre. **Mountain biking** is also good around Whangarei.

The coast about 30km east of Whangarei is very scenic. You can ride north-east through Glenbervie to Ngunguru or Matapouri Bay, or south-east to Whangarei heads. Water-based activities are popular here too. **Poor Knights Island Marine Reserve**, off the coast to the north-east of Whangarei, is said to be one of the best **diving** spots. There are also **ecotours** to the islands, themselves, which act as a sanctuary for flora and fauna – notably the prehistoric reptile the tuatara. Ask at the visitor centre for details. Tour companies can also provide information about **dolphin and whale watching**, **sea kayaking**, **scenic flights** and **fishing**.

Places to Stay The *Alpha Caravan Park* (☎ 09-438 9876, 34 Tarewa Rd) is between the city centre and the visitor centre. Tent sites are $9 per person; on-site vans cost $20/30 for a single/double and motel units are $59 a double.

Bunkdown Lodge (☎ 09-438 8886, ✉ bun kdown@ihug.co.nz, 23 Otaika Rd) is a spacious hostel charging $15 for dorms and $40 for rooms; tent sites are $9 per person. You can get a half-hour massage for $15. Bikes go in the shed. Alternatively, the *YHA* (☎ 09-438 8954, 52 Punga Grove Ave) is smaller and friendly, but it's up a steep (short) hill. Dorm beds are $15 and doubles are $34 for members.

Motel 6 (☎ 09-438 9219, 153 Bank St) is on the right as you enter town. It has studio units for $68 and self-contained apartments for $80. Bikes can be locked in a shed.

One of the few central B&Bs is the friendly *City Lights* (☎ 09-438 2390) in Vale Rd, with great views. Phone ahead to book a single/double for $40/70.

Places to Eat Check out the *Eating Out in Whangarei* guide, free from the visitor centre.

Taste Spud (☎ 09-438 1164, 3 Water St) is good value for light meals: baked potatoes, burritos, lasagne, falafel and souvlaki cost between $3 and $7. A few doors along is *Shiraz Indian Restaurant* (☎ 09-438 3112, 5 Water St) with mains from $12.50 to $16. *Caffeine* (☎ 09-438 6925, 4 Water St) does breakfast and lunch ($5 to $12) and has excellent coffee and muffins. The *Bread Basket* bakery is on the corner of Bank and Cameron Sts.

The Laughing Buddha Cafe (☎ 09-430 0730, 79 Walton St) is vegetarian, but phone first – it's not always open. *The Dickens Inn* (☎ 09-430 0406, cnr Cameron & Quality Sts) has traditional pub food. *Olivers Cafe* (☎ 09-430 0406), next door, has sourdough sandwiches and pastas from $16. *Belgrade Pizza and Pasta* (☎ 09-438 2821, 206 Bank St) has $10 pasta and pizzas from $9.

Pak 'N Save supermarket is on Curruth St and there's a *supermarket* on your way into town in the Kensington Shopping Complex.

Coromandel Peninsula

The Coromandel Peninsula has some of the North Island's finest beaches and coastal scenery. It's very much a bastion for those seeking an alternative lifestyle away from the bustle of Auckland. The serenity is briefly interrupted by hordes of Christmas holiday-makers, but even with a significant tourist industry, the locals remain very friendly and crime is practically nonexistent.

HISTORY

Maori have lived on the peninsula since the first settlers arrived and the sheltered east coast supported a large population. This was a major moa-hunting area, while fishing, sealing, bird-hunting and horticulture provided other food sources.

European settlement developed around the gold mining and gum-digging industries. Kauri timber was also in high demand for construction and ship-building during the 19th century.

Gold was first discovered in 1852. In the late 1860s mining began at Thames (becoming one of NZ's biggest towns), Coromandel, Kuaotunu and Karangahake. The Martha mine at Waihi, which opened in 1892 and operated for 60 years, has recently reopened.

NATURAL HISTORY

The Coromandel is a rugged, densely forested peninsula where rivers force their way through gorges and pour down steep cliffs to the sea. The Coromandel Range is the mountainous spine of the peninsula and the Coromandel Forest Park stretches almost its entire length, the landscape becoming more rugged and isolated farther north.

The Coromandel

Duration	5 days
Distance	259.8km
Difficulty	moderate-hard
Start/End	Thames

This ride alternates between beautiful beaches, estuaries and rugged mountain ranges. Be prepared for rough unsealed sections at times – and spend time exploring natural wonders like Cathedral Cove and Hot Water Beach. The natural beauty, laid-back lifestyle and discreet tourist industry make for delightful cycling – out of the tourist season.

Although accommodation is plentiful on the peninsula, during peak periods it's ex-

pensive and it's wise to book well in advance – including tent sites. Even during winter it pays to phone a day or two ahead – many B&Bs, especially, prefer guests to phone before turning up.

PLANNING
When to Ride

Avoid cycling the Coromandel Peninsula over the peak summer period (Christmas to late January) and during holiday weekends. It's a justifiably popular spot and you will have to share the one main road (often narrow and winding) with hundreds of holiday-makers, supply trucks and tourist buses.

The Coromandel is temperate enough to cycle year-round, but is probably most pleasant in early summer and from February to April.

Maps

The AA *Coromandel Peninsula* Leisure Map (1:200,000) features useful information about the region on the back. The area is also covered in the AA *South Auckland and Coromandel* District Map (1:350,000).

Other good maps include: the Land Information *Auckland* Terrainmap (1:250,000), which provides some topographical information; and the more basic AA road atlas.

What to Bring

Be prepared for changeable weather; rain and sun protection is essential, especially if you plan on camping or walking.

GETTING TO/FROM THE RIDE
Thames

Bus Thames is the main transport hub of the peninsula. InterCity (☎ 09-913 6100) runs a daily service between Auckland and Thames for $20 plus $10 per bike. The service continues on a circuit around the peninsula as far as Whangamata and back to Thames.

InterCity also provides a Monday to Friday service between Hamilton and Thames for $22 through Murphy Turley Buses. It runs via Te Aroha and Paeroa and connects with a service to Coromandel (don't listen to the driver if he urges you to stay on the bus to Coromandel – get on your bike and ride!).

You can finish the circuit at Paeroa and catch the daily InterCity bus from Paeroa to Tauranga, which connects with a daily service to Rotorua.

Boat The MV *Pakatoa Cat* (☎ 09-379 0066) runs a daily service between Auckland and Hannaford's Point Wharf at Te Kouma, just south of Coromandel town. The two hour trips costs $31/59 one way/return (bikes cost $10 each way). Bookings are recommended.

Bicycle From Auckland, ride Day 1 of the Seabird Coast & Hunua Ranges ride to Miranda. Thames is 30km further. Continue south along Miranda Rd and head east through Waitakaruru, Pipiroa and, at Kopu, head north to Thames (SH25).

The ride also links to Rotorua via Tauranga (take SH2 from Waihi) and to Hamilton via Te Aroha (take SH26 from Paeroa).

THE RIDE
This ride is suggested as a five day circuit to allow time to explore the area's magnificent natural attractions. Days 3 and 4 involve short distances, however, and could be combined if time is short.

Thames
Thames (population 6500) is the peninsula's gateway town. Now a modest tourist centre, during the lucrative gold and kauri days of the 19th century it was one of the country's biggest towns.

Information The Thames visitor centre (☎ 07-868 7284, ✉ tmvin@nzhost.co.nz) and bus depot is at the southern end of Pollen St. It's open daily from 8.30 am to 5 pm in summer (9 am to 4 pm on weekends during winter).

The Bank of New Zealand, National, Westpac and ANZ banks and the post office are all on Pollen St. Price & Richards bike shop (☎ 07-868 6157), 430 Pollen St, offers friendly cycling advice. Mountain bikes can be hired for $20 a day.

Things to See & Do Watch birds from the **Karaka Hide** by the mangroves (reached from Brown St) or learn about Thames' gold-mining and Maori history – the visitor centre has information about local **museums**. It also has information about **kayak** hire, **jet-boat** tours and **scenic flights**.

There is good **walking** and **mountain biking** in the Kauaeranga Valley, east of Thames. If you ride out to the DOC visitor centre on Kauaeranga Valley Rd, 13km

from town, you can pick up the pamphlet *Coromandel Recreation Information* and check where mountain bikes are permitted.

The road to the visitor centre continues (unsealed), climbing up the valley to **walking tracks** and camp sites. Transport to walks can also be arranged through Sunkist Lodge (see Places to Stay).

Places to Stay The *Sunkist Lodge* (☎ 07-868 8808, 506 Brown St) was a hotel in the 1860s. It's now a relaxed hostel with dorm beds from $14, doubles for $34 and tent sites. The manager is good for advice on cycling and tramping.

The *Brian Boru Hotel* (☎ 07-868 6523, ✉ Brian.Boru@xtra.co.nz, 200 Richmond St), also from the gold-mining era, is run by the imaginative and entrepreneurial Barbara Doyle. It has singles/doubles from $45/66 in the hotel and modern units from $95/125. Breakfast is from $5. Bikes can be stored inside the units or in a lockable garage.

Motels include the *Crescent Motel* (☎ 07-868 6506, cnr Jellicoe Crescent & Fenton St), with units from $65, and the *Rolleston Motel* (☎ 07-868 8091, 105 Rolleston St), with rooms for $70/85. Both have lock-up garages for bikes.

Places to Eat Pollen St has dozens of quaint little *coffee lounges* and *take aways* plus two bakeries – try the *Thames Bakery and Cafe* (☎ 07-868 7088), near the corner of Pollen and Richmond Sts, or the $4 baked spuds across the road. The coffee is better at *Robert Harris* (☎ 07-868 8656) in the Goldfields Shopping Centre or the stylish *Sealey Cafe* (☎ 07-868 8641), which has attractive lunch ($7.50 to $12) and evening ($19.50 to $23.50) menus. Mid-priced vegie meals are available from the *Gold Bar & Restaurant* (☎ 07-868 5548), as well as the ubiquitous steak (up to $25.50).

Day 1: Thames to Coromandel
2½-4½ hours, 56.3km
The route from Thames to Coromandel is essentially flat for the first 34km as the road winds round the coast on the narrow flat between the sea and mountains passing through a series of pretty little bays. Look out for sea birds in the Firth of Thames.

After the town of Kereta the road turns inland and upward over the shoulder of Mt

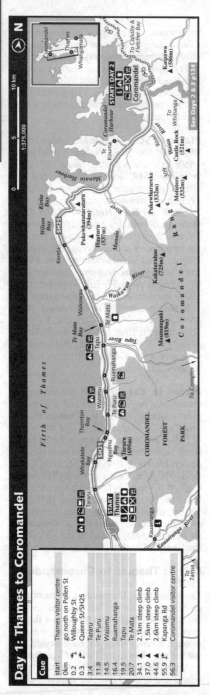

Pukewhakataratara. It climbs steeply for 2.5km to 180m, then descends and rises steeply again to 206m. Enjoy the views of Manaia Harbour and the nearby islands.

Enjoy another steep downhill run and the mangroves around Manaia Harbour, before climbing again to 160m. Once over this hill, it's a nice easy run into Coromandel township.

Side Trip: Colville & Fletcher Bay
1½-3 hours, 28km return to Colville
3-6 hours, 63km return to Fletcher Bay
This is fairly remote country (there are no shops past Colville) and Fletcher Bay is described as a real 'land's end', with deserted beaches and good forest and coastal walking. The hilly road is sealed to Colville, but mountain bikes are recommended if you're going farther north: the road is unsealed, rough and winding (though scenic!).

From SH25, head east from the Coromandel visitor centre on Kapanga Rd, which veers north, becoming the Coromandel-Colville Rd. Return via the same route.

Colville Backpackers & Farmstay (☎ 07-866 6820) and *Fletcher Bay Backpackers* (☎ 07-866 6712) both have tent sites available. The *Colville Caff* is known for its home-made pies, cakes and pastries, and there's also a *wholefood shop*.

Coromandel
Coromandel town was named after HMS *Coromandel*, which visited in 1820 to pick up a load of kauri spars for the Royal Navy. It was here on Driving Creek, 3km north of the township, that Charles Ring discovered gold in 1852. The town's population, more than 10,000 at the height of the gold rush, is less than 1000 today and noted for its alternative lifestylers.

Information The visitor centre (☎ 07-866 8598) is on Kapanga Rd, 300m north-east of the intersection with Tiki Rd. It's open daily from 9 am to 5 pm (weekend hours are 10 am to 2 pm between Easter and October). The centre has many useful leaflets on the surrounding area and takes bookings for accommodation and tours. The DOC field centre in the building has information on parks and walks.

The Bank of New Zealand on the corner of Tiki and Wharf Rds is open on weekdays between 10 am and 3 pm. There is no ATM, but EFTPOS facilities are available at the Four Square Foodmarket on Kapanga Rd.

Things to See & Do Coromandel is in the middle of a region abounding in natural beauty, scenic reserves and attractive **walking**. Pick up the DOC pamphlets *Coromandel Recreation Information* or *Walking in Coromandel* ($1 each). Walks include the Coromandel Walkway from Fletcher Bay to Stony Point and the six-hour return Mt Moehau walk, which traverses the peninsula via Mt Moehau (892m), the highest peak in the range. Coromandel Bus Services (☎ 07-866 8045) runs an on-demand service from Coromandel to Fletcher Bay, as well as special tours to walk the Stony Bay track.

Driving Creek (☎ 07-866 8703), just north of Coromandel, is a pottery run by artist and environmentalist Barry Brickell, who built a railway to transport his clay from the mountains.

Find out about Coromandel's gold-mining days at the **Coromandel Mining & Historic Museum** and the **Coromandel Stamper Battery** (☎ 07-866 8765), both on Rings Rd.

Places to Stay The *Tidewater Tourist Park* (☎ 07-866 8888, 270 Tiki Rd) is modern and clean, with views of the harbour. Tent sites cost $9 per person, dorm beds are $16, and singles/doubles are $26/36. Self-contained accommodation ranges from $70 a double for a tourist flat (own linen required) to $95 for a motel unit.

Other hostels include *Tui Lodge* (☎ 07-866 8237, 600 Whangapoua Rd), *Whitehouse Backpackers* (☎ 07-866 8468, cnr Fredrick St & Rings Rd) and *Coromandel Town Backpackers* (☎ 07-866 8327, 327 Rings Rd).

Rose Cottage (☎ 07-866 7047) on Pagitt St has simple but comfy rooms for $30/55 (more for the room with a king-size bed).

The friendly, smoke-free *Coromandel Court Motel* (☎ 0800 267 626 or ☎ 07-806 8402), behind the visitor centre, has self-contained units at $70/$110.

Places to Eat On Wharf Rd, the *Coromandel Bakehouse* has reasonable bread, pies and cakes. Ask for the organic loaf if you like a heavier bread. The arty *Assay House Craft Cafe* (☎ 07-866 7397, 2 Kaparga Rd)

does breakfast for $7, panini or burgers ($7.50) for lunch, and has reasonable espresso and a range of teas. *Chicks Takeaway* (☎ 07-866 8023) on Kapanga Rd has a good range of take-aways, from fish and chips to roast lamb and vegies ($9.90). The *Castle Rock Eatery* (☎ 07-866 8618, 22 Wharf Rd) is also reasonable value, with baked potatoes, Turkish food and pizzas (from $9.50). Treat yourself to delicious Coromandel green-lipped mussels ($8.50) at the licensed *Success Cafe* (☎ 07-866 7100). Mains here range from $16 to $22, including a vegetarian option.

You can pick up supplies at the **supermarket** on Kapanga Rd or the **natural food shop** on Wharf Rd.

Day 2: Coromandel to Whitianga
3-5 hours, 46.5km

Although Day 2 looks short, it involves some steep climbing on rough dirt roads. There is also a side trip to Whangapoua and some lovely spots to linger on Bluff Rd.

The dirt road on the steep 360m climb over the Coromandel Range is mostly hard-packed, but it's bumpy and can be slippery when wet. However, the views during the 3.5km uphill section provide a number of good excuses for rest stops!

Take care on the descent; it, too, is rough, steep and winding and has moderate amounts of traffic. Apart from the brief respite of some short sealed stretches, there is no chance to get any speed up, especially if you're using narrow tyres. Take advantage of the slow pace and enjoy the magnificent scenery.

The sealed road starts about 7.5km beyond the summit, but is soon to be extended another 4.5km. From here, the riding is back into open farmland and much easier. A good morning tea or lunch spot is at Whangapoua (see Side Trip). There's a *farm produce stall*, but no shops at Te Rerenga.

Leaving SH25 (22.2km), follow signs left to Matarangi, an out-of-place housing estate with a big stone gateway. Fortunately, there's a quick escape into more remote country by taking the first, then second right turn and veering left into Bluff Rd. There is a 2km unsealed section along Bluff Rd, but it's very pleasant riding by the rocks and water's edge. Although the road is narrow and winding, the traffic is light. (Alternatively, continue on SH25 and over a steep hill to Kuaotunu.)

Days 2 & 3: Coromandel-Whitianga-Tairua

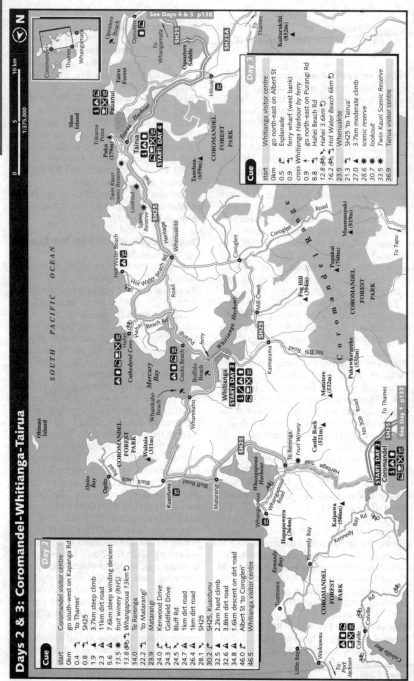

Cue — Day 2

start		Coromandel visitor centre
0km		go south-west on Kapanga Rd
0.4	⤴	'to Thames'
0.8	⤴	SH25
1.9		3.7km steep climb
2.3		11km dirt road
5.6		7.6km steep winding descent
13.5	✳	fruit winery (RHS)
13.8	⤴	Whangapoua 13km ↰
14.0		Te Rerenga
22.2	⤴	'to Matarangi'
23.9		Matarangi
24.0	⤴	Kenwood Drive
24.3	⤴	Goldfield Drive
24.5	⤴	Bluff Rd
24.7	◀	1km dirt road
26.4	◀	1km dirt road
28.1	◀	SH25
30.2	⤴	SH25, Kuaotunu
32.5		2.2km hard climb
32.6		3.8km dirt road
34.8		1.6km descent on dirt road
46.0	⤴	Albert St to Coroglen'
46.5		Whitianga visitor centre

Cue — Day 3

start		Whitianga visitor centre
0km		go north-east on Albert St
0.5	⤴	Esplanade
0.9		ferry wharf (west bank)
		cross Whitianga Harbour by ferry
0.9		go north-east on Purangi Rd
8.8	⤴	Hahei Beach Rd
12.8	✳	Hahei 3.6km ↰
16.2	✳	Hot Water Beach 6km ↰
23.5		Whenuakite
21.3	⤴	SH25 'to Tairua'
27.0		3.7km moderate climb
28.6		scenic reserve
30.7	✳	lookout
33.5	✳	Twin Kauri Scenic Reserve
36.9		Tairua visitor centre

Stop for a snack at the Kuaotunu shop before heading south for more gravel and another big hill. The 2.5km climb is only to 162m this time, but again the road is winding and the surface rough (though quite tightly packed). Being a commuter route between Kuaotunu and Whitianga, this road carries a reasonable amount of traffic, which generally travels faster than the tourists.

It's a relief to hit the sealed road again, 1.5km after the summit, and finish the descent at speed! After passing through the small township of Wharekaho (Simpson's) Beach, there's one more small hill before the flats of Mercury Bay and the town of Whitianga.

Side Trip: Whangapoua
40-60 minutes, 13km return
From the signposted turn-off, 14km east of Coromandel town, the white sandy ocean beach at Whangapoua is an easy ride around the mangroves of Whangapoua Harbour. There's no accommodation, but a *shop* is open daily and the beach walking is good.

Whitianga
Whitianga was first called Whitianga-a-Kupe (Crossing Place of Kupe) after the Polynesian explorer who landed here in 950. Around 800 years later, another great explorer, James Cook observed the transit of Mercury here and named it Mercury Bay.

Whitianga is a tourist town built on the flats surrounding Mercury Bay and the Whitianga Harbour. Much of the town fronts onto Buffalo Beach, named after HMS *Buffalo*, wrecked here in 1840.

Information The Whitianga visitor centre (☎ 07-866 5555, @ wtzvin@nzhost.co.nz),

66 Albert St, is open daily from 8.30 am to 5.30 pm in summer (9 am to 1 pm on weekends during winter).

The Bank of New Zealand and Westpac banks are on Albert St. Catch up on your email at the Heartland Deli & Cybercafe (☎ 07-866 4885) on the corner of Albert and Coghill Sts.

Whitianga Mowers and Cycles (☎ 07-866 5435), 15 Coghill St, has some parts, does repairs and hires out basic 18-speed mountain bikes.

Things to See & Do An interesting little **museum** is opposite the ferry wharf. You can **carve bone** at Bay Carving (☎ 07-866 4021), Racecourse Rd. Buffalo Beach has good **swimming** and there are interesting **walks** in the area – see the visitor centre for details on these and for information about **sea kayaking**, **windsurfing**, **fishing** or swimming with **dolphins**. Treat yourself to a **massage** at the Body Clinic (☎ 07-866 0477), 19 Albert St.

Places to Stay The central *Buffalo Beach Resort* (☎ 07-866 5854) is on Eyre St, off Buffalo Beach Rd (booking, even for tents, is recommended in summer). Tent sites cost $13 per person and chalets are $85 (own bedding required). Prices drop in the off-peak and shoulder seasons.

Coromandel Backpackers Lodge (☎ 07-866 5380, 46 Buffalo Beach Rd) has dorm beds from $16. Rooms with private kitchen are an attractive option at $19 per person – but you'll need to book ahead. The lodge has a garage.

Other hostels include the *Buffalo Peaks Lodge* (☎ 07-866 2933, 12 Albert St) – a Kiwi Experience (bus tour) stopover – and the

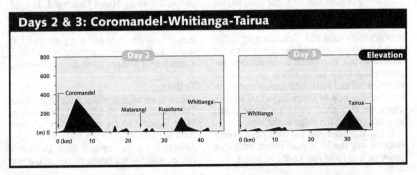

Days 2 & 3: Coromandel-Whitianga-Tairua

AUCKLAND & THE NORTH

Cats Pyjamas (☎ 07-866 4663, 4 Monk St), which also takes tents.

For B&B, *Anne's Haven (☎ 07-866 5550, 119 Albert St)* is reasonable at $35/65 for singles/doubles.

The *Seafari Motel (☎ 07-866 5263, 7 Mill Rd)*, managed by a windsurfing and kayaking instructor, is good value. Self-contained rooms are $50/90 (less in winter). There's also a spa and a garage for bike storage.

Places to Eat The *Mill Kitchen* is a good bakery and deli with pastries, home-made pies and pizza ($3 for a big slice). Opposite the visitor centre, *Rainbows (☎ 07-866 4686)* has Mexican burritos ($6), burgers and ice creams. You can't beat *Cafe Nina (☎ 07-866 5440)* for coffee; it also does weekend breakfasts (from $4.50). Evening mains (around $20) all include 'carbo hit and salad.' *Smittys Bar & Grill (☎ 07-866 4647)* has mid-priced mains and take-aways. The *supermarket* is on Albert St and there's a *bulk food shop* on Coghill St.

Day 3: Whitianga to Tairua
2-3 hours, 36.9km

Day 3 starts with a ferry ride across to Ferry Landing. It takes five minutes, and operates daily from 7.30 am to 10 pm.

The road undulates gently as it passes Maramaratotara Bay, Shakespeare Cliff, Cooks Beach and winds through semirural bushland with glimpses of a picturesque, mangrove-edged inlet.

After Cooks Beach, there are no shops until Tairua, apart from an *orchard stall* advertising devonshire teas, 2km east of the Tairua turn-off. However, don't pass this area without spending time at Hahei, Cathedral Cove and Hot Water Beach (see Side Trips).

Skirting around the hills, the road begins to climb about 5km from Whenuakite, after crossing Whenuakite Stream. It's a reasonably gradual ascent of 3.7km, reaching 220m. Two kilometres short of the top is a **scenic reserve** which, in contrast to the scrubby, regenerating bush surrounding most of the climb, is tall and lush, with a couple of walking tracks – one to Otara Bay (two hours). There are also great views out to the ocean as you're riding the ridge to the top.

It's all downhill past the **Twin Kauri Scenic Reserve** (try the 30 minute return walk to a grove of tree ferns and kauri) to Tairua.

If you're able to push on for another 15km, Hahei, close to Cathedral Cove and Hot Water Beach, is an attractive alternative finishing point.

Side Trip: Hahei & Cathedral Cove
10-20 minutes, 3.6km return

The beaches around Hahei have been described as Coromandel's finest and the two hour walk to Cathedral Cove – a giant natural arch – is one of the area's most popular. Rich in marine life, the waters and islands offshore are protected as the Te Whanganui-A Hei (Cathedral Cove) Marine Reserve.

The Hahei turn-off is 12.8km from Whitianga; Hahei is 1.8km from the turn-off. Here, you can **walk** at low tide to Cathedral Cove (leave at least two hours) or **swim** at Hahei beach. The Hahei Explorer (☎ 07-866 3910) operates **scenic tours** in an inflatable boat from Hahei through the Hahei Marine Reserve and to Hot Water Beach.

Hahei has some excellent accommodation. *Tatahi Lodge (☎ 07-866 3992)*, behind the Hahei Store, has dorms for $18, rooms for $40 and self-contained units at $125. *Hahei Holiday Resort (☎ 07-866 3889)*, right behind the beach on Harsant Ave, has tent sites for $10 per person. Or treat yourself to B&B at *The Church (☎ 07-866 3533, 87 Hahei Beach Rd)*.

Hahei's heart is a *general store* and *take away*. Behind the shop, off Grange Rd, the relaxed *Cafe Luna (☎ 07-866 3016)* is a groovy place for mid-priced meals (pizzas and pastas are $14 to $18), or just stop for cakes, coffee or home-made bread.

Side Trip: Hot Water Beach
20-30 minutes, 6km return

The Hot Water Beach turn-off is 3.5km farther south along Hahei Beach Rd. The ride from here to the beach is 3km. At Hot Water Beach, just below the sand, go two hours either side of low tide and dig your own **natural spa**. *Take care* swimming at the beach: a number of tourists have drowned here.

Tairua

Tairua is an unpretentious, little beach town. The visitor centre (☎ 07-864 7575) is on the Main Rd next to the supermarket. It's open from 8.30 am to 4.30 pm Monday to Saturday (to 2 pm on Sunday) from October to Easter, with shorter hours the rest of the year.

Things to See & Do Climb **Paku**, the old Maori *pa* (fortified village) site and landmark, whose name means 'women's breasts'. According to legend, you'll return in seven years. It also has great views.

Places to Stay & Eat The scenic *Tairua Estuary Holiday Park* (☎ *07-864 8551, 116 Pepe Rd*) has tent sites at $10 per person; cabins or on-site vans are generally $35/40 a single/double, but cost $70 during peak season. *Tairua Backpackers Lodge* (☎ *07-864 8345, 200 Main Rd*) has home-grown vegies and free-range eggs. A dorm bed is $15 and rooms are $20/34. *Hornsea House* (☎ *07-864 8536, 297 Main Rd*) is a homely old kauri farmhouse with B&B for $45/70.

The *Gazebo Cafe* (☎ *07-864 7774*) has budget-priced meals like steaks ($9) or Mexican burritos. The bakery is on the far side of town; instead, try the *Out of the Blue Cafe* (☎ *07-864 8987*) – the coffee is OK, but the berry crumble will definitely keep you going!

Day 4: Tairua to Whangamata
2-3 hours, 36.1km
After Tairua, the road undulates gently along another attractive mangrove-fringed harbour. This road can be quite busy (it links to the main route back to Thames), but the shoulder is generally OK. Take care on the single-lane bridges.

To the west lie the rugged peaks of the Coromandel Range, but (fortunately) the road turns to the south at Hikuai. Over the Tairua River is the turn-off to **Broken Hills**, where you can see relics of former gold mining and kauri-logging eras, or go walking and swimming (get the DOC *Broken Hills* brochure). There's a petrol station and toilets at this turn-off, the last before Whangamata.

The climb up the forested Tramway Gully begins after the SH25A turn-off to Thames (13.8km). The road shoulder is narrow early in the climb, but improves. There's a rest area after about 3km, not far from **Opoutere Saddle** (198m). The road descends to 100m and then undulates for several kilometres. Although it's through pine plantations, the riding is very pleasant.

The **Wharekawa Redwood Picnic Area** (24.4km) makes for a delightful lunch spot. There's a 15 minute walk through the American Redwoods, planted in the 1930s. Alter-

natively, take the turn-off to Opoutere right after the redwood forest (see Side Trip).

After passing through farming country for several kilometres (pick up supplies at the well stocked *orchard stall* south of the Wharekawa River), the route passes through the **Tairua pine forest** and then through the sprawling southern end of Whangamata.

Side Trip: Opoutere
20-30 minutes, 6km return
At undeveloped Opoutere, 3km east of SH25, is the **Wharekawa Wildlife Refuge** – breeding ground of the endangered NZ dotterel and the variable oystercatcher. There is also a fine beach and plenty of walks. From the main route, the turn-off, about 11km north of Whangamata, is signposted.

There are no shops, but *camp sites* and *YHA accommodation* are available.

Whangamata
Whangamata is a sprawling beach resort town whose population swells over the summer holiday period. It's the last beach town on the Coromandel Peninsula before you head inland, so enjoy the water!

Information The visitor centre (☎ 07-865 8340) is on Port Rd. It's open Monday to Saturday from 9 am to 5 pm and Sunday from 10 am to 4 pm (1 pm in winter).

Westpac and the Bank of New Zealand are on Port Rd, as is Whangamata Mowers & Cycles (☎ 07-865 8096), which looks like it's geared more for mowers than cycles.

Bartley Internet & Graphics (☎ 07-865 8832) is above Slipper Four Square at 712 Port Rd.

Things to See & Do North of Whangamata is Tairua Forest, great **mountain biking** country. The pine forest is privately managed by Carter Holt Harvey, which has a long-term lease on the land. You must obtain a permit (which includes a map) from the company before you ride there ($5 for two weeks), available from Whangamata and Tairua visitor centres, or from the Tairua Forest headquarters, about 6km north of Whangamata on SH25. You can also get maps here.

Whangamata has a popular **surf beach** (be careful of the strong rip) and there's some good **walking**, including guided walks in summer. Ask at the visitor centre for details

Days 4 & 5: Tairua-Whangamata-Thames

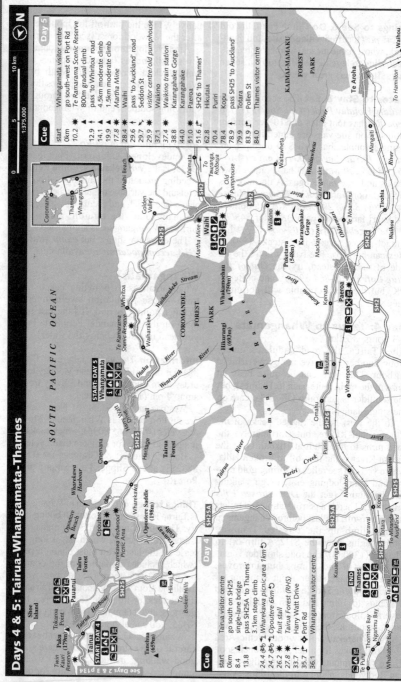

0	5	10 km

1:375,000

N

Cue — Day 5

start	Whangamata visitor centre
0km	go south-west on Port Rd
10.2	Te Ramarama Scenic Reserve
	800m gradual climb
12.9	pass 'to Whiritoa' road
14.1	4.5km moderate climb
19.9	1.5km moderate climb
17.8	Martha Mine
28.4	Waihi
29.6	pass 'to Auckland' road
29.7	Seddon St
29.9	visitor centre/old pumphouse
37.1	Waikino
37.4	Waikino train station
38.8	Karangahake Gorge
44.0	Karangahake
51.0	Paeroa
51.6	SH26 to Thames'
62.8	Hikutaia
70.4	Puriri
78.4	Kopu
78.9	pass SH25 to Auckland'
79.9	Totara
83.9	Pollen St
84.0	Thames visitor centre

Cue — Day 4

start	Tairua visitor centre
0km	go south on SH25
8.4	single-lane bridge
13.8	pass SH25A 'to Thames'
	3.1km steep climb
24.4	Wharekawa picnic area 1km
24.7	Opoutere 6km
26.2	fruit stall
27.8	Tairua Forest (RHS)
33.7	Harry Watt Drive
35.7	Port Rd
36.1	Whangamata visitor centre

and for information on **kayaking, windsurfing** or **game fishing**.

Places to Stay The pleasant *Pinefield Holiday Park* (☎ *07-865 8791, 207-227 Port Rd)* has tent sites for $11 per person ($10 in winter), standard cabins (own linen required, share facilities) at $15 per person, and cabins/flats for $45/65 a double (minimum stays apply in peak periods).

The clean and modern *Bedshed Tourist Lodge* (☎ *07-865 9580, cnr Port Rd & Mayfair Ave)* has excellent backpacker accommodation at $18 per person in a dorm ($23 over Christmas and holiday weekends), $55 for doubles and $85 for motel-style units ($120 over Christmas).

Sandy Rose (☎ *07-865 6911,* ✉ *sandyrose@ whangamata.co.nz, 122 Hetherington Rd)* is a lovely, smoke-free B&B with singles/ doubles for $65/95 and a lockable garage.

Places to Eat Whangamata has plenty of take-away joints: for meals under $10, try *La Hacienda* (☎ *07-865 8351, 630 Port Rd)*, with a Mexican menu; *Gingers Health Food and Cafe* (☎ *07-865 7265, 601 Port Rd)*; the *Carvery Cafe* (☎ *07-865 7315, 71 Port Rd)*; or pizza from the *Roundabout Takeaway* (☎ *07-865 8296, 800 Port Rd)*.

The fully licensed *Neros* (☎ *07-865 6300, 711 Port Rd)* is a trendy cafe opposite Slippers Four Square, with mains from $16 to $18, including pastas and vegetarian. *Pinky's* (☎ *07-865 9961)*, a few doors down, is similarly priced with a bar and more traditional roasts and seafood.

The *Port Road Bakery* is on the corner of Winifred Ave and Port Rd, and there is an excellent *bulk food shop* at the pedestrian crossing.

Day 5: Whangamata to Thames
4-7 hours, 84km

The climbing is all in the first third of Day 5. Leaving the coast, there's a gradual climb through Te Ramarama Scenic Reserve, before a more serious 4.5km climb up to Whiritoa/Waihi Saddle (236m). Traffic is heavier on SH2 between Waihi and Paeroa – and can be hairy through the narrow Karangahake Gorge.

Heading inland, the towns are less touristy and more industrial – this is mining country. First discovered at Waihi in 1878, gold is still mined today from **Martha Mine**.

The **Waihi visitor centre**, next to the towering old pumphouse, also houses a display and propaganda from the Waihi Gold Mining Company. Mine tours run during the week.

The spectacular **Karangahake Gorge** was the site of the gold rush in 1875. Walks in the area include a 6km walkway and tunnel through the gorge, along which you could walk your bike if traffic is unbearable (otherwise, spend an hour or two in Waikino at the eastern end of the gorge until it eases). The visitor centre at Waikino's old train station also has historical information.

Paeroa's claim to fame is the national soft drink **Lemon & Paeroa**, or L&P, which was originally made with Paeroa spring water. Though it's no longer manufactured here, every take away in the long main street advertises the drink and there's a giant L&P bottle by the SH26 turn-off to Te Aroha.

The *Belmont Bakery* and *Tui Coffee Lounge* are on Belmont Rd at Nos 15 and 18. The *Paeroa Motel* (☎ *07-862 8475)* has rooms from $25.

The last 32km along SH26 to Thames is through gently undulating farmland, with the Coromandel Range to the east.

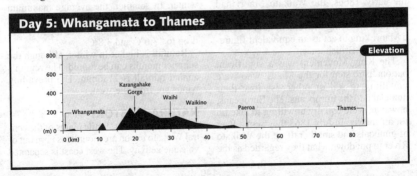

Day 5: Whangamata to Thames

Elevation

Karangahake Gorge

Waihi

Waikino

Paeroa

Thames

Whangamata

Waikato & King Country

The Waikato, one of the world's richest dairy, thoroughbred and agricultural areas, has large fertile plains with rugged mountain ranges to the south, east and west. Hamilton is the region's service centre and New Zealand's fifth largest city. The country's longest river, the Waikato, flows past on its way from Lake Taupo to the west coast of the North Island.

Further south is the historic region known as King Country, named after the Maori King Movement that developed in the Waikato during the 1850s and 1860s. King Country roughly encompasses the land to the south and west of Mt Pirongia, and south and east of Otorohanga (to Taumarunui and Lake Taupo).

Apart from the Waitomo Caves, the region is not particularly touristy; the roads are mostly quiet and some parts can feel quite remote and isolated. The west, in particular, has some beautiful rugged scenery and lots of interesting natural features. East of Hamilton, the cycle tourist is in for a taste of NZ pastoral life.

HISTORY

Prior to European colonisation, Maori used the fertile land of the Waikato region extensively for cultivation of *kumara* (sweet potato) and other crops. European missionaries introduced European crops and farming methods to the region during the 1830s and Maori began trading with European settlers in Auckland over the next decade.

However, relations between the two cultures gradually soured, largely due to the Europeans' desire to settle Maori land. By the early 1860s, the Waikato Maori had united in their dealings with the Europeans, forming the 'King Movement' and electing a Maori king to act as an equivalent figurehead to the British queen.

The King Movement was a significant nationalistic step for the Maori, who were unwilling to sell or otherwise lose their homeland to the Europeans. The Europeans, however, were equally unwilling to take no for an answer. In July 1863 they sent a fleet of gunboats and small craft up the Waikato River to put down what they regarded as the

In Summary

Area Code: ☎ 03

Highlights
- **Natural limestone formations** and **fossils** along Marokopa Road
- **Otorohanga Kiwi House** – New Zealand's largest walk-through aviary
- Stalactites and glow-worms at **Waitomo Caves**
- **Kawhia** – Puia Hot Springs and Maori culture
- **Bridal Veil Falls** on Kawhia Rd

Special Events
- **National Agricultural Fieldays** (June), Mystery Creek

Cycling Events
- **Hamilton to Whangamata** (November)

Terrain

Flat plains bounded by rugged ranges to the west and rolling hills to the east.

'open rebellion' of the Maori. After almost a year of warfare, known as the Waikato Wars, the Europeans finally won in April 1864 and the Maori retreated south to King Country, where Europeans dared not venture for several more decades.

CLIMATE

The weather in this region is generally warm to hot in summer and cool to mild in winter. In summer, the average maximum and minimum temperatures are 23.8°C and 12.7°C respectively. In winter the averages drop to 13.6°C and 3.8°C.

Rainfall is higher in winter, although the summer months can be humid. The region's annual rainfall is 1186mm. The prevailing winds are from the west.

NATURAL HISTORY

Surrounding the flat, fertile plains of the central Waikato region are mountains born out of volcanic activity. The west coast is separated

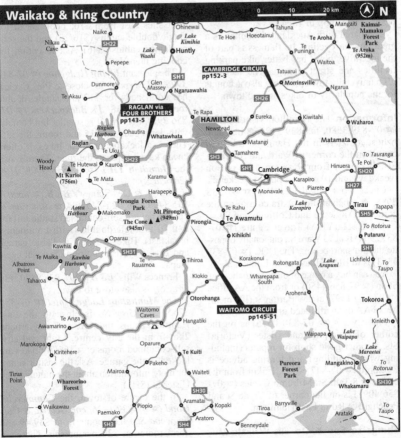

Waikato & King Country

from the plains by rugged ranges, still partly covered in dense podocarp forest. The coast is largely inaccessible, except via the wide, shallow Raglan, Aotea and Kawhia Harbours, where wading birds feed on the mudflats.

The dense bush of Pirongia Forest Park is home to the rare kokako and other birds; there are a number of walking tracks to the summit of Mt Pirongia (962m).

The Waitomo district south of Pirongia is famous for the limestone caves and rock formations that riddle the area; in fact, the Maori name Waitomo literally means 'water running out of a hole' (*wai* means 'water' and *tomo* means 'hole, or shaft').

In the Waitomo area, limestone is buried beneath the earth's surface, under layers of sandstone and mudstone. Cracks and faults have enabled surface water, containing dissolved carbon dioxide to corrode the soluble limestone, eventually forming caves and other shaped features over tens of thousands of years. Several limestone features can be seen along the Marokopa Rd. Though only small sections remain, lowland forest once covered the Waitomo's mountainous areas, while forest grew in the valleys.

GATEWAY CITIES
Hamilton

Built on the Waikato River (the only transport and communication link for early European settlers), Hamilton is NZ's largest inland city. While the area had long been settled by Maori, it was deserted when Europeans set up shop in 1864.

Compared with Auckland, Hamilton is a great city for cycling. Its flatness is part of the incentive, but it has better bike parking facilities and street signage. The fact that it's a university town probably also accounts for the popularity of bikes around town.

Information The Hamilton visitor centre (☎ 07-839 3580, fax 839 3127, ☻ hlzvin@ nzhost.co.nz) is in the Hamilton transport centre on the corner of Ward and Anglesea Sts. It's open from 9 am to 4.45 pm on weekdays and 10 am to 2 pm on weekends.

Check your email at MBE (☎ 07-838 2998, ☻ mbehamilton@xtra.co.nz), on the corner of Anglesea and Collingwood Sts.

The USIT (YHA) Travel Centre (☎ 07-839 2944) is at 73 Ward St, diagonally opposite the transport centre. The DOC (☎ 07-838 3363) is in BDO House at 18 London St.

You can buy a range of maps from the Map Shop (☎ 07-856 4450) or from the AA office (☎ 07-839 1397) at 259 Barton St (if a member of AA or an affiliated organisation).

Pins Cycles (☎ 07-838 0575) is on the corner of Liverpool and Ulster (Victoria) Sts. Another good shop for repairs (including wheel building) and touring advice is Cyclepro (☎ 07-847 5677), 1.5km from the centre at 8 Tahi St. Milremo Cycles (☎ 07-856 4092) is on the corner of Clyde St and Peachgrove Rd in East Hamilton.

Things to See & Do The **Waikato Museum of Art & History** (☎ 07-838 6606), on the corner of Victoria and Grantham Sts, includes a good Maori collection and the **Science and Technology Exhibition Centre**. Check out the **Mormon Temple** (☎ 07-847 8601) – the first to be established by the Church of Latter-Day Saints in the South Pacific. It's 7.7km from the city centre on Tuhikaramea Rd (see Day 1 of the Waitomo Circuit for directions).

Ride along the river to the huge **Hamilton Gardens** complex or go to the **Hamilton Zoo**.

The historic **paddleboat** MV *Waipa Delta* runs cruises from Memorial Park. It's best to book (☎ 07-854 7813). The visitor centre has details of other activities.

Places to Stay The *Municipal Motor Camp* (☎ 07-855 8255) on Ruakura Rd in Claudelands is 2km east of the city centre. Tent sites cost from $10; book ahead for single/double cabins ($16/25) and the self-contained cabins ($46). Ask reception for cooking utensils.

The pleasant *Flying Hedgehog* (☎ 07-839 3906, 8 Liverpool St), close to Pins Cycles, has dorm beds for $17 and singles/double rooms for $30/38. *J's Backpackers* (☎ 07-856 8934, 8 Grey St) is smaller but homely, with dorm beds for $15 and rooms for $35. There's a lockable shed for bikes. It offers cheap kayak trips on the river. There's also the *Hamilton YHA* (☎ 07-838 0009, 1190 Victoria St).

Marion & Des Slaney's *B&B* (☎/fax 07-855 3426 or ☎ 025-815 404, ☻ slaney.dm@ xtra.co.nz) is a self-contained studio loft for $40/70 a single/double (with continental breakfast). Bikes go in a lockable garage and Des, a cyclist, can provide local cycle maps.

Frances Wills' *B&B* (☎ 07-838 2120, 530 Grey St) is also close to town.

The *Manhattan Lodge Motel* (☎ 07-856 3785, 218 Grey St) is close to the East Hamilton shops, the river and only around 2km from the city centre. Light and airy, self-contained rooms cost $65/76; bikes are locked in the garage. Ask the visitor centre for more information about the motels along Ulster St (SH1).

In the centre of town, the *Commercial Hotel* (☎ 07-839 1226, cnr Victoria & Collingwood Sts) has rooms from $39/49 and dorm rooms at $20 per person. There's a shed for bikes.

Places to Eat Victoria St has a number of restaurants and cafes. *Rockets* (☎ 07-839 6422, 109 Victoria St) roasts and serves the best coffee in town, along with filled focaccias ($5.50), pizza and muffins. The *Sahara Tent Cafe & Bar* (☎ 07-834 0409, 254 Victoria St) has mains from $15, with very international fare. *Barzurk* (250 Victoria St) has gourmet pizzas for around $17 and has pastas from $14. The *Cobb & Co* (☎ 07-839 1226), adjoining the Commercial Hotel, serves breakfast lunch and dinner, with standard pub mains from $14 to $19. *Bayon Cambodian Cafe* (☎ 07-839 0947, 783 Victoria St) has mains from $8 to $15. There's also *Gilles French Bakery & Patisserie* (511 Victoria St).

For great value, try the large $6 helpings at the *Chinese Healthy Vegetarian Food* (☎ *07-838 0805)*, 100m west of the transport centre on Ward St.

The closest supermarket to the visitor centre is *Foodtown* on the corner of Bryce and Tristram Sts.

Getting There & Away The visitor centre has information bus and train services and sells tickets.

Bus Buses arrive and depart Hamilton from the transport centre on the corner of Ward and Anglesea Sts.

The Little Kiwi Bus Company (☎ 0800 759 999) runs services between Auckland and Rotorua via Hamilton. A one-way fare to Hamilton from Auckland is $17 plus $5 for a bike. InterCity (☎ 09-913 6100) runs services between Hamilton and Auckland ($27), Rotorua ($24), Thames ($22), and Wellington ($75) via Wanganui or Taupo. Bikes cost $10 per service.

Train The Tranz Scenic (☎ 0800 802 802) *Overlander* and *Northerner* (overnight) services between Auckland and Wellington stop at Hamilton. Standard one-way fares are $36 and $32, respectively. Bikes cost $10. Book well in advance to be sure of a place.

The train station is on Fraser St, about 1.8km west of the visitor centre.

Raglan via Four Brothers

Duration	2½-4 hours
Distance	46.9km
Difficulty	moderate
Start	Hamilton
End	Raglan

Raglan is Hamilton's closest beach and its harbour is one of the few spots to access the rugged west coast. The ride follows SH23, passing the Four Brothers Scenic Reserve. The return trip can be done in a day, but Raglan is definitely worth an overnight stop.

PLANNING
When to Ride
During Christmas and holiday peak seasons, the road (and Raglan) is busy with holiday-makers. Early summer and February to May are likely to be the most pleasant times of the year.

What to Bring
There are few services between Hamilton and Raglan, so carry food and water.

GETTING TO/FROM THE RIDE
Bus
Pavlovich Coachlines (☎ 07-847 5545) runs a limited weekday service between Raglan and Hamilton ($5 one way, bikes free). Buses depart from outside the visitor centre.

Bicycle
This ride links directly with the Waitomo Circuit via the rugged Kawhia Rd, which is best suited to mountain bikes. An overnight stop in Raglan is recommended. See the 'Alternative Route to Kawhia' boxed text later in the chapter.

THE RIDE
Once through the Hamilton suburbs, the road undulates gently to Whatawhata, after which the shoulder narrows and the traffic diminishes somewhat. A 3km steady climb leads to the **Four Brothers Scenic Reserve**. This popular spot is worth a stop, if only for a drink, or you can do a one hour walk. Haul your bike into the bush and lock it to a tree.

There are spectacular views of the deeply carved and denuded valley as you wind down the other side of the hill. The road continues to roll to Raglan, with some great views of the harbour on the way into town.

Raglan
Raglan (population 1550) is a relaxed, charming little town on sheltered Raglan Harbour, which is popular for windsurfing, boating and swimming. The town is world famous for its surfing. Manu Bay, an ocean beach 8km west of Raglan, is said to have the longest left-hand break in the world. Featured in the 1966 cult surfing film *Endless Summer*, this beach was where a surfer rode a wave for 10 minutes.

Information The visitor centre (☎ 07-825 0556) is at the beach end of Bow St.

Raglan Power Machinery (☎ 07-825 8889), around the corner on Wainui Rd, has basic bike parts.

WAIKATO & KING COUNTRY

Raglan via Four Brothers & Day 1: Hamilton to Kawhia

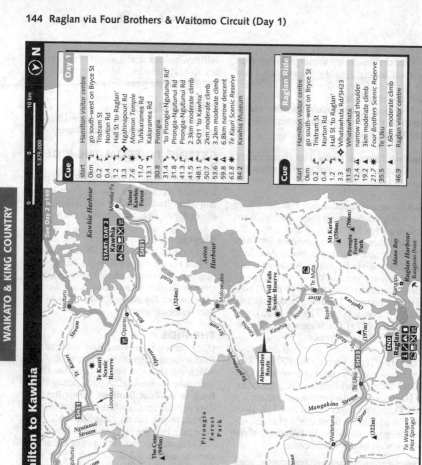

See Day 2 p149

Cue — Day 1

start		Hamilton visitor centre
0km		go south-west on Bryce St
0.2	↰	Tristram St
0.4	↱	Norton Rd
1.2	↰	Hall St to Raglan'
3.3	↱	Ngahinapouri Rd
7.6	✷	*Mormon Temple*
11.0	↱	Tuhikaramea Rd
13.1	↰	Kakaramea Rd
30.8	▲	Pirongia
31.4	↰	'to Pirongia–Ngutunui Rd'
31.8	↰	Pirongia–Ngutunui Rd
41.3	↰	Pirongia–Ngutunui Rd
41.5	▲	2.3km moderate climb
48.1	↱	SH31 to Kawhia'
50.7	▲	2km moderate climb
53.6	▲	3.2km moderate climb
59.8	▲	6.8km narrow descent
63.8	✷	Te Kauri Scenic Reserve
84.2		Kawhia Museum

Cue — Raglan Ride

start		Hamilton visitor centre
0km		go south-west on Bryce St
0.2	↰	Tristram St
0.4	↱	Norton Rd
1.2	↰	Hall St to Raglan'
3.3	✧	Whatawhata Rd/SH23
11.5	▲	narrow road shoulder
12.4	▲	3km moderate climb
19.2	✷	Four Brothers Scenic Reserve
21.7	▲	
35.5		Te Uku
	▲	1.6km moderate climb
46.9		Raglan visitor centre

Things to See & Do Visit the small **museum** on Wainui Rd, or walk down to the jetty around sunset to see the **fishing trawlers** return with the day's catch. Raglan has several **beaches**, including sheltered, safe **swimming** beaches and ocean **surf** beaches. Ask at the visitor centre for directions. The visitor centre can also tell you about **walks** in the area, including the two hour one-way climb up Mt Karioi, **harbour cruises** and other various activities such as **sky diving**.

Places to Stay & Eat The *Kopua Holiday Park* (☎ 07-825 8283) is across the estuary from town (take the path south of the jetty and cross the footbridge). Tent sites are $8 per person, but you'll need your own cooking gear. Chalets (bunkrooms) cost $20/40 for a single/double, self-contained cabins are $40 and units from $50.

Phone ahead for the pleasant and friendly *Raglan Backpackers & Waterfront Lodge* (☎ 07-825 0515, 6 Nero St). Dorm beds cost $14 and doubles $16 per person.

The colourful, friendly *Palm Beach Motel* (☎ 07-825 8153) is 1km from town along Wainui Rd. Rooms start at $75. The *Harbour View Hotel* (☎ 07-825 8010, 14 Bow St) has rooms for $35/50.

Vinnies (☎ 07-825 7273, 7 Wainui Rd) is a cheerful place with a blackboard menu. Mains cost around $16 – try the vegetarian lasagne or pizzas. *Tongue & Groove* (☎ 07-825 0027), on the corner of Wainui Rd, has good coffee, muffins, panini and mains for $16. The *bakery* opposite the visitor centre is reputed to have the best fish and chips.

The *Four Square* supermarket is on Bow St and a *bulk food store* on Wainui Rd.

Waitomo Circuit

Duration	3 days
Distance	254.3km
Difficulty	moderate-hard
Start/End	Hamilton

A scenic ride from the plains through rugged ranges to the wide, flat harbours of the west coast this ride is through some of the North Island's most remote country. Natural wonders abound en route, culminating in the magnificent glow-worm caves

at Waitomo. These caves are regarded as one of the most amazing places to see in NZ. There's a range of caving activities on offer – and it's worth spending an extra day or two here to explore them properly.

On Day 1, the main route follows a sealed road all the way from Hamilton to Kawhia. For those on mountain bikes, however, an alternative option is to ride to Kawhia via Raglan (see the Raglan & the Four Brothers ride for the route description to Raglan). From Raglan, the 'Alternative Route to Kawhia' boxed text describes the hilly route to Kawhia, 26km of which are on rough unsealed road. This option is also possible on a touring bike, but very slow.

HISTORY

The tiny town of Kawhia was one of the earliest settlements for both the Maori and Europeans, who arrived in the mid-1820s. The Tainui people regard the area as their spiritual home, having arrived here in the *Tainui* canoe during the 14th century. Both the Tainui navigators and James Cook, however, missed the narrow entrance to this large harbour the first time around.

A number of tiny townships along this ride's route were once important service centres for this relatively isolated region, both for farmers and those making the journey inland from the coast.

The Waitomo Caves had been known to the Maori for a long time, but the first European to explore it was Fred Mace, who was shown the cave in 1887 by Maori chief Tane Tinorau. Mace prepared an account (presented with a map and photographs) of the expedition for the government and before long Tane Tinorau was operating tours of the cave.

NATURAL HISTORY

Volcanic action formed a couple of dominant peaks in the area, notably Mt Karioi (756m), close to the coast south-west of Raglan, and twin peaks Mt Pirongia (959m) and The Cone (945m), to the south-east.

The area around Waitomo is riddled with limestone caves and rock formations. It's worth stopping at the series of interesting limestone formations along Marokopa Rd (Day 2). The conditions in the Waitomo Caves are almost perfect for glow-worm growth, so there is a remarkable number of them. The Waitomo Museum of Caves has further information about the geology of the area.

PLANNING
When to Ride
From November to April is the best time for this ride, when the days are long enough to spend time at places of interest and the weather is warm enough to swim. There's likely to be holiday traffic driving to the west coast, particularly between Christmas and the end of January.

Maps & Books
Pick up the interesting and free *Best of the West Heritage Trail* brochure from visitor centres for points of interest and the history of the King Country Coast.

What to Bring
Carry plenty of food and water on Day 2 – there are few places to stock up. Also bring a torch to explore the Piripiri caves.

THE RIDE
Day 1: Hamilton to Kawhia
5½-7 hours, 84.2km
The scenic ride to the sleepy port of Kawhia is likely to be a reasonably long day, but not as hard as it could be. This route is on sealed roads with some moderate climbs after Pirongia, but the alternative (see the boxed text) features 27km of dirt roads and several hard climbs.

Just outside Hamilton is a **Mormon Temple**, the first to be established in the South Pacific. The road undulates gently between farms and fields to **Pirongia**, a small town founded as Alexandra in 1864 to guard land confiscated after the Waikato Wars.

After the town the route, which has been skirting the base of Pirongia mountain, heads into some moderate hills once on Pirongia-Ngutunui Rd and into the ranges that separate the plains from the west coast. From the top of the climb beyond the SH31 junction there are fabulous views of the surrounding creased valleys and harbour. Although traffic is light, take care because the road is narrow and winding. There's a rest and **lookout** area (59.1km) and a couple of scenic reserves along the way, including the **Te Kauri Scenic Reserve** (63.8km) with marked walking tracks.

Alternative Route to Kawhia

For the more intrepid, this 53.6km alternative route to Day 1 of the Waitomo Circuit traverses the beautiful remote coastal country of Waikato on rough, partially unsealed and hilly roads. Make sure you have food and lots of water, and don't underestimate the time required to cover the unsealed section. Count on taking between five and seven hours for the whole trip.

From Raglan, backtrack up the hill for 7.6km to the Te Mata Rd turn-off. The road rolls, with one steady climb to Kawhia Rd (a sign here warns that the road is winding for the next 31km!).

At Bridal Veil Falls scenic reserve (21.4km), a pretty 10 minute walk among the ponga ferns to Bridal Veil Falls is worth the detour – you can even wheel your bike to the top of the falls. It's another 10 minutes to the swimming hole below.

The sealed road ends after Bridal Veil Falls. From here to the Kawhia turn-off is tough going, with some serious climbs made slower by the rocky, loose gravel – especially deep on the steep curves. Don't be put off: this road takes you through beautiful wild country and scenic reserves. Take your time and enjoy it!

Kawhia Harbour comes into sight a few kilometres before you hit sealed roads and civilisation again. Now all you need to do is turn right onto SH31 (48.4km) and complete the ride into Kawhia.

The Te Anga turn-off (for tomorrow's ride) is 16km from Kawhia. But for now you can enjoy 5km more downhill and a flat ride round the harbour.

Kawhia
Kawhia is a sleepy little port on the wide and convoluted Kawhia Harbour. The harbour is large, with many extensions, but its entrance is narrow – the occupants of *Tainui* canoe missing it first time down the coast, just as James Cook did in 1770.

Today, Kawhia is still easy to miss, though it gets a few fishing enthusiasts and bathers during summer.

Information The Kawhia Museum (☎ 07-871 0161), near the wharf, doubles as the visitor centre. It's open from noon to 4 pm Wednesday to Friday and 11 am to 4 pm on weekends. Otherwise, try asking at Annie's Cafe (see Places to Stay & Eat).

Things to See & Do The Kawhia Museum has interesting exhibits on the area. While here, ask for permission from a Maori elder to visit the Maketu Marae. It's a pleasant walk from the township along Karewa Beach and past Tangi te Korowhiti, the sacred Po-

hutukawa tree where the *Tainui* canoe landed (see the boxed text).

Puia Hot Springs are accessible two hours either side of low tide at Ocean Beach, 3km behind the town. Here you can dig a hole for your own natural spa. Swimming isn't advisable here; it's better to **swim** in the sheltered harbour by the town.

Places to Stay & Eat The friendly *Beachside Motorcamp* (☎ 07-871 0727, 225 SH31), where tent sites are $7 per person and cabins are $30 a double. Book ahead

The Tainui Canoe

Although it's only a small town, Kawhia has an illustrious history. It was here that the *Tainui* canoe, one of the canoes of the Great Migration of around 1350 AD, made its final landing.

Before the *Tainui* canoe departed from the Maori homeland island of Hawaiki, the priests there prophesied that it would eventually come to a favourable place where its people would make a new home, have a good life and prosper. Their prophecy went something like this:

Te Tauranga mou e Tainui	Your resting place Tainui
Ko te Taihauauru	Is the west coast
Ka whia te mataitai	(There is) an abundance of shellfish
Ka whia te ika	An abundance of fish
Ka whia te kai	An abundance of food

The priests told the leaders of *Tainui* canoe those landmarks that would indicate their new home.

The *Tainui* canoe left Hawaiki, stopping at Easter Island, Raiatea (an island in French Polynesia) and Rarotonga (the principal island of the Cook Islands) as it crossed the Pacific. It landed in New Zealand at Maketu on the Bay of Plenty, accompanied by the *Arawa* canoe. The *Arawa* canoe stopped there, its people becoming the Arawa people, a large Maori tribe that still lives in the Bay of Plenty and Rotorua areas today.

The leaders of the *Tainui* canoe – Hoturoa, the captain, and Rakataura, the expert *tohunga*, or high priest – knew that the *Tainui*'s home was destined to be on the west coast. So the *Tainui* canoe continued on. The story of how it found its final resting place is a long and heroic one.

Seeking, first one way and then another, to get to the west coast, the Tainui people finally dragged their canoe overland at Manukau Harbour, near Auckland. Setting off southwards in search of the prophesied landmarks, they journeyed all the way to the South Island, still without finding their place. They turned around and came north again, still searching, and finally recognised their prophesied new home at Kawhia Harbour.

When they landed the canoe, they tied it to a pohutukawa tree on the shore, naming the tree Tangi te Korowhiti. Although the tree is not marked, it still grows with a few other pohutukawa trees on the shoreline between Kawhia town and the Maketu Marae. At the end of its long voyage, the *Tainui* canoe was dragged up onto a hill and buried. After burying the canoe, Hoturoa and Rakataura placed sacred stones at either end to mark its resting place. Hani, on higher ground, is the stone marking the bow of the canoe, and Puna, the lower stone, marks the stern. These sacred stones are still there (behind the marae), a powerful remembrance to the Tainui people.

The prophecy did come true. Kawhia Harbour was abundant with shellfish, fish and food.

Today, the Tainui tribe extends over the entire Waikato region and surrounding districts. And Kawhia, the Maketu Marae and the burial place of *Tainui* are all most sacred.

during summer holidays. *Rosamond House* (☎ *07-871 0681)*, on Rosamond Terrace, is the historic kauri villa on the hill. B&B costs $45/65 for a single/double; evening meals can be arranged for $15. The *Kawhia Motel* (☎ *07-871 0865, cnr Jervois & Tainui Sts)* charges $57/67 for a self-contained room and will store bikes in the shed.

Annie's Cafe (☎ *07-871 0198)*, on Jervois St, opens daily and in the evenings according to demand. You can get lasagne and salad for $5, sandwiches and snacks. Evening mains are $14. There's also fresh *fish and chips* at the wharf, and a *pub* on the corner of Jervois St.

For self-caterers, there are slim pickings from the two *general stores*.

Day 2: Kawhia to Waitomo
6-7½ hours, 89.9km

Start early to allow plenty of time for exploring the rocks, caves and reserves along Marokopa Rd.

The early part of the ride is pancake flat round the harbour's edge, but becomes increasingly hilly as it crosses from one valley into the next. There are few services en route and despite several tiny settlements, civilisation feels left behind. After **Hauturu** (22.4km) the road (partially) ascends an impressive looking rocky outcrop; despite its appearance, this is not a hard climb.

The road periodically returns to the water along the convoluted edges of Kawhia Harbour. After Kinohaku (40.6km), a long climb up the valley is followed by a swift drop into the next one and a ride along the river flats to Te Anga.

Surrounded by mountains, the village of **Te Anga** is picturesque. Stop for a drink at the *tavern*, where the locals are friendly but the service is unlikely to be express.

The 10 minute return walk to the **Marokopa Falls** (59km) is worthwhile. Alternatively, 200m further on it's possible to see the falls from the side of the road. More natural beauties are in store over the next 5km. At the **Piripiri Caves** (60.6km) you can do a 10 minute (return) walk to the caves or go further to the giant oyster fossils (one hour). Bring a torch. The **Mangapohue Natural Bridge Scenic Reserve** (64.4km) has a 25 minute return walk to the giant natural limestone bridge formation, complete with stalactites and glow-worms (visible at night).

The scenery continues for the remaining ride to Waitomo, with fabulous views of the valleys and plains to the south and west. The day ends with a glorious 10km downhill run into Waitomo.

Waitomo

Waitomo is a pleasant little village that exists largely to cater for the tourists visiting the caves – and you shouldn't leave here without doing just that. Here's what the first explorers had to say:

> We had fallen upon a 'wonderland'. The sight that met our view was enchanting. Fairyland was before us. Away down, near what appeared to be its very depths was a large plateau of moss and ferns, but so far down that they appeared only small topped matter showing all the tints of green. As we looked we more than half expected to see the pixies come dancing out. This is no imagination. It was fairyland without the fairies.

> *King Country Chronicle*
> 16 December 1906

Information The visitor centre is at the Museum of Caves (☎ 07-878 7640, fax 878 6184, ✉ waitomomuseum@xtra.co.nz), which is also the post office. It's open daily from 8 am to 5.30 pm in summer (till 8 pm in January) and 8.30 am to 5 pm in winter.

Things to See & Do The **Museum of Caves** has excellent exhibits about the formation, flora, fauna and history of the caves. The $4 entry is often included in the cost for other activities.

Woodlyn Park (☎/fax 07-878 6666), 1.1km from Waitomo on Waitomo Valley Rd, is a typical NZ farm and has a show with trained farm animals. The **Ohaki Maori Cultural Centre** is about 1km east of the museum. There's a one hour walk from the car park to a **pre-European pa** (fortified Maori village) **site**.

The visitor centre has an excellent summary of the various **caving activities** on offer, from a 45 minute tour of the **glow-worm cave** to **black water rafting** and a 1½ day **adventure** involving abseiling, walking and swimming. For serious caving, contact the **Tomo Group** (☎ 07-878 7442), NZ's largest caving club; you'll pass the hut on the way down the hill into Waitomo.

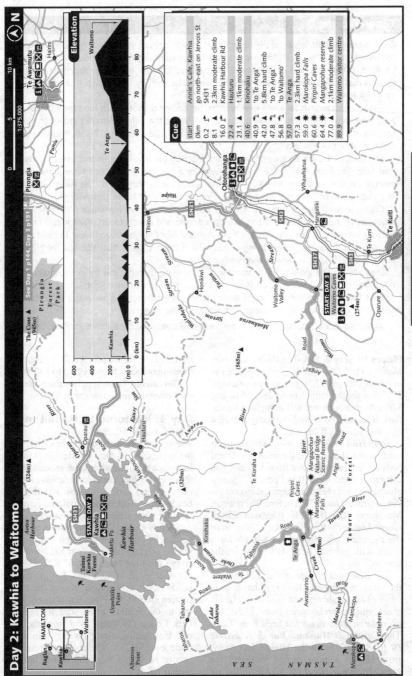

WAIKATO & KING COUNTRY

Day 2: Kawhia to Waitomo

See Day 1 p144, Day 3 p151

Elevation

Cue		
start		Annie's Cafe, Kawhia
0km		go north-east on Jervois St
0.2		SH31
8.1		2.3km moderate climb
16.0		Kawhia Harbour Rd
22.4		Hauturu
23.1		1.1km moderate climb
40.6		Kinohaku
40.9		'to Te Anga'
42.0		5.8km hard climb
47.8		'to Te Anga'
56.8		'to Waitomo'
57.0		Te Anga
57.3		2.3km hard climb
59.0		Marokopa Falls
60.6		Piripiri Caves
64.4		Mangapohue reserve
77.0		2.1km moderate climb
89.9		Waitomo visitor centre

Glow-Worms

Glow-worms are the larvae of the fungus gnat, which looks much like a large mosquito without mouth parts. The larval glow-worms have luminescent organs that produce a soft, greenish light. Living in a sort of 'hammock' suspending from an overhang, they weave sticky threads that trail down and catch unwary insects attracted by their lights. After an insect is caught it is reeled by in the thread and eaten.

The larval stage lasts for six to nine months, depending on how much food the glow-worm gets – the more food, the quicker it can mature. When the glow-worm has grown to about the size of a matchstick it goes into a pupa stage, much like a cocoon. The adult fungus gnat emerges about two weeks later.

The adult of the species may be caught and eaten by the larval glow-worm. Even if it avoids that fate, the adult insect does not live very long because it does not have a mouth; it emerges, mates, lays eggs and dies, all within about two or three days. The sticky eggs, laid in groups of 40 or 50, hatch in about three weeks to become larval glow-worms.

Glow-worms thrive in moist, dark caves, but they can survive anywhere if they have the requisites of moisture, an overhang to suspend from and insects to eat. Waitomo is famous for its glow-worms, but you can see them in many other places around New Zealand, both in caves and outdoors. Similar glow-worms exist in south-eastern Australia, but the NZ variety is a distinct species, *Arachnocampa luminosa*.

Don't touch the glow-worms' hammocks or hanging threads, and try not to make loud noises or shine a light directly on them – it causes them to dim their lights and it'll take the lights a few hours to become bright again, during which time the glow-worm will catch no food. The glow-worms that shine most brightly are the hungriest.

Places to Stay & Eat The *Waitomo Caves Holiday Park* (☎ 07-878 7639), opposite the museum, charges $7.50 per person for a tent, $20/35 a single/double in basic cabins, and $70 a double in newer self-contained tourist flats. Bikes can be locked in a garage at night or while you're off caving.

Juno Hall (☎ 07-878 7649) is on the main road, about 1km east of the museum. Dorm beds are $17, doubles are from $21 and you can pitch a tent for $10 per person. There's also rustic (and cheap) accommodation at the *Tomo Group Hut*, 1.7km before Waitomo on Marokopa Rd. *Dalziels Waitomo Caves Guest Lodge* (☎ 07-878 7641), 100m from the museum, has B&B from $40/60 for a room with private bath. Bikes go in the garage.

The *Blackwater Cafe*, about 1.5km from the museum, opposite Juno Hall has a good range of reasonably priced food like calzone, pizza, quiche or lasagne, from $3.50. It's open daily, from breakfast until 8 or 9 pm. The *Cavelands Waitomo Bar & Brasserie* (☎ 07-878 7700), in the village, has mains from $8; for a more formal meal, try the grand *Waitomo Hotel* (☎ 07-878 8204) on

the hill. Devonshire teas are $3.50 and traditional mains cost from $19.50 to $22.50.

You can buy basic supplies from the *general store* or the visitor centre.

Day 3: Waitomo to Hamilton

4½-6½ hours, 80.2km

The return ride to Hamilton briefly rejoins the route used on Day 1 (after 30.1km) before once again treading new ground. While there route has considerable undulation, there are no serious climbs and the road heads through open and populated farmland – rather tame after the previous day.

There's a short, and reasonable unsealed section as you leave Waitomo. Soon afterwards, you can take a detour to Otorohanga where the **Kiwi House** (☎ 07-873 7391) is considered one of NZ's best. The main route heads north to Pirongia, round the northeastern side of Mt Pirongia. Walkers heading to the summit often start from Forest Park Lodge (46.4km), 5km from the turn-off. Continuing along country lanes, the route joins SH23 at Whatawhata. From here, you're back into the suburbs of Hamilton within 10km.

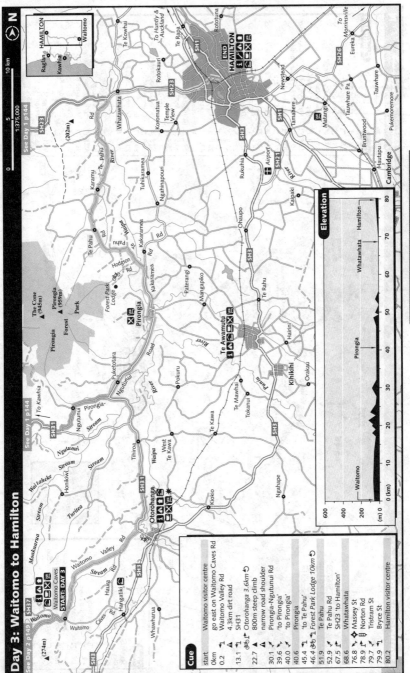

Day 3: Waitomo to Hamilton

Cue

start	Waitomo visitor centre
0km	go east on Waitomo Caves Rd
0.2	Waitomo Valley Rd
13.1	4.3km dirt road
	SH31
22.7	Otorohanga 3.6km ↺
	800m steep climb
	narrow road shoulder
30.1	Pirongia-Ngutunui Rd
39.6	'to Pirongia'
40.0	'to Pirongia'
40.6	Pirongia
45.4	'to Te Pahu'
46.4	Forest Park Lodge 10km ↺
51.9	Te Pahu
52.9	Te Pahu Rd
67.5	SH23 'to Hamilton'
68.6	Whatawhata
76.8	Massey St
78.9	Norton Rd
79.7	Tristram St
79.9	Bryce St
80.2	Hamilton visitor centre

Elevation

Waitomo — Pirongia — Whatawhata — Hamilton

0 (km) 10 20 30 40 50 60 70 80

(m) 0 200 400 600

WAIKATO & KING COUNTRY

Cambridge Circuit

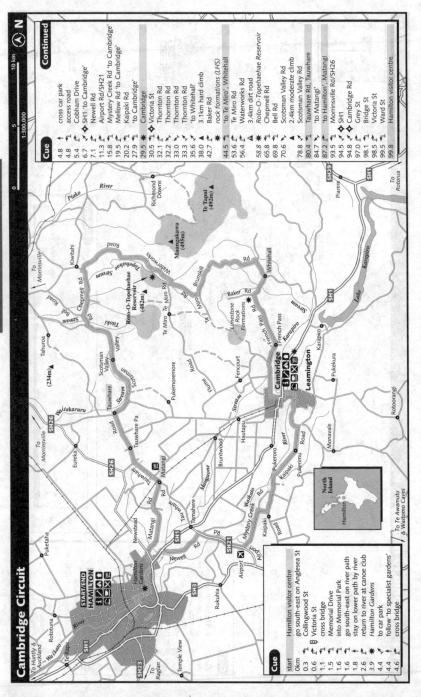

Cue		
4.8	←	cross car park
4.8	↰	access road
5.4	⬦	Cobham Drive
6.7	↱	SH1 'to Cambridge'
7.1	↳	Newell Rd
11.3	↳	Airport Rd/SH21
15.8	↳	Mystery Creek Rd 'to Cambridge'
19.5	↳	Mellow Rd 'to Cambridge'
20.2	↳	Kaipaki Rd
27.9	↰	'to Cambridge'
29.5	✳	Cambridge
30.5	↳	Victoria St
32.1	↳	Thornton Rd
32.2	↰	Thornton Rd
33.0	↳	Thornton Rd
33.3	↳	Thornton Rd
35.6	◀	'to Whitehall'
38.0	◀	3.1km hard climb
42.7	✳	*rock formations (LHS)*
44.5	↳	'to Te Miro'/Whitehall
53.6	↳	Te Miro Rd
56.4	◀	Waterworks Rd
		3.4km dirt road
58.8	✳	*Roto-O-Topehaehae Reservoir*
65.8	↰	Chepmell Rd
69.8	↳	Bell Rd
70.6	✳	Scotsman Valley Rd
		2.4km moderate climb
78.8	↱	Scotsman Valley Rd
80.4	↳	Tauwhare Rd, Tauwhare
84.7	↰	'to Matangi'
87.2	↳	'to Hamilton', Matangi
93.5	↱	Morrinsville Rd/SH26
94.5	⬦	SH1
94.8	⬦	Cambridge Rd
97.0	↳	Grey St
98.1	↳	Bridge St
98.5	↳	Victoria St
99.5	↳	Ward St
99.8	✳	Hamilton visitor centre

Cue		
start		Hamilton visitor centre
0km	↳	go south-east on Anglesea St
0.3	↳	Collingwood St
0.6	↳	Victoria St
1.1	⬦	cross bridge
1.5	↰	Memorial Drive
1.6	↳	into Memorial Park
1.6	↳	go south-east on river path
1.8	↳	stay on lower path by river
2.6	↰	return to river at canoe club
3.9	✳	*Hamilton Gardens*
4.4	↳	to car park
4.4	↳	follow 'to specialist gardens'
4.6	↳	cross bridge

Cambridge Circuit

Duration	5-8 hours
Distance	99.8km
Difficulty	moderate-hard
Start/End	Hamilton

A gentle ride through prime thoroughbred country to Cambridge becomes something of a roller coaster as you ride through the ranges to the east. This is NZ's rural idyll: rolling hills dotted with cows and sheep, narrow winding lanes – and only the occasional farmer in sight.

PLANNING
When to Ride
This ride is more pleasant during the summer and autumn months; holiday traffic is unlikely to be a problem.

GETTING TO/FROM THE RIDE
The ride begins and ends at the Hamilton visitor centre, on the corner of Anglesea and Ward Sts.

THE RIDE
The route from central Hamilton heads along the Waikato River and through **Hamilton Gardens** – worth checking out, if you have

time. Hamilton's outer suburbs quickly give way to semirural pastureland and, towards Cambridge, the thoroughbred country for which the region is famous. The 30km ride to Cambridge is mostly flat, punctuated by a couple of short sharp dips.

Cambridge, where the route again meets up with the Waikato River, is a pretty little town with a charming rural English atmosphere. The visitor centre (31.8km; ☎ 07-827 6033) is on the corner of Victoria and Queen Sts. Pick up a free copy of the *Cambridge Welcomes You* pamphlet. Stock up on food and water, since there are no services until you're nearly back in Hamilton. There are several *coffee shops* in the main part of town, as well as *bakeries*, *groceries* and *takeaways* north of Queen St, close to a couple of parks.

French's Pass (38km) is a challenging climb, the first (and hardest) in a series of roller coaster hills and dales! Look out for the **limestone rock formations** on the other side.

Waterworks Rd (56.4km) has a 3.4km section of gravel, which can be slow going on a touring bike. It passes the picturesque **Roto-O-Topehaehae Reservoir** before hitting the sealed road again.

Although it's undulating, the general trend is downwards until the turn-off to Scotsman Valley (70.6km) and the final climb for the day. Once conquered, it's an easy ride back to Hamilton.

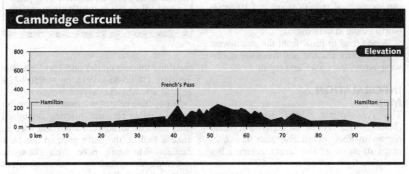

Eastern North Island

The eastern North Island contains a diverse collection of sights and landscapes, from the volcanic peaks of the Central Plateau to the rugged coastline of the East Cape and the wonderfully preserved Art Deco architecture of Napier. There are towering volcanoes, picturesque lakes, forests, beaches, towns rich in Maori culture and plenty of quiet roads – just about everything you could want for a memorable cycling adventure.

CLIMATE

The East Cape enjoys warm summers and mild winters, with an average maximum temperature in Gisborne of 24.9°C in January and 14.1°C in July. The Central Plateau has similarly warm summers, but because of its altitude (Taupo is at 360m) tends to experience colder winters than much of the North Island. Maximum temperatures in Taupo are 23.3°C in January and 11.2°C in July. Nighttime temperatures in particular can get quite low on the Central Plateau, with an average minimum for Taupo in July of 2.2°C. Snow is rare, however, below 500m.

Coastal areas of the East Cape and Central Plateau experience similar amounts of rainfall and rainy days. It rains about 115 days a year in Taupo and 111 in Gisborne, producing total rainfall figures of 1099mm and 1044mm, respectively, quite low by North Island standards.

Winds tend to blow from the south-west in the Central Plateau and from the northwest across the East Cape region.

INFORMATION
Maps

The AA *North Island* Touring Map (1:550,000) covers the Eastern North Island region in good detail and also has town maps of most of the larger centres. It's available from AA centres for $2.95.

Information Sources

There are several tourism organisations that can provide a variety of predeparture information to this area of NZ: Tourism Rotorua (🖳 www.rotoruanz.com), Destination Lake Taupo (🖳 www.laketaupo.tourism.co.nz), Eastland Tourism (☎ 06-868 6139, 🖳 www

In Summary

Area Codes
☎ **06** – Hawkes Bay, Wairarapa, Gisborne

☎ **07** – Bay of Plenty, Central Plateau

Highlights
- Volcanic peaks of **Tongariro National Park**
- **Gisborne** wineries
- The thermal wonders of **Rotorua** and **Taupo**
- **East Cape** – rugged coastline and lonely beaches

Special Events
- **Art Deco Weekend** (February), Napier
- **Air New Zealand Ironman triathlon** (March), Taupo
- **Rotorua Trout Festival** (September/October), Rotorua

Cycling Events
- **Great Lake Cycle Challenge** (November), Taupo

Terrain
Volcanic mountains and gentle uplands in the Central Plateau with low lying plains and rolling hills in coastal areas yielding to rugged ranges in the eastern interior.

.eastland.tourism.co.nz) and Hawke's Bay Tourism (☎ 06-834 1918 or ☎ 0800-429 537, 🖳 www.hawkesbaytourism.co.nz).

For cycling related information, clubs can be a valuable resource offering organised rides and a useful source of local knowledge. Take a look at the clubs page of the New Zealand Mountain Bike Web (🖳 www.mountainbike.co.nz) for a comprehensive listing of local clubs complete with current contact details.

GATEWAY CITIES
Rotorua

Rotorua (population 68,000) has been one of the North Island's top tourist destinations for well over a century. Nicknamed the

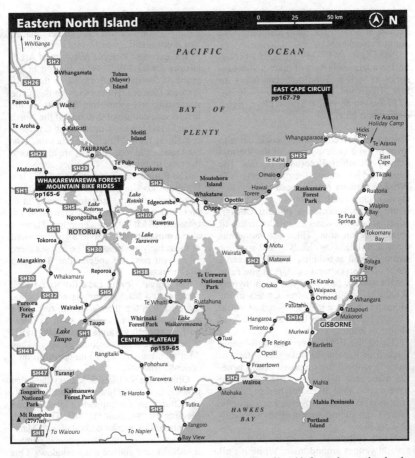

Eastern North Island

'Sulphur City', it has the most energetic thermal activity in the country, with bubbling mud pools, gushing geysers and pervasive, evil odours. Rotorua also has a large Maori population whose cultural activities are among the most interesting and accessible in New Zealand.

Rotorua is a modern bustling place with lots of entertainment and accommodation options. The constant procession of tour buses and throngs of camera-wielding visitors, however, can give the impression at times of a giant theme park.

Information Tourism Rotorua (☎ 07-348 5179, fax 348 6044) is in a Tudor-style building on the corner of Fenton and Haupapa Sts.

It has piles of local information, makes bookings for everything around Rotorua and sells both bus and train tickets. There are also showers, left-luggage facilities and a currency exchange. It's open from 8 am to 5.30 pm daily.

The post office is in Hinemoa St. The Map & Track Shop (☎ 07-349 1845), also in the complex, sells maps, hut passes, fishing licenses and provides other DOC related services. The AA office (☎ 07-348 3069) is at 1191 Amohau St.

You can check your email at the Cyber Shed (☎ 07-349 4965), at the rear of an amusement arcade at 1176 Pukuatua St, or do it over coffee at Nomads Cyber Cafe (☎ 07-348 3288), 1195 Fenton St.

There are plenty of banks with ATMs on Fenton St and in the main shopping area along Tutanekai St.

Pins Cycles (☎ 07-347 1151), 161 Fenton St, has a large selection of bikes and accessories as well as good mountain bikes for hire. Redwood Bikes (☎ 07-348 3636), 1217 Fenton St, is also a good place to rent a mountain bike.

Things to See & Do Most people come to town to get a close-up view of the **thermal activity** for which Rotorua is famous. The largest and best known thermal reserve is **Te Whakarewarewa** (pronounced faka-raywa-raywa), 2km south of town on SH30. It's home to the spectacular **Pohutu Geyser**, which shoots hot water up to 30m in the air about once an hour. There are numerous other vents billowing clouds of foul-smelling steam, as well as bubbling mud pools and a range of Maori cultural exhibits. If you're on a tight budget, however, you might bypass Whaka in favour of the free Craters of the Moon thermal area in Taupo (on the Central Plateau Tour), which is far less crowded and almost as impressive.

During the 19th century the well-heeled flocked to Rotorua to 'take the waters' in order to reap all the supposed health benefits associated with them. Today you can have a good soak at the **Polynesian Spa** off Hinemoa St in the Government Gardens. Towels and swimming costumes are available for hire.

Maori culture is on display nightly at several venues around town. While it's all

---

Performing to Schedule

How does the Lady Knox Geyser manage to perform so neatly to schedule? Simple, the geyser is blocked up with rags so the pressure builds up, then a couple of kilos of soap powder is shoved in to decrease the surface viscosity. And off it goes.

The relationship between soap powder and surface viscosity in geysers was unwittingly discovered by a group of early Europeans who thought it would be a great idea to use the hot water in the ground to wash their clothes. Needless to say they received a bit of a surprise.

---

rather commercial, attending a concert and a *hangi* (food steamed over embers placed in a hole) is still a worthwhile experience.

The excellent **Rotorua Museum of Art & History** (☎ 07-349 8334) is housed in the grand Tudor-style Bath House in the Government Gardens. The museum houses some interesting and innovative exhibits on the history and culture of this area of the North Island. The stately **Government Gardens,** containing typical English touches like croquet lawns and rose gardens, are also worth the time to explore.

The **Buried Village** (☎ 07-362 8287) is a Pompei-like site on Tarawera Rd, about 15km out of town, containing many artefacts and excavated buildings buried in ash by the 1886 Mt Tarawera eruption. There is also a **museum** which gives a good account of the cataclysmic events. The trip out there takes you past the spectacular **Blue** and **Green lakes.**

For a great view of Lake Rotorua, take a **cable car** up Mt Ngongotaha with Skyline Skyrides. On top there's a cafe, restaurant and numerous amusements such as **minigolf,** a **shooting range** and **walk trails.** When you're ready to come down you can do it on a luge, flying 900m downhill on a concrete track.

Ohinemutu is a lakeside Maori village that is home to both the historic **St Faith's Anglican Church** and the impressive **Tamatekapua Meeting House,** built in 1887. The church has a beautiful interior decorated with Maori carvings, woven tukutuku panels, painted scrollwork and stained glass windows. One of the more popular cultural displays, the Magic of the Maori Concert is held here.

There are some great spots for **whitewater rafting** around Rotorua. The most popular trips are those out to the Kaituna River, which include a plunge over the 7m Okere Falls. Kaituna Cascades (☎ 07-357 5032) pioneered the trip but all Rotorua's rafting companies come here, including River Rats (☎ 0800-333 900) and Raftabout (☎ 07-345 4652).

Scenic flights are a great way to take in some of the fantastic scenery around the town, especially the awesome chasm of **Mt Tarawera** and, further afield, the active **White Island** volcano. Volcanic Wunderflites (☎ 07-345 6079) offers trips to both; it operates from Rotorua airport. As does

Disaster on Lake Tarawera

In the 19th century, Lake Tarawera near Rotorua was a major tourist attraction. It brought visitors from around the world to see the Pink and White Terraces: large and beautiful terraces of multi-levelled pools, formed by silica deposits from thermal waters that had trickled over them for centuries. The Maori village of Te Wairoa, on the shores of the lake, was New Zealand's principal tourist resort. From here Sophia, a Maori guide, took visitors on boat trips over the lake to view the terraces, which were regarded as one of the seven wonders of the world. Mt Tarawera towered silently over the lake, although the Maori believed that a powerful fire spirit lived inside it.

One day in June 1886, Sophia took a party out on the lake, as usual, to see the terraces. As they were on the lake, they suddenly saw a phantom Maori war canoe gliding across the water, the Maori boatmen inside it paddling rapidly. It was an ancient war canoe of a kind that had never existed on this lake. It was seen by all the people in the tourist boat, both Maori and European.

To Maori people, the appearance of a phantom Maori war canoe is an omen of impending disaster. Back at Te Wairoa, an old *tohunga*, Tuhoto Ariki, said the sighting of the canoe foretold disaster. He predicted that the village would be 'overwhelmed'.

Four days later, on 10 June 1886, in the middle of the night, there were earthquakes and loud sounds and the eruption of Mt Tarawera suddenly lit up the sky, with fire exploding from many places along the top of the mountain. By the time it was finished, six hours later, over 8000 sq km had been buried in ash, lava and mud, the Maori village of Te Wairoa was obliterated, the Pink and White Terraces were destroyed, 153 people were killed, Mt Tarawera was sliced and opened along its length as if hit with a huge cleaver, and Lake Rotomahana was formed.

Excavations were carried out at Te Wairoa to rescue the survivors. The guide Sophia became a heroine because she saved many people's lives, giving them shelter in her house.

The old tohunga, however, was not so fortunate. His house was buried in volcanic ash and he was trapped inside. The Maori people working to rescue the survivors refused to dig him out. They feared he had used his magic powers to cause the eruption – he had been saying for some time that the new orientation of the villagers towards tourists and a money economy were not traditional, and that neglect of the old traditions would anger the fire spirit inside the mountain. Finally, after four days had passed, he was dug out alive by Europeans, who took him to be cared for in Rotorua. He died a week later, aged around 104.

Lakeside Aviation (☎ 07-345 4242) and the Scenic Flight Warehouse (☎ 07-345 6749). Volcanic Air Safaris (☎ 07-348 9984) does helicopter and floatplane flights departing from the Rotorua lakefront.

Places to Stay The *Cosy Cottage International Holiday Park* (☎ 07-348 3793, 67 Whittaker Rd)* has a heated swimming pool, and fishing gear and canoes for hire. Tent sites are $20 and tourist cabins cost $40; prices for two. *Acacia Park* (☎ 07-348 1886, 137 Pukuatua St)* has tent sites for $10 per person and flats from $45 for two.

The *Hot Rock* (☎ 07-347 9469, 118 Arawa St)* is a large, well equipped backpackers. Many of the rooms overlook the nice pool

area. The Lava Bar, the happening night spot in town, is in the same complex. It can create a bit of noise into the wee hours. Shared dorms start at $15, rooms sleeping four cost $17 per person and doubles cost $40.

Much quieter and smaller is *Funky Green Voyager* (☎ 07-346 1754, 4 Union St)*. Centrally located in a tranquil area, this hostel has a spacious backyard and a pleasant, sunny conservatory. Dorm beds are $15, while doubles are $36.

Other hostels worth trying include *Rotorua Downtown Backpackers* (☎ 07-346 2831, cnr Haupapa & Fenton Sts)*, *Rotorua Central Backpackers* (☎ 07-349 3285, 10 Pukuata St)* and *Kiwi Paka* (☎ 07-347 0931, 60 Tarewa Rd)*.

EASTERN NORTH ISLAND

There are literally dozens of motels lining Fenton St on the way into town. Two of the better ones are the *Bel Aire Motel (☎ 07-348 6076, 257 Fenton St)* at $60 for a double, and the upmarket *Silver Fern Motor Inn (☎ 07-346 3849, 326 Fenton St)*, charging from $115 to $150.

The best of the large hotel chains is probably the modern **Royal Lakeside Novotel** *(☎ 07-346 3888)*, by the water at the end of Tutanekai St, where rooms start at $159 for two people. *Rydges Rotorua (☎ 07-349 0099, 272 Fenton St)* has some good deals, with double rooms from $95.

Places to Eat Quite a few restaurants and cafes are clustered around the lake end of Tutanekai St. The *Thai Restaurant (☎ 07-348 6677, 1141 Tutanekai St)* has an extensive menu, serving up tasty Thai meals from around $15. Set in an attractive house, *Poppy's Villa (☎ 07-347 1700, 4 Marguerita St)* has excellent Kiwi cuisine at about $25 for a main. The *Atlas Brasserie (☎ 07-346 3888)* in the Novotel is similarly priced and features modern, imaginative dishes using local ingredients.

The *Kebab Cafe (☎ 07-348 8411, 1159 Arawa St)* serves up a mixture of tasty and reasonably priced Middle Eastern and Indian dishes. Expect to pay around $15 for dinner and $6 for lunch. Next door at the *Fat Dog Cafe & Bar (☎ 07-347 7586)* there is a good selection of salads, quiches and daily specials. *Zippy Central (☎ 07-348 8288, 1153 Pukuatua St)* is a hip little cafe, with good coffee, bagels and heaps of mountain bike magazines to read.

Self-caterers can stock up at the giant *Big Fresh* or *Pak 'N Save* supermarkets on Fenton St.

Getting There & Away There are plenty of options for getting to/from Rotorua.

Bus All major bus companies stop at the Tourism Rotorua centre (☎ 07-348 5179) on Fenton St, which also handles bookings.

InterCity has daily buses to and from Auckland ($43), Wellington ($75), Taupo ($20), Tauranga, Whakatane, Hamilton and Opotiki ($40). There are also services to Gisborne ($59) via Opotiki and Napier via Taupo. Newmans covers most of the same routes.

Buses stop at the Tourism Rotorua Centre (☎ 07-348 5279) on Fenton St, which also handles bookings.

Train The train station is at the corner of Railway Rd and Lake Rd, 1km north-west of the city centre. Tickets can be purchased at Tourism Rotorua on Fenton St. The *Geyserland Express* operates daily between Auckland and Rotorua, stopping at Hamilton and various smaller stations in between. The journey takes a little over four hours, arriving in Rotorua at 12.17 pm and departing at 1.30 pm. Fares to Auckland are $63 plus $10 per bike.

Air Air New Zealand had daily direct flights to Auckland, Christchurch, Queenstown, Taupo and Wellington, with onward connections. The Air New Zealand Travelcentre (☎ 07-343 1100) is on the corner of Fenton and Hinemoa Sts; there is also a counter at the airport (☎ 07-345 6175).

Ansett New Zealand (☎ 07-349 0146) has direct daily flights to Christchurch, Queenstown, Invercargill and Wellington, with connections to other centres. It also has a counter at the airport (☎ 07-345 5348).

The airport is about 10km out of town, on the eastern side of the lake.

Rotorua & the Central Plateau

The Central Plateau, extending from Taupo in the north and south to the snow-capped volcanoes of Tongariro National Park, lies at the heart of the North Island and is the most volcanically active area in NZ. The Taupo Volcanic Zone stretches in a line from White Island, north of the Bay of Plenty, through Rotorua and down to Tongariro National Park.

The Central Plateau volcanoes were at their most active 2000 years ago, but they still manage to put on a spectacular display from time to time. Since 1995, Mt Ruapehu has exploded in a series of eruptions, spewing forth rock and clouds of ash and steam. Lake Taupo, the biggest in NZ, is itself a remnant of a massive volcanic explosion. Rotorua is only one of three places in the world to have active geysers, the others being Yellowstone National Park in the USA, and Iceland.

HISTORY

Settlement of the Rotorua district probably began as early as the mid-14th century by descendants of the navigators from Hawaiki (the Maori ancestral homeland) who arrived in Maketu in the central Bay of Plenty in the *Arawa* canoe. Soon after their arrival they changed their tribal name to Te Arawa to commemorate the vessel that had carried them so far.

Over the next few hundred years various sub-tribes spread throughout the area and, as numbers increased, fights over territory erupted. During the 1850s and 1860s wars broke out between Te Arawa and the Waikato tribes. Te Arawa threw in their lot with the British government, gaining the backing of their troops.

With the wars virtually over by the early 1870s, European settlement took off, fuelled largely by tales of Rotorua's scenic wonders, broadcast by troops and other government personnel who had been involved in the struggle. The town's biggest drawcards were the fabulous Pink and White Terraces, considered at the time to be among the seven natural wonders of the world. Despite their destruction in 1886 during the eruption of Mt Tarawera, the travelling public maintained their enthusiasm for Rotorua, and many came instead to 'take the waters' in the hope of a cure for almost any ailment imaginable. Tourism has largely been responsible for the town's evolution over the years into a large regional centre.

The European settlement of Taupo began in 1869 during the Maori Wars when a garrison of mounted police was stationed there until the defeat of the rebel warrior Te Kooti in October of that year. The land was bought by the government from the Maori in the 1870s and the town has grown steadily since that time.

Tongariro National Park (78,651 hectares) became NZ's first national park – and only the fourth in the world – when in 1887, in order to ensure the preservation of land sacred to the Maori, Chief Horonuku of the Ngati Tuwharetoa bequeathed the entire area to the Crown for the purpose of establishing a national park. The park now also enjoys UNESCO World Heritage List status in recognition of both its cultural significance and outstanding natural features.

NATURAL HISTORY

The landscape of the Central Plateau has been shaped almost exclusively by volcanic action. The lakes surrounding Rotorua – and Lake Taupo itself – are all legacies of numerous momentous eruptions. South of Turangi, in Tongariro National Park, the snowcapped volcanic cones of Mt Ruapehu (2796m), Mt Ngauruhoe (2291m) and Mt Tongariro (1967m) form the roof of the North Island.

Early in the 20th century a decision was made to plant large tracts of pines in the area, as it was thought that the pumice soil would not lend itself to the effective rearing of sheep or cattle. Today the Central Plateau contains vast forests of plantation timber fuelling a large pulp and paper industry. There are also significant stands of native timber scattered throughout the region. Tongariro contains areas of lush podocarp forest, and red beech and rimu can be found in the Kaimanawa Forest Park.

The poor pumice soils of the high plains make it tough for plants to thrive and the areas surrounding the volcanoes are largely carpeted in alpine herbs, tussock and flax. To the east, in the rain shadow of the mountains, hardy low-growing shrubs survive in the Rangipo Desert, an area rendered barren by eruptions.

While in Tongariro you may be lucky enough to see NZ's only native mammals, the short and long tailed bats. Birds found in the region include North Island robins, fantails, parakeets and the odd *kereru* (native pigeon) or two.

Central Plateau

Duration	2 days
Distance	133km
Difficulty	easy-moderate
Start	Rotorua
End	Turangi

This is a relatively short and easy tour through the volcanic heart of the North Island. While the countryside, predominantly a mixture of trout-filled lakes and vast pine plantations, makes for very pleasant cycling, the emphasis throughout the tour is on the many attractions and activities that places along the route offer.

Rotorua has long been one of NZ's premier tourist destinations, both for its accessible displays of Maori culture and spectacular examples of geothermal activity. Taupo is a thrill-seeker's paradise with bungy jumping, jet-boat rides and tandem skydiving as well as some spectacular natural attractions. Turangi, although much smaller, offers world-class trout fishing and easy access to the magnificent Tongariro National Park, home to active volcanoes and some of the best walks in the country. It's just as well that the cycling isn't too tough, because with so much to do off the bike you'll need all the energy you can muster.

Accommodation and supplies are readily available throughout the tour. Roads are sealed and in good condition along the entire route.

PLANNING
When to Ride
While it can get quite cold in winter, it is possible to do this ride year-round. The best time to go, however, is probably between February and April, when school holiday and peak-season crowds have dissipated, but the weather is still warm and there's plenty of daylight.

What to Bring
Bring a day-pack and walking gear if you are intending to tackle the Tongariro Crossing walk from Turangi at the end of the ride.

GETTING TO/FROM THE RIDE
Rotorua
It is possible to link with the East Cape Circuit (described later in this chapter) by cycling up SH30 to Whakatane (82km), then on to Opotiki via Ohope and SH2 (50km). The first half of the Whakatane leg is very scenic as you cycle past lakes Rotorua, Rotoiti, Rotoehu and Rotoma. The second half is flat and easy, but not particularly exciting, travelling mainly through farmland and orchards.

Turangi
Bus There are several daily InterCity and Newmans services from Turangi to Taupo ($14), Rotorua ($30), Hamilton, Auckland ($58) and Wellington ($58). All buses stop

at the Turangi Bus & Travel (☎ 07-386 8918), on the corner of Ohuanga Rd and Ngawaka Place, which also sells tickets.

Bicycle It is possible to link with the Stratford Circuit (see the Southern North Island chapter). Either take SH41 to Tamarunui (65km) or SH47 to National Park (49km).

THE RIDE
Day 1: Rotorua to Taupo
4-5 hours, 83km
A fairly long, but not overly taxing day, this leg to Taupo is best described as pleasant, travelling for the most part alongside extensive pine plantations, which are prolific throughout the region. An initial stint on moderately busy SH5 is unavoidable, but thankfully there's a good width shoulder most of the time. Things improve when you turn off the highway after 34km.

This secondary route to Taupo via Reparoa is substantially quieter than SH5 and adds only minimal distance to the journey. The flat, straight road travels between fields of grazing dairy cattle, bringing you to **Reparoa** (40km). It's only a small place, but has a *dairy* and a *lunch bar*.

The scenery to Taupo is much like before, an unremarkable but pleasant landscape of fields and pine forests.

Taupo Bungy (☎ 07-377 1135) is on the right-hand side of the road on the way into town. It's a lot of fun to watch the fear on thrill-seekers' faces as they reach the point of no return. The bungy platform is also in a very scenic spot, sitting 45m above the clear, vivid aqua waters of the Waikato River.

Taupo
Lying at the north-east corner of NZ's largest lake, Taupo is a relaxed resort town famous for its giant trout and, more recently, the numerous adrenalin-pumping activities on offer in the surrounding area. It's a popular stopping-off point for most travellers heading to or from Rotorua, making it fairly lively year-round, especially during summer and in early March when it hosts the NZ Ironman triathlon. It's also the site of NZ's most popular fun ride, the 160km Round the Lake ride, held in November each year.

Information The visitor centre (☎ 07-378 9000, fax 378 9003) is on Tongariro St,

Motuarohia Island, Bay of Islands, Northland

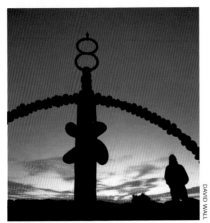

Rainbow Warrior Memorial, Matauri Bay

Cathedral Cove, Coromandel Peninsula

The Artist's Palette at Waiotapu (sacred waters) Thermal Reserve, near Rotorua, Eastern North Island

Champagne Pool, Waiotapu Thermal Reserve

Geyser, Waiotapu Thermal Reserve

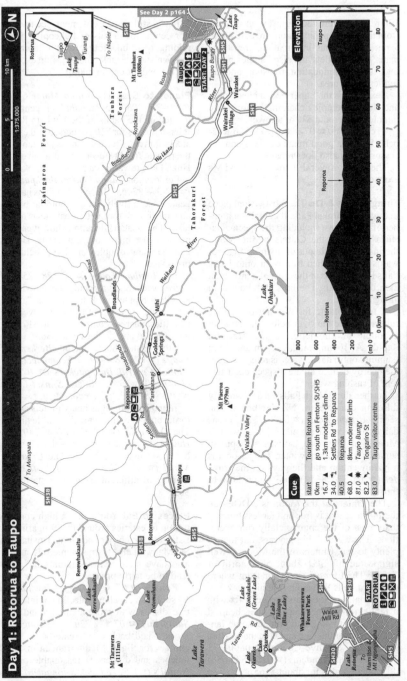

Day 1: Rotorua to Taupo

Elevation

Cue		
start		Tourism Rotorua
0km		go south on Fenton St/SH5
16.7	▲	1.3km moderate climb
34.0	⌐	Settlers Rd 'to Reparoa'
40.5		Reparoa
68.0	▲	8km moderate climb
81.0	✱	Taupo Bungy
82.5	↘	Tongariro St
83.0		Taupo visitor centre

EASTERN NORTH ISLAND

100m from where the highway turns away from the lake. Opening hours are 8.30 am to 5 pm daily. It has information, free town maps, DOC leaflets and also handles bookings for accommodation, transport and activities in the area.

Next door is the Super Loo, a clean toilet and shower complex charging $1 for a five minute shower and $1 for a towel.

Cycle World (☎ 07-378 6117), 126 Ruapehu St, has a good range of bikes and accessories and also does repairs.

There are several banks with ATMs around town.

Thing to See & Do The most visited place in town is **Wairakei Park**. It contains a number of attractions, including the spectacular **Huka Falls** and the **Craters of the Moon** thermal area. Ride out of town up SH5 towards Rotorua, then turn right onto Huka Falls Rd, which is at the crest of a hill about 2km out of town. The falls are about 5km along this road.

A track suitable for walking or cycling runs alongside the river below the falls for a couple of kilometres to the **Aratiatia Rapids**. At 10 am, midday, 2 pm and 4 pm (summer only) daily, water is released from the nearby dam to create a spectacular torrent of rushing water.

Further along Huka Falls Rd are two very different examples of NZ **riverboats**. The sedate *African Queen* (☎ 0800-727 437) has daily cruises at 11 am and 3 pm as well as Moonlight Gloworm Cruises at 9 pm in summer and 6 pm in winter. The jet-boat is a NZ invention and the guys on the *Huka Jet* (☎ 07-374 8572) sure know how to throw one around.

The **Craters of the Moon** is a DOC-run thermal area that is free and far less touristy than most of the commercially run operations. There are no big geysers, but there's plenty to see. Craters of the Moon is well signposted off SH1 about 5km north of Taupo. The turn-off is not far from where the Huka Falls Rd rejoins the highway.

Adrenalin junkies can also get a fix with a **tandem skydive**. Taupo is the cheapest place in NZ to do it and you get some fantastic views of the lake and volcanoes. Both Great Lake Skydive Centre (☎ 0800-373 335) and Taupo Tandems (☎ 025-4528 688) do tandem jumps for about $165.

If you still crave excitement, see the visitor centre for details of **helicopter rides**, **gliding**, **quad bike tours**, **Rock'n Roping** (a masochistic obstacle course), **horse treks**, **rafting** and **mountain biking**.

Places to Stay The *Taupo Motor Camp* (☎ 07-377 3080, 15 Redoubt St) is centrally located on the banks of the Waikato River. It has tent sites for $10 per person and cabins at $35 for two. Free camping is available by the river at *Reid's Farm*, 1.5km south of the Huka Falls towards Taupo.

For location, *Taupo Central Backpackers* (☎ 07-378 3206, 7 Tuwharetoa St) is hard to beat. It has a lively bar and outdoor barbecue area on the roof with great views of the lake. The upstairs location, however, can make secure bike storage a hassle. Dorms cost $15 and doubles are $40, including breakfast.

The *Rainbow Lodge* (☎ 07-378 5754, 99 Titiraupenga St) is a popular hostel with an excellent reputation. It has a sauna, a nice communal area and also books adventure activities. Shared rooms are $15 to $17, singles are $26 and doubles cost $36.

Other hostel choices include *Berkenhoff Lodge* (☎ 07-378 4909, 75 Scannell St), *Go Global Central Backpackers* (☎ 07-377 0044) in Tuwharetoa St and *Sunset Lodge* (☎ 07-378 5962, 5 Tremaine Ave).

Taupo has almost as many motels as Rotorua, but prices are generally a little higher. The *Dunrovin* (☎ 07-378 7384, 140 Heu Heu St) is an older-style motel with smart but basic units from $65. The *Courtney Motel* (☎ 07-378 8398, 15 Tui St) has a number of different sized units starting at $65.

Places to Eat You'll find a high concentration of eateries around the Tongariro St-Lake Terrace corner and along Tuwharetoa St. Many of the town's numerous motels also have their own restaurants but most tend to be fairly pricey.

Finch's (☎ 07-377 2425, 64 Tuwharetoa St) serves an excellent selection of imaginative dishes with most mains around $20. *Santorinis* (☎ 07-377 2205, 133 Tongariro St) is a laid back Greek cafe-bar, a good choice for light Mediterranean-inspired lunches and dinners at reasonable prices. *Nonni's* (☎ 07-378 6894, 3 Tongariro St) is a cafe-brasserie on the lakefront that's popular for breakfast or a coffee during the day.

There are plenty of budget options including all the usual fast food chains, most of them clustered around the lakefront. For an after hours feed, **Maxi's Diner** *(38 Roberts St)* serves up burgers, chips and the like 24 hours a day. **Holy Cow!** *(11 Tongariro St)* offers some good backpacker specials (usually advertised on the blackboard downstairs), with substantial feeds of pasta, chilli etc from $5. It's also one of the liveliest places in Taupo to get a drink.

Self-caterers can stock up at **Woolworths** on Spa Rd.

Day 2: Taupo to Turangi
2½-3 hours, 50km

While Day 2 is spent exclusively pedaling along SH1, this relatively short day is actually a lot nicer than you might imagine, skirting the picturesque shores of **Lake Taupo** much of the time. SH1 is undeniably busy, but fortunately there is a fairly broad shoulder most of the way to Turangi.

The first few kilometres out of town are spent passing rows of motels fronting Lake Taupo. There are a few small hills as you approach the outskirts of town and cycle past the airport, but the road is generally flat most of the way to Waitahanui.

The day's only major climb begins after 13km. The gradient, steep at first, gradually flattens over the course of the substantial 6km ascent. Beyond the summit the road is flanked on both sides by vast stands of plantation timber, the smell of pine filling your nostrils as you hurtle back towards the lake down **Hatepe Hill**. Back on level ground the route is particularly attractive as the highway twists and turns, shadowing the shore of the lake. Care should be taken, however, as the road becomes quite narrow in places, with large trucks taking up much of the available road space. Pull over and have a siesta by the lake at one of the numerous **picnic spots**, or if the sun is shining, strip off your gear and take a dip.

Turangi
Turangi (population 4300) lies about 4km from the southern end of Lake Taupo. It was established in 1973 to facilitate the construction of the nearby hydroelectric power station, and since that time has developed a reputation as the 'trout fishing capital of the world' for the absolute monsters that are regularly pulled from the deep. Many travellers also use Turangi as a base for exploring the magnificent Tongariro National Park.

Information The visitor centre (☎ 07-386 8999), just off SH1, is the place for information on Tongariro National Park, Kaimanawa Forest Park, trout fishing and road conditions during winter. It also sells hut passes and fishing licenses. Opening hours are 8.30 am to 6 pm daily in summer (5 pm in winter).

DOC (☎ 07-386 8607) is at the junction of SH1 and Ohuanga Rd. There are banks with ATMs in the Turangi shopping complex.

Things to See & Do It would be a shame to visit the 'trout capital of the world' without wetting a line at least once. The best months for **trout fishing** are February and March for brown trout and from June to September for rainbow trout, although you stand a good chance of catching something at any time of year. You can get a fishing licence at the visitor centre. If you really want to catch something, it's best to hire a guide for around $50 an hour, including gear. You can hire equipment from Greig Sports (☎ 07-386 7713) in the shopping mall.

River Rafting is popular and the Tongariro River has everything from Grade I (suitable for families) to Grade III rapids. The Rafting Centre (☎ 0800 101 024) on Atirau Rd is the home of Tongariro River Rafting; its five hour trip (half the time on the river) costs $75 per person.

Most people come to Turangi with the intention of doing the **Tongariro Crossing**, widely regarded as the finest one day walk in NZ. Although there are a couple of steep ascents to negotiate, the crossing is suitable for almost anyone with a reasonable level of fitness. It's still a long and tiring walk, though, taking at least five hours. Bellbird Connection, a bus service based at the Bellbird Lodge (see Places to Stay & Eat), operates a daily shuttle service from Turangi to and from the Tongariro Crossing trailheads ($20 return).

The DOC *Turangi Walks* leaflet describes a number of other excellent walks in the area.

EASTERN NORTH ISLAND

Day 2: Taupo to Turangi

EASTERN NORTH ISLAND

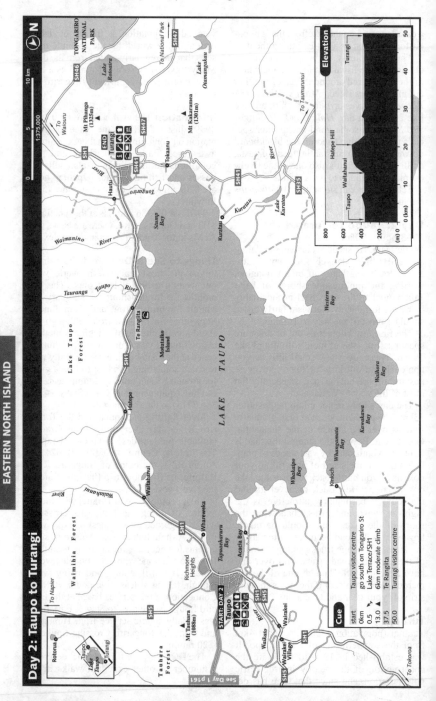

Cue

start		Taupo visitor centre
0km	↘	go south on Tongariro St
0.5		Lake Terrace/SH1
13.0	▲	6km moderate climb
37.5		Te Rangita
50.0		Turangi visitor centre

Elevation

Places to Stay & Eat The *Turangi Cabins & Holiday Park* (☎ 07-386 8754) is on Ohuanga Rd, 400m off SH41. Tent sites are $8 per person, pokey cabins are $15 per person and on-site vans are $35 for two.

Bellbird Lodge (☎ 07-386 8281, 3 Rangipoia Place) occupies several dwellings. The friendly owners operate the Bellbird Connection bus service to Tongariro and provide free transport to local walks. Dorm rooms cost $15, while doubles are $36.

There are a number of motels and lodges in town. The *Sportsman's Lodge* (☎ 07-386 8150, 15 Taupehi Rd) is good value at $50 for a double with shared kitchen and TV facilities. *Club Habitat* (☎ 07-386 7492, 25 Ohuanga Rd) is a sprawling 220-bed complex, with microbrewery, sauna and spa. Tent sites cost $7 per person, dorm beds are $15, cabins cost from $32 to $60 and motel units from $72 to $80.

Most dining options are located around the shopping complex in the centre of town. Here you'll find the *Hong Kong* chinese restaurant (☎ 07-386 7526), *Grand Central Fry* (☎ 07-386 5344), *Magee's*, *Burger King* and another couple of cafes and a bakery. *Valentino's* (☎ 07-386 8821), also near the shops, is a good Italian restaurant and a solid reminder of the many Italian workers that helped construct the nearby power station. The *Brew Haus Bar & Restaurant* (☎ 07-386 7496) in the Club Habitat Complex in Ohuanga Rd serves up a decent selection of good-value meals as well as beers brewed on site.

The shopping centre has a large *New World* supermarket.

Whakarewarewa Forest

MOUNTAIN BIKE RIDES

Beginners Trail	3.5km/easy
Challenge Trial	16km/moderate-hard
Blue Lake Trail	13km/easy-moderate
Start/End	Waipa Mill Rd car park
Circuit Trail	4km/moderate
Start/End	Radio Hut Rd

A few kilometres south-east of Rotorua is the Whakarewarewa Forest, a large area of plantation timber under the management of Fletcher Challenge Forests. Within the forest is a network of some of the best purpose-built mountain bike trails in the country. There are currently four well-signed routes to explore, ranging from the rookie-friendly 3.5km Beginners Trail to the aptly named 16km Challenge Trail.

To keep the peace with other forest users, stick to the designated mountain bike trails and only ride in the direction indicated by the arrow markers.

The Fletcher Challenge Forests visitor centre (☎ 07-346 2082) is in the forest on Long Mile Road, just off Tarawera Rd. It has displays showing the history and development of the forest and it sells drinks and copies of the trail maps.

PLANNING
When to Ride

The trails can be ridden at any time of the year, although certain sections may be temporarily off limits while logging activities are taking place. These trails are very popular with local riders, so it's best if you can ride them on a weekday.

Maps

A trail map, *Mountain Biking in Whakarewarewa*, produced by Fletcher Challenge Forests, is available from Rotorua bike shops and the Fletcher Challenge Forests visitor centre for $4. It's handy but not really a necessity, as the trails are all well-marked and fairly easy to follow.

Bicycle Hire

If you need to hire a mountain bike, get one from either Pins Cycles (☎ 07-347 1151), 161 Fenton St, or Redwood Bikes (☎ 07-348 3636), 1217 Fenton St. Both have good quality bikes with front suspension at around $20/35 for a half/full day. Fully suspended models are available at additional cost.

Redwood Bikes also conducts tours around Whakarewarewa and other local hot spots. Bikes and safety gear are included in the cost, which starts at $49 for a guided two hour ride on the Challenge Trail.

GETTING TO/FROM THE RIDE

All the trails, apart from the Circuit trail, start at the back of a car park 100m off Waipa Mill Rd. To get there head south out of Rotorua on Fenton St (SH5) towards Taupo. Turn left onto Waipa Mill Road just beyond the outskirts of town, about 3km

EASTERN NORTH ISLAND

from the city centre. The starting point is well signed on the left, a few hundred metres from the turn-off.

You can join the Circuit Trail either by riding along the Challenge Trail until you turn off Nursery Rd, or by riding about 1km from the visitor centre along Long Mile Rd, past the corralled horses, then up Nursery Rd (the gated road leading away to the left). The Circuit and Challenge Trails are signed from the top of the hill.

THE RIDES
Beginners Trail
20-35 minutes, 4km

Marked with blue arrows, the Beginners Trail involves a combination of twisting singletrack through the forest and stretches on gravel access roads and 4WD tracks. While it's unlikely to test experienced riders, there are still a few obstacles to negotiate. This is the perfect way to start your day in the forest, either as a nice warm-up or as a confidence builder for novices.

Challenge Trail
1-2 hours, 16km

Marked with orange arrows, the Challenge Trail is mountain bike bliss on twisting singletrack, with plenty of obstacles to negotiate along the way. A nice touch are the signs marked 'XXX' that warn you in advance when particularly tricky sections of the trail lie ahead. Although the Challenge Trail is the toughest of the marked tracks, it can still be ridden with care by novices. It's a good idea, though, to build up some confidence first on the Beginners and Circuit trails.

If you don't feel like riding the full distance, which can be quite hard going, there are plenty of opportunities to exit the trail as it crosses forestry roads.

Blue Lake Trail
1-1½ hours, 13km

The Blue Lake Trail, marked with brown arrows, is a fairly easy but very pleasant ride through the forest down to picturesque Blue Lake. Starting at the car park you travel predominantly on forestry roads, with some shorter sections on 4WD tracks and sealed roads closer to the lake. It is possible to continue round the lake to complete a 30km circuit that takes you back to the car park on Waipa Mill Rd (the route is shown

on the *Mountain Biking in Whakarewarewa* map). Alternatively, you can cruise back into town along Tarawera Rd.

Circuit Trail
20-35 minutes, 4km

The Circuit Trail, marked with grey arrows, is a lot of fun. Part singletrack and part BMX track, it winds its way around the forest in a 4km circuit, coinciding with the orange Challenge Trail much of the way. There are some sharp little drops and lots of tree roots and small rocks to get round, as well as a couple of fantastic high-speed banked corners. The route splits from the Challenge Trail at the start of the BMX track, a roller-coaster ride taking you over a series of steep undulations.

East Cape

Sparsely populated and remote, the East Cape is a little known region of the North Island. The small communities scattered along the coast are predominantly Maori and the pace of life is peaceful and slow. The Cape is circled by 330km of the Pacific Coast Hwy (SH35), an excellent, quiet road that is open year-round. It passes by a wild coastline of rugged little bays, inlets and coves that change aspect with the weather. On a sunny day the water is an inviting turquoise; at other times a layer of clouds hangs on the craggy mountains behind the beaches and turns everything a misty green. Fresh, clear streams flow through wild gorges to meet the sea, and during summer the coastline turns crimson with the blooming of the pohutukawa trees lining the shore.

Due predominantly to a lack of public transport, the East Cape is largely off the main tourist trail. The backpackers loss, however, is the cycle tourers gain as it is possible to explore this region of rugged beauty without having to contend with crowds of holiday-makers or cars.

HISTORY
The East Cape has a rich Maori history going back over 1000 years. Voyagers aboard the *Mataatua*, *Takitimu* and *Horoata*, sacred *waka* (canoes) of the Great Migration fleet, were largely responsible for the area's early settlement. After making landfall

at Whangaparoa, near Cape Runaway, the occupants of the *Mataatua* headed west, settling in the Whakatane district to form the Ngati-Awa tribe. Those aboard the *Takitimu*, who also landed at Whangaparoa, became the Rongowhakaata, while the *Horoata* voyagers settled in Poverty Bay, forming the Ngati-Porou tribe.

The East Cape also features in some of the earliest accounts of European contact. James Cook first stepped onto NZ soil at what is now Gisborne on 9 October 1769. It was an inauspicious first meeting – Cook's landing party was attacked and several Maori were killed in the altercation.

European settlement of the East Cape was slow. It wasn't until the 1830s that settlers from further north trickled into the area in search of farming land. At about the same time, commercial whaling ventures began in the region and missionaries also started to appear. Although settler numbers increased slowly, organised settlement was limited, due largely to Maori resistance.

When the Treaty of Waitangi was signed in 1840, many chiefs from the east coast didn't acknowledge the treaty, let alone sign it, and in the 1860s numerous battles with the Maori broke out. Even today much of the pasture land is leased from the Maori and a large part of it is under their direct control.

NATURAL HISTORY
The rugged Raukumara Range, cloaked in the Raukumara and Urutawa Forests, dominates the interior of the region. An area of largely untouched wilderness, it is significant for the diverse plant life and unique forest types it contains. Kamahi, tawa, pukatea and rewarewa are prolific at lower levels while miro, rimu, tawari and beech flourish at higher altitudes. Its relatively pristine environment, containing fewer predators than many parts of the country, harbours a number of rare and interesting animals, among them the elusive kokako (a member of the wattle bird family), *whio* (blue duck), New Zealand falcon and North Island brown kiwi.

Around the coast small sandy bays alternate with striking headlands. Pohutukawa trees, which display their magnificent crimson blooms around Christmas, can be found growing along the coastal cliffs. Fertile areas around Gisborne and Opotiki support intensive cultivation of subtropical fruit, market garden produce and even vineyards.

East Cape Circuit

Duration	6 days
Distance	473km
Difficulty	moderate-hard
Start/End	Opotiki

Parts of this tour have been described as offering the best coastal cycling in the world. While there are many worthy contenders for that crown, this is a ride that unquestionably offers an abundance of outstanding coastal scenery; the stretch between Opotiki and Hicks Bay, in particular, is a real highlight. While there aren't many substantial climbs, there is a steady succession of hills to tackle most of the way around.

It's possible to stay in fixed accommodation and buy supplies and meals throughout the tour. The road is sealed and in good condition all the way.

PLANNING
When to Ride
Long evenings, warm swimming weather and the spectacular display put on by blooming pohutukawa trees make between November and March the best time to visit, although the weather is fairly mild all year. Accommodation can get tight during the Christmas school holidays, so it's probably best to book ahead during this period.

Maps & Books
Navigation is straightforward throughout the tour. If you are looking for a map, however, the AA's *Eastland* District Map (1:350,000) shows the whole East Cape region in reasonable detail.

Be sure to pick up a free copy of the excellent *Opotiki & East Cape Holiday Guide* from the Opotiki visitor centre. It has detailed descriptions of the sights and towns encountered on the journey around the coast.

What to Bring
While fixed accommodation is always available it can be limited, and camping gear will greatly increase your options. There are some wonderful places to pitch a tent.

EASTERN NORTH ISLAND

GETTING TO/FROM THE RIDE
Opotiki

InterCity (☎ 07-315 6350) in Elliot St has daily services to/from Auckland ($66) via Whakatane and Rotorua ($40), and to/from Gisborne ($28) via Matawai.

Gisborne

Although this is a circuit ride, starting and ending at Opotiki, you can leave the ride at Gisborne if you've got limited time.

Bus InterCity (☎ 06-868 6196) has a depot at the visitor centre on Grey St. There are daily buses to Napier via Wairoa and to Auckland ($79) via Opotiki ($28) and Rotorua ($59). Newmans has a service on Friday and Saturday to Wellington via Napier ($79), also departing from the visitor centre.

Coachrite Connections (☎ 06-868 9969) has a daily bus, except Saturday, to Wairoa ($20), Napier ($35) and Hastings ($35). It departs opposite Georgie Pie on Gladstone St.

Bicycle Although they miss out on riding through the spectacular Waioeka Gorge, many cyclists who are pressed for time cycle from Gisborne to Napier via Wairoa, then take a train to Wellington. The ride south of Napier isn't terribly exciting and there aren't many good alternatives to SH2.

THE RIDE
Opotiki

Sitting at the eastern end of the Bay of Plenty, Opotiki is known as the northern gateway to the East Cape region. The town itself is fairly sleepy, but it has a wide range of services and is close to some good beaches.

Information The visitor centre (☎ 07-315 8484, fax 315 6102), on the corner of St John and Elliot Sts, is open on weekdays from 8.30 am to 4.30 pm. DOC (☎ 07-315 8484) has an office in the same building.

Things to See & Do About 7km from the town centre is **Hukutaia Domain**, which houses one of the finest collections of native plants in NZ. Many of the species on display are endangered, including a puriri tree estimated to be over 2000 years old.

Waiotahi Beach, 6km west of town on SH2, is a popular spot suitable for surfing, swimming and fishing. In town, the **Opotiki**

Museum (☎ 07-315 5193), on Church St, contains a collection of historic local items.

Places to Stay & Eat The **Opotiki Holiday Park** (☎ 07-315 6050) on Potts Ave has tent sites for $8 per person, cabins at $28 for two and tourist flats for $40. The **Tirohanga Beach Motor Camp** (☎ 07-315 7942), 7km east towards Te Kaha on SH35, has camp sites ($8 per person), and cabins and tourist flats.

Central Oasis Backpackers (☎ 07-315 5165, 30 King St) is a small and central hostel boasting a front porch with magnetic appeal. Dorm beds cost $14 and $15, while doubles are $32.

The **Ranui Motel** (☎ 07-315 6669, 36 Bridge St) has singles/doubles for $58/70, and the **Magnolia Court Motel** (☎ 07-315 8490) on the corner of Bridge and Nelson Sts charges from $73 for a double. The best choice for a basic pub room is the **Masonic Hotel** (☎ 07-315 6115) on Church St.

There are a number of take-away food places and cafes along Church St. **Aggie's** has some good vegetarian dishes and the **Flying Pig** (☎ 07-315 7618) serves up kebabs and other Middle Eastern delights. The **Masonic Hotel** (☎ 07-315 6115) has a decent but fairly pricey restaurant with traditional steak-and-chips fare. Chinese meals and take-aways are available across the road at **Vo Lee Lan** (☎ 07-315 6237).

Self-caterers will find a **Four Square** supermarket on Church St and a large **New World** store on Bridge St.

Day 1: Opotiki to Te Kaha
3½-5 hours, 69km

This is a short but fairly hilly day taking you past a succession of picturesque bays and coves.

The road east out of Opotiki is flat and fairly quiet. On a clear day there are good views out to White Island, NZ's most active volcano, billowing out clouds of steam.

At 13km the road begins to climb over a headland and across to the next bay. The descent affords some fine views across Torere Bay. Riding parallel to the coast you pass **Torere Seafoods**, a place with a big reputation for its fish and chips, before beginning the climb over to Hawai Bay.

Hawai Bay is the boundary of the Whanau-a-Apanui tribe whose territory extends north to Cape Runaway. At the far end of the bay, opposite the ***camping ground*** and ***shop***, there is easy access to the beach with river swimming possible close by. The **pebble beach**, steeply shelved and littered with driftwood, has a rugged beauty. The 5km climb out of Hawai is long and hard, but compensates with views of fantastic coastal scenery.

After crossing Motu River, SH35 heads towards the river mouth, and climbs once again before descending into Whitianga Bay (48.5km), a rocky, deep-water cove. Following another climb, the road runs close to the shore along Omaio Bay. There is a well stocked ***shop*** that makes really good hamburgers on the right at 54km.

The remaining kilometres take you past several sheltered, sandy coves and bays. There are no major climbs, but the road continues to roll along steadily, bringing you to Te Kaha (69km).

Te Kaha

Te Kaha, meaning 'to stand firm', gained its name from the local inhabitants' ability to repel the numerous advances of invading tribes. It was once a whaling centre, but now crayfish are the mainstay of the local fishing industry. Te Kaha is also a popular summer holiday destination, attracting visitors with its excellent boating and fishing.

Things to See & Do A few hundred metres north-east out of town is **Maraetai**, or Schoolhouse Bay, which has a nice sheltered sandy beach that's ideal for swimming. The **Te Kaha Golf Club** has a great outlook over the bay and reputedly offers the cheapest golf in NZ at $7 per round – hire clubs are available. The beautifully carved entrance to the Tukaki **meeting house** at the large *marae* (traditional ancestral Maori village) is also well worth a look.

Places to Stay & Eat The *Te Kaha Holiday Park* (☎ 07-325 2894), on SH35 near the golf course at the eastern end of town, is a large, well-kept motor camp. It has grassy tent sites, motel units and a 'luxury backpackers' where $15 gets you a bed in a four-person flat. The *Te Kaha Hotel* (☎ 07-325 2830) has a range of rooms and units, many with good views, starting at $65 for a double.

At pretty Whanarua Bay, 16km out of Te Kaha en route to Hicks Bay, is ***Robyn's***

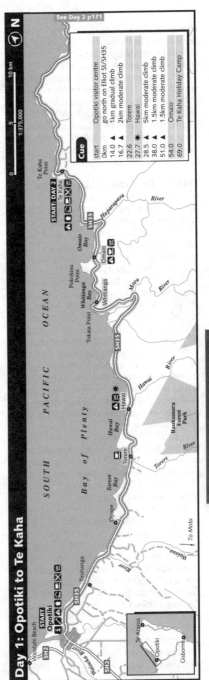

Cue		
start		Opotiki visitor centre
0km	◄	go north on Elliot St/SH35
14.0	◄	1km gradual climb
16.7	◄	2km moderate climb
22.6	◄	Torere
27.7	✳	Hawai
28.5	◄	5km moderate climb
38.0	◄	1.5km moderate climb
51.0	◄	1.5km moderate climb
54.0		Omaio
69.0		Te Kaha Holiday Camp

See Day 2 p171

Day 1: Opotiki to Te Kaha

EASTERN NORTH ISLAND

Place (☎ 07-325 2904), a small six-bed hostel close to the beach. A bed in the dorm costs $15, while a double is $35. Next door is *Rendezvous on the Coast (☎ 07-325 2899)*, a large motor camp with tent sites from $14 for two and cabins from $30.

Sit-down meals are available from the restaurant at the *Te Kaha Hotel (☎ 07-325 2830)*, while take-aways and groceries can be purchased from either *O'Brien's General Store* on SH35 near the hotel, or the *shop* at Te Kaha Holiday Park.

Day 2: Te Kaha to Te Araroa

4-6 hours, 86.5km

With few stretches of flat ground, this is a strenuous but very rewarding day. The first half, hugging the coast as far as Whangaparaoa, is particularly memorable, giving you an appreciation of why locals regard this as one of the best coastal tours in the world.

From Te Kaha the road follows the coast closely all the way to Whanarua Bay, one of the prettiest bays on the coast, before turning inland at 23.5km. The road brings you back to the Pacific Ocean at Raukokore, where a couple of **old wooden churches** stand alone on the rugged coast. The white Anglican church on the promontory, with its steeply pitched roof and flanked by Norfolk Island pines, is hard to miss. Inside, a sign explains that the fishy odour originates from a family of penguins who are living under the floorboards.

A small climb brings you round to Waihau Bay, the site of a *hotel*, *shop* and popular boat ramp. Further on is a *camping ground* that also sells drinks and hot food. The road turns inland and does not meet the coast again until Hicks Bay.

With the exception of some climbing after 55km and a moderate hill at 72km to test your tiring legs, the rest of the distance to Hicks Bay is relatively flat.

The turn-off to the small settlement of **Hicks Bay** and the backpacker hostel is on the left at 80.5km. Once known as Te Wharekahika, Hicks Bay was named after Zachary Hicks, Cook's second lieutenant on the *Endeavour*. Its natural setting is superb, as is nearby Horeshoe Bay.

If you are up to it, however, it is a good idea to make Day 3 easier by pushing on up over the hill, a testing 3km climb, and staying at Te Araroa.

Te Araroa

Te Araroa is a small settlement nestled beneath cliffs on picturesque Kawakawa Bay. There's little here beside a hotel, general store and in the grounds of the school, what is reputed to be the largest pohutukawa tree in the world. The road out to the East Cape lighthouse (22km each way), the easternmost in the world (a claim to fame applicable to just about everything in this part of the world), also starts here.

Things to See & Do For a little evening entertainment, try the **cinema** at the Te Araroa Holiday Park, which screens new-release films in a proper movie theatre, complete with surround sound.

Horse treks around the area are available through Te Puna Frontier (☎ 06-864 4862), located 6km west of town on SH35.

The beach at Hicks Bay is safe for **swimming** and a twilight dip. If you can drag yourself out of bed early enough, be among the first in the world to see the sun for the day. The proprietors of the Hicks Bay Backpackers Lodge also run **sunrise trips** to the East Cape Lighthouse.

If you're not an early riser the 42km round trip from Te Araroa to the **East Cape lighthouse** is still worthwhile in daylight, the bumpy, mostly unsealed stretch of road following the coast past lonely expanses of windswept beach. At the end of the road, ascend the steep steps to the light itself and take in the magnificent view from this most easterly of promontories.

Places to Stay & Eat There are plenty of accommodation and food options in the Te Araroa-Hicks Bay area.

Te Araroa Just over the hill on the route after the Hicks Bay turn-off is the *Te Araroa Holiday Park (☎ 06-864 4873)*, one of the only holiday parks around to have its own cinema. It also has a licensed shop, TV rooms and a communal kitchen. Tent sites are $7.50 per person, flats cost $50 for two and basic cabins cost $12 per person.

In Te Araroa itself the *Kawakawa Hotel (☎ 06-864 4809, Moana Parade)* offers pub rooms from $40 for a double. A more up-market option is *Brownlies (☎ 06-864 4748)*, a B&B set among scented gardens offering comfortable double en suite rooms,

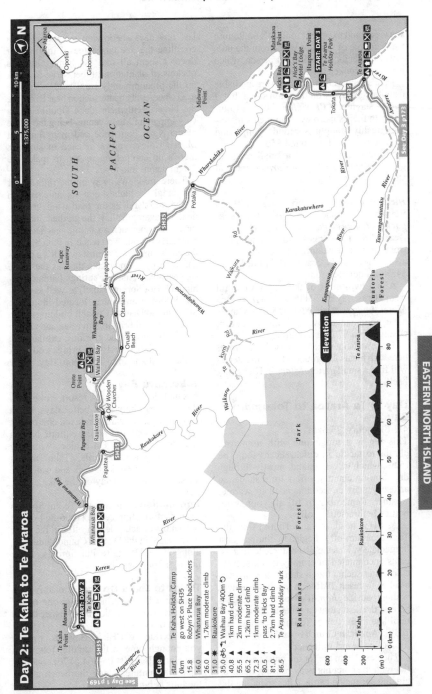

Day 2: Te Kaha to Te Araroa

Cue

start	Te Kaha Holiday Camp
0km	go west on SH35
15.8	Robyn's Place backpackers
16.0	Whanarua Bay
26.0	▲ 1.7km moderate climb
31.0	✳ Raukokore
35.0	↻ Walhau Bay 400m
40.8	▲ 1km hard climb
55.5	▲ 2km moderate climb
65.2	▲ 1.2km hard climb
72.3	▲ 1km moderate climb
80.5	↑ pass 'to Hicks Bay'
81.0	▲ 2.7km hard climb
86.5	Te Araroa Holiday Park

Elevation

EASTERN NORTH ISLAND

sea views and excellent food. It's on Pohutu Rd, a couple of minutes walk from the pub. Accommodation costs $80 per person, which includes a cooked breakfast.

Meals such as fish and chips are available from the takeaway on the main street, but if you're staying at **Brownlies**, be sure to indulge in their superb evening meals featuring freshly caught seafood, game and organic produce for around $50.

Self-caterers will find a small range of groceries at the *Te Araroa Farmers* general store on Moana Parade.

Hicks Bay Just up the dirt road from Hicks Bay is the spic-and-span *Hicks Bay Backpackers Lodge* (☎ *06-864 4731)*, on Onepoto Beach Rd. It's a small and friendly place fronting onto a beautiful beach only 50m away. The nightly cost is $15 in dorms or $45 for a double room.

About two-thirds of the way up the hill from Hicks Bay on SH35 is the *Hicks Bay Motel Lodge* (☎ *06-864 4880)*. Its units have good views overlooking the ocean, costing from $70 for a double.

There's also a decent licensed *restaurant* here with meals for around $16. Self-caterers will find a small *general store* in Hicks Bay itself.

Day 3: Te Araroa to Tokomaru Bay

4½-6½ hours, 85.5km
This leg is a tough one with numerous climbs to tackle in quick succession. The route, which travels inland, mostly through dry farming country, offers little shade, so an early start is recommended in warmer weather. Remember to fill all your water bottles before setting off.

As SH35 heads towards Tikitiki from the Te Araroa turn-off it begins to climb almost immediately. This the first of three testing ascents encountered in brutally quick succession. After such a tough start to the day it is a relief to reach **Tikitiki**, a small settlement with a roadside *shop*. It's worth stocking up here as the next store en route is not reached until late in the day at Te Puia Springs. The **Tikitiki Anglican Church** is well worth a look for its fine Maori influences.

The next 19km are for the most part fairly flat with the quiet highway passing fields of grazing sheep and cattle. After spending the

last few days shadowing the magnificent coastline the dry landscape of the interior doesn't seem all that inspiring, although pockets of plantation timber serve to break up the predominantly rural landscape. The road emerges at an intersection near Ruatoria, the largest settlement since Opotiki and a very important Maori centre, being the home of the Ngati Poru tribe and many eminent Maori. Unless you're in need of supplies there's no compelling reason to make the 2.5km detour into town.

There are views away on the right to **Mt Hikurangi**, the highest non-volcanic peak on the North Island, as the road winds its way up the Makatote Valley, the gradient increasing as you approach a summit, reached after 66km. By the time you reach Te Puia Springs the day's climbs are almost over. It's a pleasant town by a small lake that, as the name suggests has some **hot springs** (situated behind the Hot Springs Hotel) as well as a visitor information centre, located alongside SH35 in the District Council building.

After a final brief ascent relax and take in the fine views on the glorious, exhilarating 9km downhill stretch that brings you back to the coast and in to Tokomaru Bay.

Tokomaru Bay

A small coastal holiday resort, Tokomaru Bay has definitely seen better days, but it still manages to retain a relaxed charm. It's also a stronghold of Maori culture, having four active maraes. On a nice swimming beach surrounded by hills, 'Toko Bay' is the perfect place to kick back and watch the sunset after a tough day on the bike.

Information Stop in at the Te Pui Springs visitor information centre (☎ 06-864 6853) for details of activities on offer in the area. It's situated in the District Council building, alongside SH35 in Te Pui Springs, 11km north of Tokomaru Bay.

Things to See & Do The main activity in Tokomaru Bay is relaxing and one of the best places to do it is down at the nice **beach** in front of town.

If the ride from Hicks Bay hasn't given you enough time in the saddle, **Tokomaru Bay Horse Treks** (☎ 06-864 5870) conducts equine adventures along the beach and in the hills behind town.

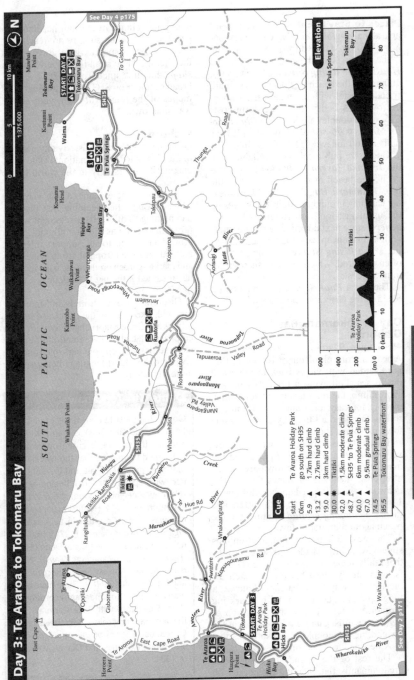

Day 3: Te Araroa to Tokomaru Bay

Cue

start	0km	Te Araroa Holiday Park
		go south on SH35
5.9	◀	1.7km hard climb
13.2	◀	2.7km hard climb
19.0	◀	3km hard climb
30.0	✳	Tikitiki
42.0	◀	1.5km moderate climb
48.7	⌂	SH35 to Te Puia Springs'
60.0	◀	6km moderate climb
67.0	◀	9.5km gradual climb
74.5		Te Puia Springs
85.5		Tokomaru Bay waterfront

Elevation

EASTERN NORTH ISLAND

Places to Stay & Eat Tent sites are available at the *Mayfair Camping Ground* (☎ 06-864 5843) on Main Rd for $7.50 per person – the office is in the general store. The *House of the Rising Sun* (☎ 06-864 5858), 100m from the beach on Potae St, is a small, friendly hostel with an enthusiastic Japanese owner. A bed in the large dorm costs $15, while doubles are $34. The *Blue Marlin Motel* (☎ 06-864 5842) on Main Rd has units at $60 for two or $45 for a single.

Good-size pub meals are available from the *Te Puka Tavern* (☎ 06-864 5466), opposite the beach at the eastern end of the bay. *Tokamaru Bay Fish 'n' Chips,* near the camping ground on Main Rd, serves up the usual fast-food assortment, while the *general store* next door does a roaring trade with its big, cheap ice-cream cones. If staying at the *Rising Sun*, an evening meal is often prepared, which you can share in for minimal cost.

There is a *Four Square* supermarket on SH35 at the Gisborne end of town.

Day 4: Tokomaru Bay to Gisborne

4½-6 hours, 91km

A heart-starting climb out of Tokomaru Bay is rewarded with views back to town and out to sea. Following a brief descent and short climb, the road levels out somewhat, making for easy, pleasant cycling through rolling farmland all the way to the seaside town of Tolaga Bay.

Tolaga Bay is a sizeable place with a few *supermarkets* and *fast-food places* on the main street. The streets in town are named after crew members of James Cook's *Endeavour*, which dropped anchor close by in 1769. It's a popular place with surfers and there's a *camping ground* right next to the beach about 3km out of town.

The next 35km is quite a strenuous stretch with little shade and several hills, thankfully none of them too large. The sea is tantalisingly close but out of reach for most of the way until reaching **Pouawa**, a long, picturesque beach with sparkling turquoise water set against a backdrop of big, brown hills. *Camping* is possible at the far end, near a couple of house buses that look destined to go no further.

The rest of the journey to Gisborne is predominantly flat, hugging the coast with only a few climbs over small headlands to negotiate. The outer suburbs are reached at **Okitu,** where a sperm whale grave marks the site of a large stranding. There's also a *shop*, the first since Tolaga Bay. A nice broad shoulder on SH35 over the final kilometres of the route will bring your all the way into town.

Gisborne

Gisborne is NZ's most easterly city and one of the closest to the International Date Line, making it the first city in the world to see the sun.

On landing here, James Cook named it 'Poverty Bay' after deciding that the area had nothing to offer. His assessment was to prove inaccurate as the rich alluvial plains around Gisborne today support intensive cultivation of subtropical fruits, vineyards and market-garden produce. Its wine industry has it earned it the tag 'Chardonnay Capital of NZ'.

Gisborne features strongly in Maori history and, like much of the East Cape region, retains a definite Maori character with great emphasis placed on the retention of culture and traditions. Keep your ears open and you will here the Maori language being spoken quite frequently.

Dame Kiri Te Kanawa

One of the most famous Kiwis of all time (in international terms) is Dame Kiri Te Kanawa, the serenely beautiful opera diva.

It's hard to imagine that this lyrical soprano who graces La Scala and Covent Garden with aplomb had her beginnings in this motley neighbourhood; she was born in Gisborne in 1944. Her first major leading role was as the Countess in *Le Nozze di Figaro* at Covent Garden (1971), and she has since embraced the roles of Donna Elvira (*Don Giovanni*), Marguerite (*Faust*), Mimi (*La Bohéme*), Amelia (*Simon Boccanegra*) and Desdemona (*Otello*). There have been many famous commercial recordings – *West Side Story* with José Carreras, and the very haunting calls across the valley of Canteloube's *Songs of the Auvergne*. She also sang at Charles and Diana's wedding in 1981.

Day 4: Tokomaru Bay to Gisborne

Cue		
start		Tokomaru Bay waterfront
0km		go south-west on SH35
1.0	◄	2.8km hard climb
36.0		Tolaga Bay
43.7	◄	1.1km hard climb
56.3	◄	3km moderate climb
64.0	◄	1km moderate climb
71.0	✳	Pouawa
77.0	◄	1km moderate climb
83.8	✳	Okitu
91.0		Gladstone Rd, Gisborne

Elevation

EASTERN NORTH ISLAND

Information The Eastland & Gisborne visitor centre (☎ 06-868 6139, fax 868 6138) is at 209 Grey St. Opening hours are from 7.30 am to 5.30 pm daily in winter, with longer hours over summer. The office has good city maps and sells tickets for InterCity buses, which depart from out the front. The DOC office (☎ 06-867 8531), 63 Carnarvon St, is open from 8 am to 4.30 pm on weekdays, although you should try the visitor centre first.

Verve cafe, 121 Gladstone St, has Internet access. There are numerous banks with ATMs along Gladstone Rd, Gisborne's main street.

Frank Allen Cycles (☎ 06-867 3677) is next to the YHA Hostel on Wainui Rd.

Things to See & Do The interesting **Gisborne Museum & Arts Centre** (☎ 06-867 3832) at 18 Stout St has numerous displays relating to east coast Maori and colonial history, as well as geology and natural history exhibits. The **Star of Canada Maritime Museum** is also in the museum complex.

There's a **statue** of 'Young Nick' (Nicholas Young, surgeon's boy on the *Endeavour*) in a little park on the river mouth. He was the first member of Cook's crew to sight NZ and was rewarded with a gallon of rum for his efforts. On the other side of the bay are the white cliffs that Cook named 'Young Nick's Head'.

Across the river at the foot of Kaiti Hill in Titirangi Domain is a **monument** to Cook, near the spot where he first set foot in NZ. A pathway from nearby **Waikahua Cottage** leads up the hill, offering panoramic **views** of the bay. At the 135m summit is the **Cook Observatory**, the world's easternmost observatory.

Also in Titirangi Domain is **Te Poho-o-Rawiri meeting house**, one of the largest in NZ. It has a richly decorated interior and its stage is framed by carved *maihi* (ornamental carved gable boards). It's open all the time, although permission (☎ 06-867 2835) should be sought before entering (see the 'Marae Etiquette' boxed text in the Facts about New Zealand chapter). The leaflet called *Tairawhiti – Heritage Trails: Gisborne District* is good for information on historic sites in this Maori ancestral land.

An interesting **walk** is the Te Kuri Walkway, a three hour walk through farmland and forest to a commanding viewpoint. The walk traverses the farm of Murray Ball, the cartoonist and creator of the famous *Footrot Flats* comic strip. It starts 4km north of town at the end of Shelley Rd.

Gisborne is a major wine-producing area, particularly known for its Chardonnay. There are a number of **wineries** within easy cycling distance of town. Wine trail maps are available from the visitor centre.

Places to Stay The *Waikanae Beach Holiday Park* (☎ 06-867 5634), in Grey St at Waikanae Beach, is well equipped. Tent sites cost $16, double cabins start from $24 and tourist units start from $55.

The *Gisborne YHA Hostel* (☎ 06-867 3269, 32 Harris St) is about 1.5km out of the centre of town. Set in a big old house in spacious grounds, you pass it on the left as you cycle in from Tokomaru Bay. Dorm beds are $15 and doubles cost $36.

The *Flying Nun Backpackers* (☎ 06-868 0461, 147 Roebuck Rd) is aptly named, being housed in an old convent. The halls of this grand old building once echoed with the voice of a young Dame Kiri Te Kanawa taking singing lessons. Dorm beds cost from $13, doubles are $37 and singles are $21.

There are lots of motels on Gladstone Rd and, closer to the beach, on Salisbury Rd. *Champers Motor Lodge* (☎ 06-863 1515, 811 Gladstone Rd), opposite the golf course, is one of Gisborne's newest, charging between $85 and $140 for two. The *Blue Pacific Beachfront Motel* (☎ 06-868 6099, 90 Salisbury Rd), opposite Waikanae Beach, has units from $85 for two.

Places to Eat There are a number of places to eat along Gladstone Rd and Peel St. *Verve* (☎ 06-868 9095, 121 Gladstone Rd) is one of the best. It's a cafe with good coffee and a relaxed ambience, serving a modern selection of main meals starting at $12. *Fettucine Brothers* (12 Peel St) serves up a good selection of pizzas and pasta, while next-door *MegaBite* is a good choice for hot lunches. *China Palace* (☎ 06-867 5037, 55 Peel St) is the most popular Chinese eatery in town and has a cheaper take away and no frills dining area out the front. *Georgie Pie* on Gladstone Rd is good for cheap, hot snacks, while *Burger Wisconsin* (☎ 06-867 6442, 26 Gladstone Rd) is a cut above your average burger joint.

EASTERN NORTH ISLAND

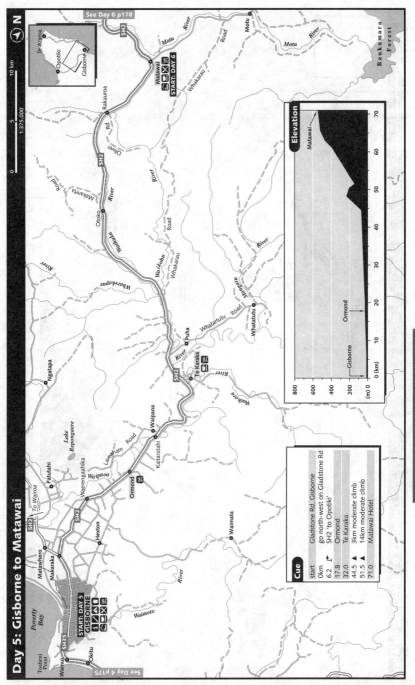

Day 5: Gisborne to Matawai

EASTERN NORTH ISLAND

See Day 6 p178

START: DAY 6

Matawai

See Day 4 p175

START: DAY 5 GISBORNE

Cue		
start		Gladstone Rd, Gisborne
0km	↰	go north-west on Gladstone Rd
6.2	↲	SH2¹ to Opotiki¹
17.8		Ormond
32.0		Te Karaka
44.5	▲	3km moderate climb
51.5	▲	14km moderate climb
71.0		Matawai Hotel

Elevation

Matawai

Ormond

Gisborne

(m) 0   200   400   600   800

0 (km)   10   20   30   40   50   60   70

EASTERN NORTH ISLAND

Day 6: Matawai to Opotiki

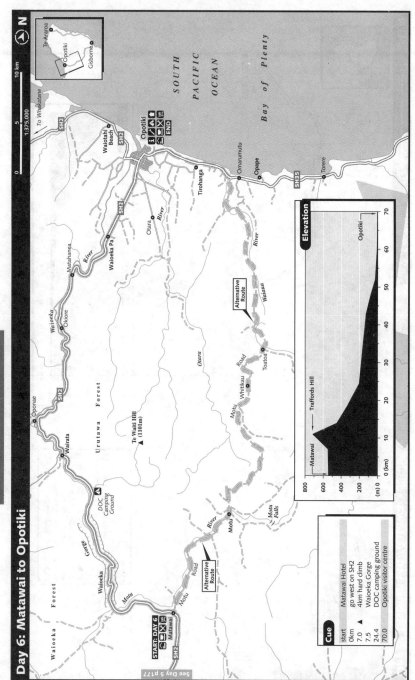

See Day 5 p.177

Cue		
start	Matawai Hotel	
0km	go west on SH2	
7.0	4km hard climb	▲
7.5	Waioeka Gorge	
24.4	DOC camping ground	
70.0	Opotiki visitor centre	

Day 5: Gisborne to Matawai
3½-5 hours, 71km

Day 5 is a shorter but quite difficult leg as most of the second half is uphill. Supply points are few and far between.

Follow the main road, Gladstone St, out of town, passing numerous motels, a racetrack and a golf course. You escape most of the traffic at Makaraka (6.2km), where you turn onto SH2, signed 'to Opotiki'. The road is straight and flat, taking you past orchards, sheep pastures and wineries.

The climbing begins at 44km, a trend that continues for the rest of the day. The initial 3km ascent is followed by a descent of similar length and a final, much longer climb into Matawai. The landscape is one of lush green pastures, with pockets of deciduous trees lining the road. If it were not for the very distinctively NZ beehive-shaped hills, you could easily be forgiven for thinking you were in the English countryside.

Matawai
Once an old sawmilling town, Matawai today is a tiny rural settlement with a hotel, dairy and petrol station.

Information The visitor centres in Gisborne and Opotiki can help with information about Matawai and the Waioeka Gorge and Scenic Reserve.

Things to See & Do There's really not much to do in Matawai, itself, except enjoy a few cold drinks in the hotel at the end of a fairly hard day. However, go for a walk around town and talk to the locals.

Places to Stay & Eat The *Matawai Hotel* (☎ *06-862 4874)*, on SH2, has basic pub rooms at $25/40 for singles/doubles. It also does a decent two-course evening meal for $15. The *Matawai Village Cafe* (☎ *06-862 4823)* is a dairy with snacks and a selection of groceries. If you still have some energy, you can press on another 24km and camp at the *DOC camping ground* at Manganuku Bridge. Stock up in Matawai.

Day 6: Matawai to Opotiki
3-4½ hours, 70km

This is a spectacularly scenic leg travelling through Waioeka Gorge.

The first few kilometres out of Matawai are relatively flat, but you begin to climb in earnest after 7km to the summit of Traffords Hill (725m). A long, spiralling descent drops you down into **Waioeka Gorge**, part of NZ's largest (1800 hectares) scenic reserve. The winding road, which closely follows the course of the Opato and Waioeka Rivers, is hemmed in by steeply sloping walls covered with thick bush. Traffic is quite light, but care is required as the route is favoured by large trucks that can consume most of the narrow road.

Just before the Manganuku Bridge at 24.4km there is a *DOC camping ground* with barbecue and toilet facilities. The predominantly downhill ride through the gorge is quite easy and very picturesque, with lots of vantage points and picnic areas along the way. You emerge back onto the coastal plain at Waioeka Pa, pedalling past the abandoned factory buildings of the old Opotiki dairy on your way into town.

Southern North Island

The southern portion of the North Island is in many ways the rural heartland of the country. From the rich dairy pastures of Taranaki to the sheep-raising properties of Wairarapa, boasting three million sheep within a 16km radius of Masterton, agriculture thrives throughout. Having said that, the landscape isn't entirely one of green fields. There are some fantastic national parks, miles of rugged coastline, mighty rivers, mountains and large areas of lonely back country to explore. Throw in the mountain biking and other considerable attractions of Wellington and it all adds up to a region well worth pedalling your way around.

The selection of rides described in this chapter showcase many of the best features of the region. Around Wellington get out and see the sights on a couple of short and easy scenic day rides around the city and harbour, or dust off your mountain bike for some great off-road rides up the Karapoti Gorge and the Rimutaka Incline, around Mt Victoria and the new Makara Peak mountain bike park. Out of the capital get a fantastic 360° view of majestic Mt Taranaki, swim at some great beaches and take in the incredibly lush pastures that make Taranaki dairy cow heaven, on the Around Mt Taranaki ride, or get away from it all and experience the solitude and rugged bush scenery of the Stratford Circuit.

CLIMATE

The weather in the Taranaki region is heavily influenced by the presence of Mt Taranaki. The region experiences warm, humid summers and mild, wet winters. The area around the mountain is one of the wettest in New Zealand, with about 7000mm of rain recorded annually at North Egmont (compared with 1584mm in New Plymouth). Moisture-laden winds from the Tasman Sea are trapped by the peak and swept up to freezing heights. New Plymouth has an average maximum temperature of 20.5°C in January and 11.3°C in July. The wind, which can be strong at times, blows predominantly from the west.

'Windy Wellington' has a deserved reputation as it is buffeted by strong westerly winds

---

In Summary

Area Codes
- ☎ **04** – Wellington
- ☎ **06** – Wairarapa, Manawatu, Taranaki
- ☎ **07** – Taumarunui

Highlights
- The magnificent cone of **Mt Taranaki**
- Rugged bush scenery along **Whanganui River Rd**
- Surf beaches at **Taranaki**
- Picturesque, cosmopolitan **Wellington**

Special Events
- **New Zealand International Festival of Arts** (March), Wellington
- **Whangamomona Republic Day street party** (October), Whangamomona
- **Taranaki Rhododendron Festival** (November), New Plymouth
- **Martinborough Wine, Food & Music Festival** (November), Martinborough

Cycling Events
- **Big Coast Ride** (February), Wellington
- **Karapoti Classic** (March), Upper Hutt

Terrain
Rolling hills throughout

funnelled through Cook Strait much of the time, particularly over winter. It is one of the cooler parts of the North Island, mild in summer (average of 21.8°C in January) and fairly cold in winter (13.3°C in July).

INFORMATION
Maps

A useful companion is the AA *North Island* Touring Map (1:550,000). It shows the whole of the southern North Island in good detail and includes street maps of the larger towns.

Information Sources

There are several tourism organisations that can provide loads of predeparture information to Wellington and southern North Island:

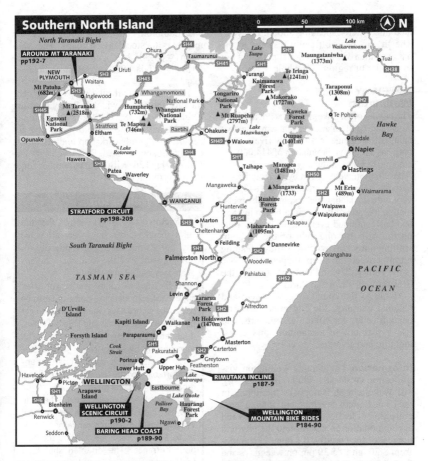

Southern North Island

0   50   100 km   N

North Taranaki Bight

AROUND MT TARANAKI pp192-7

SH4 Ohura SH4 Taumarunui SH41 Lake Taupo SH5 Lake Waikaremoana Maungataniwha (1373m) Tuai

NEW PLYMOUTH SH3 Uriti SH43 Turangi Te Iringa (1241m) Tarapaonui (1308m) SH38

Mt Patuha (682m) SH3 Inglewood Whangamomona Kaimanawa Forest Park Makorako (1727m) SH2 Te Pohue

Waitara Mt Humphries (732m) National Park Tongariro National Park Mt Ruapehu (2797m) Kaweka Forest Park Hawke Bay

Mt Taranaki (2518m) Whanganui National Park Lake Moawhango Oupae (1401m) Eskdale Napier

Egmont National Park Stratford Te Mapou (746m) Raetihi Ohakune Waiouru SH49 SH1 Maropea (1481m) SH50 Fernhill Hastings

Eltham Lake Rotorangi SH1 Taihape Mt Erin (489m) Waimarama

Opunake Hawera SH3 Mangaweka Mangaweka (1733) SH2 Waipawa Waipukurau

Patea Waverley WANGANUI Hunterville Ruahine Forest Park Takapau

STRATFORD CIRCUIT pp198-209

SH3 Marton SH54 Maharahara (1095m) Dannevirke

South Taranaki Bight Cheltenham Feilding SH1 SH2 Woodville Porangahau

TASMAN SEA Palmerston North Pahiatua SH52 PACIFIC OCEAN

Shannon Levin Tararua Forest Park SH2 Alfredton

D'Urville Island Kapiti Island Waikanae Mt Holdsworth (1470m)

Forsyth Island Paraparaumu SH1 Masterton Carterton

Cook Strait Pakuratahi SH2 Greytown Featherston

Porirua Upper Hut Lower Hutt **RIMUTAKA INCLINE** p187-9

Havelock Picton WELLINGTON Eastbourne Lake Wairarapa Lake Onoke **WELLINGTON MOUNTAIN BIKE RIDES** P184-90

Arapawa Island Palliser Bay Haurangi Forest Park

Blenheim **WELLINGTON SCENIC CIRCUIT** p190-2

SH6 Renwick Ngawi

Seddon **BARING HEAD COAST** p189-90

Totally Wellington (☎ 04-801 4000, 🖳 www .wellingtonnz.com), Tourism Taranaki (☎ 06-757 9909, 🖳 tipnet.taranaki.ac.nz/tourism) and Tourism Wairarapa (☎ 06-378 7373, 🖳 nz .com/travel/wairarapa).

For cycling related information, clubs can be a valuable resource offering organised rides and a useful source of local knowledge. Take a look at the clubs page of the New Zealand Mountain Bike Web (🖳 www .mountainbike.co.nz) for a comprehensive listing of local clubs.

Place Names

You will come across a couple of alternative place names for destinations in Taranaki and Wanganui.

The names Taranaki and Egmont are both widely used in the region. Taranaki is the traditional Maori name for the volcano and Egmont is the name James Cook gave it in 1770 in honour of the Earl of Egmont, who had encouraged his expedition. In 1986 the NZ government ruled that Mt Taranaki and Egmont are both official names for the volcano, although the former seems to be more commonly used. The national park around the mountain is Egmont National Park.

In Wanganui you will see the name spelt both with and without the letter 'h'. The difference is mainly a political issue. It was originally spelt Wanganui because the Maori tribes of the river region do not pronounce 'wh' as an 'f', contrary to most

Maori dialects. However, the sound is aspirated and strictly speaking should be 'Wh'. The 'h' has been officially restored to the name of the river and national park, but not to the city or region as a whole.

GATEWAY CITIES
Wellington

The capital of NZ, Wellington is not as big as Auckland (part of the reason why the two cities often engage in a friendly rivalry) and only has a regional population of 414,000, including 157,000 in the city itself.

Wellington, hemmed in by its magnificent harbour, began as a settlement in 1840 with very little flat land, which explains why reclamation of parts of the harbour began in 1852 and has continued ever since. The city runs up the hills on one side of the harbour, spilling into two narrow valleys leading north between the steep, rugged hills – one is the Hutt Valley and the other follows the SH1 through Tawa and Porirua.

Home to the country's government and national treasures, the city prides itself on being a centre for culture and the arts, and has a plethora of restaurants and cafes, nightlife and activities.

Information The central Wellington visitor centre (☎ 04-801 4000, fax 801 3030), 101 Wakefield St, is opposite the library in the Civic Square development. It has a large collection of leaflets detailing activities and accommodation in and around the city and the rest of the country. It's open in summer from 8.30 am to 5.30 pm on weekdays and from 9.30 am to 5.30 pm on weekends; only to 4.30 pm the rest of the year. There is also a visitor centre at the airport (☎ 04-388 5123), open until 6 or 7 pm daily and until 11.30 pm on Saturday.

The DOC visitor centre (☎ 04-472 7356, fax 471 2075) in the old government buildings facing Lambton Quay has information on walks, parks, outdoor activities and camping in the region. They also have a number of very good information sheets detailing off-road rides in the parks and reserves of the Wellington region.

The chief post office is in the Wellington train station, not far from Queens Wharf.

There are a couple of places to check your email near the Cuba St mall, including Cyberscape (☎ 04-384 1775), 115 Cuba St.

The AA centre (☎ 473 8738), 1st floor, 342 Lambton Quay, is a good place for members to stock up on maps. The Map Shop (☎ 04-385 1462), on the corner of Victoria and Vivian Sts, carries more detailed maps.

There are several bike shops in the central city, the best of which is Penny Farthing Cycles (☎ 04-385 2279), 89 Courtenay Place. It has a large range of bikes and accessories, a good workshop and also hires decent mountain bikes. Pins Cycles (☎ 04-472 4591), 126 Willis St, is another large shop worth a look.

Windy Wellington

Wellington really can get windy. When the sun's shining it can be a very attractive city, but it's not called the windy city for nothing – one of the local rock stations even calls itself Radio Windy.

At the start of winter you've got a fair chance of experiencing some gale-force days – the sort of days when strong men get pinned up against walls and little old ladies, desperately clutching their umbrellas, can be seen floating by at skyscraper height. Seriously, the flying grit and dust can be uncomfortable to the eyes and the flying rubbish can be a real mess.

One blustery day back in 1968 the wind blew so hard it pushed the almost-new Wellington-Christchurch car ferry *Wahine* on to Barrett's Reef, just outside the harbour entrance. The disabled ship later broke loose from the reef, drifted into the harbour and then sank, causing the loss of 51 lives. The Museum of Wellington City & Sea has a dramatic model and photographic display of the disaster.

Things to See & Do One of the absolutely must see places in NZ is **Te Papa** (☎ 04-381 7000, 🖥 www.museum.org.nz), the country's national museum, which opened in 1998. Down on Wellington's rejuvenated waterfront, it contains an extensive Maori collection as well as exhibits detailing the country's natural history, environment and European settlement.

Also well worth a look is the **Museum of Wellington City & Sea** (☎ 04-472 8904), on the corner of Jervois Quay and Queens Wharf.

At the north end of town on Bowen St a highly distinctive piece of architecture known as the **Beehive**, an office shaped like you-know-what is one of three adjacent buildings that form NZ's **parliamentary complex**. There are free public tours (☎ 04-471 9503) most days between 10am and 4pm. The **Wellington Zoo** (☎ 04-381 6750) has a fine collection of animals including a wide range of native species. It's 4km from the city centre at the end of the Newtown Park bus route No 10.

A good way to see the harbour is to jump on the Westpac Trust ferry (☎ 04-499 1273) for a 30 minute **cruise across to Days Bay** on the opposite shore. Several services a day also call in at **Somes Island**, a nature reserve with walking trails and nice beach areas.

A good way to get a bird's eye view of the city is to take the **cable car** up to the **Botanic Gardens**. This Wellington icon, operating since 1902, departs from an arcade just off Lambton Quay. A leisurely stroll around the botanic gardens is a good way to spend a couple of hours.

A broad **pedestrian walkway** extends along the harbour from near Queens Wharf all the way around past upmarket Oriental Bay. If you are feeling energetic there are a couple of places near Queens Wharf that rent **in-line skates**. You can also see the city from the water by taking a **kayak** out for a paddle on the harbour. Rent one from Fergs Rock 'n' Kayak (☎ 04-499 8898) at Shed 6 on Queens Wharf.

The Wellington area is excellent for **mountain biking** (see Mountain Biking in the Wellington Area section later in this chapter).

Places to Stay Camping isn't really practical in the city, but if you insist on sleeping outdoors the closest camping ground is the *Hutt Holiday Park Village* (☎ 04-568 5913, *95 Hutt Park Rd)*, 13km north-east of the city centre in Lower Hutt. Tent sites are $17 and tourist cabins cost from $30.

The *Wellington City YHA* (☎ 04-801 7280, cnr Cambridge & Wakefield Sts) is a conveniently situated, relatively luxurious hostel. Most rooms have views over the nearby harbour. Dorm beds cost from $17 and doubles are $46. *Downtown Backpackers* (☎ 04-473 8482), opposite the train station on Bunny St, is a large hostel with a big-city feel. Dorm beds are $18 and singles/doubles are $32/40.

Trekkers Hotel (☎ 04-385 2153, 213 Cuba St) is in a lively section of the city, with a good cafe, bar and travel agent in the complex. Shared rooms cost from $19, while rooms with linen are $45. There is also a locked storeroom where you can leave your bike.

Halswell Lodge (☎ 04-385 0196, 21 Kent Terrace) is a motel near the city centre with singles/doubles for $69/79 and units with spas for $120. Other similarly priced motels close to the action are the *Wellington Motel* (☎ 04-472 0334, 14 Hobson St) and the *Marksman Motor Inn* (☎ 04-385 2499, 42 Sussex St).

Top-end hotels include the *Wellington Parkroyal* (☎ 04-472 2722, cnr Grey & Featherstone Sts) and the *Plaza International* (☎ 04-473 3900, 148-176 Wakefield St), where a standard room will set you back about $300, although much better deals are usually available on weekends.

Places to Eat If you're looking for a restaurant, Courtenay Place and Cuba St have a high concentration of eateries. *Batavia* (☎ 04-801 5871, 95 Cuba St) is a cheap and cheerful Indonesian establishment serving up tasty meals of nasi lemak, beef rendang and other dishes for under $10. Close by at No 203 is *Ali Baba* (☎ 04-384 3014), a casual Middle Eastern eatery that's great for an inexpensive meal. *Cafe Globe* (☎ 04-385 2566), at No 213, in the same building as Trekkers Hotel, is a stylish cafe popular with locals and hotel guests alike. *Midnight Expresso* (☎ 04-384 7014) at No 178 is a hip coffee house with good java and wickedly tempting cakes.

Down near Courtenay Place in Blair St, traditionally Wellington's China town, a number of fashionable eateries have opened.

Here you'll find *Opera* (☎ 04-382 8654), a swish Italian-influenced place where various 'acts' (pastas and mains) are around $22. Close by are the *Exchange* (☎ 04-384 1006), at No 20, serving steaks and innovative mains for around $25, and the slightly cheaper *Beacon* (☎ 04-801 7275), at No 8.

For a filling meal on a tight budget try one of the *food courts* downtown. Most are in shopping arcades, however, so have limited opening hours. There's one in the Queens Wharf Retail Centre, another in the basement of the BNZ Centre at Willis St, Lambton Quay, and another on the ground floor of the market at James Smith Corner.

There's a large *New World* supermarket, close to the YHA hostel at 279 Wakefield St.

Getting There & Away There are plenty of options for getting to/from Wellington.

Air Air New Zealand (☎ 04-474 8950) on the corner of Panama St and Lambton Quay and Ansett New Zealand (☎ 04-471 1146) in Panama St both offer direct flights between Wellington and most larger centres around the country. A number of smaller regional airlines, such as Soundsair (☎ 04-388 2594), which flies to Picton and Blenheim (25 minutes), also serve the capital.

The 7km ride to/from the airport, located south-east of the city, is both easy and enjoyable; just follow the path along the edge of the harbour past Evans and Oriental Bays all the way into town. A number of shuttle bus companies operate between the city and the airport. Super Shuttle (☎ 04-387 8787) charges $5 for the trip into town, look for it just to the right of the main terminal ground floor exit. A taxi costs around $20.

Bus Intercity (☎ 04-472 5111) and Newmans (☎ 04-499 3261) have services to all major towns on the North Island. Buses leave from Platform 9 at the train station as well as from the Interislander ferry terminal. Tickets are available from the travel centre at the train station.

White Star (☎ 04-478 4734) has services up the west coast to Palmerston North, Wanganui and New Plymouth. Buses depart from Bunny St, opposite the train station.

Train Tranz Scenic (☎ 0800 802 802) operates three train services out of Wellington.

The overnight *Northerner* ($135 standard, $95 saver) and the daytime *Overlander* ($120/84) both run through central North Island to Auckland, while the *Bay Express* ($70/49) travels to Napier. All trains run daily except for the *Northerner*, which doesn't operate on Saturday.

The Wellington train station (☎ 04-498 3413 or ☎ 0800 802 802) is at the northern end of the city centre on Bunny St, not far from Queens Wharf. It has a travel centre selling tickets for trains, buses and ferries, as well as luggage lockers available from 6 am to 10 pm. Suburban Tranz Metro (☎ 04-801 7000) services also operate from the station.

Ferry Interislander ferries (☎ 0800 802 802) make the crossing of Cook Strait between Picton and Wellington four to five times daily. The standard fare for a one-way crossing is $46, although numerous discounts are available for advance bookings. Bikes are $10. A ticket on the faster Lynx (☎ 0800 802 802) costs $59 one way and $12 for your bike. The scenic crossing is well worth doing in daylight at least once.

The ferry terminal is about 2km north of the city centre. Cycle along the busy Aotea Quay path past the sports stadium. As the road joins the motorway, veer left then right, passing under the ramp and into the terminal complex.

Wellington Area

Although the city has the deserved nickname of 'Windy Wellington', there are plenty of good areas to get out and about on your bike. There are various mountain biking options around Wellington and in this section we look at three in particular: the Rimutaka Incline, Baring Head Coast and Karapoti Gorge rides.

In addition to mountain biking there are also several good areas to ride on-road. The diverse area of the greater city of Wellington in covered with the Wellington Scenic Circuit, which can be a fantastic ride if you can choose a wind-free day.

MOUNTAIN BIKING

Wellington is somewhat of a mecca for the NZ mountain bike scene. The country's premier off-road event, the Karapoti Classic, is held annually in the hills near Upper Hutt, and Mt Victoria, right in the heart of the city, has hosted rounds of the UCI Mountain Bike World Cup. A purpose-built mountain bike park, funded by the city council, is also under construction at Makara Peak.

While not the main focus of this guide, it would be criminal to avoid some mention of Wellington's fabulous mountain bike opportunities. As well as the areas discussed in this section, Belmont Regional Park, Mt Kau Kau, Hawkins Hill, the Akatarawa Forest and Battle Hill Farm Forest Park are all great places to ride within 30km of the city.

Credit for the popularity of off-road riding must go to the local mountain bike community and the authorities who have done a good job in accommodating mountain bikes in regional parks and recreation areas.

The Wellington Regional Council produces a range of excellent leaflets detailing off-road rides in the Wellington area. They are available from the main visitor centre in Civic Square or from the council, next door. The NZ Mountain Bike Web (🖳 www.mou ntainbike.co.nz) also has loads of information describing local rides.

If striking off into the wild, take the proper precautions. For off-road safety tips, see Riding Off-Road in the Health & Safety chapter.

Mt Victoria

You don't have to travel far from the city centre to have an off-road experience in Wellington. Mt Victoria, literally just a few hundred metres south-east of the CBD, is an oasis of urban parkland that has hosted a leg of the UCI Mountain Bike World Cup.

There are dozens of dual-use paths running through the area, mainly on the northwest side. The slog up the hill to the lookout at the top is worth it for the views alone. Access is via Palliser Rd off Oriental Parade.

Makara Peak

The Makara Peak mountain bike park, a work in progress, promises to be a real boon to the Wellington off-road scene. Like the park already in use in Rotorua, it will be purpose-built for bikes, incorporating fun features such as 'berms', jumps and 'whoopdy-doos'. Several tracks are already open and the plan is to eventually have a 50km network of trails. The project has received funding from

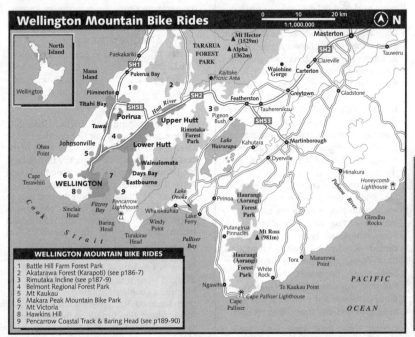

Wellington Mountain Bike Rides

0   10   20 km
1:1,000,000

WELLINGTON MOUNTAIN BIKE RIDES

1 Battle Hill Farm Forest Park
2 Akatarawa Forest (Karapoti) (see p186-7)
3 Rimutaka Incline (see p187-9)
4 Belmont Regional Forest Park
5 Mt Kaukau
6 Makara Peak Mountain Bike Park
7 Mt Victoria
8 Hawkins Hill
9 Pencarrow Coastal Track & Baring Head (see p189-90)

SOUTHERN NORTH ISLAND

the Wellington City Council, with the work being carried out by an enthusiastic bunch of volunteers.

For progress updates and more information, take a look at the Makara Peak section of the New Zealand Mountain Bike Web site.

To get there from the city centre, start at the Beehive, cycle up Bowen St to the end and then turn left, continuing up the hill on Glenmore St. Pedal past the Botanic Gardens and turn left at the small roundabout at the end. Continue through the tunnel and follow the road towards Karori, veering left at an intersection on to Karori Rd. Stay on Karori Rd, and ride past the Marsden and main Karori shops before veering left on to South Karori Rd. The park entrance is on the right about 1km down the road.

Bicycle Hire

You will, of course, need a mountain bike. If you need to rent one, both Pins and Penny Farthing have them for hire (see Information in the Gateway Cities section earlier in the chapter). Expect to pay around $30 a day for a fairly basic bike with front suspension. Better deals are available for multi-day hires.

A better option for a one-off ride may be to hire a guide. In Wellington, Mountain Bike Madness (☎ 0800 862 925) offers either guided or self-guided rides in the better known spots around town, selected to suit your ability. The bikes supplied are better than those available from the city shops and you also get safety gear and transport, making the price of around $45 self-guided and $55 guided for a three-hour ride an attractive alternative to going it alone.

The Karapoti Classic

Q: What do Superman, Darth Vader and Elvis all have in common?

If you said 'a fondness for capes', then you're absolutely right. If you answered that they've all ridden in the Karapoti Classic, then you're not far off the mark either. The Karapoti Classic is a real highlight of the New Zealand mountain bike calendar. Comprising a punishing 48km course round a single lap through the Akatarawa Forest near Upper Hutt, it's more than just another race. Since becoming an annual event in 1986 it has evolved into a tremendously popular celebration of off-road riding, attracting fat-tyre fanatics from around the country. So many people want to ride in the Karapoti, in fact, that since 1996 the race organisers have been forced to cap the number of entrants at 1000.

The Classic was the first national mountain bike race in NZ and remains one of the few big single-lap adventure-style contests around. Its status was recognised by the US magazine *VeloNews*, which named it as one of the '25 best races in the world'.

Although there are no shortage of serious riders looking to win the prestigious event, plenty of competitors fall squarely into the 'getting there is half the fun' category. Participants in recent years have included mountain bike world champions, BMX riders, grandmothers, road bikers, Darth Vader, Superman, the three Elvis', ballerinas, suit-wearing stock brokers, national politicians and even some guy with a huge ghetto blaster strapped to his back.

Karapoti Gorge

MOUNTAIN BIKE RIDE

Duration ....1-2 hours
Distance 14km
Difficulty ....easy-moderate
Start/End..............car park on Karapoti Rd

This scenic trip up the Karapoti Gorge following a branch of the Akatarawa River rates as one of the best beginner rides in the country. While it follows part of the route of the famous Karapoti Classic (see the boxed text), it is a much easier challenge.

If you're without transport the best way to get to the start is to catch a suburban train to Upper Hutt, follow (in reverse) the Rimutaka Incline ride to the SH2, then ride about 1km in the direction of Masterton, turning left onto a side road signed 'to Waikanae', about 500m beyond the Rimutaka Tavern. Ride along this narrow, quiet road through the hills for a couple of kilometres and turn off onto Karapoti Rd, crossing the Akatarawa River. About 2km further on the road comes to a car park and the start of the trail.

THE RIDE

The track is in good condition most of the way, but gets progressively narrower and rougher as you ride deep into the gorge, following the river upstream. The trail climbs steadily but the gradient is very gentle, making for easy, enjoyable cycling perfect for off-road rookies. A couple of stream crossings keep things interesting, as does the wonderfully lush regenerating bush. After passing McGhies Bridge the trail comes to a grassy clearing. This is a good spot to take a break before turning around and enjoying the downhill run back to the car park.

Rimutaka Incline

MOUNTAIN BIKE RIDE

Duration .... 2-3 hours
Distance 41.2km
Difficulty .... moderate
Start .... Featherston
End .... Upper Hutt

This scenic off-road ride through the Rimutaka Range follows the route of the historic railway line. Ride it either as an enjoyable Wellington day trip or as an alternative to the SH2 on your way to or from the capital.

HISTORY

The Rimutaka Incline railway opened in 1878. Its Fell locomotives struggled up the steep gradients until the line's closure in 1955 brought about by the opening of a new 8.8km tunnel through the hills. The Rimutaka Incline was the steepest railway line in NZ, with a vertical drop of 265m in less than 5km.

While in Featherston, take the opportunity to stop in at the Fell Engine Museum (☎ 06-308 9379), on the corner of Lyon and Fitzherbert Sts. It contains a magnificently restored Fell locomotive, the only one remaining, which used three rails to assist it in the arduous climb up and over the Rimutaka Incline. Lots of photographs and other memorabilia provide a historical perspective that really enhances the ride that travels over the same route.

PLANNING

A front light or torch (flashlight) will come in handy in the tunnels and grab a snack and top up your water bottles in Featherston.

GETTING TO/FROM THE RIDE
Featherston

Train There are several daily Tranz Metro (☎ 04-801 7000) Wairarapa Connection trains to Featherston departing from Wellington central train station. The trip takes about an hour and costs $8.50. Bikes are $4 and travel in the guard's van.

Upper Hutt

Train Upper Hutt is serviced by the Tranz Metro (☎ 04-801 7000) suburban rail network. There are frequent connections to/from Wellington central train station. Your bike goes with you in the passenger carriage, so it's best to travel outside peak hours.

Bicycle It's possible to cycle from Upper Hutt to Wellington on the SH2, but while plenty of commuter cyclists use the route, it is a very busy road and not at all enjoyable to ride on. The train is a much better option.

THE RIDE

Not far out of Featherston, turn off the SH2 and onto the Western Lake Rd signed to Lake Ferry. The route is fairly flat, passing through bland coastal farming land. After 9.7km a signed turn-off leads you down a short stretch of gravel road to the start of the trail. An old station shelter contains a few plaques detailing the history of the route.

The first few kilometres along the track are by far the roughest, travelling over a rocky narrow path through thick bush. If you are on a touring bike you will probably have to get off and push at some stage. Things get a lot easier when the trail reaches **Cross Creek**, the site of another station shelter. The old rail bed is clearly distinguishable and now resembles a grassy path about 2m wide. It is quite good to cycle on but is rocky in places.

As to be expected of a former railway line, the gradient is constant but gentle and you steadily gain height as the pathway snakes its way through the hills of the Rimutaka Range. The first of four tunnels is encountered after 15.4km. It's only about 100m in length and can be safely ridden through once your eyes have had time to adjust. A short distance on another tunnel is reached after the incline rounds a bend known as Siberia Gully, a part of the track

SOUTHERN NORTH ISLAND

Rimutaka Incline

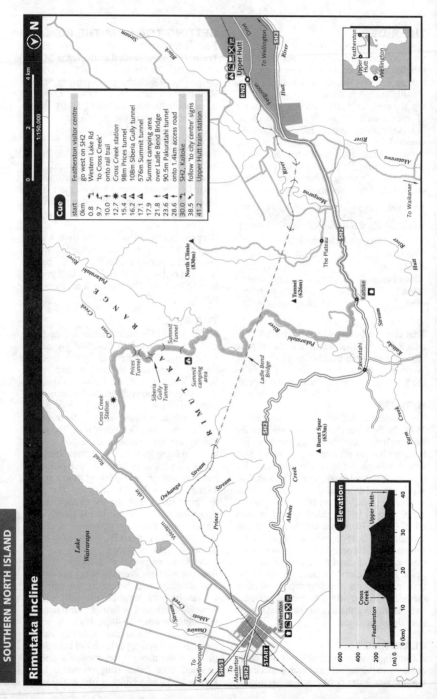

Cue		
start		Featherston visitor centre
0km		go west on SH2
0.8	⌐	Western Lake Rd
9.7	∟	'to Cross Creek'
10.0		onto rail trail
12.7	✳	Cross Creek station
15.4	▲	98m Prices tunnel
16.2	▲	108m Siberia Gully tunnel
17.1	▲	576m Summit tunnel
17.9	◀	Summit camping area
21.8	↑	over Ladle Bend Bridge
23.6	▲	90.5m Pakuratahi tunnel
28.6	↑	onto 1.4km access road
30.0	↑	SH2, Kaitoke
38.5	↘	follow 'to city centre' signs
41.2		Upper Hutt train station

Elevation

particularly prone to strong crosswinds – so strong in fact that in 1880 a fully loaded train was blown from the rails.

The longest of the tunnels is the Summit Tunnel, a 576m-long shaft of darkness which emerges at the route's high point. Apart from the pinprick of light at the end, it's very dark, so watch out for the puddles! At the summit there is another station shelter and a nice grassy *camping area* surrounded by pine trees. The track is much better for cycling on from this point, resembling a hard-packed gravel road.

The descent is a real joy and is just gradual enough so that you don't have to touch the pedals as you travel between large stands of plantation timber. There is another *camping area* with toilets off to the side of the Ladle Bend Bridge (21.8km).

By the entrance to the final tunnel (73m) a large concrete box marks the opening of a long ventilation shaft for the 8.8km tunnel, 116m below the surface, that rendered the old Rimutaka route obsolete.

Beyond the Pakuratahi Tunnel the route flattens and opens out into a mixed landscape of grazing land and pine forests, reaching a gate marking the end of the route at 28.6km.

The access road emerges onto the busy SH2 at Kaitoke and climbs briefly before descending and rolling the rest of the way (following signs to the town centre) into Upper Hutt.

Baring Head Coast

MOUNTAIN BIKE RIDE

Duration	2-3 hours
Distance	37km
Difficulty	easy-moderate
Start/End	Days Bay

This great Wellington day trip combines a scenic ferry crossing with an enjoyable coastal ride by the harbour along the rugged, windswept beaches of Cook Strait to Baring Head. Unless you fancy pushing your bike along the soft sand for a couple of kilometres, you have to return the way you came.

It used to be possible to continue the ride around Baring Head, inland towards Featherston and back to Wellington via the Rimutaka Incline. Private property restrictions

across a small stretch of land near Turakirae Head unfortunately prevent cyclists from riding that way any more. It is now only possible once a year on the organised Big Coast mountain bike ride, held in late February, when about 1000 touring enthusiasts gather for the weekend event.

PLANNING
What to Bring

The route goes to a very exposed part of the coastline, so take a warm top and a raincoat along even if the sun is shining.

GETTING TO/FROM THE RIDE
Days Bay

The Westpac Trust ferry (☎ 04-499 1273) has several daily sailings across the harbour to Days Bay near Eastbourne. The trip takes about 30 minutes and costs $7 each way. Bikes are free. The ferry sails from a pier at Queens Wharf; the last ferry leaves Days Bay at 7 pm.

THE RIDE

From the Days Bay jetty the road follows the coast before turning inland through the shopping precinct in Eastbourne. Once on Muritai Rd you travel briefly through a nice residential area before hitting the coast again after 3.8km. A little further on a boom gate at the start of the Pencarrow coastal track blocks vehicle access, leaving you free to enjoy the rugged coastal scenery in a traffic-free environment. The road turns to gravel, but is still in good condition and fine for touring bikes.

At Pencarrow Head you cycle past a **lighthouse** and a not-so-pleasant sewage outfall pipe. The coastline is very rugged with rocky cliffs away to the left and windswept vegetation and the waters of Cook Strait to the right. With only the sound of the gravel beneath your tyres and not a soul in sight, it is hard to believe you are just a handful of miles from downtown Wellington.

The track becomes progressively rougher and sandier around 16.5km and gets pretty much unrideable on a touring bike as it approaches **Baring Head**, a headland containing a large rocky outcrop popular with local climbers looking to hone their skills. The rocks also provide welcome shelter if the wind is blowing hard, as it often is.

SOUTHERN NORTH ISLAND

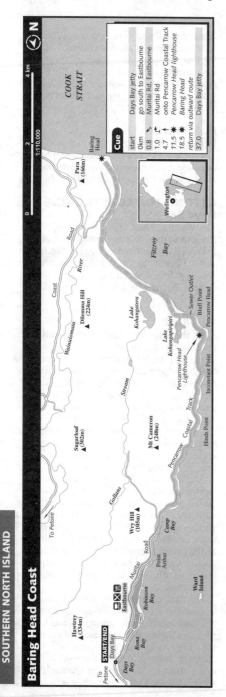

Baring Head Coast

SOUTHERN NORTH ISLAND

COOK STRAIT

	Cue	
start		Days Bay jetty
0km		go south to Eastbourne
0.8	↗ ←	Muritai Rd, Eastbourne
1.0	←	Muritai Rd
4.7		onto Pencarrow Coastal Track
11.5	✳	Pencarrow Head lighthouse
18.5	✳	Baring Head
return via outward route		
37.0		Days Bay jetty

A walk along the wonderfully windswept and secluded beach provides a nice break off the bike prior to the return trip back to the ferry pier. Backtracking may seem a little boring, but at least the wind is bound to be with you at some stage.

Wellington Scenic Circuit

Duration .... 2-2½ hours
Distance 38km
Difficulty .... easy
Start/End .... Te Papa museum

This scenic introduction to Wellington, provides some great views of the 'Windy City' and harbour. It also describes the route (in reverse) from the airport, surely one of the most accessible by bike anywhere in the world.

PLANNING
Maps
Navigation is pretty straightforward for this ride; it follows the coast much of the way. However, Wises' *Wellington City Handi Map* (1:31,250) shows the route in good detail and is likely to prove useful on other excursions about town.

THE RIDE
From **Te Papa museum** the broad walkway follows the waterfront round to Oriental Parade, a wonderful harbour-front promenade lined with fine million-dollar homes and apartments. The small **beach** next to the Freyberg Pool is a great place to take a dip and soak up the sun when the weather is warm. This stretch of path is always very popular with walkers and rollerbladers, so you might find it easier to cycle on the road; just watch for cars reversing.

The pedestrians thin out as you round Point Jerningham, the flat road hugging the water's edge on its way out towards the airport. Traffic is surprisingly light given the proximity to the city centre. If you feel like some excitement, jet skis are available for hire at **Greta Point**.

After passing the yacht club at Evans Bay, the road comes out onto busier Cobham Dr, although a good cycle path continues along the shore. Traffic diminishes considerably as the main road turns inland and you follow

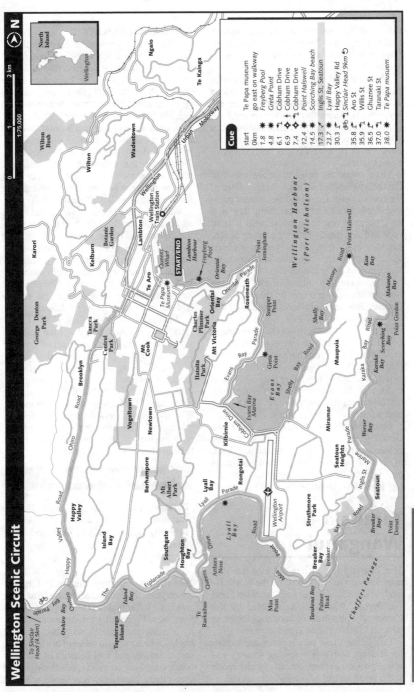

Wellington Scenic Circuit

N

North Island
Wellington

0 1 2 km
1:75,000

Cue

start	Te Papa museum
0km	**✷** go east on walkway
1.8	**✷** Freyberg Pool
4.8	**✷** Greta Point
6.1	◇ Cobham Drive
6.9	**↰** Cobham Drive
7.4	**↱** Cobham Drive
12.4	**✷** Point Halswell
14.5	**✷** Scorching Bay beach
17.3	**↰** Inglis St, Seatoun
23.7	**↱** Lyall Bay
30.3	**↰** Happy Valley Rd
	♺ Sinclair Head 9km ↻
35.8	**↰** Aro St
35.9	**↰** Willis St
36.5	**↰** Ghuznee St
37.0	**↰** Taranaki St
38.0	**✷** Te Papa musuem

SOUTHERN NORTH ISLAND

the coast past an outcrop of fuel storage tanks. Large low-flying jets making their final approach to the nearby airport are a spectacular sight.

The quiet harbour-side road is wonderful for cycling with only the occasional carload of gawking sightseers to interrupt your enjoyment. It passes through a military base then continues out to **Point Halswell**, a windy vantage point affording some tremendous views back to the city and across to Somes Island.

Once round the point there are views of Eastbourne nestled on the opposite shore of the harbour and also of the occasional passing Cook Strait ferry. **Scorching Bay** is a nice place to rest for a while with a good *cafe* and very pretty little swimming beach. Looking at the tranquil surrounds, it's hard to believe you are only minutes away from the centre of NZ's capital city.

After travelling inland briefly through Seatoun the road emerges by the coast near Breaker Bay and continues round the back of the airport to **Lyall Bay**, a popular local surf spot. The road follows the picturesque coastline all the way to the small settlement of Owhiro Bay. From here you can opt either to turn inland back towards the city, or extend the ride by following the coast round to Sinclair Head, a scenic 9km return trip, travelling mostly on a sandy 4WD track best suited to mountain bikes.

Once on Happy Valley Rd, the route climbs gently, travelling alongside a creek before emerging, surprisingly quickly, back in suburbia at Brooklyn. A scenic downhill past Central Park brings you back into the city just off Willis St. Te Papa isn't far away.

Taranaki & Wanganui

The Taranaki region juts out into the Tasman Sea on the west coast of the North Island, about halfway between Auckland and Wellington. Wanganui, dominated by the historically important Whanganui River, is between Taranaki and Wellington.

Combined these two regions are superb for touring, with awe-inspiring scenery, national parks, beaches, (mostly) quiet roads and a good spread of towns and services.

NATURAL HISTORY

Mt Taranaki is the dominating natural feature of the region. The massive cone of the mountain, a dormant volcano that looks remarkably like Japan's Mt Fuji, rises some 2518m above the lush green dairy pastures of the countryside. Egmont National Park (33,534 hectares), the second oldest in NZ, surrounds the mountain. The high rainfall and mild coastal climate of the area supports a lush rainforest on the lower slopes. Further up the mountain, tall *rimu* (red pine) and *kamahi* (black birch) trees give way to dense subalpine shrubs and alpine herbs, some of which are unique to the park.

Wanganui is a region of numerous rivers and countless valleys, the best known being the Whanganui River, which winds its way 392km from its source on the flanks of Mt Tongariro to the Tasman Sea. By virtue of its status as the longest navigable waterway in the country, it has historically played a large part in the settlement of the region and the interior of the North Island.

Whanganui National Park (74,231 hectares) covers a large portion of the countryside. It contains the largest tract of lowland forest in the North Island, consisting chiefly of rata, NZ honeysuckle *(rewarewa)*, rimu, tawa, kamahi and kowhai and other podocarp species, with beech dominant on the ridge tops. Tree ferns are also abundant. Bird species such as *kereru* (native pigeon), *piwakawaka* (fantail), tui, *toutouwai* (robin), *riroriro* (grey warbler) and *miromiro* (tomtit) can also be seen and heard.

Around Mt Taranaki

Duration	3 days
Distance	145km
Difficulty	easy-moderate
Start/End	New Plymouth

This short tour through the fertile Taranaki countryside is dominated by the towering cone of Mt Taranaki. The three day circuit from New Plymouth provides an opportunity to study the majestic mountain from all angles. The route also takes in the laid-back seaside towns and surf beaches of the west coast, travelling on quiet roads through lush green dairy pastures synonymous with the region. There are also plenty of diversions off the bike, including a number of excellent walks in Egmont National Park, including the walk to the mountain's summit.

PLANNING
When to Ride
Summer is the best season to cycle, especially if you are planning to climb Mt Taranaki. The warm weather and long days also allow full advantage to be taken of the excellent beaches along the west coast.

GETTING TO/FROM THE RIDE
New Plymouth
Air Air New Zealand Link (☎ 06-757 3300), 12-14 Devon St, has direct flights to Auckland, Hamilton, Nelson, Wanganui and Wellington, with onward connections.

Bus InterCity (☎ 06-759 9039) stops at the Travel Centre on the corner of Queen and King Sts. There are several buses daily heading north to Hamilton and Auckland and south-east to Wanganui and Palmerston North, with connections to Wellington, Gisborne and Napier. White Star (☎ 06-758 3338) operates two daily services (except Saturday) to Wellington via Wanganui and Palmerston North ($65). The bus departs from outside the Avis office at 25 Liardet St.

Bicycle It is possible to get to New Plymouth from Turangi, the end point of the Central Plateau ride (see the Eastern North Island chapter) by cycling 62km on the SH41 to Taumarunui, then following the Stratford Circuit ride, featured later in this chapter, in reverse. The route from Stratford to New Plymouth is described on Day 3 of this ride.

THE RIDE
New Plymouth
The principal centre of the Taranaki region, New Plymouth (population 66,500) is a bustling city boasting the only deep-water port on the west coast. With Mt Taranaki as a backdrop (though usually obscured by low cloud), magnificent parks and plenty of accommodation and dining options, it makes a good base for exploring Egmont National Park and the surrounding region.

Information The New Plymouth visitor centre (☎ 06-759 6080, fax 759 6073) at the corner of Liardet and Leach Sts is open from 8.30 am to 5 pm on weekdays and 10 am to 3 pm on weekends. The staff are helpful and the informative brochures, *New Plymouth Options* and *Taranaki for Free*, are worth picking up.

DOC (☎ 06-758 0433, fax 758 0430), 220 Devon St West, is open from 8 am to 4.30 pm on weekdays. A number of banks with ATMs and a good bike shop, Cycle Inn (☎ 06-758 7418), can be found along the main drag, Devon St.

Things to See & Do Even though New Plymouth is renowned for its superb **parks**, it's hard not to be surprised at just how nice they are. Just 10 minutes walk from the centre of town, **Pukekura**, which first opened in 1876, and **Brooklands**, a private estate bequeathed to New Plymouth in 1934, offer 49 hectares of manicured gardens featuring some superb water features.

Also well worth a look is the **Taranaki Museum** (☎ 06-758 9583) in Ariki St which has a collection of Maori artefacts, wildlife exhibits and an early colonists exhibition. The **Govett-Brewster Art Gallery** on the corner of Queen and King Sts is a renowned contemporary art gallery with a good reputation for its adventurous shows.

In summer, **boat trips** out to the Sugar Loaf Islands Marine Park are a popular attraction. The islands, eroded volcanic remnants, are a refuge for seabirds, NZ fur seals and other marine life. Seal numbers are at their greatest from June to October. Chaddy's Charters (☎ 06-758 9133) run island cruises, departing from Lee Breakwater. There are also some excellent beaches close to town. East End and Fitzroy Beaches at the eastern end of the city are both patrolled and nice places to spread out your towel.

Places to Stay The *Fitzroy Beach Holiday Park (☎ 06-758 2870, 1D Beach St)* is next to a good surfing beach, 3.5km east of the centre. Tent sites are $8 per person, while cabins are $38 and on-site caravans are $33.

The YHA-associate *Egmont Lodge (☎ 06-753 5720, 12 Clawton St)* is a quiet, friendly hostel in large grounds. The owner, who kindly bakes a chocolate Egmont cake for guests each evening, is helpful and knowledgeable about the area. The only down side is that the hostel is a five minute ride

SOUTHERN NORTH ISLAND

Around Mt Taranaki

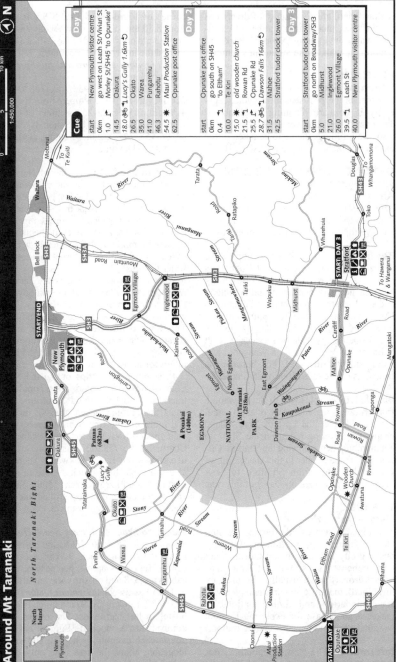

Cue

Day 1

start		New Plymouth visitor centre
0km		go west on Leach St/Vivian St
1.0	↵	Morley St/SH45 'to Opunake'
14.5		Oakura
18.0	⚲ ↵	Lucy's Gully 1.6km ↺
26.5		Okato
35.0		Warea
41.0		Pungarehu
46.3		Rahotu
54.5	✳	Maui Production Station
62.5		Opunake post office

Day 2

start		Opunake post office
0km		go south on SH45
0.4	↵	'to Eltham'
10.0		Te Kiri
15.0	✳	old wooden church
21.5	↵	Rowan Rd
25.5	↵	Opunake Rd
28.7	⚲ ↵	Dawson Falls 16km ↺
31.5		Mahoe
42.5		Stratford tudor clock tower

Day 3

start		Stratford tudor clock tower
0km		go north on Broadway/SH3
5.0		Midhurst
21.0		Inglewood
26.0	✳	Egmont Village
39.5	↵	Leach St
40.0		New Plymouth visitor centre

(1.5km) from the centre of town. Dorm beds are $15, singles $25 and doubles $36. You can also pitch a tent.

Much more central is **Shoestring Backpackers** (☎ 06-758 0404, 48 Lemon St), a well equipped, friendly place in a stately old home. Dorm beds cost $14, singles are $20 and doubles $32.

There are plenty of motels in town. The **Central Motel** (☎ 06-758 6444, 86 Eliot St) is small but convenient with units from $60. The **Cottage Mews** (☎ 06-758 0404, 50 Lemon St), next door to Shoestring Backpackers, is modern and good value with tidy rooms from $60.

Balconies (☎ 06-757 8866, 161 Powderham St) and **Treehouse** (☎ 06-757 4288, 75 Morley St) are both excellent B&Bs charging from $50.

Places to Eat To satisfy a cyclist-sized appetite try the good-value, $10 smorgasbord of Chinese, Thai and Indonesian dishes at the **Asian Wok** (☎ 06-758 1828, cnr St Aubyn & Dawson Sts). You can also order off the menu. **Steps Restaurant** (☎ 06-758 3393, 37 Gover St) is a popular Mediterranean place offering good lunches and dinners and a pleasant atmosphere. For a genuinely French experience try **Andre's L'Escargot** (☎ 06-758 4812, 37 Brougham St), a local favourite and award winner in a historic building. Mains cost from $25.

There are plenty of fast-food places in town mainly scattered along Devon St. Try **Burger Wisconsin** at No 144 or the **El Condor Pizzeria** at No 170, a trendy little Argentinian pasta place with tasty pizzas at around $14 for a medium.

Self-caterers will find a **Pack 'N Save** at the City Centre Mall on Gill St.

Day 1: New Plymouth to Opunake

3-4 hours, 62.5km

Day 1 is a relatively easy ride that will have you craning your neck to take in the fabulous scenery on both sides of the road as you cycle between Mt Taranaki and some of the best surf beaches in NZ.

The outskirts of town are reached after a rolling 5km. The SH45 is fairly quiet and has a good broad shoulder for much of its length, making the first part of the ride through coastal grazing pastures very pleasant, especially if you are fortunate enough to glimpse Mt Taranaki without its usual shroud of cloud cover. There is a saying around these parts that if you can see the mountain it's going to rain, and if you can't it's already raining!

About 10km out of town the highway meets the ocean and begins running parallel with it. The road is fairly straight and there are no major hills to tackle, but the gently undulating terrain ensures that there is always something for your legs to do. The small seaside town of **Oakura** is reached after 14.5km. It is famed for its beautiful beach, which is ideal for swimming and a popular spot with surfers and windsurfers.

Eighteen kilometres out of Oakura is an access road to the left leading up to **Lucy's Gully**, one of the few places where exotic trees are being maintained in a national park. There is a nice picnic area surrounded by lush vegetation and it is also the starting point for a couple of good walks into the Kaitake Ranges. It's a worthwhile detour, but the steep 800m-long climb up the access road is tough going.

Back on the main route, the road climbs gradually for a while and then begins a steady roller-coaster-like series of dips, rising and falling around 20m each time. The road is flanked by lush green dairy pastures and there are occasional views away to the ocean.

The terrain beyond Okato is much flatter than earlier in the day, making the remainder of the ride fairly easy going.

Learn more about the region's energy industry at the hard-to-miss **Maui Production Station's visitor centre** (☎ 06-761 8604), about 8km before Opunake. The Maui A platform, 35km offshore, is visible through a large set of binoculars at the centre.

Opunake

Opunake (population 2100) is the largest town on the west side of the mountain. It's well known for its good fishing as well as the fine black sand beach in Opunake Bay, a peaceful place that's good for swimming and surfing.

Information The visitor centre (☎ 06-761 8663) is in the Egmont Public Library and Cultural Centre on Tasman St, the main street. Also on Tasman St is Collins Sports

Centre (☎ 06-761 8778), which has a small selection of bikes and accessories.

Things to See & Do If the weather is warm, a **swim** down at the black sand beach at Opunake Bay, regarded as the best in south Taranaki, is hard to beat.

Places to Stay & Eat Right on the beach, the ***Opunake Beach Camp Resort*** *(☎ 06-761 8235)* has tent sites for $8 per person and dorm beds for $14. In town, the ***Opunake Motel & Backpackers Lodge*** *(☎ 06-761 8330, 36 Heaphy Rd)* has single/double units for $55/70 and dorm beds in a large house out the back for $18. Good pub beds are available at the ***Opunake Club Hotel*** *(☎ 06-761 8213, 100 Tasman St)* at $25/50 for a single/double.

For food, the ***Club Hotel*** *(☎ 06-761 8213)* or get a feed at ***Opunake Chinese Takeaways*** *(☎ 06-761 8087, 37 Tasman St)*. Self-caterers can stock up at ***Beau's Foodmarket*** *(77 Tasman St)*.

Day 2: Opunake to Stratford

2½-3½ hours, 42.5km

Just out of town, turn left off the SH43 onto Eltham road, a quiet rural thoroughfare that begins to climb steadily but gently. Looking at the countryside, it's not hard to appreciate why Taranaki is one of the premier dairying regions in NZ. Even in summer the grass appears incredibly lush and green, evidence of the area's high rainfall courtesy of the rain shadow cast by the mountain. For the black-and-white dairy cattle grazing in the fields it must seem like cow heaven.

After 10km the road continues to ascend as you pass by a few scattered buildings forming the settlement of Te Kiri. At 15km, an **old wooden church** stands alone at the roadside, the towering presence of Mt Taranaki forming a spectacular backdrop. After turning onto Rowan Rd, cycle directly towards the mountain, the gradient of the route increasing as you scale its lower slopes. On a clear day (rare) the Fuji-like cone, which nearly fills your entire field of vision, is an awesome sight.

Not long after the turn onto the Opunake Rd, the route passes the turn-off to Dawson Falls on the left (see Side Trip) and reaches the high point for the day a couple of kilometres further on at Mahoe. The final

rolling downhill stretch to Stratford is easily covered, bringing you out onto the SH3 close to the centre of town.

Side Trip: Dawson Falls

1-1½, 16km return

Dawson Falls is a popular recreation area in Egmont National Park, with many fine short walks. A 20 minute walk brings you to the waterfalls themselves, a spectacular 18m cascade over an ancient lava flow. Dawson Falls is also the starting point for the more difficult of the two main routes to the summit of Mt Taranaki, a 10 hour return walk requiring some technical climbing skills.

From the turn-off onto Upper Manaia Rd from the main route, it's approximately 8km uphill to the car park and DOC visitor centre (☎ 025 430 248). Although the ride there is quite tough, Dawson Falls is a worthwhile trip and, given the brevity of the main route, you should still have plenty of time to make it to Stratford.

If you want to stay overnight, there's accommodation near the visitor centre available at either the comfortable Swiss-style ***Dawson Falls Tourist Lodge*** *(☎ 06-765 6100)* or cheaper ***Konini Lodge*** *(☎ 025 430 248)*, operated by the DOC.

Stratford

Named after the birthplace of William Shakespeare, most of the streets in Stratford bear some reference to one of his plays. A large town, known as the gateway to the Egmont National Park, Stratford is a good base for exploring the region but has few attractions of its own likely to distract you for long. It is also the starting point for the Stratford Circuit ride.

Information The visitor centre (☎ 06-765 6708) is at the southern end of town on Broadway (SH3), the main street. It's open from 9 am to 5 pm weekdays and 10 am to 2 pm on Saturday. InterCity and Newmans buses also stop here.

The DOC centre (☎ 06-765 5144) is on Pembroke Rd, heading up to Mt Taranaki.

If you plan on tramping in Egmont National Park there are two DOC visitor information centres on the mountain, offering maps and advice on the weather and track conditions. The North Egmont visitor centre (☎ 06-756 0990), on the eastern slopes of

Mt Taranaki at the end of Egmont Rd, is the most visited. On the southern slopes, the Dawson Falls visitor centre (☎ 025-430 248) is on Upper Manaia Rd.

Bike spares and accessories are available from Excelsior House (☎ 06-765 6254), at 184 Broadway.

Branches of the ANZ and Bank of New Zealand (with ATMs) can also be found on the main street.

Things to See & Do The **Taranaki Pioneer Village** on the SH3 1km south of the centre is a four-hectare outdoor museum with 50 historic buildings. Some are transplanted originals, while others are recreations containing an array of historic artefacts.

Stratford also has a number of manicured **parks and gardens**. Ngaere Gardens, 5km south of town on the SH3, is an English-style park complete with ponds, fountains and 100-year-old chestnut trees. Hollard Gardens is also well worth a look. The visitor centre has details. If you fancy a **swim** there is a nice heated public indoor pool on Page St.

There are also plenty of **great walks** in the Stratford area and Egmont National Park. In town choose from the Carrington Walkway, which starts on Regan St West and follows the Patea River (2 hours), or the Three Bridges Trail, an easy 20 minute hike also along the river bank, through King Edward Park. The Stratford visitor information centre has details.

The national park itself contains a number of excellent walking possibilities. The hike to the summit of Mt Taranaki is popular, but challenging and thanks to the highly changeable weather, not without its hazards. There are two main routes. The safest and most direct takes off from the North Egmont visitor centre (6-8 hours return), while the other, starting at the Dawson Falls visitor centre (see Side Trip earlier) requires more technical skills (7-10 hours return). The three to five day 55km round-the-mountain track is another justifiably popular trek. There are a number of huts en route. Contact the DOC's Stratford Field Centre (☎ 06-765 5144) on Pembroke Rd, or the DOC visitor centres at North Egmont (☎ 06-756 0990) and Dawson Falls (☎ 025-430 248) for further information as well as track and weather conditions.

Places to Stay & Eat The *Stratford Holiday Park* (☎ 06-765 6440), in Page St, has tent sites at $9 per person, cabins from $33 (for two) and dorm beds in a good backpacker bunkhouse for $16.

The *Broadway Motel* (☎ 06-765 7308, 65 Broadway North) has units set in park-like surroundings from $72 for two people, while budget pub beds are available at the *New Commercial Hotel* (☎ 06-765 6364), on Broadway.

During the day there are a number of food places along Broadway to choose from, mainly fish and chip takeaways and old-fashioned country cafes. After dark, however, the selection is somewhat limited. Choices include *Garwah* (☎ 06-765 6402), a Chinese restaurant and take away, *Lucky's*, the *Axemen's Inn* (☎ 06-765 5707) and the *Stratford Food Hut* (☎ 06-765 8663). *Berties Bakery* is a good place to refuel on pies and sausage rolls during the day.

The *New World* supermarket is on Ragan St.

Day 3: Stratford to New Plymouth

2-2½ hours, 40km

The ride to New Plymouth is mostly downhill, passing through the region's rural heartland, a landscape of distinctive grassy hills populated by herds of content dairy cattle. The SH3 carries more traffic than the SH45, but the shoulder is good most of the way.

Not long after leaving Stratford you pass through the small settlement of Midhurst and, after a series of rolling descents, arrive in the sizeable town of Inglewood (21km). Kids at heart will want to check out the **Fun Ho! National Toy Museum** (☎ 06-756 7030), in Rata St, which contains an impressive collection of NZ-made metal toys.

Continuing on the SH3 the downhill run through the lush Taranaki countryside continues. At Egmont Village the main road into the national park leads away to the left. There is a good farmstay here, *The Missing Leg* (☎ 06-752 2570, 1082 Junction Rd), which offers transport to the upper slopes. Dorm beds cost $13.

Cycling through the outskirts of New Plymouth you pass by the horse-racing track and a number of motels scattered along Eliot St (SH3), before coasting downhill into the centre of town.

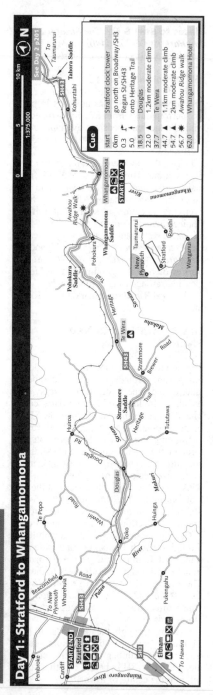

Cue

start		Stratford clock tower
0km	↑	go north on Broadway/SH3
0.3	↳	Regan St/SH43
5.0		onto Heritage Trail
18.5		Douglas
22.0	▲	1.2km moderate climb
37.7	◀	Te Wera
44.7	◀	1.1km moderate climb
54.7	◀	2km moderate climb
56.7	✳	Awahou Ridge walk
62.0		Whangamomona Hotel

Stratford Circuit

Duration..7 days
Distance.....................................447.9km
Difficulty...........................moderate-hard
Start/End.....................................Stratford

This tour takes you into parts of NZ well off the tourist track. It is characterised by long stretches of quiet, isolated road, small towns and some terrific bush and rural scenery. The leg from Stratford following the SH43 Heritage Trail to Taumarunui, continuing down the magnificent river road to historic Wanganui is a real highlight. From Wanganui you have the option of heading further south towards Wellington or completing the circuit to Stratford via Hawera on the SH3.

PLANNING
When to Ride
Taranaki and Wanganui are not subject to as big an influx of summer holiday-makers as some other regions, so summer, with its warm weather and long days, is probably the pick of the seasons. Things can get a little chilly over winter, especially if camping out along the river road.

Maps & Books
Make sure to pick up a copy of the *Taranaki and SH43 Heritage Trail* leaflet from the Stratford visitor centre. It is a valuable companion on the ride, describing historical points of interest along the route to Taumarunui. The *Whanganui River Road* leaflet, available from the visitor centre in Taumarunui, is also worth getting hold of.

What to Bring
Because of the relatively large distance between supply points, make sure to carry plenty of water as well as enough food to munch on during the day. Between Days 4 and 5, unless you are staying at the Flying Fox, there are no shops en route and you will need to carry enough food for two days.

GETTING TO/FROM THE RIDE
Stratford
Bus InterCity (☎ 09-913 6100) and Newmans (☎ 0800 777 707) buses stop at the Stratford visitor centre on Broadway (SH3)

at the southern end of town. There are daily services from New Plymouth and Wellington (via Wanganui and Palmerston North).

Bicycle The route from New Plymouth is described in the Around Mt Taranaki ride earlier in this chapter, although you'll need to reverse the directions.

Wanganui
Air Air New Zealand Link (☎ 06-345 4089), 133 Victoria Ave, has daily direct flights to Auckland and Wellington, with onward connections. The airport is located 4km south of town.

Bus InterCity (☎ 06-345 4433) and Newmans (☎ 06-345 5566) both operate services north to Auckland via Hamilton and to New Plymouth. Heading south, buses go to Palmerston North and on to Wellington and Napier, leaving from the Wanganui Travel Centre at the top end of Ridgway St. White Star (☎ 06-345 7612) has services to New Plymouth, Palmerston North and Wellington, departing from outside the Avis office at 161 Ingestre St.

Bicycle It is possible to link this tour with the Central Plateau ride in the Eastern North Island chapter by cycling 46km on the SH47 to Turangi from National Park (Day 3 of this ride) or 62km on the SH41 from Taumarunui (Day 2).

THE RIDE
Stratford
See Stratford (pp196-7) in the Around Mt Taranaki ride earlier in this chapter for information about accommodation and other services.

Day 1: Stratford to Whangamomona
3½-5 hours, 62km
Day 1 takes you away from Taranaki dairy country and into the back country, where sheep and beef cattle rule the roost. Traffic on SH43 is generally very light as it rolls along throughout the day, although there are three significant hills to tackle. Make sure to stock up with food and drinks before setting off from Stratford as there are no shops en route today and the selection available in Whangamomona is pretty limited.

The first few kilometres out of town are slightly downhill, bringing you to a display board marking the start of the SH43 Heritage Trail after 5km. Throughout the ride to Taumarunui, teal-and-yellow signs mark places of historical interest along the route, described fully in the Heritage Trail leaflet.

The road is very quiet, rolling gently through a landscape filled with the grassy beehive-like hills found throughout the region. Beyond Douglas the terrain becomes hillier and you start the ascent of **Strathmore Saddle** after 22km. From the summit there are great views on a clear day back to Mt Taranaki and ahead to the distant volcanic peaks of the Central Plateau.

The route passes by the *Te Wera Camp* (☎ *06-762 3859*) at 37.7km. Its multitude of small cabins are mainly intended for school groups but the public, even cyclists, are welcome. After the climb over Pohokura Saddle there are several fairly flat kilometres before the major climb of the day to Whangamomona Saddle begins (54.7km). The landscape changes to lush beech and podocarp forest. At the summit there is a small picnic area as well as the start point of the **Awahou Ridge Track**, a nice three-hour forest walk.

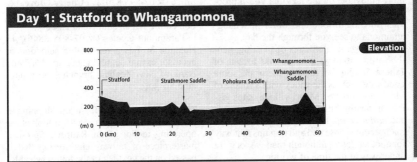

Day 1: Stratford to Whangamomona

SOUTHERN NORTH ISLAND

The descent brings you most of the way into the near ghost town of Whangamomona, a faded outpost with plenty of character, offering the only food and lodging in the area.

Whangamomona

The grand tour of Whangamomona doesn't take long. There are a few scattered houses, some long-closed businesses, a tearoom and historic hotel. The town has been in steady decline since the great flood of 1924, but gained notoriety in 1989 when it declared itself a republic after a change in regional boundaries meant it was no longer part of Taranaki.

Places to Stay & Eat A camping ground is about 600m behind the Whangamomona Hotel. In keeping with the rest of the village it has seen better days, but there is plenty of space to pitch a tent ($8). There are also a few dilapidated cabins and a couple of resident peacocks. Pay at the hotel.

Rooms are available at the *Whangamomona Hotel* (☎ 06-762 5823) at $45 per person for dinner, bed and breakfast. Rowdy crowds are definitely not a problem here.

The hotel is also the only place to get an evening meal. The *tearoom* across the road has a small selection of pies, soft drinks and other snacks to stock up on for lunch.

Day 2: Whangamomona to Taumarunui

5-6 hours, 87.2km
This is a challenging but rewarding ride, with a number of significant climbs and a sizeable stretch of unsealed road. The scenery, however, is fantastic, especially through the Tangarakau Gorge, made all the more enjoyable by the fact that you'll probably only see a handful of cars all day. Stock up with enough food and water in Whangamomona to see you through the day.

After several kilometres of twisting, gently rolling road you begin the ascent of **Tahora Saddle**. At the top there are some good views across the valley with a couple of Maori *pa* (fortified Maori village) sites visible on nearby hilltops. There is also a *cafe* and *motor camp*. Following the descent, the road becomes unsealed and remains that way for another 25km, although road works were under way at the time of writing.

The road climbs gently and not long after passing the turn-off to Bushlands Holiday Park you cycle through the 180m-long Moki Tunnel, arriving at the entrance to the **Tangarakau Gorge** a short distance later. The gorge is wonderfully scenic, the road running alongside the river below sheer limestone walls festooned with lush ferns and other vegetation. You continue to climb gently most of the way through it, the ascent steepening as you approach the far end. The road emerges back into farming country after 36.5km.

For much of the remaining distance to Taumarunui you cycle through a landscape of undulating, rocky pastures, with a number of sizeable climbs keeping your heart rate high and providing some great views over the King Country to the distant volcanic peaks of the Central Plateau.

Approaching Taumarunui the road drops down, travelling beside the Whanganui River and below Herlihy's Bluff before climbing through the outskirts, a final welcome descent bringing you into the centre of town.

Taumarunui

Taumarunui (population 6630) is a quiet town at the confluence of the Whanganui and Ongarua Rivers. In winter it operates as a ski town, but it is really too far from the snow to be convenient. In summer it is a popular access point for people setting off on canoeing trips down the Whanganui River.

Information The Taumarunui visitor centre (☎ 07-895 7494, fax 895 6117) is at the train station on Hakiaha St in the centre of town. Pick up a copy of the *Whanganui River Road Pamphlet*, which details points of interest found on the route south of Raehiti. The DOC office (☎ 07-895 8201) at Cherry Grove, beside the river, is the place to go for information on the Whanganui National Park.

Paramount Cycles (☎ 07-895 8846), 48 Hakiaha St, has a reasonable selection of accessories and spares. There are ANZ and Bank of New Zealand branches on Manuaute St.

Things to See & Do It's worth stopping in at the visitor centre just to take a look at the operating model of the **Raurimu Spiral**, a masterpiece of railway engineering that is passed on the next leg of the tour. The centre

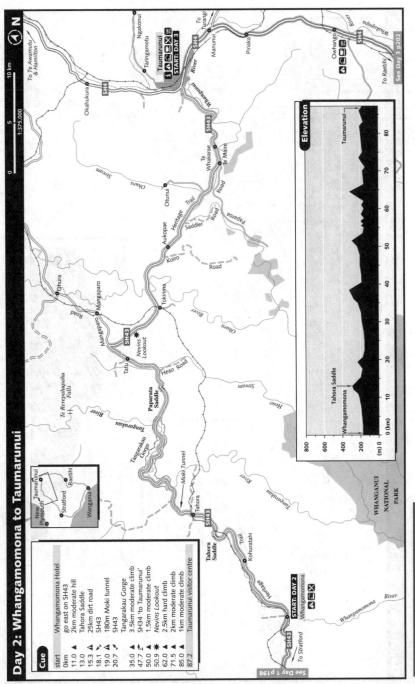

Day 2: Whangamomona to Taumarunui

Cue		
start		Whangamomona Hotel
0km		go east on SH43
11.0	◄	2km moderate hill
13.0	◄	Tahora Saddle
15.3	◄	25km dirt road
18.1	↘	SH43
19.0	↗	180m Moki tunnel
20.7	↗	SH43
35.0		Tangarakau Gorge
47.7	↵	3.5km moderate climb
50.0		SH34 'to Taumarunui'
50.9	✴	1.5km moderate climb
62.0	◄	Nevins Lookout
71.5	◄	2.5km hard climb
85.0	◄	2km moderate climb
87.2	◄	1km moderate climb
		Taumarunui visitor centre

SOUTHERN NORTH ISLAND

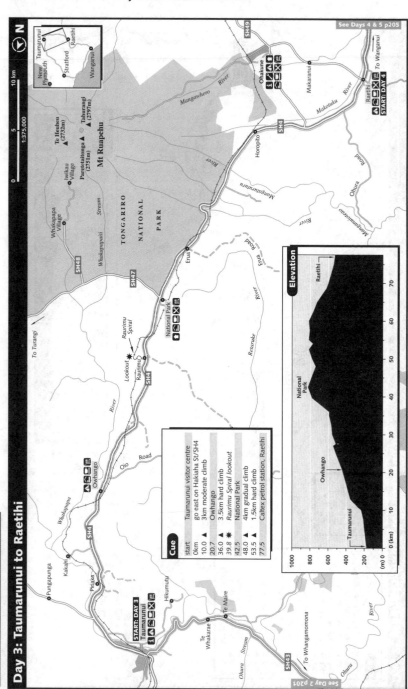

SOUTHERN NORTH ISLAND

Day 3: Taumarunui to Raetihi

See Days 4 & 5 p205

START: DAY 4

START: DAY 3

See Day 2 p201

Cue

start		Taumarunui visitor centre
0km		go east on Hakiaha St/SH4
10.0	▲	3km moderate climb
20.7		Owhango
36.0	▲	3.5km hard climb
39.8	✳	Raurimu Spiral lookout
42.5		National Park
48.0	▲	4km gradual climb
53.5	▲	1.5km hard climb
77.5		Caltex petrol station, Raetihi

Elevation

also has suggestions for some **walks** in the area. A nice short one is the tramp along the path running east beside the Whanganui River from Cherry Grove to the holiday park about 3km away.

Places to Stay & Eat The *Taumarunui Holiday Park (☎ 07-895 9345)* is situated next to the Whanganui River, just off the SH4 about 3km east of town. Tent sites cost $8 and cabins are available for $29. The *Taumarunui Alpine Inn & Backpackers (☎ 07-895 3478, cnr Marae & Miriama Sts)*, a large pub named to attract ski groups, has dorm beds from $16 and clean, comfortable doubles from $44. *Kelly's Motel (☎ 07-895 8175, 10 River Rd)* is comfortable and reasonable value with double units from $70.

The *Main Trunk Cafe (☎ 07-895 6544)*, on Hakiaha St, is a bright red 1913 train carriage fitted out as a cheerful cafe. It's open 24 hours, serving up a menu of burgers, fish and chips, sandwiches and the like. There are a number of takeaways and cafes along Hakiaha St, including two *Chinese restaurants* and the *Rivers II Cafe*, a good coffee bar with an excellent selection of vegetarian dishes. The *Pinnacles Restaurant* at the Taumarunui Alpine Inn is licensed and reasonably priced.

Self-caterers will find a *New World* supermarket on Hakiaha St.

Day 3: Taumarunui to Raetihi
4½-6 hours, 77.5km
The first few kilometres out of town are fairly flat, but it isn't long before you begin to climb, a trend that continues throughout the first 60km of the ride. Traffic is light, although quite a high proportion of it consists of large trucks. After a hill at 10km the road continues to gently ascend all the way up to the winter ski town of Owhango.

The road takes a somewhat more direct route up Spiral Hill than the railway line, requiring a fairly stiff climb over 3.5km to reach the summit. There is a lookout just off the road that provides a view of the famed **Raurimu Spiral**, a piece of engineering hailed as a 'wonder of the world' when it was completed in 1908. The railway spiral's three horseshoe curves allowed the main lines coming south from Auckland and north from Wellington to finally be joined.

The road continues to climb gently from the top, bringing you into the high country

of the central volcanic plateau. As you approach the village of **National Park** there are fine views across to the lofty peaks of Mt Ruapehu, Mt Tongariro and Mt Ngauruhoe.

The village is a popular base for the ski crowd in winter and in summer attracts trampers setting off to do the fabulous Tongariro Crossing and other walks in nearby Tongariro National Park. It's on the main north-south rail line and has a good selection of hostel and lodge accommodation available if you feel like staying on.

The route descends slightly from National Park, before climbing steadily again to around 52km, after which the alpine grasses of the high country give way to thick native vegetation as the road drops down beside the Manganuioteao River. You climb again for several kilometres, reaching a high point at 60km, from where the remaining distance into Raetihi is predominantly downhill, making for an easy end to a tough day.

Raetihi
Out of the ski season, Raetihi is a small, sleepy place with many vacant shops mixed in with those still doing business along the main thoroughfare.

Information Some services, including the visitor centre (☎ 06-385 4805), 38 Seddon St, close down over summer.

If you want to stay more than one night, the town of Ohakune, 11km to the east, is a better option, boasting more facilities and a better choice of accommodation. Contact the Ruapehu visitor centre (☎ 06-385 8427), 54 Clyde St, Ohakune, for more information.

Places to Stay & Eat The *Raetihi Motor Camp (☎ 06-385 4176)*, on SH4 in town, has tent sites for $10. The *Raetihi Ruapehu Hotel (☎ 06-385 4016)* is a pub with several motel units priced at $55. Pub rooms are a little cheaper at $35 for a single. The *Country Classic Lodge (☎ 06-385 4511, 14 Ameku Rd)* offers comfortable rooms in a large heritage building at $80 a double.

There are a couple of *cafes* and *takeaways* on Seddon St and the *Caltex petrol station* also sells a range of snack food. Filling *pub meals* are available from the Raetihi Ruapehu Hotel.

Self-caterers will find a *Four Square* supermarket on Seddon St.

SOUTHERN NORTH ISLAND

Day 4: Raetihi to Otumaire
4½-6 hours, 67km

Day 4 sees you join the Whanganui River Rd, a bumpy byway that shadows the mighty Whanganui River (NZ's longest navigable waterway), passing through the magnificent bush land scenery of the Whanganui National Park. Long stretches of rutted unsealed road and numerous hills can make the going tough, but this day spent pedaling alongside the river, surrounded by hills carpeted in native forest, is sure to be a highlight of any tour.

Stock up with food for the next two days as there are no shops along the way.

The road out of Raetihi is very quiet and the sense of solitude grows the further you pedal out of town. The first few kilometres are through fairly flat grazing country. The gravel road, starting at 14km, is generally quite hard-packed and in good condition, but is corrugated in places, making for some bone-jarring descents.

Pipiriki is a tiny historic settlement nestled along the banks of Whanganui River at the start of the Whanganui River Road. It's worth stopping to take a look at the **Colonial House Museum** ($1 admission), which has lots of pictures and exhibits detailing the history of the settlement and the Whanganui River.

There are great views of the river throughout the day. At the end of a descent after 40km you come to **Hiruharama** (Jerusalem). Stop in and take a look at the historic church, the interior of which contains a mix of traditional Maori and Catholic religious artefacts.

After passing through Ranana (London), a bigger outpost along the road, you come to the **Kawana Flour Mill**. A restored example of one of the several mills that used to process wheat grown along the Whanganui.

Otumaire
The Otumaire area is not so much a settlement as a collection of places to stay. There are no shops and only one place to eat.

You can pitch a tent at the *Kauika Camp Site* (☎ *06-342 8133*) behind the *marae* at Ranana (46km) for $6, and at the DOC-run *Otumaire Camp Site* (67km).

The best place to stay, however, and certainly one of the most unusual, is the *Flying Fox* (☎ *06-342 8160*), a superb get-away on the opposite bank of the river. Access is normally via a flying fox, although the cableway

crossing ($2.50) is a less life-threatening alternative with your bike. You can sleep in a loft above the brewhouse for $20 per person. B&B plus dinner is $50, or you can camp for $8. Make sure to ring ahead; look for the house-shaped mailbox by the roadside.

Day 5: Otumaire to Wanganui
2½-3 hours, 37.2km

In contrast to Day 4, this ride back on the bitumen passes quickly, providing plenty of time to have a look at the numerous attractions that await in Wanganui.

A tough 2.5km climb up Aramoana (Hill Sea) begins at around 85.5km, providing views from the summit on a clear day of Mt Ruapehu. Just as the enjoyable 2km descent ends, the road emerges at the SH4, marking the end point of the river road.

The remaining 14km into Wanganui are rather dull, but at least the route is fairly flat.

Wanganui
Boasting many fine old buildings and a rejuvenated city centre, Wanganui is an attractive clean city that has done an excellent job preserving the remnants of its colonial past. Conspicuous displays of civic pride such as the flower baskets hanging from the balconies of restored historic and Art Deco buildings along the main street, Victoria Ave, serve to enhance the town's considerable appeal.

Information The Wanganui visitor centre (☎/fax 06-345 3286) is on Guyton St. The staff are very helpful and there's a great model of the area.

The DOC office (☎ 06-345 2402), on the corner of Ingestre and Hill Sts, is a good source of information on the Whanganui National Park and the river road.

Numerous banks (and ATMs) are represented along Victoria Ave. The Wanganui Pro Cycle Centre (☎ 06-345 3715) is at 199 Victoria St.

Things to See & Do Wanganui has several fine **parks and gardens** close to the city centre. Pleasant **Queens Park** is also Wanganui's cultural centre, containing both the **Serjeant Art Gallery** and the **Wanganui Regional Museum** (☎ 06-345 7443), one of the largest and best in the country. It houses a fine collection of Maori exhibits as well as colonial and wildlife displays.

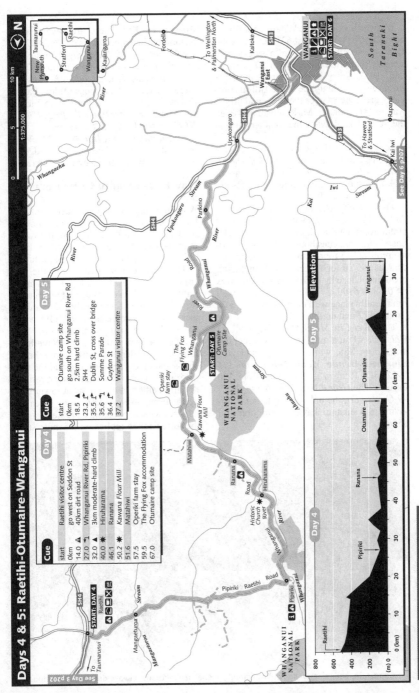

Days 4 & 5: Raetihi-Otumaire-Wanganui

Day 4

Cue	
start	Raetihi visitor centre
0km	go west on Seddon St
14.0 ⚠	40km dirt road
27.0 ↰	Whanganui River Rd, Pipiriki
32.0 ⚠	3km moderate-hard climb
40.0 ✳	Hiruharama
46.1	Ranana
50.2 ✳	Kawana Flour Mill
51.6	Matahiwi
57.5	Operiki farm stay
59.5	The Flying Fox accommodation
67.0	Otumaire camp site

Day 5

Cue	
start	Otumaire camp site
0km	go south on Whanganui River Rd
18.5 ⚠	2.5km hard climb
23.2 ↰	SH4
35.5 ↰↱	Dublin St, cross over bridge
35.6 ↰↱	Somme Parade
36.4 ↱	Guyton St
37.2	Wanganui visitor centre

Elevation

Day 4

Day 5

SOUTHERN NORTH ISLAND

It's worth visiting the **Whanganui River-boat Centre** (☎ 06-347 1863), beside Taupo Quay, to see the *Waimarie*, a side-paddle steamer that plied the river for 50 years up until 1952. Entry is free. Across the river from town, a ride up the **Durie Hill** lift provides great views over the town and all the way to Mt Taranaki, Mt Ruapehu and even the South Island, when the weather is clear.

Places to Stay The closest place to town to pitch a tent is the *Avro Motel & Caravan Court* (☎ 06-345 5279, 36 Alma Rd), about 1.5km west of the city centre. Tent sites are $8 per person and flats are $59.

The friendly *Riverside Inn* (☎ 06-347 2529, 2 Plymouth St), by the river on the left 100m over the bridge into town, is part YHA hostel and part guesthouse. The cost is $16 in dorms or $35 for a double. The guesthouse charges $45/60 for a single/double including breakfast. Close by is *Tamara Backpackers* (☎ 06-347 6300, 24 Somme Parade), a well run friendly place with dorm beds from $14, singles $22 and doubles $30.

The *River City Motel* (☎ 06-343 9107, 57 Halswell St) on a quiet tree-lined street has units from $65, while the large and well equipped *Avenue Motor Inn* (☎ 06-345 0907, 379 Victoria Ave) charges from $70 for two. The *Grand Hotel* (☎ 06-345 0955, 99 Guyton St), the only old-style hotel surviving in Wanganui, has singles/doubles for $55/65.

Places to Eat There are several good restaurants in town. *Cables* (☎ 06-348 7191, cnr Victoria Ave & Ridgeway St) has plenty of atmosphere with mains at around $25.

Easier on the pocket is *Jabies Kebabs (160 Victoria Ave)*, where various Middle Eastern dishes cost around $7. Further up Victoria Ave you'll find a *McDonald's*, *Pizza Hut* and *KFC* clustered close to one another.

The *Rutland Arms Inn* (☎ 06-347 7677), in a restored historic building on Ridgeway St, is one of Wanganui's best pubs for a meal.

Day 6: Wanganui to Hawera
5-6 hours, 89km

After the last few days of back roads and bush scenery, the leg to Hawera along the SH3 can seem a bit pedestrian, the rolling road passing through a pleasant but unexciting landscape of hilly grazing pastures.

The road climbs gently for the first stretch out of town. Traffic is reasonably light and the shoulder is decent much of the way. There aren't any really big climbs to tackle, but the route is pretty hilly with a continuous series of ups and downs.

After 44.5km you come to **Waverley**, a fair-sized settlement with a number of shops and other facilities. Beyond the town the route is relatively flat, but soon resumes its hilly pattern; a nice descent towards the ocean bringing you down into Patea, the largest town encountered en route. Look for the **Aotea canoe replica** on the main street.

Come rain, hail, sleet or snow, Wanganui's posties (circa 1930s) always delivered the goods.

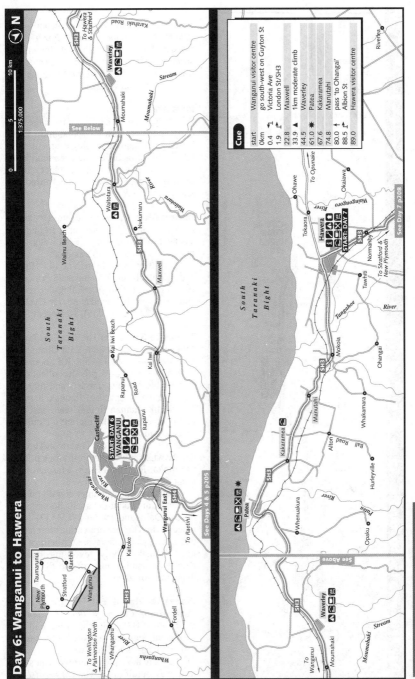

Day 6: Wanganui to Hawera

N

0   5   10 km
1:375 000

Cue		
start		Wanganui visitor centre
0km		go south-west on Guyton St
0.4	↰	Victoria Ave
1.9	↰	London St/SH3
22.8	▲	Maxwell
33.9	▲	1km moderate climb
44.5		Waverley
61.0	✳	Patea
67.6		Kakaramea
74.8		Manutahi
80.0	←	pass 'to Ohangai'
88.5	←	Albion St
89.0		Hawera visitor centre

SOUTHERN NORTH ISLAND

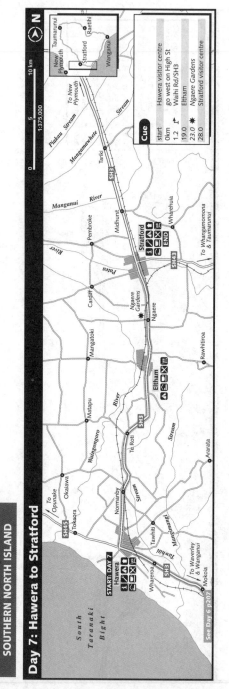

Day 7: Hawera to Stratford

Cue		
start		Hawera visitor centre
0km		go west on High St
1.2	↲	Waihi Rd/SH3
19.0	✳	Eltham
23.0	✳	Ngaere Gardens
28.0		Stratford visitor centre

The road climbs gently but steadily from Patea. Look for the ***Ohanga Farm Backpackers*** (80km) sign on the right for an early accommodation option. There are some nice views across to the ocean and Mt Taranaki as you approach Hawera.

Hawera

Primarily a service centre for the large local dairy industry, Hawera (population 8400) isn't a particularly engaging destination but has plenty of facilities and accommodation options, making it a good place for an overnight stay. Some of the local attractions are worth a look.

Information The visitor centre (☎ 06-278 8599), 55 High St, is dead easy to find as it sits next to the imposing 51.5m water tower that dominates the town's skyline.

There is an ANZ branch at 145 High St and a Bank of New Zealand at 73 Princes St. A modest selection of cycling accessories and spares can be found at Seaver Cycles & Mowers (☎ 06-278 6046), 18 Regent St.

Things to See & Do The excellent **Tawhiti Museum** (☎ 06-278 6839), on Ohangai Rd near the corner of Tawhiti Rd about 4km from town, houses a private collection of remarkable exhibits, models and dioramas covering many aspects of Taranaki heritage. The lifelike human figures were cast from real people around the region; it's quite an unusual museum.

About 2km north of Hawera on Turuturu Rd are whats left of the pre-European **Turuturumokai Pa**. The Tawhiti Museum has a great detailed model of it.

Taranaki is dairy country and if you want to learn more about the area's dominant industry, **Dairyland** (☎ 06-278 4537) is the place to do it. There are various interactive and audiovisual displays, and believe it or not, Taranaki's only revolving licensed cafe. Dairyland is just off the SH3 about 2km south of town.

Places to Stay & Eat The ***King Edward Park Motor Camp*** (☎ 06-278 8544) on Waihi Rd (SH3), adjacent to the park and municipal pool, has tent sites at $8 per person and charges $28 for two.

There are a couple of farm-stay hostels a little way out of town. The ***Ohangai Farm***

Backpacker (☎ *06-272 2878*) on Urupa Rd in Ohangai (follow the signs from the turnoff on the SH3 about 9km before Hawera) is a working dairy farm with a well equipped bunk house in the paddocks. The cost is $14 in good four-bed rooms or $32 for twin rooms. You can also arrange for a pick-up from town. *Wheatly Downs* (☎ *06-278 6523*) on Ararata Rd (the extension of Tawhiti Rd), about 4km beyond Tawhiti Museum, has dorm beds for $15, singles for $30 and doubles for $40.

The *Furlong Motor Inn* (☎ *06-278 5136, 256 Waihi Rd*) is a comfortable motel with a decent restaurant and units from $73.

There are quite a few places around town to get a meal. *Morriesons Cafe Bar* (☎ *06-278 5647, 60 Victoria St*) has inexpensive, good food served in tasteful surroundings, while the *East Ocean Chinese Restaurant* (☎ *06-278 3010, 26 Union St*) is BYO and also does take-aways. For something tasty but cheap *Kreative Kebabs* (☎ *06-278 5552, 135 High St*) has kebabs ($7.50), of course, as well as a good selection of gourmet burgers. *Aunties Cafe* (☎ *06-278 6535, 79 High St*) does a good cooked breakfast sure to juice you up for the day.

Day 7: Hawera to Stratford
1½-2 hours, 28km

This final short stage of the tour takes you through Taranaki dairy country, providing good views of Mt Taranaki throughout the day. The first few kilometres are spent clearing the outskirts of town. Although there are no major hills, the road gains height steadily all the way to Stratford. The SH3 is moderately busy.

After 20km you come to **Eltham**, a dairying centre famous for its excellent cheeses. Information on the town is available from the Public Library on High St. Just down the road, about 5km short of Stratford alongside the SH3, are the **Ngaere Gardens**, a very pleasant English-style park. It is a great place to relax for a while before embarking on the final few kilometres of the tour.

Marlborough & Nelson

MARLBOROUGH & NELSON

Sitting at the top of the South Island, Marlborough and Nelson are often overlooked as destinations in their own right by travellers scrambling south towards the mountains, fjords and glaciers for which the South Island is renowned. Locals, however, are well aware of the region's special appeal, making it a favourite domestic destination.

Blessed with some of the best weather in the country, beaches, vineyards, a magnificent coastline, cosmopolitan towns and world class wilderness areas like Abel Tasman National Park, Marlborough and Nelson have a lot to offer, especially for cyclists. The roads are mostly quiet, the scenery is varied and beautiful, and the terrain is not too testing.

HISTORY

The Maori began to migrate to the South Island during the 16th century, and among the first to arrive in Nelson were the Tumatakokiri. By 1550 this tribe occupied most of the province, as Abel Tasman found out to his cost when he turned up in 1642 at what he later named Murderers' Bay. Other tribes followed the Tumatakokiri, settling at the mouth of the Waimea River. The Tumatakokiri remained supreme in Tasman Bay until the 18th century, when the Ngati-apa from Wanganui and the Ngai Tahu – the largest tribe in the South Island – got together in a devastating attack on the Tumatakokiri, who virtually ceased to exist as an independent tribe after 1800.

The Ngati-apa's victory was short-lived because between 1828 and 1830 they were practically annihilated by armed tribes from Taranaki and Wellington, who sailed into the bay in the largest fleet of canoes ever assembled in New Zealand.

By the time European settlers arrived, no Maori lived at Te Wakatu – the nearest *pa* (fortified Maori village) being at Motueka – and the decimated population that remained in the area put up no resistance. The first Pakeha (the name given to whites or Europeans by the Maori) settlers sailed in response to the advertisements by the New Zealand Company, set up by Edward Gibbon Wakefield to systematically colonise the country. His grandiose scheme was to trans-

plant a complete slice of English life from all social classes. In reality 'too few gentleman with too little money' took up the challenge and the new colony foundered in its infancy.

Although the area was visited by Abel Tasman in 1642 and several times by James Cook between 1770 and 1777, Marlborough's European settlement was brought about by an overflow of colonists from Nelson. In 1840 the opportunistic and unscrupulous New Zealand Company tried to settle part of the Wairau Plain (now part of Marlborough) after buying the rights from the widow of a trader who claimed he had bought the land from the Maori in exchange for a 16 pound cannon (now on display in Blenheim). The Maori disputed the sale and in 1843 the chiefs Te Rauparaha and Te Rangihaeata arrived from Kapiti to resist survey operations. They were met by an

In Summary

Area Code: ☎ 03

Highlights
- **Farewell Spit Bird Sanctuary**
- **Abel Tasman National Park** and **Marlborough Sounds**
- Marlborough wineries

Special Events
- **Wine Marlborough Festival** (February), Blenheim
- **Nelson Arts Festival** (September)
- **Nelson Jazz Festival** (December)
- **Havelock Mussel Festival** (December)
- **The Gathering** (New Year's Eve), Takaka Hill – electro-funk dance rave

Cycling Events
- **Rainbow Rage** (March/April), St Arnaud

Terrain
Low lying plains in the east interspersed with ranges and valleys fanning from the interior towards the sea; increasingly rugged in the west; rolling hills and plains in central coastal areas.

armed party from Nelson led by Arthur Wakefield and Police Magistrate Thompson. The party was greeted peacefully by the Maori but during a brief skirmish precipitated by the settlers, Te Rangihaeata's wife was shot. The enraged Maori attacked, killing 22 of the Nelson party including Wakefield and Thompson. The whole event came to be known as the Wairau Massacre.

In March 1847, Wairau was finally bought and added to the Nelson territory and it was not long before settlers from Nelson and elsewhere flocked to the area. When Wairau settlers realised, however, that money from land sales in their area was being used to develop the Nelson district, they petitioned for independence. The ap-

peal was successful and the colonial government called the new region Marlborough, approving one of the two settlements, Waitohi (now Picton), as the capital. At the same time, the other settlement, known as 'The Beaver', was renamed Blenheim. After a period of intense rivalry, the capital was transferred peacefully to Blenheim in 1865.

CLIMATE

The Marlborough and Nelson regions enjoy some of the best weather in NZ. Blenheim holds the crown as the sunniest town in the country, averaging 2470 hours of sunlight a year. The weather is generally mild year-round with maximum temperatures in summer around 23°C, getting down to 13°C

over winter. Nelson experiences an average of 94 rain days and 985mm of rain a year, while the drier Blenheim averages 689mm over 78 days. Contrast this with Westport on the west coast, which gets 168 rainy days and 2245mm annually.

The prevailing breezes are north-westerly near the coast, tending south-westerly further inland. Areas bordering Cook Strait are particularly prone to strong winds.

Cycling is possible year-round but autumn (from March to May) is probably the pick of the seasons for its combination of mild temperatures, dry days, lighter winds and lack of holiday crowds.

NATURAL HISTORY

Marlborough and Nelson contain a diverse collection of landscapes and habitats, reflecting their variety of coastal, rural and mountainous areas. The interior is punctuated by a series of ranges and valleys fanning out towards the sea.

The Marlborough Sounds, an area of convoluted and beautiful waterways, contains patches of coastal podocarp forest and is home to numerous species of birds including the tui, bellbird, tomtit, Australasian gannet and shearwater.

The Wairau Plains around Blenheim are largely given over to sheep farming and wine production, while to the west and south-west, large tracts of native forest remain in the Mount Richmond Forest Park and Nelson Lakes National Park. Around Nelson huge tracts of plantation timber are cultivated in the Golden Downs Forest.

Geologically, the hills to the west of Tasman Bay rank with those of Fjordland as being some of the oldest in NZ. NZ's smallest national park, Abel Tasman, lies on the north-west side of Tasman Bay and features magnificent coastal scenery and patches of lush rainforest. Further inland there are marble gorges, sinkholes, numerous caves and large tracts of beech forest containing all five native beech species.

Adjacent to Abel Tasman is Kahurangi National Park, one of NZ's newest and, at over 400,000 hectares, largest national parks. Incorporating the Tasman Mountains, it is an area of rugged beauty covered in bush with tracts of beech, rimu and other podocarps.

The north-west tip of the Nelson region contains Farewell Spit. Formed over a period of 10,000 to 14,000 years, it's NZ's largest sand spit and a renowned bird sanctuary of international importance. It is home to over 90 species of birds including a gannet colony and tens of thousands of migratory godwits, knots and curlews that arrive from Siberia each summer.

INFORMATION
Maps & Books

Pathfinders *Nelson, Blenheim Picton* (1:250,000) map shows the area covering both tours in excellent detail. It also incorporates 1:25,000 town maps and an enlargement of the Nelson area. The AA *Nelson and Marlborough District Map* (1:350,000) is also very good.

The Treasured Pathway: A Guide to the Marlborough Nelson Heritage Highway ($24.95), by Simon Noble, gives a detailed historical account of places of interest along the heritage highway running between Picton and Farewell Spit. Most of the routes correspond with those of the tours described here, making it a worthwhile companion for anyone with a particular interest in the region's past.

Information Sources

Destination Marlborough (☎ 03-577 5520, 🖳 www.destination.co.nz/marlborough/) and Tourism Nelson (☎ 03-548 2304, 🖳 webnz .com/nelson/) are the regional tourism bodies and best equipped to provide predeparture information.

There are information centres in most of the larger towns throughout the region that can supply maps of the local area and information on activities, accommodation and transport. They also often serve as the bus station. The main information centres are found in Picton, Blenheim, Nelson, Motueka and Takaka.

DOC is the best place to get information on national parks and scenic reserves. It produces a range of excellent pamphlets and maps detailing walks and other activities in parks throughout the region. It also sells hut passes and can provide details of local conditions such as tidal information for the Abel Tasman National Park. Many visitor centres, especially over summer, have a DOC officer on hand; otherwise you can contact their offices directly in Picton, Havelock, Nelson, Motueka and Takaka.

There is often no substitute for local knowledge. Cycling clubs can provide detailed information on local conditions, touring routes and organised rides. Local clubs include the Nelson MTB Club and the Golden Bay MTB Club; for current contact details take a look at the clubs page of the New Zealand Mountain Bike Web (🖳 www .mountainbike.co.nz).

GATEWAY CITIES
Nelson

The city of Nelson (population 51,000) has a deserved reputation as one of NZ's top travel destinations. Blessed with some of the best weather in the country as well as proximity to fine beaches and national parks, Nelson is a great place to 'lay back' for a while. The city itself is pleasant, bright and cosmopolitan, with an active arts and crafts community, a number of shady parks and no shortage of good cafes, pubs and restaurants.

Information The Nelson information centre (☎ 548 2304, fax 546 9008) is on the corner of Trafalgar and Halifax Sts. It's open from 8.30 am to 6 pm daily in summer, and from 8.30 am to 5 pm weekdays and 10 am to 4 pm on weekends in winter.

During summer a DOC officer is on hand at the information centre to handle inquiries concerning national parks and walks in the Nelson area. A full range of DOC pamphlets is also available. The main DOC office (☎ 546 9335) is at 186 Bridge St.

Internet access is available at Boots-Off at 53 Bridge St, or at coin operated terminals in Chez Eelco at 296 Trafalgar St and Subway at 40 Bridge St. There are plenty of banks with ATMs on Trafalgar St, Nelson's main shopping thoroughfare.

Kelvin's Cycles (☎ 548 2851), 109 Rutherford St, is small but has a very good workshop. Stewart's Cycle City (☎ 548 1666) and Cycle Logic (☎ 545 7573) are just round the corner on Hardy St. The best place to rent a bike is Natural High (☎ 546 6936), 52 Rutherford St. A decent front suspension mountain bike costs $30 a day; camping gear and kayaks are also for hire.

Things to See & Do Strolling around the compact city centre and soaking up the relaxed atmosphere from a street-side cafe table are good ways to appreciate Nelson's charm. There are, however, quite a few specific attractions worth seeing.

The traditional symbol of Nelson is its Art Deco **cathedral**, situated in pleasant parkland at the top of Trafalgar St. Close by is **South St**, home to a row of restored workers cottages dating from 1863. Of prime interest is the **South St Gallery** on the corner of South St and Nile St West, noted for its extensive collection of fine pottery.

Nelson boasts a number of parks and gardens including **Queens Gardens** and the **Botanic Gardens**, where the lookout at the top of Botanical Hill marks NZ's exact geographical centre.

Adjoining Queens Gardens on Bridge St is the **Suter Art Galley**. It has a few interesting lithographs and paintings as well as changing exhibitions and musical and theatrical performances. Its Stage Two theatre also shows a selection of **cult and classic films**. Mainstream releases can be seen at the State Cinema multiplex at 91 Trafalgar Street.

Nelson is a mecca for adventure activities. The most popular is a **quad bike tour** along farmland and high-country trails with Happy Valley Tours (☎ 545 0304). You can also go **white-water rafting** or **riverbugging** with the Rapid River Adventure Company (☎ 545 0332) or Ultimate Descents (☎ 546 6212). Half/full-day trips cost around $70/105. **Tandem parachute jumps** can be arranged through Tandem Skydive Nelson (☎ 548 7652) at $185 per person.

The local hills, covered in vast timber plantations, contain some great **mountain bike trails**. Natural High (see Information) conducts guided adventures on tracks selected to suit your ability level. A half-day tour including bike hire, helmet and transport costs $35.

Places to Stay The *Tahuna Beach Holiday Park (☎ 548 5159, 70 Beach Rd)* is situated out towards the airport, 5km from the city centre, and has its own supermarket. There are plenty of secluded tent sites for $18, cabins from $28, tourist flats from $50 and motel units from $60; prices are for two.

The modern and comfortable *Nelson Central YHA (☎ 548 8817, 57 Rutherford St)* has dorm beds costing $18 and singles/ doubles for $28/40. There's also a secure room to store bikes. Also well equipped is *Paradiso Backpackers (☎ 546 6703, 42 Weka St)*, in a lovely old building about a five minute ride from the centre of town, and with a swimming pool, spa and sauna. Seven or eight-bed dorms with mezzanines cost $16, four-bed dorms are $17 and twins and doubles are $38.

Other hostels worth trying include *Tasman Towers (☎ 548 7590, 10 Weka St)* and *Bumbles (☎ 548 2771, 8 Bridge St)*.

Central and reasonably priced motels include the *Lynton Lodge Motel (☎ 548 7112, 25 Examiner St)*, with double rooms from $70, and the *Trafalgar Lodge Motel (☎ 548 3980, 46 Trafalgar St)*, which has units starting at $68 and B&B accommodation for $35 per person. For a real pampering try *Cambria House (☎ 548 4681, 7 Cambria St)*, a luxury-plus B&B charging from $165.

Places to Eat The wealth of local produce, particularly seafood, makes dining out in Nelson a pleasure. Deep-sea fish such as orange roughy and hoki, scallops from Tasman and Golden Bays and mussels from nearby Havelock can all be enjoyed, washed down with locally produced wines and beers.

A number of cafes are located at the top end of Trafalgar St near the Cathedral. *Chez Eelco (☎ 548 7595)*, No 296, is a Nelson institution, serving everything from coffee and croissants to main meals. It is particularly famed for its delicious mussel chowder. Other good choices close by include *Pomeroy's (☎ 548 7524)* and the *Metro Cafe (☎ 546 7530)*.

The *Victorian Rose (☎ 548 7631, 281 Trafalgar St)* is a popular English-style pub with street-side tables, a wide variety of beers on tap and a range of good-value meals. Vouchers for discounts on meals are often available at local hostels.

For vegetarian selections, *Zippy's (☎ 546 6348, 276 Hardy St)* is a funky place with decor based on the 1970's cartoon character. A few doors down, the *Land of the Pharaohs (☎ 548 8404)* serves kebabs and other Middle Eastern delights for under $15. *Yaza (☎ 548 2849, 117 Hardy St)* is the place to go for good-value breakfasts.

A number of restaurants specialising in local seafood are clustered along the waterfront on Wakefield Quay. Choose from *Quayside (☎ 548 3319)*, *Scrub Coaster* or the *Boatshed (☎ 546 9783)*.

For burgers reputed to be the biggest in NZ check out the *Roadside Diner*, a big white pie cart that has been serving fast food in Nelson since 1933.

Self-caterers will find a *New World* supermarket at Montgomery Square, and a *Big Fresh* on Halifax St.

Getting There & Away There are plenty of options for getting to/from Nelson.

Bus Most buses serving Nelson stop and pick up from the Nelson information centre. InterCity (☎ 548 1539) and Newmans (☎ 548 2581) have a depot at 27 Bridge St.

InterCity buses run daily to Picton and Christchurch and to Greymouth via Murchison and Westport. Newmans also has daily buses to Picton and Christchurch.

The main shuttle services to Picton and Blenheim are Kiwilink (☎ 0800 802 300) and Knightline (☎ 547 4733). Each charges $19 one way between Nelson and Picton and an additional $10 per bike. Nelson Lakes Transport (☎ 548 6858) services St Arnaud and Murchison.

Abel Tasman Coachlines (☎ 548 0285), 27 Bridge St, provides transport to Motueka, Kaiteriteri, Marahau (Abel Tasman Track), Takaka and the Heaphy Track, while Kahurangi Bus (☎ 525 9434) runs daily services from Nelson to Collingwood ($32, $10 per bike) and most towns in between.

Air The Air New Zealand Travelcentre (☎ 546 3100) is on the corner of Trafalgar and Bridge Sts. There are direct flights to Wellington, Auckland, Christchurch and New Plymouth, with connections to other cities. Ansett (☎ 0800 267 388) also has direct flights to Wellington and Auckland. Flight Corporation (☎ 547 8175) flies from Nelson to Wellington daily except Saturday, charging $80. Discounted fares to Wellington are sometimes available for as little as $49; check hostel notice boards for availability.

Bicycle The most direct route to Nelson from St Arnaud and Picton is via Rai Valley, Canvastown and Havelock (109.5km). For details of the ride, see Days 4 & 5 of the Marlborough Explorer ride – to do this you'll need to follow the cue sheet directions in reverse.

Marlborough Explorer

Duration	.5 days
Distance	.331km
Difficulty	.moderate
Start/End	.Picton

This tour is a great introduction to the South Island, taking in a variety of stunning landscapes. You'll experience Marlborough's world-renowned vineyards, beautiful Lake Rotoiti, bustling Nelson and the breathtaking coastal scenery of the Marlborough Sounds. With sealed roads, a mixture of shorter and longer legs, and good accommodation options every day, this is an ideal ride for those new to touring or looking to build some fitness before heading for more challenging terrain further south.

The Molesworth and Rainbow Rd rides, featured in boxed texts later in this chapter, are well worth considering for suitably equipped tourers looking for a real off-road, big sky experience. The two rides combined can be substituted for the Blenheim-St Arnaud leg of this tour.

NATURAL HISTORY

The first taste of the South Island for most visitors is the picturesque waterways of the Marlborough Sounds on the approach to Picton. The Sounds contain patches of grassy farmland, regenerating forest, coastal podocarp forests and stands of mature beech. Bird life is also prolific with tui, bellbird, silvereye, tomtit, shining cuckoo and morepork all found in the forest areas. Waders and sea birds such as Australasian gannet, shearwater and tern can be seen in tidal areas and the outer islands.

Blenheim lies on the Wairau Plains, a contrasting landscape to the Marlborough Sounds. Much of the land is given over to sheep farming, timber plantations and vineyards, although the Wairau Lagoons to the east are home to over 70 species of birds.

The Richmond Range and 177,109 hectare Mount Richmond Forest Park dominates the area between Blenheim and Nelson. The forest contains a wealth of native timbers including beech, rimu, totara and miro as well as bird species such as kaka, yellow-crowned parakeets and blue ducks (*whio* in Maori).

To the south is the Nelson Lakes National Park, a beautiful wilderness area of glacial lakes, beech forests and mountains, forming the northern extremity of the Southern Alps. The landscape was created by the Alpine fault and glacial action during the last ice age, evidenced by the characteristic long valleys found throughout the park. All five native species of beech flourish at varying altitudes and tui, bellbird and kea, the large alpine parrot, may be seen.

The area around Nelson is dominated by plantation timber, with extensive tracts cultivated in the hills near town and in the Golden Downs Forest.

PLANNING
What to Bring

Accommodation is available at the end of each stage, however, between Renwick and St Arnaud (Day 2) there are few places to pick up supplies, so take a packed lunch and carry plenty of water.

GETTING TO/FROM THE RIDE
Picton

Ferry Interislander ferries (☎ 0800 802 802) cross Cook Strait between Picton and Wellington four to five times daily. The three hour journey is well worth doing in daylight as the approach to Picton through the narrow waterways of Tory Channel and Queen Charlotte Sound is very scenic. The standard fare for a one-way crossing is $46 although discounts are available for advance bookings. Bikes are an additional $10. No special preparations are required, just wait at the designated point outside the terminal and ride onto the train deck when instructed to do so. Bikes are placed in a small storage area off to one side – lash it to the railing to prevent it falling during the crossing.

A ticket on the faster Lynx (☎ 0800 802 802) costs $59 one way and $12 per bike.

Air Soundsair (☎ 573 6184) has a regular service to/from Wellington. The short flight costs $55 and operates about six times a day. Transport between Picton and the airstrip at Koromiko, 8km out of town, is included in the price. There are also flights to Blenheim.

Bus InterCity (☎ 573 7025) has a service between Picton and Christchurch ($40 plus $10 per bike) with connections to Dunedin

MARLBOROUGH & NELSON

and Invercargill. Another route between Picton and Nelson goes via Blenheim and Havelock with connections to Greymouth and the glaciers. At least one bus daily on each of these routes connects with the Picton ferry. Newmans (☎ 578 2713) has one bus daily in each direction between Christchurch and Nelson. Both companies operate from the Picton ferry terminal.

Smaller companies including Atomic Shuttles (☎ 573 6855), South Island Connections (☎ 578 9904) and Compass Coachlines (☎ 578 7102) also run services to/from Christchurch, charging around $30 plus $10 per bike. Book at the information centre.

Kiwilink (☎ 0800 802 300) and Knightline both run services between Blenheim and Nelson, stopping at Picton. The Picton to Nelson fare is $19 plus $10 per bike. Sounds to Coast (☎ 0800 802 225) has shuttles three days a week to Greymouth via St Arnaud.

Train The *Coastal Pacific* between Picton and Christchurch, via Blenheim and Kaikoura, operates daily in each direction. A standard fare costs $72. The train connects with the ferry and a free shuttle service is provided between the train station and ferry terminal on both sides of the strait. This trip is highly recommended for its coastal scenery.

Nelson
See the Gateway Cities section (p214) earlier in this chapter for information on Getting to/from Nelson.

THE RIDE
Picton
The North Island ferries dock in the picturesque port of Picton (population 4000), nestled at the head of Queen Charlotte Sound. It's a hive of activity when the ferries are in and during the peak of summer, but rather sleepy any other time.

Information The Picton visitor centre (☎ 573 7477, fax 573 8362), on the foreshore 200m from the ferry terminal, is open daily from 8.30 am to 7.30 pm (5 pm in winter). DOC (☎ 573 7582) also has a booth in the centre.

The Bank of New Zealand is at 56 High St. Renee's Petrol Station (☎ 573 6725), on the corner of Kent St and Wairau Rd, has a small selection of cycling spares.

Things to See & Do On the water, between the information centre and the ferry wharf, you can explore the *Edwin Fox*, a historic sailing ship reputed to be the oldest wooden merchant vessel afloat in the world. Visitors preferring to stick to dry land should take a look at the excellent **Picton Museum**, on the foreshore below London Quay. It houses a range of interesting exhibits including a Dursley Pederson bicycle built around 1890 – imagine touring on that!

The Picton area provides some excellent opportunities for **walking**. The information centre and DOC have maps and leaflets detailing several walks near town and further afield. An easy 1km track runs along the eastern side of Picton Harbour to Bob's Bay, where there is a BBQ area in a sheltered cove. The **Snout Walkway** carries on along the ridge from the Bob's Bay path and has great views of the length of Queen Charlotte Sound. Allow three hours for the walk.

Picton is also the main base for longer trips out to the **Queen Charlotte Track**, a 67km-long trail connecting historic Ship Cove with Anakiwa. This increasingly popular track passes through lush coastal forest, giving spectacular views of Queen Charlotte and Kenepuru Sounds. A number of Picton based boat operators will drop you off at the Ship Cove start point for around $30. The visitor centre has details.

The track is also open to **mountain bikes**, except during December and February when the Ship Cove to Kenepuru Saddle section is off limits. Although you should allow two to three days to ride the entire track, the Ship Cove to Kenepuru Saddle (27km) and Mistletoe Bay to Anakiwa (12.5km) sections are excellent day rides.

Numerous companies offering **boat cruises**, **fishing** and **sea kayak** trips around the Marlborough Sounds operate from the Picton waterfront. See the visitor centre for details.

Places to Stay The *Blue Anchor Holiday Park* (☎ 573 7212, 70-78 Waikawa Rd), only 500m from the centre of town, has tent sites for $18 per person, cabins from $32 and tourist flats from $55.

The *Villa* (☎ 573 6598, 34 Auckland St) is a well equipped, popular hostel in a fine renovated villa. Dorm beds are from $17, and doubles or twins are $44 (breakfast included). The attentive owners make this place special. The closest hostel to the ferry, **Baden's Picton Lodge** (☎ 573 7788, 9 Auckland St), 200m from the ferry terminal, adjacent to the train station, has dorm beds for $15 and twins and doubles for $36.

Other hostels include the **Bavarian Lodge Backpackers** (☎ 573 6536, 42 Auckland St), **Wedgewood House YHA** (☎ 573 7797, 10 Dublin St) and **Juggler's Rest** (☎ 573 5570, 8 Canterbury St).

The central **Tourist Court Motel** (☎ 573 6331, 45 High St) is a basic motel with studio units from $54 for two. Top of the line is the **Picton Beachcomber Inn** (☎ 573 8899, 27 Waikawa Rd) with units from $75.

Good pub rooms, many with great sea views, can be found at the centrally located **Terminus Hotel** (☎ 573 6452, 1 High St), where rooms with private facilities cost $45/75 for singles/doubles.

Places to Eat Straightforward pub meals from $8 to $10 are available from the **Terminus** (☎ 573 6452), **Federal** (☎ 573 6077) and **Oxley** (☎ 573 7195) hotels, while a cluster of more upmarket restaurants can be found on High St. The **Marlborough Terranean** (☎ 573 7122, 31 High St) offers a Mediterranean inspired menu featuring local seafood. Next door, **Le Cafe** (☎ 573 5588) is also justifiably popular.

For a more price-conscious dining experience try the **Kiwi Takeaways** (☎ 573 5537), near the corner of the Quay and Wellington St, or stock up on pies and sausage rolls at the **Picton Bakery** (☎ 573 7082, 34 Auckland St).

Day 1: Picton to Renwick
1½-2½ hours, 39.5km

This is a short and easy ride leaving plenty of time for a late start or leisurely afternoon tour of the vineyards.

Following a short climb out of Picton the route travels up the valley, passing through pleasant farming land populated by flocks of grazing sheep and flanked by plantation timber covered hills. The SH1 has a nice broad shoulder and is reasonably quiet most of the time, but can get busy for short periods when the ferries are in. Beyond Tuamarina the valley opens out through a string of small settlements, reaching **Blenheim** (population

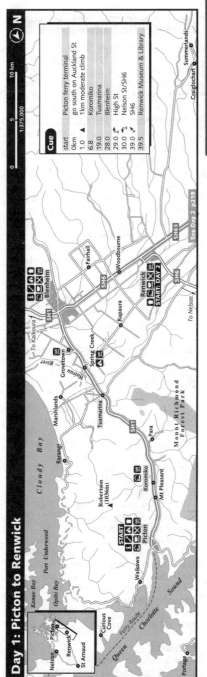

Cue		
start		Picton ferry terminal
0km	◄	go south on Auckland St
1.0	▲	1km moderate climb
6.8		Koromiko
19.0		Tuamarina
28.0		Blenheim
29.0	↰	High St
30.0	↱	Nelson St/SH6
39.0	↴	SH6
39.5		Renwick Museum & Library

Day 1: Picton to Renwick

Molesworth Rd Ride

The 198km Molesworth Rd is a unique three day off-road cycle tour through the South Island high country. Starting in Blenheim and finishing at Hanmer Springs, this tough ride on gravel roads takes you through New Zealand's largest farm (180,000 hectares) and across an imposing landscape of towering mountains, deep valleys and huge grassy flats.

Vehicle access is only available during a six week period in January and February, although access for cyclists is possible outside this time with permission from the station manager (contact The Manager of Molesworth Station, Landcorp, Awatere Valley, Blenheim). The Molesworth Rd ride can be combined with the Rainbow Rd ride (see the 'Rainbow Rd Ride' boxed text) to form an extended off-road tour of around 330km.

An excellent DOC pamphlet ($1) on Molesworth Station and the surrounding area is available from the visitor centre in Blenheim.

26,000), the largest town in the Marlborough region, after 28km.

While not as picturesque as Picton, Blenheim has a good range of services including an excellent visitor centre (☎ 578 9904, fax 578 6084), 2 High St. In addition to tips on accommodation options, pick up information about Renwick here, as well as a copy of the *Marlborough Winemakers' Wine Trail Guide*.

Blenheim also has a good bike shop, Spokesman Cycles (☎ 578 0433), 61 Queen St, and several banks on Market St.

Although much smaller than Blenheim, Renwick is the best place to finish the day as it is situated right in the heart of the vineyards, has an excellent hostel and a night here shortens the otherwise long leg to St Arnaud on the second day. You pass a number of **vineyards** on SH6 during the final easy 10km to Renwick.

Renwick

Renwick's main attraction is its proximity to the wineries that make Marlborough known to wine lovers the world over. There are more than 20 of them within a 5km radius of town.

Information Information on Renwick and surrounds is available from the Blenheim information centre (☎ 578 9904), 2 High St.

Things to See & Do No visit to the Marlborough region would be complete without a visit to a vineyard and, using Renwick as a base, there's no shortage of them to choose from. A variety of wine styles are produced in the area but without doubt the region is best known for its superb Sauvignon Blancs. Most of the wineries are open daily for tastings and some, such as **Highfield**, **Hunter's** and **Allan Scott**, also have restaurants. Plan your journey using one of the wine trail maps available from the Blenheim information centre and local businesses.

Places to Stay & Eat Watson's Way Backpackers (☎ *572 8228, 56 High St)*, on the right as you cycle into town, is an excellent purpose-built hostel in a pleasant garden setting. Shared rooms are $18 per person and the one double is $40 (including a simple breakfast). Tents can also be pitched in the grounds.

The *Airport Motel (☎ 0800 767 797, 46 High St)* is the only motel in town. It has modern studio and two-bedroom units from $75.

On High St, *Woodbourne Tavern (☎ 572 8007)* serves good-value pub meals with dinner specials from $5. *Percy's Takeaways (☎ 572 8098)* offers the usual fast food assortment. If you've had your fill of wine, the *Cork & Keg (☎ 572 9328)*, on Inkerman St, is an English-style pub serving up an assortment of excellent house-brewed beers as well as snacks and light meals.

Self-caterers can stock up at the *Supervalue Supermarket* on High St.

Day 2: Renwick to St Arnaud
4½-7 hours, 92.5km
Day 2 is quite long, and climbs to over 700m. Most of this altitude, however, is gained quite gradually, making it an easier day than it may first appear. There is little shade and few supply points along the route so pack a lunch and carry plenty of water.

Leaving Renwick, traffic is light and the road is straight and seemingly flat, although

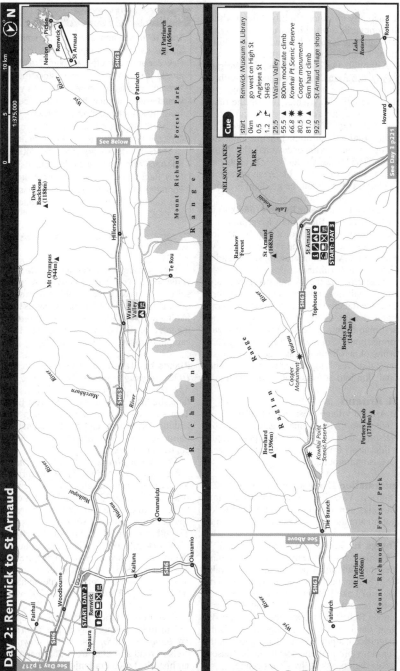

Day 2: Renwick to St Arnaud

Cue		
start		Renwick Museum & Library
0km	←	go west on High St
0.5	↗	Anglesea St
1.2	↱	SH63
25.5	◄	Wairau Valley
55.5	◄	800m moderate climb
66.8	✳	Kowhai Pt Scenic Reserve
80.5	✳	Cooper monument
81.0	◄	6km hard climb
92.5	◄	St Arnaud village shop

it's actually climbing slightly. After a while the vineyards around Renwick give way to drier grazing land with views away to hills in the Mount Richmond Forest Park.

Although there's not much in **Wairau Valley** (25.5km), a petrol station with a *store* provides the final opportunity to stock up until St Arnaud. Just up the road there is a tavern adjoining a spartan looking camping ground. Beyond town, the route continues through grazing land, interrupted only by the occasional pine plantation. The broad Wairau River is visible at times away to the right. A short climb (55.5km) is the signal the gradient is about to become more noticeable.

Kowhai Point Scenic Reserve (66.8km) is on the banks of the Wairau River and is a pleasant spot for lunch or a rest. It has picnic tables and toilets and is one of the few points along the route offering some shade. *Camping* is permitted.

After crossing the Wairau River there are a few small ups and downs to tackle before the route flattens out. A **monument** (80.5km) marks the site of John Henry Cooper's (the first man to introduce sheep to the Wairau) former home. Soon after, the route begins a tiring 6km climb through attractive lush vegetation reaching a summit at 88km. The final 5km into St Arnaud is all downhill.

St Arnaud

St Arnaud village, nestled on the shores of Lake Rotoiti, is the main gateway to the Nelson Lakes National Park, a picturesque wilderness area of glacial lakes, beech forests and mountains.

Information The DOC visitor centre (☎ 521 1806), in View Rd, has lots of information on walks and activities in and around Lake Rotoiti and the Nelson Lakes National Park.

Things to See & Do The area around St Arnaud provides some magnificent opportunities for **walking**. A popular three day walk from St Arnaud takes you along the eastern shore of Lake Rotoiti to Lake Head and up to the beautiful alpine Lake Angelus, returning via Roberts Ridge and the Mt Robert ski field. On a clear day this ridge walk affords magnificent alpine views all along its length. For more information on walks in the Nelson Lakes region, ask at the visitor centre.

Rainbow Rd Ride

The 116km ride from St Arnaud to Hanmer Springs has gained a reputation as one of New Zealand's best off-road tours. It follows an old pylon road and former stock route through spectacular alpine scenery. As you would expect of a ride through the mountains, there's a lot of climbing involved, especially if starting out in Hanmer Springs. Typically, it takes two to three days to ride.

There is also an organised adventure ride/race along the route called the 'Rainbow Rage', held annually in late March. For more information on the route, consult the Rainbow Rd pamphlet ($1) produced by DOC.

There are also a number of very nice **short walks** on a well signed network of paths skirting the lake. Lake Rotoiti also provides other recreational opportunities such as **trout fishing** and **paddling**. Kayaks can be hired at the edge of the lake in the Kerr Bay DOC camping ground (see Places to Stay & Eat).

Places to Stay & Eat There are excellent *DOC camping grounds (☎ 521 1806, fax 521 1896)* with hot showers, kitchens and fantastic lake views at Kerr and West Bays. Tent sites cost $7 per person. Camp sites and lodges are also scattered throughout the national park – contact the DOC visitor centre for details.

The *Yellow House (☎ 521 1887)*, on the left as you enter town, is a comfortable YHA-associate hostel charging $15 per person in a dorm and $34 for doubles. It's close to Lake Rotoiti, has a bike storage area, a spa pool and hires out walking equipment. The other backpacker option is the *Alpine Chalet (☎ 521 1869)*, a large, clean hostel. Dormitory beds cost $16, singles are $40 and doubles $45. It's right in the centre of town in the same complex as the upmarket *Alpine Lodge Motel (☎ 521 1869)*, where rooms start at $95.

If you don't fancy back-tracking up the hill in the morning, stay at the *Tophouse (☎ 0800 867 468)*, about 3km down the Nelson road and 8km from St Arnaud. It's an historic 1880s era building that's now a

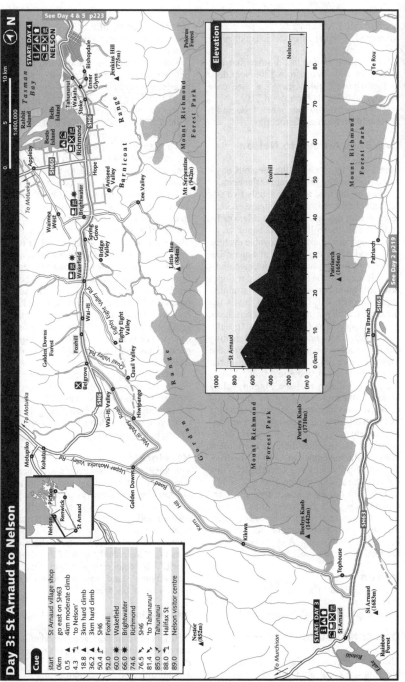

Day 3: St Arnaud to Nelson

Cue

start		St Arnaud village shop
0km		go east on SH63
0.5	◄	4km moderate climb
4.3	◄┐	'to Nelson'
18.8	◄	3km hard climb
36.2	◄	3km hard climb
50.4	◄┘	SH6
52.0		Foxhill
60.0	✳	Wakefield
66.0	✳	Brightwater
74.6		Richmond
76.5	⸜	SH6
81.4	⸝	'to Tahunanui'
85.0	⸝	Tahunanui
88.0	◄┐	Halifax St
89.0		Nelson visitor centre

Elevation

See Day 4 & 5 p223

START: DAY 4
NELSON

START: DAY 3
St Arnaud

See Day 2 p219

comfortable B&B charging $45 per person (dinner $15), with self-contained cottages at $80 a double.

The *Alpine Lodge* has a smart bar and restaurant with mains from $20. Next door at the *Alpine Chalet*, there's a nice cafe serving tasty meals for around $10.

The *petrol station* has snack food and a reasonable selection of groceries.

Day 3: St Arnaud to Nelson
4-6 hours, 89km

Start Day 3 by retracing the previous day's route back up the hill towards Blenheim.

Once on the road to Nelson, only two significant climbs remain and both are encountered during the first half of the ride. Traffic is light and the rolling terrain and views across the valley make for enjoyable cycling.

Around 35km the road climbs again but you could be forgiven for thinking otherwise. It seems to the naked eye as if it slopes downhill quite considerably. Your straining legs, however, will confirm that this is not the case. It really is quite a bizarre sensation.

The busier SH6 (50.4km) is a straight, moderately busy and rather uninteresting road. Fortunately it's slightly downhill and their are more things to distract you off the route. The town of Wakefield (60km) has a number of shops, and the **Pigeon Valley Steam Museum**, containing an interesting collection of vintage machinery, is close by.

The road continues through more strung-out settlements, passing a succession of orchards. In Brightwater there's a **monument** marking the birthplace of Lord Rutherford, the Nobel-prize winning scientist who discovered the atomic nucleus.

The SH6 becomes busier through Richmond (76.5km) as the bypass joins the main road. It continues through Stoke before reaching the coast at **Tahunanui**, an old-time beachside holiday spot. A cycle lane makes the final kilometres most enjoyable.

Nelson
See the Gateway Cities section (pp213-14) earlier in this chapter for information about accommodation and other services in Nelson.

Day 4: Nelson to Havelock
3½-5 hours, 74.5km

The first 10km of the day are flat, the road hugging the coast alongside the waters of Nelson Haven. Traffic is heavy at first but steadily diminishes as you get further from Nelson.

Heading inland the route is flat for 3km before commencing the first and smallest of three significant climbs. This first relatively short climb is a good warm-up for the much longer ascent of Whangamoa Saddle (16km). Although the gradient is quite gentle, the road climbs for a considerable 7km.

The straight high-speed descent levels out at around 29km, where a grassy **picnic area** offers a good spot to take a break. There are a few more kilometres of easy pedalling before the final big climb of the day over the Rai Saddle, a 6km ascent that steepens as you near the summit.

Rai Valley is reached as the descent ends. There's a **store** with a decent selection of food and drinks, a small **supermarket** and a **pub**. Once out of town the road rolls gently through pleasant farming country, before reaching Pelorus Bridge (55km). The **scenic reserve**, which contains a remnant pocket of lush vegetation, is a great spot to take a break off the bike or to stay as an alternative to Havelock. The *DOC camping ground* has tent sites for $14 and two person cabins for $24.

The last 20km to Havelock are fairly flat, mostly following the Pelorus River. You pass through Canvastown, so named because of the tent city it spawned during the gold rush, then cycle beside Pelorus Sound for the final stretch in to Havelock.

Havelock
This small town of 500 people was once the hub of the timber milling and export trade and later became the service centre for gold mining in the area. Today it has a thriving harbour and is the place to catch a boat to more remote parts of the Marlborough Sounds. Its main claim to fame these days is as the 'Greenshell Mussel Capital of the World'. In celebration, larger than life 'mussel men' stand atop the roofs of buildings on the main street.

Information The Havelock Outdoors Centre (☎ 574 2114), on the main street (SH6), books transport, accommodation and activities in and around town. It's open daily from 8 am to 5 pm. DOC (☎ 574 2019) has a small office on Mahakipawa Rd.

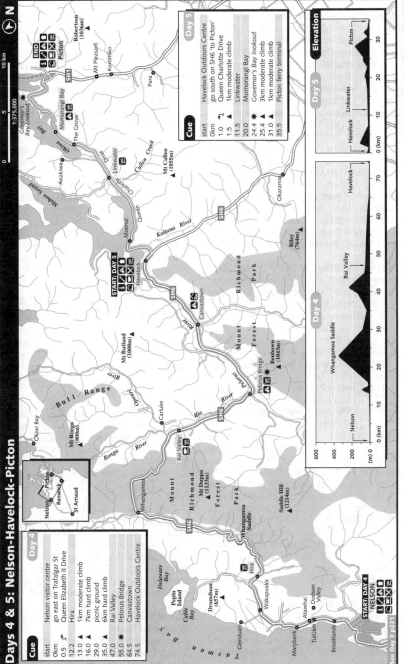

Days 4 & 5: Nelson-Havelock-Picton

Cue

Day 4

start		Nelson visitor centre
0km		go east on Trafalgar St
0.5	↱	Queen Elizabeth II Drive
12.2		Hira
13.0	▲	1km moderate climb
16.0	▲	7km hard climb
29.0		picnic ground
35.0	▲	6km hard climb
47.0		Rai Valley
55.0		Pelorus Bridge
64.5		Canvastown
74.5		Havelock Outdoors Centre

Cue

Day 5

start		Havelock Outdoors Centre
0km		go south on SH6 'to Picton'
1.0	↰	Queen Charlotte Drive
1.5	▲	1km moderate climb
11.5		Linkwater
20.0		Momorangi Bay
24.4	✳	Governor's Bay lookout
25.4	▲	3km moderate climb
31.0	▲	1km moderate climb
35.5		Picton ferry terminal

Elevation

Day 5

Day 4

Things to See & Do There's little in the town itself, but there are a number of activities on offer in the Havelock area. Havelock Fishing Charters (☎ 574 2190) can organise **charter boats** and water taxis. There are a variety of good **walks**, including the four-hour return trip to **Takorika Summit**. The half-hour walk to Cullen Point provides good views of Havelock and the sunset. An excellent two day walk is the **Nydia Track** from Kaiuma to Duncan Bay.

The Maritime Park Wilderness Company (☎ 574 2114) offers **sea-kayaking** trips (and independent rentals) from Havelock. Beachcomber Cruises takes passengers on the **Pelorus mail boat**, stopping at isolated homesteads to deliver mail and supplies. The Outdoors Centre takes bookings for the mail boat tours around the **mussel farms**, snapper **fishing trips** and **cruises** on a 40ft kauri launch.

Places to Stay & Eat The *Havelock Motor Camp* (☎ 576 2339), next to the marina on Inglis St, has tent sites for $7 per person and cabins from $25 for two.

The *Rutherford YHA Hostel* (☎ 574 2104), at the Blenheim end of the main street, is a quiet and comfortable hostel housed in an old schoolhouse dating back to 1881. A bed in a large but well partitioned dorm costs $15. Doubles start at $32.

The *Havelock Garden Motel* (☎ 574 2387, 71 Main Rd) charges from $55 to $73 for two, while the *Pelorus Motor Inn Hotel* (☎ 574 2412), on the same road, also boasts a restaurant and a pub, and has units for $60.

If you want to sample the local delicacy at its freshest and cooked to perfection try *Mussel Boys* (☎ 574 2878, 73 Main Rd). The mussels are served steamed or grilled with a variety of flavourings for around $10 a serve. The mussel chowder is also excellent. The *Pelorus Hotel* (☎ 574 2684), on the marina, has counter or restaurant meals, while lighter meals are available from the *Pelorus Jack Cafe* (☎ 574 2640), also on Main Rd.

Self-caterers can stock up at the *Havelock Foodmarket*.

Day 5: Havelock to Picton
1½-2½ hours, 35.5km
This short day allows plenty of time to enjoy the breathtaking scenery along the route and still arrive in Picton in time for the early afternoon ferry.

Not far out of Havelock the route crosses a bridge over the Kaituna River and start to climb. The descent that follows is an absolute joy, just steep enough to ensure that you need not touch the pedals but so gradual that the benefits the modest climb are extended over several very picturesque kilometres above the azure waters of Pelorus Sound.

After about 8km of bliss the road turns inland towards **Linkwater** (11.5km). There's little here but you can buy a cold drink at the *petrol station*. The road is flat and straight as it passes through some nice rural countryside, meeting the water again at Okiwa Bay. The road rises and falls sharply as you drop into and climb out of a series of delightful little bays. At the **Governor's Bay lookout** there are fantastic views over the sparkling waters of the sounds as well as a walk trail leading to the beach below. The sight of pretty Picton and the ferry terminal below, on the final sweeping descent into town, makes for a memorable finish to the ride.

Farewell Spit

Duration	3 days
Distance	153km
Difficulty	moderate
Start	Nelson
End	Farewell Spit

This short three-day tour takes in the relaxed seaside towns of Tasman and Golden Bays to Farewell Spit, a bird sanctuary of international significance at the north-west tip of the South Island. The riding is generally pretty easy with the one glaring exception of Takaka Hill, a 15km endurance test just outside Motueka.

There are also a couple of side trips off the main route well worth doing, including a ride to Marahau at the start of the Abel Tasman track and a short detour to see the crystal clear waters of Pupu Springs. Unfortunately, the road to Farewell Spit is a dead end, so unless you fancy reliving the tour in reverse, catch the bus back from Collingwood.

PLANNING
When to Ride
It's possible to ride this tour year-round, although from late February to May is probably the best time to cycle, with mild

Wellington looking towards Days Bay

Incredible Mt Taranaki, Southern North Island

Abel Tasman National Park, Nelson

Silver beech forest in Kahurangi National Park, Nelson

weather, light winds and fewer crowds than during the peak summer months. The gannet nesting season at Farewell Spit starts in mid-January and ends around Easter.

GETTING TO/FROM THE RIDE
Nelson
See the Gateway Cities section (p214) earlier in this chapter for information on Getting to/from Nelson.

Collingwood
Kahurangi Bus (☎ 525 9434) runs a daily shuttle bus service from Collingwood to Nelson, leaving from the post office and stopping at most towns in between. The adult fare to Nelson is $32 and bikes are an additional $10.

THE RIDE
Day 1: Nelson to Motueka
2-3 hours, 47km
The route out of Nelson is cyclist-friendly with a broad bike lane running along the waterfront to Tahunanui. After this the road turns away from the water and soon after joins a busier road, taking you through Stoke and Richmond. After joining SH60 navigation is a breeze as this is the road the route follows for the rest of the tour.

The next 15km on SH60, a much quieter road than SH6, are mostly straight and flat, passing through a pleasant but unremarkable landscape of market gardens, wineries and orchards. Around 30km there are a number of small climbs as the route travels between orchards. The town of Mapua, off the route to the right, is home to NZ's first clothes-optional holiday park. The road passes through Ruby Bay then runs briefly alongside the waters of Tasman Bay before climbing away from the coast once more.

Jester House (39.8km) is an off-beat cafe where the main attraction is a collection of **tame eels**. These slippery looking creatures come right out of the water to take food straight from your hand. It's quite a sight! Beyond Jester House the route passes through Tasman, then follows Moutere Inlet for the remainder of the journey into Motueka.

Motueka
Surrounded by rich horticultural land supporting green tea, hops and fruit growing industries, Motueka is a sizeable, laid-back town and a popular summer holiday destination. It's situated close to both the Abel Tasman and Kahurangi National Parks, making it a popular base for walkers. Its cosmopolitan inhabitants include many potters, artists and craftspeople.

Information The visitor centre (☎ 528 6543, fax 528 6563), 13 Wallace St, is open from 8.30 am to 7 pm daily in summer (5 pm in winter). Bookings for assorted national park trips can be made through Abel Tasman National Park Enterprises (☎ 528 7801), 234 High St.

DOC (☎ 528 9117), on the corner of High and King Edward Sts, is the best place for information on the Abel Tasman and Kahurangi national parks.

Hollidays Cycle Centre (☎ 528 9379), 277 High St, is well stocked. If you fancy a walk in the national parks tents and backpacks can be hired from Coppins Great Outdoor (☎ 528 7296), 255 High St. Most hostels rent out sleeping bags and cooking gear.

You can check your email at Cyber World (☎ 528 0072), 15 Wallace St, or grab some cash from an ATM at the High St branches of ANZ and the Bank of New Zealand.

Things to See & Do Most visitors to Motueka come to visit the **Abel Tasman National Park**, a coastal wilderness area blessed with golden-sand beaches lapped by clear, bright blue water. There are various walking tracks in the park but the most popular, and justifiably so, is the **coastal track**. This 51km, three to four-day walk starting at Marahau, 17km north of Motueka, passes through pleasant bush overlooking some of the prettiest beaches imaginable. The track operates on a Great Walks pass system – the cost is $12 per person in huts and $6 for camp sites ($6 for huts or camp sites from June to October). During summer the huts can be overcrowded, so it's wise to bring a tent. The pass is available from either the information centre or DOC in town.

Another popular way to explore Abel Tasman is by **sea kayak**. Paddling allows you to avoid overcrowded huts and camp sites and is a stunning way to see the coast. Most of the kayaking companies operate out of Marahau but provide free transport

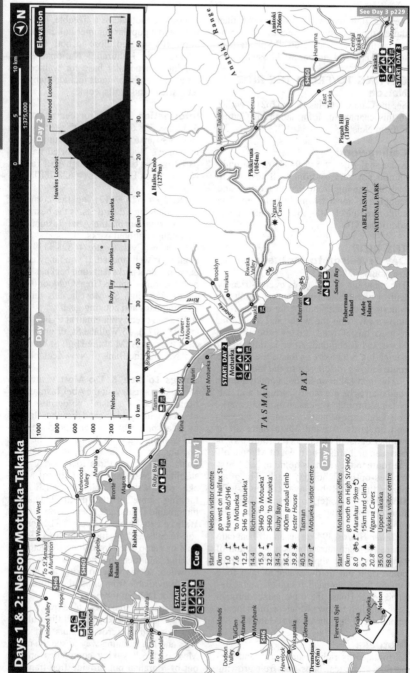

Days 1 & 2: Nelson-Motueka-Takaka

Elevation

| Day 1 |
| Day 2 |

Cue

Day 1

start		Nelson visitor centre
0km		go west on Halifax St
1.0	↰	Haven Rd/SH6
7.6	↰	'to Motueka'
12.5	↰	SH6 'to Motueka'
14.4		Richmond
15.9	↱	SH60 'to Motueka'
32.8	↱	SH60 'to Motueka'
34.5		Ruby Bay
36.2	▲	400m gradual climb
39.8	✳	Jester House
40.5		Tasman
47.0	↰	Motueka visitor centre

Day 2

start		Motueka post office
0km		go north on High St/SH60
8.0	🚲	Marahau 19km ↻
9.7	▲	15km hard climb
20.8	✳	Ngarua Caves
35.0		Upper Takaka
58.0		Takaka visitor centre

Farewell Spit

from Motueka. The Ocean River Adventure Company (☎ 527 8266) conducts one to five-day guided trips starting at $90 per person. It also rents out sea kayaks. As does Abel Tasman Kayaks (☎ 0800 527 8022) at Marahau. In Motueka, try the Sea Kayak Company (☎ 528 7251), 506 High St.

Places to Stay The well equipped *Fernwood Holiday Park* (☎ 528 7488, 519 High St), sandwiched between SH60 and High St South, has tent sites at $13 for two and good four-person cabins for $30.

The *White Elephant* (☎ 528 6208, 55 Whakarewa St) is a good backpackers in a big, comfortable old house. It charges $16 per person in dorms and $40 for doubles including linen. It also has tent sites for $9. Other hostels include the friendly *Twin Oaks Cottage* (☎ 528 7882, 25 Parker St) and the *Motueka YMCA Hostel* (☎ 528 8652, 500 High St), on the southern edge of town.

Basic pub rooms are available at the centrally located *Post Office Hotel* (☎ 528 9890, 122 High St) at $30/45 for a single/double. The *Troubadour Motel & B&B* (☎ 528 7318, 430 High St) charges $52/72 for the B&B while motel units start at $70 a double. The town's best motel is the *Equestrian Lodge Motel* (☎ 528 9369, 2 Avalon Court), with units from $75 to $90.

Places to Eat There are numerous dining options along Motueka's endless main street. The *Post Office Hotel* (122 High St), serves filling pub meals with a salad bar for around $10. *Hot Mama's* (☎ 529 7039, 105 High St) is a hip(py) cafe with good coffee and reasonably priced light meals. It's also licensed and has live music on weekends.

A step up the gastronomic ladder is the *Gothic Gourmet* (☎ 528 6699, 208 High St), occupying an old Methodist church in the centre of town. Its innovative meat and vegetarian dishes would be notable anywhere. A town favourite is the *Bakehouse Cafe* (☎ 528 6111, 21 Wallace St), a European-style cafe with a bar that serves up great pizza and Italian food. Self-caterers will find *New World* and *Supervalue* supermarkets on High St.

Day 2: Motueka to Takaka
3-4½ hours, 58km
This day is dominated by the long slog up Takaka Hill, also known as 'Marble Moun-

tain' for the stone that is still quarried there. The climb is punishing but thankfully, once conquered, the remainder of the day's ride is downhill. If it all seems a bit too hard, it's possible to catch a lift to the summit with Kahurangi Bus (☎ 525 9434).

The route's first 10km are flat, passing through numerous fields of fruit crops and crossing the Motueka River and passing through the town of the same name.

The 15km, 800m ascent of Takaka Hill is not overly steep and traffic is fairly light and slow moving. Just keep an eye out for trucks; at times they threaten to completely fill the narrow road on sharp bends.

Around 18km the route flattens a little as the landscape opens out into an unusual mixture of scrub and grazing land. **Hawkes Lookout**, which lies at the end of a short path, affords some sweeping views. Drinks are available at the adjacent *craft gallery*.

A short distance later is **Caves Lookout**, where a short access road leads away to the **Ngarua Caves** (☎ 528 8093). The caves are open from 10 am to 4 pm daily, except Friday; it's also closed from mid-June to August.

Caves Lookout is something of a false summit as the descent that begins there is short lived and the road begins to climb again. The road is much straighter and the gradient quite gradual from this point, with the summit tantalisingly visible in the distance. Finally, after 25km a sign reading 791m signals the top.

Stop to take in the fine views down the Takaka River Valley to Takaka and Golden Bay from **Harwood Lookout** (25.4km). This is a popular spot for paragliders who can often be seen soaring above. The descent is 5km shorter than the climb, making for a steep and exhilarating descent.

The terrain starts to level out at 35km on the outskirts of **Upper Takaka**. Smoked fish lovers can indulge at a roadside stall. The rest of the way into Takaka is fairly easy going through lush grazing pastures.

Side Trip: Marahau
1½-2½ hours, 19km return
This pleasant ride takes you past some fabulous swimming beaches out to Marahau and the start of the Abel Tasman coastal track, returning inland through the hills. It would also make an enjoyable day trip if you want to spend an extra day at Motueka.

About 8km out of Motueka, turn right at the turn-off signposted to Kaiteriteri. Once off SH60 the route is quiet and flat at first, but you soon encounter a number of small climbs, reaching Kaiteriteri after 13km. **Kaiteriteri**, a popular summer holiday spot, has a beautiful beach with golden sand and clear green water. It's a fantastic spot to take a dip and relax for a few hours. If you end up wanting to stay longer, the large, well equipped *Kaiteriteri Beach Camp (☎ 527 8010)* is just across the road.

Beyond Kaiteriteri the deserted road climbs steadily through native bush for about 3km before an exhilarating, twisting descent brings you to an intersection. Turn right and pedal alongside Otuwhero Inlet for the remaining few kilometres into Marahau.

Marahau is the principal gateway for the Abel Tasman National Park as well as the starting point for the popular **coastal track walk**. A number of sea kayak operations are based here (see Things to See & Do in Motueka earlier in this chapter). **Horse treks** and, believe it or not, **llama safaris** are also available. Follow the road to the end to reach the coastal track trailhead where there's an information kiosk and the excellent *Park Cafe*. Just across the way is the *Barn Backpackers (☎ 527 8043)*, a popular hostel with a commune feel. A dorm bed costs $15 and twins/doubles are $38. There are also plenty of tent spaces ($8.50) and, for something different, hammocks, a house-truck and a native American tepee.

On the return journey, cycle back alongside the inlet for 3km, but continue straight ahead instead of going left at the Kaiteriteri turn-off. After the intersection the road begins to climb, gently at first then progressively steeper. The ascent continues for a scenic but tiring 4km, bringing you to the summit at around 31km. Mid-way through the twisting descent a board on the side of the road marks the start of the **Rimu Valley walking track**, a pleasant 40 minute, 1.4km walk through a remnant patch of native coastal forest. It's a worthwhile detour if you're keen. The descent finishes at the SH60, turn right to continue on Day 2's route to Takaka.

Takaka

The small town of Takaka (population 1250) is the last settlement of any real size on the journey to Farewell Spit. It's the major centre for the beautiful Golden Bay area, and for such a small place is quite cosmopolitan. A lot of 'children of the 60s' and artists call Takaka home.

Information The visitor centre (☎ 525 9136) is on the left as you enter town. It's open from 9 am to 5 pm daily in summer and from 10 am to 4 pm over winter. The DOC (☎ 525 8026), 62 Commercial St, has lots of information on Farewell Spit, Pupu Springs and the nearby Abel Tasman and Kahurangi National Parks.

Takaka's bike shop, the Quiet Revolution (☎ 525 9555), 7 Commercial St, has a reasonable selection of gear and is a good source of local knowledge. Pick up the *Golden Bay Fat Tire Fun* leaflet detailing off-road rides in the area.

There is a Bank of New Zealand at 57 Commercial St and a Westpac Trust ATM further up the street.

Things to See & Do There are few specific attractions in town, but with a reasonable selection of shops and a couple of good cafes, it's easy enough to spend an hour or two browsing along Commercial St. An interesting selection of local arts and crafts is on display in the **Artisans' Shop** cooperative next to the Village Theatre. There's also a small **museum**, open daily.

Places to Stay & Eat The closest camping ground is the *Pohara Beachside Holiday Park (☎ 525 9500)* at Pohara, 10km away.

The *Shady Rest Hostel (141 Commercial St)*, a friendly, roomy but rather basic place occupying a large historic home, has an enthusiastic, slightly eccentric owner – you can't ring ahead as it's a 'Telecom Free Zone'. A bed in the large dorm costs $15 per person. The *River Inn (☎ 525 8501)*, 3km west of town on the route to Collingwood, is an old pub-turned-backpackers with better standards of accommodation, charging $15/30 for singles/doubles.

Takaka's newest and best motel is *Anotoki Lodge (☎ 525 8047, 147 Commercial St)*, which has modern units from $74 to $110; pub beds are available at the *Junction Hotel (☎ 525 9207, 15 Commercial St)* for $32/50.

There are a number of fast food places and fancier eateries strung out along Commercial St. The *Dangerous Kitchen (☎ 525 8686)*, at

No 48, is a cafe-pizza bar offering an imaginative array of gourmet pizzas. The *Whole Meal Cafe* (☎ 525 9426), at No 60, is very popular and has a varied selection of reasonably priced all-day and evening meals. A notch up in the gourmet stakes is *Milliways* (☎ 525 9636, 90 Commercial St), a relaxed place with mains starting at around $18.

Day 3: Takaka to Farewell Spit
2-3 hours, 48km

This is another short and fairly easy day allowing plenty of time to relax on the beach and soak up the natural beauty of the area. After 4km of flat terrain the route crosses a bridge over the Waikoropupu River, where a road leading away to the left marks the turn-off for the short and very worthwhile side trip to Pupu Springs (see Side Trip).

The SH60 is ideal for cycling; virtually traffic-free as it rolls through a mixture of pleasant rural countryside and native bush. There are some fine views out across hilly fields to the ocean from **Golden Bay lookout** (12km).

Several more small climbs follow until the route reaches an intersection (26km) by the coast. The tiny town of **Collingwood** (population 250) is about 1km away to the right. The tours to Farewell Spit and shuttle buses back to Nelson leave from Collingwood, making it a good alternative destination, especially for those seeking motel accommodation.

Turn left to continue to Pakawau, Puponga and Farewell Spit. After another 400m turn right over a bridge and cycle along a flat deserted road running parallel to a tidal area by the coast. Big fat hills loom ahead but fear not, the road skirts them, remaining flat for the rest of the journey.

The *Innlet* hostel (35km), off to the left, is probably the best place to stay in the Farewell Spit area, although there are a couple more options closer to Cape Farewell in Pakawau and Puponga.

Side Trip: Pupu Springs
1 hour, 6km return

Reputedly boasting some of the clearest water in the world, Te Waikoropupu (Pupu) Springs, the largest fresh water springs in NZ, are just a short detour off the main route to Farewell Spit. The turn-off is on the left, 4km out of Takaka, just over Waitapu Bridge.

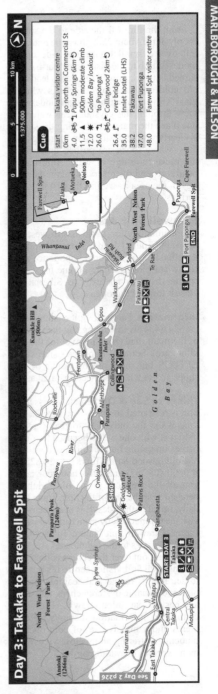

Cue	
start	Takaka visitor centre
0km	go north on Commercial St
4.0 🚲 ↖↑	Pupu Springs 6km ↻
11.5 ◀	500m moderate climb
12.0 ✱	Golden Bay lookout
26.0 ↖↑	'to Puponga'
	🚲↖ Collingwood 2km ↻
26.4 ↳↑	over bridge
35.0	Innlet hostel (LHS)
38.2	Pakawau
47.0	Port Puponga
48.0	Farewell Spit visitor centre

Day 3: Takaka to Farewell Spit

From the turn-off the ride to the springs is only 3km. About 2km down the road, turn left over a small bridge and ride up the modest climb to the visitors car park. A well signed network of walking tracks leads past old gold diggings to the springs where a glass viewing area allows an underwater view through the crystal clear waters. In one place the main vent feeding the springs is clearly visible, resulting in 'dancing boulders' where rocks are pushed upwards by the powerful surge of water. Information boards around the reserve explain the geology of the area as well as the history of the springs.

Farewell Spit Area

The main attraction in this north-west corner of the South Island is Farewell Spit. It's a wetland of international importance and a renowned bird sanctuary, home to over 90 species from as far away as Siberia. The closest town is Puponga.

Information Farewell Spit visitor centre (☎ 524 8454) is in Puponga, at the very end of the main road (rough gravel for the final kilometre). Some of Puponga's stores have EFTPOS but there are no banks or bike shops so get what you need in Takaka.

Things to See & Do Vehicle access to the Spit is restricted so unless you fancy a very long walk, the only way to really get out onto it is with one of the licensed tour companies operating out of Collingwood.

Collingwood Safari Tours (☎ 524 8257 or ☎ 0800 808 257) runs a five hour tour, taking you all the way out to the old lighthouse perched near the end of the Spit. Tours leave daily, timed to the tides. It is also licensed to visit the **Gannet colony** from early January to Easter. Farewell Spit Nature Tours (☎ 524 8188) also goes to the lighthouse.

Looking out over the eel grass flats from the **Farewell Spit visitor centre** it's possible to see many waders and seabirds such as pied and variable oystercatchers, turnstones and eastern bar-tailed godwits. The visitor centre has information displays, refreshments and a massive set of coin operated binoculars offering an up close view of the many species of wading birds.

Also in Puponga is Cape Farewell Horse Treks (☎ 524 8031), offering a range of **horse-riding** trips including a three hour trek to Wharariki Beach. **Wharariki Beach** is a worthwhile 20 minute walk from the Puponga car park. It's a wild place with unusual dune formations, two craggy, rock islets just out from shore and a seal colony at its eastern end.

Places to Stay The *Collingwood Motor Camp* (☎ 524 8149), on William St, has tent sites at $18 for two and cabins for $32. Closer to Farewell Spit, the *Pakawau Beach Park* (☎ 524 8327), 12km from the Collingwood turn-off, has tent sites at $18 for two. Large cabins with cooking facilities are $44 and motel units are $79. Nearest of all to the Spit at Puponga is *Farewell Gardens* (☎ 524 8445), charging $9 for tent sites, $39 for self-contained flats and $22.50 for a twin room, all per person.

The *Innlet* (☎ 524 8040), 9km from the Collingwood turn-off on the Puponga road, is a friendly hostel and a great place to just hang out. Comfortable beds in renovated share rooms are $16, doubles are $40, and there is also a self-contained cottage sleeping six for $90. There are some nice walks in the surrounding native bush and the beach is only a short walk away.

In Collingwood try the *Collingwood Motel* (☎ 524 8224) on Haven Rd, it has units from $65 for two, or the newer and marginally cheaper *Pioneer Motel* (☎ 524 8109) on Tasman St.

Places to Eat Dining options are pretty limited. On Tasman St in Collingwood, the *Collingwood Tavern* (☎ 524 8160) serves reasonable bistro meals until 8.30 pm from Monday to Thursday and 9 pm over the weekend. Food is also available from the *Collingwood Cafe* (☎ 524 8114) until around 8 pm daily. The best restaurant in the area is the *Old School Cafe* (☎ 524 8457), opposite the motor camp at Pakawau. The decor of the building matches its former calling and scallops and other local seafood are featured on the menu (mains around $20).

Self-caterers will find a reasonable selection of groceries at the *Pakawau Beach Park* and the *Collingwood Store*, on Tasman St.

Canterbury

Canterbury extends from Kaikoura in the north to the Waitaki River in the south, and inland to the Southern Alps as far as Lewis Pass, Arthur's Pass and Mt Cook. Containing the major city, Christchurch, and two-thirds of the South Island's population, Canterbury has the densest road network and traffic. Fortunately, the traffic congregates in the urban centres, leaving long stretches of peaceful road just begging to be cycled.

The low rainfall and mostly level terrain in the eastern parts make for easy cycling, winds permitting (see Climate). There is spectacular mountain and coastal scenery as well as an immense variety of activities to enjoy, including whale and dolphin-watching, bungy jumping and jet-boating, thermal springs and mountain biking.

Rides in this chapter take in Canterbury's varied cycling environments. Starting with the flat city and suburbs of Christchurch, rides go into the volcanic Port Hills, popular for mountain biking, north to Kaikoura for marine mammal watching and breathtaking coastal views, and to Hanmer Springs with more wonderful mountain bike terrain as well as thermal springs. Another ride explores the foothill towns of the dividing range west and south of Christchurch, finishing at the beach in Timaru. The Mackenzie Country route takes you through New Zealand's 'Outback', further south. Two harder, adventurous rides are the Southern Alps Circuit, which crosses the South Island's mountain spine in both directions between Christchurch and Greymouth, and the Banks Peninsula Circuit visiting French-influenced Akaroa via the long, steep, sometimes unsealed slopes of the extinct volcanoes near Christchurch.

HISTORY

Prior to European settlement, waves of Polynesian immigration brought a Maori population of anywhere from 6000 to 10,000 to the South Island. The dominant tribe was the Ngai Tahu.

The first Europeans to spend time on the South Island were sealing gangs that plundered the seal colonies from 1792 to supply the fashion markets of the northern hemisphere. Whalers followed including the

In Summary

Area Code: ☎ 03

Highlights
- Marine mammals off **Kaikoura**
- **Hanmer Springs** thermal baths
- **Arthur's Pass National Park** walks
- The scenery of **Banks Peninsula**
- The French influence of **Akaroa**
- **Timaru** and its fine-sand beach

Special Events
- **Country Music Festival** (January), Geraldine
- **Festival of Arts & Plants** (November), Geraldine
- **Heritage Festival** (November), Oamaru
- **Christmas & New Year Festival**, Caroline Bay (Timaru)

Cycling Events
- **Coast to Coast multi-sport race** (February), West Coast to Christchurch
- **Le Race** (March), Christchurch to Akaroa
- **Port Hills Mountain Bike Classic** (November/December), Christchurch

Terrain
It ranges from vast, dead-flat plains around Christchurch to the mountains of the Southern Alps in the west; hilly terrain lies to the north (Kaikoura Ranges) and south-west (Mackenzie Country), while the volcanic Port Hills and Banks Peninsula are to the south.

Frenchman Jean Langlois, commanding the *Cachalot*. He saw potential for a French colony on the Banks Peninsula and in 1838 made a deed of purchase with some Ngai Tahu living at present day Lyttelton. French colonial ambitions were narrowly thwarted by the British who rushed to raise the Union Jack at Akaroa just days before the French arrived. Captain Lavaud and a group of 57

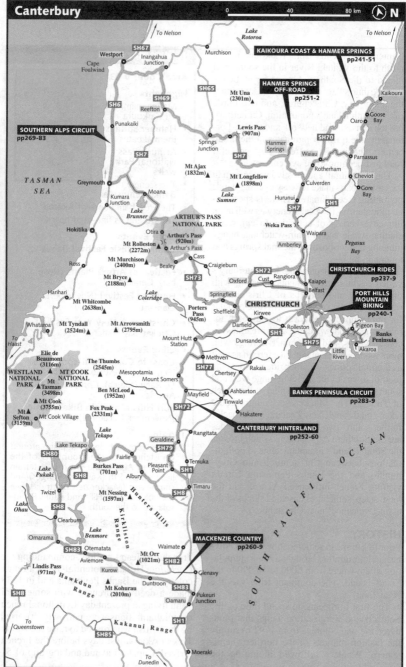

Canterbury

0   40   80 km   N

KAIKOURA COAST & HANMER SPRINGS
pp241-51

HANMER SPRINGS
OFF-ROAD
pp251-2

SOUTHERN ALPS CIRCUIT
pp269-83

CHRISTCHURCH RIDES
pp237-9

PORT HILLS
MOUNTAIN
BIKING
pp240-1

BANKS PENINSULA CIRCUIT
pp283-9

CANTERBURY HINTERLAND
pp252-60

MACKENZIE COUNTRY
pp260-9

CANTERBURY

To Nelson

Lake
Rotoroa

To Nelson

Westport
Cape
Foulwind
Inangahua
Junction

SH67

Murchison

Mt Una
(2301m)

SH6
SH69
SH65

Reefton

Lewis Pass
(907m)

Kaikoura

Goose
Bay

Oaro

Punakaiki

SH7

Springs
Junction

Hanmer
Springs

SH70

Waiau

Parnassus

SH7

Rotherham

Cheviot

Gore
Bay

Mt Ajax
(1832m)

Mt Longfellow
(1898m)

Culverden

TASMAN
SEA

Greymouth

Moana

Lake
Sumner

Hurunui

SH7

SH1

Kumara
Junction

Lake
Brunner

ARTHUR'S PASS
NATIONAL PARK

Weka Pass

Waipara

Pegasus
Bay

Hokitika

Otira

Arthur's
Pass
(920m)

Arthur's
Pass

Amberley

Mt Rolleston
(2272m)

Ross

Mt Murchison
(2400m)

Bealey

Cass

Craigieburn

SH72

Oxford
Cust
Rangiora

Kaiapoi
Belfast

Mt Bryce
(2188m)

SH73

Harihari

Mt Whitcombe
(2638m)

Lake
Coleridge

Springfield

CHRISTCHURCH

Sheffield

Kirwee

Pigeon Bay

Whataroa

Mt Tyndall
(2524m)

Mt Arrowsmith
(2795m)

Porters
Pass
(945m)

Darfield

Rolleston

SH1

SH75

Banks
Peninsula

To
Haast

Mount Hutt
Station

Dunsandel

Little
River

Akaroa

Elie de
Beaumont
(3116m)

WESTLAND
NATIONAL
PARK

MT COOK
NATIONAL
PARK

The Thumbs
(2545m)

Methven

SH77

Chertsey

Rakaia

Mt
Tasman
(3498m)

Mesopotamia
Mount Somers

Mt Cook
(3755m)

Ben McLeod
(1952m)

Mayfield

Ashburton

Mt
Sefton
(3159m)

Mt Cook Village

Fox Peak
(2331m)

Tinwald

Hakatere

Lake
Tekapo

SH72

Geraldine

Rangitata

SOUTH PACIFIC OCEAN

Lake Tekapo

Fairlie

SH79

Temuka

SH80

Burkes Pass
(701m)

Pleasant
Point

SH1

Lake
Pukaki

SH8

Albury

Timaru

Twizel

Mt Nessing
(1597m)

SH8

Lake
Ohau

SH8

Clearburn

Lake
Benmore

Omarama

SH83

Otematata

Waimate

Aviemore

Mt Orr
(1021m)

SH82

Lindis Pass
(971m)

Hawkdun
Range

Kurow

Glenavy

Duntroon

SH83

SH8

Mt Kohurau
(2010m)

Pukeuri
Junction

Oamaru

To
Queenstown

Kakanui Range

SH1

SH85

To
Dunedin

Moeraki

Kirkliston
Range

Hunters Hills

French and German passengers landed to settle present-day Akaroa on 17 August 1840. To this day, French family names are still prominent in that community.

Also among Canterbury's first settlers were two young Scottish brothers, William and John Deans, who established a farm at Riccarton, near today's central Christchurch, early in the 1840s. Their cottage is now a museum in Deans Bush Reserve.

The prosperity of the Ngai Tahu was destroyed by inter-island warfare and disease epidemics from 1830. The final indignity was the 'purchase' of their land by the British – at Akaroa in June 1848, tribal chiefs signed a deed turning over to the British Crown 20 million acres of Canterbury and Otago for a mere UK£2000. Ngai Tahu claims before the Treaty of Waitangi Tribunal have only recently been settled.

NATURAL HISTORY

The mountains along Canterbury's western boundary supply alluvial material making up the plains. Jutting eastwards are extinct volcanoes that form the Banks Peninsula. These once rose to 3000m, but, over millions of years, have sunk. The sea has flooded part of the craters to form deep sheltered bays, now Lyttelton and Akaroa harbours. The peninsula was first charted by James Cook in February 1770. Deceived by the then swampy low lying land surrounding it, Cook named it Banks Island after botanist Joseph Banks.

CLIMATE

Canterbury is in the rain shadow of the Southern Alps and receives less than one-sixth of the rainfall of the West Coast (around 750mm compared to 5000mm!). Year-round temperatures are generally mild (winter average 6°C) to warm, although solar radiation can be intense and shade hard to find in the treeless inland. Christchurch's December to February average temperature is around 17°C.

On summer afternoons, cool north-easterly sea breezes are common close to the coast, while occasional southerly changes can bring days of cold south-westers and rain. Warm, dry north-westerly winds are a cyclist's nightmare during east-west mountain traverses. These winds originate in the Roaring Forties over the Southern Ocean and, after dumping their moisture on the West Coast and Alps, swing round and gather speed and heat as they descend to the south-east. They can blow strongly for several days. Local cyclists advise not to attempt to ride against them but to delay your journey north-west, or else turn around and go with the flow.

INFORMATION
Maps

The InfoMap 1:500,000 series titles *The South* and *North Meets South* cover the South Island and are adequate for navigating sealed roads, but lack detail for more remote, unsealed routes.

The AA in Christchurch has 1:350,000 scale maps of the region that are very useful for cycling. They're free to members of AA or affiliated motoring associations.

For mountain biking, 1:50,000 maps published by Land Information New Zealand and costing around $13 are most useful. While each only covers a small area, they have good contour detail (20m intervals) and accurately show most trails. They are widely available through most outdoor shops and some bike shops.

Be aware that place names on maps are no guarantee that any services exist at a location. Also, some are not identified with the same name on the ground. For example, try finding Windy Point on SH7 between Lewis Pass and Hanmer Springs. If you can't, don't worry, you haven't missed a thing! (It's a car park identified by a sign saying 'Lake Sumner Forest Park, Hope River Entrance'.)

Single-Lane Bridges

Canterbury, in common with other regions of the South Island, has many single-lane road bridges. Some are several hundred metres long. Be certain oncoming vehicles can see you when on the bridge and, if they are not waiting for you to clear the span, that you can avoid them. (Brightly coloured cycling clothes are excellent in this situation and generally.) On the longer bridges, passing bays allow avoidance space (and photo opportunities) and it would be polite to let any following traffic, as well as oncoming vehicles, pass here rather than hold them up.

Information Sources

Trail Blazers (☎ 366 6033, fax 366 6173), 86 Worcester St, Christchurch, offers multi-lingual advice (in Japanese, Mandarin and Cantonese) to cyclists. It also conducts tours and hires out touring bikes.

Advice about routes and local conditions is available from the Canterbury Recreational Cycle Club (☎ 337 1151), which also runs social rides on Tuesday evening and Sunday year-round, and the Canterbury Mountain Bike Club (☎ 337 1466).

GATEWAY CITIES
Christchurch

Centrally located on the east coast of the South Island, Christchurch is the focus of the island's road, rail and air networks. It is often described as the most English city in NZ. The tranquil Avon River bisects it and its street and suburb names reinforce the mother-country connection of this thoroughly modern South Pacific city.

Founded in 1850, it has developed from a gentrified, devoutly religious farming community into a 330,000-strong multicultural centre. A vibrant cafe scene and cultural offerings give it life at all hours.

The lack of hills and compact nature of the city make cycling the ideal means of personal transport, particularly for the visitor. Bicycles can be hired at several locations (see Information). The network of cycle routes, lanes and facilities is relatively recent, but caters to a large population of cyclists. To a newcomer, the city and its traffic may appear benign, but local cyclists know there is much more that needs to be done to satisfy their needs and encourage others out of their cars.

Information The Christchurch-Canterbury tourism and visitor centre (☎ 379 9629, fax 377 2424, ✉ info@christchurchtourism.co .nz), on the corner of Worcester St and Oxford Terrace, is open from 8.30 am to 5 pm on weekdays (4 pm on weekends) and takes bookings for accommodation and tours. Pick up a copy of the *Free Official Christchurch Visitors Guide*.

DOC (☎ 379 9758) at 133 Victoria St has information on national parks and outdoor attractions on the South Island.

The post office is in the south-west corner of Cathedral Square. The AA (☎ 379 1280), 210 Hereford St, has 1:350,000 scale maps of the region that are very useful for cycling if you're a member of AA or an affiliated motoring association.

Christchurch cyclists are well served by bike shops, with several on Colombo St, which runs north-south through the city. Some of the better shops include the touring

The Speedy Cycle Works (circa 1912), formerly of Manchester St, Christchurch.

specialists Cycle Trading Co (☎ 366 3760), 27 Manchester St, and Cyclone Cycles & Mowers (☎ 332 9588 or ☎ 332 9573), 245 Colombo St, which hires off-road mountain bikes from $23 for four hours ($50 with full suspension) or from $30 per day ($75 with full suspension).

John Bull Cycles (☎ 377 2058), on the corner of Colombo and Tuam Sts, offers short and longer term touring bike hire. A mountain bike with slick tyres, racks and pannier bags costs from $100 for seven days to $400 for 12 weeks. One-way hire is available for an extra $35.

Things to See & Do Many of the attractions of Christchurch, such as historic buildings and parks, can be seen on the Christchurch Parks & Gardens and Beaches & Hills rides in this chapter.

At the heart of the city is Cathedral Square. It is dominated by **Christ Church Cathedral**, consecrated in 1881. For $4 you can see the historical display and climb 133 steps up the 63m-high spire to the bells and viewing balconies.

Cathedral Square is the haunt of **The Wizard**, a genuine NZ eccentric who spouts forth his opinions on fine days in the summer months. His put-downs of hecklers are artful.

Grab a copy of the free *Central City Walks* brochure from the visitor centre or ride the **tram** on the 2.5km inner city circuit from the square past the Arts Centre and gardens. Drivers provide comprehensive, entertaining commentary.

Next to the airport on Orchard Rd is the **International Antarctic Centre** (☎ 358 9896). As well as the hands-on exhibits and video presentations, you can endure polar conditions in the 'Snow and Ice Experience'.

The **Canterbury Museum** (☎ 366 5000), on Rolleston Ave, is at the entrance to the Botanic Gardens. Particularly interesting are the early colonist exhibits, the Antarctic discovery section and the Maori gallery.

The **Robert McDougall Art Gallery** (☎ 365 0915), behind the museum, and has an extensive collection of NZ and international art.

Ferrymead Historic Park (☎ 384 1970) is at 269 Bridle Path Rd, Ferrymead. Set in a re-creation of an Edwardian village, it is a working museum of transport and technology with locomotives, model railways, machinery and old household appliances.

The largest marae in NZ, **Nga Hau e Wha** (The Four Winds; ☎ 388 7685) is at 250 Pages Rd, 6km north-east of the city. It is a multicultural facility open to all. There are carvings, weaving and paintings on display in the *whare nui* (meeting house) and *whare whananga* (house of learning).

Air Force World (☎ 343 9532) is on the old RNZAF Base at Wigram on Main South Rd, one of the earliest air bases in the country. It has displays on the history of flight in NZ, a special WWII section and even a flight simulator in which you can pretend to pilot an A4 Skyhawk jet.

Aerial sightseeing is offered by Garden City Helicopters (☎ 358 4360). Options include city and harbour flights, a farm visit with horse trekking, and a three hour Akaroa flight including lunch. Flights operate daily and start at $45 per person.

Places to Stay The *Showground Motor Camp (☎ 338 9770, 47 Whiteleigh Ave)* is conveniently close to the train station, 3km south of the city centre. Tent sites are from $10 and cabins range from $15 to $49. Spartan in appearance, it's not a place where you'll want to spend much time.

Meadow Park Holiday Park (☎ 352 9176, 39 Meadow St) is off Main North Rd, 5km north of town in Papanui. Tent sites are $20 for two, cabins start at $33 and there are tourist flats from $50.

One other conveniently located motor park is *Amber Park Caravan Park (☎ 348 3327, 308 Blenheim Rd)*, 4km south-west of the centre. Tent sites cost $18 and tourist flats with en suites are from $46; prices for two.

There are two YHA hostels in Christchurch. The *City Central YHA (☎ 379 9535, ✉ yhachch@yha.org.nz, 273 Manchester St)* has dorm beds for $19. Doubles cost $42. *Rolleston House (☎ 366 6564, ✉ yhachrl@ yha.org.nz, 5 Worcester Boulevarde)* is a smaller place, opposite the Arts Centre and just 700m from the Cathedral Square. Dorm beds cost $17 and twin rooms are $38.

Other popular hostels are *Vagabond Backpackers (☎ 379 9677, 232 Worcester St)*, with dorm and share-room beds from $14 and doubles for $17.50; and *Foley Towers (☎ 366 9720, 208 Kilmore St)*, which has dorm beds from $13 and doubles from $17.

B&B operators are scattered all over the city and suburbs. A comprehensive list is available from the visitor centre. Examples in the city area include *Armagh Lodge (☎ 366 0744, fax 374 6359, 257 Armagh St)*, which charges around $60/80 for a single/double with full breakfast, and *Croydon House (☎ 366 5111, fax 377 6110, 63 Armagh St)*, charging around $60/90, also with breakfast.

Many Christchurch motels charge between $70 and $100 a double. Bealey Ave, close to the city centre, has a number, and Papanui Rd has more, including upmarket accommodation.

Downtown hotels include the *Ambassador (☎ 366 7808, 19 Manchester St)*, just a short walk south of the centre. Attractive original features include leadlight windows. Rooms start at $40/60, with continental breakfast included. The *Excelsior (☎ 366 9489, cnr High and Manchester Sts)* has old double rooms for $45 ($55 with en suite).

Top-bracket hotels include *Chateau on the Park (☎ 348 8999, cnr High & Manchester Sts)*, *Quality Hotel Durham (☎ 365 4699, cnr Durham & Kilmore Sts)*, *Quality Hotel Central (☎ 379 5880, 776 Colombo St)*, and *Noah's (☎ 379 4700, cnr Worcester St & Oxford Terrace)*. All charge upwards of $150 a night.

Places to Eat Almost any cuisine you could desire is available in downtown Christchurch. There is *Mythai (☎ 365 1295, 84 Hereford St)* for great Thai food, *Raj Mahal (☎ 366 0521, cnr Manchester & Worcester Sts)* for Indian, *Sala Sala (☎ 366 67551, 84 Oxford Terrace)* for Japanese, *Bardellis Deli Cafe (☎ 353 0000, 89 Cashel St)* for Mediterranean, *Il Felice (☎ 366 7535, 56 Lichfield St)* for Italian, *Alva Rados (☎ 365 1644, cnr Manchester & Worcester Sts)* for Mexican and *Chung Wah II (☎ 379 3894, 63 Worcester St)* serves Chinese. Wander around the city and along Colombo St to find more.

Dux de Lux (☎ 366 6919, cnr Hereford and Montreal Sts) caters for vegetarians and seafood lovers and has an on-site brewery.

Excellent coffee is available at the popular street-front *Vesuvio Cafe (☎ 365 4183, 182 Oxford Terrace)*. For pub food, the *Oxford on Avon (☎ 379 7148, 794 Colombo St)* is popular for its atmosphere and hearty cheap meals, from breakfast (starting at 6.30 am) through to dinner and late night snacks. It closes at midnight.

Getting There & Away As the major city on the South Island, access to Christchurch can be by air, bus or train.

Air Christchurch's international and domestic airport is about 11km north-west of the city. Numerous door-to-door shuttle services, such as Super Shuttle (☎ 365 5655) and Carrington (☎ 352 6369), operate to and from the airport carrying luggage and bicycles in enclosed trailers. The cost to the city is around $10 and your bike travels free.

Air New Zealand (☎ 353 4899) is the main international and domestic carrier. Daily direct flights go between Christchurch and Auckland, Blenheim, Dunedin, Hokitika, Invercargill, Mt Cook, Nelson, Queenstown, Te Anau, Timaru and Wellington, with connections to most other centres. It can also book Air Chatham flights to the Chatham Islands.

Ansett New Zealand (☎ 371 1146) has direct flights to Auckland, Dunedin, Invercargill, Palmerston North, Queenstown, Rotorua and Wellington.

Bus InterCity (☎ 379 9020) is the main South Island carrier (buses depart from the corner of Moorhouse and Fitzgerald Aves). It runs services north to Kaikoura and Blenheim and south to Queenstown via Mt Cook, and south along SH1 to Dunedin, with connections to Invercargill, Te Anau and Queenstown.

Newmans (☎ 374 6149) buses stop at the visitor centre on Oxford Terrace. It has daily buses to Dunedin and to Nelson via Kaikoura and Picton. Mt Cook Landline (☎ 348 2099) buses go to Queenstown via Mt Cook, departing from 47 Riccarton Rd.

The West Coast is sadly neglected by the major bus companies, but Coast to Coast Shuttle (☎ 0800 800 847) and Alpine Coach & Courier (☎ 0800 274 888) have daily services to Greymouth or Hokitika via Arthur's Pass. Other shuttles are Ko-Op (☎ 366 6633) to Greymouth and East West (☎ 0800 500 251) to Westport.

Train Christchurch's train station (☎ 0800 802 802) is at Addington, near the south-west corner of Hagley Park. Tranz Scenic trains link the city with Invercargill, Dunedin and other points south, Greymouth and other points west, and Kaikoura and Picton in the north. The Interislander ferry

(☎ 0800 802 802) from Picton connects passengers with the North Island.

Bicycles travel in the baggage car, space permitting, for a flat $10 charge regardless of distance.

Christchurch Region

Christchurch is a very cycle-friendly city and boasts many great areas to ride. These rides can be done at any time the weather is favourable, although it is best to avoid busy commuter-traffic periods.

Maps & Books
City by Cycle ($7.95) is a 100 page booklet describing many of Christchurch's scenic, commuter and mountain bike routes. It includes the pull-out 'Christchurch Cycle Map' of bike routes, which can be used in conjunction with the book's sometimes vague ride directions to explore the city.

Christchurch Parks & Gardens

Duration	1½-2½ hours
Distance	15.8km
Difficulty	easy
Start/End	Cathedral Square

Sample some of the best sights of Christchurch on this tour of suburban parks, gardens and historic buildings. This ride works well combined with Christchurch Beaches & Hills, which takes you out to the coast and the Port Hills.

THE RIDE
From Cathedral Square cycle west through Hagley Park to **Mona Vale Homestead** in Fendalton. This grand Elizabethan-style homestead (built in 1900) is set among 5.5 hectares of richly landscaped gardens, ponds and fountains on the bank of the Avon River. From here, the route follows quiet streets and cycle paths through **Riccarton Bush Reserve**, the last remnant of the Kahikatea forest that once covered Canterbury, passing stately **Riccarton House** and **Deans Cottage**, Christchurch's oldest existing building. After cruising through the **University of Canterbury**, you'll visit **Ilam Homestead**, a

shady garden oasis with meandering gravel paths and little bridges across the Avon.

Swing back to the city past Christchurch Boys High School and through little Daresbury Park. Going south along Harakeke St, the route crosses its outward path and, via Kilmarnock St, re-enters North Hagley Park at the crossing of Deans Ave. Cycleways lead to Rolleston Ave after which it's necessary again to share city streets that can be busy with cars, buses and trucks.

Christchurch Beaches & Hills

Duration	2½-3½ hours
Distance	45.9km
Difficulty	moderate
Start/End	Cathedral Square

This ride contrasts flat central Christchurch and its eastern suburbs with the spectacular hilly remnant volcano to the south near Lyttelton. It follows from the Christchurch Parks & Gardens ride that loops west of the city.

THE RIDE
From near Cathedral Square in the centre of town, cycleways and quiet roads follow the so-very-English Avon River's banks to the coast. At sandy **New Brighton Beach**, pounded by the relentless swells of the South Pacific Ocean, there is the opportunity for swimming, surfing or sunbathing. The route turns south behind the dunes before returning inland past the Avon estuary where the shallows, part of **Te Huingi Manu Wildlife Refuge**, are a haven for water birds.

To this point, the ride has been almost totally flat but that suddenly changes at Mount Pleasant Rd with a testing 5.5km ascent past glorious homes into the Port Hills. At the junction with Summit Rd (350m), there is a drinking water tap adjacent to the driveway on the left. The route stays high, winding and undulating along the crater rim, with panoramic views extending across the Canterbury Plains to the Southern Alps.

At the *Sign of the Kiwi*, a restaurant built in 1917 perched atop Dyers Pass, there are stunning city views from its lookout. A thrilling descent follows back to sea level, leading to a flat, straight run along Colombo St back to Cathedral Square.

CANTERBURY

Christchurch Parks & Gardens

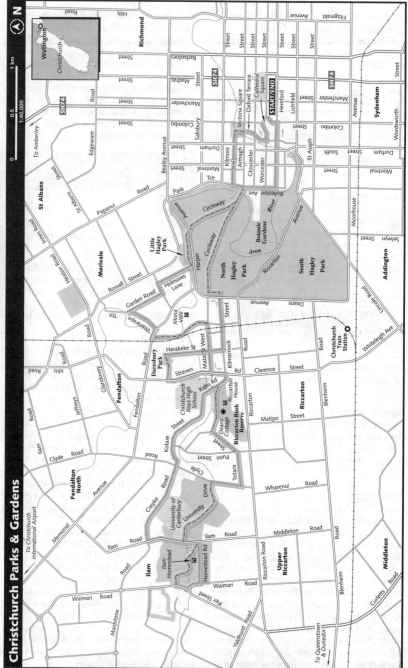

Christchurch Beaches & Hills

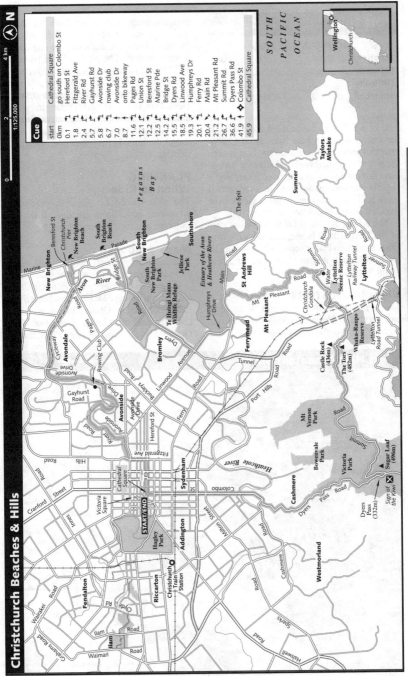

CANTERBURY

Cue	
start	Cathedral Square
0km	go south on Colombo St
0.1	Hereford St
1.8	Fitzgerald Ave
2.4	River Rd
5.7	Gayhurst Rd
5.8	Avonside Dr
6.7	rowing club
7.0	Avonside Dr
8.7	onto bikeway
11.6	Pages Rd
12.1	Union St
12.2	Beresford St
12.5	Marine Pde
14.2	Bridge St
15.5	Dyers Rd
18.5	Linwood Ave
19.3	Humphreys Dr
20.1	Ferry Rd
20.4	Main Rd
21.2	Mt Pleasant Rd
26.7	Summit Rd
36.6	Dyers Pass Rd
41.9	Colombo St
45.9	Cathedral Square

CANTERBURY

Port Hills

MOUNTAIN BIKE RIDE
Duration ....2-2½ hours
Distance 16km
Difficulty.....................................moderate
Start/End.........................Cathedral Square

The Port Hills and Summit Rd are the focus for many mountain bike rides from Christchurch – local bike shops are the best source for more. This short outing features a strenuous climb from sea level to over 300m, and a slightly challenging downhill on a very rutted track back. In between are great views over the Canterbury Plains and Southern Alps.

The Kennedys Bush Track is used as part of the Port Hills Classic, one of NZ's original mountain bike events, which began in 1986. Although it hasn't been run for a few years, it may be resurrected.

NATURAL HISTORY
The Kennedys Bush area is part of the long term, six stage Hoon Hay Valley Arboretum project. This involves the removal of grazing animals, gorse and broom from the slopes, and the protection of tussock areas, followed by pine planting to stabilise soil and control weed regrowth. The pines will be harvested in 2026 and natural vegetation allowed to expand into some of the pine forestry zone. Eventually the bush will expand to cover the Hoon Hay Valley. By 2100 your kids will be able to cycle through pristine natural forest all the way from Christchurch's outskirts to the top of the hills. In the meantime, keep to the existing tracks.

PLANNING
When to Ride
The ride should be possible year-round whenever conditions are dry so that the trails are not too slippery or boggy.

Maps & Books
Detailed topographical maps should not be necessary, but a map to get to the start may be.

Bike shops can supply copies of the Christchurch trail guide, *Flat City Mountain Biking* ($2), published by Ground Effect, which details this and other trails in the Port Hills, Godley Head and Bottle Lake Plantation.

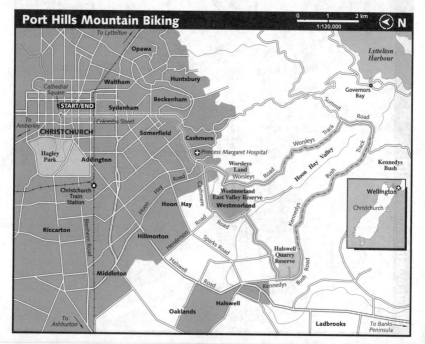

THE RIDE

The ride begins in Cathedral Square. Head south on Colombo St. From the roundabout at its southern end, ride west along Cashmere Rd all the way to the end, turning left onto Kennedys Bush Rd. Pass the old quarry and climb past houses to a turning area and the start of the track.

This hard-packed 4WD track traverses open fields dotted with thorny gorse. Eight fences with stiles interrupt the cycling, but at least give you a chance to catch your breath and appreciate the developing panorama. The track beyond stile No 7 – before it veers left and levels off – is perhaps the steepest part of the climb. After about 5km, you've reached 370m altitude. Another fence and stile allows you to reach Summit Rd, where you go left.

Ride 1.4km on the sealed road to a cattle-grid and turn left onto Worsleys Rd, just beyond. There is a fine view of Lyttelton on your right. The bitumen terminates after 300m at three gates. The centre one is labelled 'Worsleys Road Track'. Go through and plummet down a very steep, very rutted 4WD track, hard-packed if it is dry, diabolically slippery if not.

It is only 2.5km before sealed road appears again, but in that distance you lose 230m altitude. The descent continues quite steeply on the bitumen, although there are parallel off-road opportunities.

When you reach the intersection of Worsleys, Cashmere and Hoon Hay Rds, turn right on Cashmere and follow it back to the roundabout at Colombo St. It is a 4km ride from here back to Cathedral Square.

Kaikoura Coast & Hanmer Springs

Duration	6 days
Distance	512.8km
Difficulty	hard
Start/End	Christchurch

Rolling hills, the spectacular Kaikoura Coast and thermal springs are major natural attractions of this ride. It is worthwhile allowing a rest day in both Kaikoura and Hanmer Springs for marine mammal-spotting trips (book ahead), mountain biking and thermal-spring bathing.

Where possible the route avoids the coastal SH1 and other busy roads, but SH7 has considerable truck traffic thundering between Christchurch and Nelson or the West Coast. There is about 9km of good gravel remaining to be sealed on the inland SH70 to Kaikoura, and these are a few climbs of moderately difficulty on both the inland road and on the coast road (SH1) south towards Cheviot.

Day 1 is a long ride at over 120km. If desired, the trip could be broken at Culverden (99.5km) or Rotherham (112.1km) where there are places to stay and eat. Alternatively, the distance can be cut by taking the Coastal Pacific train (☎ 0800 802 802) departing Christchurch daily at 7.30 am to Rangiora (standard fare $19) or Waipara ($22). A bike costs a flat $10 regardless of the distance to be travelled and, because space is limited, should also be booked when reserving a seat.

A good side trip is the 20km return cycle from Cheviot to the coast at Gore Bay. Near here are the Cathedral Cliffs, historic Port Robinson and a lovely coastal walk with panoramic views across Pegasus Bay from the Kaikoura Range to Banks Peninsula.

HISTORY

The inland Kaikoura road was the original route north from the Canterbury Plains. The coastal highway and railway came later due to the terrain difficulties that required tunnels to be built for both, south of Kaikoura.

NATURAL HISTORY

The ride traverses an interesting variety of terrain including the alluvial Canterbury Plains; the bare, rounded limestone outcrops of the Weka Pass; and some moderate coastal and inland hills, often with spectacular mountain backdrops. The Seaward Kaikouras, the Amuri Range and the Hanmer Range are the dominant mountains.

PLANNING
When to Ride

Ride in the months outside winter, when precipitation peaks can bring snow even to low altitudes, and outside the height of summer (mid-December to mid-February), when the heat can be oppressive and holiday-makers far too numerous.

Maps

The single sheet InfoMap 1:500,000 series title *North Meets South* conveniently covers the ride and is adequate for navigating the route.

AA's 1:350,000 maps (available free to motoring association members at 210 Hereford St, Christchurch), cover the route in two sheets – Lewis Pass & Arthur's Pass map and the next sheet north.

GETTING TO/FROM THE RIDE
Bicycle

This ride connects to the Canterbury Hinterland tour (which circles west and south from Christchurch to Timaru) and to the Southern Alps Circuit (following the same route between Hanmer Springs and Ashley). Both rides are described later in this chapter.

THE RIDE
Day 1: Christchurch to Waiau

6½-10 hours, 123.5km

This is a long but relatively easy ride since it is mostly flat. An early start is advisable though. There is not a lot to distract from the cycling, other than regular settlements with shops and tearooms but, with a tailwind, the ride's a blast! If there is a headwind on this largely exposed, treeless route, the public transport option is recommended. The one significant climb, past the bare, rounded limestone outcrops of Weka Pass (71.9km; 179m), is gentle and is rewarded with a good downhill.

Amberley is the last town with an ATM before Kaikoura.

You encounter considerable traffic but no hills while traversing Christchurch's northern suburbs and industrial precincts. Once across the Waimakariri River and the northern motorway on Tram Rd, traffic drops to a trickle. Beyond Rangiora and across the Ashley River you begin to enjoy long stretches of near-zero traffic. Stands of neatly trimmed conifers shelter the adjacent fields from winds.

The first significant climb is after Waipara Junction, at the start of the Weka Pass Railway (for details of the two hour trip on the steam train, see Day 5). The relatively gentle 6km ascent of rocky **Weka Pass** finishes just before Waikari, outward terminus of the railway, where there are *refreshment rooms*. Next landmark, 13km towards Culverden, is

the historic *Hurunui Hotel*, built of local limestone and licensed continuously since 1860. Meals and accommodation are also available.

Only a few short hills stand between here and Waiau, making for a fast trip, barring unfavourable winds. If the distance is too great, accommodation is available at *Culverden Motels (☎ 315 8350)* on SH7, while the *Rotherham Hotel (☎ 315 6373)* on SH70 has rooms at $20 per person. Meals are available or there is a *general store* in the street opposite.

Watch out on the way into Waiau – there is a very long single-lane bridge with passing bays across the river.

Waiau

This small rural service centre nestles on the Amuri Plain between the braided Waiau River and the hills of the Amuri Range. It features a mixture of Victorian and more recent buildings. **Cob Cottage**, built in the late 1870s, is the town museum.

Places to Stay & Eat The *Waiau Motor Camp (☎ 315 6664)* is in Highfield St (first left after the bridge into town). Situated in a bare and uninviting expanse of ground, it is inexpensive and well equipped. Tent sites are $5 per person and cabins, sleeping one to six, are $12 per person. The homey *Waiau Backpackers (☎ 315 6283, 4 Leslie St)* has rooms sleeping two to four for $12 per person. Diagonally across the road, *Waiau Hotel (☎ 315 6003)* charges $25/40 for a single/double; bar meals and snacks are available.

The only other food outlets in town are the *tearooms* (with takeaways) and *Four Square* supermarket, both on Lyndon St (SH70).

Day 2: Waiau to Kaikoura

4½-7 hours, 86km

This interesting route features some moderate climbs, but is not complicated: simply stay on SH70 until it intersects with SH1. There are no services en route and just under 9km of gravel to traverse. Don't forget to bring enough food to last the day.

The first 20km climbs 250m to the Mt Lyford ski village turn-off. You may find yourself the inadvertent shepherd of a mob of sheep or cattle. If so, ride slowly up the edge of the road, making some noise, and the herd will clear for you.

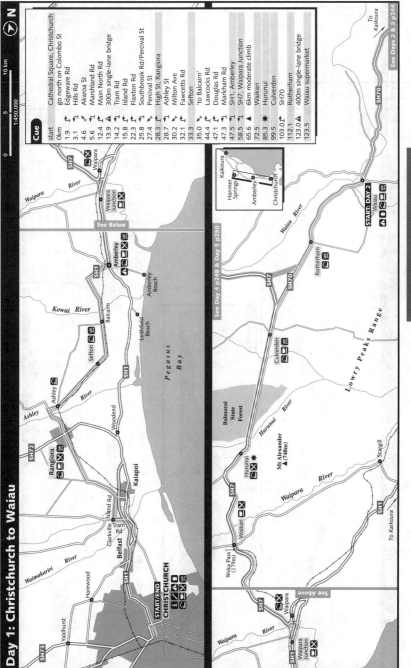

Day 1: Christchurch to Waiau

CANTERBURY

Cue	
start	Cathedral Square, Christchurch
0km	go north on Colombo St
1.9	Edgeware Rd
3.1	Hills Rd
4.6	Akaroa St
5.6	Marshland Rd
12.4	Main North Rd
13.9	300m single-lane bridge
14.2	Tram Rd
15.8	Island Rd
22.3	Flaxton Rd
25.8	Southbrook Rd/Percival St
27.4	Percival St
28.3	High St, Rangiora
28.7	Ashley St
30.2	Milton Ave
32.1	Fawcetts Rd
33.3	Sefton
35.0	'to Balcairn'
44.4	Lawcocks Rd
47.1	Douglas Rd
47.3	Markham Rd
47.5	SH1, Amberley
58.5	SH7, Waipara Junction
65.6	6km moderate climb
72.5	Waikari
85.3	Hurunui
99.5	Culverden
103.0	SH70
112.1	Rotherham
123.0	400m single-lane bridge
123.5	Waiau supermarket

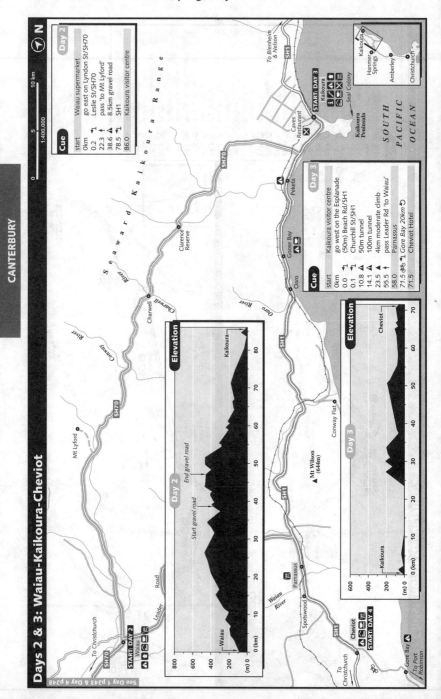

CANTERBURY

Days 2 & 3: Waiau-Kaikoura-Cheviot

See Day 1 p243 & Day 4 p248

Day 2

Cue

start		Waiau supermarket
0km	↱	go east on Lyndon St/SH70
0.2	↰	Leslie St/SH70
22.3	←	pass 'to Mt Lyford'
38.6	←	8.5km gravel road
78.5	↑	SH1
86.0	↱	Kaikoura visitor centre

Day 3

Cue

start		Kaikoura visitor centre
0km	↱	go west on the Esplanade
0.0	↱	(50m) Beach Rd/SH1
0.1	↰	Churchill St/SH1
10.8	←	50m tunnel
14.1	←	100m tunnel
23.5	←	4km moderate climb
55.5	↑	pass Leader Rd 'to Waiau'
58.0		Parnassus
71.5	↰⤴ ↱	Gore Bay 20km ↩
71.5		Cheviot Hotel

Elevation — Day 2

Elevation — Day 3

The last two-thirds of the journey winds between lumpy hills. After 35km a fast descent wipes off 150m of altitude. At the Conway River bridge engage a low gear to regain height back on the other side of the valley, where the sealed road ends. Good gravel on a hard-packed base and a steep descent combine for some thrills until climbing resumes and finding traction becomes harder. Enjoy the challenge because this last 8.5km gravel section should be sealed by mid-2000.

At another high point, around the 50km mark, you pass the boundary of the Hurunui district, entering that of Kaikoura. Two long sweeping descents and some sharp uphills bring the sea within sight, 6km before SH1 junction. A couple of kilometres to your left is *Caves Restaurant*, selling fast food and meals, the first services on the road since Waiau. Kaikoura town centre is another 3km ahead.

Kaikoura

The town (population 3000) has a spectacular location beneath towering and often snowcapped mountains on the edge of a peninsula jutting into the sea. Its main trade is the tourism generated by local scenic and natural wonders. Nearly every second building in town has some accommodation or service function.

Information The visitor centre (☎ 319 5641, fax 319 6819, ✪ kbzvin@nzhost.co.nz) is on the beach side of West End, next to a car park. Kaikoura All Sports (☎ 319 5370), 21 West End, is the bike shop.

Things to See & Do While the coastal waters' abundant whales, dolphins and seals attracted early European settlers to hunt and kill, the only hunting these days is in aircraft and boats to watch these fascinating creatures in their natural habitats (see the boxed text). Several companies run **whale-watching** and **swim with the dolphins** tours. The visitor centre can give further details and make bookings.

Land-based activities include **rafting**, **horse trekking** and **skiing**. Get details at the visitor centre. **Cave tours** depart from the Caves Restaurant (☎ 319 5023) on SH1 daily. The visitor centre will guide you to the area's many **walks**, from 30 minutes to

half or full-day tramps. Along the Peninsula Walkway are several **New Zealand fur seal colonies** where you can get up close and personal with the natives. (But *don't feed them* and give them some space – they are big and can bite.)

Sealside Gallery (☎ 319 6416), 4 West End, a cooperative of local artists working with glass, wood, clay and paint, is worth a look.

Places to Stay Kaikoura township has three motor camps. Modern *Searidge Holiday*

Watching Marine Mammals

Several companies run trips to watch marine mammals, including:

Whale Watch Kaikoura (☎ 0800 655 121) is in the old train station building on the ocean front. Its three boats often sight sperm, pilot and, sometimes, killer whales, dusky dolphins, seals, albatross and petrels. Tours daily, weather permitting. The cost is $95 for a thrilling three hours.

For $85, Dolphin Encounter (☎ 0800 733 365), 58 West End, will take you swimming with the playful dusky dolphins at 6 am, 9 am or 1 pm daily (again subject to weather). A wet suit and equipment are supplied, all you need to bring is your swimsuit and a towel. For people who just like to watch, it's $48. The same company runs an ocean (pelagic) birdwatching tour called Ocean Wings that costs $60.

Wings Over Whales (WOW; ☎ 0800 226 629) flies out of Kaikoura airport and lets you 'see the whole whale' as well as appreciate the rugged coast. The cost is $95. AirTours Kaikoura (☎ 0800 524 566) offers scenic flights from $55.

If that's not excitement enough, there is always Shark Dive Kaikoura (☎ 0800 225297 or ☎ 319 6888), on Beach Rd, adjacent to Act One Pizza, where you come face to face with 'Jaws' from the safety of a shark cage. The price is $110 (the minimum age for participants is 12 years). Times for the tour are 8 am and 1 pm daily with the season starting in December and finishing in April or May, depending on water temperature.

Park (☎ *319 5362, 34 Beach Rd)*, across the line from the train station, has the best facilities and a spacious site. Tent sites are $8.50 per person, a two berth cabin is $33 ($48 with en suite) and holiday flats are $58. Across the road and slightly closer to the centre of town, *A1 Kaikoura Motels & Holiday Park* (☎ *319 5999, 11 Beach Rd)* has a cramped, noisy site with poorer facilities. Tent sites are $10 for one. There are some cabins (from $30), tourist flats (from $50) and backpacker beds (from $15).

Other facilities include *Esplanade Holiday Park* (☎ *319 5947, 128 Esplanade)*, almost 1km east of the business area, *Peketa Motor Camp* (☎ *319 6299)* on SH1, 8km south of Kaikoura, and *Goose Bay Camping Ground* (☎ *319 5348)*, 16km south.

Backpacker hostels are numerous but most close in winter, so check first. *Cray Cottage* (☎ *319 5152, 190 Esplanade)* is deservedly popular. Dorm beds cost $17, twins are $19. *K's* (☎ *319 5538, 11 Churchill St)* has doubles for $20 per person. *Top Spot* (☎ *319 5540, 22 Deal St)*, along a path near the post office, has dorm beds for $16 and doubles for $20. The large *Planet Backpackers* (☎ *319 6972, 86 West End)* has dorm beds from $16, doubles cost $20 and singles cost $24. The *Maui YHA Hostel* (☎ *319 5931, 270 Esplanade)* is a long way east, but has an attractive location with modern facilities. Dorm beds cost $17 per person and doubles $40. Ask at the visitor centre for others.

Notable among plentiful B&Bs is *The Old Convent* (☎ *319 6603, cnr Mt Fyffe & Mill Rds)*, a well preserved 1911 building, is 3.6km from town. It charges from $50 to $120, depending on the standard of room, and features genuine French cuisine. The visitor centre can recommend other B&Bs in the area.

Motels mostly charge from $70 and up for two. Find a selection along the Esplanade facing the ocean. Try *Norfolk Pine Motel* (☎ *0800 106 706, 124 Esplanade)*, nonsmoking *Anchor Inn Motel* (☎ *0800 720 033, 208 Esplanade)*, *Blue Seas Motels* (☎ *0800 507 077, 222 Esplanade)* or the *Panorama Motel* (☎ *319 5053, 266 Esplanade)*. The *White Morph Motor Inn* (☎ *0800 803 6662, 92 Esplanade)* is more expensive but offers discounts to AA and affiliates members and has a licensed restaurant.

Places to Eat Food outlets cluster on West End. Crayfish is a popular menu item in several restaurants and takeaways. As well as pubs serving standard fare, there is *Aromas* (☎ *319 5221)*, a stylish cafe with outdoor seating, excellent coffee, good cakes and quiche. *Why Not Cafe* (☎ *319 6486)* serves tasty home-made food but in small portions. *Hislops Wholefood Cafe* (☎ *319 6971, 33 Beach Rd)* uses organically grown ingredients. *Sonic* (☎ *319 6414)* on the Esplanade is, as its name suggests, music oriented; it has reasonable prices and food till late.

A *supermarket* and *dairy* are near the railway overpass and there's another *supermarket* on the Esplanade.

Day 3: Kaikoura to Cheviot
4-6½ hours, 71.5km

Day 3's ride is, of necessity, all on hilly SH1, which can sometimes be busy – listen and watch for occasional trucks – but is always scenic. There's only a couple of very limited supply points – tearooms at Goose Bay and a store (closed Sunday) a couple of hundred metres off the route at Parnassus – follow signs onto the parallel old road. It is advisable to carry some snack food from Kaikoura.

The day begins spectacularly. Ride a narrow corridor between hills and the edge of the ocean, all the while spotting fur seals, birds and whale-watching boats close to shore. As the highway leaves the coast beyond **Goose Bay**, a couple of moderate climbs take you into forest 200m above sea level before the country becomes open and rolling towards Cheviot.

Make sure you take the time to visit Gore Bay, with its Cathedral Cliffs and coastal walkway.

Side Trip: Cheviot to Gore Bay
2-3 hours, 20km return

The Gore Bay round trip takes you gently down to the coast and back. There is one steep hill up to the cliffs viewpoint. Thereafter you stay high to visit Port Robinson lookout and the start of the coast walking track. You needn't walk far to get huge views encompassing all of Pegasus Bay, with Kaikoura Range to the north and Banks Peninsula to the south.

Leave town on McQueens Rd opposite the Four Square supermarket, turning right after 300m onto Gore Bay Rd. This quiet road meanders along the floor of a narrow, treed valley, gently descending for 8km east of Cheviot. At Gore Bay there are two *camping grounds* costing $10 for two. At the end of the village, the road turns away from the beach and up a steep hill. It reaches 140m, where a **lookout** is signposted off to the right. From the lookout, you'll see how siltstone erosion gullies have produced a landform resembling a buttressed cathedral wall, hence the name **Cathedral Cliffs**.

A further short climb takes you to Port Robinson Rd. Ride 300m on gravel and park at a gate. The walking track on the other side takes you to a **viewpoint**, from where the ruins of Port Robinson and an old slipway are visible. The track descends to water level and follows the shore at low tide to Manuka Bay near the Point Gibson lighthouse. Instead of following the track, however, return to your bike and cycle back up the gravel road, turn left and ride another 800m south to Manuka Bay Rd. Follow this to another gate and take the short walk towards the point, where great views across Pegasus Bay unfold.

Return to Cheviot via your outward route.

Cheviot

A rural service centre, Cheviot has the essentials to satisfy touring cyclists' overnight needs.

Information Services include a hardware store, a petrol station that is also the post office, and a pharmacy.

Places to Stay & Eat The *Cheviot Motel* (☎ *319 8607, 4 Ward Rd)*, run by an expatriate Dutch cycle tourist couple, is in a quiet farm setting. It has tent sites for $7 per person, an on-site van ($25 for two), cabin ($30) and motel rooms from $50. There is a kitchen, swimming pool and laundry.

Cheviot Hotel (☎ 319 8616) on SH1 at the north end of town has camping, charging $6 per person for a tent site, but there is no campers' kitchen. Hotel rooms are $58 for two with en suite.

Two *tearooms*, a *takeaway*, *butcher* and a reasonably well stocked *supermarket* are the extent of food suppliers, although the Cheviot Hotel does meals.

Day 4: Cheviot to Hanmer Springs
6-8 hours, 95.4km

This day involves some backtracking over Days 1 & 3. A mostly flat day's riding is in store through open agricultural country. However, there is one short, sharp hill as you leave Cheviot and another on SH7A, the last leg into Hanmer Springs. The only services on the way are at Waiau and Rotherham. All roads are sealed and in good condition.

Follow the meandering Leader River on undulating, picturesque Leader Road. This offers some challenge in terms of hills, climbing to 230m at the saddle where Leader Rd East becomes Leader Rd West. Winds can be a problem.

Pause at the top of the hill before Waiau for views across the braided Waiau River. After Rotherham, take the 'short cut' to SH7, continuing up to the Hanmer Springs turn-off.

Hanmer Springs

Hanmer Springs (population 600), the main thermal resort on the South Island, is about 10km off SH7. As you cycle in, you could mistake the town for a Swiss alpine village with its chalets perched on the grassed mountainside beneath towering conifers and firs.

Hanmer's thermal springs are by legend a piece of the fires of Tamatea, dropped from the sky after an eruption of Mt Ngauruhoe. Renowned for more than a century, the springs are open to bathers daily.

Apart from the hot pools, it's a popular locale for mountain biking and other adventure activities (but it's much more relaxing than Queenstown).

Information The visitor centre (☎ 315 7128 or ☎ 0800 733 426, fax 315 7658, @ hanvin@nzhost.co.nz) is on Amuri Ave, near the thermal pool and close to the corner of Jacks Pass Rd. It is open daily from 10 am to 5 pm (closed Christmas Day).

There is a part-time Bank of New Zealand in the shopping mall on Conical Hill Rd, open from 10 am to 2 pm on Monday, Wednesday and Friday.

Things to See & Do Just walking around town is a relaxing experience. A must-do is the 30 minute walk to the top of **Conical Hill** (549m).

CANTERBURY

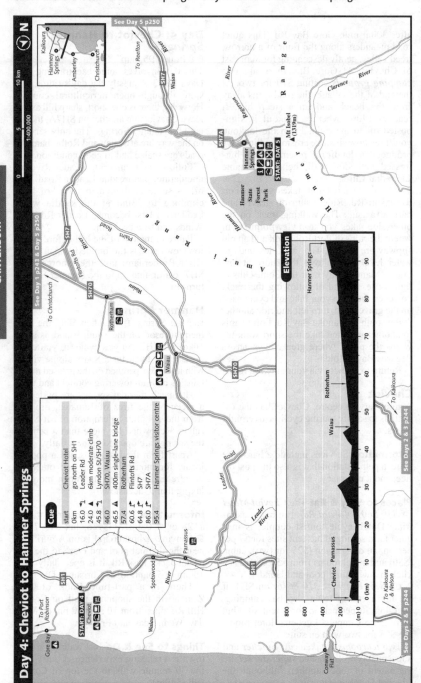

CANTERBURY

Day 4: Cheviot to Hanmer Springs

Cue

start	0km	Cheviot Hotel
		go north on SH1
16.0		Leader Rd
24.0		6km moderate climb
45.8		Lyndon St/SH70
46.0		SH70, Waiau
46.5		400m single-lane bridge
57.4		Rotherham
60.6		Flintofts Rd
64.8		SH7
86.0		SH7A
95.4		Hanmer Springs visitor centre

Elevation

(m) 800 600 400 200 0

(km) 0 10 20 30 40 50 60 70 80 90

Cheviot Parnassus Waiau Rotherham Hanmer Springs

See Day 1 p243 & Day 5 p250

See Days 2 & 3 p244

START: DAY 5

Hanmer Springs

Hanmer State Forest Park

Mt Isobel ▲ (1319m)

H a n m e r   R a n g e

A m u r i   R a n g e

Rotherham

Waiau

Parnassus

Spotswood

Cheviot

START: DAY 4

Gore Bay

Conway Flat

To Port Robinson

To Christchurch

To Reefton

To Kaikoura & Nelson

To Kaikoura

SH7

SH7A

SH70

SH1

Waiau River

Leader River

Leader Road

Emu Plains Road

Flintofts Rd

Lyndon St

Rotherton River

Clarence River

N

0   5   10 km

1:400,000

Kaikoura
Hanmer Springs
Amberley
Christchurch

Mountain bikers will be on cloud nine with the variety of trails available to them (for one option, see the Hanmer Springs Off-Road ride later in this chapter). Dust 'n' Dirt (☎ 315 7233) on Conical Hill Rd hires mountain bikes (front or dual suspension) and offers guided downhill trips.

Mountain bike trails are signposted in the nearby pine plantations, about 1km east of town – walkers and horse riders may also be in the forests, so keep an eye out and be considerate.

Other activities on offer include: **forest walks**, **horse treks**, **jet-boating**, **rafting**, **bungy jumping** from the Waiau Bridge (which you cross just after turning off SH7) and winter **snow skiing**. Ask at the visitor centre for details.

Places to Stay Modern and central, the *Pines Motor Camp* (☎ 315 7152) on Jacks Pass Rd charges $7 per person for tent sites. On-site caravans are from $30 and standard cabins from $34. *Mountain View Holiday Park* (☎ 315 7113) is on Bath St on the way into town. Tent sites are $9 per person. Standard cabins cost $35, en suite cabins $49 and tourist flats $59, all for two.

The YHA hostel, *Hanmer Springs Forest Camp* (☎ 315 7202, ✉ hanmer.forest.camp@ xtra.co.nz), 2.8km east on Jollies Pass Rd, has beds in old forestry workers' cabins. Adults pay $14 each. Tent sites cost $8 per person.

Motels in town include the bottom-end *Willowbank* (☎ 315 7211), on Argelins Rd, with units from $55 to $75; *Forest Peaks* (☎ 315 7132), on Torquay Terrace, with doubles from $60; *Aspen Lodge* (☎ 315 7224, 24 Jacks Pass Rd) with rooms from $79 to $105 for two; and the *Alpine Garden* (☎ 315 7332), on Leamington St, with doubles from $79 to $115. The luxurious *Alpine Lodge* (☎ 315 7311) on Harrogate St has doubles from $75 and 'executive units' with circular beds and spa baths for up to $180.

B&Bs include the *Shining Cuckoo Guest House* (☎ 315 7905) on Cheltenham St, which charges $25/55 a single/double. Next door, *Cheltenham House* (☎ 315 7545) has higher standards and prices – $100/120 for rooms with bathroom. *Glen Alvon Lodge* (☎ 315 7475) on Amuri Ave charges $60/75. It also has motel units with kitchens for $85 to $125 for a double.

Places to Eat The *Old Post Office* (☎ 315 7461, 2 Jacks Pass Rd) serves hearty NZ fare with mains from $21 to $26.

PT's Famous New York Pizza in the shopping mall serves up unusual combinations from $10 to $24. Try the 'NZ Sunday Roast' pizza with Canterbury lamb, broccoli, potato, pumpkin, mushroom and mint conserve topping, or 'Sweet Voca' with smoked chicken, cream cheese, apricot conserve and toasted almonds!

Also in the mall are several cafes serving coffee and light meals, including *Village Plus* (☎ 315 7124), *Scruples* (☎ 315 7214) and *Keith's* (☎ 315 7274), which has vegetarian dishes and mains for $11 and up. Along Conical Hill Rd, *Mel & Lou's* (☎ 315 7182) has basic takeaways or light, sit-down meals.

A *Four Square supermarket* is in the mall if you are self-catering. It is also the post office.

Day 5: Hanmer Springs to to Amberley
4½-7 hours, 88.9km
Retrace your path of the previous day, gently descending to the Flintofts Rd turn-off, but then continue on SH7 to Culverden and Waipara Junction, this time you get to enjoy the long sweeping downhill from Weka Pass.

From Waipara, you can take the two hour trip on the **Weka Pass Railway** (☎ 314 6813) if it's a steaming day. Follow signs to the railway along Waipara's main street (left off SH7 at the Waipara Junction Hotel and turn left after the railway crossing). Steam trains run on the first and third Sunday each month and on Sunday and Monday of most long weekends.

If you choose to break your journey here, one option is *Waipara Sleepers* (☎ 314 6708), made up of old railway guards' vans with four beds costing $15 per person and double rooms for $50 (tent sites are also available).

Amberley
Amberley is the main service centre on SH1 between Kaikoura and the Ashley River. It has limited accommodation and food outlets, but it does have a Westpac bank with an ATM, on the east side of main street (SH1) in the town centre.

CANTERBURY

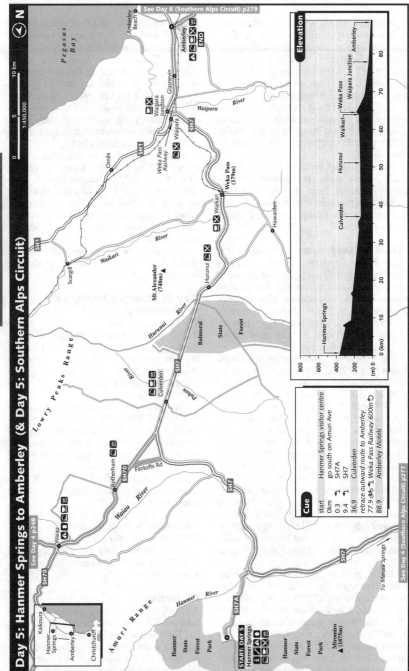

Day 5: Hanmer Springs to Amberley (& Day 5: Southern Alps Circuit)

CANTERBURY

See Day 6 (Southern Alps Circuit) p279

See Day 4 p248

See Day 4 (Southern Alps Circuit) p277

N

0   5   10 km
1:450,000

Elevation

800
600
400
200
(m) 0

0 (km)   10   20   30   40   50   60   70   80

Hanmer Springs
Culverden
Hurunui
Waikari–Weka Pass
Waipara Junction
Amberley

Cue

start		Hanmer Springs visitor centre
0km	↑	go south on Amuri Ave
0.3	↰	SH7A
9.4	↰	SH7
36.9		Culverden
		retrace outward route to Amberley
77.9	↶	Weka Pass Railway 600m ↰
88.9		Amberley Motels

Pegasus Bay

Amberley Beach
Amberley
END
Glasnevin
Waipara Junction
Waipara
Waipara River
Weka Pass Railway
Omihi
SH1
Weka Pass (179m)
Scargill
Waikari
Waikari River
Mt Alexander (748m) ▲
Hurunui
Hawarden
River
Hurunui River
Balmoral State Forest
Lowry Peaks Range
River
Culverden
Pahau
SH7
Rotherham
Flintofts Rd
Waiau River
Waiau
SH70
SH7A
SH7
Hanmer River
Amuri Range
Hanmer State Forest Park
START DAY 5 Hanmer Springs
Hanmer State Forest Park
Miromiro ▲ (1875m)
To Maruia Springs

Kaikoura
Hanmer Springs
Amberley
Christchurch

Places to Stay & Eat The *Amberley Motels* (☎ 314 8550, 124 Main North Rd) has tent sites from $10, cabins for $38 and motel rooms from $55. There's a *dairy-takeaway* 200m north, but it's not open late.

Day 6: Amberley to Christchurch
2½-3 hours, 47.5km
Return to Christchurch via the outward route of Day 1 (pp242-3).

Hanmer Springs Off-Road

MOUNTAIN BIKE RIDE

Duration	1½-2 hours
Distance	20km
Difficulty	easy-moderate
Start/End	Conical Hill Rd

This ride is a good introduction to the mountain bike trails around Hanmer Springs. The trails are virtually flat on the small circuit south of Jollies Pass Rd, before you climb steadily into the foothills of the Hanmer Range on gravel road. A short but difficult climb on singletrack brings you to Jolliffe Saddle, then there is some great singletrack descending back towards Jollies Pass Rd.

THE RIDE
Roll downhill from Dust 'n' Dirt and take the first left onto Jollies Pass Rd. Cross Dog Stream and, up the short hill opposite the DOC HQ, find the slightly obscure Herdmans Rd signposted behind a barrier. This gravel road runs straight for a few hundred metres to meet Mansfield Rd. Turn right here and follow the vehicular track as it gently descends and swings left to parallel Dog Stream for 200m. Now a blue-coloured mountain bike trail sign points you 90° left. The trail turns to singletrack and twists through the forest with a few stutter bumps, roots and overhanging blackberries lying in wait. There is one tricky creek crossing that you can walk if you're worried about breaking yourself or your bike.

Recrossing Mansfield Rd, the trail weaves its way back to Jollies Pass Rd. Turn right and ride another few hundred metres to a left turn onto McIntyre Rd. This is another gravel forest road that bends right, becoming Mullans Rd and climbing steadily. As

CANTERBURY

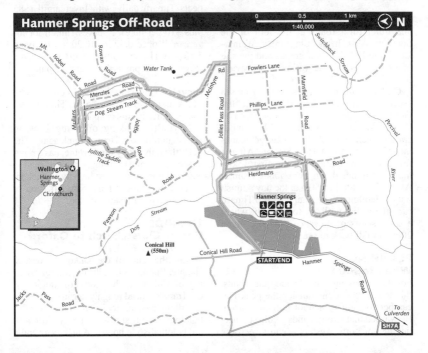

the road becomes steep, take a trail on the left marked as Jolliffe Saddle Track. Follow it up to the saddle for good views over pine forest and clear-felled areas.

Return down the steep, rutted singletrack taking care on the tight switchbacks, and take the right fork, signposted as Dog Stream Track. This is an easy downhill singletrack. At the next fork, take the right branch. Go round a log barrier before Jolliffe Rd, cross the road, negotiate the next barrier and continue gently winding down through pleasant forest.

At the next road junction, turn left and head past Camp Track back to Jollies Pass Rd. Turn right here to go straight back to town, or take Herdmans Rd, first on the left, and do it all again!

Canterbury Hinterland

Duration	4 days
Distance	285km
Difficulty	moderate
Start	Christchurch
End	Timaru

This four day ride features easy gradients and quiet rural roads at the foot of the Southern Alps. It takes in Ashley, Waimakariri and Rakaia River gorges and the site of NZ's (or perhaps the world's) first heavier-than-air flight.

On Day 1 the route rises gently from sea level at Christchurch to 200m at Ashley Gorge. A gentle upward trend continues on Day 2, with a descent followed by a moderately steep climb at Rakaia Gorge, reaching 380m at Mount Hutt Station. After a few minor undulations in the first 15km, the route trends down from about 370m at Alford Forest to just 50m at the day's finish point, Geraldine. The final day into Timaru is virtually flat until the town itself, where a short series of nuisance hills rise about 20m and fall back to sea level.

PLANNING
When to Ride
For those seeking solitude and quiet roads, this tour is best done outside the peak December to January school holiday season. Be warned that strong winds – cold southerlies or hot north-westers – can sweep the

Canterbury Plains for days at a time. Avoid them, if possible, by rescheduling the ride.

Maps
The single sheet InfoMap 1:500,000 series title *North Meets South* conveniently covers the ride and is adequate for navigating the route.

AA's 1:350,000 Canterbury map, available free to motoring association members at 210 Hereford St, Christchurch, covers the route in slightly better detail than *North Meets South*.

GETTING TO/FROM THE RIDE
Timaru
Bus InterCity and Newmans buses stop at the Timaru train station, connecting to Christchurch, Dunedin, Queenstown and Te Anau. The booking centre (☎ 688 3597) is at the station. Shuttle services, such as Atomic (☎ 322 8883), Ko-op (☎ 366 6633) and Southern Link (☎ 379 9991), connect with Christchurch or Dunedin with fares of around $20 plus $10 per bike.

Train The *Southerner* (☎ 0800 802 802) connects Timaru daily with Invercargill ($85 plus $10 per bike) and Christchurch ($36 plus $10 per bike). It leaves Timaru for Invercargill once daily at 10.20 am (arriving 5.15 pm). The one daily train to Christchurch leaves at 3.13 pm, arriving at 5.15 pm.

Bicycle This ride links directly to the Mackenzie Country ride at Timaru described later in this chapter.

If you're thinking of riding back to Christchurch from Timaru, think again. The SH1, the only really direct route, has a reputation as the most boring section of road in NZ, and one of the most heavily trafficked. In case that doesn't put you off, you're likely to have a headwind, too.

THE RIDE
Day 1: Christchurch to Oxford
3½-5½ hours, 63.4km
Follow the route of the Kaikoura Coast & Hanmer Springs ride to the overbridge crossing of Christchurch's northern motorway. On Tram Rd, head roughly north-west across the plain past agricultural and 'lifestyle' holdings. The first town is pretty Cust with old colonial-style houses. A *takeaway* and a

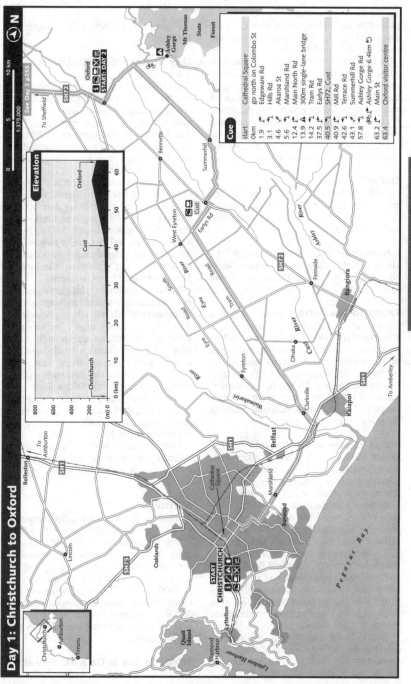

Day 1: Christchurch to Oxford

CANTERBURY

Cue

start		Cathedral Square
0km		go north on Colombo St
1.9	⤴	Edgeware Rd
3.1	⤴	Hills Rd
4.6	⤴	Akaroa St
5.6	⤴	Marshland Rd
12.4	◄	Main North Rd
13.9	⤴	300m single-lane bridge
14.2	⤴	Tram Rd
37.5	⤴	Earlys Rd
40.5		SH72, Cust
40.9	⤴	Mill Rd
42.6	⤴	Terrace Rd
43.1	⤴	Summerhill Rd
57.8	⤴	Ashley Gorge Rd
	⤴	Ashley Gorge 6.4km ↻
63.2	⤴	Main St
63.4		Oxford visitor centre

Elevation

Oxford

Cust

Christchurch

800
600
400
200
(m) 0

0 (km)   10   20   30   40   50   60

pub offer the makings of a picnic, which you could eat at a table in the pleasant domain (to the left off Mill St).

Riding out of town past a deer farm, you encounter the first hill of the day on Summerhill Rd. It's innocuous – a 60m gain over 2.2km. There is one more gentle climb before **Ashley Gorge** which, with its attractive camping ground, is 3.2km to the right at the next terminating T-junction.

Oxford is about 6km to the left after this junction, along a low-traffic road.

Oxford

Its industry based on sawmilling until the start of the 20th century, Oxford is now a quiet farm service centre with many historic buildings.

Information The visitor centre (☎ 312 4014) is in the Waimakariri District Council offices at 34 Main St. Hours are 8.30 am to 5 pm.

Things to See & Do There are **walks** in nearby State Forests and at Ashley Gorge, and **mountain biking** in the Lees Valley. Other activities include **fishing** and **horse riding** as well as **water sports** such as jet-boating on the Waimakariri River. Attractive buildings and 'lifestyle' residences make up the town. There are **handicraft shops** and a **historical museum** detailing the town's sawmilling past.

Places to Stay & Eat The *Ashley Gorge Motor Park* (☎ 312 4099) is 9km from town. Tent sites are $7 per adult, and self-contained cabins (sleeping five) cost $44. Dorms are available at $12 per adult.

Country Life B&B (☎ 312 4167), which is on High St near Main St, charges $30 per person with shared bathroom or $35 in a self-contained unit. Beds in a sleep-out are $20. A three course dinner (by arrangement) is $20. Just opposite, *Glenariff B&B* (☎ 312 4678) charges $60 a double and also offers a $20 dinner. At the south-western end of High St, the *West Oxford Hotel* (☎ 312 4582) does B&B for $35 per person. Bikes can be stored overnight in the lock-up garage.

Oxford is not overflowing with restaurants, but the *Oxford Country Cottage Restaurant* (☎ 312 4424, 51 Main St) makes up for the lack of choice with friendly service

and good meals. There's also a *supermarket* opposite.

Day 2: Oxford to Methven
4-6 hours, 81km

The SH72 out of town is quiet, although the majority of the traffic can be trucks. There are some single-lane bridges; the longest, across the Eyre River, is more than 100m. The flatness of the Canterbury Plains to your left contrasts with the ruggedness of the cloud-wrapped or snow-fringed mountains on your right.

You soon cross the scenic 'Waimak' (Waimakariri) River on a narrow, high-level bridge and then the railway line at Waddington. A zig and a zag here keep you on the 'Inland Scenic Route', SH72. Twelve kilometres on, at Coalgate, a *pub* offering meals may be an opportunity for a comfortable lunch stop; otherwise, continue for 3km to a *shop* at tiny Glentunnel.

The route continues with gentle gradients in a peaceful agricultural landscape with the occasional roadside stall offering organic produce – vegies, honey, eggs – but no sizable town. Windwhistle, an appropriately named locality if you encounter a dreaded southerly or north-wester, consists of just a petrol station that is closed at weekends. After a sweeping descent to the **Rakaia River** crossing just beyond, you'll probably see jet-boats ready to take thrill-seekers up and down the gorge. Join in if you wish, or get a free view of the show from the elevated bridge.

Over the next 4km you regain almost 200m as you gasp at the surrounding mountain panorama, soon reaching the Methven turn-off.

Methven

A small town, Methven is quiet for most of the year, but comes alive in the ski season.

The visitor centre (☎ 302 8955) is at 93 Main St, next to the Bank of New Zealand. It is open from 9 am to 5 pm daily and 7.30 am to 6.30 pm during the ski season.

There is an ATM in the shopping mall down the lane from the visitor centre. Big Al's Ski & Sports (☎ 302 8003), in the mall near the corner of Forest Dr and Main St, is the bike shop.

Things to See & Do Aside from skiing, Methven is a centre for **hot air ballooning**

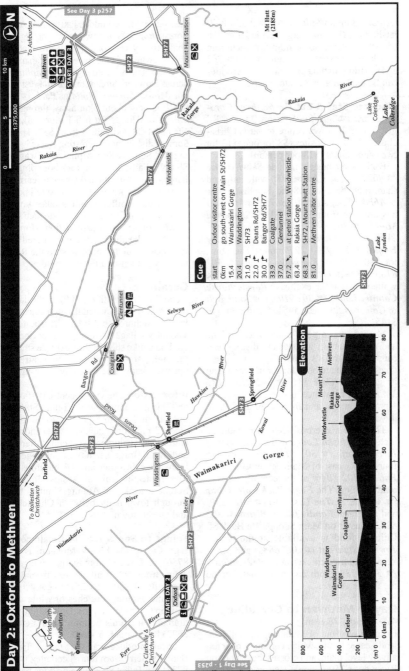

Day 2: Oxford to Methven

CANTERBURY

See Day 3 p257

To Ashburton

Methven
START: DAY 3

Mt Hutt
(2185m)

Mount Hutt Station

SH72

SH77

Rakaia Gorge

Rakaia River

Rakaia River

Lake
Coleridge

Lake
Coleridge

Windwhistle

SH77

Selwyn River

Lake
Lyndon

Glentunnel

Bangor Rd

Coalgate

Deans Road

SH73

Springfield

Hawkins River

Kowai River

SH73

Waimakariri Gorge

Sheffield

SH73

SH77

Darfield

To Rolleston &
Christchurch

Waddington

Bexley

River

Waimakariri

River

SH72

To Clarkville &
Christchurch

Eyre River

START: DAY 2
Oxford

See Day 1 - p253

Cue

start	Oxford visitor centre
0km	go south-west on Main St/SH72
15.4	Waimakariri Gorge
20.4	Waddington
21.0	SH73
22.0	Deans Rd/SH72
30.0	Bangor Rd/SH77
33.9	Coalgate
37.0	Glentunnel
57.2	at petrol station, Windwhistle
63.4	Rakaia Gorge
68.3	SH72, Mount Hutt Station
81.0	Methven visitor centre

N

0   5   10 km

1:375,000

To Ashburton
Christchurch
Ashburton
Timaru

Elevation

Oxford	
Waddington	
Waimakariri Gorge	
Coalgate	
Glentunnel	
Windwhistle	
Rakaia Gorge	
Mount Hutt	
Methven	

800
600
400
200
(m) 0

0 (km)   10   20   30   40   50   60   70   80

(Aoraki Balloon Safaris, ☎ 0800 256 837) **jet-boating** (Rakaia Gorge Scenic Jet, ☎ 318 6515) **abseiling, horse riding, parachuting** (Rock+Ice Adventure Group, ☎ 0800 762 564), **rafting, fishing** and **walking**. Activities can be booked at the visitor centre.

Places to Stay & Eat The *Methven Caravan Park* (☎ 302 8005) is on Barkers Rd just out of the town centre towards Christchurch. It has tent sites ($8 for one, $13 for two) and cabins ($13 per person).

Backpacker hostels include *Skiwi House* (☎ 302 8772, 30 Chapman St) with dorm and share-room beds for $18 and doubles for $19.

Abisko Lodge (☎ 302 8875, 74 Main St) has doubles from $62 to $100. *Sherwood Motels* (☎ 302 8977, 199 Main St) charges $100 and *Methven Mount Hutt Holiday Homes* (☎ 302 9200, 29 Patton St) has rooms for $80 to $120. *Koromiko Lodge* (☎ 302 8165, 182 Main St) has doubles for $75, while rooms at the exclusive *Powderhouse Country Lodge* (☎ 302 9105, cnr South Belt & Cameron Sts) start at $125 and go up to $145.

Methven has a good range of cafes, bars and restaurants in its business district. Because of the town's popularity as a ski destination, some are open longer in winter than in summer – *Cafe 131* (☎ 302 9131, 131 Main St), for instance, is open from 9 am to 4 pm in summer and from 7 am until 'late' in winter.

There are numerous licensed restaurants including *Abisko Lodge* in the town centre; *Birches Cafe* (☎ 302 8116) on Forest Dr, four blocks east of Main St; and the *Blue Pub* (☎ 302 8046) at the central, six-way road junction. The *Eagle Rock Cafe & Bar* (☎ 302 8222), *The Last Post* (☎ 302 8259) and *Vee Tee's Family Bar & Bistro* (☎ 302 8252) cluster on Main St opposite Bank St. Chinese food is available at the *China Town Restaurant* (☎ 302 8882) and pizza, kebabs and fried chicken at *Uncle Dominic's* (☎ 302 8237), both are in the mall behind the visitor centre.

Day 3: Methven to Geraldine
4½-7 hours, 78.6km
Heading west out of Methven, rejoin the Inland Scenic Route, which continues on a relatively level plain, and crosses the Ashburton River on a 250m single-lane bridge with a passing bay in the middle. Pause at the Alford Forest *shop* to watch two moas grazing nonchalantly by the road. (They are made of chicken wire and other pieces of scrap metal.)

There is possible emergency *camping* just across Bowyers Stream bridge at a rest area, but *Mount Somers Holiday Park* (☎ 303 9719) is only about 5km away, through the village on Hoods Rd (off Patton Rd). Tent sites cost $8 and cabins from $32. The **Mt Somers** district has interesting **walks** including Mt Somers Sub-Alpine Walkway and Sharplin Falls, as well as **rock hounding** and **fishing**. A *restaurant* and *tavern* offer meals.

An imperceptible descent past tall hedges of carefully coiffed conifers takes you towards Mayfield, with a poorly stocked *shop*, a *pub*, pottery and petrol station. Hope not to have a headwind; the unsheltered road runs dead straight south-west to the Rangitata River, then into lively Geraldine.

Geraldine
Geraldine (population 2300) is the largest town you'll have cycled through since leaving Christchurch, but it has the feel of a country village. It offers most services, including a bike shop in the next side street on the right, south of the visitor centre. It's open weekdays and Saturday morning.

Information The visitor centre (☎/fax 693 8597) is in the main street, Talbot St, and is open from 8 am to 5 pm weekdays and 10 am to 2 pm (often later) on weekends. The enthusiastic volunteer weekend staffers, Pat and John Braggins, have comprehensive knowledge of quiet and adventurous cycling routes to suit all tastes. InterCity, Southern Link and Atomic Shuttles travel through town daily between Christchurch and Queenstown.

Things to See & Do The Geraldine Vintage Car & Machinery Museum (☎ 693 8756), on Lower Talbot St, has vintage cars dating from 1905. Call the crew from Rangitata Rafts (☎ 0800 251 251) to get very wet on some exciting stretches of white water with up to Grade 5 rapids. Only slightly less dramatic are Jim's Salmon Safaris (☎ 693 8622) by jet-boat or 4WD.

Local produce can be tasted free at Barker's Berry Barn tourist complex (☎ 693 97271) on Talbot St, while a working beehive

Mt Cook National Park, Canterbury

Dusky dolphins, Kaikoura Coast

Lyttelton Harbour, Canterbury

Mt Cook over Lake Pukaki, Canterbury

NEIL IRVINE

Tekapo-Pukaki Canal Road, Canterbury

DAVID WALL

Port Hills mountain biking trails, Christchurch

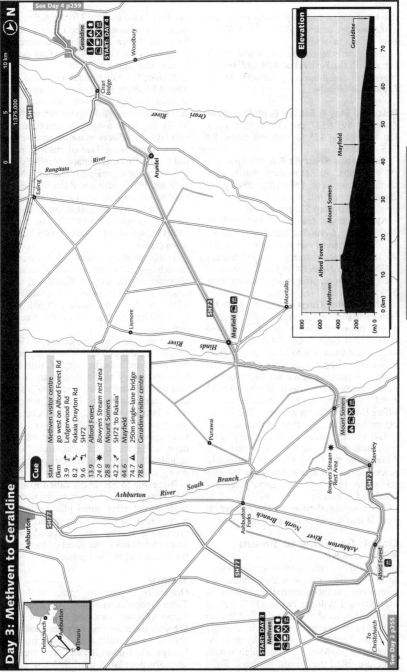

Day 3: Methven to Geraldine

CANTERBURY

See Day 4 p259

See Day 2 p255

N

0   5   10 km

1:375,000

Elevation

(m) 0   200   400   600   800

0 (km)   10   20   30   40   50   60   70

Methven   Alford Forest   Mount Somers   Mayfield   Geraldine

Cue

start	0km	Methven visitor centre
		go west on Alford Forest Rd
3.9		Ledgerwood Rd
8.2		Rakaia Drayton Rd
9.6		SH72
13.9		Alford Forest
24.0		Bowyers Stream rest area
28.8		Mount Somers
42.2		SH72 'to Rakaia'
44.6		Mayfield
74.7		250m single-lane bridge
78.6		Geraldine visitor centre

Christchurch
Ashburton
Timaru

Ashburton

SH72

SH1

Ealing
Rangitata River
Arundel
Otari Bridge
Geraldine
Woodbury
START: DAY 4

Orari River

Lismore

Hinds River

Mayfield
SH72

Montalto

Punawai

Ashburton River   South Branch
North Branch
Ashburton Forks
Ashburton River

Bowyers Stream Rest Area

Mount Somers
SH72
Staveley

Alford Forest

START: DAY 3
Methven

To Christchurch

can be observed and its products purchased at the Honey Corner (☎ 693 9771) on Woodbury Rd, north of town.

Geraldine is renowned for an active craft scene with the **Festival of Arts & Plants** in November and a three day **Country Music Festival** in January.

Places to Stay & Eat The *Geraldine Motor Camp (☎ 693 8147, cnr Cox & Hislop Sts)* has tent sites at $15 for two and cabins for $15 per person.

Raukapuka Roost B&B & Backpackers (☎ 693 7665, 90 Main North Rd) is 2km north of town. The 1884 *Olde Presbytery Backpackers (☎ 693 9644, 13 Jollie St)* has double rooms from $20 per person.

Motels include *Andorra (☎ 693 8622, 16 McKenzie St)*, *Geraldine Motel (☎ 693 8501, 97 Talbot St)* and *Four Peaks (☎ 693 8339, 28 McKenzie St)*, charging from $60 and up.

The *Crown Hotel (☎ 693 8458)*, opposite the visitor centre, offers budget rooms from $25 per person.

The Crossing Guest Lodge (☎ 693 9689) is in a luxuriously restored 1908 English manor house on Woodbury Rd, 2km from town. B&B costs from $80 to $117 for a single, and from $96 to $147 for a double; it has an in-house licensed restaurant and plenty of parking space for bicycles and gear. *Heron Rose Guest House (☎ 693 8343, 29 Cox St)*, a 1930s character home, offers B&B at $75 for a double. The visitor centre has details of other B&Bs nearby.

Get cheap, quick eats at the busy cafe-style *bakery (cnr Talbot & Cox Sts)*. The *Village Inn (☎ 693 8458)* has reasonably priced meals. *Robbie's Tearooms (☎ 693 8338)* on Talbot St is a good place for breakfast or snacks.

For resupply, there is a *supermarket* on Peel St that's open seven days.

Day 4: Geraldine to Timaru
4-5 hours, 62km

An easy day's ride starts from Geraldine, following tiny minor sealed roads and passes close to the **memorial** to pioneer aviator Richard William Pearse (1877-1953). The obscure local man was the first British citizen to fly in a powered heavier-than-air machine. The date is believed by some to have been 31 March 1903, which would have pre-dated the Wright brothers' flight

by almost nine months. His aircraft crashed near the site now occupied by its pedestal-mounted replica and a plaque commemorating the event. Timaru's airport at Levels is named after him.

A short flat ride brings you to the aptly named **Pleasant Point**, well equipped with shops and bakeries. Information is available at the district council service centre (☎ 615 9537) on Domain Ave. On weekends and holidays the **railway museum** runs vintage steam trains along 3km of track from the old station towards Timaru. Nearby points of interest are a working blacksmith, Maori rock art, Parr's Mill and Raincliff Reserve (ask at the council service centre for details). There is a delightful, shady *domain camping ground (☎ 614 7723)* on the left of SH8 about 1km towards Timaru from the town centre.

Traffic increases steadily, but the gently descending SH8 has a good surface and shoulder all the way to Washdyke, at the junction with SH1, where free guided tours of the **DB Mainland Brewery** (☎ 688 2059) in Sheffield St take place on weekday mornings.

The next 5km into the centre of Timaru on SH1 are through unprepossessing industrial areas and suburban sprawl, with a few hills and heavy traffic thrown in. A short side trip to **Caroline Bay**, one of NZ's safest, most scenic swimming beaches, which attracts huge crowds to its annual Christmas and New Year festival. More than 20 hectares here have been developed into gardens, a fairground and play areas, with a soundshell, aviary, roller-skating rink and diving raft.

Returning to SH1, now called Evans St, ride along Timaru's main accommodation strip. Motel after motel plus backpacker hostels tout for business, with garish signs promising luxury and 'bargain' prices. More motels are in the street on the right at the next set of traffic lights.

Timaru

Originally Te Maru, or 'place of shelter', Timaru (population 27,000) was a haven for Maori travellers canoeing along the coast. Whalers were the first European settlers in about 1838, followed by pastoralists George and Robert Rhodes. The area was sparsely populated until 1859 when the

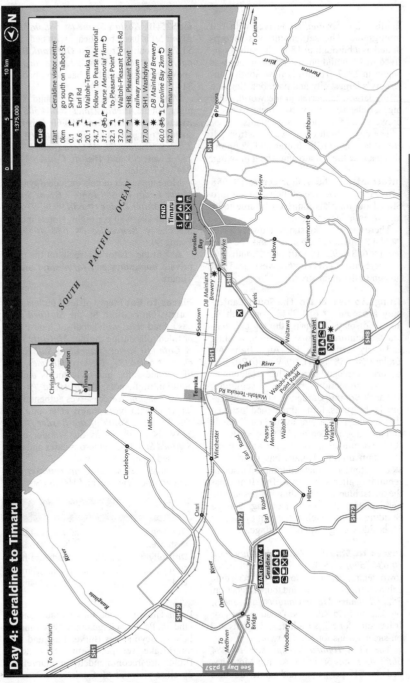

Day 4: Geraldine to Timaru

CANTERBURY

Cue

start	Geraldine visitor centre
0km	go south on Talbot St
0.1	SH79
5.6	Earl Rd
20.1	Waitohi-Temuka Rd
24.7	follow 'to Pearse Memorial'
31.1	Pearse Memorial 1km
32.1	'to Pleasant Point'
37.0	Waitohi-Pleasant Point Rd
43.7	SH8, Pleasant Point
	railway museum
57.0	SH1, Washdyke
	DB Mainland Brewery
60.0	Caroline Bay 2km
62.0	Timaru visitor centre

English ship, *Strathallan*, arrived with 120 immigrants. The settlement was incorporated as a borough in 1868, the railway arrived in 1876 and an artificial harbour was begun in 1877. Timaru is now South Canterbury's largest city and port, boasting one of the largest tanneries in the world, NZ's biggest cheese factory, two meat works, a brewery and food processing plants.

The city is built on a lava flow from Mt Horrible. Its fertile hinterland supports sheep and cattle, potato and wheat growing.

Information The visitor centre (☎ 688 6163) is at 14 George St, between Stafford St and the train station. Get the free town map to assist navigation.

There are two bike shops: Howes Cycles (☎ 684 8900) at 127 Church St and The Cyclery (☎ 688 8892) in Stafford St South.

There are ATMs at the Westpac Trust branch in the main street.

Things to See & Do The South Canterbury Museum (☎ 684 2212), on Perth St, houses displays featuring the region's natural and cultural history, including whaling and early settlement. The **Aigantighe Art Gallery** (☎ 688 4424), 49 Wai-iti Rd, in a historic house and garden, has a large public art collection including sculpture. Timaru's **Botanic Gardens** on Queen St feature herbs, roses, ferns, threatened local native species plus a bird aviary, duck ponds and playground. **Centennial Park** on Otipua Rd is a natural area popular for walking and mountain biking. Timaru has many substantial stone and brick buildings, a result of rebuilding after a disastrous fire. It also has the oldest bluestone building in the southern hemisphere, the 1870 **Landing Service Building** on the beach at the foot of George St, beside George Rhodes' cottage.

Places to Stay The *Selwyn Holiday Park* (☎ 684 7690), on Selwyn St, 2km north of the town centre, has tent sites for $8 per adult, cabins from $25 for two and tourist flats from $52. *Glenmark Motor Camp* (☎ 684 3682), on Beaconsfield Rd, is 3km south of the city. It has sites for $8 per adult, and cabins and on-site caravans for $25 for two.

The YHA *Timaru Backpackers* (☎ 684 5067, 42 Evans St) in the Anchor Motel has beds for $17 per person and singles/doubles

for $25/40. *Kosta's Scone* (☎ 688 0871, 24 Evans St) is basic but cheap, with beds from $12 and doubles from $30. *Old Bank Backpackers* (☎ 686 9098, 232 Stafford St), above the Old Bank bar, has dorm beds for $14 and doubles for $36.

Most motels charge from around $70 a night, but the *Anchor Motel* (☎ 684 5067, 42 Evans St) has rooms from $50/60. Other reasonable places include *Bay Motel* (☎ 684 3267, 9 Hewling St), *Al Casa* (☎ 684 7071, 131 Evans St) and *Wai-iti Court* (☎ 688 8447, 5 Preston St).

More upmarket motels include *Baywatch Motor Lodge* (☎ 688 1886, 7 Evans St) and *Ashley Motor Lodge* (☎ 688 9939, 97 King St), both over $80 per night. Hotels include the classy *Benvenue* (☎ 688 4049, 16 Evans St).

Ask at the visitor centre about the many private *homestays* and *farm stays* around Timaru.

Places to Eat Plenty of food outlets offer variety. On Stafford St, the *Stafford Mall* has a food court with kebabs, Chinese food or filled rolls during the day. *McGinty's Bar & Cafe (10 Variety Lane)* and *Sail & Anchor (☎ 688 8177, 18 Royal Arcade)*, both offer good-value pub-style meals and are popular nightspots. *Casa Italia (☎ 684 5528, 2 Strathallan St)* serves authentic Italian food with pasta mains at around $17. The Tex-Mex *South of the Border (☎ 688 5189)* is at 88 Evans St. Wander along *Stafford St* to find numerous cafes and other licensed restaurants.

A large, well stocked *supermarket* is on the corner of Victoria and Heaton Sts.

Mackenzie Country

Duration	4 days
Distance	315.9km
Difficulty	moderate-hard
Start	Timaru
End	Oamaru

From Timaru, scenic minor roads lead inland via Pareora Gorge to pretty, somnolent Fairlie. Beyond lies Burkes Pass and stunning Lake Tekapo, from where scenic flights are recommended for marvellous, up-close views of Mt Cook.

The wide open inland – NZ's 'Outback' – featuring long distances between tiny towns, is dotted with huge hydro lakes and is populated mostly by sheep. East of Omarama there is an alternative route option visiting some of the region's big dams. A day of near constant downhill finishes at historic Oamaru where the nightly penguin parade is a must-see.

PLANNING
When to Ride
This ride is best from October to March, although try to avoid crowds and traffic during the school holidays from Christmas through January.

Maps
The single sheet InfoMap 1:500,000 series title North Meets South conveniently covers the ride and is adequate for navigating the route outside towns. The AA *South Canterbury & Mount Cook* (1:350,000), available free to motoring association members at 210 Hereford St, Christchurch, covers the route with good detail outside towns.

Use the free town map from the Timaru visitor centre to assist in finding the way out of town.

GETTING TO/FROM THE RIDE
Timaru
Bus InterCity and Newmans buses stop at the Timaru train station, linking Timaru with Christchurch, Dunedin, Queenstown and Te Anau. The booking centre (☎ 688 3597) is at the station.

Shuttle services such as Atomic (☎ 322 8883), Ko-op (☎ 366 6633) and Southern Link (☎ 379 9991), connect with Christchurch or Dunedin for around $20 plus $10 per bike.

Train The *Southerner* (☎ 0800 802 802) leaves Timaru daily at 10.20 am for Invercargill ($85 plus $10 per bike, seven hours)

CANTERBURY

The Legend of Jock McKenzie

A legend this rightly is – many subsequent investigations have only helped to cloud or con-fuse the truth. It is thought that James (Jock) McKenzie was born in 1820 in Scotland. In his short time in this country (date of arrival unknown), possibly only two years, he achieved great notoriety. In March 1855 he was caught near present-day Mackenzie Pass in possession of 1000 sheep which had been stolen from the Levels run, north-west of Timaru.

It was believed at the time that he had stolen the sheep to stock a run he had purchased in Otago and that he was aided only by his remarkable dog, Friday. He was captured near the pass by the Levels overseer and two Maori shepherds. He escaped and made his way to Lyt-telton where, while hiding in a loft, he was recaptured by a police sergeant. He was then tried for sheep stealing and sentenced to five years imprisonment. Throughout the trial McKenzie had pleaded not guilty and, nine months after the trial, he was granted a pardon. He had, re-putedly, escaped from prison three times during his nine month incarceration, always pro-claiming his innocence. Even the then superintendent of Canterbury, James Fitzgerald, remarked: 'I am inclined to believe his story.' Popular myth had it that he was then ordered to leave the country, but there is no evidence to back this belief.

Lyttelton's town clock now covers the foundations of the jail that once held McKenzie; he was interned here after the only supreme court trial ever held in the town. It is believed by some that McKenzie's 'treasure' – well, his savings anyway – are concealed in a bush near Edendale, 39km north of Invercargill. He supposedly selected the bush as it was *tapu* (sacred) to the local Maori. As legend has it, McKenzie was only pardoned on the condition that he leave New Zealand for ever – so he never returned to pick up his savings.

If you're heading to Timaru via Mackenzie Pass you will see a monument erected near the spot where McKenzie was apprehended, although no-one really knows the exact spot. The pass is said to be named after McKenzie as the discoverer, but it is now believed that it had appeared on an earlier map in the late 1840s. Similarly, there is no proof that he had ever purchased land in Otago to stock with either stolen or bought sheep. Little is known of his later life and the date of his death is a mystery.

and Christchurch ($36 plus $10 per bike, two hours) at 3.13 pm.

Bicycle This ride follows on directly from the Canterbury Hinterland ride.

Oamaru

Bus InterCity and Newmans buses link Oamaru with Christchurch, Queenstown, Dunedin, and Te Anau. Book by telephoning ☎ 688 3597. Shuttle services such as Atomic (☎ 322 8883), Ko-op (☎ 366 6633) and Southern Link (☎ 379 9991), also connect with Christchurch or Dunedin.

Train The *Southerner* (☎ 0800 802 802) connects Oamaru daily with Invercargill ($75 plus $10 per bike) and Christchurch ($51 plus $10 per bike). Discounted fares are available.

Bicycle An adventurous link to the Central Otago Circuit ride (see the Otago & Southland chapter) takes you from Oamaru towards Weston and Ngapara, then south through the Kakanui Mountains via Danseys Pass on well maintained gravel to Naseby and Ranfurly. There is a *motor camp* (☎ 431 2564) at Danseys Pass.

Don't do this when a southerly change is imminent or you risk being caught in a blizzard on the 935m pass.

THE RIDE
Day 1: Timaru to Fairlie

3½-6 hours, 67km

The ride starts with an undulating route, starting at sea level. Climbing and descending a series of hills out of Timaru, the route reaches the tiny village of Cave (111m) via very quiet, scenic roads through Pareora Gorge. Thereafter it's a gentle, steady climb to Fairlie at an altitude of 250m.

Stock up on anything you need before leaving Timaru – the town has the last real supermarkets before Oamaru.

The suburban streets of Timaru give way to rolling rural hills. Ride west with views of the emerald Pacific to one side and brown, misty mountains to the other. You encounter some steep grades through **Pareora Gorge**. Along the way is a **memorial** to George Bertram Baker (1895-1971) who devoted himself to the destruction of the rabbit infestation in NZ. As you ride on,

you'll note that much more needs to be done to solve the problem.

Cave, which is off the route to the right, has a *general store* and is conveniently located for lunch opposite a shady park. Nearby limestone caves are noted for **rock art** attributed to pre-Maori inhabitants (ask for directions at the shop). Cave has the last services before Fairlie, other than the *pub* at Albury.

On leaving Cave, a sign announces your entry to 'Mackenzie Country'. The scenery does not change – the entire route is on exposed and shadeless roads. Surfaces are good and there is little traffic other than the occasional tour bus heading for Mt Cook.

Fairlie

This small town (population 850) was named in 1865 after the birthplace in Scotland of the town's first hotel owner. Close to the base of Burkes Pass, it is 'the gateway to the Mackenzie Country', as the wide open inland to the west is known. Avenues of trees are a legacy of the early residents.

Information The Sunflower Centre (see Places to Stay & Eat) is the visitor centre.

Things to See & Do The colonial **Mabel Binney cottage** and **Vintage Machinery Museum** are just west of the town centre.

Places to Stay & Eat The *Gateway Holiday Park* (☎ 685 8375) is on Allandale Rd (SH79), a short distance from the centre. Tent sites are $8 per person, and cabins and on-site vans $30/35 for two, respectively. The *Gladstone Grand Hotel* (☎ 685 8140, 43 Main St) has rooms from $25 per person and serves meals. Two motels, *Aorangi* (☎ 685 8340, 26 Denmark St) and *Rimuwhare Country Retreat* (☎ 685 8058, 53 Mt Cook Rd), have units from $60 and the latter has a restaurant.

B&Bs near town are *Fontmel* (☎ 685 8379) on Nixons Rd and *Braelea* (☎ 685 8366) on SH79, both 3km from Fairlie's centre and charging from $70 for a double. *Kimbell Motel* (☎ 685 8819), 9km towards Lake Tekapo on SH8, has doubles from $55 per night (meals are available).

The *Sunflower Centre* (☎ 685 8258) on the way into town from Cave is a wholefood eating house and health shop with a speciality 'vegieburger' and traditional fare.

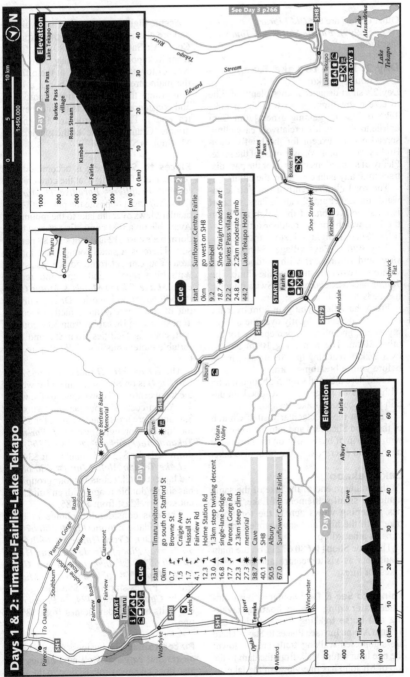

Days 1 & 2: Timaru-Fairlie-Lake Tekapo

CANTERBURY

Elevation

Day 2

Fairlie — Kimbell — Ross Stream — Burkes Pass village — Burkes Pass — Lake Tekapo

Cue — Day 2

start		Sunflower Centre, Fairlie
0km		go west on SH8
9.2		Kimbell
18.7	✴	*Shoe Straight roadside art*
22.2		Burkes Pass village
24.8	▲	2.2km moderate climb
44.2		Lake Tekapo Hotel

START: DAY 2
Fairlie

Cue — Day 1

start		Timaru visitor centre
0km		go south on Stafford St
0.7		Browne St
1.5		Craigie Ave
1.7		Hassall St
4.1		Fairview Rd
12.3		Holme Station Rd
13.0	◄	1.3km steep twisting descent
16.8		single-lane bridge
17.7		Paeora Gorge Rd
22.3	▲	2.3km steep climb
27.3	✴	*memorial*
38.7		Cave
40.1		SH8
50.5		Albury
67.0		Sunflower Centre, Fairlie

Elevation

Day 1

Timaru — Cave — Albury — Fairlie

START
Timaru

Other outlets are the *Old Library* restaurant *(☎ 685 8999)*, *Fairlie Stores* and *Tom's* for fast foods.

Day 2: Fairlie to Lake Tekapo
2½-4 hours, 44.2km

Day 2's short distance allows plenty of time to take a joy flight or go walking at Lake Tekapo. Despite gaining a net 470m from Fairlie to Tekapo, it's a relatively easy climb spread evenly, except for the briefly steep Burkes Pass (26.8km), over most of the route. Plenty of stupendous views after the pass distract from any pain caused by the climb.

The road climbs gently from Fairlie towards the rather anticlimactic Pass, so short is its steep section. At the 18km mark, on the left, watch for the outdoor artwork entitled 'Shoe Straight' – it stops traffic!

Tiny **Burkes Pass** village (540m) has a *shop* and *restaurant* with outdoor tables where you can refresh before the climb. The *Yodler* backpackers, run by a Swiss migrant, has beds for $14.

From the village you gain 60m over the next 2km, descend slightly over the following 300m, and climb imperceptibly for another 300m. The remaining 100m gain is over 2.2km, reaching the 709m pass almost before you're breathing hard.

From here the road stays high, undulating with views to jagged, snowcapped mountain peaks beyond Lake Tekapo.

Roll past the spectacularly sited Church of the Good Shepherd and into the township with its strip of businesses on the north side of the road overlooking the turquoise lake.

Lake Tekapo

At the southern end of the lake of the same name the small settlement of Lake Tekapo has sweeping views across the torquoise lake with the hills and snowcapped mountains as a backdrop.

The Hide Shop (☎ 680 6721), on the main road, acts as visitor centre and has basic bikes for hire.

Things to See & Do Popular activities include **water skiing, fishing, boating, kayaking** and **horse trekking**. Book at the Lake Tekapo Alpine Inn (see Places to Stay). There are signposted **walking trails** around town: the one hour return walk from the dam to the top of Mt John has fine views of the lake.

Scenic flights over the Alps are available and are cheaper from Tekapo than from Mt Cook. Air Safaris (☎ 680 6880) has flights from Tekapo airport, an easy 3km pedal west of town on SH8. Book at the office in the main street. Because it books a lot of tour groups there are sometimes spare seats and considerable discounts for independent travellers. The standard fare for the 50 minute 'Grand Traverse' of the glaciers and Mt Cook is $210.

Places to Stay There is accommodation 'exclusively for cyclists' at the conveniently located *Pedallers' Paradise (1 Aorangi Crescent)*, right opposite the pub, with spectacular views over the lake to the mountains. Available on a first come, first served basis, dorm beds cost $12 and tent sites $8 per person. There is a small lounge and kitchen area. You can get route advice, assistance with bike repairs and send and receive email. *Lake Tekapo Motels & Motor Camp (☎ 680 6825)* on Lakeside Dr is a fair way out of town, but in an attractive location. Tent sites are $18, cabins from $32, cottages with cooking facilities from $58 and comfortable motel units from $75; all prices for two.

The *Tekapo YHA Hostel (☎ 680 6857, fax 680 6664)* is on Simpson Lane, also west of the town centre and down towards the water. The dorm costs $15 per person, twins cost $36 and there are some tent sites for $9. Up the hill on Aorangi Crescent, *Tailor-made Tekapo Backpackers (☎ 680 6700)* has dorm beds for $15 and doubles for $34.

Lake Tekapo Alpine Inn (☎ 680 6848), the largest hotel, caters for tour groups and has single/double rooms with en suite and a cooked breakfast from $60/85.

There is considerable choice in B&B accommodation: *homestay (☎ 680 6703, 3 Pioneer Dr)*, *Creel House (☎ 680 6516, 36 Murray Place)*, *Freda du Faur House (☎ 680 6513, 1 Esther Hope St)* and *Charford House (☎ 680 6888, 14 Murray Place)*. Prices start from $60/85.

The *Chalet (☎ 680 6774, 14 Pioneer Dr)* has units and holiday homes from $85 for two.

Places to Eat The business area has *takeaways* and *cafes*, as well as a *bakery* that also does takeaway meals, next to the hotel.

The Alpine Inn has several restaurants including the *Garden Buffet* with hot buffet lunches from $15 and dinners from $30. Others cater to Asian tourists with the *Kohan Japanese* doing sashimi from $20. *Jade Palace* (☎ 680 6828) is a cheap Chinese restaurants.

Day 3: Lake Tekapo to Omarama
5-8 hours, 86.5km

Today you ride on absolutely shadeless roads through the NZ 'outback'. Spectacular mountain views accompany you everywhere. There is very little traffic along the tourist route beside the hydro canal to Lake Pukaki.

Should you not have seen enough of Mt Cook from the ground or the air, you can get closer by adding a day or two to the trip and turning onto SH80 just after Lake Pukaki. It is 55km from the turn-off to Mt Cook village, but there is a good *camping ground* at Glentanner, 33km up the road, which you could use as a base.

The only town on today's route is Twizel (population 1200), which, with its numerous *food outlets* in a central mall (follow the signs), is a convenient lunch spot. Cycle accessories are also available in the central mall. Twizel is about the only place you will see many trees together today. This former hydro village has reinvented itself as a tourist town with the slogan 'Town of Trees'.

Two kilometres south of Twizel is the turn-off to Lake Ruataniwha Recreation Park, which has *camping* facilities. The rest of the way to Omarama is quite flat and the road goes straight ahead for many kilometres at a time. Part of the way is through a wide valley used for sheep grazing, below bare brown tussocky hills. It can get very hot.

Omarama
Omarama is 'Merino Country'; there are only 400 people, but many more sheep.

Information The visitor centre (☎ 438 9610, fax 438 9694) opens daily from 10 am to 4 pm from September to April, but closes the rest of the year. For advice on the area, also try the Caltex petrol station (☎ 438 9870) on Main St.

Things to See & Do Stop in Twizel if you'd like to try **helibiking** (☎ 0800 435 424). As the name suggests, you fly to the top of a mountain and descend on a mountain bike. Trips are priced from $65.

The **Paritea**, or Clay Cliffs, formed by the active Osler fault line, are down a dirt road 15km from Omarama; entry is $5. Similar formations can be seen for nothing from SH8 a few kilometres south towards Lindis Pass.

Omarama has a worldwide reputation for **gliding** due to the area's thermals and was once the venue for the world championships. Alpine Soaring (☎ 438 9600) offers 20-minute flights for around $140.

Places to Stay & Eat The *Omarama Holiday Park* (☎ 438 9875) has tent sites for $19, basic cabins from $32, on-site vans from $37 and tourist flats for $59; all prices are for two. *Omarama Hotel* (☎ 438 9713) has single/double rooms from $30/55. The *Ahuriri Motel* (☎ 438 9451), with similar prices, is 500m along the road to Oamaru.

The Briars (☎ 438 9615) is a homestay 2km north of Omarama offering B&B at $40/70. *Omarama Station* (☎ 438 9821) has a farm stay on its busy sheep station, 1km from town ($55/85).

There are two tearooms serving light meals and a small general store in the town centre.

Day 4: Omarama to Oamaru
7½-10 hours, 118.2km

Day 4 follows the Waitaki Valley, mostly descending to the coast, making the longer distance less onerous. Brown, tussock grass-covered hills again dominate the scene. In the first 5km you climb over a small range of hills, getting a fine view of the southern part of Lake Benmore, NZ's largest artificial lake at 75 sq km.

The road follows the lake's shore for some distance, passing a *domain camping ground*, then climbs 140m in 5km over Ahuriri Saddle.

Otematata, which has a good *general store*, is the turn-off for Lake Aviemore (see Side Trip).

The main intermediate town on the route is **Kurow** (52km), where you are welcomed by the cute 'Hay People'. This larger-than-life family of figures is made of hay bales planted in a park on main street. You can buy souvenir Hay People T-shirts at the first cafe.

CANTERBURY

CANTERBURY

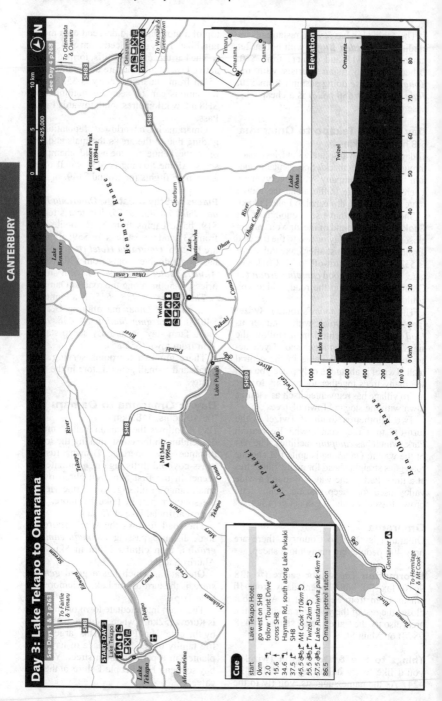

Day 3: Lake Tekapo to Omarama

See Days 1 & 2 p263

To Fairlie & Timaru

To Faitlie & Timaru

SH8

START: DAY 3
Lake Tekapo

Lake Alexandrina

Edward Stream

Tekapo River

Tekapo River

Canal

Mary Burn

Fraser Canal

Tekapo Canal

Maryburn

Frchman Creek

Mt Mary (995m)

Lake Pukaki

Pukaki Canal

Pukaki River

Twizel
i ⌂ X ⛽ ⊖

Twizel River

Lake Benmore

Ohau Canal

Benmore Range

Benmore Peak (1894m)

Clearburn

Lake Ruataniwha

Ohau River

Ohau Canal

Lake Ohau

SH8

Omarama
⌂ ⛽ X ⊖
START: DAY 4

SH83

To Otematata & Oamaru

See Day 4 p268

To Wanaka & Queenstown

N

0   5   10 km
1:425,000

Timaru
Omarama   Oamaru

Ben Ohau Range

Glentanner ⌂

To Hermitage & Mt Cook

Tekapo River

Pukaki River

Twizel River

Cue		
start	Lake Tekapo Hotel	
0km	go west on SH8	
2.0	follow 'Tourist Drive'	←
15.6	cross SH8	←
34.6	Hayman Rd, south along Lake Pukaki	↰
37.5	SH8	↰
45.5	Mt Cook 110km	⟳
55.6	Twizel 2km	⟳
57.5	Lake Ruataniwha park 4km	⟳
86.5	Omarama petrol station	⟳

Elevation

Lake Tekapo	Twizel	Omarama

1000 (m) 800 600 400 200 0

0 (km) 10 20 30 40 50 60 70 80

Should you wish to break the journey here, the *Kurow Holiday Park* (☎ 436 0725, 76 Bledisloe St) has on-site vans and cabins or there's the *Kurow Motel* (☎ 436 0850, 55 Bledisloe St). The Kurow community centre (☎ 436 0812) has details of *homestays*.

Further down the valley is **Duntroon**, which has a *domain camping ground*, the *Duntroon Tavern* (☎ 431 2850) and a *cafe*. It is also the turn-off to Danseys Pass. To minimise hills and distance to Oamaru, continue on SH83 to Pukeuri and take SH1 for the last 8km into Oamaru.

Side Trip: Lake Aviemore
2½-3½ hours, 27km return
This is more an alternative route than a side trip, but it can be worth it there is traffic on SH83. Take the turn-off to Lake Aviemore at Otematata. The detour takes you via **Benmore Dam** and along the northern shore of **Lake Aviemore**, rejoining SH83 at Aviemore. There's a *lodge* and *camping ground* (☎ 438 7826) in town and numerous camping options at *domain camping grounds* on the lake shore. This adds 15km to the trip to Oamaru, but is quiet and scenic, however, a steep climb to the dam wall and numerous undulations make it demanding.

Oamaru
Established in the 1850s, Oamaru (population 13,500) is now a prosperous town with imposing buildings made of beautiful local limestone in its historic port precinct. The Oamaru steam train rolls through during school and public holidays. Among other events at heritage celebrations in November are penny farthing races. The town is renowned for its nearby colonies of little blue and yellow-eyed penguins.

Information Oamaru's visitor centre (☎ 434 1656), on the corner of Thames and Itchen Sts, near the historic area, is open from 9 am to 5 pm weekdays and 10 am to 4 pm weekends. Martyn's (☎ 434 8416), 45 Thames St, is a friendly and helpful bike shop.

Things to See & Do Visiting the **penguins** is a must. The little blue penguins nest around the harbour. From a grandstand at the end of Waterfront Rd, watch them come ashore and waddle up to their burrows in a disused quarry. Their 'show' appears each night at dusk from September to February ($8). It is amazing to see some of them scale a cliff to reach their front doors.

Yellow-eyed penguins, among the world's rarest, nest at Bushy Beach on Cape Wanbrow, within walking distance of town. You view them from a specially constructed hide. **Tours** leave the car park on Bushy Beach Rd in the evening; the visitor centre has details.

The 1876 **public gardens** on Severn St (at SH1's railway crossing) feature a Japanese bridge across the creek, oriental and fragrant gardens, and superb rhododendron, cactus and azalea displays.

Places to Stay The *Oamaru Gardens Holiday Park* (☎ 434 7666) is in a quiet location on Chelmer St, adjacent to the public gardens. Tent sites are $9 per person, while flats are $50 and cabins start from around $30. *Waitaki Mouth Motor Camp* (☎ 431 3880) is north of town near the Waitaki bridge on SH1. Tent sites cost $7 per person and cabins are $14 per adult.

Red Kettle YHA Seasonal Hostel (☎ 434 5008, cnr Reed & Cross Sts) is open from the end of September to May or June. Dorm beds are $14 and doubles $32.

CANTERBURY

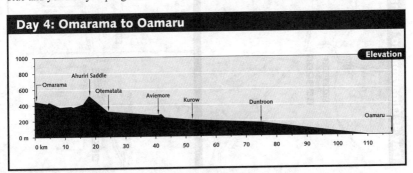

Day 4: Omarama to Oamaru

CANTERBURY

Day 4: Omarama to Oamaru

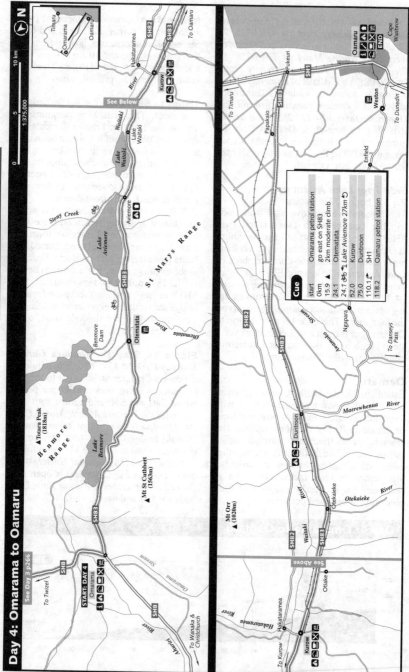

Cue		
start	0km	Omarama petrol station
	15.9 ▲	go east on SH83
		2km moderate climb
	24.1	Otematata
	24.1 ⚲	Lake Aviemore 27km ↻
	52.0	Kurow
	75.0	Duntroon
	110.1 ↰	SH1
	118.2	Oamaru petrol station

There are numerous rural homestay B&B establishments within 5 to 20km of town. Check with the visitor centre for details.

Alpine Motel (☎ 434 5038, 285 Thames St) has units sleeping up to seven from $65 for two. Nearby, the *Thames Court Motel (☎ 434 6963, 252 Thames St)* has doubles for $70. The *Tui Motels (☎ 437 1443, 469 Thames St)* and *Avenue Motel (☎ 437 0091, 473 Thames St)* have basic doubles from around $55.

Places to Eat Oamaru's restaurants, tearooms and takeaways are concentrated along Thames St. *Emma's Cafe* at 15 Thames St is the trendiest and reputedly has the best coffee in town. Next door, *Bridge Cafe (☎ 434 8827)* attracts an older clientele. Multinational fast-food outlets are on Thames St.

The very fashionable *Last Post* restaurant *(☎ 434 8080)* is in the town's first post office on Thames St, near the museum. Mains start from about $20. The *Star & Garter (☎ 434 5246)*, on Itchen St, has a heritage theme, with a pianola, and has a blackboard menu with mains (also from $20). The restored stone *Criterion Hotel (☎ 434 6247)* on Tyne St is a heritage watering hole. It's only open on Friday.

Southern Alps Circuit

Duration	8 days
Distance	692.4km
Difficulty	hard
Start/End	Greymouth

This classic, strenuous tour makes a double crossing of the central spine of the South Island. The suggested route includes some of the best scenery on the west coast and four high mountain passes. The route climbs from sea level at Westport to 680m at Rahu Saddle, drops to near 400m, then climbs over 907m to Lewis Pass before descending again to near sea level. On the return leg, you pedal up the 945m Porters Pass and stay above 500m for nearly 70km. Cruising over Arthur's Pass at 920m, you plummet down a narrow, winding ribbon of bitumen to return to sea level again near Greymouth.

A new viaduct is being built in Otira Gorge to bypass the unstable slope crossed by the steepest section of the old Arthur's Pass road. The slope on the viaduct will still be 1:8 or 12.5% for a kilometre or more. Be thankful you are going downhill, but check your brakes before you do!

HISTORY

The Southern Alps were well known to the Maori who used the passes to move *pounamu* (greenstone) from Westland. Settlers explored the eastern side of the mountains first in the 1850s in search of grazing land. In 1864 Arthur Dobson surveyed Arthur's Pass as a quick route to the west coast, and a rugged coach road was put through in the terrible winter of 1865.

The coal and timber trade demanded a railway, which was completed with the opening of the 8.6km Otira tunnel in 1923. After this people began to take the train to Arthur's Pass for skiing, walking and climbing. Arthur's Pass area became a national park in 1929 and tramping clubs built huts in the back country.

NATURAL HISTORY

The Southern Alps straddle the edges of two tectonic plates. Earthquakes are common. Glaciation during the last Ice age smoothed the bedrock creating narrow U-shaped valleys. Erosion crumbles mountain ridges, producing scree slopes and gravelly river beds.

Braided rivers like the Waimakariri are habitats for birds like the wrybill and black-fronted tern, while mountain beech forest, dominating the eastern side of the mountains, is home to bellbirds, fantails, robins, brown creepers, tom-tits and grey warblers. Otira Gorge is home to a small, endangered population of great spotted kiwi, and the mischievous kea, a mountain parrot, is common.

On the wetter western side, mixed podocarp forest has luxuriant understorey shrubs, tree ferns, mosses and lichens. Rata flowers colour Otira Gorge a magnificent bright red in January and February. Above the tree line, snow tussock and alpine meadows contain plants and insects adapted to harsh conditions.

PLANNING
When to Ride

November to March is the best period for this ride. Winter daytime temperatures in

CANTERBURY

the Alps can be below zero; a hot summer's day may be in the high 20s, but dramatic changes of weather are common. Frequent north-westerly air flows bring heavy rain and winter snow to the west of the ranges. Check weather reports for up-to-date information on road conditions.

What to Bring
Warm clothing and waterproof garments are essential. A low-geared touring bike is ideal – all roads are sealed.

GETTING TO/FROM THE RIDE
Greymouth
Bus InterCity (☎ 379 9020) has daily services from Nelson, Westport and the glaciers. Coast to Coast Shuttle (☎ 0800 800 847), Alpine Coach & Courier (☎ 762 6332) and Ko-op Shuttles (☎ 366 6633) connect with Christchurch.

Train The once-daily Tranz Alpine from Christchurch (at 9 am) to Greymouth (1.25 pm) costs $79 plus $10 per bike.

Bicycle You can start the ride at any point. Various other rides link to the Southern Alps Circuit, including the West Coast, Kaikoura Coast & Hanmer Springs and Canterbury Hinterland.

THE RIDE
Greymouth
Now the largest city on the west coast (population 10,000), Greymouth was also the site of Mawhera, the biggest Maori settlement in the region in the 1840s. In 1860 Greymouth was where Europeans 'bought' the west coast from the Maori for UK£300. From 1863 gold drove development until the expansion of the coal and timber industries ensured Greymouth's viability.

Information The visitor centre (☎ 768 5101, fax 768 0317, ☻ gmnvin@nzhost.co.nz) is in the cinema complex at the intersection of Herbert and Mackay Sts. It's open seven days a week. Get the free colour town map to assist navigation.

There are two bike shops in town, both are nearby on Mackay St: Mann Security & Cycles (☎ 768 0255) at No 25, and Graeme Peters Cycles (☎ 768 6559), a few doors east at No 37.

Things to See & Do The visitor centre can book you into a free tour of **Monteith's Brewing Co** (☎ 768 4149) on which you can sample the product. Tours are at 10.30 am and 1.30 pm, Monday to Thursday.

History House Museum (☎ 768 4028) has a collection of memorabilia and historic photographs of the west coast in the 1880 period County Council Chambers on Gresson St.

At the Jade Boulder Gallery (☎ 768 0700), on the corner of Guinness and Tainui Sts, you can watch **jade-carvers** at work and see displays of **greenstone sculptures** and jewellery.

Surfing and **swimming** are best at Karoro, Cobden Beach (North Breakwater) and at Seven-Mile Beach at Rapahoe, 11km north of town.

There are a number of good short **walks** around town. The steep King Park and Lions Walks, each about two hours return, leave Mount St and Weld St, respectively, on either side of Cobden Bridge and climb to lookouts, from where you can see far along the coast. To the south on a clear day, beyond a great sweep of beach, are the outlines of Mts Cook and Tasman.

You can get an even higher viewpoint on a **Westcoast Scenic Flight** (☎ 768 0407), or go into **Taniwha Cave** with Wild West Adventures (☎ 0800 223 456) on a 5½ hour trip involving floating on inner tubes through a glow-worm gallery and down a rapid. Heritage **Jet Tours** (☎ 0800 668 355) has trips up Grey River to the Brunner Mine site, and **Dolphin Watch** (☎ 0800 929 991) runs sea tours spotting Hector's dolphins and seals.

Ten kilometres south of town on Rutherglen Rd is the replica 1860s gold rush village, **Shantytown**, which offers steam train rides, gold-panning, horse and cart rides, and has more than 30 buildings on display. A licensed cafe and bar are open daily.

From Shantytown you can follow signs to Woods Creek Track, one of Westland's most rewarding **walks**. This easy 45 minute circuit takes you past mining relics, tunnels and dams, on bridges across streams and through virgin rimu forest and native bush regrowth.

Places to Stay Two camping grounds serve Greymouth: *Greymouth Seaside Holiday Park* (☎ 768 6618), 2.5km south of the centre on Chesterfield St; and *South Beach Motor Park* (☎ 762 6768), about 5km south

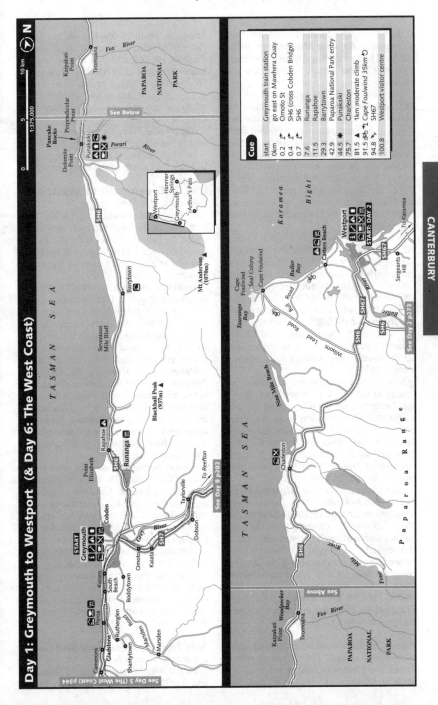

Day 1: Greymouth to Westport (& Day 6: The West Coast)

Cue		
start	Greymouth train station	
0km	go east on Mawhera Quay	
0.2	Omoto St	
0.4	SH6 (cross Cobden Bridge)	
0.7	SH6	
7.6	Runanga	
11.5	Rapahoe	
29.3	Barrytown	
42.9	Paparoa National Park entry	
44.5	Punakaiki	✳
75.7	Charleston	
81.5	1km moderate climb	▲
91.5	Cape Foulwind 35km ↺	⮌
94.8	SH67	⤷
100.8	Westport visitor centre	

CANTERBURY

of the town centre. More pleasant, however, is the smaller *Rapahoe Motor Camp (☎ 762 7025)*, 11km north. Right behind the beach, it charges $7 per person for a tent site and has free washing machines.

The *Kaianga-Ra YHA Hostel (☎/fax 768 4951, 15 Alexander St)* is a large one-time Marist Brothers' residence with four-bed dorms at $15 per person or a 10 bed dorm in a former chapel for $13. Doubles are $36. *Noah's Ark Backpackers (☎ 768 4868, 16 Chapel St)* is also an ex-monastery. It charges $15 in dorms and doubles or $35 in twins. The *Duke Backpackers (☎ 768 9740, cnr Guinness & Albert Sts)* is a converted hotel. Dorm beds are $14 per person and single rooms $20.

A few kilometres out of town at Taylorville, near the Brunner Mine site, is the *Old School Lodge (☎ 762 5522)*. Dorm accommodation is $15 and tent sites $8 per person.

Central B&Bs include *Ardwyn House (☎ 768 6107, 48 Chapel St)*, where a good single/double with cooked breakfast is $40/70; *Rosewood (☎ 0800 185 748, 20 High St)*, with rooms from $50/85; and *Shakespeare House (☎ 768 4646, 43 Shakespeare St)* in an early 19th century villa where a room is $65/85.

Motels are numerous but expensive, although in the off-peak season lower prices may be negotiable. Try *Willowbank Pacifica Lodge (☎ 768 5339)*, 3km north of Cobden Bridge, for doubles from $78; *Riverview Motel (☎ 768 6884)*, on Omoto Rd, 2km from the centre, with units from $65; and *Greymouth Motels (☎ 0800 220 032, 195 High St)* with units from $70.

Upmarket motels are the *Highpark Motor Inn (☎ 0800 844 846, 90 High St)* with rooms from $90 and the newer *Alpine Rose (☎ 768 7586, 139 High St)*, charging from $85.

The number of hotels in central Greymouth is a reminder of its gold rush history. Most offer only basic accommodation, the cheapest being *Railway (☎ 768 7023)* on Mawhera Quay – rooms are from $17/34. *Revingtons (☎ 768 7055, 46 Tainui St)* once hosted Queen Elizabeth II, but most customers are now backpackers paying from $20.

Places to Eat Standard cafes and sandwich places include *Tides Cafe* on Albert St and the *Chantilly* sandwich bar on the Mall at Mackay St. *Make 'n' Bake* on

Tainui St, south of Mackay St, has good-value filled rolls, muffins and bread. *Bonzai Pizzeria (☎ 768 4170)* is a very popular lunch-time spot at 29 Mackay St. It serves 16 varieties of pizza priced from $11 to $22 plus good cakes and coffee. Light meals are served in the licensed *Jade Rock Cafe (☎ 768 4636)*.

Supervalue Plus supermarket is on Guinness St behind the visitor centre. *New World* is on High St near the Greymouth Seaside Holiday Park south of the town centre.

Day 1: Greymouth to Westport
6-8 hours, 100.8km

This ride, gently undulating for the most part, passes the amazing rock formations called the Pancake Rocks at Punakaiki. The road then hugs the coastline with sea stacks and surf at arm's reach most of the way to Westport.

From Greymouth it is an easy 11km ride to the coast at Rapahoe. Beautiful vistas unfold as you ride north – wide bays are flanked by steep hills and salt spray sweeps inland. About 29km from Greymouth is Barrytown; from here the road curves inland slightly around grazing fields on the coastal plain.

Paparoa Park Motel is at the entrance to **Paparoa National Park**, commanding a view across a bay to Dolomite Point. After a descent and return climb, you reach the start of the short walk to the **Pancake Rocks** and **blowholes**. There's a *cafe* and *takeaway* on the right-hand side of the road making it a convenient lunch stop.

Further north, the one-time gold-mining town of **Charleston** (75.7km) is at the bottom of a snaking descent. A shadow of its booming past, the village has a *pub*, *motor camp*, *cafe* and *motel*. You can book 'underworld' rafting trips at the office next to the pub. Guide, Glen White, a national-level racing cyclist, is keen to take other cyclists on this and other trips through the local caves.

Attractive green-clad limestone hills roll north of Charleston. There is some shade, but climbs are exposed to the afternoon sun. An option is to turn off SH6 about 9.3km before Westport to Cape Foulwind.

Side Trip: Cape Foulwind Seal Colony
2-3 hours, 35km return

Turn left onto Wilsons Lead Rd from SH6 and ride 15km, following the signs, to visit

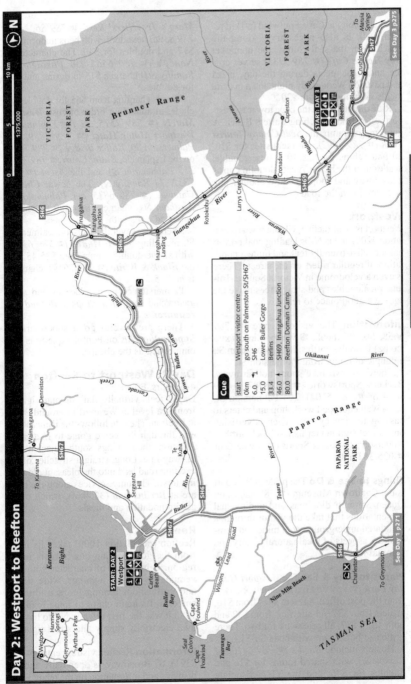

Day 2: Westport to Reefton

CANTERBURY

Cue

start	Westport visitor centre
0km	go south on Palmerston St/SH67
6.0	SH6
15.0	Lower Buller Gorge
33.4	Berlins
46.0	SH69, Inangahua Junction
80.0	Reefton Domain Camp

See Day 3 p275

See Day 1 p271

START: DAY 3
Reefton

START: DAY 2
Westport

the seal colony at Cape Foulwind (a 1km return walk is also necessary). Along the beach from the seal colony, the upmarket *Bay House Cafe* (☎ 789 7133) serves coffee and light meals during the day, pizza and pasta on Wednesday night and a la carte meals with mains from $20.

Ride directly from the cape towards Westport, after 14km reaching Carters Beach. A good motor camp, the *Seal Colony Tourist Park* (☎ 789 8002), with tent sites for $10/20 and cabins for $28/40 a single/double, nestles near the beach. A cafe doubling up as a takeaway and shop, open till about 7 pm, is 250m down the road.

Westport

Westport is an attractive, vibrant town (population 4200) and is NZ's leading coal port. It has a cyclist-friendly feel and quite a population of regular riders on the streets. There is even a velodrome in Victoria Square. Toilets, picnic tables and shady trees make the square a good place to relax.

Information The visitor centre (☎ 789 6658, fax 789 6668, ✉ westport.info@xtra .co.nz) is on the north side of Brougham St, a couple of doors from Palmerston St.

There are two bike shops not far away. Becker's Sportsworld (☎ 789 8787, ☎ 789 8854 or ☎ 789 5102), 204 Palmerston St, has a well equipped workshop and caters to passing touring cyclists, even advertising on a street sign in German. A block north is Anderson's Cycles & Sports (☎ 789 6293 or ☎ 025 383 630).

Things to See & Do The pride of Westport is the Coaltown Museum (☎ 789 8204), on Queen St, with dioramas and audiovisual presentations that take the visitor through a simulated coal mine and demonstrate aspects of local natural history and colonial life.

Places to Stay & Eat The *Westport Holiday Park* (☎ 789 7043, 31 Domett St), 1km from the post office, has tent sites from $16, chalets from $27, on-site vans from $32 and units from $37; all prices are for two. There is a basic bunkroom with beds for $12.

Hostels include *Bazil's* (☎ 789 6410, 54 Russell St), with shared rooms for $16 and doubles for $36; and the YHA-associate

Marg's Travellers' Rest (☎ 789 8627, fax 789 8396) next door, with beds in dorms for $17 and doubles for $40. The characterful *Nancy's* (☎ 789 6565, cnr Pakington & Romilly Sts) charges $15 in dorms and $34 for doubles.

Motels charging from $65 for doubles include, in ascending order of cost, *Westport Motels* (☎ 789 7575, 32 the Esplanade), *Westport Motor Hotel* (☎ 789 7889, 207 Palmerston St), *Buller Bridge* (☎ 789 7519) on the Esplanade, *Buller Court* (☎ 789 7979, 235 Palmerston St) and the *Ascot* (☎ 789 7832, 74 Romilly St). The newer *Chelsea Gateway* (☎ 789 6835, cnr Palmerston & Bentham Sts) charges from $80 to $140 if you need a spa bath.

There are several hotels on Palmerston St, including the *McManus* (☎ 789 6304), with single/double rooms from $25/45, and the *Black & White* (☎ 789 7959), charging from $25/50.

Palmerston St is the place to find *takeaways* and *sandwich shops*, *pub food* and *restaurants*.

There are several good supermarkets. *Supervalue Plus* on Fontblanque St is recommended as the cheapest.

Day 2: Westport to Reefton

4-6 hours, 80km

Day 2 feels virtually flat, although it rises from sea level at Westport to around 200m at Reefton. The ride follows the Buller River east through its scenic gorge to Inangahua Junction, then swings south adjacent to a railway line. Long, straight stretches of unexciting road lead into the pleasant old mining town. The only services along the route are at *Berlins pub* (33.4km), which offers accommodation and meals.

Reefton

Reefton (population 1000) takes its name from the gold-bearing quartz reefs in the region. It has a lot of character with old, veranda-style shop awnings, wide streets and craft shops among more traditional emporia. Its main claim to fame is that in 1888 it was the first town in NZ to have its own electricity supply and street lighting.

Information Reefton visitor centre (☎ 732 8391), 67 Broadway, is open daily and has displays and information on the many walks

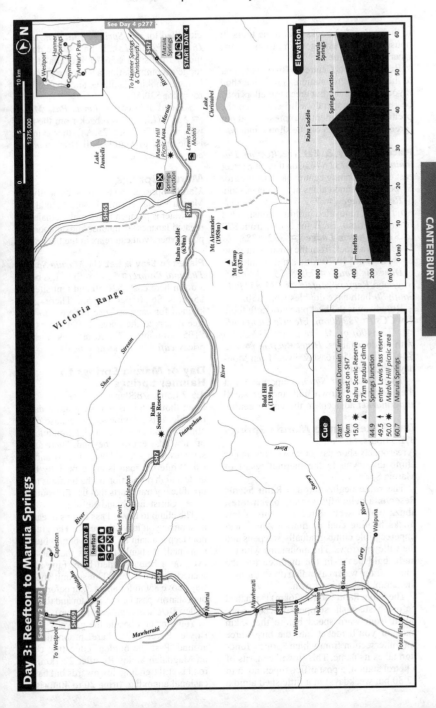

Day 3: Reefton to Maruia Springs

See Day 2 p273

See Day 4 p277

START: DAY 3 Reefton

START: DAY 4 Maruia Springs

Rahu Saddle (630m)

Victoria Range

Springs Junction

Marble Hill Picnic Area

Lewis Pass Motels

Lake Christabel

Lake Daniells

Mt Alexander (1958m)

Mt Kemp (1637m)

Bald Hill (1191m)

Rahu Scenic Reserve

Crushington

Blacks Point

Capleston

To Westport

Waitahu

Waiuta

Maimai

Mawheraiti

Waimaunga

Hukarere

Ikamatua

Waipuna

Totara Flat

SH65 · SH7 · SH69

Inangahua · Mawheraiti River · Grey River · Slaty River · Shaw Stream

To Hammer Springs & Christchurch

Maruia River

Westport · Greymouth · Hanmer Springs · Arthur's Pass

10 km · 1:375,000

CANTERBURY

Cue

Cue		
start		Reefton Domain Camp
0km		go east on SH7
15.0	✹	Rahu Scenic Reserve
	▲	17km gradual climb
44.9		Springs Junction
49.5	✦	enter Lewis Pass reserve
50.0	✹	Marble Hill picnic area
60.7		Maruia Springs.

Elevation

Rahu Saddle · Springs Junction · Maruia Springs · Reefton

1000 · 800 · 600 · 400 · 200 · 0 (m)

0 (km) · 10 · 20 · 30 · 40 · 50 · 60

in the region and books coal mine tours. It houses an interesting re-creation of the Quartzopolis Mine.

Reefton Sports Centre on Broadway, next to the Mobil petrol station, is the bike shop if you're desperate, but green travellers may be reluctant to spend cash here given the prehistoric sentiments expressed about 'greenies' in notices on the shop window.

Places to Stay & Eat The *Reefton Domain Camp* (☎ *732 8477)*, on the main street east of the shopping centre, has tent sites for $7 per person and cabins at $16 per person. *Reef Cottage* (☎ *732 8440, 51 Broadway)* is in a renovated building constructed from local rimu. B&B for two is from $70 to $100. *Quartz Lodge* (☎ *732 8383, 78 Sheil St)* is a block from the town centre and does B&B at $40/70 for a single/double.

Dawsons Hotel (☎ *732 8406, 74 Broadway)* and *Reefton Motels* (☎ *732 8574, 11 Smith St)* both have doubles from $50.

Broadway is the best place for cafe food. Try *CCs* (☎ *732 8066)*, *Electric Light Cafe* (☎ *732 8406)* or *Al Fresco* (☎ *732 8513)* with outdoor tables. *Hotel Reefton* (☎ *732 8447)* offers a '$6 roast & 5 veg' from Monday to Saturday.

There is a *Four Square* supermarket at the entrance to town and another small *supermarket* adjacent to the visitor centre.

Day 3: Reefton to Maruia Springs
3½-5 hours, 60.7km

A reasonably short day's ride with one major climb takes you to the thermal resort of Maruia Springs.

The route begins through **Rahu Scenic Reserve**, a delightfully shady beech forest abuzz with insects, birds and only a few trucks hauling coal or timber. An almost imperceptible climb gradually steepens and the valley narrows. The mountains with the high, bald peaks in the distance are the source of the water cascading down through the damp, lush undergrowth.

The 680m **Rahu Saddle** (36km) is reached before a steepish, stepped descent. Ease down from warp speed before the 45km mark or you'll rocket into the busy three way intersection from which **Springs Junction** takes its name. This 'town' consists of a petrol station, a post office (open noon to 12.30 pm weekdays) in a little shed amid a

gravelled lot and *Springs Junction Alpine Inn* (☎ *523 8813)*. It has single/double motel rooms for $56/70 and chalet-style lodge accommodation across the road with lounge, cooking facilities and shared bathroom for $30/50.

Around 3km east is *Lewis Pass Motels* (☎ *523 8813)*, set well back from the road, with rooms from $55/75. A farther 2km east is the entry to Marble Hill *DOC camping and picnic area*.

Maruia Springs
Maruia Springs township is basically the Maruia Springs Thermal Resort. Natural thermal water is pumped into a male/female segregated Japanese bathhouse and outdoor rock pools where you can relax in the hot water.

Places to Stay & Eat The *Maruia Springs Thermal Resort* (☎ *523 8840)* is it. A bed in a dorm here costs $26.50 and tent sites are $5 plus $6.50 per person. There is no kitchen for campers' use but you do have free access to the pools. Hotel rooms cost $105 a double. The resort has a rather pricey *cafe* for snacks and meals.

Day 4: Maruia Springs to Hanmer Springs
4½-7 hours, 78.3km

Even though this is not the longest day of the ride, it is a taxing stage because of the climb up to Lewis Pass and the undulating, often windswept road beyond. There are no services of any kind between start and finish. While the road is not especially busy, quite a high proportion of the traffic is made up of heavy transports that use the route between Christchurch and Nelson.

The climb to **Lewis Pass** begins in earnest as soon as you leave the resort. The grade is not steep – a gain of 320m in 6km – but it is sustained. It should take less than an hour even on a heavily laden bike. Fine alpine scenery awaits at the 907m summit and you stay above 850m for about 3km before dropping sharply past Foleys Stream and the Deer Valley *DOC camping area* (9.5km).

You are soon beside the gravelly bed of Boyle River with bare mountains all around. Pass the outdoor education centre on Magdalen Valley Rd after 22.7km. The road is still trending downwards but has occasional annoying, tiring 20 to 40m rises.

CANTERBURY

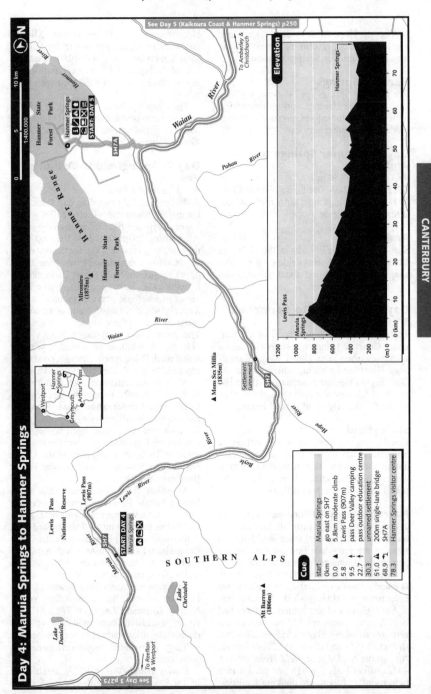

Day 4: Maruia Springs to Hanmer Springs

See Day 3 p275

See Day 5 (Kaikoura Coast & Hanmer Springs) p250

Cue		
start	Maruia Springs	
0km	go east on SH7	
0.0	5.8km moderate climb	◀
5.8	Lewis Pass (907m)	←
9.5	pass Deer Valley camping	
22.7	pass outdoor education centre	◀
30.3	unnamed settlement	
51.0	200m single-lane bridge	◀
68.9	SH7A	⤴
78.3	Hanmer Springs visitor centre	

After the Hope River bridge (41km) there are longer, steeper climbs almost all the way to the Hanmer Springs turn-off.

Hanmer Springs
See Hanmer Springs (pp247-9) in the Kaikoura Coast & Hanmer Springs ride earlier in this chapter for information about accommodation and other services.

Day 5: Hanmer Springs to Amberley
4½-7 hours, 88.9km
See Day 5 (pp249-50) of the Kaikoura Coast & Hanmer Springs ride for a map and description of this ride.

Amberley
See Amberley (pp249-51) in the Kaikoura Coast & Hanmer Springs ride earlier in this chapter for information about accommodation and other services.

Day 6: Amberley to Springfield
5-7 hours, 96.1km
The day's route follows Day 6 of the Kaikoura Coast & Hanmer Springs ride as far as Ashley, then joins Day 1 of the Canterbury Hinterland ride at Ashley Gorge. At Waddington the routes separate – there is a gentle climb westwards to Springfield. Pray the north-westerly wind is not blowing!

Springfield
Considering its size, the small village of Springfield has a good range of accommodation and services that make it a very convenient point to attack Porters Pass. The petrol station is the post office.

Places to Stay & Eat For *camping*, stop off 1.4km before town; turn off Domain Rd (north of SH73). Water, toilets and 50c coin showers are provided. Tent sites are $6 per person; the caretaker drives in to collect fees.

Smylie's Accommodation (☎ 318 4740, ✉ email@smylies.co.nz), on the left as you enter town on SH73, is a YHA hostel in one of Springfield's oldest homes. A dorm bed is $17, twin rooms are $20 per person and self-contained motel units $55 for a double. Breakfast ($5) and dinner ($12) are served. Just up the road, *Springfield Hotel* (☎ 318 4812) offers beds for $18 per person in a twin room and there are cooking facilities.

Hotel rooms are $30 per person. Midday and evening meals are available. *Springfield Store Motel* (☎ 318 4840) on the north side of the highway has a motel room sleeping four at $60 a double ($15 for each extra adult).

The *shop* has basic groceries at a hefty premium and is also a tearoom. Up the road past the petrol station is the attractive *Te Kowai Cottage Cafe*.

Day 7: Springfield to Arthur's Pass
5½-8 hours, 83.6km
A challenging but rewarding day starts with the major Porters Pass climb – 530m gain in 19km – with the final kilometre *very* steep. After losing 250m altitude in the next 9km, the route stays above 500m for the rest of the day. Constant undulations, reaching 800m near Craigieburn State Forest Park, make it a tiring ride. Balancing this, tremendous views of awesome gravelly mountains give a special sense of isolation and of a human's insignificance in these impressive highlands. The final 10km to Arthur's Pass village (740m), all uphill, is on a scenic, winding forest road. Bring lunch – there is no shop of any kind before Bealey Hotel (72.9km).

After descending to Lake Lyndon the road levels briefly, then continues down to **Castle Hill Conservation Area**. Here, 30 million-year-old limestone outcrops, popular with climbers, have been sculpted by erosion and groundwater weathering. Set aside in 1976, this was part of the Castle Hill Sheep Station owned by the Porter Brothers from 1858.

At 36km from Springfield, the Cave Stream Scenic Reserve, a picnic area with toilets, is a convenient place for a break. Four kilometres later is a turn-off signposted to an 'Enviromental (sic) Education Centre', then **Craigieburn Recreation Area** with more picnic facilities, plus camp sites, toilets, shelters and walking trails in the forest park.

Undulations ease where beautiful Lake Pearson mirrors the surrounding peaks. Nearby, *Grasmere Lodge* (☎ 318 8407), offering 'exclusive accommodation' ($900 a double!) by prior reservation, nestles beneath hulking, crenellated mountains streaming with scree.

Bealey Hotel (☎ 318 9277), established in 1865, is 10.7km south-east of Arthur's

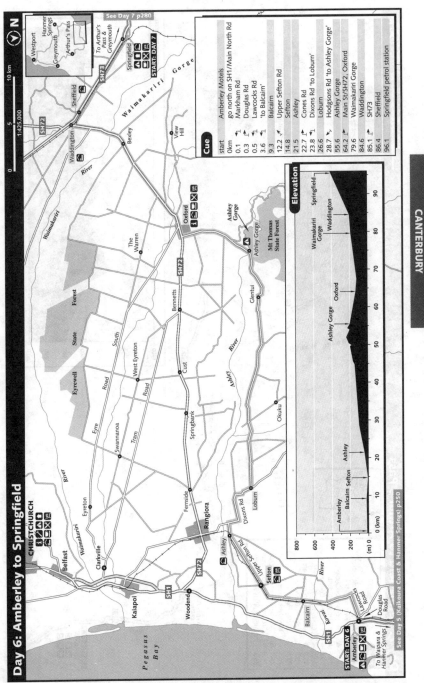

Day 6: Amberley to Springfield

CANTERBURY

Cue	
start	Amberley Motels
0km	go north on SH1/Main North Rd
0.1	Markham Rd
0.3	Douglas Rd
0.5	Lawcocks Rd
3.6	'to Balcairn'
9.3	Balcairn
12.2	Upper Sefton Rd
14.8	Sefton
21.5	Ashley
22.7	Cones Rd
23.8	Dixons Rd 'to Loburn'
26.6	Loburn
28.7	Hodgsons Rd 'to Ashley Gorge'
55.6	Ashley Gorge
64.2	Main St/SH72, Oxford
79.6	Waimakariri Gorge
84.6	Waddington
85.1	SH73
86.4	Sheffield
96.1	Springfield petrol station

Elevation

See Day 5 (Kaikoura Coast & Hanmer Springs) p250

CANTERBURY

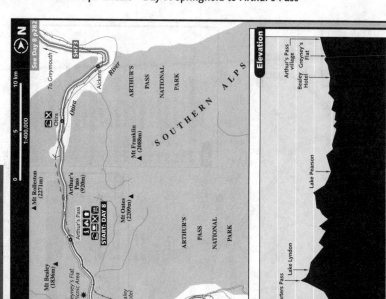

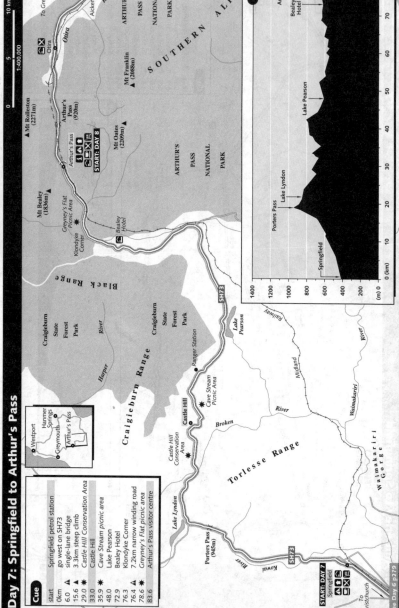

Day 7: Springfield to Arthur's Pass

Cue		
start		Springfield petrol station
0km	▲	go west on SH73
6.0	▲	single-lane bridge
15.6	▲	3.3km steep climb
29.0	✳	Castle Hill Conservation Area
33.0	▲	Castle Hill
35.9	✳	Cave Stream picnic area
48.0		Lake Pearson
72.9		Bealey Hotel
76.3		Klondyke Corner
76.4	▲	7.2km narrow winding road
78.6	✳	Greyney's Flat picnic area
83.6		Arthur's Pass visitor centre

Elevation

See Day 8 p.282

See Day 6 p.279

Pass village and has motel units for $75 a double and beds in a 'budget lodge' for $18 per person. Bistro meals are available. In 1993 a rumour, 'confirmed' by some German tourists, spread around the country that a live moa had been seen here. Today the moa still stands stonily on the hill adjacent to the hotel.

Eight kilometres before Arthur's Pass village is Klondyke Corner *DOC camping ground* with toilets, a shelter shed and hordes of sandflies. Tent camping is free, the right price. *Greyney's Flat*, 2km farther west, has similar facilities.

The following section of narrow road though quite nice as it climbs through magnificent beech forest has a bad traffic accident record. Be particularly careful when traffic approaches from both directions at once.

Arthur's Pass

The village (740m) is in a canyon-like valley beneath the towering mountains of Arthur's Pass National Park, 4km from the top of the pass.

Information The visitor centre (☎ 318 9211) is open from 8 am to 5 pm daily. It has information on all the park walks and displays of historical and environmental interest inside its spacious building. The train station is just south of the visitor centre, on the right as you ride into town.

Things to See & Do Activities in the area are centred on **walking** in the national park. One of the must-see sights is the 130m-high **Devils Punchbowl Falls**, a one hour return walk from the village. (You'll see a glimpse of it on the right as you cycle out of town.) Steep tracks from town take you to high peaks for 360° views. Get the latest weather information from the visitor centre and register there if you are doing any walks; remember to also sign in again when you return. In January there is a program of **guided walks**, evening **talks** and **slide shows**.

Places to Stay & Eat Accommodation is in heavy demand from November to March, so book well ahead or arrive early if you're camping. Sites at the basic *public shelter* cost $3 per person. There is running water that must be treated, and a flush toilet. More salubrious camping is possible at the YHA and Mountain House.

The *YHA Hostel* (☎ 318 9230) in the village centre has beds at $15 per night or $36 for a double room. Tent sites are $8 per person. Opposite, the popular *Mountain House backpackers* (☎ 318 9258) has shared rooms and dorms for $16 per person. Tent sites are $9 per person. Campers can use the kitchen, lounge, bathroom and the washing machine. From May to September you can stay three nights for the price of two.

At the southern end of the village is *Snowgrass Cabin* (☎ 318 9238). Sleeping four, it is fully self-contained and costs $60 for two plus $8 for each extra adult. A couple of hundred metres on, the *Alpine Motel* (☎ 318 9233) has doubles at $70 and studio rooms from $65, plus a family unit that sleeps six for $78 a double. The *Chalet* (☎ 318 9236) at the northern end of town offers B&B for $100.

You can eat at the *Arthur's Pass Store & Tearoom* or in the *Chalet Restaurant* (☎ 318 9236), which has a cheaper coffee bar beyond its restaurant area. *Oscar's Haus* has a cafe and bar that is the social focus of the town.

Day 8: Arthur's Pass to Greymouth
5-8½ hours, 104km

Lots of downhill thrills are in store early in the day, then the terrain is flat with a few minor undulations along the Lake Brunner Tourist Drive. The first 4km to the 920m pass are not too tough, especially as you are fresh. When the viaduct bypassing the unstable road route (built in 1865) is complete at **Otira Gorge**, it will be all downhill from the pass.

Take your time; there is much to see and you have put in a lot of effort to get here. There are rushing rivers to watch, inquisitive keas at Otira Gorge, lookouts, *tearooms* at Otira and accommodation and meals at the *Otira Hotel*.

Be careful on the steep downhill – 550m in 9km on a narrow, twisting road with more than enough traffic.

At Kellys Creek a *DOC camping ground* has a shelter shed and toilets. The long pedestrian bridge across the river 3km farther on is a **memorial** to Brian Morrison, one of three boys drowned while crossing the flooded stream in 1966.

The next settlement, **Jacksons**, a whistle-stop on the transalpine railway, has a *pub*

CANTERBURY

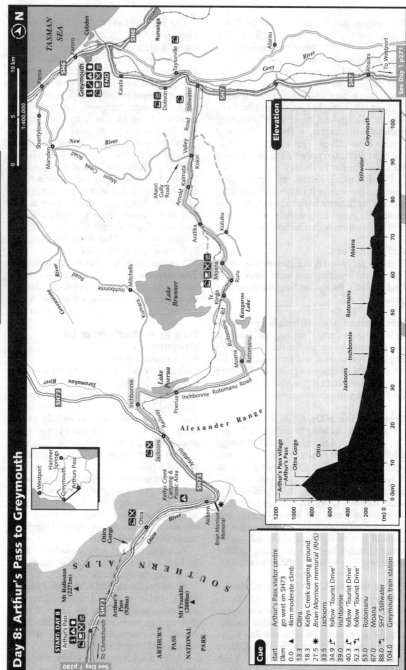

Day 8: Arthur's Pass to Greymouth

Cue		
start		Arthur's Pass visitor centre
0km	◀	go west on SH73
0.0	◀	4km moderate climb
13.3		Otira
18.3	✳	Kellys Creek camping ground
21.5		Brian Morrison memorial (RHS)
33.5		Jacksons
34.9	↰	follow 'Tourist Drive'
39.0		Inchbonnie
40.3	↱	follow 'Tourist Drive'
52.3	↰	follow 'Tourist Drive'
53.0		Rotomanu
67.0		Moana
88.0	↰	SH7, Stillwater
104.0		Greymouth train station

serving food and drinks and *Mountain View Cabins*, fully self-contained budget accommodation. Just over 1km on is the start of the Lake Brunner Tourist Drive that meanders along a generally level valley floor through meadows and beside little lakes.

Moana, the next centre with any services, has an expensive *cafe* overlooking Lake Brunner, a *hotel* advertising 'Cyclists special, $10 beds', and *Lake Brunner Motor Camp* (☎ 738 0600) with a petrol station and shop, at the top of a hill on the way out. A little further on is the **Moana Zoo, Kiwi House & Conservation Park**, which operates a captive breeding program for the endangered kiwi. *Lake Brunner Country Motels* (☎ 738 0144) are adjacent.

There are no more services until the outskirts of Greymouth. The road gets busier, passing through industrial townships like Stillwater, which has only a *pub*. The **Brunner Mine site**, scene of NZ's worst mining disaster, is visible between Stillwater and Greymouth.

Banks Peninsula Circuit

Duration	4 days
Distance	168.4km
Difficulty	hard
Start/End	Christchurch

This beautiful but *very* demanding hilly tour will test your stamina at climbing and skill at descending on gravel. It is not recommended as a first loaded tour, but is best left until late or last in an extended tour of the South Island (or of the whole country) when you have the necessary fitness. Daily distances are short because of the severe terrain. Highlights include the often cloud-shrouded Summit Rds, extinct volcanoes, spectacular views and exciting descents.

Travelling some of the most scenic roads in Canterbury involves repeated gain and loss of altitude, plus a challenging stretch of gravel road on the outward leg. Most of the roads carry very little traffic. Allow at least one full day for sightseeing in Akaroa.

The ride takes in Lyttelton, the South Island's main port, and Akaroa, Canterbury's oldest settlements and one of its most fascinating with its tangible French atmosphere. Akaroa Harbour is the place to take a cruise

to see Hector's dolphins (the world's smallest dolphin species) at play.

Much of the route is exposed to sun and wind, which can add to the degree of difficulty, and clean drinking water on the road is hard to come by.

HISTORY

The Banks Peninsula was called by the Maori Pataka o Rakaihautu (Rakaihautu's Great Storehouse), because of its importance to them as the southernmost location for cultivation of *kumara* (Polynesian sweet potato).

The return journey follows the route of a 200km, two day road race formerly held from Christchurch to Akaroa and back. It was won in 1937 by William Hall, father-in-law of the Akaroa visitor centre's manager, Beth Hall. In those days all the roads were gravel and riders had to carry their own repair equipment.

The Akaroa race (now known as Le Race) was revived in March 1999 with a 100km road and mountain bike event open to the public, from Christchurch into and through the Port Hills and Banks Peninsula on the Summit Rds. It looks set to be an annual event. Contact Events Co (☎ 377 7704), PO Box 28089, Christchurch, for entry details or more information.

PLANNING
When to Ride

The ride is possible most of the year, although the Summit Rds are bleak, windswept and can be snow-covered in winter. Early autumn is recommended for settled weather. It can be hot on the exposed slopes of the Summit Rd in mid-summer.

Akaroa's average temperatures are reasonably mild: 17°C in summer and 8°C in winter. The area gets three to four frosts on average each winter. Rainfall averages 990mm per annum, fairly evenly spread across the seasons.

Maps & Books

Akaroa: A Short History, by Steve Lowndes, gives a local's fascinating insight into this unique NZ town and is available at the visitor centre for $14.95.

AA's 1:350,000 *Canterbury Map*, available free to motoring association members at 210 Hereford St, Christchurch, covers the route adequately, but better detail is shown on the Land Information series 1:250,000 map entitled *Christchurch*.

GETTING TO/FROM THE RIDE
Akaroa
Bus The Akaroa Shuttle (☎ 0800 500 929) operates between Akaroa and Christchurch, departing from the Akaroa visitor centre daily at 8.30 am, 2.15 and 4.30 pm from December to March, at 8.30 am and 4 pm in November and April, and on a reduced schedule the rest of the year. The fare for the 1½ hour trip is $15 per person ($25 return) and $3 per bicycle, space permitting.

THE RIDE
Day 1: Christchurch to Pigeon Bay
3-6 hours, 47.7km

This adventurous day's ride uses spectacular but isolated roads on the Banks Peninsula. Self sufficiency is essential if riding the full distance to Pigeon Bay. There is nowhere to get food after Diamond Harbour or reliable water after Purau. Indoor accommodation options are also nonexistent after Purau Motor Camp (22.2km), which has cabins. The only place to stay at Pigeon Bay is the very basic DOC camping ground, so a tent is an asset.

After a flat ride from the centre of Christchurch to the Avon estuary there is a steep 5.5km climb to Summit Rd in the Port Hills. The views make the effort worthwhile, as does the subsequent descent to Lyttelton via Evans Pass. **Lyttelton** is your last chance to buy anything you still need for the trip. There is a good *bakery* and a *supermarket* in London St, straight ahead from the junction of Sumner Rd and Oxford St (on entering town).

Cross Lyttelton Harbour by scheduled ferry; the scenic 15 minute trip costs $3.60 per person plus $1 per bicycle. It's best to load and unload your own bike – strap it to the railing on the ferry's roof behind the exhaust funnel (while holding your breath). Don't leave it to the captain to tie it for you even if he says he will; the consequences of it going overboard don't bear thinking about! Convenient ferry departures from Lyttelton to Diamond Harbour are 9.30 and 11 am on weekdays and 10.30 am and 12.30 pm on summer weekends and public holidays. Phone Lyttelton Harbour Cruises Ltd (☎ 328 8368) for other departure times. Services run subject to weather and harbour conditions.

Diamond Harbour has only a small *general store* near the top of the climb from the wharf. Just west of Diamond Harbour is the *Bergli B&B* (☎ 329 9118), which offers backpacker accommodation at $14 per person, a $40 unit suitable for a family, or B&B at $45/70 for a single/double.

Follow the signs to **Purau**, where the *motor camp* (☎ 329 4702) has tent sites for $9 per person and cabins from $40 to $55 for two.

For those with the recommended camping equipment and the energy to continue, there is waterfront *DOC camping* at Pigeon Bay, about 25km away (13km unsealed up and down a major hill). Facilities are poor – only toilets and water that has to be boiled before drinking. The site fee is $7.

Day 2: Pigeon Bay to Akaroa
2-2½ hours, 22.6km

From Pigeon Bay there is another long climb to the Summit Rd, from sea level to 370m in 7km. Akaroa Harbour, NZ's first marine mammal sanctuary, is a spectacular sight from this junction.

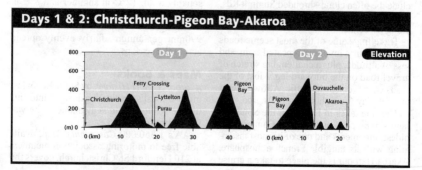

Days 1 & 2: Christchurch-Pigeon Bay-Akaroa

After a thrilling descent to SH75, 1.5km west of Duvauchelle, the final 10km in Akaroa is on undulating, rather than mountainous roads. (The earlier in the day you arrive, the less traffic you will encounter on the busy highway.)

Akaroa

The main town on the Banks Peninsula, Akaroa (population 1000) is surrounded by high hills, the eroded summits of a giant volcanic crater. The volcano may once have risen as much as 3000m above sea level, but over millions of years it has sunk and the sea has flooded part of the crater to form a deep sheltered bay, Akaroa Harbour (Akaroa literally means 'long harbour' in Maori). The town sits on the edge of the bay, 8km from the ocean.

To commemorate the town's origins, many street names were converted to French by the council in 1968 (see History at the beginning of this chapter).

Information The Akaroa visitor centre (☎/fax 304 8600), open from 10 am to 5 pm daily, is in the post office building on the corner of Rues Lavaud and Balguerie. The petrol station has limited bicycle spares and repair equipment.

Things to See & Do The visitor centre has a free brochure, *Akaroa Historic Village Walk*, which will guide you on a 1½ to 2 hour tour of the township's characterful wooden **buildings** and **churches**. This can be extended to take in the **Britomart memorial** on Greens Point, which commemorates the raising of the British flag six days before the arrival of the French, and a **walk** through the native Garden of Tane. The visitor centre can provide details of other **walks** – such as that to the Onawe Peninsula, the ancient heart of the volcano – as well as brochures on visits to historic homes and special gardens in Akaroa.

The **Akaroa Museum** (☎ 304 7614), on Rue Lavaud, has a 15 minute audiovisual show on the history of the Banks Peninsula and displays colonial memorabilia. **Langlois-Eteveneaux Cottage**, one of the oldest houses in NZ and partly fabricated in France, is in the museum complex.

A great way to see the peninsula's volcanic features is on a **harbour cruise** (☎ 304 7641).

These depart daily from the Main Wharf. You may see the endangered Hector's dolphin, white-flippered penguins and a wide range of birdlife in volcanic caves. Dolphin Experience (☎/fax 304 7866), 61 Beach Rd, offers three-hour trips to swim with the **dolphins**. If **fishing** is your thing, phone Bluefin Charters (☎ 304 7866) for a range of trips including **diving**.

Guided or supported multi-day **walks** are also available. The Southern Bays Track (☎/fax 329 0007) is three days and two nights from the coast at Lake Forsyth to Okuti Valley Scenic Reserve. The 35km (two or four day) Banks Peninsula Track takes you from Onuku, south of Akaroa, to Mt Vernon Lodge around the spectacular volcanic coastline. Bookings (☎ 304 7612) are essential.

Bayline Services (☎ 304 7207), 108 Rue Jolie, runs the fascinating 110km **Eastern Bays Scenic Mail Run**. This 110km rural delivery service departs from the visitor centre at 8.20 am from Monday to Saturday taking mail, newspapers, supplies and up to eight passengers to the remote settlements on the peninsula, with photo stops and commentary. It costs $20, returning to Akaroa at 1 pm. The company's three hour Harbour and Inner Bays Scenic Drive takes in the Barrys Bay cheese factory, French Farm winery, Wainui and Mt Bossu, also for $20.

Places to Stay & Eat The *Akaroa Holiday Park* (☎ 304 7471), off Old Coach Rd at the crest of the hill before town, has tent sites for $18, on-site caravans for $32, cabins from $42 and flats from $56; all prices are for two. *Chez la Mer* (☎ 304 7024) on Rue Lavaud in a historic garden cottage is the central backpacker hostel. Dorm beds are $16 per person and singles/doubles are from $22/36. *Lavender Hill B&B* (☎ 304 7082, 1 Lighthouse Rd) charges $60/80. *La Rive Motel* (☎ 304 7651, 1 Rue Lavaud) offers rooms at $80 per double. Six kilometres south of town beside the bay is the popular *Onuku Farm Hostel* (☎ 304 7612), a 340 hectare sheep farm with in-house accommodation ($15), a summer hut ($10) or tent sites ($8). Kayaks and bikes are available for guests' use. *Mt Vernon Lodge* (☎ 304 7180), 2km from town on Rue Balguerie, has budget accommodation from $15 per night and chalets and cabins from $70. The visitor centre has details of other accommodation.

CANTERBURY

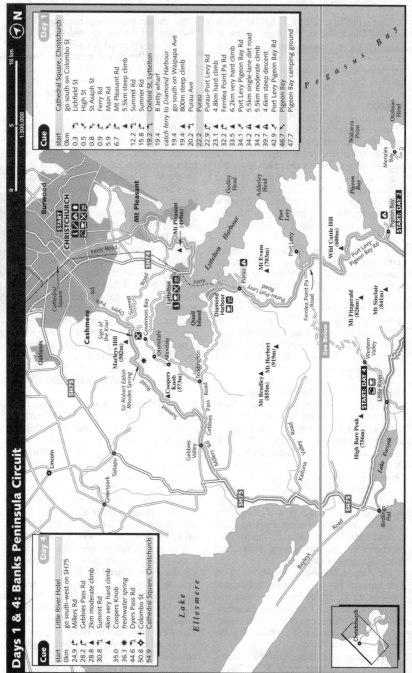

Days 1 & 4: Banks Peninsula Circuit

CANTERBURY

Day 1

Cue	
start	Cathedral Square, Christchurch
0km	go south on Colombo St
0.3	Lichfield St
0.5	High St
0.8	St Asaph St
0.9	Ferry Rd
5.9	Main Rd
6.7	Mt Pleasant Rd
12.2	5.5km steep climb
15.8	Summit Rd
19.2	Sumner Rd
19.4	Oxford St, Lyttelton
19.4	B Jetty wharf
	catch ferry to Diamond Harbour
19.4	go south on Waipapa Ave
20.2	800m steep climb
20.2	Purau Ave
22.2	Purau
22.9	Purau–Port Levy Rd
23.1	4.8km hard climb
32.2	Fernlea Point Pa Rd
33.5	6.2km very hard climb
34.1	Port Levy Pigeon Bay Rd
34.2	5.5km single-lane dirt road
34.2	5.5km moderate climb
39.7	4.6km steep descent
42.9	Port Levy Pigeon Bay Rd
46.7	Pigeon Bay
47.7	Pigeon Bay camping ground

Day 4

Cue	
start	Little River Hotel
0km	go south-west on SH75
24.9	Millers Rd
28.2	Gebbies Pass Rd
28.8	2km moderate climb
30.8	Summit Rd
	4km very hard climb
35.0	Coopers Knob
36.3	freshwater spring
44.6	Dyers Pass Rd
50.8	Colombo St
54.9	Cathedral Square, Christchurch

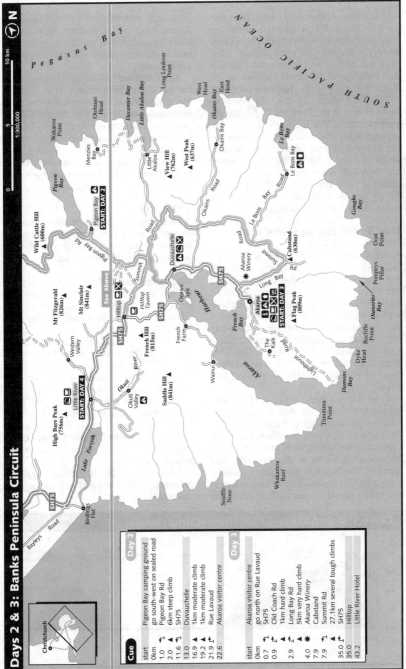

Days 2 & 3: Banks Peninsula Circuit

CANTERBURY

Christchurch

N 1:300,000
0 5 10 km

Cue

Day 2

	km		
start			Pigeon Bay camping ground
0km	⌐		go south-west on sealed road
1.0	⌐	◄	Pigeon Bay Rd
2.0			6km steep climb
11.6	⌐		SH75
13.0			Duvauchelle
16.9		◄	1km moderate climb
19.2		◄	1km moderate climb
21.9	⌐		Rue Lavaud
22.6			Akaroa visitor centre

Day 3

	km		
start			Akaroa visitor centre
0km			go north on Rue Lavaud
0.7	⌐	⌐	SH75
0.9	⌐	◄	Old Coach Rd
			1km hard climb
2.9	⌐	◄	Long Bay Rd
			5km very hard climb
4.0		✶	Akaroa Winery
7.9	⌐	◄	Cabstand
7.9	⌐		Summit Rd
			27.1km several tough climbs
35.0	⌐		SH75
35.0			Hilltop
43.2			Little River Hotel

Pegasus Bay

SOUTH PACIFIC OCEAN

Wild Cattle Hill (600m) ▲

Mt Fitzgerald (826m) ▲

Mt Sinclair (841m) ▲

High Bare Peak (756m) ▲

Lake Forsyth

Birdlings Flat

Bayleys Road

SH75

Western Valley

Little River

START: DAY 4

Okuti River

Okuti Valley

French Hill (815m) ▲

Saddle Hill (841m) ▲

Wainui

Akaroa Harbour

The Kaik

Lighthouse Road

Reclffe Point

Dyke Head

Damons Bay

Timutimu Point

Whakamoa Reef

Snuffle Nose

French Farm

French Bay

Akaroa

START: DAY 3

▲ Flag Peak (809m)

Long Bay

Akaroa Winery ✶

Summit Rd

Cabstand (630m)

Goughs Bay

Goat Point

Pompeys Pillar

Otanerito Bay

Le Bons Bay

Le Bons Bay Road

West Peak (637m) ▲

Okains Bay

Okains Bay Road

View Hill (762m) ▲

Little Akaloa

Little Akaloa Bay

Decanter Bay

Long Lookout Point

West Head

East Head

Wakaroa Point

Menzies Bay

Pigeon Bay

Pigeon Bay Road

START: DAY 2

Duvauchelle

Hilltop Tavern

Hilltop

SH75

Summit Road

See Above

Otohuao Head

A selection of the more expensive eateries is on Beach Rd, 500m south of the visitor centre near the main wharf. The *Akaroa Bakery* is the place for good pastries, filled rolls and coffee, or you can eat excellent fish and chips at the tables overlooking the harbour in front of the *Akaroa Fish Shop*.

For good value, try the $10 breakfast (until 11 am) at the *Turenne Cafe*, near the visitor centre on Rue Balguerie. You can also get reasonably priced lunches here while you log on to the Internet. Nearby is the licensed *Dolphin Cafe & Bar* (☎ 304 7658), which has tasty fish and chip and salad or steak dishes starting from around $10. *C'est La Vie* (☎ 304 7314, 33 Rue Lavaud) is a vegetarian eatery with a BYO licence.

Day 3: Akaroa to Little River

3½-6 hours, 43.2km

Stunning scenery is the order of the day's ride with panoramic views over the Banks Peninsula from both sides of the Summit Rd. Ocean bays appear to the north-west while the long, thin inlet of Akaroa Harbour with its backdrop of brown hills dominates the view to the south-east. The price to pay for such scenic delight is a major climb from sea level to about 630m in just over 6km, followed by continuing undulations most of the way to Hilltop above Little River.

From Akaroa there is first a 1km climb on the Old Coach Rd then a farther 5km very steeply on Long Bay Rd to Summit Rd. On the way, you pass the **Akaroa Winery**, open daily for tastings and tours, and there are widening views of the peninsula and harbour. The Summit Rd appears tantalisingly close for some time as it snakes across the range ahead. Clouds often graze the

ridge tops, with wisps of vapour descending to near road level. Columnar basalt formations break through the bush, giving the peaks an untidy hairstyle like dreadlocks gone wrong.

The **Cabstand** (630m), as the junction at the top of the climb from Akaroa is called, has a fine view to Goughs Bay with its prominent headlands. The Summit Rd to your left continues to climb briefly but settles into a rolling routine as it climbs along the crater rim to join SH75 at Hilltop. Here is your first opportunity since Akaroa to buy refreshments. The *Hilltop Tavern* offers snacks but not accommodation.

Little River

A straggling village, Little River is at the bottom of an exciting 6km downhill run. It is a convenient place to break your journey and refresh for the hills ahead.

Places to Stay & Eat Left off SH75 and 4.3km into the Okuti Valley, following sings first along Kinlock Rd then left onto Okuti Valley Rd, is *Birdlands Holiday Park* (☎ 325 1141). Tent sites here are $21 for two with 50c metered showers. Two cabins are also available, sleeping up to six at $20 per adult. Campers have free entry to the bird 'sanctuary'. If you love your birds imprisoned, you'll be in heaven here.

The *Little River Hotel* (☎ 325 1007) is at the southern end of town on SH75. It offers accommodation and meals. Before the town is *Jasmine Cottage Organic Garden Cabin Stay* (☎ 325 1137), an attractive house with beautiful gardens.

Food options are limited to a *bakery*, *takeaway*, *cafe* and a *pub*, all on the main street (SH75).

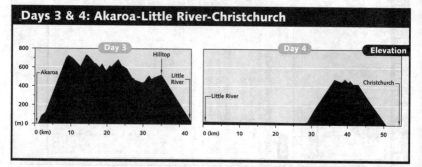

Days 3 & 4: Akaroa-Little River-Christchurch

Day 4: Little River to Christchurch

4-7½ hours, 54.9km

From Little River the route continues for 25km on the flat, exposed and relatively busy main road, passing **Lakes Forsyth** and **Ellesmere**, the latter with its introduced Australian black swans and other waterbirds. The only shop all the way to the restaurant at Dyers Pass is Kaituna Orchard's *fruit & vegetable stall*, which also sells ice creams and drinks.

There's a moderate hill after 30km and after Gebbies Pass begins the hard 4km climb towards Coopers Knob. The last 1.5km is a solid, bottom-gear grind, but with ever-improving views.

The **Sir Robert Eaton Rhodes Spring** (36.3km) was donated by the said gentleman in 1914, commemorated by a 'Summit Road Society' marker.

From the spring, it's pretty much downhill or flat – well, there might be a couple of short ups here and there – back to Christchurch, but don't rush. Diversions are many – views from lookouts are breathtaking and you can take short walks through remnant forest, visit the **visitor centre** in Victoria Park or pause at the *Sign of the Kiwi* restaurant near Dyers Pass.

From Dyers Pass it's a fun descent to the roundabout at the southern end of Colombo St, then a straight, flat run back into the heart of Christchurch.

CANTERBURY

Otago & Southland

Covering almost one-third of the South Island, Otago and Southland form a very diverse area. The open spaces of sparsely settled, hilly and dry central Otago contrast the lush, level agricultural areas around Invercargill in the south and the forested Catlins coast to the east. Its history steeped in gold, the region's economy is now driven by hydroelectricity generated from damming mighty rivers like the Clutha and from the 'black gold' of its collieries.

Southland's main centre is Invercargill, the southernmost city in New Zealand and the gateway to Stewart Island, the Catlins and Fiordland. The second largest city on the South Island, Dunedin is also the main centre of Otago.

Visiting cyclists can experience lively Queenstown and Wanaka with their adventure activities, quaint old gold towns like Naseby and Arrowtown and the vibrant university city of Dunedin, where Otago Peninsula provides a backyard playground. There's also the fascinating Taieri Gorge scenic train journey and the Central Otago Rail Trail to enjoy.

Main access routes to the region are SH1 from Christchurch in the north and SH6 from the west coast via challenging, scenic Haast Pass. The Southern Scenic Route is a popular tourist link that travels around the coast from Dunedin to Invercargill then turns inland to Te Anau, Milford Sound and Queenstown.

Distances between urban centres and services in this part of the South Island can be large, sometimes involving difficult terrain and gravel roads, especially in the Catlins. Everywhere, spectacular scenery rewards a cyclist's efforts.

HISTORY

The region's early Maori history was particularly bloody, with a three-way feud between Otago Peninsula tribes at the end of the 18th century. Disease raged after European sealers and whalers began operating until, by 1848, the Maori population had fallen to a very low level. European settlers arrived at Port Chalmers in March 1848 to found a Presbyterian settlement.

Gold rushes, which began with discoveries about 120km inland in 1861, shaped the early European history of Otago. It became the richest province in the colony and the powerhouse of its economy. Gold wealth produced splendid public buildings in Dunedin, now one of the best preserved Victorian and Edwardian cities in the southern hemisphere. The University of Otago, NZ's first, was established in Dunedin in 1869.

Bluff, south of Invercargill, claims the title of oldest European town in NZ – there has been a settlement there continuously since 1824.

NATURAL HISTORY

Oamaru, the Otago Peninsula and the Catlins are all renowned wildlife areas featuring little blue penguins, yellow-eyed penguins, albatross and seal colonies, as well as pods of dolphins. The Marine Aquarium at Portobello gives insight into the complex marine life found on the coast and the Otago Peninsula. White-fronted terns can also be seen in the area, but you'll need to be lucky to see the rare Stewart Island cormorant.

Harrier hawks are a common sight in the skies of the interior, while the spotted skink may be seen basking on sun-warmed rocks.

One of the larger native lizards, it is unique to the South Island.

Introduced varieties are now virtually the only trees in the interior and, in autumn, deciduous species provide colourful displays.

CLIMATE

Otago and Southland experience a range of climates, from temperate coastal to continental in the interior. Central Otago suffers climatic extremes, with the highest summer temperatures and lowest winter temperatures in NZ; the town of Ophir has the country's highest annual temperature range, 55°C. One winter the temperature in Ophir plummeted to a national record of -22°C. In winter ponds and dams on the Maniototo

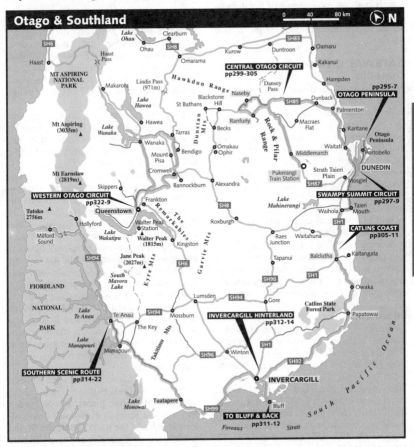

Plain freeze, which permits ice skating and the game of curling. Snow is possible at higher elevations at any time.

Otago's clear blue skies and the increasingly large atmospheric ozone 'hole' combine to allow intense solar ultra-violet radiation to reach the ground. Thunderstorms are a common feature of the Strath Taieri plain and huge storm clouds, locally dubbed the 'Taieri Pet', tower over the Rock & Pillar Range.

The prevailing wind is from the west, with July and August the least windy months.

While central and north Otago are among the driest regions in NZ, with average rainfalls frequently less than 600mm, Fiordland, on the west coast, is extremely wet. It rains on more than half the days of the year in Milford Sound, which receives an average annual rainfall of more than 6500mm.

GATEWAY CITIES
Dunedin

At the head of fiord-like Otago Harbour, Dunedin's position attracted Maori settlers more than 400 years ago. Today it is home to 120,000 people, making it the South Island's second city. The influence of its original Scottish settlers is still strong – *Dun Edin* is Celtic for Edinburgh. Robbie Burns' statue stands in the city centre and bagpipes herald traditional haggis ceremonies where his poetry is recited. Whisky is produced at the local Wilson's distillery. Scottish Week, in mid-March, is when the city celebrates its founders' origins.

Soaring cathedral spires, the much photographed Flemish Renaissance-style train station, a private 'castle', heritage university buildings and a neo-gothic convent are among the city's architectural highlights.

Information The visitor centre (☎ 474 3300, fax 474 3311, ✆ visitor.centre@dcc .govt.nz) is in the town hall at 48 The Octagon, in the centre of the city. It's open daily from 8.30 am to 5 pm weekdays and 9 am to 5 pm on weekends, and operates extended hours over summer. You can book tours, travel (with InterCity, Tranz Rail and on the Interislander ferry) and accommodation here. *Focus on Dunedin* is a useful free guide.

DOC (☎ 477 0677) has a shop at 77 Lower Stuart St.

Lower Stuart St is the city's bike shop hub. Cycle Surgery (☎ 477 7473, fax 477 6129), at No 67, is a busy but friendly place to hire mountain bikes for the various nearby trails. Hire costs range from $25/day for a rigid bike, $30 for front suspension models and slightly more for dual suspension. In the next block towards The Octagon is Brown's Avanti Cycle Centre (☎ 477 7259), at No 109. Opposite Cycle Surgery is R&R Sport (☎ 474 1211), which has a wide range of sporting equipment and mountain bikes.

Across town in Filleul St, the department store Smiths City (☎ 479 2514) has a bicycle section which offers cycle service as well as sales.

Things to See & Do Weekday tours of **Wilson's Whisky Distillery**, on George St, can be booked at the visitor centre. **Speight's Brewery** (☎ 477 9480), 200 Rattray St, is one of the smallest in NZ. Tours run Monday to Thursday. The boutique **Emerson's Brewery** (☎ 477 1812), 4 Grange St, also has tours.

Dunedin has several interesting museums. **Otago Museum**, on the corner of Great King and Union Sts (free entry), has excellent displays on Maori and Pacific culture. It also features NZ's natural history with exhibits ranging from penguins to the extinct moa. An interactive Discovery World exhibit (admission fee) will entertain children. The **Settlers Museum**, 31 Queens Gardens, displays Otago's social history from the Maori to Scottish pioneers, gold miners and latter day business entrepreneurs. **Dunedin Public Art Gallery**, in The Octagon, is NZ's oldest and features works of many famous painters. The University of Otago welcomes visitors to its **Geology Museum** (☎ 479 1100), which has displays of minerals and fossils, and the **Hocken Library**, which has an extensive collection of books, manuscripts, paintings and photographs relating to NZ and the Pacific.

Dunedin's Botanic Garden, open daily on the slopes of Signal Hill to the north of the city, features native plants, a rock garden and a world renowned rhododendron collection. Also to the north is **Baldwin St**, the world's steepest street (see 'The Ultimate Challenge' boxed text).

The Ultimate Challenge

Dunedin boasts the world's steepest street, Baldwin St. With a maximum gradient of 1:1.266, this short road has much in common with a parabola – it gets steeper the higher you go. Test your strength riding up, and your brakes *before* you try descending.

Baldwin St is on the way into town on the Central Otago Circuit. To reach it from town, ride 2km along Great King St from the city and veer right along North Rd for 1km – it's on your right. A souvenir shop nearby on North Rd sells the official T-shirt ($20).

Otago Harbour Cruises (☎ 477 4276) runs boat trips from Rattray St wharf, visiting fur seal, shag and gull colonies, and the albatross colony at Taiaroa Head.

A bike provides convenient transport to many of the **walks** around the charming city, with its features like historic staircases, and the peninsula's hills, stone walls, secluded beaches, tidal inlets and volcanic landforms. Overlooking the city, Mt Cargill (676m; with the TV tower) and Signal Hill (393m), both a few kilometres to the northeast, are popular **lookouts**. As is Flagstaff (668m), on Pineapple Walk to the northwest (see the Swampy Summit Circuit map on p298). To access the Mt Cargill walk, cycle up the North East Valley and through Normanby to Bethunes Gully. A side track leads to **The Organ Pipes**, a stratified basalt columnar formation. The walkways and tracks are well signposted. Details are available from the visitor centre.

Places to Stay Conveniently and attractively located, *Leith Valley Touring Park* (☎ 467 9936, 103 Malvern St) is just north of the city centre. Tent sites are $9 and on-site vans $30 per person, while tourist flats are $55 for two. Several walks start from the gate. Other camping grounds are further from the action. *Tahuna Motor Park* (☎ 455 4690) is near the beach at St Kilda, giving easy access to the Otago Peninsula. Tent sites are $18 and cabins start from $32; prices for two.

Elm Lodge (☎ 474 1872, 74 Elm Row) has doubles and twins from $17 per person and dorm beds from $14. The YHA-associate

Stafford Gables (☎ 474 1919, 71 Stafford St) has beds for $16 per person.

There are several B&Bs in central Dunedin. *Castlewood* (☎ 477 0526, 240 York Place) has singles/doubles from $60/80. *Magnolia House* (☎ 467 5999; 18 Grendon St, Maori Hill) is 2km out of town in a house built in 1910 and in a native bush setting. It charges $55/80.

Relatively cheap hotels include the small *Statesman* (☎ 477 8411, 91 St Andrew St), which has rooms from $40/70, including breakfast; and the central *Law Courts Hotel* (☎ 477 8036, 65 Stewart St), with en suite rooms from $50/75.

Several convenient motels line Dunedin's main drag, George St. The *Allan Court Motel* (☎ 477 7526, 590 George St), *Alcala Motor Lodge* (☎ 477 9073, cnr George & David Sts), and *Farry's Motel* (☎ 477 9333, 575 George St), all charge between $76 and $100 a double. *Garden Motel* (☎ 477 9333, 958 George St) is cheaper with rooms from $60 a double.

Places to Eat Lunch time *sandwich places* cluster around Moray Place and along George St. *Governors* (438 George St) is popular with students for its low prices and is open from early morning to late at night.

Log on at *Arc Internet Cafe & Bar* (135 High St), which is popular with backpackers and musos for its good coffee, meals, entertainment and free Internet access. The *119 Coffee Shop* (119 Stuart St) serves all-day breakfasts, flavoursome soups and sandwiches.

For good value pub food, try the *Albert Arms Tavern* (cnr George & London Sts) and the *Captain Cook Hotel* (cnr Albany & Great King Sts).

The licensed *A Cow Called Berta* (☎ 477 2993, 199 Stuart St), in a Victorian terrace house, serves Swiss country-style cuisine (open from 6 pm). *High Tide Waterfront Restaurant* (☎ 477 9784, 29 Kitchener St) has views of the harbour and a menu emphasising local seafood.

Getting There & Away There are plenty of options for getting to/from Dunedin.

Bus InterCity (☎ 477 8860), 599 Princes St, has services to Christchurch, Invercargill

OTAGO & SOUTHLAND

($40), Queenstown ($28) and Te Anau ($58). There is a $10 charge for bicycles but space for them is not guaranteed. Special discounted fares are available.

Atomic Shuttles (☎ 477 4449) run daily services from Dunedin train station to Christchurch (5½ hours, $30), and Queenstown (4¼ hours, $30). Bicycles cost $10 each.

Train Tranz Rail (☎ 0800 802 802) has a daily service, *The Southerner*, each way linking the city with Invercargill (3¼ hours, $51 plus $10 per bike) and other points south, and Christchurch (5¼ hours, $74 plus $10 per bike) to the north.

Invercargill

NZ's (but certainly *not* the world's) southernmost city is the commercial heart and transport hub of Southland as well as the gateway to Stewart Island. Around 53,000 people call Invercargill home. Built with wide, spacious streets in a grid pattern on a flat plain, the city is gradually opening to tourism and fighting the perception of the rest of NZ that it is dull and backward.

Information The visitor office (☎ 214 6243, fax 218 9753, ✉ tourismandtravel.inv ercargill@thenet.net.nz) is in the remarkable Queens Park pyramid, which also houses the museum, art gallery and the Tuatara House (see Things to See & Do).

The DOC office (☎ 214 4589), on the 7th level of the State Insurance Building in Don St, has details of walks on Stewart Island.

Invercargill has several bike shops: Wensleys Cycles (☎ 218 6206), on the corner of Tay and Nith Sts, Gladstone Cycles (☎ 218 8822), 420 Dee St, and Big on Bikes, (☎ 214 4697), 254 Elles St. The chain store Smiths City (☎ 218 2033), on the corner of Yarrow and Deveron Sts, also offers bike shop services.

Things to See & Do Within the central city is the very English **Queens Park**, 80 hectares of botanic gardens with an aviary and small animal park, duck ponds, rose gardens and a tea kiosk. Inside the pyramid (entry free) in the park is the **Southland Museum**, which has natural history, technology and Maori galleries, and an art gallery with temporary and touring exhibitions. It also

has a fascinating 'Beyond the Roaring Forties' audio-visual exhibit on NZ's sub-antarctic islands. Best of all, it has the **Tuatara House**, displaying NZ's fossil-like reptile, the tuatara.

Anderson Park is a beautiful Georgian-style house 7km from town. Ride north on North Rd towards Queenstown and turn right to follow McIvor Rd for 3km. The route is signposted. Built in 1924, the house is now used as an art gallery.

The **water tower** at the eastern end of Leet St is an Invercargill landmark. Built in 1889, the 40m tower has great views of the surrounding countryside. You can climb it on Sunday afternoons for $1. Get the key from next door on other days.

Other watery entertainment can be had at the Splash Palace, as **Southland Aquatic Centre** on Elles Rd is known, or **Oreti Beach**, a long sweep of sand 9.5km west of town.

City historic walks are shown on a leaflet from the visitor centre. Visit Thomson's Bush on Queens Dr, the last remnant of the forest once covering the Invercargill area, about 3.5km north of the chief post office.

On Tiwai Point, the opposite side of the harbour from Bluff, is Comalco's huge **Tiwai aluminium smelter**, the eighth largest in the world. Annually it processes 500,000 tonnes of aluminium oxide shipped from Queensland, producing nearly a quarter of a million tonnes of aluminium and providing 1500 jobs for Invercargill. Power comes from the purpose-built Lake Manapouri hydroelectric power station. Free guided tours are available; book at the visitor centre or phone ☎ 218 5494 well in advance. You need to make your own way there; it's about a 45km return journey.

Places to Stay Pleasant and inexpensive, but well out of town near Oreti Beach, the *Beach Road Motor Camp (☎ 213 0400)* has tent sites for $6, cabins from $13 and tourist flats for $27 (all per person). Central, but fairly grim, is *Invercargill Caravan Park (☎ 218 8787)* in the A&P Showgrounds on Victoria Ave. It's closed during show time, the first two weeks of December. At other times, tent sites cost $15 and chalets with tea making facilities are $34; both for two. Beds in a bunkroom cost $10.

Southern Comfort Backpackers (☎ 218 3838, 30 Thomson St), about 1km from the chief post office, is highly rated by guests. Doubles cost $18 per person while dorm beds cost $16. The *Invercargill YHA (☎ 215 9344; 122 North Rd, Waikiwi)* has beds for $15.

B&B accommodation is available in two central locations. *Aarden House (☎ 215 8825, 193 North Rd)* charges from $40/65 a single/double, while the larger hotel-like *Montecillo Lodge (☎ 218 2503, 240 Spey St)* has rooms from $76/96. About 5km along the road to the airport is *The Oak Door (☎ 213 0633; 22 Taiepa Rd, Otatara)*, with doubles for $60.

Gerrard's Hotel (☎ 218 3406, cnr Esk & Leven Sts) is an ornate former railway hotel built in 1896 with a good restaurant. Rooms start from $40/60 and breakfast costs an extra $10.

Invercargill's many motels are similarly priced. Try the *Aachen Motel (☎ 218 8185, 147 Yarrow St)* or *Ashlar (☎ 217 9093, 81 Queens Dr)*; doubles start from $75.

The best (and most expensive) hotel in town is the *Ascot Park (☎ 217 6195, cnr Tay St & Racecourse Rd)*, which has an indoor pool. Motel units cost from $92 and deluxe hotel rooms from $145.

Places to Eat Along Dee St and around the city centre you'll find a selection of *fast food* and *sandwich places*. Try the *Cod Pot (136 Dee St)* for good fish, chips and Bluff oysters in season. Pizzas are good value at *Da Vinci's (300 Dee St)*. The pyramid housing the visitor centre in Queens Park has a good *cafe*.

Plenty of pubs serve food – the better ones are the *Homestead Cobb & Co (cnr Dee & Avenal Sts)* the *Waikiwi Family Inn*, to the north on Bainfield St, and *Molly O'Grady's* in the Kelvin Hotel, Kelvin St.

One of Invercargill's original licensed cafe bars, *Zookeepers Cafe (☎ 218 3373, 50 Tay St)* promises zaniness, good coffee and long hours (10 am till late) seven days a week. Light meals such as lasagne cost around $13, and steaks from $16. Next to the cinema complex the *Frog 'n' Firkin (☎ 214 4001, 31 Dee St)* has a restaurant and bar that serves inexpensive lunches and dinners from Monday to Saturday until late.

Local seafood is a specialty at *HMS Kings Restaurant (☎ 218 3443, 82 Tay St)*. Open daily for lunch and dinner, it is decked out like an old sailing ship. Mains, from about $20, feature oysters, whitebait, blue cod and salmon. Check opening times for the *Bungalow Restaurant (☎ 214 3116)*, on Ythan St. This training restaurant of the Southland Polytechnic offers lunch for $10 and dinner $25.

Getting There & Away There are plenty of options for getting to/from Invercargill.

Bus InterCity buses (☎ 218 1837) has services from the train station daily to Te Anau ($30), Dunedin ($20), Queenstown ($33) and Christchurch ($43). Bikes cost $10, if space is available.

Spitfire Shuttle (☎ 218 7381) has services to Te Anau ($29), and Atomic Shuttles (☎ 322 8883) goes to Wanaka ($35). Both charge $10 for bikes. The Bottom Bus (☎ 471 0292) specialises in the Catlins/Southern Scenic Route ($80), running three days a week between Dunedin and Te Anau via Invercargill.

Train Tranz Rail (☎ 0800 802 802) has a daily service to Christchurch (9 hours, $117 plus $10 per bike) departing at 8.25 am; the corresponding service from Christchurch arrives at 5.15 pm.

Otago Peninsula

Duration	3-4½ hours
Distance	68.6km
Difficulty	moderate
Start/End	Dunedin train station

Otago Peninsula is the most accessible wildlife area on the South Island with royal albatross, little blue penguin, yellow-eyed penguin and fur seals all to be seen in various locations. This route visits Portobello on the way to Taiaroa Head, where attractions include historic Fort Taiaroa and the albatross colony. It then returns to Dunedin via Highcliff Rd, with its coastal panoramas. An optional detour travels to Larnach Castle, Dunedin's best-known building.

PLANNING
When to Ride
This half-day ride can be done any time the weather is favourable. It is best timed to avoid busy commuter traffic periods, such as during summer school holidays.

OTAGO & SOUTHLAND

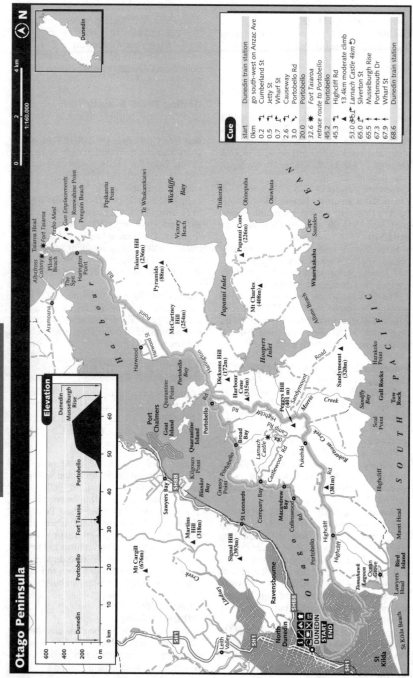

OTAGO & SOUTHLAND

Otago Peninsula

Elevation

Cue	
start	Dunedin train station
0km	go south-west on Anzac Ave
0.2	Cumberland St
0.5	Jetty St
0.7	Wharf St
2.6	Causeway
3.0	Portobello Rd
20.0	Portobello
32.6	Fort Taiaroa
	retrace route to Portobello
45.2	Portobello
45.3	Highcliff Rd
	13.4km moderate climb
53.0	Larnach Castle 4km
65.0	Silverton St
65.5	Musselburgh Rise
67.3	Portsmouth Dr
67.9	Wharf St
68.6	Dunedin train station

Queenstown and Lake Wakatipu, Otago

Mitre Peak mirrored in Milford Sound, Southland

Mt Aspiring National Park, Otago

Otago Central Rail Trail, Otago

The Criterion hotel, Oamaru, Otago

Skippers Canyon, near Queenstown

World's steepest road, Baldwin St, Dunedin

GETTING TO/FROM THE RIDE

For transport to/from Dunedin, see the Getting There & Away section (pp293-4) under Gateway Cities earlier in the chapter.

THE RIDE

The trip out to the peninsula is an easy, flat, very scenic ride, but the return route climbs a 13km hill. The main road out to Taiaroa is narrow and lacks a shoulder, but is relatively quiet outside commuter-traffic times. It clings desperately to the edge of the harbour without even a guardrail to separate traffic from a watery doom. Don't get distracted.

Barely a ripple appears in the road in the first 20km to Portobello, but a few undulations arise as the route heads across country. Near the tip of the peninsula it descends from an unaccustomed 60m into the Taiaroa Head visitor centre car park at the end of the sealed road. Pause at the crest to spot **fur seals** reclining on the beach below.

Originally known to the Maori as Pukekura, **Taiaroa Head** was a natural refuge and defensive position. Maori occupation culminated in a fortified village, or *pa*, on the headland. From 1885, tension between Britain and Russia over the Russian invasion of Afghanistan led to a scheme to defend NZ's major ports and Taiaroa Head became a European fortress. An emplacement of retractable 150mm guns (with an 8km range) served as a deterrent to Tsarist Russian invasion. (It worked!)

Ninety minute tours of the **fortifications** as well as the nearby **royal albatross colony**,

Taiaroa's Royal Albatross

Royal albatross arrive to breed at Taiaroa from September. They build nests in early November and lay one 500g white egg. Each parent incubates the egg in shifts of two to eight days over 11 weeks – one of the longest incubation periods of any bird.

Chicks hatch in late January or early February. They're not fully fledged until the following September, when they leave the colony to spend three to six years at sea. They may return to Taiaroa with a mate to breed. The parents also leave and spend a year at sea before returning to breed again.

costing $25, can be booked at the visitor centre (☎ 478 0499) on the Head.

From Tairoa Head the route retraces its the outward journey to Portobello (45.3km). From the junction in the centre of the village, Highcliff Rd takes off to the left (uphill). The climb reaches a ridge with views to the Pacific Ocean and the bays of the Peninsula's southern shore.

At 53km is a turn-off to **Larnach Castle** (☎ 476 1616), a 4km return journey that includes a gentle climb. Dunedin's best known building stands as testament to the wealth that once resided in the city. Built by politician and merchant JWM Larnach in 1871 at a cost equivalent to about $25 million today, it features a mish-mash of architectural styles. The building and gardens can be viewed daily between 9 am and 5 pm ($10 adult).

The route continues on high for 5km, passing grazing fields bounded by attractive dry stone walls, then begins a rapid descent into the suburban sprawl of Dunedin.

Swampy Summit Circuit

MOUNTAIN BIKE RIDE

Duration	3-4 hours
Distance	30km
Grade	moderate-hard
Start/End	The Octagon, Dunedin

The very scenic Swampy Summit Circuit ride is sure to test your fitness and skills. All this from a mountain bike ride that starts a mere 15 minute ride from downtown Dunedin.

The Pineapple Walk also starts from the 'Bull Pen'. Avoid the temptation to ride this 'walkers only' route.

PLANNING
When to Ride

The route should be negotiable year-round whenever conditions are dry. However, you're less likely to suffer frostbite on descents outside June to August.

Maps & Books

Bike shops have copies of the free Dunedin City Council brochure *Mountain Bike Rides in Dunedin*, which briefly describes half a dozen or so possible trips in the region, including this one.

OTAGO & SOUTHLAND

Swampy Summit Circuit

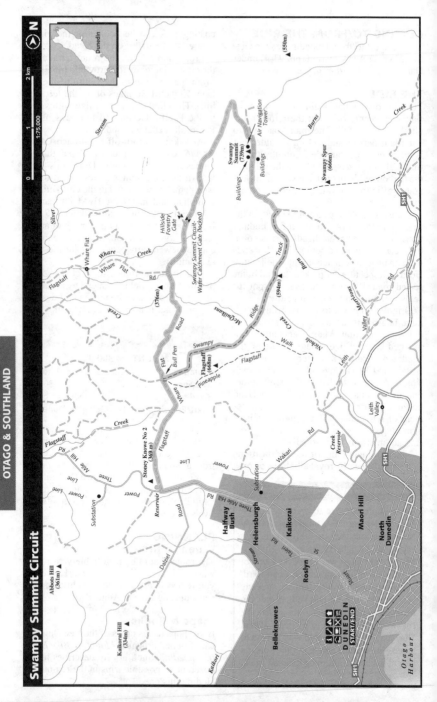

What to Bring

Carrying water, repair equipment, snack food and a jacket is recommended.

THE RIDE

This one-day mountain bike ride tests fitness and skills on an interesting range of surfaces from sealed to gravel road and rutted 4WD track, with some strenuous climbing thrown in.

Climbing begins in earnest immediately. From The Octagon, ride up steep Stuart St to the suburb of Roslyn, gaining about 140m in 1.5km, then drop down into Kaikorai Valley. Climb again on Taieri Rd, following it until it becomes Three Mile Hill Rd. About 400m after passing Dalziel Rd (on the left), Flagstaff Whare Flat Rd appears on the right (5km), at just over 300m altitude. It is signposted to Whare Flat. Follow it, riding over a crest and onto a gravel surface after 200m.

Cycle uphill for about 10 minutes. A corrugated road travels through pine forest to a crest, 500m above sea level, which leads to a clearing and car park, the 'Bull Pen'. (The outward path rejoins here at the end of the circuit.)

Continue straight ahead and descend for 1km or so on a gravel switchback road. At the first Y-junction (290m altitude) take the right fork and ... you guessed it, start climbing again. At the next fork, ignore the Hillside Forestry gate and continue uphill on the right fork again. Soon another gate appears with a sign 'Swampy Summit Circuit – Water Catchment'.

The gravel road zigzags across the mountain face, reaching a junction in sight of an air navigation installation. Go right again, following Swampy Ridge Track, past two Aviation Department structures on the summit (739m). At the next fork, veer right once more, staying on Swampy Ridge Track. This descends for a few hundred metres, then branches; take the right fork, following a rough track across a saddle and climb to a sign pointing to Whare Flat Rd, further uphill and to the right.

The rough track continues up, and up, to a crest from which the Bull Pen is visible. It's still a rocky ride down to there but, after turning left onto the gravel Flagstaff Whare Flat Rd, it only takes 15 minutes to rocket back to The Octagon.

Central Otago Circuit

Duration	4 days
Distance	233km
Difficulty	hard
Start/Finish	Dunedin

This four-day ride into central Otago (also known as the 'outback') starts with a scenic train journey through the spectacular terrain to the north-west of Dunedin. The riding begins at the rail siding of Pukerangi and travels in the shadow of the Rock & Pillar Range through quiet gold rush towns before winding its way back to the coast at Palmerston. The final day affords spectacular views of the coastline on quiet roads back into Dunedin.

On Day 2 you can choose to ride on a sealed road or take a rail trail. This gently graded, gravel trail is a former railway route, now managed by the DOC. Day 3 also starts with a 15km section of gravel road.

HISTORY

The Otago Central Rail Trail has been created along the route of the closed Central Otago railway line. Only a 20km section between Ranfurly and Ida Dam remains unfinished; when complete, the rail trail will run from Middlemarch to Clyde, 9km beyond Alexandra.

The ride's return route, SH85 (known as the Pig Root), was a major access to the goldfields during the 1862 Dunstan rush. The wagon teams' era on this mountainous, then often muddy and hellish track, ended when the railway from Dunedin reached Middlemarch in 1892. Less than a century later, in 1990, the railway era ended too.

PLANNING
When to Ride

You can ride any time from October to April, but try to avoid the hottest days, usually in January, as water is hard to find and shade is even scarcer.

See Getting to/from the Ride for operating times for the Taieri Gorge Limited tourist train, which forms the first part of this ride.

Maps & Books

The InfoMap *The South* (1:500,000) has adequate detail for roads in the area, while the

AA *Otago* map (1:350,000) is slightly more detailed.

Leaflets describing the Otago Central Rail Trail are available from DOC in Dunedin and Alexandra (☎ 448 8874) and at many visitor centres.

What to Bring

You'll need a mountain bike to ride the deep, loose-packed gravel of the rail trail; the gravel roads on Days 1 & 3 can be ridden on a touring bike. Trail users will also need to be self-sufficient for food and water as there are no shops along the route between towns.

GETTING TO/FROM THE RIDE
Dunedin

For transport to/from Dunedin, see the Getting There & Away section (pp293-4) under Gateway Cities earlier in the chapter.

Pukerangi

Train The Taieri Gorge Limited tourist train leaves Dunedin once a day from February to December, except Christmas Day. In January school holidays it runs twice a day. Timetables are available from Dunedin visitor centre or the train station (☎ 477 4449, ✉ reserve@taieri.co.nz).

The final destination is usually Pukerangi (2 hours), 58km from Dunedin and the highest point on the line, but on Sundays from October to January the afternoon run goes 19km further to Middlemarch (2½ hours). The adult fare is $34/53 one way/return to Pukerangi or $37.50/59 to Middlemarch. Bikes are carried free.

Bicycle An adventurous link to the Mackenzie Country ride travels from Naseby (end Day 2) to Oamaru over Dansey Pass (see the ride description in the Canterbury chapter for details).

THE RIDE
Day 1: Pukerangi to Middlemarch

1-1½ hours, 19km

The ride to Middlemarch from Pukerangi 'station' – where there is only a railway shed, a siding and, across the tracks, a farm – is quite straightforward and enjoyable after the train journey. Although the route starts out unsealed, after about 1km (mostly

downhill) the sealed road begins. There's a shared road/rail bridge to negotiate, but it's unlikely you'll meet a train. A further 5km of unsealed road leads to SH87, just south of **Sutton**, from where it's only another 8km through open country to Middlemarch.

Middlemarch

The small settlement of Middlemarch (population 400) nestles below the Rock & Pillar Range at the northern terminus of the Taieri Gorge railway. It is also at the southern end of the Otago Central Rail Trail, a long narrow recreation reserve for mountain biking, walking and horse riding managed by the DOC.

The Railhead store (☎/fax 464 3762) acts as the visitor centre.

The **Strath Taieri museum** has a display of NZ's first submarine. Ask at the store for details of opening times. Explore the Rock & Pillar Range on **mountain bike trails** from Kinvara (see Places to Stay & Eat).

Places to Stay & Eat The *Blind Billy's Holiday Camp* (☎ 464 3355), in Mold St, has guest facilities in old railway carriages. Tent sites are $8 per person, motel rooms $65 a double ($10 per extra adult). *Strath Taieri Hotel* (☎ 464 3800), in Snow Ave, has rooms for $45 a double and serves meals. The proprietors of the Railhead store, which is also a *tearoom/restaurant*, also run a *self-catering lodge*. Rates are $25/45 for a single/double or $15 each for groups of 10 or more. *Kinvara* (☎ 464 3089), about 10km north of town, has cabin accommodation for $15 per person. Farm stays in the area are *Stonehurst* (☎ 464 3831) and *Gladbrook* (☎ 464 3888), both on Gladbrook Rd.

Day 2: Middlemarch to Naseby

5-7 hours, 67km

The sealed road to Ranfurly parallels Rock & Pillar Range on SH87, traversing rolling farmland and rocky hills. It's very dry country in the hot months of January and February and there's a couple of long climbs en route.

The alternative route from Middlemarch to Ranfurly along the Otago Central Rail Trail is on gently graded, gravel and about 5km less than the sealed road. If the gravel proves too tedious there are many bail-out opportunities to return to the sealed road.

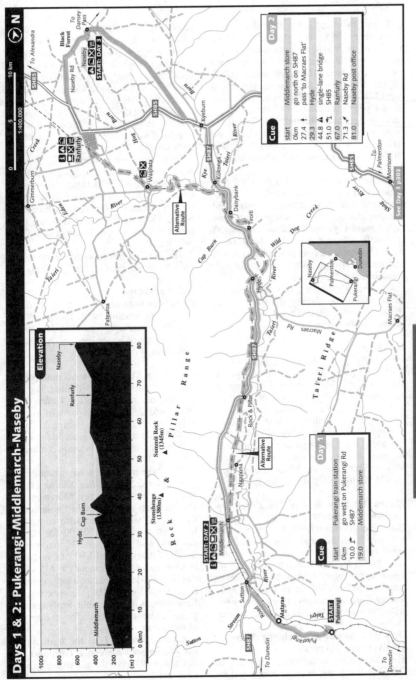

Days 1 & 2: Pukerangi–Middlemarch–Naseby

See Day 3 p303

OTAGO & SOUTHLAND

Elevation

	Day 2
Cue	
start	Middlemarch store
0km	go north on SH87
27.4 ↑	pass 'to Macraes Flat'
29.3	Hyde
44.8 ◭	single-lane bridge
51.0 ↰	SH85
67.0	Ranfurly
71.3 ↙	Naseby Rd
81.0	Naseby post office

	Day 1
Cue	
start	Pukerangi train station
0km	go west on Pukerangi Rd
10.0 ↰	SH87
19.0	Middlemarch store

The trail was opened in three stages from November 1995. The section to Hyde (29.3km) is rough in parts with bridges decked and rideable except for one which can be bypassed. There are toilets (BYO paper) at the Rock & Pillar station, 15km from Middlemarch and at Hyde. The 14km from Hyde to Daisybank (43.3km) features three bridges and a **tunnel** with fine stonework. After Daisybank the trail crosses the Taieri River on the 96m-long **Waipiata Bridge**. Waipiata (58km) has a hotel and toilet facilities.

Ranfurly, service centre for the Maniototo region, is a town of 850 people. Its attractively **restored train station** has displays and audiovisuals on railway history. There are stores, *takeaways* and *restaurants* nearby. At *Ranfurly Motor Camp (☎ 444 9144, 3 Reade St)* tent sites cost $15, cabins are $25 and tourist flats are $50; all prices for two. Bunk beds are $15 per person.

On the day's final leg, near the top of the gentle climb into Naseby, the route passes the aptly named **Black Forest**, a pine plantation established in 1900.

Naseby

Once the largest gold mining town on the Maniototo plain, Naseby is now a quaint, sleepy village. Many restored commercial buildings evoke the gold rush atmosphere. The town's slogan is '2000 feet above worry level' and it proclaims itself the 'smallest borough in NZ at the highest altitude'.

Naseby has a **museum** and the surrounding area is great **walking** country. From May to September the Maniototo **Ice Rink** (☎ 444 9270) is used for winter sports.

Places to Stay & Eat The *Larchview Camping Ground (☎ 444 9904)*, on a tree-clad hill overlooking town, has tent sites for $15, cabins for $28 and self-contained cottages from $35; all prices for two. The *Ancient Briton Hotel & Motel (☎ 444 9992)*, on Lever St, has rooms from $22 per person or motel rooms from $68 for two. The friendly *Stables Cafe*, on the next block, serves excellent toasted sandwiches and other snacks.

Day 3: Naseby to Palmerston
4½-6½ hours, 78km

The surrounding countryside for much of Day 3 is harsh and bumpy, dominated by stark, dry hills with tussock grass cover. There is no shelter from sun or wind and no services before Dunback (70.1km). Traffic is light though it increases towards the coast. A fair proportion is smelly double-trailer stock transporters rushing loads of sheep and cattle to their doom.

The challenges start from the minute you leave Naseby, with a 14.6km-long unsealed stretch of road that joins SH85 just west of Kyeburn (18.9km).

From here a series of increasingly strenuous undulations begin, peaking at **Red Cutting Summit** (640m; 34.1km), above Pigroot Creek. At Dead Horse Pinch Historic Reserve a **plaque** (39.9km) pays tribute to the horses that sometimes died from the tough job of pulling wagons to the central Otago goldfields.

The ups and downs continue from here, with the downs winning, but it's a tiring ride.

Palmerston

Palmerston is a small community straddling SH1 at its junction with the 'Pig Root' (SH85). Dominating the hill at the entrance to the town is St James Presbyterian Church, built in 1874 of local stone.

Places to Stay & Eat Accommodation and food options are very limited. The true-to-name but noisy *Pleasant Valley Camp (☎/fax 465 1370)*, 3.5km south of town on SH1, has tent sites for $8, backpacker bunks for $12 and cabins for $15; all prices are per person. Also in a noisy location is a *hotel* at the SH1/SH85 junction.

The Palmerston area has several farm stay options. *Shag Valley Station (☎ 465 0821)*, on SH85 between Morrisons and Dunback, has been owned by the same family since 1864. Doubles with continental breakfast cost from $70/100 for singles/doubles, and dinner is $30 per person. South of town, just off SH1 at Goodwood, is *Centrewood Homestead (☎ 465 1977)*, offering B&B in a wing of a large colonial-style house for $80/100; dinner costs $30. Reservations are advisable. Seals and penguins can be seen within a five minute walk of the house.

Locomotion No 1, at the train station, and *McGregor's Bakery & Tearooms (126 Ronaldsay St)* have the usual fare of takeaway meals.

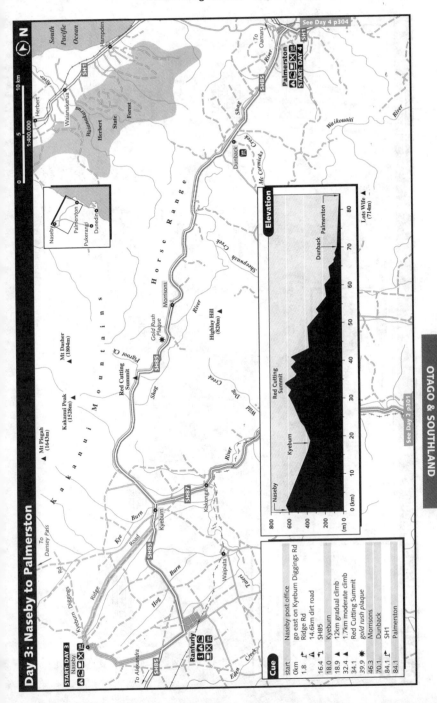

Day 3: Naseby to Palmerston

Cue		
start		Naseby post office
0km	→	go east on Kyeburn Diggings Rd
1.8	←	Ridge Rd
16.4	←	14.6km dirt road
		SH85
18.0	◄	Kyeburn
18.9	◄	12km gradual climb
32.4	◄	1.7km moderate climb
34.1	◄	Red Cutting Summit
39.9	✳	gold rush plaque
46.3		Morrisons
70.1		Dunback
84.1	↱	SH1
84.1		Palmerston

OTAGO & SOUTHLAND

OTAGO & SOUTHLAND

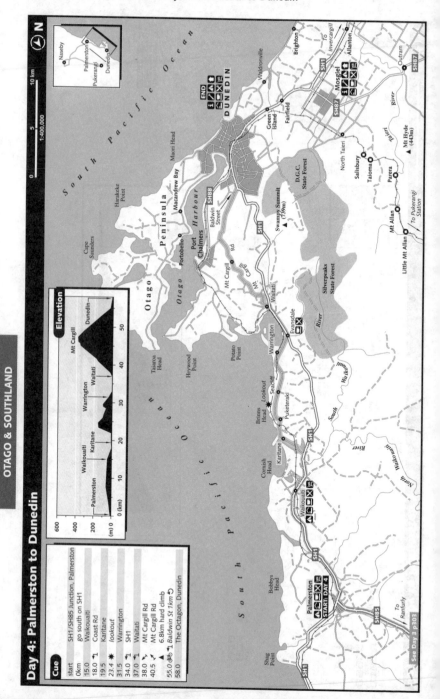

Day 4: Palmerston to Dunedin

Cue

start	SH17/SH85 Junction, Palmerston
0km	go south on SH1
15.0	Waikouaiti
18.0 ⤴	Coast Rd
19.5 ⤴	Karitane
23.4 ✳	lookout
31.5	Warrington
34.0 ⤴	SH1
37.0 ⤴	Waitati
38.0 ⤴	Mt Cargill Rd
40.5 ◣	Mt Cargill Rd
	6.8km hard climb
55.0 ⬤↤↳	Baldwin St 1km ⟲
58.0	The Octagon, Dunedin

Elevation

Mt Cargill
Waitati
Warrington
Dunedin
Waikouaiti
Karitane
Palmerston

1:400,000

0   5   10 km

N

Day 4: Palmerston to Dunedin
3½-5 hours, 55km

Day 4 is dominated by the dramatic Otago coastline, the surrounding hills and the South Pacific Ocean. The route follows the coast in part but more often it'll be the vast green and blue views from the day's climbs (especially Mt Cargill) that capture your imagination.

The metre-wide shoulder of SH1 provides a comfortable separation from the constant traffic until, after Waikouaiti (15km), the route turns off to follow the more scenic coast. This also bypasses the long, steep climb of Kilmog Hill. The coast road undulates, twists and zigzags across the railway line, returning to SH1 on the south side of the hill next to shallow Blueskin Bay, where you find the Evansdale *tearooms*.

After Waitati, the smooth, wide shoulder is deemed too dangerous for cyclists. A small bicycle route sign indicates the narrow, steep and sinuous road over Mt Cargill as the way into Dunedin. On the climb, beautiful views of rolling forested hills and fields unfold behind. The reduction in traffic means the sounds of bleating sheep and chirping birds dominate. Powerful scents of conifer and eucalypt plantations alternately transport you to Europe and Australia. Below, to the left, is Otago Harbour and Port Chalmers. Soon Dunedin comes into view, its buildings and houses sprawled untidily across the hillsides ahead like the covers on an unmade bed.

On the way into town, test your strength on Baldwin St, the world's steepest hill (see Things to See & Do in Dunedin at the start of the chapter).

The Catlins Coast

Duration	3 days
Distance	269.1km
Difficulty	hard
Start	Dunedin
End	Invercargill

The Catlins is a rugged region brimming in natural beauty: podocarp forests and populations of marine mammals and bird life. Despite being an increasingly popular tourist area, the Catlins still has that laid back, out-of-the-way feel. A wedge of rolling hill country between the mouths of the Clutha and Mataura Rivers, it is a challenging area to cycle, with significant hills, stretches of awful gravel road, big distances and detours required to reach points of interest.

It is also an area that takes time explore its many capes, beaches, cliffs, waterfalls and natural sites. The three-day suggested riding time of this ride could be supplemented by extra days off the bike at scenic locations like Nugget Point and Porpoise Bay.

HISTORY
The Catlins bears the (misspelt) name of the New South Wales (before Australia became a federation) whaling captain who first assessed the area's development potential. In 1840, Edward Cattlin was sent to navigate the river now named after him and found the South Island's most accessible forests. The beech trees were soon being logged and shipped out of Hinahina on the broad stretch of river called Catlins Lake. Townships dwindled as sawmilling declined after the best stands of timber had been cut; logging ended in 1887. The area is now quieter than it was more than a century ago. Most of the surviving forests on the hills and in the lowland valleys are protected in reserves and the scars left by logging are healing.

PLANNING
When to Ride
The Catlins is the most southerly part of the South Island, so expect lower temperatures and be ready for rain. It is advisable to check daily weather forecasts to avoid being caught by a southerly change – it'll be a strong headwind, particularly on the exposed run from Fortrose to Invercargill. Because distances are relatively long and road surfaces sometimes poor, it's a good idea to ride in the months from October to March when daylight hours are at a maximum.

What to Bring
Camping gear will be useful if staying at the more isolated, off-route attractions of the Catlins. Low gearing and wide, sturdy tyres are an advantage on the deep gravel of the area's many unsealed, hilly roads.

GETTING TO/FROM THE RIDE
For transport to/from the ride, see the Getting There & Away sections (pp293-5) under Gateway Cities earlier in the chapter.

OTAGO & SOUTHLAND

OTAGO & SOUTHLAND

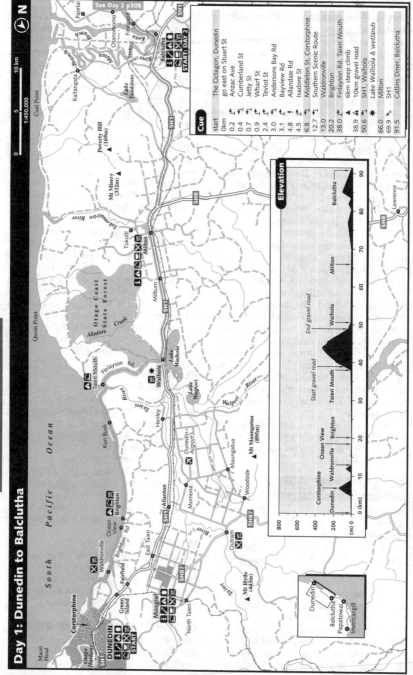

Day 1: Dunedin to Balclutha

Cue

start	The Octagon, Dunedin
0km	go east on Stuart St
0.2	Anzac Ave
0.4	Cumberland St
0.7	Jetty St
0.9	Wharf St
2.4	Teviot St
3.0	Andersons Bay Rd
3.1	Bayview Rd
4.8	Allandale Rd
4.5	Isadore St
6.8	Middleton St, Corstorphine
12.7	Southern Scenic Route
13.0	Waldronville
20.2	Brighton
38.0	Finlayson Rd, Taieri Mouth
	6km steep climb
38.9	10km gravel road
50.6	SH1, Waihola
66.0	Lake Waihola & wetlands
	Milton
69.9	SH1
91.5	Catlins Diner, Balclutha

Elevation

Bicycle This ride links with the Southern Scenic Route and the Invercargill Hinterland rides at Invercargill.

THE RIDE
Day 1: Dunedin to Balclutha
6-8½ hours, 92km

NZ road authorities deserve condemnation for their worse-than-third-world treatment of cyclists leaving Dunedin. The wide shoulders of the 'motorway' section of SH1 are off limits, according to signs, but no information is provided on any alternative route. There *is* a better way, though hillier. It's superbly scenic as the route reaches the beach and follows the coast, with only minor undulations, to Taieri Mouth.

The day's ride starts with some steep climbing through the southern suburbs of Dunedin, before descending to the coast at Waldronville (13km). From Taieri Mouth (38km) the next 10km are on gravel, with a stiff 5km climb, then a winding descent on a loose surface. Views from the top are worth the effort. From Waihola (50.6km), where the route joins SH1, to Balclutha are only three noticeable hills.

Over the hill, **Waihola** has a welcome *takeaway food shop* and Lake Waihola is a good **fishing spot**. At *Lake Waihola Holiday Park* (☎ *417 8908*), tent sites cost $8, and cabins $16 per person. Rare NZ birds frequent the nearby Sinclair Wetlands – ask at the shop for directions. From here, SH1 has a fair-to-good shoulder all the way to Milton (66km). The pleasant rural idyll continues to Balclutha.

Balclutha
The largest town in South Otago, with a population just over 4000, Balclutha features an impressive concrete arch bridge over the Clutha River. The town receives about 650mm of rain a year, evenly spread.

The visitor centre (☎ 418 0388, fax 418 1877, ✉ cluthadistrict@cluthade.govt.nz), 63 Clyde St, is open from 10 am to 4 pm on weekdays and 1 to 4 pm on Sunday.

South Otago Cycles & Sports (☎ 418 0370), 61 Clyde St, is the place to head for repairs and touring advice.

The **museum**, 1 Renfrew St, showcases a collection of 10,000 old farm and household implements, giving an idea of just how much things have changed over the years.

Places to Stay & Eat The *Naish Park Motor Camp* (☎ *418 0088, 56 Charlotte St)* has sites for $16 and cabins from $22 for two. Beds at *Balclutha Backpackers* (☎ *025 291 7466, 20 Stewart St)*, next to the Catholic school, cost $18 per person. *Rosebank Lodge* (☎ *419 1490, 265 Clyde St)* has twin or double rooms from $80. Motel rooms are also available at *Highway Lodge Motel* (☎ *418 2363, 165 Clyde St)*. Studio units cost $70 and one-bedroom suites $75.

B&B accommodation is available at *Balcairn* (☎ *418 1385)*, a sheep farm on Blackburn Rd, 22km north of Balclutha. Doubles cost from $70.

The *265 Restaurant* in the Rosebank Lodge has a menu featuring locally caught salmon and trout. The *Hotel South Otago*, a string of *takeaways* and a *supermarket* are along Clyde St (SH1).

Day 2: Balclutha to Papatowai
3-5 hours, 58km

Day 2 is a relatively short ride, all on sealed road and with only three relatively climbs. For much of the day the road parallels the coastal range of hills cloaked in lush, dense forest. A couple of optional side trips can add gravel and extra kilometres. The first, to Nugget Point, leaves the route 7km outside Balclutha (see Side Trip).

Owaka, the only significant town in the Catlins, with 400 people, has a variety of hostel and motel accommodation. The *Catlins Diner* (☎ *415 8392, 3 Main St)* doubles as the store and visitor centre. Other eating places include the *Lumber Jack Cafe & Bar* (*3 Saunders St)* and *Catlins Inn* (*21 Ryley St)*.

From Owaka, an 8km (return) side trip on sealed road leads to tranquil town of **Pounawea**, which has *camping* and is set on Catlins Lake.

On a steep descent about 8km before Papatowai, there's a walking track to **Matai & Horseshoe Falls**. It's a very worthwhile 20 minute return walk through cool native bush full of bird life to the pretty cascades.

Side Trip: Nugget Point
2-3 hours, 31.5km return

Nugget Point is named for the sea stacks – the **Nuggets** – off the coast from the photogenic **historic lighthouse**. Also at the point is the

OTAGO & SOUTHLAND

Day 2: Balclutha to Papatowai

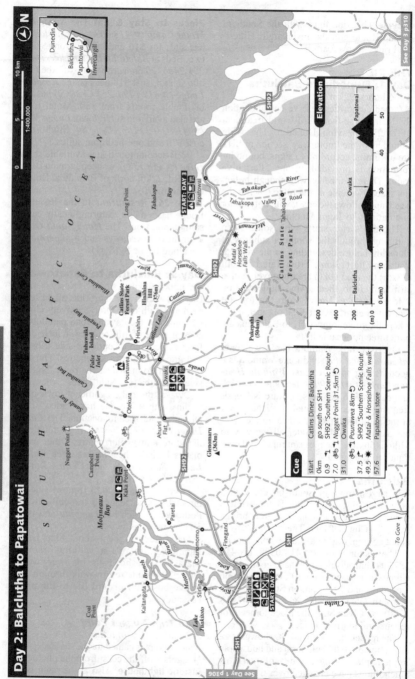

Elevation

Cue		
start	Catlins Diner, Balclutha	
0km	go south on SH1	
0.9	SH92 'Southern Scenic Route'	↰
7.0	Nugget Point 31.5km	⟳
31.0	Owaka	
37.5	Pounawea 8km	↱
49.5	SH92 'Southern Scenic Route'	↰
49.5	Matai & Horseshoe Falls walk	✳
57.6	Papatowai store	

OTAGO & SOUTHLAND

Nuggets Wildlife Reserve, where you can see fur, elephant and leopard seals, sea lions, penguins and sea birds. The unsealed road loops back to the main route at Ahuriri Flat.

The only accommodation at Nugget Point is a B&B right on the water. *Nuggets Lodge* (☎ 412 8783) is run by the wildlife reserve's honorary ranger. Doubles cost from $90.

The route passes the holiday settlement of **Kaka Point**, which has several accommodation options. There's the *camping grounds* (☎ 412 8818, 21 Esplanade) and the *Nugget View Motels* (☎ 412 8602, ✉ nugview@ catlins.co.nz; 11 Rata St, Kaka Point), which also has a backpackers hostel, has budget doubles for $75 and more luxurious rooms for $95.

Papatowai

Not so much a town as a convenient place to break your journey beside the Tahakopa River, Papatowai consists of little more than a store-come-post centre, the Trading Post, with a motor camp and motel behind.

Papatowai is the base for **wildlife tours** in the nearby forests. Ask at the Trading Post.

Places to Stay & Eat The *Papatowai Motor Camp* (☎ 415 8500) has tent sites for $12 (for two) and cabins from $15 per person. *Scenic Highway Motel* (☎ 415 8147), behind the store, has rooms from $50/60 per single/double. Fantastic views and sunsets, and backpacker beds from $18, are available at the aptly named *Hilltop* (☎ 415 8028), 1.5km from the main road along Tahakopa Valley Rd.

South of Papatowai on SH92, *Chaslands Farm Motor Lodge* (☎ 415 8501) has cabins from $50 a double.

The *Trading Post* (☎ 415 8147) can supply meals, sandwiches, snacks and tea and coffee.

Day 3: Papatowai to Invercargill

7½-10 hours, 120km
Already a long day, Day 3 is made harder by two significant stretches of unsealed road. However, camping grounds or other accommodation at Waikawa (35.2km) and Curio Bay (42.3km) provide opportunities to break the journey. None of the hills today is especially difficult and the high point is only about 200m, though loose gravel can make the going tough.

Well-maintained gravel road begins in the first kilometre from Papatowai and continues with only very brief sealed respites (at bridges) for the next 23km. Watch for wheel-munching gaps at the bridge 7km down the road. Stay away from the road edges where the gravel is deepest and you're steering against the camber that tries to take you off to the side.

Florence Hill allows a fine view of sweeping, surf-pounded Tautuku Bay. Industry here began with a whaling station that operated from 1839 to 1845 and a sawmill that opened at the turn of the 20th century and closed in 1917. The bush has now hidden the evidence of both sites.

Cathedral Caves, named for their resemblance to an English cathedral, are only accessible at low tide. Tide tables are posted at the turn-off from SH92 (11.2km), but may be out-of-date. It's a 2km detour followed by a 40 minute walk, each way.

In Waikawa (35.2km), at the old church, Dolphin Magic (☎ 246 8444) offers **dolphin-watching boat trips**, which cost from $45. The backpackers, *Waikawa Holiday Lodge* (☎ 246 8552), has beds from $15.

The next 7km around Porpoise Bay to Curio Bay motor camp is a tough ride with deep gravel and short steep pinches. After passing the road to Haldane, the brief section of road to Curio Bay is appalling for cycling but it is (just) bearable. The locals have organised a petition to get the council to seal the road, so it can't be good for motorists either! The *motor camp* has a small *store*. The next services are not until Mokotua, 77.7km away.

Porpoise Bay, visible from the motor camp, is where **Hector's dolphins** can sometimes be seen body surfing in the shore break. It's possible to swim with them; ask at the store about obtaining wet suits. Nearby, at low tide, a Jurassic era petrified forest emerges, providing evidence of NZ's connection with the Gondwanaland supercontinent about 160 million years ago.

Another **petrified forest** is visible at Slope Point, most southerly point on the South Island, a 10km-return side trip on gravel off Otara-Haldane Rd.

Perhaps the hardest sustained climb is on Otara-Haldane Rd, 15km of which is unsealed and where loose gravel reduces traction on the steep grade. From Otara, the last 50km is downhill or flat. Although this part

Day 3: Papatowai to Invercargill

OTAGO & SOUTHLAND

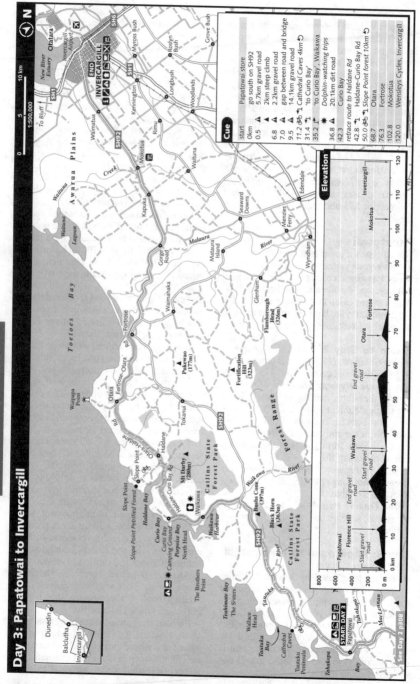

of the road is exposed to wind, in summer chances are it will be a north-east sea breeze to provide a tail wind into Invercargill.

To Bluff & Back

Duration	3½-5½ hours
Distance	60km
Difficulty	easy-moderate
Start/Finish	Invercargill

Bluff has much of interest, from historic buildings to the ultra-kitsch of Fred & Myrtle's Paua Shell House, 'Land's End' and the Stirling Point signpost, as well as the fishing fleet and port. This ride can be done in half a day or you can take your time and spend all day. All roads are sealed and the only real hill is to the lookout at Bluff, where you will need your lowest gear, and powerful brakes for the descent.

HISTORY
Bluff, settled by Europeans since 1824, has developed into the main port for Southland, handling 1.5 million tonnes of cargo each year. It is home to the Bluff oyster fleet, which dredges the delicacy from Foveaux Strait.

NATURAL HISTORY
The 14,500 hectare Awarua Wetlands, on the way to Bluff, is the largest area of protected wetland in southern NZ. Waituna Lagoon and Awarua Bay are recognised as important feeding and nesting areas for migratory birds from the northern hemisphere.

PLANNING
When to Ride
The ride should be possible all year, but it's unlikely you'll encounter a nice enough day to want to do it in the depths of winter.

Take winds into account as the route is exposed – avoid riding into a southerly and beware of a strong north-easter on the way back. A good road shoulder ensures you have plenty of room if you encounter heavy traffic (unlikely).

THE RIDE
The route takes very quiet, wide streets through the suburbs of Invercargill to join

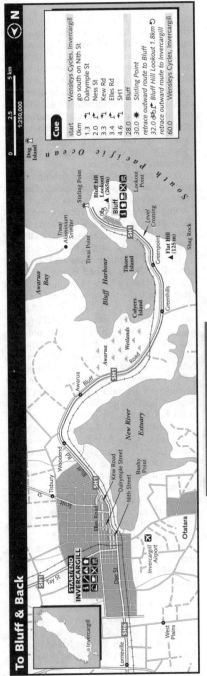

Cue

start		Wensleys Cycles, Invercargill
0km	⬏	go south on Nith St
1.3	⬏	Dalrymple St
2.0	⬏	Ness St
3.3	⬏	Kew Rd
3.4	⬏	Elles Rd
4.6	⬏	SH1
28.0		Bluff
30.0	✷	Stirling Point
		retrace outward route to Bluff
32.0	☍⬆	Bluff Hill Lookout 1.8km ↻
		retrace outward route to Invercargill
60.0		Wensleys Cycles, Invercargill

OTAGO & SOUTHLAND

To Bluff & Back

the fairly busy SH1 on the outskirts of town. The highway has a reasonable, though not especially wide, shoulder all the way to Bluff. However, be alert for impatient motorists in oncoming cars overtaking vehicles without waiting for you to pass.

Bluff, population 2100, has an unprepossessing air about it, although it doesn't look that inviting as you cycle in across the acutely angled railway crossing and past the fuel storage tanks, which cut off the water views for their neighbours across the road. Fortunately, it gets better.

Town attractions include fishing factory tours, boat cruises, and good **seafood restaurants**. Bluff's Festival Week and **Fishing Contest** in late February underlines the importance of the sea to its community. Foveaux Souvenirs & Antiques (☎ 212 8305), 74 Gore St, acts as the visitor centre.

The **Bluff Maritime Museum** is on Foreshore Rd. The **Paua Shell House**, 258 Marine Pde, with its huge collection of shells from around the world, is beyond the business area on the right. Just look for the garish fountain, huge paua shell and oversize clock in the front yard. Entry is by donation and it's open from 9 am to 5 pm daily.

Continue on SH1 (Marine Pde) from Paua Shell House to **Stirling Point**, latitude 46° 32'S. It's known as NZ's 'Land's End', not because it's the most southerly point in the South Island (Slope Point has that distinction) but because it is the start/finish of SH1, which goes all the way (with a short, wet gap) to Cape Reinga at the top of the North Island. (But surely the 'down under' Kiwis have it upside down? As the point with the higher latitude, Bluff should be the country's 'John O'Groats'; all the more so with the Scottish influence pervading Otago and Southland.) A famous signpost at the point gives distances to major world centres and to places in NZ.

When you've seen enough, backtrack to Bluff.

The **Foveaux Walk** goes 6.6km along the coast to Ocean Beach. You can turn off after about 1km and return by the 1.5km **Glory Track** through beautiful bush.

Opposite the *Property Arcade Backpackers* (☎ 212 8074, 120 Gore St) is the road to the wharf where the **Stewart Island** *Foveaux Express* catamaran (☎ 212 7660) departs. The one-hour crossing costs $74 return.

For one of the best panoramas in Southland, take the challenge of cycling up to **Bluff Hill Lookout** (265m). From the backpackers, take Lee St, Bandon St and Flagstaff Rd 2.5km steeply uphill. The 360° views extend to Stewart Island and across the harbour to Invercargill and Oreti Beach. Control your speed on the descent.

Invercargill Hinterland

Duration	2 days
Distance	146.8km
Difficulty	easy-moderate
Start/End	Invercargill

This pleasant ride, with neither major hills nor especially dramatic scenery, explores the small towns in the farming country around Invercargill. It can be done as a two day tour staying overnight at Nightcaps or Wreys Bush, or as a long, unladen one day ride. It uses mostly minor roads or lightly trafficked highways, all of which are sealed.

PLANNING
When to Ride
Traffic will be light year-round except on SH6 during the winter ski season and during summer school holidays. Cold southerly blows can occur year-round and are best avoided (study the weather forecast).

THE RIDE
Day 1: Invercargill to Nightcaps
4-6 hours, 73.1km

Invercargill's traffic subsides by the time you reach Wallacetown. The Southern Scenic Route (SH99) carries little more than tourist traffic, usually travelling at moderate speed. From Waimatuku the route follows the railway line, which runs as far as Ohai. This lonely ribbon of steel sees one train each way each day carrying coal from the collieries around Nightcaps and Ohai.

Thornbury is a sleepy village with a pub, a tannery trading post and a vintage machinery museum.

On the way through the lush, gently rolling agricultural country to Otautau you pass the bizarrely named and isolated **Gropers Bush Public Library**, established in 1880. **Otautau**, on the 'Inland Scenic Drive', is a sizeable town, somewhat desperately proclaiming

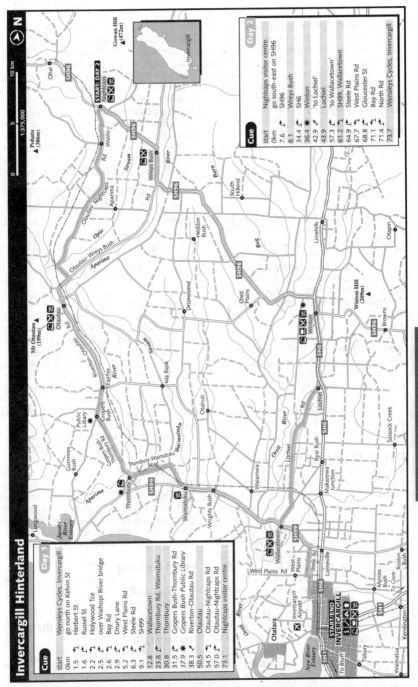

Invercargill Hinterland

Cue	Day 1	
start		Wensleys Cycles, Invercargill
0km		go north on Kelvin St
1.5	↰	Herbert St
1.6	↱	Russel St
2.2	↱	Holywood Tce
2.5	↙	over Waihopi River bridge
2.6	↰	Bay Rd
2.9	↱	Drury Lane
5.2	↱	West Plains Rd
6.3	↱	Steele Rd
9.1	↱	SH99
12.8		Wallacetown
23.8	↰	Thornbury Rd, Waimatuku
30.8		Thornbury
31.5	↱	Gropers Bush–Thornbury Rd
37.9	✳	Gropers Bush Public Library
38.3	↘	Riverton–Otautau Rd
50.5		Otautau
54.5	↱	Otautau–Nightcaps Rd
57.0	↰	Otautau–Nightcaps Rd
73.1		Nightcaps visitor centre

Cue	Day 2	
start		Nightcaps visitor centre
0km		go south-east on SH96
7.6	↰	SH96
8.1	↱	Wreys Bush
34.4	✳	Winton
36.4	↘	"to Lochiel'
42.9	↘	Lochiel
43.9		'to Wallacetown'
57.3	↰	SH99, Wallacetown
61.2	↱	West Plains Rd
64.9	↰	Steele Rd
67.7	↱	Gloucester St
68.8	↱	Bay Rd
71.1	↰	North Rd
73.7		Wensleys Cycles, Invercargill

OTAGO & SOUTHLAND

itself 'the heart of western Southland'. It's a rural service town with some substantial buildings suggesting a more prosperous past.

Distant craggy peaks draw closer and closer towards Nightcaps. High tension power line towers march across the landscape, carrying electricity to the Tiwai Point aluminium smelter.

Nightcaps

Nightcaps is a small settlement with an attractive streetscape.

If the visitor centre in the craft shop on somnolent SH96 is closed, ask at the store across the road.

Places to Stay & Eat Nightcaps' *Railway Hotel* (☎ 225 7332) is about it for accommodation and dining options. Rooms cost $30/40 per single/double and meals are available. Nightcaps' *domain camping ground* is at the bottom of the short hill from the pub but, while there is plenty of level tent space, there are currently no amenities. The publican said, 'They're trying to get it up and running again'.

About 8km further along SH96 is *Wreys Bush Hotel* (☎ 225 7651), where a double with breakfast costs $38.50 and the proprietor said, 'They've been trying to get Nightcaps camping ground up and running for the last four years'.

Nightcaps has a *supermarket* on the main street, as well as the *store* and a *takeaway* opposite the pub.

Day 2: Nightcaps to Invercargill
4-6 hours, 73.7km

Another gentle day of riding, Day 2 goes through level or pleasantly rolling agricultural countryside. There is no hill worthy of the name. The route features quiet roads as well as expansive views to the foothills of the Alps. The only place where traffic may be encountered before the outskirts of Invercargill is on the 8.5km section of SH6 from just north of Winton to Lochiel.

The promotion leaflet for the bustling township of **Winton** shows a picture of a cycle race on the main street (SH6) and includes cycle touring as one of the various pastimes in the area. However, there's little evidence that cycling is a major activity in this farm service centre that, because of its mild climate, is a popular retirement venue

for Invercargillians. Winton has other charms, including **historic buildings**, inviting tearooms, a good ***supermarket*** and a **shady park** with picnic tables. The Oreti River is a highly recommended **fishing spot**.

The SH6 south of Winton has a narrow shoulder. Although it leads directly back to Invercargill, it's much more enjoyable to leave the traffic behind and follow our route through the back streets. Turn off through Lochiel and take the little trafficked road to Wallacetown. Shelter belts of conifers will provide some relief if a headwind picks up.

Southern Scenic Route

Duration	3 days
Distance	307.7km
Difficulty	hard
Start	Invercargill
End	Milford Sound

Ride the Southern Scenic Route via scenic Lakes Manapouri and Te Anau to stunning Milford Sound, home of NZ's most famous walk, the Milford Track. The 22km fiord is breathtaking, and its often still waters reflect the sheer peaks that rise all around it.

Besides its natural beauty, the area is renowned for its swarms of sandflies and abundant rainfall, an average of 5500mm per year or 15mm *per day* (more than half an inch in imperial parlance). Think yourself lucky if the sun is shining; enjoy the spectacular, thundering waterfalls if not.

PLANNING
When to Ride

The route should be rideable at least from October to mid-April. Tourist traffic, including many coaches, is heaviest in December and January, which can be a problem in those winding and narrow sections of the road.

What to Bring

Good lights are advisable for the Homer Tunnel. Sandflies and mosquitoes can be a problem in the area.

GETTING TO/FROM THE RIDE
Invercargill

For transport to/from Invercargill, see the Getting There & Away section (p295) under Gateway Cities earlier in the chapter.

Bicycle This ride begins where the Catlins Coast ride ends.

Milford Sound/Te Anau
Bus InterCity (☎ 249 7505) has daily services between Milford and Queenstown (4½ hours, $55 plus $10 per bike) via Te Anau ($28 plus $10 per bike).

Change at Te Anau for other destinations. InterCity's three hour service to Invercargill costs $37. The trip to Christchurch (10½ hours, $116) goes via Dunedin (4½ hours, $58). Bikes cost $10 extra.

Topline Tours (☎ 249 8059) runs a 10 am shuttle service from Te Anau to Queenstown (2½ hours, $35 plus $10 per bike).

Packages that combine the Milford Track walk, kayaking and transporting you and your bike back to Te Anau are available. Te Anau Holiday Park (see Places to Stay in Te Anau) will mind your gear and organise this package. Track Net (☎ 249 7777), operating out of Te Anau Holiday Park, runs shuttle buses year round that can transport cyclists and bicycles out of Milford ($35 plus $5 per bike).

Bicycle If you want to ride to Queenstown there are two options. SH94 takes a long route (about 200km) between Te Anau and Queenstown through rolling, unpopulated country. After cutting across to SH6 from Mossburn (which has a store and restaurant), the road alongside Lake Wakatipu is without a shoulder, busy, narrow and winding.

A shorter (about 128km) and more adventurous two-day connection to Queenstown goes via South Mavora Lake on unsealed road. This route is only suitable for mountain bikes. The InfoMaps *Walter Peak* and *Te Anua* (1:50,000) cover the route.

Turn left off SH94 about 34km from Te Anau (after The Key), from where the road climbs gradually for 36km towards South Mavora Lake. A DOC camping ground is 5km off the road near the north end of South Mavora Lake. Water is available from the lake and the camping ground has a toilet, but there are no other services on the route.

From the lake it is mostly downhill, on rough road beside the Von River, to Walter Peak Station. From here the steamer TSS *Earnslaw* takes passengers across Lake Wakatipu to Queenstown every two hours

from 11 am to 7 pm between October and mid-April. The one-way fare is $20 (bikes free).

THE RIDE
Day 1: Invercargill to Tuatapere
5-6½ hours, 85.7km
Day 1 follows the sealed Southern Scenic Route from Invercargill. There are no hills to speak of but plenty of striking coastal scenery and panoramas over Colac and Te Waewae Bays. Heading roughly south-west to Riverton and beyond leaves you exposed to strong winds. If a southerly change has arrived or is due, it is advisable to delay your departure a day or so, if possible, or to break the journey at Riverton.

This attractive town of 1500 people dates from the early sealing and whaling days. Proclaiming itself the 'Riviera of the South', **Riverton** (38km) has good beaches and a range of accommodation and food options. Information is available from the Riverton Rock (☎ 234 8886) at 136 Palmerston St.

About 22km west of Riverton, *Hillcrest Holiday Park (☎ 234 5129)* caters to cyclists and backpackers. It has tent sites for $8 per person and bunks for $16. **Orepuki**, 6km beyond, now consists of just a *pub* and a tiny, poorly stocked *store* on a side street. The town is mostly decaying old buildings with verandah awnings.

For the rest of the way the undulating road snakes past farms, fields and views of Te Waewae Bay's crashing surf and gravelly beaches and the cloud capped coastal range inland. **Hector's dolphins** and **southern right whales** are sometimes seen in the bay.

Tuatapere
Tuatapere has a unique claim to fame: it's the 'sausage capital' of NZ. The local sausage factory, in small, nondescript premises at one end of town, turns out a tonne of handmade sausage per week. The town is also the most south-westerly in NZ, and its 740 inhabitants are the last in the country to see the sunset each day in summer. Tuatapere is at the end of the 'Down Under' version of Route 66, State Highway 99. Formerly relying on logging, the town is now diversifying into tourism.

Information The visitor centre (☎ 226 6349) is in Main St.

OTAGO & SOUTHLAND

OTAGO & SOUTHLAND

Day 1: Invercargill to Tuatapere

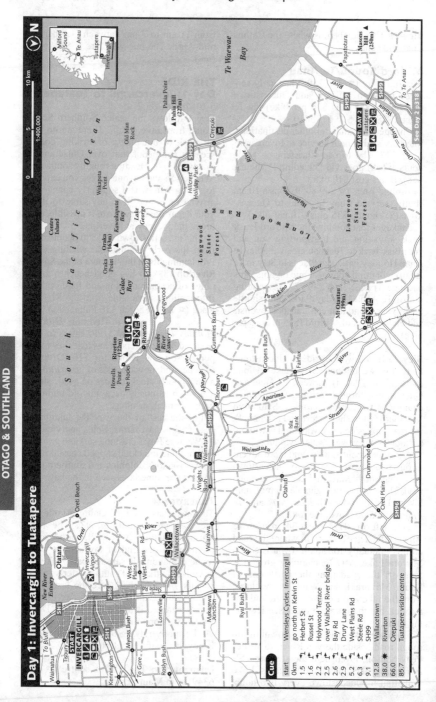

Cue		
start	Wensleys Cycles, Invercargill	
0km	go north on Kelvin St	
1.5	Herbert St	
1.6	Russel St	
2.2	Holywood Terrace	
2.5	over Waihopi River bridge	
2.6	Bay Rd	
2.9	Drury Lane	
5.2	West Plains Rd	
6.3	Steele Rd	
9.1	SH99	
12.8	Wallacetown	
38.0	Riverton	
66.0	Orepuki	
85.7	Tuatapere visitor centre	

START DAY 2 Tuatapere

See Day 2 p318

Things to See & Do Farming and timber milling are Tuatapere's main industries and the effectiveness of the woodchoppers is demonstrated by the small remnant of native forest in the town's domain – once most of the area looked like this.

The visitor centre has information on many activities. **Jet-boat rides, helicopter flights** and transport for walkers can be arranged through the centre.

The **Tuatapere Wild Challenge**, a multi-sport event involving kayaking, mountain biking and running, is held in January. Details are available from the visitor centre.

Places to Stay & Eat The small *Tuatapere Motor Camp* (☎ 226 6397), in the attractive domain near the river, has tent sites for $6 per person. *Five Mountains Park* (☎ 226 6418, 14 Clifden Rd) offers budget twin rooms from $26 and has some tent sites. *Waiau Hotel* (☎ 226 6409, 49 Main St) has doubles from $80, which includes breakfast.

Waiau Hotel also serves good country meals and Tuatapere sausages. *Takeaway shops* and a *supermarket* are on Main St.

Day 2: Tuatapere to Te Anau
6-8 hours, 102km

Day 2's route is long but it's over generally easy terrain with plenty of scenic and historic interest.

Clifden is the gateway to a short loop road detour to the **historic suspension bridge**, opened to traffic on 5 April 1899. The only traffic using it nowadays is on foot or bicycle. A basic *domain camping area* is at the northern end of the bridge; it has a toilet and water.

From Clifden the road rises gently and almost imperceptibly. The road then climbs again before it steepens after the Monowai turn-off to climb **Jericho Hill** (54.2km), which has good views to the mountains ahead.

Manapouri (82.3km) could be a good place to stop to shorten the day's distance. The name of the neighbouring lake is actually a cartographer's mistake. Manapouri (a corruption of *manawapora* or 'sorrowing heart') belonged to another lake; its real name was *Moturau*, which aptly translates as 'lake of a hundred islands'. Public outrage in the 1960s saved the lake from hydroelectric overdevelopment. The town is now a popular centre for **trips, cruises**

and **walking expeditions** to Doubtful Sound and the Fiordland area. The spectacular lake is the second deepest in NZ and is surrounded by bare topped mountains with native forest on their lower slopes.

Fiordland Travel (☎ 0800 656 502) is the visitor centre and tour operator. Kayak and dinghy hire is available at Adventure Charters (☎ 249 6626), next to the garage. Tiny *Manapouri Glade Motor Park* (☎ 249 6623), accessed by a road opposite the post office/store, is beautifully located by the lake and has tent sites at $16 for two people.

Possum Lodge (☎ 249 6660, 3 Waiau St) is a good backpackers, with share rooms for $16 per person and doubles for $18.

In Manapouri, Ruth and Lance Shaw offer *B&B* (☎/fax 249 6600, @ eco@xtra.co.nz) in self-contained cottages for $50/70 a single/double. They also operate a 20m charter vessel on the Fiordland Coast, and can transport bikes (by road) from Manapouri to Bluff for cruise passengers from Doubtful Sound.

The final 20km to Te Anau is lined by thick forest, which obscures any views.

Te Anau
Te Anau township, on the lake of the same name, is the tourist gateway to Milford Sound. The lake was gouged out by a huge glacier thousands of years ago and takes its name from the caves discovered on its western shore, Te Ana-au (meaning 'cave of rushing water').

With 2800 people, many more tourists and a huge variety of activities, Te Anau is a lively, spectacularly located town.

Information The busy Te Anau visitor centre (☎ 249 8900, fax 249 7022) is in the Fiordland Travel office, by the waterfront on the corner of Te Anau Terrace and Milford Rd.

The DOC office, the Fiordland National Park visitor centre (☎ 249 7924) is at the Manapouri end of Lake Front Dr, and can provide information on walks and camp sites in the area. It houses the Great Walks Booking Desk (☎ 249 8514, fax 249 8515).

The post office is in the centre of town on Milford Rd. Several banks are near the corner of Mokonui St and Milford Rd. An ATM is outside the bank near the supermarket in Milford Rd.

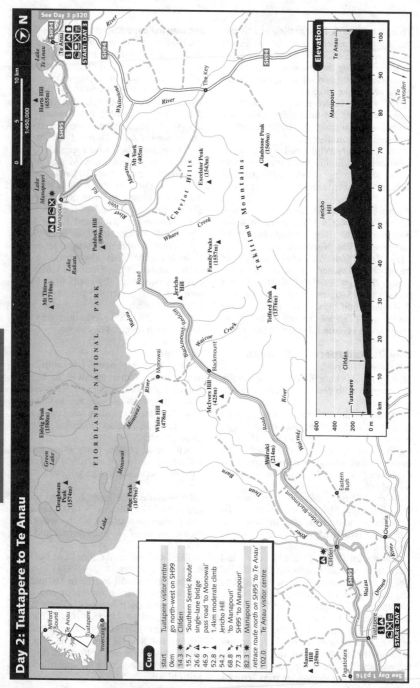

OTAGO & SOUTHLAND

Day 2: Tuatapere to Te Anau

Elevation

Cue		
start		Tuatapere visitor centre
0km		go north-west on SH99
14.3	❋	Clifden
15.7	◢	'Southern Scenic Route'
26.6	◢	single-lane bridge
46.9	↑	pass road 'to Monowai'
52.8	◢	1.4km moderate climb
54.2		Jericho Hill
68.8	◣	'to Manapouri'
77.3	◢	SH95 'to Manapouri'
82.3	❋	Manapouri
		retrace route north on SH95 'to Te Anau'
102.0		Te Anau visitor centre

The bike shop is Ferris's Cycle & Mowers (☎ 249 7460), 197 Milford Rd, on the outskirts of town.

Things to See & Do Te Anau is the jump-off point for the **Milford Track** and other walks such as the Kepler, Dusky, Routeburn and Hollyford. Ask the DOC office for details (see Information). Te Anau Holiday Park (see Places to Stay) will store gear and bicycles for walkers for $2 per bag and $5 per bicycle. The staff can also organise transport packages to Milford Sound and will do one-way pick ups (see Bus in Getting to/from the Ride).

The classic four-day **Milford Track** walk can only be done in the direction from Lake Te Anau to Milford Sound between late October and mid-April. Bookings are essential as walker numbers are limited. Accommodation is only in huts, to protect the environment and ensure the track is not overcrowded. You can walk independently or as part of a guided tour. A dated permit ($90/45 per adult/child) is required from DOC; book as far ahead as possible – even several months. Transport to the start, at the northern end of the lake, and back from Milford Sound costs extra. Book through the Great Walks Booking Desk (see Information).

The DOC-run **Te Anau Wildlife Centre** is just before town on the road from Manapouri. Landscaped grounds and natural enclosures house numerous birds, including the rare takahe, one of NZ's flightless birds and thought extinct until a colony was discovered in 1948. This is a good opportunity to identify birds you may see on walks.

Te Ana-au Caves on the western side of the lake were known to the Maori but not found by Europeans until 1948. Accessible only by boat, the 200m of active cave system has waterfalls, whirlpools and a glow-worm grotto in the inner reaches. Walkways and punts take visitors into the heart of the caves on daily 2½ hour trips. Book at Fiordland Travel (☎ 0800 656 501).

Kayaking trips in Milford Sound are offered by Fiordland Wilderness Experiences (☎ 249 7700, ✉ fiordland.sea.kayak@clear.net.nz), 66 Quintin Dr.

Waterwings Airways (☎ 249 7405), Air Fiordland (☎ 249 7505) and Southern Lakes helicopters (☎ 249 7167) operate **scenic** flights over the fiord from either Te Anau or from Milford Sound.

Cruises on Lake Te Anau and trips to Milford and Doubtful Sound are popular. From November to April, when the Milford Track is open, Fiordland Travel's MV *Tawera* runs from Te Anau Downs to Glade House ($40/10 per adult/child), the start of the Milford Track.

Places to Stay The *Fiordland Holiday Park* (☎ 249 7059), 2.5km from town on Milford Rd (200m past Upukeroa River bridge), offers serenity away from tourist hordes and has good modern facilities. Tours to Milford Sound pick up from the gate. Tent sites cost $7 per person, basic cabins cost from $20 up to around $60 for the best ones, and on-site vans from $28. Centrally located *Mountain View Holiday Park* (☎ 249 7462, 128 Te Anau Terrace) is on a small suburban block with limited tent sites at $20, cabins from $39, en suite units for $60 and motel units from $75; all prices for two. The large *Te Anau Holiday Park* (☎ 249 7457, 1 Te Anau-Manapouri Rd), near the DOC office on the way into town, has tent sites for $19, cabins from $39, tourist flats from $70 and motel units from $75; all prices for two. A bunkhouse has beds for $15.

At least a dozen DOC camping grounds are off SH94 towards Milford before the Homer Tunnel; the first is 17km out of Te Anau at Ten Mile Bush. These are listed in the pamphlet *Conservation Camp Sites*, available from all DOC offices. It costs around $3 per night to stay at each camp site.

Hostels include the large *Te Anau Backpackers Lodge* (☎ 249 7713, 48 Lake Front Dr). Beds in shared rooms and dorms cost $16, while doubles cost $18 per person. *Te Anau YHA Hostel* (☎ 249 7847, 220 Milford Rd) has spacious grounds, full amenities (including laundry) and offers gear storage. Dorm beds cost $16 per person, doubles are $38.

Several B&Bs are central. In increasing order of cost, they include: *Matai Lodge* (☎ 249 7360, 42 Mokonui St), *The Cats Whiskers* (☎ 249 8112, 2 Lake Front Dr), *House of Wood* (☎ 249 8404, 44 Moana Crescent) and *Shakespeare House* (☎ 249 7349, 10 Dusky St). Prices start from around $60/80 for a single/double.

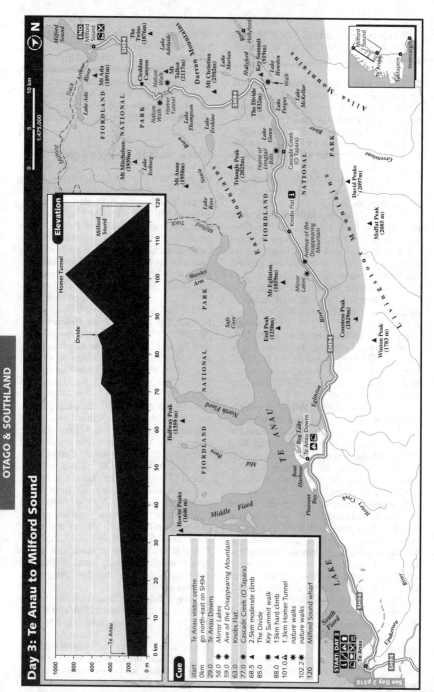

Day 3: Te Anau to Milford Sound

Cue

start	ℹ️	Te Anau visitor centre
0km		go north-east on SH94
29.0		Te Anau Downs
58.0	✸	Mirror Lakes
59.0	✸	Ave of the Disappearing Mountain
63.0	ℹ️	Knobs Flat
77.0	▲	Cascade Creek (O Tapara)
68.5	▲	2.5km moderate climb
85.0	✸	The Divide
88.0	✸	Key Summit walk
101.0	⛰️	13km hard climb
102.2	✸	1.3km Homer Tunnel
	✸	nature walks
	✸	nature walks
120		Milford Sound wharf

Elevation

Te Anau — Homer Tunnel — Divide — Milford Sound

OTAGO & SOUTHLAND

Motel rooms start at around $80 a double. Try the **Edgewater XL Motel** (☎ 249 7258, 52 Te Anau Terrace) or **Anchorage Hotel** (☎ 249 7256, 47 Quintin Dr). Many others have similar or higher prices. Top end options include **Te Anau Travelodge** (☎ 249 7411), on Te Anau Terrace in the town centre, with rooms from $120.

Places to Eat For ordinary snacks and sandwiches served among uninspiring decor and a tourist crush, visit the **Pop Inn** on the lake front.

Head along Milford Rd for a better selection of restaurants and takeaways. Arguably the best restaurant in town, and one which is reasonably priced, is **La Toscana** (☎ 249 7756, 108 Milford Rd). It serves pasta dishes for around $15, excellent pizzas for about $18 and has a good range of desserts. The **Olive Tree Cafe** (☎ 249 8496, 52 Milford Rd) is very good and has similar prices.

Keplers (☎ 249 7909), also on Milford Rd, serves venison, lamb and seafood dishes for around $20. Offering similar fare and at similar prices are **Hollywood Boulevard Cafe** and **Henry's**, a bistro at the Te Anau Travelodge (see Places to Stay). Get your teeth into good value steaks and grills at the **Settlers Steakhouse** or the **Ranch**.

Day 3: Te Anau to Milford Sound
7-9½ hours, 120km

The stretch of road to Milford Sound is simply spectacular. There are many fascinating sights as the road climbs steadily to the Divide. After a descent comes a challenging 13km climb culminating at the Homer Tunnel. The road plunges into this dark 1.2km subterranean passage, emerging into Cleddau Canyon and twisting steeply downwards all the way to the Sound.

If you have time to do this ride it is very worthwhile; if not, it's best to take a one day bus tour (see Things to See & Do in Milford Sound) – this will also overcome the problem of low roadside shrubbery that blocks at lot of scenery at cyclist-level. The return trip to Te Anau from Milford Sound is not so attractive with its climb through the damp Homer Tunnel. Bus transport out is available (see Getting to/from the Ride earlier in the chapter).

With camping gear, and sufficient food, this long trip can be broken at any of the DOC camping grounds along the road to Milford Sound. (Get the leaflet showing the locations from the DOC office in Te Anau.)

The first part of the ride is through undulating farmland atop the lateral moraine of the glacier that gouged out Lake Te Anau. At 16km the road enters a patch of mountain beech forest and passes the **Te Anau Downs harbour** (29km), where boats run to the start of the Milford Track. At Te Anau Downs, the popular **Grumpy's Backpackers** (☎ 249 8133) has beds from $16 per person in dorms to $22.50 in doubles.

About 6km after Te Anau Downs the ride enters **Fiordland National Park** and the Eglinton Valley, studded with more patches of beech – red, silver and mountain – between the alluvial flats and meadows.

Interesting sights on the way are the **Mirror Lakes** (58km), where the glassy surface perfectly reflects the surroundings, and the **Avenue of the Disappearing Mountain** about 1km later. On this long straight, the mountain ahead, Consolation Peak in the Darran range, seems to disappear below the horizon when approached. (Unfortunately, due to the growth of its trees, the Avenue of the Disappearing Mountain is itself disappearing.) At Knobs Flat, 5km beyond Mirror Lakes, a **visitor centre** has exhibits on the area, toilets and water. **O Tapara**, more commonly known as Cascade Creek (77km), is home to long-tail bats, NZ's only native land mammal.

The vegetation changes significantly nearer the **Divide** (85km) the lowest east-west pass across the Southern Alps. A good shelter here is used by walkers starting or finishing the Routeburn and Greenstone tracks. About an hour's brisk walk leads to **Key Summit**, the source of three river systems – the Hollyford, Greenstone/Clutha and Eglinton/Waiau – which radiate to the west, east and south coasts of the island.

From the Divide, the road falls into the beech forest of the Hollyford Valley before rising to the east portal of the **Homer Tunnel** (101km). At each portal there are short **nature walks**, with plaques describing alpine species found here. Cheeky keas frequent the area; keep a close eye on your gear as these beautiful drab-green parrots' strong beaks can rip saddles, panniers, clothing and destroy plastic containers.

OTAGO & SOUTHLAND

Named for Harry Homer, who found the Homer Saddle in 1889, the tunnel was begun in 1935 to provide Depression-era employment. The 1270m rough hewn shaft plummets steeply from east to west, emerging into the spectacular **Cleddau Canyon** on the Milford Sound side. Traffic travels slowly through the tunnel – cyclists may be able to engage the services of a friendly following driver to light the way for them.

Above the beech forest just before Milford, it might be possible to glimpse Mt Tutoko (2746m), Fiordland's highest peak.

Milford Sound

The 22km-long sound, (strictly speaking, a fiord, since it was carved by a glacier) is breathtakingly beautiful. Dominated by Mitre Peak (1695m), Milford's calm water mirrors the mountains that rise all around. In wet weather the cliffs are ribboned with waterfalls and the mist and rain creates a haunting atmosphere.

This scenery attracts large numbers of tourists and the wharf resembles an international passenger terminal with its constant bus and ferry arrivals and departures.

Information The ferry terminal has an information desk (☎ 249 7419) with brochures on the area; cruises can be booked here. The terminal has a display on the area's history.

Things to See & Do A cruise is a must and provides the chance to see wildlife such as dolphins, sharks, seals and penguins. Trips 'n' Tramps (☎ 249 7081) offers a variety of bus trips from Te Anau to Milford Sound incorporating cruises and walks. Fiordland Travel (☎ 249 7419) has 1½ hour cruises, which travel to the **underwater reef observatory** moored at Harrison Cove. Milford Wanderer cruises are longer at 2½ hours. Overnight cruises are also offered between 1 October and 30 April. Red Boat Cruises (☎ 0800 657 444), the biggest operator on the sound, has similar itineraries. The cruises are enormously popular. Despite there being a total of more than a dozen cruises daily in the summer months, it is advisable to book a place a few days ahead.

Places to Stay & Eat The *Mitre Peak Lodge* caters only to those who do the guided walk on the Milford Track. The only other place to stay is the hostel-style *Milford Lodge* (☎ 249 8071), about 2km before the ferry wharf, off the main road. Tent sites cost $9 per person, and a bed in a musty bunkhouse for $18. Singles/twins cost from $30/40. Cheap meals are served in a good dining area, and there's a kitchen for guests.

Mitre Peak Lodge runs the *Mitre Peak Cafe*, which serves coffee and snacks but closes at 5pm. The *Shark in the Bar* next door serves little else other than pies and beer.

Western Otago Circuit

Duration	3 days
Distance	205.5km
Difficulty	moderate-hard
Start/End	Queenstown

Starting in NZ's adventure capital, Queenstown, this ride takes the Crown Range Rd (SH89; the country's highest highway) to visit Wanaka, Cromwell and other old gold towns. Passing river gorges, brilliantly coloured lakes and wide open spaces, this ride includes a challenging climb and a descent on a scenic gravel road on Day 1. Enjoy the excitement of the challenging section while you can; the road is expected to be fully sealed by 2002.

HISTORY

Maori moa hunters lived in the Otago region from the 10th to the 14th century until habitat destruction and extinction of the moa forced them to the coast. Pressure to find sheep grazing country brought Europeans to the area after John Thomson found the way across Lindis Pass. All the suitable farming area around Lakes Wanaka and Wakatipu was taken up by the 1860s. The discovery of gold below the junction of the Clutha and Kawarau Rivers in 1862 diverted attention from pastoral pursuits and brought an influx of prospectors to the area. The stone buildings, gold mining equipment and machinery, and piles of tailings found throughout the region are a legacy of this era. Cromwell is at the centre of the old Otago Goldfields, which were active until 1910.

NATURAL HISTORY

The rugged, dry schist plateau of central Otago lies in the rain shadow of the Southern

OTAGO & SOUTHLAND

Alps. Cromwell only receives about 400mm of rain per year; however, the area was not always as arid and barren as it now appears. Only about 1500 years ago a thick scrub covered the land with remnant forest of matai and totara. The fires of the moa hunters, followed by sheep grazing and rabbit invasion, successively denuded the vegetation and eroded the soils.

The long narrow lakes of the area are glacial in origin. Lake Wakatipu is unusual, having 'tides' of 150mm due to changes in air pressure. Maori beliefs say the tides are created by the beating of the heart of a giant demon below the water.

PLANNING

This ride can be cut from three to two days. To do this, ride from Queenstown to Wanaka on Day 1 (as outlined). Leave year gear in Wanaka and then ride the loop to Cromwell and through the Kawarau Gorge unladen. To get back to Wanaka from here, either ride back via Day 1's route or catch a shuttle bus from near Arrow Junction (see Getting to/from the Ride).

When to Ride

The Crown Range Rd (SH89) can be closed by winter snowfalls, but otherwise the route should be accessible most of the year. Best times will be October and March to April when temperatures and UV radiation are milder.

GETTING TO/FROM THE RIDE
Queenstown

Air It is possible to fly with a bike into and out of Queenstown airport, 8km east of town. Air New Zealand (☎ 442 4600) and Ansett New Zealand (☎ 0800 800 146) run daily direct flights to Christchurch, Auckland, and smaller destinations on both main islands.

Bus All major operators have services to Queenstown from other main South Island centres; see Getting to/from the Ride for the Southern Scenic Route.

Wanaka Connexions (☎ 0800 879 926) runs shuttles between Queenstown and Wanaka. To condense Days 2 & 3, leaving gear in Wanaka, arrange for a shuttle pick up from near Arrow Junction (see Planning). The last shuttle of the day to Wanaka leaves Queenstown at 5 pm and arrives at the

Crown Range Rd (SH89) turn-off on SH6 between 5.15 and 5.30 pm. Don't be late!

Bicycle See the Southern Scenic Route for details on routes between Te Anau and Queenstown.

Wanaka

Bus InterCity buses travel daily between Queenstown and the west coast glaciers via Haast Pass, stopping at the Wanaka. The bus depot (☎ 443 7885) is at 84 Ardmore St, opposite Cliffords. Wanaka Connexions (☎ 0800 879 926) runs a scheduled service between Queenstown and Wanaka via Queenstown airport. It costs $25 per person plus $10 per bike, which is carried on a 'bike beak' at the back of the van. It *will* get dusty.

Bicycle The West Coast ride in the Westland chapter starts at Wanaka.

THE RIDE
Queenstown

White explorers found the Queenstown area deserted when they first arrived in the 1850s, although evidence shows prior Maori occupation. Sheep farmers followed, but when two shearers found gold in 1862 prospectors rushed to the region. At the height of the mining boom, four paddle steamers and many other craft plied the waters of Lake Wakatipu. When gold petered out by 1900 the population had dropped from thousands to a mere 190.

Now the self-styled 'adventure capital of the world', Queenstown has a permanent population of 7500 and a stunning setting beside Lake Wakatipu and the Remarkable Range. Unfortunately, the hustle for the tourist dollar and threat of overdevelopment mar the town's character. The cycle tourist seeking peace and quiet will be disappointed. On the other hand, the cycle tourist wishing to party has come to the right place.

Skiing is the main winter activity, but in summer plenty of substitute adrenalin activities are on offer for those with the money to pay for them. High prices for everything (including food) is another stunning feature of modern Queenstown.

Information The Queenstown Travel & Visitor Centre (☎ 442 4100, fax 442 8907, ✉ qvc@xtra.co.nz), in the Clocktower Centre

OTAGO & SOUTHLAND

on the corner of Shotover and Camp Sts, is the town's genuine visitor centre. It's a very busy place, open from 7 am to 7 pm during summer. The other 'information centres' are merely activity booking offices keen to relieve you of money.

The DOC office (☎ 442 7933), on Shotover St opposite the Trust Bank, has information on walks and natural attractions in the area. It's open Monday to Saturday from 8 am to 7 pm in summer.

Queenstown has a number of banks and moneychangers.

A good bike shop, Dr Bike (☎ 442 8883), is at the top of the mall, opposite the post office. It hires out older front/dual-suspension mountain bikes from $30/40 half-day, or $40/60 for the day. More recent models are an extra $5 for a half-day or $10 for the day. Trail maps and advice are included, but keep in mind that the people giving the advice are probably super-fit elite mountain bike racers. If *you* aren't, the trail is harder than *they* think.

Things to See & Do The list of activities available is virtually endless – just browse the shopfronts along Shotover St. A good start is to take the steeply inclined – and priced – **Skyline Gondola** to the summit of the hill overlooking town. It operates from 10 am to 9 or 10 pm daily. The views are thrilling. If you have the energy, save your money and **walk** or **ride** to Skyline through the forest on the steep unsealed vehicle track from Lomond Crescent. A good cafeteria-style *restaurant* is at the top. The travel & visitor centre can guide you to the many other free walks and rides in the area.

The **Queenstown Motor Museum** below the lower gondola terminal has a collection of old cars, motorcycles and a MiG-21 jet on show. Next door to the gondola terminal, the **Kiwi & Birdlife Park** has a nocturnal kiwi house and a growing program of raising endangered species. Kea and the rare black stilt are on display in the landscaped grounds.

Steam railway fans can get a fix near Queenstown. At Kingston, off SH6 on the southern end of Lake Wakatipu, the *Kingston Flyer* (☎ 248 8848, fax 248 8881) runs twice daily from 1 October to 30 April to Fairlight and back, a total of around 30km. InterCity buses stop at Kingston on their run between Te Anau and Queenstown.

Cycling activities are offered by Gravity Action (☎ 442 8178), including a combined **mountain bike & rafting** experience in Skippers Canyon and on the Shotover River, or a **mountain biking & bungy** (off the 102m high 'Pipeline') package.

Places to Stay Though noisy and crowded, the *Queenstown Motor Park* (☎ 442 7252) is conveniently located at the end of Man St, up a steep hill less than 1km from the centre. Tent sites cost $11 per person. Cabins start from $30, tourist flats from $56 and motel units cost $90; all prices for two. About 8km away, the tired *Frankton Motor Camp* (☎ 442 2079) has tent sites for $8.50 for one; cabins are $32 and self-contained tourist flats cost from $40 to $50 – both for two.

The large *Queenstown YHA* (☎ 442 8413, ✉ yhaqutn@yha.org.nz, 88 Lake Esplanade) is right by the lake. Dorm beds cost $18; double rooms cost from $40.

Queenstown is full of good backpacker hostels; ask at the tourist & visitor centre for a full list. Highly rated backpacker hostels include: *Alpine Lodge* (☎ 442 7220, 13 Gorge Rd), which has beds in dorms for $17 and, in doubles, for $20; and *Scallywags Guesthouse* (☎ 442 7083, 27 Lomond Crescent), with beds in shared rooms for $20 and, in doubles, for $25.

Dozens of B&B establishments operate in the Queenstown/Arrowtown/Arrow Junction triangle. Ask for details at the travel & visitor centre.

Queenstown motels are expensive, but prices fluctuate with the seasons. Cheapest are the *Colonial Village* (☎ 442 7629, 100 Frankton Rd) with rooms from around $75, and the *Alpine Sun* (☎ 442 8482, 14 Hallenstein St), which is slightly dearer.

Upmarket hotels include the *Sherwood Manor Hotel* (☎ 442 8032, 335 Frankton Rd), which has good facilities and well-appointed doubles from $100.

Places to Eat Queenstown has a thriving restaurant scene serving a wide range of cuisines. Cafes and takeaways along Shotover and Beach Sts include the *Bakery (11 Shotover St)*, serving baked food, sandwiches and pizza 24 hours a day. The Beach St shopping centre's *food hall* has a selection of stalls, including Thai and Japanese, and is open from 9 am to 9 pm.

The crowded *Cow Restaurant* has served pasta and pizza on Cow Lane for 23 years, so it must be doing something right. *Little India Bar & Tandoor (11 Shotover St)* is popular for its reasonably priced traditional vegetarian and non-vegetarian dishes.

Among the better more expensive eateries is *Roaring Megs (☎ 442 9676, 57 Shotover St)*, established in 1982, in a historic gold mining cottage. Serving what is described as 'NZ cuisine with Swiss and French inspiration', it opens at 6.15 pm. *Trellises Restaurant*, in Mountain View Lodge on Frankton Rd, opens daily from 6 pm and serves standard NZ main courses, pasta and salads.

Despite its size, the town doesn't have a large supermarket. The nearest things are the *Queenstown Supermarket* on the mall or the *Alpine Food Centre* on Shotover St. The cheapest and largest *supermarket* is at Frankton, about 8km away.

Day 1: Queenstown to Wanaka
5-6½ hours, 75km
A challenging climb to 1100m on a sandy surface followed by a long gravelly downhill is the main feature of Day 1.

Gorge Rd out of Queenstown is busy and undulating at first but has only one really noticeable hill, after the **Shotover River** bridge, where jet boats charge back and forth in the narrow gorge.

The attractive, well-preserved gold mining village of **Arrowtown** (19km) features a beautiful avenue of deciduous trees and a main street with wooden buildings resembling the set for a classic western movie.

Part way up the steep climb of the Crown Range, a **scenic lookout** (27.7km) gives classic views of the winding ribbon of road clinging to the edge of the precipice and across the Kawarau River valley. The sandy surface, starting 4km after the lookout, makes the final 3km of the climb a struggle for traction and control.

From the summit, the unsealed road continues for 14.7km, descending steadily without hairpin bends but with more loose gravel and corrugations. The scenery is not as exciting, but there's no time to look around – it is essential to concentrate on your line and speed around bends and to keep the bike pointing in the right direction.

For the rest of the way to Cardrona the route follows a narrow valley of the pretty Cardrona River between lowish, brown, tussocky hills. The river switches back and forth under the road 11 times at numbered bridges.

Cardrona has the feel of a one-horse western town, emphasised by the big American car parked outside the Cardrona Hotel sporting police markings and the satirical (read with a Kiwi-accent) number plates 'SHERUF'. Next to the hotel in another ancient weatherboard building is a small museum containing period items. Accommodation and food is available at the *Cardrona Hotel (☎/fax 443 8153)*, the only service provider on the route between Arrowtown and Wanaka.

Another 12km along the sealed, gently descending SH89 is the access track to the **Pisa Conservation Area**. A seven hour return walk goes to **Little Criffel Peak** (1341m). The road into Wanaka has superb views to Mt Aspiring (3030m), 'the Matterhorn of NZ'.

Wanaka
Laid-back Wanaka (population 2200) is a breath of fresh air after the hype of Queenstown. Most of the same activities and similar stunning scenery are here, but the pace and prices are (s)lower. The town is the gateway to Mt Aspiring National Park and surrounding ski areas.

Information The visitor centre (☎ 443 1233, fax 443 9238) is in the Mt Aspiring National Park visitor centre (☎ 443 7660) on Ardmore St. It's open from 8 am to 4.45 pm weekdays and 9 am to 4.30 pm on weekends. The DOC counter is the place to inquire about walks.

The Adventure Centre (☎ 443 9422), 99 Ardmore St, books most activities (see Things to See & Do). It is open from 8.30 am to 6 pm in summer.

Wanaka has several well-equipped bike shops. Good Sports (☎ 443 7966, ✉ goodsports@xtra.co.nz), in Dunmore St opposite the New World supermarket, plans to hire suspension mountain bikes for $30 to $50 per day. Staff can also advise where to ride and organise transport to the national park. Ask about their Cardrona bike/hike trip. Cycles & Mowers (☎ 443 7259) is around the corner at 3 Helwick St. Racers Edge/Planet Snow (☎ 443 7882; ✉ racers.edge_wanaka@xtra.co.nz), on the lakefront at

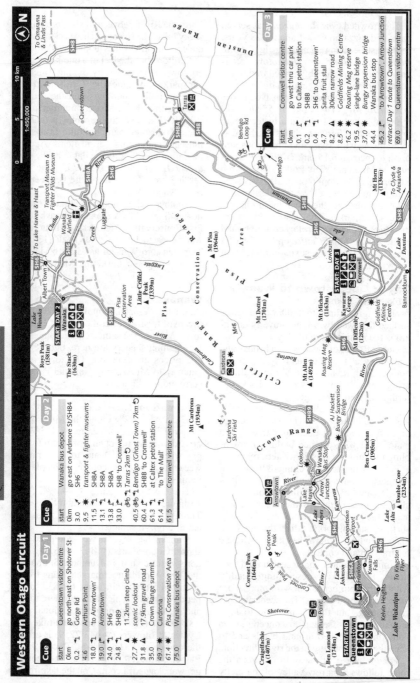

Western Otago Circuit

Day 1

Cue		
0km		Queenstown visitor centre
	↱	go north-east on Shotover St
0.2	↱	Gorge Rd
4.6		Arthurs Point
18.0	↱	'to Arrowtown'
19.0	↰	Arrowtown
24.0	↱	SH6
24.8	↰	SH89
27.7	▲	11.2km steep climb
31.8	✳	scenic lookout
35.0	▲	17.9km gravel road
49.7	✳	Crown Range summit
61.4	✳	Cardrona
75.0		Pisa Conservation Area
		Wanaka bus depot

Day 2

Cue		
start		Wanaka bus depot
0km	↱	go east on Ardmore St/SH84
3.0	↱	SH6
9.5	✳	transport & fighter museums
11.5	↰	SH8A
13.1	↰	SH8A
13.8	↱	SH8A
33.0	↱	SH8 'to Cromwell'
	⟲	Tarras 2km ↰
40.5	↰	Bendigo (Ghost Town) 7km ⟲
60.4	↱	SH8B 'to Cromwell'
61.3		at Caltex petrol station
61.4	↰	'to The Mall'
61.5		Cromwell visitor centre

Day 3

Cue		
start		Cromwell visitor centre
0km		go west thru car park
0.1	↱↱	to Caltex petrol station
0.2	↱↱	SH8B
0.4	↱↱	SH6 'to Queenstown'
4.7	▲	Sarita fruit stall
8.2	▲	30km narrow road
8.5	✳	Goldfields Mining Centre
16.2	▲	Roaring Meg reserve
19.5	▲	single-lane bridge
37.0	✳	Bungy suspension bridge
44.4		Wanaka bus stop
45.2	↱	'to Arrowtown', Arrow Junction
		retrace Day 1 route to Queenstown
69.0		Queenstown visitor centre

the corner of Ardmore and Helwick Sts, also offers bike shop services.

Things to See & Do The Day 3 route passes several of Wanaka's main attractions, including the **New Zealand Fighter Pilots Museum**, which hosts Warbirds over Wanaka, an airshow held every second Easter (even years) – see Day 3 for further details.

You can try **skydiving** with Tandem Skydive Wanaka (☎ 443 7207) at the Wanaka airfield. The view from 2800m, and dropping, is a buzz. **Paragliding** is slightly less expensive – try Wanaka Paragliding School (☎ 443 9193).

DOC's *Wanaka Walks* brochure outlines 11 **walks** around the town, ranging from easy 30-minute jaunts beside the lake to more exhausting treks such as the one up Mt Roy, which starts 6km from town on the Mt Aspiring road. This 8km track winds every step of the way, but has stunning views of Mt Aspiring. Mountain bikers can also use the track (see Information).

To take the work out of **mountain biking**, Alpine Mountain Biking (☎ 443 8943) offers 4WD or helicopter trips to high altitudes between November and April. It provides the transport up and you enjoy the descent.

Book other activities, including **kayaking, parapenting, rock climbing, white-water sledging, rafting** and **canyoning** through the Adventure Centre (see Information).

Places to Stay The *Wanaka Motor Park* (☎ 443 7883, 212 Brownston St) is to the left off SH89 at the entrance to town. Tent sites cost $9 per person and there is a special, shady camping area without car access for walkers and cyclists. Cabins cost $30, and tourist flats from $50; both for two.

The other motor camps are well out of town, as are the DOC camp sites. Check with the information centre.

Wanaka YHA Hostel (☎ 443 7405, 181 Upton St) has a relaxed, friendly atmosphere and is open all day. Gear and bike storage is available. Beds cost $15 in dorms or $18 per person in doubles. *Holly's Hostel (☎ 443 8187, 71 Upton St)* gets an excellent rating from backpackers. It is very close to the centre of town and has beds in dorms for $16 and, in doubles, $18 per person. *Wanaka Bakpaka (☎ 443 7837, 117 Lakeside Rd)* is opposite the jetty on the northern side of Roy's Bay, with great views of the lake and mountains. Mountain bikes, kayaks and canoes can be hired. Dorms or shared rooms cost $16 per person, doubles cost from $34.

The best among a dozen or so B&B establishments in and around Wanaka are *Williman's (☎ 443 9333, ✉ williman@voyager.co.nz, 15 Norman Terrace)*, charging $40 per person per night, and *Te Wanaka Lodge (☎ 443 9246, ✉ tewanakalodge@xtra.co.nz, 23 Brownston St)*, which operates as a ski lodge in winter. It serves a gourmet buffet breakfast and charges $120 single, $130 a double or $160 in a semi-contained cottage that sleeps three.

Cheaper motels include *Archway Motel (☎ 443 7698, 64 Hedditch St)*, which has doubles from $70. *Edgewater Resort Hotel (☎ 443 8311)*, on Sargood Dr, is an upmarket option offering rooms from $150.

Places to Eat Wanaka is well appointed with eating houses. There are a couple of standard takeaways on Ardmore St near the Mall. Other places worth trying include *Paddy's (☎ 443 7645, 21 Dunmore St)*, a

Day 1: Queenstown to Wanaka

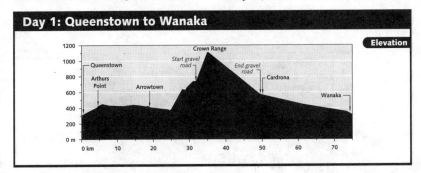

popular family restaurant with reasonable food, including vegetarian options, at equally reasonable prices; the **Tuatara Pizza Co** (☎ *443 8186, 76 Ardmore St)* for interesting pizzas; or nearby **Relishes** (☎ *443 9018, 1/99 Ardmore St)*, an excellent cafe. For more up-market dining, try **Ripples** (☎ *443 7413)*, in Pembroke Mall, with seafood dishes and good views from an alfresco verandah.

Not to be missed is **Wanakai** (☎ *443 7795, 199 Ardmore St)*, on the waterfront. It serves fabulous chunks of fruit pies and large servings of imaginative vegetarian and non-vegetarian cafe style mains at reasonable prices.

The well-stocked **New World supermarket** on Dunmore St is open daily.

Day 2: Wanaka to Cromwell
3½-5 hours, 61.5km

The longest and steepest climb of the day is the hill out of Wanaka from the lake past the shops – it 'climbs' about 30m over its 1km length. The good sealed road, with minimal traffic, to Cromwell passes two museums at the airfield. First is the **Wanaka Transport Museum** (9.5km), which includes a section on bicycles. Next door is the fascinating **New Zealand Fighter Pilots Museum**, where many lovingly restored, airworthy war planes are displayed. You can even fly in a WWII Mustang fighter, but if you have to ask the price you can't afford the $2000.

There are no services on the route, so a worthwhile side trip (at 33km) is the easy 2km return trip to Tarras' **tearooms** and **store**, where you're likely to meet other cyclists coming down from Lindis Pass.

The route follows the Clutha River, crossing the wide, strongly flowing stream on a steel box girder bridge, then taking the eastern side of the valley beneath bare brown hills. Snowy peaks are now visible behind. There is no shade anywhere along the road.

At 40.5km is the Bendigo Loop Rd (which eventually loops back onto the route); 6km to the left, up a steep unsealed grade on the western slopes of the Dunstan Range, is Bendigo and the beginning of a well-marked **ghost town walk** past tunnels, crumbling dwellings, shafts and old stamper batteries.

Rocky outcrops herald the headwaters of **Lake Dunstan**, where plenty of water birds wade in the shallows. The rest area nearby has toilets.

The route crosses the Clutha again on the substantial Deadmans Point Bridge to reach Cromwell.

Cromwell
This modern town of 2600 people, once dependent on gold, now makes money from stone fruit production. The massive fruit bowl beside the road near the town centre is testament to this. Roadside stalls on SH6 sell apricots, peaches, nectarines, plums, cherries, apples and pears. Picking and packing takes place in January and February.

Information The visitor centre and museum (☎ 445 0212, fax 445 1319) is in the mall, just off SH8B (turn left at the Caltex petrol station). It's open from 10 am to 4 pm daily. The Caltex petrol station has basic bike bits.

Things to See & Do Cromwell is at the centre of the Old Otago goldfields. The **museum** in the visitor centre (see Information) displays local mining artefacts and has a section on Chinese miners. Nearby are several gold-mining ghost towns and working

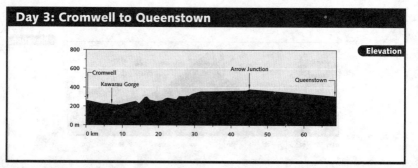

Day 3: Cromwell to Queenstown

Terminal face of Fox Glacier, Westland National Park, Westland

Picturesque Lake Wanaka, Otago

Mount Tasman from Fox Glacier, Westland

Pancake Rocks at Dolomite Point, near Punakaiki, Westland

Weathered ice formations, Franz Josef Glacier, Westland

exhibitions of mining techniques. **Bannockburn**, 9km south of Cromwell over the Bannockburn bridge, features a 2½ hour walk around water races, dams, shafts and remains of mud brick buildings. Self-guiding maps are available at the visitor centre.

On Melmore Terrace, beside the lake on the south side of town, is Old Cromwell, a row of historic buildings housing craft shops. The buildings were carefully moved and restored before the original Cromwell site was submerged by the dammed waters of Lake Dunstan.

Places to Stay & Eat The *Cromwell Holiday Park (☎ 445 0164, 1 Alpha St)*, just down from Deadmans Point Bridge, has tent sites for $18, cabins from $28 to $45 (with en suites), tourist flats for $55, and motel units for $65; all prices for two. It has a store, and sporting facilities (including a golf course) are nearby.

The *Chalets (☎ 445 1399, 102 Barry Ave)*, once the dam workers' quarters, are now well-equipped budget accommodation. Each chalet has its own communal lounge, kitchen and bathroom facilities and a number of singles/doubles with washbasin for $20/30.

Motels include the *Twin Rivers Motel (☎ 445 0035 or ☎ 0800 267 268, 69 Inniscort St)*, with rooms from $68 to $75, and *Gateway Lakeside Motel (☎ 445 0385, 45 Alpha St)*, which charges $65 a double. It may be possible to negotiate better prices outside peak season.

Several B&B establishments operate in the Cromwell area, most a few kilometres out of town (the visitor centre has details). One in town is the very welcoming *Cottage Gardens (☎ 445 0628, ✉ eco@xtra.co.nz, 3 Alpha St)*, next to the motor camp. Singles/twin rooms with family share bathroom cost $40/50, or $55/70 with private en suite. You can have your washing done, torn clothes mended and even have grazes and blisters patched. Prices include supper at night and a good breakfast.

A three course dinner, at a day's notice, costs $20 per person.

Licensed *restaurants*, *cafes* and *takeaways* cluster around the mall in the town centre. Near Old Cromwell is a *dairy* and a *pub*.

Day 3: Cromwell to Queenstown
4-5½ hours, 69km

Spectacular gorge scenery is the attraction along the Kawarau River. Between about the 8km and 38km points, the road is quite narrow and winding with almost no shoulder. SH6 carries lots of coaches at times, which can be unnerving with their size, speed and closeness. There are no major hills, though the road undulates, rising gradually towards Arrow Junction. The side trips provide opportunities to visit gold mining ghost towns.

Several fruit stalls offer refreshment. The *Sarita stall*, beside the road about 4.7km from Cromwell, has toilets and picnic tables sheltered by poplars. The stalls further on do not have these facilities.

In Kawarau Gorge, the **Goldfields Mining Centre** (8.5km) is reached via a footbridge spanning the gorge. Rather high-priced tours of mining relics are offered.

At 16km is a small but active hydroelectric installation opposite the aptly named **Roaring Meg Recreation Reserve**.

Closer to Queenstown is a **suspension bridge** built in 1880 to access the Wakatipu goldfields. It was used until 1963, but now has a new lease on life as the launching point for bungy jumps. View for free from the sidelines if you don't want to take the plunge towards the swirling, emerald green waters. Further on there are vineyards and wineries.

If not shuttling from Arrow Junction to Wanaka (see Getting to/from the Ride), either retrace the outward route via Arrowtown or stay on busier SH6 and SH6A directly to Queenstown, which will save about 8km.

OTAGO & SOUTHLAND

Westland

Westland is one of New Zealand's wildest, wettest and most wonderful places to cycle. Comprising the South Island's narrow coastal strip between the Southern Alps and the Tasman Sea, it's an isolated region of rocky beaches, bush-clad hills, glaciers and towering peaks. While Fox and Franz Josef Glaciers are the most popular sights, there are many other fascinating features on view, including mighty Mt Cook, huge lakes in the south and interesting towns like Hokitika.

Finding your way could hardly be simpler, the only ride in this chapter follows SH6 from Wanaka up the west coast to Greymouth and then continues north to Westport.

HISTORY

The area was sparsely settled by Maoris in pre-European days. Groups moved through in search of food and carried prized greenstone across the mountain passes to other regions.

The first European to sight the west coast was Dutch navigator Abel Tasman in 1642. It was nearly 130 years before the next visit, when James Cook sailed the *Endeavour* north along the coast in February 1770.

Sealers visited the coast from the early 1800s, but the dense vegetation and uninviting weather hampered land exploration and white settlement. The discovery of gold in the late 1850s was the spur to development. The Arthur's Pass coach road was completed in 1865 and by 1867 about 30,000 prospectors had flocked to goldfields along the Buller River and Lake Brunner.

From 1861, timber exploitation saw *kahikatea* (white pine), *matai* (black pine) and silver beech rafted down the rivers and lakes to the gold-mining areas for use as pit props, while flax milling took place in the Makarora valley for three decades from 1890.

After gold-mining declined, many of the prospectors who remained turned to coal-mining, the timber industry and farming. The coastal bush was hacked back but always threatened to reclaim open spaces. Now, scattered throughout the thick bush and by rivers, is the rusted debris of a century of exploitative industry.

NATURAL HISTORY

The Alpine Fault running the length of the west coast is a major geological feature shaping Westland. The two tectonic plates carrying different sections of the earth's crust continue to slide past one another, causing earthquakes along their junction. One of these earthquakes caused landslips in 1968 that dammed the Buller River in its gorge near Inangahua. The resulting flood forced people to evacuate as water banked up behind the slip and overflowed the river's banks downstream when it broke through.

Haast Pass, at just over 560m, is one of the lowest passes on the main Southern Alps divide. The contrast between the rainforest on its western side and the lakes and open spaces to the east is amazing. On the valley slopes atop the pass, subalpine scrub dominates the first 100m above the tree line, with tall snow tussocks and herbs at higher altitudes.

Before white settlement, the lower flats of the Makarora River were covered by cabbage trees, flax shrubs and ferns. Remnants of the original vegetation are preserved in Mt Aspiring National Park.

The Haast region is the centre of a major wildlife refuge where some of the biggest

0   40   80 km

KAHURANGI
NATIONAL
PARK

▲ Mt Domett
(1615m)

Oparara
Karamea

▲ Mt
Kendall
(1751m)

*Karamea
Bight*

SH67

*To
Nelson*

SH6

Seddonville
● Hector
Granity

Westport
Cape
Foulwind
● **Buller**

Denniston
Buller Gorge

Murchison

*Lake
Rotoroa*

Charleston

▲ Mt
Uriah

Inangahua
Junction

SH69

SH65

SH6

**PAPAROA
NATIONAL
PARK**

Punakaiki

Reefton

Springs
Junction

Barrytown ● ▲ **Mt Ryall**

Ikamatua

▲ Mt Kemp
(1637m)

Lewis
Pass
(907m)

Runanga
● Stillwater
Nelson Creek

Greymouth ●
Brunner

Shantytown

Kumara
Junction

*Lake
Brunner*

▲ Mt Ajax
(1832m)

To Christchurch

**ARTHUR'S PASS
NATIONAL
PARK**

*Lake
Sumner*

Hokitika ●

Otira

Ross

▲ Mt Rolleston
(2272m)

)(Arthur's Pass
(920m)
▲ Arthur's Pass

Pukekura

Mt Bryce
(2188m) ▲

▲ Mt Murchison
(2400m)

*Paketeraki
Range*

Oxford

Okarito ● Whataroa
Harihari

▲ Mt Whitcombe
(2638m)

Newton Peak
(2545m) ▲ ▲ Mt Arrowsmith
(2795m)

*Lake
Coleridge*

SH73

Sheffield

**WESTLAND
NATIONAL
PARK** ~

Franz Josef
Glacier

Fox Glacier

Mt Cook
(3754m)
▲

**MT COOK
NATIONAL
PARK**

Mount Hutt
Station

To Christchurch

Karangarua

Bruce Bay

Mt Sefton
(3157m) ▲ ▲ Mt Cook Village

Mount
Somers

SH1

Lake Paringa

Knights Point

Mt Ward
(2646m) ▲

SH80

*Lake
Tekapo*

*Lake
Pukaki*

SH72

● Ashburton

Haast Junction

Okuru

Jackson
Bay

Mt Brewster
(2519m) ▲

Haast Pass
(562m)

SH6

Burkes
Pass
(701m)

Geraldine

SH79

Fairlie

SH8

**Te Wahipounamu
World Heritage
Area**

*Lake
Ohau*

Mt Pollux ▲
(2542m)

Makarora

SH8

Hunters Hills

● Timaru

SOUTH

Mt Aspiring
(3035m) ▲

*Lake
Hawea*

Omarama

*Lake
Benmore*

SH1

PACIFIC

**MT ASPIRING
NATIONAL
PARK**

*Lake
Wanaka*

Lindis Pass
(971m)

Kurow

SH83

OCEAN

Wanaka

Lake
Hawea

SH8

*Hawkdun
Range*

To Queenstown

To Dunedin ● Oamaru

THE WEST COAST
pp332-45

THE WEST COAST
pp332-45

WESTLAND

stands of rainforest survive alongside some of the most extensive wetlands. The kahikatea swamp forests, sand-dune forests, seal and penguin colonies, kakas, the Red Hills and vast sweeps of beach have ensured the preservation of this hauntingly beautiful place as a UNESCO World Heritage List site. In the forests of rimu with their flaming red flowers, birdlife abounds. You may see fantails, bellbirds, native pigeons (kereru), falcons, kiwis and moreporks.

Because of their steepness, Fox and Franz Josef Glaciers (13 and 11km long, respectively) are unique at this latitude in terms of how close to sea level they descend. The glaciers fluctuate according to snowfall, advancing when snow accumulates at the top faster than the ice melts at the bottom and retreating when the opposite is the case. Nowadays Franz Josef's foot is about 10km inland, but during the last Ice age it extended right to the coast.

Along the valleys leading to the glaciers are piles of terminal moraine left during halts in the early 1600s, mid-1700s and around 1825, and the ice-cold streams leaving the caves at each face appear to steam with condensing vapour.

CLIMATE
Westland could aptly be called 'Wetland' with its lush rainforest supported by an average annual rainfall often quoted in metres rather than millimetres. The rain is driven by strong westerlies of the Roaring Forties and the wettest place is Roaring Billy on the Haast River. Here, 22km from the coast, the average annual rainfall is 5840mm and rain falls, on average, every second day. By contrast, Makarora, at the eastern foot of Haast Pass, receives an average 2440mm in 125 days – still more than enough from a cyclist's point of view.

Despite the deluge, Westland enjoys as many sunshine hours as the region around Christchurch. Much of the downpour falls as snow on the high peaks, becomes ice and feeds the massive glaciers.

INFORMATION
Maps
The North and *North Meets South* editions of the InfoMap 1:500,000 series, published by the Department of Survey and Land Information, cover the South Island.

The West Coast

Duration	6 days
Distance	563.7km
Difficulty	hard
Start	Wanaka
End	Westport

Starting amid mountain-ringed lakes, this ride crosses the Southern Alps via atmospheric Haast Pass and follows the grey-rock coastline north on the narrow coastal plain. The winding SH6 is flanked by mountains and affords views to lofty Mts Cook and Tasman along the way.

There is a remarkable contrast between the vegetation on Days 1 & 2. Bare rocky hills in the rain shadow of the Divide give way to lush forests beyond Makarora. After the descent from Haast Pass, long flat stretches alternate with sharp climbs. Rewarding views reveal the restless Tasman Sea crashing on a battered coastline.

To the north, Fox and Franz Josef Glaciers and the towns of Hokitika, Greymouth and Westport beckon the traveller. Each is worth exploring. Adding further interest are the pancake stacks of Punakaiki Rocks, bizarre road-and-rail bridges and lots of wildlife spotting opportunities.

This trip involves long days with climbing – and the probability of bad weather. However, it is possible to do the ride over a greater number of shorter days. With this in mind, accommodation options between the suggested stops have been included.

HISTORY
The ride crosses Haast Pass, an old Maori route used by Charles Cameron, a Scottish gold-miner and explorer, in January 1863. Later the same month, Julius von Haast, with four companions, followed it from Wanaka to the west coast and back in nonstop rain.

The road over Haast Pass was not begun until 1929 and it took 31 years to link Wanaka and Haast townships. Only in 1965 was it pushed through to Paringa, to complete the (now-sealed) SH6.

PLANNING
When to Ride
The weather is most favourable for cycling in summer, especially December and January,

but this is also when crowds are biggest. From May to September days are often mild and clear, giving mountain views but no crowds.

What to Bring

Waterproof everything! Genuinely waterproof clothing and panniers are essential, while mudguards (fenders) are an advantage.

GETTING TO/FROM THE RIDE
Wanaka

See the Western Otago Circuit ride (p323) in the Otago & Southland chapter for information on getting to/from Wanaka.

Westport

Bus InterCity (☎ 789 7819) runs daily services between Nelson and the glaciers via Westport. Services leave from Craddock's petrol station on Palmerston St.

Other buses make daily return trips between Westport and Greymouth (two hours) with a rest stop at Punakaiki's Pancake Rocks. White Star (☎ 789 6200) and East-West Express (☎ 789 6251) run shuttles to Christchurch with fares around $40. Cunninghams (☎ 789 7177) makes the run north to Karamea for the Heaphy Track.

Bicycle This ride joins the Southern Alps Circuit (see the Canterbury chapter) at Greymouth. You can either do the entire ride or return to Greymouth from Reefton along the Grey River valley on SH7.

THE RIDE
Wanaka

See Wanaka (pp322-9) in the Western Otago Circuit ride in the Otago & Southland chapter for information about accommodation and other services.

Day 1: Wanaka to Makarora

4-6½ hours, 64.4km
The first half of Day 1 has numerous short but tiring climbs beside Lake Hawea and across The Neck to Lake Wanaka, which can be made harder by a north-westerly wind. If the wind is strong, chances are it is raining hard at Haast Pass and beyond. The scenery is dramatic the whole way to Makarora.

For a short distance along **Lake Hawea** the road passes between a cliff to the left and a precipice dropping to the lake from

the right-hand edge of the road. The exposed, often wind-blown road climbs to the 405m saddle called **The Neck** and then descends to travel above **Lake Wanaka**. Now the cliff is on your right and the precipice on your left. Dark, jagged mountains cleft by chasms loom across the ruffled water.

From the head of the lake, the route enters the Makarora valley. Shelter from the wind takes the form of the excellent *Country Cafe*, 4km before the township. This is also where tourist coaches disgorge their loads for compulsory 15-minute breaks.

Makarora

At the gateway to the Haast Pass for northbound travellers, tiny, isolated Makarora has a frontier feel. With a permanent population of only 30, there is accommodation for about 140 others. Half the places on a given night are likely to be taken by Kiwi Experience 'bus-packers' who have a deserved reputation for partying until all hours.

Information The Makarora DOC visitor centre (☎ 443 8365), on the highway in the village, has information on the area and should be consulted before undertaking any walks.

Things to See & Do Makarora is the base for one of NZ's great outdoor adventures, the **Siberia Experience**, a thrill-seeking extravaganza including a light-plane flight, three-hour walk through a remote mountain valley and a jet-boat trip down a river valley. The trip runs from mid-October to mid-April, operated by Southern Alps Air (☎ 443 8372).

Jet-boating trips into Mt Aspiring National Park are cheaper than runs on the Shotover River. A one hour, 50km jaunt with Wilkin River Jets (☎ 443 8351) costs about $50.

The area has lots of **walks**. There's a 20 minute nature walk around town and the Blue Pools River Walk where you can see huge rainbow trout. A 1½ hour walk along the Old Bridle Track takes you from the top of Haast Pass to Davis Flat. Because of avalanche danger and the unpredictability of weather, harder walks should not be undertaken without proper preparation. See the DOC for details and advice.

Places to Stay & Eat The *Makarora Tourist Centre* (☎ 443 8372), behind the

WESTLAND

Day 1: Wanaka to Makarora

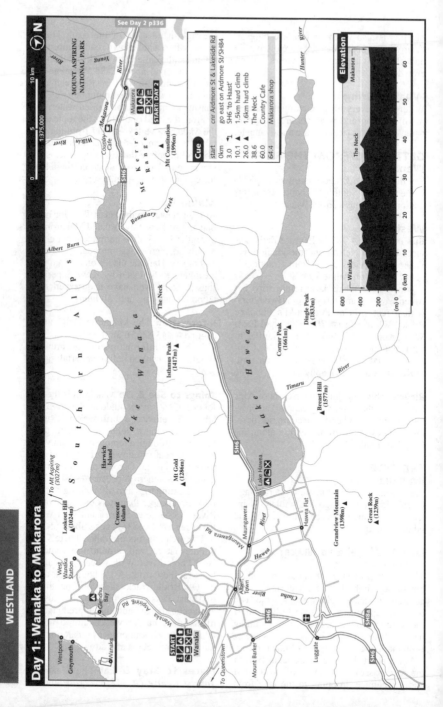

Cue	
start	cnr Ardmore St & Lakeside Rd
0km	go east on Ardmore St/SH84
3.0	SH6 'to Haast'
10.1	1.5km hard climb
26.0	1.6km hard climb
38.6	The Neck
60.0	Country Cafe
64.4	Makarora shop

The West Coast?

Which way should you ride the west coast of the South Island? This vexed question really has no definitive answer. There is a lot of luck (or is it good timing?) required to get favourable wind and weather. Face it, you are going to get a headwind and rain somewhere, so it might as well be on the west coast.

The proprietor of the Hokitika bike shop maintains the way to go is north to south.

'We don't get much wind on the west coast', he told me, clearly unconcerned by, or unaware of, the 30km/h zephyr that had blown me into town, and which had the many southbound cyclists cursing. 'The views are better going south, the mountains sweep around and you see them the whole time', he added.

Many foreign tour companies apparently agree with him. Backroads, the big US operator, runs its trips from Picton or Nelson south along the west coast to Queenstown. Perhaps this is to allow participants to build endurance on the gentler terrain in the north before meeting serious climbs. Or perhaps it's because direction doesn't matter so much if there's a sag wagon for exhausted cyclists.

If you spend a week or so cycling on the west coast you will experience a great variety of weather conditions, some likely to seem extreme. Riding here is a character-building experience as much as anything else. Be philosophical if it is raining and adopt the maxim once espoused to me by a British Columbian cyclist in Vancouver (on another wet west coast): 'If you don't ride in the rain, you don't ride'. And think about this: it only rains on the west coast, *on average*, every second day. At least you should be able to find indoor accommodation and wait it out.

The same tactic can be used to beat the wind. Of course, sitting tight on a fine day and not going anywhere just because the wind is in your face might be considered 'chicken', but you *could* pretend you are planning to stay and see the area's sights, until your accuser is out of sight.

In the end though, as you lounge inside before a roaring fire after you have emptied litres of water from your panniers (damn that 'reverse Gore-Tex' fabric!), dried your clothing and shoes and disposed of your stinking socks in the garbage skip, you will look back on the headwind and rain that blasted you off the road at Knights Point as a rite of passage.

If you are going north, the high pressure system parked east of the North Island that has been sending wind and rain your way will eventually move further east. The next south-westerly change will push you north, probably under clear skies, while cyclists heading south will have their turn to curse, or freeze, on a mountain pass under snow. It all balances out.

Neil Irvine

tearooms, has self-contained chalets in a bush setting from $70 for two. Cabins and $40 for two and tent sites $8.50 per person.

B&B accommodation is available nearby at *Larrivee Homestay* (☎ 443 9177), down a private drive next to the DOC visitor centre. In an unusual two-storey octagonal house built with local stone, wood and recycled materials, doubles cost from $80 to $120.

There are *DOC camping grounds* on SH6 at Cameron Flat and Davis Flat, 14km and 17km north of Makarora, respectively. Facilities consist of only a pit toilet; water can be obtained from a nearby stream but should be treated before drinking.

Makarora tearooms, open from 8.30 am to 8.30 pm, has light meals and snacks plus a grocery store for basic supplies.

Day 2: Makarora to Haast Junction

5-7½ hours, 81.6km

Despite its long distance, Day 2 is relatively easy. After the first 18.6km, it's virtually all downhill until the 31km mark, where the road levels off, meandering beside the gravelly bed of the Haast River, and finally emerges from the forest at the coastal village of Haast. As there are no services of any kind on the day's route, riders should ensure they carry, at least, enough food for lunch.

After the boundary of **Mount Aspiring National Park**, damp and mossy beech trees cloak the hillsides. Roadside signs identify attractive side valleys, although these may be invisible through mist, rain or low cloud across the river.

WESTLAND

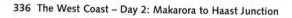

WESTLAND

Day 2: Makarora to Haast Junction

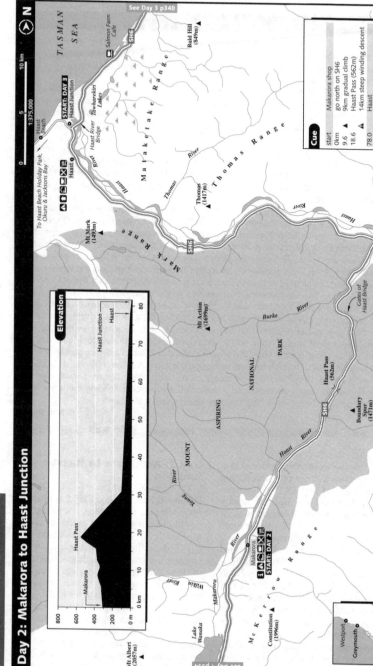

Cue

start	Makarora shop
0km ▲	go north on SH6
9.6 ▲	9km gradual climb
18.6 △	Haast Pass (562m)
78.0	Haast
81.6	World Heritage Hotel

14km steep winding descent

Elevation

Makarora — Haast Junction — Haast

See Day 3 p340

The gradient steepens slightly but the main climb to **Haast Pass** is only 3km and is soon conquered. Take time at the top to absorb the atmosphere of the forest and perhaps walk a few hundred metres of the Old Bridle Track. Under the dense, dripping, claustrophobic canopy of beech, out of view of any sign of human civilisation, you perhaps gain some appreciation of the conditions encountered by the early European explorers.

The descent from the pass is much steeper on the western side. There are several cattlegrids at angles across the road that should be approached with caution, especially if it is wet. A tremendous number of waterfalls thunder beside, or, in heavy rain, onto the road all the way to Haast village.

The bitumen ribbon twists wildly in a headlong plunge to the **gates of Haast bridge**, one of several single-lane bridges with torrents coursing beneath them. After about 10km of thrilling downhill through a thickly forested valley, the grade eases. A few short ups reverse the general down trend, but it's easy riding (weather aside) beside the broad Haast River to the coast.

Haast & Haast Junction

The small village of Haast is a rather strung out collection of buildings and settlements; the northern extremity of which (and where the day's ride ends) is officially known as Haast Junction. Centred around the estuary of the Haast River, 120km south of Fox Glacier, it provides the first services since Makarora. It's advisable to book indoor accommodation ahead of time in case, due to bad weather, camping is impractical and beds are in strong demand.

Information The South West New Zealand World Heritage visitor centre (☎ 750 0809, fax 750 0832), on the southern bank of the river at the junction of SH6 and Jackson Bay Rd in Haast Junction, has displays and information on the area.

Things to See & Do South West Penguin (☎ 750 0824) has tours to see a colony of **Fiordland crested penguins**. These medium-sized penguins stand 50 to 70cm tall and have a yellow crest running over each eye.

The visitor centre has information on other activities including **scenic flights, canoeing, fishing** and **diving** for crayfish.

Places to Stay & Eat The *Haast Beach Holiday Park* (☎ 750 0860) is at Okuru, 11km south of the Haast River bridge on the Haast-Jackson Bay Rd. Bunk beds are $13 per person. Tent sites are $16, cabins cost from $30 and motel units from $65.

Wilderness Backpackers (☎ 0800 750 029), 3km before the bridge and 200m off SH6 on the left, has dorm beds for $15 and doubles for $17.50 per person. *Haast Highway Accommodation* (☎ 750 0703) is a YHA-associate hostel charging $15 to $18 per person. There are also tent sites but you may not be allowed to pitch if the manager decides it will rain too much overnight.

Heritage Park Lodge (☎ 750 0868), next door to Wilderness Backpackers, has motel units from $80. *Erewhon Motels* (☎ 750 0817), 4km south of Haast on the Haast-Jackson Bay Rd, has units from $80. The *Haast World Heritage Hotel* (☎ 750 0828), near the bridge over Haast River, has doubles from $90 and singles from $40. The restaurant has a good menu and reasonable prices.

In the township, *Smithy's Tavern* (☎ 750 0034) and the *Fantail Tearooms* serve light meals and there's a small *supermarket*.

Day 3: Haast Junction to Fox Glacier

7-10 hours, 118.6km

The windy ride over the long single-lane bridge across Haast River is followed by 4km of sheltered road between thick stands of rainforest. For the next 3km the road is at the back of dunes in sight of the turbulent Tasman, with nothing to stop the blast of the Roaring Forties. The sharp angle of the trees to the right of the road indicates the strongest wind comes from the west to south-west.

After 15.5km some seriously steep hills begin. While only low, the three in succession are tiring and, when combined with gusty winds, can make progress very slow. It's worth a break at the **Knights Point lookout**, which has a shelter, an excellent view and an informative display.

The terrain might be cycle-friendly the rest of the way to Fox Glacier and traffic light, but SH6 is not especially wide, has poor lines of sight and has little shoulder, so be alert to the simultaneous approach of tour buses from both directions – it'll be close!

In the event of bad weather forcing a shortened day, there is accommodation available

WESTLAND

at Lake Paringa. On SH6 is the *Lake Paringa cafe (☎ 751 0894)*, which also has cabins and a seven-bed motel-style share room with en suite bathroom for a flat tariff of $65. The next services are at *Salmon Farm Cafe*, 7km north at Waituna Creek, and there is a *farm stay B&B* 800m along Condons Rd near Bruce Bay. *Pine Grove Motels (☎ 751 0898)*, 35km south of Fox Glacier on SH6, has self-contained units for $40 for two and budget cabins for $15 per person.

Three long, elaborately engineered single-lane suspension bridges span raging torrents of cloudy water between the Karangarua River and the Fox River. Just after the third bridge is the turn-off to Fox Glacier.

Side Trip: Fox Glacier
30 minutes, 8km return
Fox Glacier, like Franz Josef, is in a period of advance. Since 1985 it has advanced about 1km and now averages about 40cm per day. It is named after NZ prime minister Sir William Fox, who visited it in 1872.

The 4km ride on gently graded, smooth gravel is like cycling into a refrigerator as cold air drains down the valley from the glacier – it's great on a hot day! From the car park at the end of the road, a short walking track goes to the base of the glacier. Guided walks onto the glacier are organised by Alpine Guides (☎ 781 0825).

Fox Glacier
Fox Glacier village is on SH6, 4.6km north of the turn-off to the glacier. It is a small service centre nestled at the base of the steep climb to Cook Saddle.

The visitor centre (☎ 751 0807, fax 751 0858), in the centre of town, is open daily from 8.15 am to at least 6 pm.

Things to See & Do The visitor centre presents **slide shows** on summer evenings and has displays on the glaciers and the natural environment. Also pick up the leaflets detailing short **walks** around the ice. Take an evening walk to the **glow-worm grotto**, a couple of minutes from the centre of the village.

About 3km west of the village is the turn-off to **Lake Matheson** and one of the most famous panoramas in NZ. An hour on a boardwalk takes you round the lake to see unforgettable postcard views of the mountains and their reflections. The best time is in the still of early morning. Further down this road is isolated **Gillespies Beach**, with a few houses and a three hour return walk along the black sand to a seal colony.

Aerial sightseeing trips are expensive, but the views are superb. Operators include Glacier Helicopters (☎ 0800 800 732), Mt Cook Airline (☎ 751 0812), Helicopter Line (☎ 751 0767) and Fox Glacier Helicopter Services (☎ 751 0866).

Guided **glacier walks** are run by Alpine Guides (☎ 751 0825). Tours leave the village at 9.30 am and 2 pm daily.

Places to Stay The *Fox Glacier Holiday Park (☎ 751 0821)* is on Lake Matheson Rd, 800m from the middle of town. Tent sites are $18 for two. Bunks cost from $12 per person, double cabins from $30 and motel units from $65.

Ivory Towers (☎ 751 0838), on Sullivan Rd, has dorm beds for $16 and doubles for $20. *Fox Glacier Inn & Backpackers (☎ 751 0022, 39 Sullivan Rd)* offers dorm beds for $16, share rooms for $17 and twins from $18.

Farm stays and B&Bs in the area charge between $60 and $80. Try *Reflections Lodge*

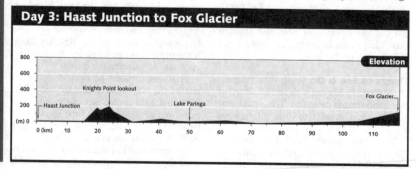

Day 3: Haast Junction to Fox Glacier

Fox & Franz Josef Glaciers

Glaciers always advance, they never really retreat. Sometimes, however, the ice melts even faster than it advances and, in that case, the terminal, or end, face of the glacier moves back up the mountain and appears to be retreating.

With Fox and Franz Josef, the great mass of ice higher up the mountain pushes the ice down the valleys at prodigious speeds but – like most glaciers in the world – this past century has been a story of steady retreat and only the odd short advance.

The last great Ice age of 15,000 to 20,000 years ago saw these two glaciers reach right down to the sea. Since then warmer weather has probably seen them retreat even further than their current position. In the 14th century a new 'mini ice age' started and for centuries Fox and Franz Josef Glaciers advanced, reaching their greatest extent around 1750. The terminal moraines from that last major advance can be clearly seen on both glaciers. In the 250 years since then, the glaciers have steadily retreated and the terminal face is now several kilometres back from its first recorded position in the late 19th century or even from its position in the 1930s.

From 1965 to 1968 the Fox and Franz Josef Glaciers made brief advances of about 180m, and in 1985 they once again started to advance and have been moving forward steadily and fairly dramatically ever since. Nobody is quite sure why this advance is taking place. It could be cooler or more overcast summers, or it could be the result of heavy snowfalls 10 or 15 years ago, which are now working their way down to the bottom of the glacier.

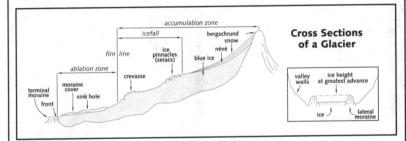

Cross Sections of a Glacier

Useful Terminology

ablation zone – where the glacier melts

accumulation zone – where the snow collects

bergschrund – large crevasse in the ice near the headwall or starting point of the glacier

blue ice – as the accumulation zone or névé snow is compressed by subsequent snowfalls, it becomes firn and then blue ice

crevasses – as the glacial ice moves down the mountain it bends and cracks open in crevasses as it crosses obstacles

dead ice – as a glacier retreats, isolated chunks of ice may be left behind (sometimes these can remain for many years)

firn – partly compressed snow on the way to becoming glacial ice

glacial flour – the river of melted ice that flows off glaciers is a milky colour from the suspension of finely ground rocks

icefall – when a glacier descends so steeply that the upper ice breaks up in a jumble of ice blocks

kettle lake – lake formed by the melt of an area of isolated dead ice

lateral moraine – walls of debris formed at the sides of the glacier

névé – snowfield area where firn is formed

seracs – ice pinnacles formed, like crevasses, by the glacier passing over obstacles

terminal – the final ice face at the end of the glacier

terminal moraine – mass of boulders and rocks marking the end point of the glacier, its final push down the valley

WESTLAND

Day 3: Haast Junction to Fox Glacier

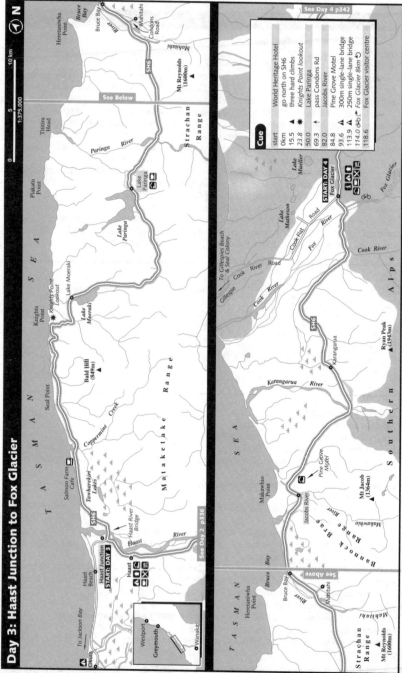

WESTLAND

Cue

start	0km		World Heritage Hotel
	15.5	▲	go north on SH6
	23.8	✳	three hard climbs
			Knights Point lookout
	50.0		Lake Paringa
	69.3	↟	pass Condons Rd
	82.0		Jacobs River
	84.8		Pine Grove Motel
	93.6	⋀	300m single-lane bridge
	113.9	⋀	250m single-lane bridge
	114.0	⌖↱	Fox Glacier 8km ↻
	118.6		Fox Glacier visitor centre

See Day 4 p342

(☎ 751 0707), **Roaring Billy Lodge** (☎ 751 0815) and **Homestyle** (☎ 751 0895).

The **Fox Glacier Hotel** (☎ 751 0839), in the centre of the village, has budget rooms from $38. **Lake Matheson Motels** (☎ 751 0830), 750m down Cook Flat Rd, charges $80 a double. **Alpine View Motels** (☎ 751 0821), next to the holiday park, charges $64, and the **Rainforest Motel** (☎ 751 0140, 15 Cook Flat Rd) has units from $70.

Places to Eat There is good vegetarian food at the **Cone Rock Cafe**, and the **Hobnail Cafe** (☎ 751 0005), in the Alpine Guides Building in the village centre, has sandwiches and light meals.

Locals like the western-theme **Cook Saddle Saloon & Cafe** (☎ 751 0700, cnr SH6 & Cook Flat Rd). Mains of seafood, steak and venison start at around $16. Try the cosy restaurant in the **Glacier Country Hotel** (☎ 751 0847), opposite the Alpine Guides Building, for atmosphere and an open fire, or sit with a beer in the central **Fox Glacier Hotel** (☎ 751 0839) lounge and talk about the day's riding.

Fox Glacier Store in the town centre has a reasonable selection of essentials.

Day 4: Fox Glacier to Harihari
5-7 hours, 87km

Fox Glacier village sits at the base of a series of hills that line the route to Franz Josef.

The road is quiet, gradients are steady, not severe, and there are good views back to the river flats. Rainforest-clad slopes with stark mountain peaks are all around, many with clefts caused by landslips. Bellbirds punctuate the silence with their chimes. Torrents of water descend from the often cloud-wrapped peaks. It's a marvellous place to cycle and the descents between the saddles are magic.

Near Franz Josef village, a tremendous flow of ice can be seen tumbling from the mountain top: **Franz Josef Glacier** (see Side Trip).

The **South Westland Triathlon** (☎ 753 4091, fax 753 4072) is held between Franz Josef and Whataroa in late February each year. For information on activities around **Franz Josef**, ask at the DOC visitor centre (☎ 752 0796) in the centre of town.

Accommodation options at Franz Josef village are similar to those at Fox. The **Franz Josef Holiday Park** (☎ 752 0766) is on the left 500m before town. Hostels on Cron St, 100m east of the main road, include the **YHA** (☎ 752 0754, ✉ yhafzjo@yha.org.nz) and **Chateau Franz** (☎ 752 0738), while the **Franz Josef Lodge** (☎ 752 0712) is on SH6 at the northern end of the village. The more expensive, motel-style **Mountain View Accommodation** (☎ 752 0735) is 200m north of the centre.

Shops at Franz Josef have a good selection of food supplies and there's a choice of decent restaurants.

As you cycle out of Franz Josef past the town's petrol station, feel smug that you don't need any – the price here is reputedly the highest in NZ.

North of Franz Josef the road is virtually flat until the climb over **Mt Hercules**. It runs below cloud-shrouded mountains through majestic forest, past attractive lakes.

Before Mt Hercules is **Whataroa** (54km) with a **shop-tearooms**, **pub** and **motel**. This is the base for tours (☎ 753 4120 or ☎ 0800 523 456) to the **white heron sanctuary** in the Waitangi Roto nature reserve on the coast. There's also camping, cabins and motel accommodation available.

Side Trip: Franz Josef Glacier
30 minutes, 8km return

The access road to the glacier, at the entrance to the village, is somewhat rougher and more corrugated than the road to Fox Glacier, but is of similar length. It's a longer walk to the lookout – 30 minutes each way across gravelly moraine – but you can get closer here than at Fox. The view of the mighty river of ice is awe-inspiring and not to be missed.

The DOC-run Franz Josef visitor centre (see the ride description) has details of many guided and do-it-yourself walks near the glacier.

Harihari
The small town of Harihari, 33km north of Whataroa, hit the headlines in 1931 when Australian Guy Menzies completed the first solo flight across the Tasman Sea from Sydney. His aircraft, the *Southern Cross Junior*, crash-landed in the nearby La Fontaine swamp and he made an undignified exit headfirst into the mud from the upturned plane. Still, he had made the trip in 11¾

WESTLAND

WESTLAND

Day 4: Fox Glacier to Harihari

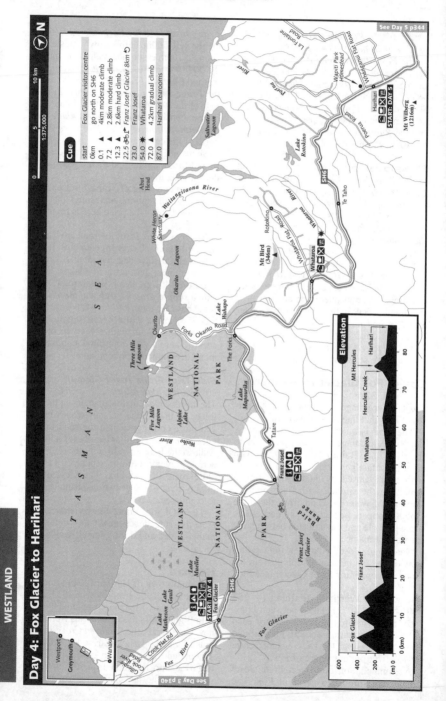

Cue

start	Fox Glacier visitor centre	
0km	go north on SH6	
0.1	4km moderate climb	▲
7.2	2.8km moderate climb	▲
12.3	2.6km hard climb	▲
22.5	Franz Josef Glacier 8km	↻
23.0	Franz Josef	
54.0	Whataroa	✴
72.0	4.2km gradual climb	▲
87.0	Harihari tearooms	

See Day 5 p344

See Day 5 p344

See Day 3 p340

Elevation

hours, 2½ hours less than fellow Australian Charles Kingsford Smith and his crew in 1928.

Things to See & Do The two to three hour Harihari Coastal Walkway (also called the Doughboy Walk) is a local attraction, with a lookout over the coastline, forest and mountains. You can **walk** up into the Wilberg Range near the town (20 minutes return). There's also an old gold-miners pack track, rivermouth **fishing** for trout and salmon, as well as the opportunity to explore the estuaries and wetlands of the Poerua and Wanganui Rivers. Go **bird-watching** for native parakeets, herons, penguins, kakas and a variety of migratory wading birds.

Places to Stay & Eat The *Tomasi Motels* (☎ *0800 753 3116)*, on SH6, is the accommodation of choice for cyclists in town. Beds in cabin-style rooms with bath cost $15 per person and there is a communal combined kitchen-lounge area. Motel rooms cost $60 for two, plus $15 per extra adult.

The *Harihari Motor Inn (☎ 753 3026)*, across SH6, has motel units costing $70 for two, bunk beds for $15 per person and a hot spa pool, but no kitchen facilities.

On the way into Harihari, on the left side of SH6 just before Wanganui Flat Rd, is the *Wapiti Park Homestead (☎ 753 3074, ✉ wapitipark@minidata.co.nz)*, a B&B on a deer farm. Standard doubles with private bathroom are $110 or there's a room with king-size bed and ensuite for $165. Three course dinner costs $30 per person.

Harihari has a *tearoom* and a *fish and chip shop*. The *Harihari Motor Inn* has pub meals, a *restaurant* and *takeaways*.

Day 5: Harihari to Greymouth
6½-9 hours, 111.3km

Day 5 is a long one, mostly through thick rainforest, with many undulations but only one real climb after pretty Lake Ianthe.

The first supply point, tiny **Pukekura**, nestles amid hills cloaked in incredibly dense, tall forest. The village features the touristy **Bushmans Centre** with its restaurant and, suspended from the front of the building, a giant sandfly. It won't bite, but the many little ones here will.

For cheap accommodation, cross the road to *Cafe Ianthe (☎ 755 4032)* and ask about the adjacent cabins and on-site caravan.

Towards Ross, up a hill on a short access road from the main route, there is a trig point, a **monument** to the early surveyors' role in the development of Westland. Views extend across a swampy, tussocky plain to the coast and there are picnic tables.

NZ's largest gold nugget, the 2.8kg 'Honourable Roddy', was found in 1907 at the historic gold town of **Ross**, which still mines the precious metal today. Grimmond House,

---

Annoying Wildlife

Westland is headquarters for the most annoying of New Zealand wildlife: the sandfly. For those who haven't yet met them, sandflies are nasty little biting insects, smaller than mosquitoes. Unfortunately, the ease with which they can be killed is far outweighed by the numbers in which they attack. Any exposed skin is a target for orbiting clouds of these tiny winged demons. Their stinging bites leave itchy red welts that can remain sore for days. Insect repellent is

only partly effective; total cover-up is the best defence. Keep your tent tightly zipped because they will squeeze through any opening. Don't be surprised if the inside of your fly (an appropriate term) is covered with the insects when you wake on a Westland morning. Don't be put off visiting, though: while the phenomenal west coast rain is falling, it is quite effective at discouraging sandflies.

WESTLAND

Day 5: Harihari to Greymouth

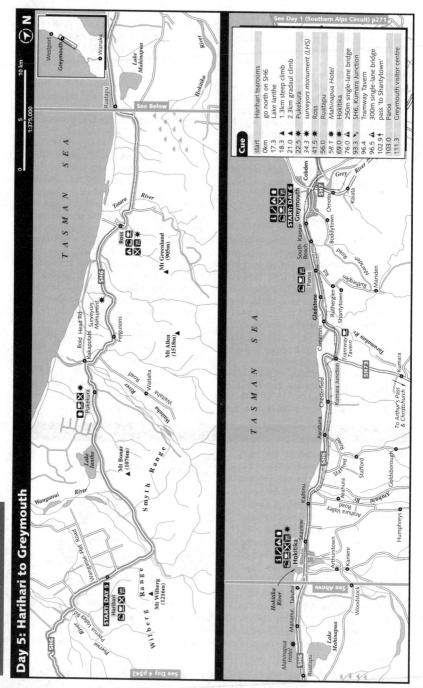

See Day 4 p342

See Day 1 (Southern Alps Circuit) p271

Cue		
start		Harihari tearooms
0km		go north on SH6
17.3	▲	Lake Ianthe
18.3	▲	1.3km steep climb
21.0	▲	2.3km gradaul climb
22.5	✳	Pukekura
34.3	✳✳	surveyors monument (LHS)
41.5	✳✳	Ross
56.0		Ruatapu
58.1	✳✳	Mahinapua Hotel
69.0	⚠	Hokitika
76.0	⚠	250m single-lane bridge
93.3	⤷	SH6, Kumara Junction
96.4	⚠	Tramway Tavern
96.5	⚠	300m single-lane bridge
102.9	↑	pass 'to Shantytown'
103.0		Paroa
111.3		Greymouth visitor centre

See Below

See Above

Greenstone

Greenstone is big in Hoki. Historically, greenstone – or jade – was much treasured by the Maori who used it for decorative jewellery (tiki) and for carving their lethal weapons (the flat war clubs known as *mere*). Since greenstone is found predominantly on the west coast, expeditions undertaken by the Maori to collect it not only took months but were also dangerous. Working the stone with their primitive equipment was no easy task either, but they managed to produce some exquisite items.

MARTIN HARRIS

The legend of Tamatea explains why there are differing types of greenstone in the South Island. Tamatea's three wives were either abducted by Poutini (a fear-inspiring spirit, or *taniwha*) or they deserted him. At Anita Bay he found Hinetangiwai, one of his wives, turned into greenstone and, when he wept his tears entered it, giving it its flecked appearance, hence the stone's name of *tangiwai* (water of weeping). When travelling north he heard voices in the Arahura Valley and went to investigate. His companion, Tumuaki, breached *tapu* (sacred law) by putting his burnt fingers in his mouth while cooking, so Tamatea was not able to find his other wives. Like Hinetangiwai, the other wives were turned into greenstone – *auhanga* and *pounamu*.

once the Bank of New Zealand, is now the visitor centre. There is a small **Miner's Cottage museum** at the beginning of two goldfield walkways (each taking up to two hours). The current working gold mine is nearby and you can look down on the operations.

The town's atmospheric *Empire Hotel* (☎ 755 4005, 19 Aylmer St) has bar meals and accommodation. Around the corner on Gibson St, the *Ross Motel* (☎ 755 4022) has units at $58 a double.

The *City Hotel* has a dining room and there's also the *Nicada Tearooms* on the main street.

The strangely lifeless saw-milling town of **Ruatapu,** 14km from Ross, has no services at all. Just 2.1km to the north on SH6, which now has a good shoulder, is *Mahinapua Hotel* (☎ 755 8500), familiar to TV viewers from advertisements for Mainland cheese. It is overrun by bus loads of Kiwi Experience tourists, so don't expect to get a bed.

The **craft shops** of Hokitika are this town's biggest attraction. Many are on Tancred St, most selling greenstone jewellery and artefacts. Hokitika Cycles & Sports (☎ 755 8662) is at 33 Tancred St.

North of Hoki, the road continues flat past grey surf beaches on open plains next to a railway line. The wind can be merciless here.

NZ road builders' obsessive economy with single-lane bridges, perhaps born of a Scottish heritage, reaches its zenith at the 200m-long one-lane bridge over the Arahura River. It carries not only two-way motor (and bicycle) traffic on its span, but also trains loaded with moss, timber and dairy products.

The attractive but dinged box girder bridge at Taramakau River is similar but is 300m long. Beside this bridge is the *Tramway Tavern*, a good food and drink stop that also offers free camping out back.

The ride to Greymouth is on an increasingly busy road, so the wide shoulder is a blessing.

On the outskirts, you pass the turn-off to the replica gold-rush village **Shantytown**, and the start of a string of motels and other accommodation options. *Paroa Motel/Hotel* (☎ 762 6860), on SH6, has twin units for $75 and budget units for $25.

Greymouth

See Greymouth (pp270-2) in the Southern Alps Circuit in the Canterbury chapter for information about accommodation and other services.

Day 6: Greymouth to Westport
6-8 hours, 100.8km
See Day 1 (pp271-2) of the Southern Alps Circuit in the Canterbury chapter for a map and description of this ride.

WESTLAND

Glossary

This glossary is a list of Maori and English terms you will come across in New Zealand.

AA – New Zealand Automobile Association; the organisation that provides road information and roadside assistance

afghan – popular homemade chocolate biscuit

All Black – a member of NZ's revered national rugby union team (the name comes from 'All Backs', which the press called the NZ rugby team on an early visit to England)

Aoraki – Maori name for Mt Cook, meaning 'the cloud piercer'

Aotearoa – Maori name for NZ; literally 'land of the long white cloud'; jokingly translated as 'land of the wrong white crowd'

bach – a holiday home, usually a wooden cottage (pronounced 'batch'); see also *crib*

baths – swimming pool, often referred to as municipal baths

Beehive – Parliament House in Wellington, so-called because of its distinctive shape

black-water rafting – rafting or tubing underground in a cave or *tomo*

boozer – a public bar

box of birds – an expression meaning 'on top of the world', usually in response to 'How are you?'

bro – literally 'brother'; usually meaning mate, as in 'just off to see the bros'

bush – heavily forested areas

Buzzy Bee – a child's toy as essential to NZ child development as dinosaur models; a wooden bee dragged along by a string to produce a whirring noise

BYO – bring your own (drinks and/or alcohol)

Captain Cooker – a large feral pig, introduced by James Cook and now roaming wild over most of NZ's rugged bush land

CHE – not the revolutionary but Crown Health Enterprise (regional, privatised health authorities)

chillie bin – cooler; esky; large insulated box for keeping food and drink cold

choice – fantastic; great

crib – the name for a *bach* in Otago and Southland

dairy – a small corner store which sells just about everything, especially milk, bread, the newspaper and ice cream; a convenience store

Dalmatian – a term applied to the predominantly Yugoslav gum diggers who fossicked for kauri gum (used as furniture polish) in the gum fields of Northland

DOC – Department of Conservation (or *Te Papa Atawhai*); the government department that administers national parks and thus all tracks and huts

domain – an open grassed area in a town or city, often the focus of the civic amenities such as gardens, picnic areas and bowling clubs

doss house – temporary accommodation

farm stay – accommodation on a typical Kiwi farm where you are encouraged to join with in the day-to-day activities

fiscal envelope – money set aside by the NZ government to make financial reparation for injustices to Maori people since the Treaty of Waitangi

football – rugby, either union or league

Godzone – the way locals refer to New Zealand (God's own country)

good as gold, good as – very good

greenstone – jade, pounamu

haka – the traditional challenge; war dance

hakari – feast

handle – a beer glass with a handle

hangi – oven made by digging a hole and steaming food in baskets over embers in the hole; a feast of traditional Maori food

hapu – sub-tribe or smaller tribal grouping

hard case – an unusual or strong-willed character

Hawaiki – the unknown place in the Pacific from where the Maori tribes (the original seven waka) came

heitiki – carved, stylised human figure worn around the neck, often a carved representation of an ancestor; also called a *tiki*

hoa – friend

hokey pokey – a delicious variety of ice cream with butterscotch chips

hoki – a fish common in fish and chip shops

homestay – accommodation in a family house where you are treated (temporarily, thank God) as one of the family

hongi – Maori greeting; the pressing of noses and sharing of life breath

hui – gather; meeting

huntaway – a loud-barking sheep-herding dog, usually a sturdy black-and-brown hound

Ika a Maui, Te – the North Island

Instant Kiwi – state-run lottery

Interislander – the ferry that makes the crossing across Cook Strait between the North and South islands

'Is it what!' – strong affirmation or agreement; 'Yes isn't it!'

iwi – a large tribal grouping with lineage to the original migration from Hawaiki; people; tribe

jandals – sandals; flip-flops; thongs; usually rubber footwear

judder bars – bumps in the road to make you drive slowly; speed humps

K Rd – Karangahape Rd in Auckland

ka pai – good; excellent

kai – food; any word with kai in it has some food connection

kainga – village; pre-European unfortified Maori village

karakia – prayer

kaumatua – highly respected members of a tribe; the people you would ask for permission to enter a marae

kina – sea urchins; a Maori delicacy

kiwi – the flightless, nocturnal brown bird with a long beak which is the national symbol; the New Zealand dollar; a New Zealander; a member of the national rugby league team; an adjective to mean anything of or relating to NZ

kiwi bear – the introduced Australian ringtailed possum; also called an opossum

kiwi fruit – a small, succulent fruit with fuzzy brown skin and juicy green flesh; a Chinese gooseberry

koe – you (singular)

koha – a donation

kohanga reo – schools where Maori language and culture are at the forefront of the education process; also called 'language nest' schools

koutou – you (plural)

kumara – Polynesian sweet potato; a Maori staple food

kunekune – another type of wild pig introduced by Chinese gold-diggers in the 19th century

Kupe – an early Polynesian navigator, from Hawaiki, credited with the discovery of the islands that are now NZ

league – rugby league football

lounge bar – a more upmarket bar than a public bar; called a 'ladies bar' in some countries

mana – the spiritual quality of a person or object; authority of a chief or priest

manaia – a traditional carving design; literally means 'bird-headed man'

manuhiri – visitor; guest

Maori – indigenous people of New Zealand

Maoritanga – Maori culture

marae – sacred ground in front of the Maori meeting house; also used to refer to the traditional ancestral village of a tribe

Maui – an important figure in the mythology of the Maori

mere – flat, greenstone war club

metal/metalled road – gravel road

MMP – Mixed Member Proportional; a cumbersome electoral system used in NZ and Germany; a limited form of proportional voting

moko – facial tattoo

Mongrel Mob – a large, well-organised and mainly Maori bikie gang

Moriori – an isolated Polynesian group; inhabitants of the Chatham Islands

motor camp – usually well-equipped camping grounds with tent sites, caravan and campervan sites, on-site caravans, cabins and tourist flats

motorway – freeway or expressway

naiad – a rigid hull inflatable boat (used for dolphin swimming, whale-watching etc)

ngati – people; tribe (in the South Island; Ngai)

nifty-fifty – 50cc motorcycle

nui – carved ceremonial poles of peace and war

NZ – the universal appellation for New Zealand; pronounced 'enzed'

o – of

pa – fortified Maori village, usually on a hill top

Pacific Rim – a term used to describe modern NZ cuisine; cuisine with an innovative use of local produce, especially seafood, with imported styles

Pakeha – Maori for a white or European person; once derogatory, and still considered so by some, this term is now widely used for white New Zealanders

pakihi – unproductive and often swampy land on South Island's west coast; pronounced 'par-kee'

papa – large blue-grey mudstones; the word comes from the Maori for the Earth Mother

paua – abalone; tough shellfish pounded, minced, then made into patties (fritters), which are available in almost every NZ fish and chip shop

peneplain – area worn almost flat by erosion

pig islander – derogatory term used by a person from one island for someone from the other island

pillocking – 'surfing' across mud flats on a rubbish-bin lid

Plunket – an adjective describing the Plunket Society's services to promote the health of babies eg Plunket rooms (baby clinics), Plunket nurses (baby nurses)

polly – politician

ponga – the silver tree fern; called a bungy (pronounced 'bungee', with a soft 'g', in parts of the South Island)

powhiri – a traditional Maori welcome onto the marae

quad bikes – four-wheel farm bikes

Rakiura – literally 'land of glowing skies'; Maori name for Stewart Island, which is important in Maori mythology as the anchor of Maui's canoe

Ratana – a Protestant Maori church; adherents of the Ratana faith

rigger – a refillable half-gallon plastic bottle for holding draught beer

scrap – a fight, not uncommon at the pub

section – a small block of land

silver fern – the symbol worn by the All Blacks on their jerseys, representative of the underside of a ponga leaf

singletrack – off-road trail only wide enough for a bike

switchback – hairpin bend typically found on steep mountain roads or trails

Tamaki-makau-rau – the Maori name for Auckland

tane – man

tangata – the people

tangata whenua – people of the land; local people

taniwha – fear-inspiring water spirit

taonga – something of great value; a treasure

tapu – sacred; forbidden; taboo

tarseal – sealed road; bitumen

te – the

Te Kooti – a prominent Maori rebellion leader

Te Papa Atawhai – Maori name for DOC

tiki – short for *heitiki*

tohunga – priest; wizard; general expert

tomo – hole; entrance to a cave

tramp – walk; trek; hike; a more serious undertaking than an ordinary walk, requiring some experience and/or special equipment

tua tua – shellfish

tuatara – a prehistoric reptile dating back to the age of the dinosaurs (perhaps 260 million years)

tukutuku – wall panellings in marae and churches

varsity – university

VIN – Visitor Information Network; the umbrella organisation of the visitor information centres and offices

wahine – woman

wai – water

Wai Pounamu, Te – Maori for the South Island

waiata – song

Waitangi – short way of referring to the Treaty of Waitangi

waka – war canoe

Watties – the NZ food and canning giant; New Zealand's answer to Heinz, until Heinz took over the company

whakapapa – genealogy

whare – house

whare runanga – meeting house

whare taonga – a treasure house; a museum

whare whakairo – carved house

whenua – the land

wopwops – remote ('in the wopwops' is out in the middle of nowhere)

LONELY PLANET

You already know that Lonely Planet produces more than this one guidebook, but you might not be aware of the other products we have on this region. Here is a selection of titles which you may want to check out as well:

New Zealand
ISBN 1 86450 122 7
US$21.99 • UK£13.99 • 169FF

Tramping in New Zealand
ISBN 0 86442 598 8
US$17.95 • UK£11.99 • 140FF

Auckland
ISBN 1 86450 092 1
US$14.95 • UK£8.99 • 110FF

South Pacific
ISBN 0 86442 717 4
US$24.95 • UK£15.99 • 190FF

Kiwi Tracks
ISBN 0 86442 787 5
US$12.95 • UK£6.99 • 95FF

South Pacific phrasebook
ISBN 0 86442 595 3
US$6.95 • UK£4.99 • 50FF

Healthy Travel Australia, NZ & The Pacific
ISBN 1 86450 052 2
US$5.95 • UK£3.99 • 39FF

Available wherever books are sold

LONELY PLANET

Guides by Region

L onely Planet is known worldwide for publishing practical, reliable and no-nonsense travel information in our guides and on our web site. The Lonely Planet list covers just about every accessible part of the world. Currently there are fifteen series: travel guides, Shoestrings, Condensed, Phrasebooks, Read This First, Healthy Travel, Walking guides, Cycling guides, Pisces Diving & Snorkeling guides, City Maps, Travel Atlases, Out to Eat, World Food, Journeys travel literature and Pictorials.

AFRICA Africa on a shoestring • Africa – the South • Arabic (Egyptian) phrasebook • Arabic (Moroccan) phrasebook • Cairo • Cape Town • Cape Town city map • Central Africa • East Africa • Egypt • Egypt travel atlas • Ethiopian (Amharic) phrasebook • The Gambia & Senegal • Healthy Travel Africa • Kenya • Kenya travel atlas • Malawi, Mozambique & Zambia • Morocco • North Africa • Read This First Africa • South Africa, Lesotho & Swaziland • South Africa, Lesotho & Swaziland travel atlas • Swahili phrasebook • Tanzania, Zanzibar & Pemba • Trekking in East Africa • Tunisia • West Africa • Zimbabwe, Botswana & Namibia • Zimbabwe, Botswana & Nambia Travel Atlas • World Food Morocco**Travel Literature:** The Rainbird: A Central African Journey • Songs to an African Sunset: A Zimbabwean Story • Mali Blues: Traveling to an African Beat

AUSTRALIA & THE PACIFIC Auckland • Australia • Australian phrasebook • Bushwalking in Australia • Bushwalking in Papua New Guinea • Fiji • Fijian phrasebook • Healthy Travel Australia, NZ and the Pacific • Islands of Australia's Great Barrier Reef • Melbourne • Melbourne city map • Micronesia • New Caledonia • New South Wales & the ACT • New Zealand • Northern Territory • Outback Australia • Out To Eat – Melbourne • Out to Eat – Sydney • Papua New Guinea • Pidgin phrasebook • Queensland • Rarotonga & the Cook Islands • Samoa • Solomon Islands • South Australia • South Pacific • South Pacific Languages phrasebook • Sydney • Sydney city map • Sydney Condensed • Tahiti & French Polynesia • Tasmania • Tonga • Tramping in New Zealand • Vanuatu • Victoria • Western Australia
Travel Literature: Islands in the Clouds • Kiwi Tracks: A New Zealand Journey • Sean & David's Long Drive

CENTRAL AMERICA & THE CARIBBEAN Bahamas, Turks & Caicos • Bermuda • Central America on a shoestring • Costa Rica • Cuba • Dominican Republic & Haiti • Eastern Caribbean • Guatemala, Belize & Yucatán: La Ruta Maya • Jamaica • Mexico • Mexico City • Panama • Puerto Rico • Read This First Central & South America • World Food Mexico
Travel Literature: Green Dreams: Travels in Central America

EUROPE Amsterdam • Amsterdam city map • Andalucía • Austria • Baltic States phrasebook • Barcelona • Berlin • Berlin city map • Britain • British phrasebook • Brussels, Bruges & Antwerp • Budapest city map • Canary Islands • Central Europe • Central Europe phrasebook • Corfu & Ionians • Corsica • Crete • Crete Condensed • Croatia • Cyprus • Czech & Slovak Republics • Denmark • Dublin • Eastern Europe • Eastern Europe phrasebook • Edinburgh • Estonia, Latvia & Lithuania • Europe on a shoestring • Finland • Florence • France • French phrasebook • Germany • German phrasebook • Greece • Greek Islands • Greek phrasebook • Hungary • Iceland, Greenland & the Faroe Islands • Ireland • Italian phrasebook • Italy • Krakow • Lisbon • London • London city map • London Condensed • Mediterranean Europe • Mediterranean Europe phrasebook • Munich • Norway • Paris • Paris city map • Paris Condensed • Poland • Portugal • Portugese phrasebook • Portugal travel atlas • Prague • Prague city map • Provence & the Côte d'Azur • Read This First Europe • Romania & Moldova • Rome • Russia, Ukraine & Belarus • Russian phrasebook • Scandinavian & Baltic Europe • Scandinavian Europe phrasebook • Scotland • Slovenia • Spain • Spanish phrasebook • St Petersburg • Switzerland • Trekking in Spain • Ukrainian phrasebook • Venice • Vienna • Walking in Britain • Walking in Ireland • Walking in Italy • Walking in Spain • Walking in Switzerland • Western Europe • Western Europe phrasebook • World Food Italy • World Food Spain
Travel Literature: The Olive Grove: Travels in Greece

INDIAN SUBCONTINENT Bangladesh • Bengali phrasebook • Bhutan • Delhi • Goa • Hindi & Urdu phrasebook • India • India & Bangladesh travel atlas • Indian Himalaya • Karakoram Highway • Kerala • Mumbai (Bombay) • Nepal • Nepali phrasebook • Pakistan • Rajasthan • Read This First: Asia & India • South India • Sri Lanka • Sri Lanka phrasebook • Trekking in the Indian Himalaya • Trekking in the Karakoram & Hindukush • Trekking in the Nepal Himalaya
Travel Literature: In Rajasthan • Shopping for Buddhas • The Age Of Kali

LONELY PLANET

Mail Order

Lonely Planet products are distributed worldwide. They are also available by mail order from Lonely Planet, so if you have difficulty finding a title please write to us. North and South American residents should write to 150 Linden St, Oakland CA 94607, USA; European and African residents should write to 10a Spring Place, London, NW5 3BH; and residents of other countries to PO Box 617, Hawthorn, Victoria 3122, Australia.

ISLANDS OF THE INDIAN OCEAN Madagascar & Comoros • Maldives • Mauritius, Réunion & Seychelles

MIDDLE EAST & CENTRAL ASIA Bahrain, Kuwait & Qatar • Central Asia • Central Asia phrasebook • Dubai • Hebrew phrasebook • Iran • Israel & the Palestinian Territories • Israel & the Palestinian Territories travel atlas • Istanbul • Istanbul City Map • Istanbul to Cairo on a shoestring • Jerusalem • Jerusalem City Map • Jordan • Jordan, Syria & Lebanon travel atlas • Lebanon • Middle East • Oman & the United Arab Emirates • Syria • Turkey • Turkey travel atlas • Turkish phrasebook • Yemen
Travel Literature: The Gates of Damascus • Kingdom of the Film Stars: Journey into Jordan • Black on Black: Iran Revisited

NORTH AMERICA Alaska • Backpacking in Alaska • Baja California • California & Nevada • California Condensed • Canada • Chicago • Chicago city map • Deep South • Florida • Hawaii • Honolulu • Las Vegas • Los Angeles • Miami • New England • New Orleans • New York City • New York city map • New York Condensed • New York, New Jersey & Pennsylvania • Oahu • Pacific Northwest USA • Puerto Rico • Rocky Mountain • San Francisco • San Francisco city map • Seattle • Southwest USA • Texas • USA • USA phrasebook • Vancouver • Washington, DC & the Capital Region • Washington DC city map
Travel Literature: Drive Thru America

NORTH-EAST ASIA Beijing • Cantonese phrasebook • China • Hong Kong • Hong Kong city map • Hong Kong, Macau & Guangzhou • Japan • Japanese phrasebook • Japanese audio pack • Korea • Korean phrasebook • Kyoto • Mandarin phrasebook • Mongolia • Mongolian phrasebook • North-East Asia on a shoestring • Seoul • South-West China • Taiwan • Tibet • Tibetan phrasebook • Tokyo
Travel Literature: Lost Japan • In Xanadu

SOUTH AMERICA Argentina, Uruguay & Paraguay • Bolivia • Brazil • Brazilian phrasebook • Buenos Aires • Chile & Easter Island • Chile & Easter Island travel atlas • Colombia • Ecuador & the Galapagos Islands • Healthy Travel Central & South America • Latin American Spanish phrasebook • Peru • Quechua phrasebook • Rio de Janeiro • Rio de Janeiro city map • South America on a shoestring • Trekking in the Patagonian Andes • Venezuela
Travel Literature: Full Circle: A South American Journey

SOUTH-EAST ASIA Bali & Lombok • Bangkok • Bangkok city map • Burmese phrasebook • Cambodia • Hanoi • Healthy Travel Asia & India • Hill Tribes phrasebook • Ho Chi Minh City • Indonesia • Indonesia's Eastern Islands • Indonesian phrasebook • Indonesian audio pack • Jakarta • Java • Laos • Lao phrasebook • Laos travel atlas • Malay phrasebook • Malaysia, Singapore & Brunei • Myanmar (Burma) • Philippines • Pilipino (Tagalog) phrasebook • Read This First Asia & India • Singapore • South-East Asia on a shoestring • South-East Asia phrasebook • Thailand • Thailand's Islands & Beaches • Thailand travel atlas • Thai phrasebook • Thai audio pack • Vietnam • Vietnamese phrasebook • Vietnam travel atlas • World Food Thailand • World Food Vietnam

ALSO AVAILABLE: Antarctica • The Arctic • Brief Encounters: Stories of Love, Sex & Travel • Chasing Rickshaws • Lonely Planet Unpacked • Not the Only Planet: Travel Stories from Science Fiction • Sacred India • Travel with Children • Traveller's Tales

Index

Text

For a listing of rides, see the Table of Rides (pp4-5)

Bold indicates maps.

Boxed Text

ABOUT LONELY PLANET GUIDEBOOKS

Lonely Planet published its first book in 1973 in response to the numerous 'How did you do it?' questions Maureen and Tony Wheeler were asked after driving, busing, hitching, sailing and railing their way from England to Australia.

Written at a kitchen table and hand collated, trimmed and stapled, *Across Asia on the Cheap* became an instant local bestseller, inspiring thoughts of another book.

Eighteen months in South-East Asia resulted in their second guide, *South-East Asia on a shoestring*, which they put together in a backstreet Chinese hotel in Singapore in 1975. The 'yellow bible', as it quickly became known to backpackers around the world, soon became the guide to the region. It has sold well over half a million copies and is now in its 10th edition.

Today an international company with offices in Melbourne (Australia), Oakland (USA), London (UK) and Paris (France), Lonely Planet has an ever-growing list of books and other products, including: travel guides, walking guides, city maps, travel atlases, phrasebooks, diving guides, wildlife guides, healthy travel guides, restaurant guides, world food guides, first time travel guides, condensed guides, travel literature, pictorial books and, of course, cycling guides. Many of these are also published in French and various other languages.

In addition to the books, there are also videos and Lonely Planet's award winning Web site.

Some things haven't changed. The main aim is still to help make it possible for adventurous travellers to get out there – to explore and better understand the world.

At Lonely Planet we believe travellers can make a positive contribution to the countries they visit – if they respect their host communities and spend their money wisely. Since 1986 a percentage of the income from each book has been donated to aid projects and human rights campaigns.

> Lonely Planet gathers information for everyone who's curious about the planet – and especially for those who explore it first-hand. Through guidebooks, phrasebooks, activity guides, maps, literature, newsletters, image library, TV series and Web site we act as an information exchange for a worldwide community of travellers.

LONELY PLANET OFFICES

Australia
PO Box 617, Hawthorn, Victoria 3122
☎ 03 9819 1877 fax 03 9819 6459
✉ talk2us@lonelyplanet.com.au

USA
150 Linden St, Oakland, CA 94607
☎ 510 893 8555 or ☎ 800 275 8555 (toll free)
fax 510 893 8572
✉ info@lonelyplanet.com

UK
10a Spring Place, London NW5 3BH
☎ 020 7428 4800 fax 020 7428 4828
✉ go@lonelyplanet.co.uk

France
1 rue du Dahomey, 75011 Paris
☎ 01 55 25 33 00 fax 01 55 25 33 01
✉ bip@lonelyplanet.fr
🖥 www.lonelyplanet.fr

World Wide Web: 🖥 www.lonelyplanet.com *or* AOL keyword: lp
Lonely Planet Images: ✉ lpi@lonelyplanet.com.au